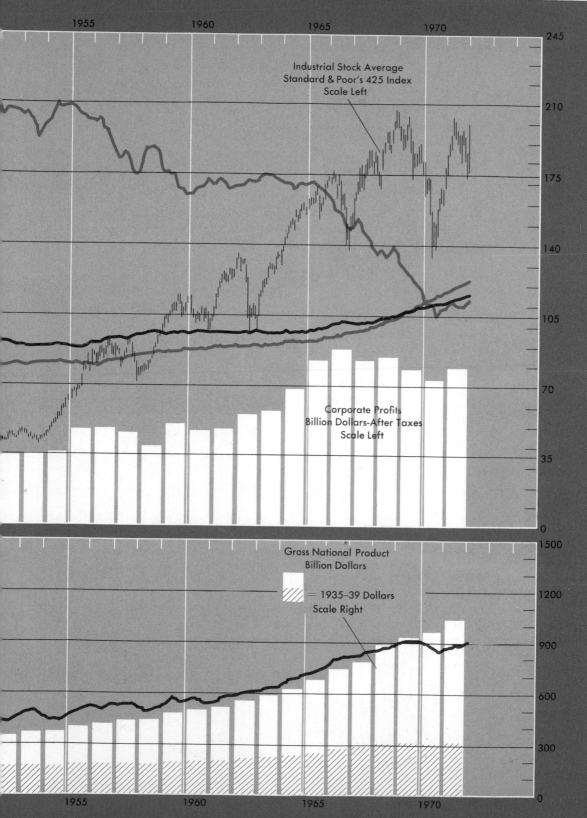

introduction to
modern business

sixth edition

introduction

PRENTICE-HALL, INC., Englewood Cliffs, New Jersey

to modern business

ANALYSIS AND INTERPRETATION

VERNON A. MUSSELMAN

Professor of Business Education
University of Kentucky

EUGENE H. HUGHES

Professor and Dean, Emeritus,
University of Houston
and
Labor Arbitrator
Sacramento, California

Library of Congress Cataloging in Publication Data

MUSSELMAN, VERNON A
    Introduction to modern business.

    Bibliography: p.
    1. Business. I. HUGHES, EUGENE HARLEY, 1908-
joint author. II. Title.
HF5351.M86 1973   658.4   72-3562
ISBN 0-13-488163-X

introduction to modern business
ANALYSIS AND INTERPRETATION

sixth edition

VERNON A. MUSSELMAN and EUGENE H. HUGHES

PRENTICE-HALL INTERNATIONAL, Inc., London
PRENTICE-HALL OF AUSTRALIA, Pty. Ltd., Sydney
PRENTICE-HALL OF CANADA, Ltd., Toronto
PRENTICE-HALL OF INDIA Private Limited, New Delhi
PRENTICE-HALL OF JAPAN, Inc., Tokyo

contents

preface

In a business world that is constantly changing, collegiate textbooks about business need to be revised frequently. This sixth edition of *Introduction to Modern Business: Analysis and Interpretation* has been completely revised, as have all supplementary materials—business cases, problems and projects, objective tests, *Instructor's Manual,* and the *Study Guide and Workbook.* Visual aid transparency masters, a valuable teaching device, are a new supplement to the text.

In preparing this sixth edition, our objectives were manifold:

1. To update statistical and economic data and expand on those topics that have increased in importance since the previous edition.
2. To include new developments pertinent to business education at the college level.
3. To make the text an ever more effective teaching instrument; teaching aids, among them tables, charts, graphs, and other illustrations, have been increased in number.

4. To make the chapter material reveal more of what business really is and how it actually works, so that the reader has at hand a comprehensive analysis of the business field.

Other objectives—already well established in previous editions—are: to provide up-to-date career information about business occupations; to increase the student's ability to analyze problems; and to expand his business vocabulary as a foundation for further study of business and related fields.

The twenty-three chapters of this book are grouped into six major sections, with each section treated as a study unit. For example, Part Five, "Quantitative Controls for Decision Making," includes accounting as a tool of management, research and statistical methods for decision making, quantitative analysis, data processing, and data processing equipment for computer programming.

Chapter One is rewritten to include a greater discussion of the role of the American system of free markets as this system relates to the law of supply and demand and as it operates in a changing economic environment. The expanding role of government in business is emphasized. Chapter Two is devoted to a new subject, a discussion of ecology, pollution, conservation, and the responsibility of business to help improve our environment. Chapters Fourteen and Fifteen of the previous edition, which dealt with manufacturing (purchasing, processes, and controls), have been combined in this edition without detracting from the importance of the production function. The chapters on advertising and personal selling have been combined, too. Chapter Twenty-three, "International Business," has been updated. It discusses the significance of growing business interests in tariffs and trade quotas, the European Common Market, the devaluation of the American dollar, and the impact of devaluation on the U.S. balance of trade deficits and the American economy.

The sixth edition continues to use color as an aid to teaching and learning. Chapter introductions, summaries, problems, projects, business cases, and vocabulary review tests have been revised. The chapter discussion questions, formerly located at the end of a chapter, now appear throughout each chapter to help students relate more effectively to the subject matter as it is being discussed. A revised *Study Guide and Workbook* features business readings from magazines and newspapers. These readings will enlarge the student's understanding of business by exposing him to a variety of original ideas. Throughout both the textbook and the study guide, the authors have made use of the behavioral sciences to identify the structure of the business firm, not only as an economic group, but also as a social organization subject to environmental change. Discussion of causes and effects of specific cultural, legal, social, and economic changes helps to clarify the role of business and its responsibility to society. The business organization is made up of individuals who are subject to motivation, interaction, and leadership. In short, the authors have attempted to provide in this edition the text teachers want.

Once again, the authors are indebted to friends far too numerous to list. A special debt of gratitude, however, is due the following people and their organizations: King C. Torgesen, District Manager, Social Security Administration, Department of Health, Education, and Welfare, Sacramento, California; Vernon G. Huwaldt, Account Executive, Merrill Lynch, Pierce, Fenner & Smith, Inc., Sacramento, California; Paul H. Gilman, F.S.A., Associate Actuary, Cal-Western Life Insurance Company, Sacramento, California; Jordan B. Dell'Era, Vice-President and Manager, Marketing Administration, Crocker National Bank, San Francisco, California; Stephen Kirchner, Assistant Vice-President, Crocker National Bank, San Francisco, California; Peter H. Langer, Capital Research and Management Company, Los Angeles, California; J. E. Weaver, Vice-President and Manager, Wells Fargo Bank, Woodland, California; Alvin W. Vogtle, Jr., President, The Southern Company, Atlanta, Georgia; L. I. Dietz, President, East End State Bank, Houston, Texas; M. R. Crockard, Senior Vice-President and Manager, International Banking Division, Bank of the Southwest, N.A., Houston, Texas; Stanley M. Rice, Vice-President, Sales, United Business Service, Boston, Massachusetts; R. Thomas Willson, Vice-President, American Iron and Steel Institute, New York; William McSherry, Manager, News Department Services, *The Wall Street Journal,* Dow Jones & Company, Inc., New York; Rowena Wyant, Manager, Business Economics Department, Dun & Bradstreet, Inc., New York; John L. Cobbs, Editor, *Business Week,* New York; Dr. Hilton D. Shepherd, Shepherd Associates, Fort Worth, Texas; and C. Ed Carlisle, Manager, American Pyramid Companies, Inc., Louisville, Kentucky.

We also wish to express appreciation to our colleagues for their suggestions: Dr. Z. S. Dickerson, Professor of Business Education, Madison College, Harrisonburg, Virginia; Dr. Russell Johnston, Professor of Business, Virginia Commonwealth University, Richmond, Virginia; Chester A. Schriesheim, Community College of Baltimore, Baltimore, Maryland; Dr. Harold R. Steinhauser, Chairman, Division of Business, Rock Valley College, Rockford, Illinois; Norman Carniel, Business Department, Queensborough Community College of the City University of New York, Bayside, New York; Professor Jerome M. Peschke, Professor of Business Technology, University of Houston, Houston, Texas; Dr. Joel Dauten, Professor, Arizona State University, Tempe, Arizona; and Norman D. Nichols, Texarkana, Texas.

We are indebted to the staff of Prentice-Hall, Inc., especially Chester Lucido, acquisitions editor and Assistant Vice-President, with whom we consulted regarding plans for this revision; James Bacci, our College Division production editor whose patience and guidance we sincerely appreciate; Judy

Winthrop for her creative contributions as the designer of this edition; Barbara Cassel for her invaluable help in all phases of production work; Joyce Perkins and Colette Conboy for editorial assistance; and, of course, Rita DeVries, our very competent copyeditor, who really helped make this a more readable book.

VERNON A. MUSSELMAN
EUGENE H. HUGHES

*business
and
its environment*

american business and our economic system

CHAPTER ONE

This is a study of American business, a social institution that exerts a broad influence on people's work and lives. Business furnishes employment for a major segment of our working population, and it provides goods and services for all the people. In our study we are concerned with the business system per se and the way it functions within the economic environment.

Anything as varied and changing as business poses many problems—and these problems can be solved best by those who are adequately prepared to deal with them. This book about business is designed to help the student to confidently and capably face the challenges—and take advantage of the opportunities—that lie before him in his chosen profession.

You will find that this book covers many areas within the broad field of business. The area to which you will be introduced first is economics, because business and economics are mutually complementary. This first chapter will introduce you to a formal study of business and the relationships that exist between business and the economic system.

No viable economic system can remain static and still meet the needs of society. So in addition to studying current trends, we shall be concerned with changes and future developments. What you learn here will be not only of interest to you now but of value to you throughout your lifetime as you broaden your experiences in the business world.

WHAT ECONOMICS IS ABOUT

Economics is everybody's business. We need a working knowledge of this subject for several reasons. First of all, we use economic information in our everyday life. More important, business problems require a broader knowledge of our entire economic system. We need to understand the relationship between our ability to produce goods and services and our methods of selling them. History teaches us how similar problems have been solved in the past. Economics should help us solve our business problems of the present and the future. A knowledge of the basic economic principles forms the basis for a better understanding of our business system.

Economics is generally said to be concerned with wants and resources. However, without man there would be no wants and no need to manage the resources. So *economics* may be defined as the study of the means by which man manages resources to meet his material needs and wants. These resources consist of those things needed to produce an abundance of goods, made available at prices people can afford to pay.

An understanding of economics is important to all of us, because the subject relates directly to man's behavior as he struggles to earn a living. Economics is concerned with production, distribution, and consumption of goods and services. It is also concerned with the way people organize themselves in order to work together to meet their wants. Because resources are limited, they must be conserved or managed in such a way as to make them go further and last longer. In other words, we must *economize* in our use of resources, and thus the term *economics*.

In most societies, goods and services in themselves have little value; their accumulation in warehouses makes no contribution to the welfare of the people. What is important is that our business system should enable individuals to satisfy at least some of their needs and wants. The process of creating goods and services is called *production*, and using them to satisfy wants is *consumption*.

The Means of Production

The wants of society are practically unlimited. The more a person has, the more he seems to want; and the things men want are no longer supplied free by nature. Raw materials must be processed before they are usable, labor must be exerted to process them, tools must be employed in the processing—and all of this must be financed. The means of production, then, consist of land, labor, capital, and technology. Or we might well use the terms *material, men, money, and machines.*

Natural Resources. The greatness of the American economy has resulted to a large degree from our ability to obtain necessary supplies of raw materials for productive processes from the natural resources at our disposal. These natural resources include—in addition to the land—navigable streams, lakes, forests, minerals, and oil. We are more nearly able to satisfy our demands for these resources from within our own boundaries than is any other country, with the possible exception of the Soviet Union.

Historically, we have had plenty of clean, pure water and fresh air. But with industry developed to its current level, we are now polluting our air, lakes, and rivers at an alarming rate. Ecologists and conservationists have called our attention to this situation, and both federal and state governments have become concerned. Our manufacturing industries are spending billions of dollars to protect our air and water resources, an undertaking that is essential to the health of our people and the preservation of wildlife. This subject has become so important that the entire next chapter is devoted to it.

The rich soil in many regions of the country is a resource that makes possible the raising of huge agricultural harvests. We have almost 400 million acres of farm-crop land, a half billion acres of pasture, and almost a half billion acres of commercial forests. In recent years, our farms have produced considerably more food and fiber than we can use.

Climate is another very important asset to commerce and industry, and again our country is extremely fortunate. Most regions of the United States enjoy growing seasons that last long enough to permit the cultivation and harvesting of valuable crops. We have an annual rainfall ranging from 20 to 60 inches in our principal crop-producing regions, and even in some regions of scant rainfall, crops are successfully grown by means of irrigation. Our winters are usually not so severe as to hinder business to any marked degree, and all our principal harbors are usable throughout the year.

The Labor Supply. The American labor force is derived from a population that embraces many different nationalities, religions, social strata, and economic backgrounds. Since 1900, our population has increased sevenfold, and the official estimate of the U.S. Bureau of the Census for January 1971—a population of 206 million persons—represents an increase during the preceding ten-year period of 27 million. The makeup of the total population is shown in the accompanying chart.

Until the first U.S. census was taken in 1790, little had been done to identify the economic characteristics of our people. That first census, however, revealed that over 70 percent of the population in this country were active in some form of agriculture. Since that date, this percentage has decreased continuously, until today only 6 percent of our people earn their living by working on farms.

Manufacturing had become significant by the time of that first census,

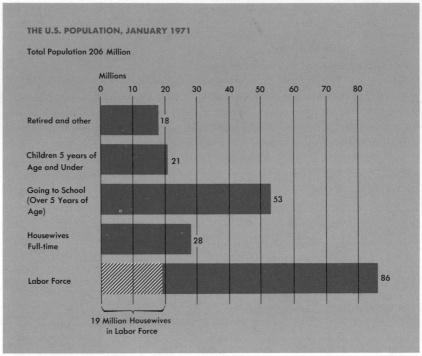

THE U.S. POPULATION, JANUARY 1971

Total Population 206 Million

Source: U.S. Bureau of the Census

TodAY 6 out of 10 mAnk,

and by 1900 it provided employment for 31 percent of our working force. Today, our total labor force numbers more than 80 million Americans, with approximately 26 percent engaged in manufacturing occupations. Slightly over one-fifth are employed in wholesale and retail trade, and 16 percent are employed by government.

There has been a significant shift in the structure of our employed labor force. Whereas at the turn of the century only three out of ten workers were providing services for others, by 1970 more than half were engaged in service occupations, and it is estimated that by 1980, seven out of ten employed persons will be engaged in rendering services rather than in the production of goods. Between the end of World War II and 1970, almost 4 million new jobs were provided in the goods-producing industries, but during this same period more than 21 million persons were added in service occupations—see the chart on the opposite page.

Machines. Industrial development occurred very rapidly in this country, with machines replacing hand labor in numerous types of operations. In fact, machines are the dominant factor in industry today; mechanization has given way to automation, with some sophisticated machines directing and controlling other machines. An entire petroleum-pumping station may be so completely automated that only one person, or no person at all, is needed to man the station. Human effort is employed largely in planning, directing, supervising, and inspecting operations. Technological advancement has been extremely rapid, making possible the tremendous growth in the national product that we have experienced.

Capital Financing. Mass production requires mass capital financing, and the people of this nation have always raised sufficient capital to finance our business firms. America possesses great wealth, and ownership of American business is widespread. More than 33 million Americans own shares in our many corporations; the American Telephone and Telegraph Company alone has more than 3 million stockholders. In addition, we have more than 9 million businesses that are owned by individual proprietors and over 300,000 partnerships. Capital expenditures for plant and equipment alone now exceed $100 billion annually.

Because of the unfavorable balance of payments, the administrative branch of the U.S. government has discouraged the outflow of cash to other countries. As a result, American corporations have developed their overseas investments to the point where there is hardly such a thing as an "American corporation." Many of our industrial giants generate as much as 30 to 50 percent of their total sales from their overseas properties. The United States leads the field of the creditor nations of the world, and our rapid growth as an industrial nation was possible only because we were able to finance it.

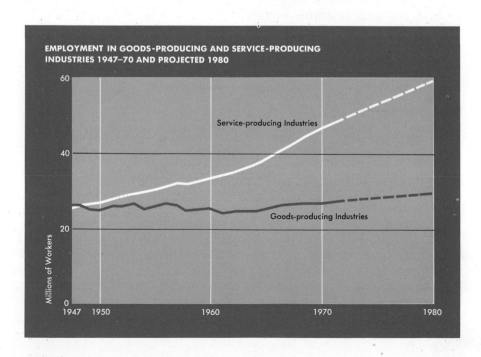

EMPLOYMENT IN GOODS-PRODUCING AND SERVICE-PRODUCING INDUSTRIES 1947–70 AND PROJECTED 1980

MAKING ECONOMIC DECISIONS

Scarcities in natural and human resources limit man's ability to satisfy all his needs and wants. *The presence of unlimited wants in the face of scarcity is the primary economic problem of every society.* The fact of scarcity—limited resources—has always plagued mankind; its very existence serves to challenge man's ingenuity and spur him to increase his economic competence and efficiency.

Solving the problem of the utilization of scarce resources to satisfy unlimited wants involves the establishment of an economic system. Thus men organize so as to work together for the common good of all. In deciding how to utilize the nation's resources, the people of any nation must answer some very fundamental questions regarding their economic scheme. These basic questions are:

1. What goods are to be produced—what capital goods, what consumer goods? Who determines what goods are to be produced?[1]
2. How are these goods to be produced—how do we organize our resources to produce them?
3. Who will receive and use the goods and services that are produced? How should they be distributed? Who will buy them, and at what price?

The manner in which these questions are answered determines the relative roles of private and governmental leadership. As they are answered and implemented, a nation's economic goals become established, and a method of achieving those goals can be developed.

In democratic countries, economic decisions are made by millions of individuals. In socialistic countries, where the major industries are owned collectively (by the government), economic decisions are made by "the people's government." In authoritarian and communist societies, economic decisions are made by a dictator and his few trusted advisers.

Later in this chapter, you will see that in America the economic organizational pattern is based on private enterprise and competition in the marketplace. In this country, planning and control of industrial production and distribution are determined by the management teams of individual companies. But in the Soviet Union there is central planning and control by the government for all industry. There, the nation's rulers decide the type of transportation facilities to be used in any location, the amount and kinds of consumer goods to be manufactured, and even the types of work various persons are to perform.

In the United States, wage scales are largely determined through collective bargaining between labor unions and company management teams. In the

[1]Capital goods are those used in industry to produce other goods—examples are supplies, machinery, and equipment.

Soviet Union, the wage scale is set by the government. The profit mechanism has in the past been absent in the Communist economic scheme, but recent reports indicate that some aspects of the profit incentive have been introduced in Russia.

Choice and Decision Making

Making a choice necessitates selecting from among one's alternatives. It also implies that a business or an individual is faced with more than a single opportunity from which to choose. The correct choice means selection of the best alternative or choice of the preferred opportunity, and to make correct choices one needs a set of guidelines or criteria to follow. When making choices, one wishes to maximize a certain interest or desire. This might be earnings (or profits) or it might be satisfaction and enjoyment. In choice making, the law of economics dictates that for a given degree of satisfaction, one will choose the cheapest alternative, or in the case of identical costs, one will choose the greatest satisfaction. To illustrate: A business, when selecting between two pieces of equipment of equal cost, will choose the one that affords the greatest efficiency of operation or the largest output; a government, when selecting from among aircraft of comparable performance and capability, will choose the cheapest.

Setting Individual and National Goals

Individual Goals. By now it should be obvious to the reader that an economy without direction would function very poorly—or maybe not at all—and that a nation's people must work together for the benefit of the greatest number. In America, each individual is free to a great degree to run his own economic affairs. To begin with, he may choose the type of work in which he wishes to engage—assuming, of course, a willingness and the ability to prepare and qualify for such work. In fact, he may choose either to go into business for himself or to work for someone else. He is free to spend or to save his earnings, according to his own personal desires. Yet in all of this, each individual is but a part of the whole, and what he does is limited, for he is not free to ignore or tread upon the rights of others.

In the United States and in other parts of the free world, the individual exerts his influence upon the system by voting, both at the polls and in the marketplace. We have in this country a private-enterprise economy operating within a democratic political framework. Economic freedom and political freedom go hand in hand, complementing and reinforcing each other; and economic, social, and political freedoms make possible the setting and the achievement of one's economic goals.

Collective Goals. In addition to individual needs, mankind has a group of collective wants, such as education, highways, national defense, and a variety of social-welfare benefits. Some of our economic goals in the United States are high wages, stable prices, a high return on investments, conservation of natural resources, increased production of goods, protection by the government, freedom from government regulation, and greater cooperation between management and labor groups.

Just as an individual's goals give direction to his planning and effort, the choice of goals by society gives direction to the national economy. But society's goals are not altogether consistent with one another; indeed, they may often be in direct conflict. For example, an attempt to maintain stable prices may run contrary to the desire for higher wages and dividends. The desire for increased consumption may conflict with the idea of conserving natural resources. New industry in the local community would provide more jobs for local workers, but it might decrease the quality of the environment by polluting the air or water. Increased technological development may cause, at least temporarily, increased unemployment. And free trade among the industrial nations conflicts with the desire for protection through import duties. Although we cannot reconcile completely the attainment of these conflicting national goals, we can agree that *the overriding economic objective of the American people is the desire for an ever-rising living standard—a higher level of personal income and consumption—subject to conditions that provide for individual and national advancement and freedom of choice.* All this is also conditional upon the maintenance of an environment that enables us to live a good life.

Discussion Questions

1. *Identify any conflicts between the desire for maximum profits on the part of business and the conservation policies of government. Explain.*
2. *How do you account for the fact that many countries have abundant natural resources and available labor but have made little or no progress in industrial development?*
3. *Several of our national goals are in conflict with one another. What criteria should be followed in resolving such conflicts?*

A SYSTEM OF "FREE MARKETS"

Under a private-enterprise economy, goods are exchanged in the marketplace. Persons who own goods offer to sell them through competitive bidding at the highest price the goods will bring. At the same time, those who wish to buy these goods hope to secure them at the lowest possible price. In order for a sale to be completed, the seller and buyer must reach an agreement on the price of the good. A *market*, then, may be defined as *a place where sellers and buyers exchange goods (or services) for an agreed-upon price.*

The existence of a free market means that an entrepreneur may purchase his merchandise, his fixed assets, and his labor at a fair price. It means, too, that he may borrow needed capital at a fair price. But it also means that the persons he employs receive a fair price for their services. And the consumer can get full value for the dollars he spends for the commodities he buys.

When the market system is free of external controls, it serves as the nerve center of business, ordering that certain types of goods be produced and distributed. But nowhere is a market completely free of "imposed" restrictions. Were it entirely free, some person or company might gain an upper hand and, through unfair practices, drive competitors out of business. With a monopoly of the market secured, prices might be raised to unreasonably high levels, to the detriment of the best interests of society. So you will see, as you progress through this book, that governments have imposed certain controls on the American market system. But basically, the functioning of American capitalism depends primarily on the theory of making economic decisions through "free markets."

The free-market system offers several advantages. In the first place, it ensures that goods will be produced efficiently. It also rewards workers for outstanding performance and thereby provides an incentive for them to do their best. Furthermore, it makes for flexibility, for every transaction is important, and it immediately effects specific adjustments in the economy.

The Law of Supply and Demand

In a system of free markets, the ideal situation is that of maintaining a balance between the supply and the demand for any commodity.

When a new good is produced, a market for it must be created. At first, the price of the article is relatively high, because only a few are available. As the demand for the new product increases, however, the number produced is increased to meet it, and the unit cost is reduced. And as the unit price decreases, more people can afford to purchase the good, so the demand increases further. The demand will vary according to the price; under a system of free markets, there will be a balance between the supply and the demand at any given price. The law of supply and demand functions best under a free-market system where government interference is minimal.

The choices people make when they buy goods create a greater demand for certain products than for others. This demand triggers the production of more goods similar to those "chosen." Decisions to buy these goods are not only votes for them, but votes against other goods. This is called "voting in the marketplace." Consumers, by deciding how to spend their income, decide how our resources are to be used, and which factories and stores are to survive and prosper and which to fail. It is through competitive bidding in the marketplace that we determine the answers to the questions raised earlier.

Specialization—Individual and Regional

An inevitable result of the free-market system is the development of specialization. Specialization began as far back as when the industrial development of our country was in the handcraft stage. The man who could make shoes better than other men could spend all his producing hours making shoes. Then he exchanged his surplus production with the silversmith and the clothier for their surplus goods, which they could make better and faster than he could.

As the use of machines greatly increased one's productive output, specialization in industry became the rule rather than the exception. Men could specialize not only in shoe production but in operating machines that made soles, or uppers, or that sewed parts together. The scope of a man's operations became more narrow than ever before. Each man developed an expertness at his specific task.

In the same way that persons became specialists, regional specialization developed. The climate, especially temperature and rainfall, determined the kinds of crops that were produced in specific areas. In this country there developed the corn belt, the cotton- and wheat-growing areas, and the large pasture or grazing areas. Mining and smelting became the principal industries in regions where coal, iron ore, and copper deposits were discovered. Where high-grade clays abounded, pottery and brick factories flourished. Manufacturing started in New England, where water power and financing existed, then spread to other areas.

Today some countries are still predominantly agricultural, while others, like West Germany, Japan, and the United States, are known for their industrial development. And within the principal industrial regions, specialized types of manufacturing have prospered, such as that of watches in Switzerland, chemicals and dyes in Germany, and cameras and binoculars in Japan.

Individuals, regions, and countries specialize in those types of endeavors that are most profitable for them. The result is that everyone benefits through the exchange of the surplus goods that are the fruits of total production.

Discussion Questions

4. *What are the requirements of a "free market"?*
5. *How is price related to supply and demand?*
6. *How does specialization enhance a nation's economic development?*

THE FOUNDATIONS OF CAPITALISM

Certain factors are essential to any private-enterprise economic system. They are sometimes called the *foundations of capitalism.* In a very real sense, they constitute the democratic foundations of our economic system. Goods and services are produced by businesses with reasonable freedom from government controls. Profit serves as the reward for one's risking his time, effort, and capital in a business. Our economic system, called *capitalism,* is based on private ownership and the right to make a profit. Free enterprise assumes that the individual is the best-qualified judge of his own interests. And an economic system that sponsors this philosophy makes it possible for people to pursue those interests that achieve the most not only for the individual, but also for the welfare of society.

These economic rights are intimately related to other freedoms that characterize American democracy—social and political freedoms. Without the right of private enterprise, we could not be sure of a free press. No single freedom stands alone, and no one freedom alone can make a free society. Every type of freedom is interrelated with, and interdependent upon, all other freedoms. The economic foundations of the private-enterprise system truly constitute one of the foundation blocks of our democratic way of life.

Right to Property Ownership

Private enterprise is built around the use of private property. By *private enterprise* we mean the system under which individuals are free to carry on business with their own capital, experience, and desire to succeed, without the aid of the government or other subsidizing agencies. Under private enterprise, land, buildings, and factories are owned by private individuals or groups of individuals. Our right to own property is guaranteed by the Fifth and Fourteenth Amendments to the Constitution. In fact, the preservation of this right is an essential function of our government. Many laws have been enacted to protect our ownership rights to property against theft, confiscation, and embezzlement.

The right of ownership of property includes the right to control its use, to sell it, or to give it to another. Most of the property in this country—farms, homes, factories—is owned by individuals, not by the government.

The right to ownership serves as an incentive to care for, to preserve, and to improve the wealth of the nation. Most of us take better care of our personal possessions than we do of the property of others. This right also encourages individuals to acquire more property. A person's awareness that he may retain the earnings of his labor serves as an incentive for him to try to increase the amount he owns. As a result, not only does he profit personally, but society in general gains as well. The right of property ownership is fundamental to a free-enterprise economy.

The Profit Incentive

The individual's opportunity to gain from his ownership and use of property encourages him to go into business. And in attempting to improve his own economic position, he renders valuable services to others. The hope of making a profit is the chief incentive for venturing into a business operation. *Profit* is the return to the businessman in excess of his cost of operations—that is, the amount by which his income exceeds his costs and expenses.

An *entrepreneur* is a person who assumes the risk and management of a private enterprise. He faces the possibility of losing money, of course, instead of making a profit. Since he risks his time, money, and effort, many argue that he should be allowed to make as large a profit as he can. Others feel that he should be restricted to making only a "fair and reasonable" profit. Just what constitutes a fair and reasonable profit, however, is difficult to decide—many factors enter the picture. At any rate, the entrepreneur is entitled to an interest return on his investment. He should enjoy a margin of profit to cover possible losses in future years, and a reward for his efficiency and ingenuity in management.

The opportunity to try to make a profit is one of the foundations of our private-enterprise system, and the danger of suffering a loss is one of the risks assumed by every entrepreneur.

The Opportunity to Compete

Private enterprise under the capitalist system inevitably leads to competition. *Competition* is the practice of trying to get something that is being sought by others under similar circumstances at the same time. The ground rules and ethics of competitive practices are set up by the members of society. From many angles, competition is good for both businessmen and consumers. Self-interest encourages businessmen to ask high prices; but when many competitors are bidding for the same business, price reductions ultimately enter the picture. In addition, the aggressive characteristics of one dealer may make him more efficient than another; thus, under competition, managerial practices tend to be kept on a high plane of efficiency.

Competition operates in the market in many ways. To begin with, producers compete with one another for the best raw materials at the lowest prices. They also compete for the best factory locations and for the most efficient and productive workers. Wholesale and retail establishments also vie with one another for qualified employees and for the most desirable locations.

Some industrial firms compete principally with rival business enterprises that manufacture identical or similar products. Toolmakers exemplify this type of competition, for they must manufacture products to meet specifications. They attempt to meet or beat their competitors by making a better-quality or a better-designed product, and by giving better service.

Competition also prevails among firms that produce or sell different but related products. Manufacturers of one line of toys are competing with producers of other toys and games for a share of the recreation market. Similarly, a radio station competes with both newspapers and television stations for advertising.

Probably the most active area of competition among entrepreneurs is that of price, for they engage in a ceaseless attempt to gain a price advantage over their competitors through effecting lower costs or increasing the efficiency of management.

Competition among entrepreneurs usually benefits consumers in several ways. It leads to better service, for example. In an attempt to gain a service advantage over a competitor, a business owner may air-condition his place of business, extend credit to his customers, deliver merchandise to their homes. Competition also leads to better products for the consumer and tends to eliminate inefficient entrepreneurs. The businessman who cannot meet the competition—who fails to provide better service or to produce a better product or a cheaper one—soon goes out of business.

Freedom of Choice and Contract

Freedom of choice is the right of every person in a free-enterprise society. Each of us is free to decide whether to become an entrepreneur or to work for someone else. We have the privilege of choosing whether to manufacture goods ourselves or to distribute goods that others have produced. We can choose the type of goods we will produce or sell, and we can make our own decisions regarding our place of residence and employment.

We also enjoy freedom of choice as consumers in a private-enterprise system. We have the right to decide whether to buy, where and when and how much to buy, and whether the product or service is worth the price being asked.

Another privilege enjoyed by members of a free society is *freedom of contract,* which is simply the right of every entrepreneur, worker, property owner, and consumer to bargain with another. This freedom includes the right to exchange goods and services on terms that are acceptable to all parties concerned.

Discussion Questions

7. *Some persons hold that the "right to own property" is the keystone in the foundation of capitalism. Do you agree or disagree? Explain.*
8. *What are the economic freedoms that we enjoy in this country?*

APPRAISING
OUR ECONOMIC ACHIEVEMENTS

How would you set about determining whether an economic system had done well or poorly? This is usually measured in terms of production growth and the equity with which the fruits of production are shared by the people of the nation. Let us examine America's economic system—capitalism—to see how well it has fulfilled these two objectives.

Our Economic Growth

There are several measures of economic growth, but the one most commonly used is the gross national product.

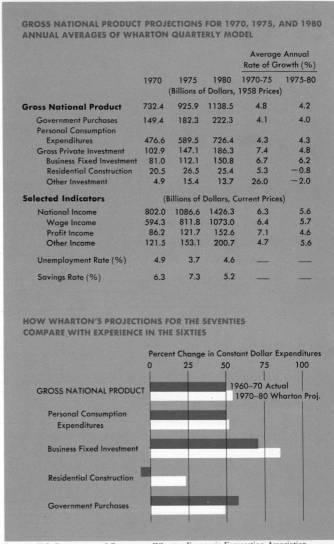

GROSS NATIONAL PRODUCT PROJECTIONS FOR 1970, 1975, AND 1980 ANNUAL AVERAGES OF WHARTON QUARTERLY MODEL

	1970	1975	1980	Average Annual Rate of Growth (%) 1970-75	1975-80
	(Billions of Dollars, 1958 Prices)				
Gross National Product	732.4	925.9	1138.5	4.8	4.2
Government Purchases	149.4	182.3	222.3	4.1	4.0
Personal Consumption Expenditures	476.6	589.5	726.4	4.3	4.3
Gross Private Investment	102.9	147.1	186.3	7.4	4.8
Business Fixed Investment	81.0	112.1	150.8	6.7	6.2
Residential Construction	20.5	26.5	25.4	5.3	−0.8
Other Investment	4.9	15.4	13.7	26.0	−2.0
Selected Indicators	(Billions of Dollars, Current Prices)				
National Income	802.0	1086.6	1426.3	6.3	5.6
Wage Income	594.3	811.8	1073.0	6.4	5.7
Profit Income	86.2	121.7	152.6	7.1	4.6
Other Income	121.5	153.1	200.7	4.7	5.6
Unemployment Rate (%)	4.9	3.7	4.6	—	—
Savings Rate (%)	6.3	7.3	5.2	—	—

HOW WHARTON'S PROJECTIONS FOR THE SEVENTIES COMPARE WITH EXPERIENCE IN THE SIXTIES

Percent Change in Constant Dollar Expenditures

0   25   50   75   100

GROSS NATIONAL PRODUCT
1960–70 Actual
1970–80 Wharton Proj.

Personal Consumption Expenditures

Business Fixed Investment

Residential Construction

Government Purchases

Sources: U.S. Department of Commerce; Wharton Economic Forecasting Association

The Gross National Product. By gross national product (GNP), we mean the total market value of all the finished goods produced and the services rendered in the economy in one year. In a way, this serves as an index of the degree to which our output is growing (measured in terms of market value). It is the most comprehensive measure we have of what we produce. The GNP increased from $504 billion in 1960 to $785 billion in 1967, and we achieved a trillion-dollar economy (our GNP passed the trillion-dollar mark) in 1971.

Important

Test

Our economic growth is generally considered to be good. Sometimes we read that the growth rate in such countries as Japan is much greater than that in the United States. When interpreting comparative growth rates, however, we must take into consideration the age span of a country's industrial development. Growth rates are greatest during the early years of industrial expansion. As a nation's industrial development matures, it is harder to attain the same rate of growth as was achieved in the infancy period of development. The general trend of our economic development is shown by the Forbes business index illustrated below.

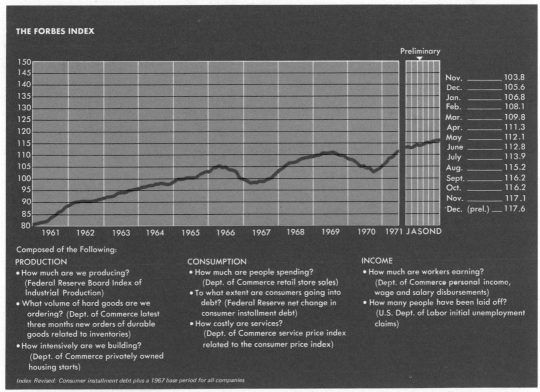

THE FORBES INDEX

Preliminary

Nov.	103.8
Dec.	105.6
Jan.	106.8
Feb.	108.1
Mar.	109.8
Apr.	111.3
May	112.1
June	112.8
July	113.9
Aug.	115.2
Sept.	116.2
Oct.	116.2
Nov.	117.1
Dec. (prel.)	117.6

1961 1962 1963 1964 1965 1966 1967 1968 1969 1970 1971 J A S O N D

Composed of the Following:

PRODUCTION
• How much are we producing? (Federal Reserve Board Index of Industrial Production)
• What volume of hard goods are we ordering? (Dept. of Commerce latest three months new orders of durable goods related to inventories)
• How intensively are we building? (Dept. of Commerce privately owned housing starts)

CONSUMPTION
• How much are people spending? (Dept. of Commerce retail store sales)
• To what extent are consumers going into debt? (Federal Reserve net change in consumer installment debt)
• How costly are services? (Dept. of Commerce service price index related to the consumer price index)

INCOME
• How much are workers earning? (Dept. of Commerce personal income, wage and salary disbursements)
• How many people have been laid off? (U.S. Dept. of Labor initial unemployment claims)

Index Revised: Consumer installment debt plus a 1967 base period for all companies

Source: *Forbes Magazine,* February 1, 1972

Investment in Plant and Equipment. The economist uses the term *capital* to refer to industry's productive equipment. By reinvesting profits in new plants and equipment, we increase the amount invested in these business assets, which are essential to all basic manufacturing operations. Continuous capital improvements and expansion are essential to increased industrial production. The amount of capital expenditures is one of the most closely watched economic indicators. It varies directly in relation to the national economic trend—that is, spending by industry of large sums for capital improvements and expansion is considered an index of a favorable economic climate. When capital expenditures are curtailed, the economy lags. Fortunately, the recent history of American industry has been one of rapidly expanding capital investment. This, of course, means increased capacity to produce.

Private spending for capital goods more than doubled from 1961 to 1969—a rise from $47 billion a year to $99.3 billion, as shown on the accompanying chart. When this is discounted because of inflation, it represents a rise of 78 percent, or $7\frac{1}{2}$ percent increase per year. The repeal of the 7 percent investment tax credit in 1969 had a dampening effect on capital spending, so that the total amount spent in 1970 and 1971 (in constant dollars) was less than for the year 1969. Capital spending in the United States has averaged close to 10 percent of gross national product; in no year has it been less than 9 percent or more than 11 percent. See the chart on the page opposite.

Productivity. *Productivity means output achieved in relation to input*—the amount of materials and labor consumed to produce goods and services. Increased output makes for higher wages, shorter hours, lower prices, and a greater return to the business owner. There are two ways of measuring productivity: by means of the average hourly output per worker, and in terms of national income per man-hour (one man times one hour equals one man-hour).

The average worker today produces approximately six times as much as the average worker produced 100 years ago. This ratio is based on dollar value in terms of constant (not fluctuating) purchasing power.

One of the important results of increased expenditures for plants, equipment, and research is a greater output per man-hour of labor. Output per man-hour has advanced during the last three decades at a rate of approximately 3.1 percent per year.

Personal Income

The *total national income* differs from the GNP in that it represents the amount left after subtracting the costs of maintaining the nation's productive capacity. *National personal income* represents the total earnings of all the people in the form of wages or salaries, profits, interest, dividends, and royalties. This amount has continually increased from year to year. The growth in national

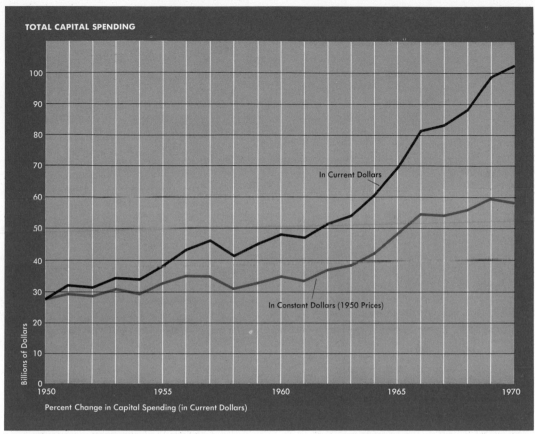

TOTAL CAPITAL SPENDING

In Current Dollars

In Constant Dollars (1950 Prices)

Billions of Dollars

Percent Change in Capital Spending (in Current Dollars)

Source: Maurice Berson for *Fortune Magazine,* June, 1971

income in recent years, as well as the different components that make up personal income, is shown in Table 1.1, page 21.

But any increase in the size of the employed working force would result in a corresponding increase in their total earnings. What is most important is the degree to which the income per worker has been increased.

Growth in Per Capita Income. *Per capita income* is an average figure computed by dividing the total national income by the total population. *Real income* is income that has been adjusted to account for fluctuations in prices and in the buying power of the dollar. Our *real per capita* income has increased during the past century at a rate varying between 2 and 3 percent per year.

Distribution of Income. Average family income rose to $10,001 in 1970. It has risen approximately 7 percent per year on the average for the last ten years. We can calculate the average income per person, but how many

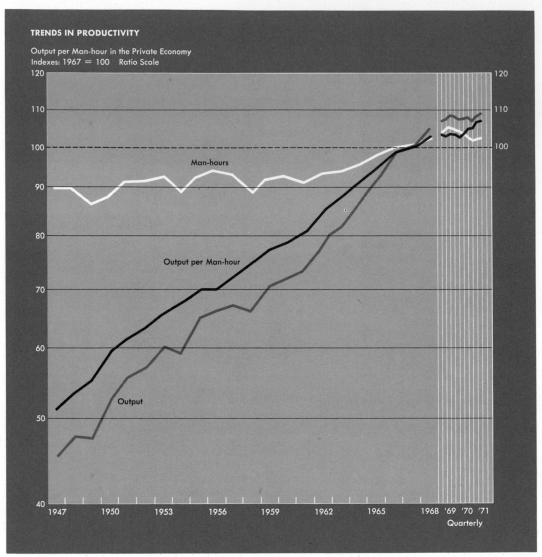

TRENDS IN PRODUCTIVITY

Output per Man-hour in the Private Economy
Indexes: 1967 = 100   Ratio Scale

Man-hours

Output per Man-hour

Output

1947   1950   1953   1956   1959   1962   1965   1968 '69 '70 '71
Quarterly

Source: The National Industrial Conference Board, No. 1675, October 1, 1971

persons receive this average figure? How is the national income distributed; how is it shared by the population as a whole? There has been a significant shifting of more and more persons into the middle-income brackets—people who are earning enough to buy more than the basic essentials of life. With few exceptions, income per customer unit in terms of real purchasing power has increased steadily for the last thirty years.

Upward Shift in Distribution of Income. As the average annual family income increases, the number of families whose income places them in the

TABLE
1.1
SOURCES OF PERSONAL INCOME, 1960–1970

In billions of dollars

Averages	Wages, Salaries, and Related Income*	+	Pro- prietors' Income	+	Income from Rent, Interest, and Dividends	+	Income from Transfer Payments**	−	Personal Contributions for Social Insurance	=	Personal Income
1951–1955	198.4	+	41.2	+	33.5	+	14.5	−	4.2	=	283.4
1956–1960	257.3		45.2		46.6		24.1		7.3		366.0
1961–1965	331.0		51.8		65.5		35.5		11.5		472.3
1966–1970	491.5		64.4		98.6		59.5		23.0		691 0
Annual											
1960	282.8		46.2		52.7		28.6		9.3		401.0
1965	377.6		57.3		77.5		39.9		13.4		538.9
1966	415.2		61.3		84.4		44.1		17.8		587.2
1967	445.4		62.1		90.5		51.8		20.5		629.3
1968	489.7		64.1		98.6		59.1		22.8		688.7
1969	536.6		66.8		106.4		65.1		26.0		748.9
1970ᵖ	570.5		67.6		113.1		77.6		27.8		801.0

Source: U.S. Department of Commerce.
Note: Parts may not add to totals due to rounding.
ᵖ Preliminary.
* Related income, which is called "other labor income" by the Department of Commerce, includes compensation for injuries, employer contributions under private pension and related programs, and other items, such as the pay of military reservists and directors' fees.
** Transfer payments include benefit payments made under government (federal, state and local) social security, unemployment and veterans' programs, and miscellaneous payments by business.

lower income brackets decreases. Accompanying this shift there is a marked increase in the number whose income places them in the upper brackets.

The effect of these changes can be seen in the two graphs on the accompanying page, which show the percentage of family units in the different income categories in 1968. The largest concentration of units is found in the $10,000-and-over income class, which contains approximately 42 percent of all consumer units.

Stability. The history of economic development has always been characterized by cyclical periods of change. The four phases of cyclical behavior are prosperity, decline, recession, and recovery. The smaller the span between the high and low points of the cycle, the better the economic system. The recent history of the United States has been generally one of prosperity punctuated periodically with minor recessions or adjustments.

Discussion Question

9. *What, in your opinion, is the best single index when judging the success of a nation's economic system?*

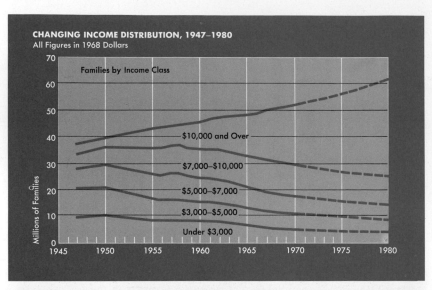

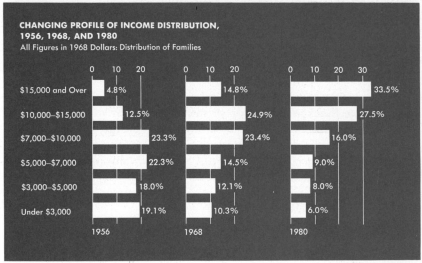

Source: The National Industrial Conference Board, *1971 Financial Facts Yearbook*

THE CHANGING FUNCTIONS
OF AMERICAN BUSINESS

Business in America has never been static—each generation has witnessed rapid strides forward. The last generation saw the large corporation become the dominant force in American capitalism. Today we are seeing several transformations occurring simultaneously—the exceedingly strong influence of organized labor, the decentralization and diversification of business operations, the separation of ownership and control, and the increasing recognition of the social responsibility of big business.

The Extent of Corporate Bigness

There are various ways of comparing large and small business—the number of enterprises, the gross value of assets, the number of persons employed, and the amount of sales, gross income, or net income.

Our immediate concern has to do with the degree to which corporate bigness sets the tone for the private-investment sector of the national economy. There are about the same number of partnerships as corporations, and proprietorships outnumber corporations by more than nine to one. Yet the total profits before taxes for all corporate business in the United States is almost twice as much as that for all nonincorporated businesses (proprietorships and partnerships combined).[2] Corporations employ almost as many people as the rest of the economy combined, including federal, state, and local governments.

We are living in not only a corporate society, but a society of large corporations. It is the activities of the corporate giants in industry that we watch with the greatest concern and interest. To bear out this contention, one has only to observe the news featured in the business section of such periodicals as *Business Week* or *Time*. Most of the space and stories are devoted to big business—mergers of already huge corporations, labor negotiations in the giant industries such as steel or automotive, changes in the executive officers of the major corporations, fluctuations on the stock markets. Only infrequently is some unique accomplishment of an individual proprietor given recognition.

The problems of an economy dominated by large corporations differ in type and magnitude from those of an economy made up predominantly of small business enterprises. At this point, we are merely noting that the pattern of business in the United States is being set by large corporations. The details of the corporate form of organization, and its operational structure, are discussed in later chapters.

The Growing Influence of Organized Labor

The history of organized labor in the United States is a record of the increasing importance of labor's role in determining economic policy. Labor unions, with their 20 million members, constitute a tremendous influence in both business and politics. Like many industries, they maintain effective lobbies in both houses of Congress, indorse candidates for public office, and contribute liberally to the treasuries of their favorite political parties. They have funds

[2]The U.S. Treasury Department has estimated the number of businesses in 1967 to be 9.2 million proprietorships, 918,000 partnerships, and 1.5 million corporations. Source: *Statistical Abstract of the U.S.,* 1971, p 459.

available to support hundreds of thousands of their members during prolonged strikes—strikes that, at least in the transportation, automotive, steel, or coal industries, attract widespread public attention and create interest on a national scale.

The internal government of some of our largest unions has on a number of recent occasions been the subject of court action. The question of anti-monopoly labor legislation is continually being raised. The degree to which labor should share in profits has not yet been settled. Whether labor should be guaranteed a minimum number of weeks of work or given an annual wage is still being debated at important collective-bargaining sessions.

Like large corporate businesses, large, powerful labor unions give rise to large and important economic problems that are difficult to solve. Whether they will be solved during the present generation remains to be seen.

Decentralization and Diversification

Businesses that *decentralize* are businesses that locate their factories and offices in different places instead of concentrating them at one site. The modern trend is to decentralize, because adjacent properties and buildings are generally too expensive, particularly when a business's headquarters are located in a big city. Also, in the case of a serious riot or a bombing attack, an entire business might be wiped out if it is concentrated in one place.

Businesses that *diversify* are those that launch out into new areas of manufacturing or service. Companies that once made only radios have found it economically wise to manufacture washers, dryers, and refrigerators as well. They have done this either by creating and producing their own new lines of goods and building new facilities, or by buying out manufacturers of the goods in which they are interested.

Often a healthy business will buy out one that is suffering losses, in order to acquire its line of products. In the bargain, the surplus funds of the healthy business aid the weak one, and the latter's losses provide a tax credit for the former.

Separation of Ownership and Control

The owner-entrepreneur of the small-business, proprietorship-partnership era has yielded, as has already been noted, to the corporation. Since anyone may buy shares in a corporation, the ownership of today's business is widely held. For example, there are more than 3 million persons who own stock in American Telephone and Telegraph but the management of financial assets and the determination of sales policy fare best when they are entrusted to experts. Thus the corporate form of business organization has led to the separation of ownership and control in our American business enterprises. Not only is this true, but today the leading investors in stocks are the trustees of pension funds, mutual funds, investment banks, and insurance companies. These groups vote on behalf of their stockholders; thus, even the right to vote has been transferred from the real owners to these investing groups.

This separation of ownership from control has given impetus to the growth of what might be called *professional management.* Professional managers are specialists who are employed to operate and manage business enterprises. The idea men who develop the operational plans and procedures for getting jobs done make up what is termed *middle management.* Those who make policy decisions and supply the executive leadership to business organizations constitute the highest level of professional management. We shall look more fully at the types, organizational structures, and functioning of management in later chapters.

The Social Responsibility of Big Business

The making of a profit has always been considered legitimate, for a business institution's very existence depends on its making a profit. Likewise, the idea of service is an accepted function of business. A business makes a profit for itself by rendering a service for others. In addition, a business is supposed to serve society *well*—that is, it should provide well-paid jobs for its employees, and yield a profit to its owners commensurate with the risks involved.

All this worked fairly well, with no serious problems, under the owner-entrepreneur business system. But under the corporate form of business organization—especially large corporations—the best interests of all facets of society are sometimes difficult to serve. A firm's economic responsibility may come in conflict with its social responsibility. This situation is perhaps best illustrated by the dependence of a local community on a single large corporation located there. Should the management decide that survival necessitates a move to a new community where tax or labor advantages exist, serious problems will arise for the community. Many residents, perhaps a good number of whom own stock in the firm, will lose their jobs, and the tax loss will seriously affect the community's economy. Persons who have deep roots in the community will have to move to a new community—perhaps even a new state—if they choose to remain with the firm.

The company responsibility for maintaining a healthy environment has come to the fore in recent years. Industrial firms must include, in their planning and their budgets, measures aimed at pollution prevention and control. Business management must observe federal, state, and local regulations, as well as the public pressure from citizens. Pollution abatement has become perhaps business's foremost concern in the area of social responsibility. All this points up the complexity of the social responsibility of a corporate economic society and reflects the changing nature of American business in today's economy.

It has given rise to new and unsolved problems in our kaleidoscopic society—problems in which ownership, labor, and government all have tremendous stakes.

Multinational Character

more than one nation

There is hardly such a thing today as an "American business enterprise" among our leading corporations, if by that we mean one that does business only in the United States. In fact, most American corporations' foreign sales are growing at a much faster rate than their domestic sales. The General Motors Corporation, which is known largely for its sale of American-made cars in America, reported that during 1970, its overseas operations accounted for 14 percent of its total sales. Standard Oil Company of California, in its 1970 Annual Report, shows that only one-fourth of its oil production is from the United States; about 70 percent is from the Eastern Hemisphere; and slightly over 40 percent of its sales of petroleum products are in the Eastern Hemisphere. The Continental Oil Company reported that during 1970, U.S. sources contributed $99.2 million to company income out of a total income from petroleum sales of $149.6 million.

During the five-year period from 1966 through 1970, American investments abroad increased by 35 percent, while foreign investments in the United States increased 55 percent. Direct American investments in Great Britain and continental Europe in 1969 totaled $19.4 billion. Meanwhile, British and European investments in the United States were $8.5 billion. According to U.S. Department of Commerce figures, investments of U.S. companies abroad totaled $77.4 in 1970. Total sales in Western Europe made by overseas subsidiaries of American firms in 1968 amounted to $25.8 billion.

Some of the best-known major European-based corporations doing business in the United States include the Dutch Shell Petroleum Company, the Phillips Company (electrical appliances, including Norelco shavers), the Anglo-Dutch Unilever Company (which owns Lever Brothers), the Swiss Nestlé Company, and the British Beecham Company (maker of Brylcreem and MaClean's toothpaste). Some of the well-known Japanese firms are Honda Motors, Matsushita Electric, Toyota, and Nissan. Foreign and American corporations are interrelated through joint ownership of other corporations.

So we see that American industry is continually expanding its investment and business interests outside the continental United States, while capital from other countries is being invested in businesses in this country. The pace of this trend toward corporations becoming multinational is quickening.

The Increased Role of Government

Government has always had a stake in American business. Governments are supported by taxes, and large amounts of taxes are paid by businesses.

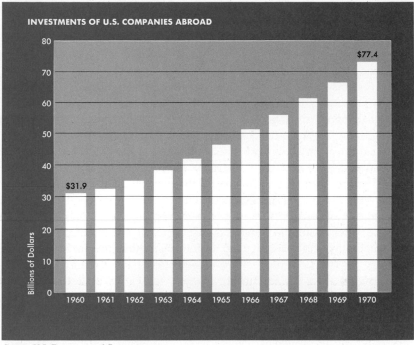

INVESTMENTS OF U.S. COMPANIES ABROAD

Source: U.S. Department of Commerce

Businesses pay taxes on the property they own and on the profits they earn. In the financial sense, then, whatever is good for business is good for the government.

The U.S. government has never taken a *laissez-faire* (let alone) attitude toward business, although in the early years of our country its influence upon the economic system might have been appropriately described by the phrase, "the working of the invisible hand of government." Then, as the economy grew and businesses became large and complex, the activity of the federal government in the affairs of business increased. At first the government exercised largely the functions of supervision, inspection, and minor regulation, but with the passing of the years, its regulatory aspects were intensified. In recent years, its influence in some instances might be described by the word "control."

Perhaps one of the most notable instances of government interference in business in recent history occurred in April 1962. President Kennedy became quite concerned over certain price increases that had been instituted by the steel industry and the possible inflationary effect these increases might have on the economy. He immediately sent a message to the presidents of twelve major steel companies, asking them not to raise the price of steel. He threatened to withdraw from the market any government purchases of steel from those companies that raised their prices. The result was that impending price increases were cancelled, and those that had already been put into effect were rolled back to their previous levels. Since that date there have been frequent occurrences of price regulation and rollbacks. President Johnson caused the aluminum industry to roll back its price increases during the spring of 1966. Again in January 1971, President Nixon "jawboned" the steel industry into a rollback on announced price increases on steel products.

It seems to have become standard policy for the federal government to use its powers to encourage capital spending when it has felt business has needed to be spurred, and to discourage it when the economy has appeared to be expanding too rapidly. During the fall of 1966, the rules regarding depreciation allowances and write-offs were tightened in an effort to curtail plant expansion and cool off the apparent overheated boom in the economy. Then in January 1971, President Nixon reversed this policy by liberalizing allowable depreciation rates on new construction, in order to encourage capital spending to stimulate business and the economy.

In 1969, Congress passed sweeping revisions in the Tax Code. One of the chief purposes was to plug loopholes in the law that permitted many wealthy persons to avoid paying income taxes. Another was to broaden the tax base. Among the important changes was a reduction in the depletion allowance on crude oil and gas recovery from $27\frac{1}{2}$ percent to 22 percent. This change was of tremendous significance to the oil and gas industries, because it increased their expenses and reduced profits. At the same time that Congress was debating these tax changes, the special panel that had been appointed by President Nixon to make recommendations regarding import quotas on petroleum products was in the midst of its deliberations. The uncertainties associated with what their recommendations might be, together with the question of how severe the change in the depletion allowance would be, added to the woes of the petroleum industry during this period. It was almost impossible for management in this essential industry to plan for the future using normal extrapolation procedures.

Under President Johnson, wage negotiation teams were called to Washington on numerous occasions to carry on their dealings under the close scrutiny of the administrative branch of the federal government. Guidelines for wage and price increases have become commonplace, and prices are no longer determined strictly through competitive bidding in the marketplace. It may very well be that this increased role of the government in business represents one of the most significant changes on the American business scene today.

The most recent example of government interference in business is the 90-day price and wage freeze imposed by President Nixon effective August 15, 1971. This 90-day period was followed on November 15 by Phase II of the program which was labeled by some as a "controlled thaw." Under this program a Pay Board was appointed to regulate wage raises. (This board had fifteen members—five representing the public, five representing business, and five representing labor.) There was also a Price Commission to regulate and control price and rent increases.

The primary objective of the Pay Board and the Price Commission was to bring inflation under control. Both had to work within guidelines and directions from the President's Cost of Living Council. Under the directive from the Cost of Living Council companies whose annual sales exceed $100 million must receive advance approval before raising prices. All wage and fringe benefit settlements affecting more than 5,000 employees must have prior approval of the Pay Board. (Some 1,300 companies, accounting for almost half of all sales in this country, were included in this group to receive close surveillance.)

This whole action represents a definite shift away from the "free market system" discussed earlier in this chapter and toward a "planned economy." Of course, it was anticipated that this would be a temporary measure and that the need for such severe controls would not be prolonged.

Discussion Questions

10. *How far can we go in holding big businesses responsible in the social and economic life of any particular community?*

11. *Why has the government increased its activity in the affairs of private business?*

THE NEW ECONOMICS

We have just seen some of the ways that the role of the federal government in the business affairs of the nation has taken on special significance in recent years. One of the foremost advocates of the increased role of government in business was John Maynard Keynes. Lord Keynes, writing in the 1930's, was one of the first to show that government has not only the ability but also the responsibility to exercise its influence to increase a nation's production, employment, and income. He held that this could be accomplished without destroying the basic freedoms of private enterprise or restricting competition, arguing that the government can go a long way toward maintaining continuing prosperity through tax increases and reductions, the easing and tightening of credit, and the exercising of restraint in budgetary matters. His idea was to use these activities on the part of government to supplement those of the private sector of the economy, particularly in the areas of capital and consumer spending, investment, and production. He argued that the government should furnish the incentive, but that private businesses and consumers should decide whether to spend, and when, where, and for what to spend.

Classical Economic Theory

Keynesian economic theory differed radically in its basic concepts from theories of earlier economists. Prior to Keynes, the leading economists presumed that the economy was held in balance by certain natural forces that counterbalanced one another. The French economist Jean Baptist Say, for example, advanced the theory that a nation's production facilities would just naturally create enough income to purchase the goods manufactured. He argued that any excess in demand would correct itself automatically. And Adam Smith argued that if wages rose too rapidly, business would dismiss workers to cut down on labor costs, and that this reduction would continue until a point was reached where business would again hire more workers.

The New Theory

Keynes showed that economic history did not bear out these theories, but actually refuted them. He pointed out that for many years the economic cycle had fluctuated from boom to bust, and that prosperity based on inflation had invariably led to deflation, recession, and depression. Keynes reasoned that if employers reacted to decreased demand by laying off workers and/or reducing wages, the end result could only be less income to buy fewer goods, thus decreasing demand and curtailing production. He advocated that "the remedy for the trade cycle is not to be found in abolishing booms and keeping us permanently in semi-slump; but in abolishing slumps and thus keeping us permanently in a quasi-boom." His formula for bringing this about was to maintain a constant high level of total demand—demand for investment, as well as for consumption. His plan called for the government to come to the aid of the private sector of the economy whenever that sector fell off.

The key elements in the Keynesian theory are:

1. If left to make its own adjustments in wages and prices, a market economy might come into balance, but it would not necessarily balance out at the full-employment level.
2. The level of employment essentially depends on the amount of income that business and consumers combined spend for goods.
3. If consumers withhold money from spending, and if at the same time industry curtails capital-expansion investment, the economy may settle into a low-employment level.
4. To correct low economic levels, government must increase the purchasing power in the money system. It might do this by loosening credit, by decreasing taxes, or by increasing its own spending.

Keynes stated that the economy should be evaluated in its totality, not piecemeal; that all the many forces at work in the total economic structure—production, prices, income, profits, interest, and so on—should be measured and considered as a whole. He looked upon money as a means to an end, not as the end itself; money was to be used to achieve economic objectives, rather than being treated as a valuable possession.

The economists who have advised our presidents since the establishment of the Council of Economic Advisers by Congress in 1946 have for the most part been followers of Keynesian economic theory. The economic policies of our federal government during the past decades have frequently been referred to as "the new economics."

SUMMARY

Economics is concerned with the utilization of a country's resources in meeting man's wants. Because natural resources are scarce and man's wants seem to have no limits, the wise management and conservation of these resources constitutes one of our basic problems. Deciding how to organize to use these resources leads the people of every country to develop some type of an economic system, and choice making becomes important in formulating such a system. Both individual and collective goals must be considered, and sometimes they are in conflict with one another.

In the United States, the basic decision-making process rests with the people. The economic system they developed is called capitalism. It is essentially a private-enterprise economy, resting squarely on the individual's right to private ownership of property. Other basic tenets of capitalism are profit motivation, competition, and freedom of choice and contract. Together these factors form a basis for the political and social freedoms we enjoy in this country.

The heart of a private-enterprise economy is its system of free markets. This means that goods and services are exchanged in the open market through competitive bidding. Supply and demand are kept in balance through the system of pricing; when the price becomes too high, persons refuse to buy goods, thus signaling a reduction in the supply. Decision making in buying, called "voting in the marketplace," is the means by which each person plays a significant role in helping to decide how a nation's resources are to be used.

How well any economic system functions must be assessed in relation to several factors. Increased production alone is not a reliable index, for it does not take into consideration the increase in population. To measure the efficiency of an economic system, output must be measured in relation to input; this is called productivity. Another criterion of a system's success is equitability in distributing the fruits of production—how widely and to what degree the masses of workers share in the goods produced. The free-enterprise economic system ranks high, since the people in capitalistic nations enjoy the highest standards of living found anywhere in the world.

The basic functions of the American economy have undergone some significant changes, resulting in corporate bigness and dominance, increased influence of organized labor, decentralization and diversification of industry, absentee ownership, and growing social responsibility of big business. People everywhere are insisting that industry cease polluting the air, water, and land. Other important changes are the internationalizing of American business at an ever-increasing rate.

Economic theories have changed in recent years, giving emphasis to a greater role of government in business. The father of this new economic theory was John Maynard Keynes. Today, most of the leading public and private economists follow the theories advanced so forcefully by Lord Keynes.

VOCABULARY REVIEW

Match the following vocabulary terms with the statements that follow.

a. Capitalism   f. Economics   j. Market
b. Competition   g. Entrepreneur   k. Personal income
c. Consumption   h. Free market   l. Productivity
d. Decentralization i. Gross national product   m. Real income
e. Diversification

1. The study of the manner in which the people of a nation use their resources to satisfy their wants
2. The using of goods and services to meet people's needs
3. A place where buyers and sellers exchange goods
4. The buying and selling of products through competitive bidding
5. The term generally used to refer to a free-enterprise economic system
6. A person who risks his capital by investing in a business in the hope of earning a profit
7. An attempt to secure something that is also being sought by others
8. The total value of all the goods and services produced in a nation during a one-year period
9. The output of goods achieved in relation to the amount of labor and materials required to produce them
10. The earnings of people, counting wages, interest, dividends, and royalties
11. The amount of a person's income, stated in terms of what goods and services it will buy
12. The scattering of a firm's buildings in a variety of geographical areas
13. The broadening of the scope of a company's operations by producing several different lines of goods

PROBLEMS AND PROJECTS

1. Name two types of business that depend heavily on natural resources, two where labor plays the most important role, and two that depend in some special way on capital.
2. How would you assess your local community (county) as to the adequacy of raw materials, labor, capital, and technology?
3. Assume that you are to assess the current trend in the American economy. Name six factors that you consider important in indicating this trend. (Example: rate of unemployment)
4. Take a sounding on the present trend of the nation's economy, using the six factors named in Problem 3, and state what you consider to be the current state of the economy.
5. What types of businesses appear to you to be less susceptible to cyclical fluctuations than others?
6. How would you describe a capitalistic economic system?

A BUSINESS CASE

Case 1-1   Responsibility for Clean Water

An article that appeared in the August–September 1969 issue of *Natural History* includes the following paragraph:

> Take the case of the pollution of Lake Erie. The runoff of phosphate fertilizers from hundreds of Ohio farms has had a significant role in the pollution of the lake. The phosphates (and nitrates) became nutrients for a fantastic growth of algae in the lake—accelerating the natural process called eutrophication. The western basin of Lake Erie is covered, during the summer, with an 800-square-mile mass of algae, two feet thick. This tremendous algae growth, in turn, removes much of the oxygen from the water, which makes life impossible for the more desirable forms of life (game, fish, etc.), and also makes swimming a messy and risky business. As a result, the value of Lake Erie as a recreational resource has declined tragically.

In addition to the poisons from soil erosion, the lake is being polluted by wastes from industrial plants and sewage disposal from the large municipalities that border on it.

What do you see as the solution to this problem? Here are some starters—react to these and suggest others.

1. The Maumee River dumps about three tons of silt per minute into Lake Erie at Toledo. Would you forbid the use of fertilizers on the farms in the area surrounding the lake? Would you require the farm owners bordering on the rivers that empty into the lake to build a waterway, terraces, and settling basins to trap the soil being lost into the rivers?

2. The Bethlehem Steel Corporation recently spent $23 million to control its pollution of Lake Erie at its Lackawanna plant near Buffalo. What is the extent of social responsibility on the part of big business here? Is it reasonable to ask industry to spend this sum to keep the lake water clean? Should all manufacturing plants dumping industrial waste into the lake be required to stop polluting or close their factories?

3. Cities that border on Lake Erie, such as Cleveland and Toledo, pollute the lake through their sewage-disposal plants. They have been warned by state and federal agencies to stop polluting the lake. It would cost their cities hundreds of millions of taxpayer dollars to comply with the clean-environment regulations imposed upon them. Therefore, the appropriate city officials have not taken adequate steps to stop pollution of Lake Erie and have blamed red tape and agencies other than themselves for the delays. How far should state and federal government authorities go in enforcing standards? How far should the federal government go in supplying funds to help bring about compliance on the part of the city agencies?

4. The citizens and businesses of the cities create the waste-disposal problem. They are also the ones who profit from the clean water in the lake. Can you justify assessing whatever tax revenue is needed to solve their part of the problem?

social responsibilities of business to our environment

CHAPTER TWO

In a message to Congress, President Nixon made a special plea to restore harmony between man and his environment. For too long, man has watched his environment deteriorate. Although he has made great strides in providing new and improved material benefits, an occupation that has required most of his time, he has simultaneously become his own enemy by polluting his environment. What has happened is in part the fault of business, for putting too much emphasis on the profit motive and too little on human-welfare values. Now people are asking whether the American environment may not be on the brink of a catastrophe.

According to Alvin Toffler, "Pesticides and herbicides filter into our foods. Twisted automobile carcasses, aluminum cans, nonreturnable bottles and synthetic plastic form immense kitchen middens in our midst as more and more of our detritus resists decay."[1]

[1] Alvin Toffler, *Future Shock* (New York: Random House, Inc., 1970), p. 380.

On land and at sea, the existence of living organisms is threatened. Our urban centers are overpopulated, thereby threatening to consume food and oxygen faster than they can be replaced. Our lakes and streams are becoming contaminated, and as a result the ecology of water life is being destroyed by foreign substances. Pollution is becoming a global problem; the longer this condition exists, the greater the losses will be.

Billions of dollars, it is estimated, will be needed to clean up the environment in this country. Although funds are beginning to flow from government and private business, critics charge that progress is still too slow. Our purpose here is to help you obtain an understanding of the nature of the problem and the methods being employed to solve it.

MEANING OF MAN'S ENVIRONMENT

Man is a product of his environment. In nations with advanced technology, such as the United States, it is not easy to understand how much environment relates to man's existence. To comprehend fully the meaning of the business environment, one must look not only at business itself, but also at the total environment within which business operates.

We have become accustomed to such an abundance of material goods that we have taken for granted that they would continue without interruption. But we have failed until recently to take cognizance of the fact that our natural resources are deteriorating at an alarming rate. As a nation, we have put great stress on the need for a high rate of economic growth, yet as we build more factories, we increase the contamination of our air and water. Once our water and air were clean and free; now they are either polluted or scarce. At stake in our struggle for conservation of our environment are those values that give us a quality of life many other nations still do not have.

We are also concerned about what is happening to our business environment, because we live in a business-oriented society. Moreover, besides being the main user of our natural resources, business is a dominant force in our social system. Business is the source of most of our goods and services, the employer of most of the population, and the originator of many of our pollutants.

The dictionary defines *environment* as the total of all the external forces affecting living organisms. This means that environment is composed of the natural resources and man's cultural modifications of them. On the other hand, *business environment* relates to the total of all things external to enterprises and industries that affect their organization and operation. The term *society* refers to the social system, composed of interacting groups whose members have cultural patterns, mores, and goals. Since the business firm is part of society, it is natural that society should be interested in the welfare of business and that business should be interested in the welfare of society.

Business in a Pluralistic Society

During the early history of its development, business was conducted in a very simple manner. Business firms were small, and the total economic environment of business provided the livelihood for a small population. The family was the central group around which most activities were planned. Even the role of government was minimal, and the sole proprietorship was the predominant form of business ownership. Trade between nations was small.

The business firm is the focal point today for the many environmental forces that come to bear on business in general. Business is complex, competitive, and comprehensive, with many diverse groups attempting to influence businessmen in their decisions. This total involvement of business within the community is referred to as *community relations,* an all-inclusive term in which "good relations" with all parties in the community is the goal.

Today's Pluralistic Society. The unique development of modern business is its affiliation with a pluralistic society. The accompanying diagram depicts the wide variety of organizations that comprise pluralism in our society. In this society there are many power centers, each with some degree of automony, but none entirely independent. This means that business is a joint venture with many of these organizations. With this relationship goes a sense of business responsibility for community values, general welfare, and general integrity.

Many people criticize the "establishment" because, among other reasons, they feel that it has produced great wealth for a few while allowing poverty to exist on a large scale. It is a fact that too many people in this country still go to bed hungry or do not have an adequate diet. Some corporate directors and managers have been more interested in achieving the profit objective at any price than in helping to make a community a better place to live. This has caused broad areas of conflict that raise the following questions:

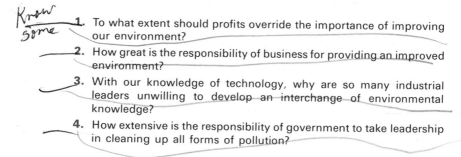

1. To what extent should profits override the importance of improving our environment?
2. How great is the responsibility of business for providing an improved environment?
3. With our knowledge of technology, why are so many industrial leaders unwilling to develop an interchange of environmental knowledge?
4. How extensive is the responsibility of government to take leadership in cleaning up all forms of pollution?

Young people are among those who seek answers to these questions. They reflect a pervasive attitude that questions whether our social order is in proper balance. They see great affluence on the one hand and a deteriorating environment on the other—a condition they regard as illogical.

BUSINESS AS PART OF A PLURALISTIC SOCIETY

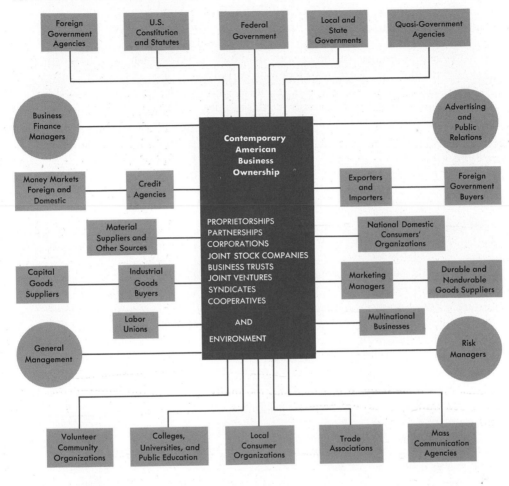

Discussion Questions

1. *In a pluralistic society, what relation does business have to other sectors of society?*
2. *How do you explain the reluctance of certain segments of society to accept their responsibility for improving the quality of life?*

POLLUTION:
AN ENVIRONMENTAL PROBLEM

There is now widespread agreement that massive efforts must be exercised to improve our environment. Clean air is essential. Our water supply has been impaired by industrial pollution, by inadequate sewage treatment, and even by insecticide poison runoffs. The public has become increasingly aware of what is happening to the air and water so essential to its existence and of the problem of dealing with trash, garbage, and abandoned vehicles.

Legislative bodies are beset with demands to start crash programs for dealing with the various forms of pollution. Pollution does not respect geographical boundaries. Not only do nations pollute beyond their borders, but efforts to control pollution can distort international understanding and trade. The Rhine River has become an international sewer; the Baltic is regarded as a dying sea. Several of the Great Lakes are being filled with unsafe raw pollutants. When one political entity permits dumping untreated wastes in a river or lake that flows through another country, the downstream area will become polluted regardless of whether the nation downstream requires proper disposal of its own effluent.

Relationship of Ecology to Pollution

Regardless of man's progress, he still cannot exist for very long without the help of microorganisms to maintain the health and fertility of plants and animals. For example, bread comes from wheat grown in soil requiring air and sunlight. In a biosphere, energy from the sun activates living processes; chemicals from air, water, and soil act as building blocks for living organisms.

The total relationship between these living organisms and the environment is recognized by the concepts of *biotic communities* and ecosystems. A *biotic community* is a collection of different species of plants and animals inhabiting a common area. Each species is considered to have effects upon others. And when these biotic communities are combined with their physical environment, this is called an ecosystem. Fish, for example, are end products of food chains in aquatic ecosystems. The study of ecosystems and their status is known as *ecology*. What happens to ecosystems determines what will happen to people. The air that man breathes, the water he drinks, the food he eats, and the sunlight that warms him are all part of his physical and biological environment. An understanding of ecology and ecosystems is basic to conservation. Constant pollution will ultimately result in an ecological imbalance that will become a threat to life.

Major Forms of Pollution

Water and air were once clean; now they are polluted. The three areas of pollution are (1) air, (2) water, and (3) solid-waste disposal. Each presents a threat to the existence of the biotic community.

Air Pollution and Its Sources. Air pollution has generally increased since 1969 in the United States, even though emissions from automobiles, a

Courtesy Standard Oil Co. of New Jersey

Coke and chemical plants just west of Pittsburgh.

major source, have apparently reached their peak level. The Council on Environmental Quality (CEQ), which is responsible for defining and setting air pollution standards, estimates that more than 215 million tons of air pollutants are released annually to destroy the ecology. Recent federal government estimates report the damage to crops and livestock caused by air pollution in a single year as approximately $500 million, with another $100 million worth done annually to painted steel surfaces as a form of corrosion. In addition, it is estimated that pollution from the air causes an $800 million expenditure annually to refurbish fabrics. Note that these costs do not include the expense of medical care required by people who suffer from pollutants.

The five major air pollutants are carbon monoxide, sulfur oxides, hydrocarbons, nitrogen oxides, and particles. Particulate pollutants are composed mainly of carbon, ash, oil, and grease, and microscopic amounts of metallic substances.

As you can see from the accompanying graph, the main sources of air pollutants are emissions from transportation equipment (mostly automobiles); forest fires; industrial processes; fuel combustion from stationary plants; miscellaneous sources, such as plant life and refuse incineration; and solid waste, such as particles.

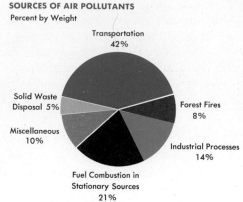

SOURCES OF AIR POLLUTANTS
Percent by Weight

Transportation 42%

Forest Fires 8%

Industrial Processes 14%

Fuel Combustion in Stationary Sources 21%

Miscellaneous 10%

Solid Waste Disposal 5%

Source: National Air Pollution Control Administration, U.S. Department of Health, Education, and Welfare

An air-pollution crisis occurs more often during the daytime, when air temperatures decrease from the ground upward. This is known as a *temperature inversion.* The result is to block the upward direction of the flow of warmer air from the ground and thus trap polluted air in areas where the greatest amount of human activities are concentrated.

Air pollution is not only dangerous to health but affects adversely other elements of biotic communities. For example, air pollution from the Central Valley in California has been known to damage pine trees in the Sierras, more than 100 miles away.

Ways to Reduce Air Pollutants.   Essentially, there are at least three ways to eliminate or control emissions into the atmosphere:

1. Design equipment that does not produce pollutants in sufficient amounts to be harmful.
2. Develop new products that do not destroy the ecology, and discontinue those products that are contaminating the environment.
3. Enact at the state and federal levels stronger laws to force individuals and companies to conform to existing control standards of what is released as waste.

Combustion produces most of the air pollution. Although some of the most severe forms of air pollution are derived from chemical processes used in certain industries, the most prevalent pollutants are from the burning of coal, fuel oil, and gasoline. In heavily industrialized and heavily populated areas, smog becomes a major problem of health. The automobile is a major source of air contamination. The gasoline engine emits large amounts of unburned or partially burned hydrocarbons, carbon monoxide, nitrogen oxides, and other organic compounds that are contained in fuel additives and in lubricating oils. At the present time, over 100 million automobiles are sources of air pollution. The antipollution devices required of automobiles cover only about one-half the total vehicles now in use. (Not all the states have strict laws requiring antismog controls on motor vehicles.)

The following chart, based on a nationwide survey, shows in millions of tons per year the various kinds of emissions released into the air by transportation, industrial processes, and stationary sources. Stationary sources include power plants, and industrial processes include such plants as petroleum refineries, pulp mills, iron and steel mills, and nonferrous metal smelters.

Water Pollution. Water as a natural resource has the quality of being inexhaustible; however, water of usable quantity and quality, available at the right place and at the right time, is not inexhaustible. Much of the water pollution is the result of its use by business and individual citizens.

When water first appears on the surface of the earth in the form of rain, hail, sleet, or surface condensation, it becomes useful as a natural resource. What happens to it as it flows into lakes and dams or becomes part of a river system may be the beginning of a pollution problem. The components of water pollution are complex and varied and consequently often hard to identify. One of the main sources of water pollution is the flow of contaminated sewage into lakes, streams, and rivers. Apart from the health hazard, disposal of sewage in watercourses presents other problems too. Where there is a high concentration of organic waste, disease results and most forms of aquatic life are destroyed.

Another source of water pollution is the disposal of wastes from industry,

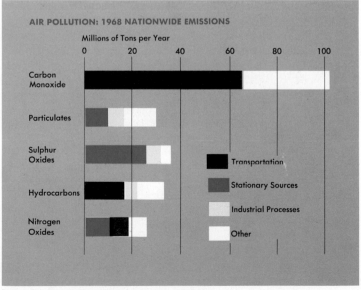

Source: U.S. Department of Health, Education, and Welfare

ranging from canning and food-processing plants to steel mills, mines, and chemical plants. The development of nuclear energy as a power source has brought a new source of pollution—radioactive contamination of both water and air, far more dangerous than many other forms of pollutants.

The most direct dangers from water pollution are from disease-causing organisms found in human and livestock sewage, and synthetic organic chemicals such as pesticides, which flow into water-storage facilities and rivers. Both Lake Erie and Lake Michigan absorb wastes from sewage released by cities along their shorelines; this has made them the nation's most spectacular sewer outfall. In the harbors of most of the large seaports of the world, water pollution has become a major problem.

Federal estimates made in 1971 indicate that about 30 percent of the total population are served by sewer systems providing what is called "adequate" treatment.[2] In addition, about 32 percent of the population have sewer service that is considered inadequate, and 5 percent are served by sewer systems without treatment plants. For the remaining 33 percent of the total population, there are no sewer systems at all.

The need considered most critical is to replace existing inadequate treatment facilities of sewage and to install treatment plants in urban and rural areas that have no sewage-processing plants. The lowest authoritative price tag fixed by President Nixon for the cost of improving municipal sewage treatment plants and adding new ones through 1974 is about $12 billion. The U.S. Water Quality Office (WQO) estimates that industry must spend $3.3 billion during the next five years to treat water that is now flowing into streams and lakes.

State and federal authorities are finding it a slow process to work out suitable water-quality standards as a prelude to obtaining nationwide support from municipalities and private enterprises, so they can begin these programs—which will most likely be financed by federal funds.

Ways to Reduce Water Pollution. Experts agree that there are four possible ways to eliminate or reduce water pollution:

1. Install modern sewage-treatment plants and improve those in operation.
2. Develop less damaging substitutes for substances now causing pollution.
3. Use recycled water from treatment plants that is considered fit for consumption as a means of economizing on the use of water.
4. Reduce the flow of unintentional polluted runoffs, such as from agricultural projects using harmful pesticides.

[2] The term "adequate" describes secondary treatment in which undesirable solids are settled out in the treatment process, oxygen-hungry components are largely neutralized, and disease-causing bacteria are destroyed. However, this tends to leave a sludge that creates a solid-waste disposal problem.

Environmental protectionists see an ecological disaster unless pollution is eliminated. Industry contributes far more water pollution than is derived from domestic wastes, with the major responsibilities resting with the chemical, food, paper, and primary metals plants. Furthermore, the volume of industrial water wastes (runoff water) is increasing more rapidly than municipal sewage, a situation that is caused by the rise in per capita output of goods. At the same time, however, most industrial-waste water can be treated with existing technological processes. Some industries are learning that water pollution can be reduced by changes in the production processes now in use. As an example, the conversion in the pulp and paper industry to the kraft pulping process significantly reduced the volume of undesirable chemical content subject to disposal.

Solid-Waste Pollution. What to do with solid-waste materials has always been a problem for mankind. No longer is the simple solution of burning garbage possible in urban areas, because of the air-pollution problem it creates. As a result, the disposal of solid wastes is the third form of pollution problem.

What is meant by solid-waste materials? These wastes include an assortment of products that are no longer usable. Among them are all kinds of junk, including bottles, metal cans, automobile bodies, tires, plastic containers, agriculture and mining wastes, newspapers, and radioactive wastes from uranium mines.

The United States produces about 4.4 billion tons of solid wastes annually. As indicated in the accompanying graph, there are four main sources of solid wastes, with agricultural activities representing the largest source. Mineral wastes rank second, residential and commercial third, and industrial plants are fourth.

The corrective action in solving the solid-waste disposal problem is not merely the screening of junkyards as eyesores, but, as with air and water

SOURCES OF SOLID WASTES
Million Tons

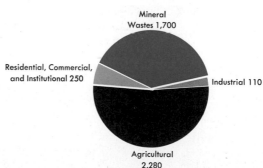

Mineral Wastes 1,700

Residential, Commercial, and Institutional 250

Industrial 110

Agricultural 2,280

Sources: U.S. Department of Health, Education, and Welfare; U.S. Department of Interior

Every day is recycling day in American steel mills. Today's cans, cars, and carpet tacks and many other products, are made from scrap metal that would otherwise pollute the environment.

Courtesy American Iron and Steel Institute, New York, N.Y.

pollution, a matter of finding long-term solutions. One of these is the reclaiming of these materials through a process called *recycling*, which is a means of reconverting waste materials into usable products by reclaiming existing values. At the present time, industries are beginning to recycle a variety of materials to help solve the waste-disposal problem. Here are some examples:

1. A plant in New Jersey was able to produce 400,000 tons of newsprint from used newspapers by the recycling process, at a cost of $7 per ton less than the cost of producing paper from virgin pulp.

2. The aluminum industry reports 75 million cans were gathered for recycling during the first quarter of 1971.

3. The use of scrap metals—iron and steel, aluminum, lead, and other materials—helps to salvage substantial amounts of metal heretofore discarded as junk.

4. Glass bottles and jars have been ground into a powder, and with other solid materials, used as a basis for highways.

Some idea of the amount of metals that are recycled from scrap waste is indicated in the following chart, which shows that lead tops the list for the percentage of consumption that is reclaimed from scrap.

RECLAIMED "WASTE"–A MAJOR SOURCE OF RAW MATERIALS

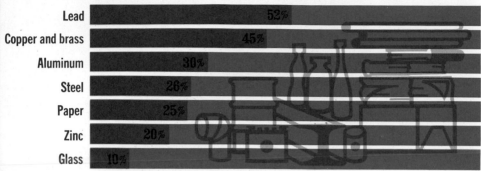

Per cent of U. S. consumption produced from scrap

Lead	52%
Copper and brass	45%
Aluminum	30%
Steel	26%
Paper	25%
Zinc	20%
Glass	10%

AS RECYCLING of cans, bottles, papers and other solid wastes catches on as a way to fight pollution, authorities predict a growing proportion of America's demand for raw materials will be met by reprocessed wastes.

Source: National Association of Secondary Material Industries; Scrap Iron and Steel Institute; Glass Container Manufacturers Institute. Reprinted from *U.S. News & World Report,* June 7, 1971. Copyright © 1971, U.S. News & World Report.

Discussion Questions

3. *Why is there so much interest in solving pollution problems now as compared with a decade ago?*
4. *Which of the three forms of pollution is the most difficult to correct and which costs the most to improve?*
5. *If the pollution problem is so acute, why can't the government take more drastic action to bring about stronger controls?*

THE DYNAMICS OF POLLUTION-CONTROL FACTORS

One of the dynamic factors in bringing about pollution control is the rapid growth of our population, a trend that is felt in both the city and the country-side. The concentration of people in urban areas adds to the cost of building more sewage-disposal plants, the cost of recycling more disposable waste, and the cost of eliminating additional pollutants from the air.

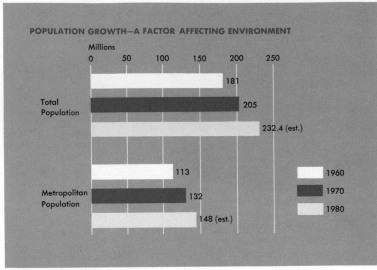

POPULATION GROWTH—A FACTOR AFFECTING ENVIRONMENT

Source: U.S. Department of Commerce

Impact of Population Growth on Pollution

As you can see in the population-growth chart above the total U.S. population is expected to reach 232.4 million by 1980. At the same time, the population of metropolitan areas will increase from 132 million in 1970 to an estimated 148 million by 1980. That is, about 70 percent of all Americans will be living in metropolitan areas, where concentration is already too high for a completely satisfactory way of life. Today, the figure is 66.6 percent. In number, almost all of the growth by 1980 will be in the suburbs while central cities will scarcely increase their population. Without control over population increase, all other efforts at conservation must inevitably become ineffective.

If increasing population is a villain in our struggle against pollution, then why not take action to control the number of persons added to the annual population? The answer, of course, is that any effective method of control would undoubtedly create other problems more difficult to solve than most of our existing ones in the area of environmental development. For example, each new family unit is a market for new consumer goods. But if the number of new units were intentionally reduced, this might have an adverse impact on our economy.

Proposals to Control Population Growth. Several proposals aimed at control of population growth have been offered in recent years. In the more technically advanced countries, most of these involve mechanical and chemical methods of birth control. One of the most effective has been the use of birth control pills. Other control methods involve income tax incentives—for example, imposing a limit on child-dependency deductions; using a sliding scale of exemptions, such as $1,000 for the first child, with a scaling down to none for the fourth and successive children; enactment of a "child tax" law; and granting benefits and allowances to couples who remain childless. "Zero population growth"—that is, holding the line at the present figure—has been cited as the goal.

Other Proposals to Reduce Pollution

In addition to the control of population, several other approaches to the problem of reducing the nation's pollution have been made:

1. Enactment of excise taxes on polluting materials such as coal, sulfur, plastic containers, and lead, and also on the use of such resources as land, oil, and electric power.

2. Payment of subsidies and tax incentives—tax forgiveness and accelerated depreciation—for companies that install pollution control equipment; also, loans and cash payments to firms that are able to reduce the amount of pollutants they produce.

3. Levying of fees for discharging specific amounts of pollutants against producers of the effluent materials, as well as the consumers of the products they produce.

4. Passage of direct-regulation legislation, including enforcement procedures for maintaining standards, licenses, and permits.

These proposals are extremely controversial. Environmentalists feel that any changes made would, in effect, give a business the right to pollute, since they would never be set high enough to induce effective restrictions. Industry is opposed to any imposition of effluent charges on the ground that they are an unfair financial burden.

Everybody wants to reduce pollution in order to improve the national health, but not all persons are willing to pay the cost. In a recent poll, people were asked if they would be willing to pay $15 more in federal taxes if that amount were to be used for pollution control. By a two-to-one vote, younger Americans said they would, but two-thirds of those over the age of 50 opposed such a tax. When the same question was put to those considered to have better-than-average education, the vote for the tax was nearly two-to-one in favor of it, while those with less-than-average education opposed the tax by a similar margin.

Inasmuch as pollution problems differ in the various states, it is unlikely that the most effective method of reducing pollution is to leave the matter up to individual states. Also, some states can afford to spend more than others to solve these pollution problems. In recent months, much of the impetus to improve the environment has come from the federal government, which has taken the lead in enacting laws to establish guides and standards for various forms of controls applicable to all the states. At the same time, private industry is beginning to step up its spending to clean up its own environmental pol-

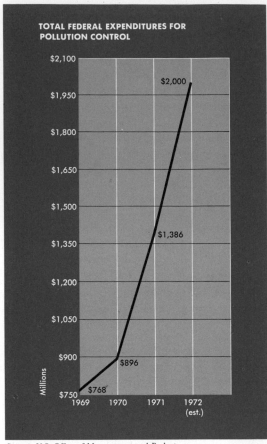

TOTAL FEDERAL EXPENDITURES FOR POLLUTION CONTROL

Source: U.S. Office of Management and Budget

lutants, although, as one executive of a major oil and chemical company stated, "Many of us have the money already set aside to spend on cleaning up this dangerous level of pollution, but we are not going to spend it until *all* of us are forced to do the same."

Since 1969, expenditures by the federal government to control pollution have increased annually, as indicated by the accompanying chart. However, the amounts expended by the government thus far are still considerably less than many experts have estimated to be required if progress is to be achieved. According to an estimate made by the Council on Environmental Quality, the cost for cleaning up the environment by 1975 will be $105.2 billion. These expenditures include outlays by both private industry and government.

Pollution-Control Legislation

The earliest law enacted by Congress pertaining to pollution was the Refuse Act of 1899, which forbids discharge of refuse, except in liquid form, from streets and sewers into navigable waters without a permit from the Corps of Engineers. According to the *New York Times,* the Justice Department demonstrated little interest in enforcing this act until 1970, when eight large companies were charged with dumping waste mercury into navigable waters in several states. Seven of these companies were among the 500 largest corporations, and four of them were listed in the top 100.

Water Resources Planning Act of 1965. This law created a Water Resources Council (WRC) and river basin commissions. The law authorized establishment of national air-quality standards and emission standards for both stationary air-pollution sources and automotive vehicles. The act further requires each state to submit plans for achieving national air-quality standards. Those states that have not previously submitted an acceptable plan for state standards will have one imposed upon them by the federal government.

Solid Waste Disposal Act of 1965. This law authorizes a program to develop methods of solid-waste disposal, including garbage, paper, and scrap metal. It also provides technical assistance to state and local governments in solid-waste disposal programs.

Water Quality Act of 1965. This act gives states the option of setting water-quality standards or having the federal government fix such standards, to be approved by the U.S. Department of the Interior.

Clean Water Restoration Act of 1966. Funds are authorized for grants to states, cities, and counties to develop improved methods of waste treatment, including water purification, sewer design, and actual construction of treatment plants. The need for this type of development is far greater than the funds available to create them.

Air Quality Act of 1967. In January 1967, President Johnson, in his message to Congress, urged the adoption of legislation to strengthen the nation's research and control efforts. The Air Quality Act of 1967 provided for a systematic effort to deal with air pollution on a regional basis. It established coordinated action at various levels of government and segments of industry.

National Environmental Policy Act of 1970. This law requires Congress to specify the kinds of environmental factors to be considered in land-use planning and requires the agencies to indicate how they were taken into account.

Clean Air Amendment of 1970. More stringent air-quality measures are included in this act than in any previous legislation. For automotive vehicles, carbon monoxide and hydrocarbon emission standards have been set for 1975 compliance, when 90 percent of nitrogen oxides must be eliminated from auto exhausts. Funds amounting to $1.1 billion were earmarked for a three-year period for research. This act also created the Environmental Protection Agency.

Water Quality Improvement Act of 1970. This law strengthened water pollution laws—particularly pollution by oil—and requires installation of marine sanitation devices to control sewage from vessels. Stiff penalties for noncompliance are provided.

Resources Recovery Act of 1970. This act calls for a greatly expanded program to improve solid-waste disposal. It also transferred the solid-waste program from the Department of Health, Education and Welfare to the Environmental Protection Agency.

Test

Discussion Questions

6. *What effect does an expanding population have on environmental pollution?*
7. *Explain how payment of subsidies by government, tax incentives, and accelerated depreciation for companies that install pollution control equipment would help to reduce pollution.*
8. *Why is the effectiveness of pollution control so highly dependent upon federal legislation?*

THE SOCIAL RESPONSIBILITY OF BUSINESS

Business functions by public consent, and its underlying purpose is to serve the needs of society to the satisfaction of society. Business has carried out its basic economic responsibilities so well largely because of the dynamic performance of the private enterprise system. Among business leaders themselves, there is a renewed plea nowadays for a strong emphasis on "social responsibility" by corporate leaders. The fact is that the public expects business leadership to contribute a good deal more toward achieving the goals of a good society.

Reasons for Emphasizing Social Responsibility

There are several reasons for the continuing emphasis on social responsibility. One is the insistence of public opinion that business be more responsive to its community responsibilities.

A second is that the various parts of society are now bound together in a manner requiring more dependence on other parts. As society faces more complex problems, a new social dependency develops.

A third reason is the realization by businessmen that they share a great responsibility in determining attitudes and values, and that therefore, they cannot afford to withdraw into isolation and avoid these social responsibilities. The issue is whether society must arbitrarily determine the responsibilities of business by law or allow business to regulate itself.

Some businessmen are in doubt as to how much social responsibility should be accepted by their companies, especially in areas of pollution. Others advocate that businesses have a responsibility to engage in both political and community activities. Still others see this responsibility as purely a social role.

In a speech to the Association of National Advertisers on October 31, 1968, C. W. Cook, chairman of the board of the General Foods Corporation, stressed that American business must accept involvement with the social issues, because it is "in our own best interest to make our American system work better and more equitably; involvement because business bears the obligation of leadership; and, most importantly, involvement because it is right."[3]

Anyone who regularly reads periodicals about our environment must be aware of the great amount of attention that is given to the subject of pollution. Business is being challenged to lead the way in helping to end the destruction of the environment so as to improve the quality of life in urban and rural areas. As one writer put it, "Business is on the 10-yard line in the fight against pollution." Management teams are puzzled in some instances as to how to approach the problem in a way that will bring about substantial benefits to society and the environment, but at the same time not consume large proportions of profits.

There are those who contend that social responsibilities should be shared by all individuals and not chiefly by corporations. After all, they argue, the environment belongs to everyone and includes all sectors of society.

Discussion Questions

9. *What is the meaning of the "social responsibility" of business to society?*
10. *What are the reasons for emphasizing the social responsibility of business?*

WHAT BUSINESS IS DOING ABOUT POLLUTION

For years the idea that business has a responsibility apart from the one to its owners was not embraced by many businessmen. Times seem to be changing. Now more businessmen have broadened their concept of responsibility for improving the plight of the ecology; and a massive program to restore the environment has been sent to Congress by the administration, calling for close cooperation between government—at both state and federal levels—and business.

[3] Clarence C. Walton, ed., *Business and Social Progress* (New York: Praeger Publishers, Inc., 1970), p. 134.

A Program of Action

At its plant on the tiny Tittabawassee River in Midland, Michigan, the Dow Chemical Company employs 8,000 persons and produces 3 billion pounds of chemical products a year. A tour of the company's plant at Midland shows that its concern over continuing pollution runs deep. The company has launched an attack on pollution by:

1. Establishing recycling of raw materials
2. Attaching the same emphasis to pollution as to personal injury, explosion, or fire
3. Continuing to maintain environmental patrols to look for hazards

One of the major improvements at the Midland plant is a system of devices that can sense contaminants in the cooling water and immediately divert polluted water into a 50-million gallon pond, where it is treated and cleaned so that it may be diverted back into the Tittabawassee River. This system costs approximately $800,000.

Another major project, which the Dow Company initiated in 1970, was the building of 28 cooling towers in the Midland plant at a cost of $7 million. The aim is to eventually discontinue dumping into the Tittabawassee River completely. The coal-burning electrical plants at Midland are due to be replaced by 1975 by two nuclear-reactor plants, which will not give off any forms of air pollution such as fly ash. The company's giant bottle-melting rotary kiln at Midland, which was adequate for 1960 air pollution standards, is being reconstructed to meet the current emission standards.

General Motors budgeted a record $150 million expenditure in the United States in 1971 to help fulfill its commitment to take the automobile out of the air pollution problem as soon as possible. This expenditure was in addition to $64 million spent in this country by the company to control industrial air and water pollution. A 1,300-foot supplementary sewer system has been installed at the company's Lakewood, Georgia plant. Following primary treatment, the industrial waste water is diverted into the city of Atlanta's disposal system, thus eliminating any possibility of the plant's polluting public streams.

The Goodyear Tire and Rubber Company has committed nearly $12 million to renovating pollution controls at thirteen of its plants. A completely new water-treatment facility has been installed at the Akron plant. The Company expects to have spent $32 million on pollution control by 1975.

The Commonwealth Edison Company, at its Lemont, Illinois, generating station, has installed a $7 million air-cleaning unit to remove both dust and sulphur dioxide. The company is spending about $400 million to construct a nuclear generating station at Zion, Illinois. This plant will eliminate air pollutants formerly produced by coal-burning units.

The Republic Steel Company installed during 1971 some of the most effective environmental-control systems ever constructed. For example, in Chicago the company built three new waste water terminal plants and a giant cooler to cool and filter electric furnace emissions. In Cleveland, Republic constructed the largest private facility in Ohio for quality control of processing 100 million gallons of water per day.

President Charles B. McCoy of the du Pont Company announced plans to spend more than $300 million on air- and water-pollution control in the United States over a three-year period. Costs will be equally divided between construction and installation of control facilities and the expense of operating existing facilities and future controls.

The Procter & Gamble Company allocated $30 million for pollution-control equipment at its various plants in the United States, and the company reports that it will invest another $49 million during the next five years. The greatest source of air pollution reported by P&G is from its synthetic detergent cellulose pulp and paper manufacturing plants. Various kinds of pollution-control equipment, including cyclone separators, electrostatic precipitators, and scrubbers, have been installed.

A car shredder capable of smashing 600 automobiles a day into pint-sized chunks has been developed by the General Electric Company. This machine can help to make abandoned cars a rare sight in cities and along highways. General Electric is also exploring a process that uses bacteria to convert paper trash into a high-protein food for livestock. The company is perfecting a new kind of municipal incinerator for the complete combustion of trash with virtually no air pollution.

A model $101 million, four-year plan devised by the International Paper Company aims to upgrade pollution controls at each of its 18 primary pulp and board mills, to equip them with the best possible controls. Other paper companies have launched similar programs.

Almost overnight, the market for antipollution equipment has exploded into a $5-billion-a-year industry. Among the new devices is a nontoxic product to be sprayed on oil slicks; within minutes, it produces a still gel that captures spilled petroleum so that it can be scooped up with a suction pump. Another is a new plastic bottle that can be burned without generating toxic fumes. One company sells a solid-waste-disposal plant that pulverizes various kinds of refuse continuously without creating odors.

Discussion Questions

11. *What evidence exists to show that business is increasing its cooperation to government to improve the quality of life?*

12. *When a company is confronted with a pollution problem involving an existing law, what are some of the factors it must consider in making its decision to meet the issue?*

SUMMARY

Pollution in all its forms is a major problem for society. It is damaging crops and exposing humans to health hazards. Failure to meet the issues and take corrective action can seriously damage or even destroy society, as evidenced by what has already happened to the ecology. The chief forms of pollution are in the air, in water, and from waste materials.

The growth of population is a major contributor to pollution problems, especially in crowded urban areas where there is a high population density. A policy of control of national population growth would be helpful, but it would also create other problems, equally difficult to solve.

The degree of pollution is closely related to that of congestion, and pollution is not subject to political boundaries. A westerly wind may sweep across the nation carrying its pollutants. Consequently, a coordinated approach cutting through political lines is essential.

The purpose of most of the existing antipollution legislation is to establish standards that industry must meet in correcting existing pollution; to create legal authorities responsible for administering federal funds and standards; and to appropriate funds to be used to improve equipment and facilities.

The billions of dollars that must be spent by business and government to clean up the environment are beginning to flow, but critics charge progress is too slow on the part of business, owing to lack of acceptance of social responsibility. Society is critical of business because it does not accept more responsibility to work with government to improve the environment. Critics charge business with putting too much emphasis on the profit objective and not enough on recognizing the need to clean up the environment for the benefit of society.

The facts show that giant companies are beginning to make massive expenditures to meet the existing legislative standards pertaining to pollution. At the same time, other large companies that are also fighting pollution are receiving federal grants in one form or another where improvements involve natural resources. Proposed federal expenditures to control or eliminate pollution are expected to exceed $2 billion annually.

VOCABULARY REVIEW

Match the following vocabulary terms with the statements below:

a. Biotic communities
b. Business environment
c. Community relations

d. Ecology
e. Environment
f. Ecosystem

g. Recycling
h. Society

1. The total of all the external forces affecting the living organisms around us
2. The total involvement of business within the community, in which good relations with all parties in the community is the goal
3. A social system consisting of interacting groups whose members have cultural patterns, mores, and goals

4. The total of all things external to enterprises and industries that affect their organization and operation
5. The study of ecosystems to determine their status and how they function
6. A collection of different species of plants and animals inhabiting a common area
7. A community of biotic communities combined with the physical environment
8. A means of reconverting waste materials into usable products by reclaiming existing values

PROBLEMS AND PROJECTS

1. Recently, the Western Michigan Environmental Action Council asked Joseph L. Sax, Professor of Law, University of Michigan, to draft a model environment law that would be presented to the Michigan legislature for enactment. The bill empowered any person or organization to sue any private or public body and to obtain a court order restraining conduct of an activity that might impair, destroy, or pollute such resources as air and water. The proposed law was considered by some as unprecedentedly far-reaching; nevertheless, it was introduced in both houses. Months passed without a hearing on the bill. When it was finally scheduled for a hearing, hundreds of people came from all over the state, and the hearing had to be transferred to a larger meeting room. Groups of all kinds indorsed it, including lawyers, labor unions, and students. The governor finally signed the measure into law.
   a. What, in your opinion, was the purpose of this law?
   b. Why was there so much interest in it?
2. The ENRO Corporation proposes to develop a new industrial park about 35 miles from Cleveland, near Lorain, Ohio. Fifteen industrial companies have tentatively agreed to lease ground and build manufacturing plants in the park. An estimated 10,000 workers would be employed during the first two years, and another 15,000 in the following three years. Almost one-third of the factories will be owned by existing companies, and the remaining two-thirds are to be new companies. The proposed park is located about four miles from the closest residential area. County zoning laws restrict residential homes in an industrial park. The public utility company serving the city of Cleveland has agreed to supply electricity to the park. Gas lines are also available throughout the district. The park area is part of an unincorporated township.
   a. What are some of the precautions the industrial-park developers can take to prevent water and air pollution?
   b. Which government agencies are likely to be responsible for enforcing antipollution regulations and laws?

A BUSINESS CASE

Case 2-1   A Court Order Gives New Life to the Ecology

Until recently, some corporate managers believed that the pursuit of profits was adequate justification for most of their actions, provided they were not acting illegally. However, this has now been changed as a result of a ruling handed down by the U.S. Court of Appeals in the District of Columbia, which may eventually make corporate managers more responsive to the social concern of shareholders.

A group of stockholders proposed an amendment to the corporate charter of the Dow Chemical Corporation, to wit, "Napalm shall not be sold to any buyer unless that buyer gives reasonable assurance that the substance as produced by the Dow Chemical Corporation will not be used on or against human beings." This group, known as the Medical Committee for Human Rights, asked the company to submit the amendment at the next stockholder's meeting.

The company argued against the amendment in a letter to the Securities and Exchange Commission. The commission advised the company that no objection would be raised if the corporation omitted the proxy statement, on which the amendment would be printed for the meeting.

The Medical Committee then sued to force the SEC to order Dow to include the proxy containing the amendment. In its decision, the court ruled that the SEC was without the right to make this decision, and further that it was the responsibility of the shareholders, not the commission, to decide how to handle an amendment at the meeting, as well as to decide on the use of the proxy form.

1. What was the issue in this case, as it related to pollution?
2. What was the basis of the court's decision?
3. Do you concur in the opinion? Why?

our legal environment and business ethics
CHAPTER THREE

Almost since the beginning of mankind, societies have relied heavily on laws to mediate the relationships among men. These laws are the framework, so to speak, for enforcing the rules under which people live. Not all rules are law, but virtually all law is based upon rules. These rules are part of our legal system which consists of procedures devised for formulating such laws, for applying them, and for interpreting them.

William Pitt, First Earl of Chatham, the famous English statesman, once said, "Where law ends, tyranny begins." One function of law is to establish order. Another is to settle disputes. Still a third is to provide protection.

Business administration consists of making decisions, and the decisions involved in a business transaction almost always have legal implications. It is unwise to make such decisions without first having gained an insight to one's legal rights and to the rules of conduct. When business disputes arise—and they often do—they have to be settled by the due process of law, not by force or any other illegal means.

To anyone contemplating a business career, a basic understanding of legal terms and principles is very important. Such knowledge will at least help you to avoid common legal blunders when signing a contract, forming a partnership, buying merchandise—in fact, when engaging in any of a host of business activities. An understanding of the law can help you, too, to determine when you must seek expert legal counsel. In any courtroom situation, you would do well to recall the old saying, "A man who serves as his own lawyer has a fool for a client."

This chapter is also concerned with business ethics, which is closely related to law. There are some business practices that, although not in direct violation of the law, are not necessarily in harmony with existing laws. The regulation of these practices is left to voluntary groups of people who band together for their own protection and adopt a code of ethics, the standard of behavior they have agreed to follow.

THE NATURE AND PURPOSE OF LAW

Before starting our exploration of the relationship of law to business, let's review briefly the nature of law, its classifications, and some of its history.

What Is Law?

Law may be defined as a body of rules, statutes, legal codes, and regulations that are enforceable by the courts. Blackstone, in his *Commentaries on the Laws of England,* states that law is "a rule of civil conduct prescribed by the supreme power of a state, commanding what is right and prohibiting what is wrong."

When the scientist refers to a specific law of science, he is concerned with a rule that is applied consistently. When a judge interprets a law, he, too, is dealing with a rule that should be applied consistently by society. Laws applied to common business transactions come under the heading of *business* or *commercial law.* These are also codes and statutes that are enforceable by the courts. The enforcement of legal rules would be impossible were it not for the fact that members of society are willing to subordinate themselves to a higher authority approved by a political unit such as a state.

Classification of Laws

Over the years, our laws have been developed under a legal system that includes both *civil law,* derived from legislative statutes, and *common law,* which consists of precedents based on court decisions. The broad scope of the law gives rise to several classifications. The two major categories are *substantive law* and *procedural law.*

Substantive Law. Substantive law is that part of the law that defines, creates, and regulates the individual's legal rights. Laws pertaining to contracts, property, sales, crimes, and the Constitution are classified as substantive law.

Substantive law may be further subdivided into *public law* and *private law*. Public law deals with the relation of the government to the individual and with the creation and operation of governments. Within the scope of public law, we find such subcategories as *constitutional law,* which deals with the legal principles of the Constitution; *administrative law,* which is concerned with the mechanics by which governments carry out their legal functions; and *criminal law,* which defines conduct deemed a crime against the government.[1]

Laws that are concerned with the rights and liabilities between private individuals, partnerships, corporations, and other organizations are called *private laws.* In addition, there are private laws having to do with wrongs of a noncontractual nature known as *torts.*[2] Examples of torts include false arrest, false imprisonment, deceit, slander, and libel. Some understanding of the law of torts is important to the businessman, because he needs to know which civil conduct, apart from any considerations of contracts, society denounces as socially undesirable or unreasonable, and for which torts the courts may impose monetary liability in the form of damages.

Procedural Law. This classification of the law, sometimes referred to as *adjective law,* has to do with the procedural machinery required to enforce personal rights and duties. Included under procedural law are such matters as court pleadings, court jurisdiction, decrees, evidence, and administrative decisions. Procedural or adjective law is the body of rules that regulate the conduct of a lawsuit.

Origin of the Law

For centuries, our Western civilization has developed under two legal systems. The older system is the Roman or civil law, which was founded in the Roman Empire. Continental Europe and most of the countries colonized by the European nations (except those now under communism) live under Roman or civil law. The English-speaking countries and the nations colonized by them live under the English or common-law system.

---

[1] Crimes are classified as either *felonies* or *misdemeanors.* A *felony* is a criminal offense punishable by imprisonment in a state penitentiary in excess of one year, or by death. A *misdemeanor* is also considered a criminal offense, but not as severe as a felony. It carries either a fine or imprisonment, or both. Imprisonment for conviction of a misdemeanor is generally not in a state penitentiary but in a city or county jail, and generally for less than one year.

[2] A *tort* is a civil (private) wrong (other than a breach of contract) that may result in legal action. A tort is also a violation of a private duty that may result in damages to the injured party. Damage, then, is an essential element of the tort. Both slander and libel are examples of torts. Slander consists of publication or communication of defamatory spoken words or gestures. Libel is a wrong against an individual in the form of written defamation, or in print, picture, or some other visual form.

Legal Sources. In the United States, there are two main sources of law. One is the unwritten body of principles known as *common law,* which is based mainly on court decisions that become precedents to be followed in cases of a similar nature. (This is known as the doctrine of *stare decisis.* By this doctrine the judge, in effect, *makes* law—in the sense that the principles he enunciates may be followed by other judges.) The source of most of our laws pertaining to contracts, property, and agency relationships is common law.

The other source of law is *statutory law.* This is written law, consisting of formal declarations or enactments (statutes) by various government bodies and agencies. These statutes, together with the federal and state constitutions, make up what is commonly known as *law by enactment.*

Constitutional law is regarded as superior to statutory law, and statutory law is considered higher than common law. Hence, common law applies only to those instances where there are no written laws applicable to the situation. On the other hand, such organizations as corporations, partnerships, and trusts are forms of ownership subject to statutory laws, as are many other activities in business.

Under the Constitution of the United States, each state has the right to enact its own laws. State laws are often lacking in uniformity, and this makes trade between states confusing. To bring about greater uniformity, the National Commission of Uniform State Laws has recommended model laws to the states for uniform adoption. Among the first of the model laws proposed was the Uniform Limited Partnership Act. Other uniform codes that have been adopted include the Uniform Negotiable Instruments Act, the Uniform Sales Act, the Uniform Bills of Lading Act, the Uniform Conditional Sales Act, and the Uniform Stock Transfer Act, the Uniform Warehouse Receipts Act, and Uniform Trust Receipts Act.

Uniform Commercial Code. During the last decade, there has been a trend toward the adoption of a single uniform code, applicable to many kinds of business transactions and replacing some of the existing codes in order to accomplish uniformity in all the states. The code that embraces the major areas of commercial law is the Uniform Commercial Code (UCC), generally referred to briefly as "the Code."

The Code is the result of a project sponsored by the National Conference of Commissioners on Uniform State Laws and by the American Law Institute. At this writing only one jurisdiction, Louisiana, has failed to adopt it. Since the UCC embraces the major areas of commercial law, it expressly provides that in the states where it is adopted, it will replace the several Uniform Acts, including several of those mentioned above.[3]

Specifically, the UCC regulates general sales, negotiable instruments,

---

[3]The purposes of the UCC are (1) to encourage uniform laws among the states to cover the broad field of commercial transactions, (2) to simplify and modernize laws governing commercial transactions, and (3) to permit expansion of commercial practices.

implied warranties, warehouse receipts, trust receipts, bills of lading, stock transfer, and certificates of deposit.

The latest edition of the UCC is known as the 1962 Official Edition commonly found in law libraries. It should be noted that the exact interpretations of the Code will not be found in the Code, but rather in the court decisions interpreting the Code.

The Court System

A *court* is a tribunal created by government for the purpose of hearing and deciding on matters properly brought before it. It may give redress to the injured by enforcing some kind of punishment against the wrongdoer. It may direct compliance with the law or prevent wrongs from occurring. There are various levels of courts in both the federal and state systems. Jurisdiction and organization of courts are regulated by constitutional and statutory provisions.

The Constitution of the United States, while ordaining the Supreme Court, provides a good deal of discretion to Congress to establish and administer the judicial power through legislation. The federal system of courts is provided for by Article III, Section 1: "The judicial power of the United States shall be vested in one Supreme Court, and such inferior courts as the Congress may from time to time ordain and establish." The Supreme Court is the only federal court established by the Constitution and not by Congress, although Congress determines the number of justices. The federal system of courts, as shown on the chart on page 62, reveals the relationship of the Supreme Court to other courts in the federal judicial system.

State Courts. The state system of courts is similar to the federal system. Most states have a *state supreme court* or *supreme court of errors,* which is followed in rank order by a *superior court,* the highest state trial court with general jurisdiction. Some states refer to the superior court as their *circuit court* or *district court.* Sixteen states have an intermediate *appellate court* between the state supreme court and the superior court. The *county court* is the lowest level that has jurisdiction in both civil and criminal cases. In cities, it is customary to have *municipal courts,* presided over by a municipal justice or magistrate. The lowest-level state court is that of the justice of the peace or police magistrate, who handles petty offenses and traffic violations.

Remedies at Law and at Equity

Through the system of courts, society provides redress (justice) to any person who believes he has suffered from a legal wrong. The alleged injured person, the *plaintiff,* is the one who brings the action against the accused, known as the *defendant.*

The American system of jurisprudence operates under a dual system of

THE FEDERAL COURT SYSTEM OF THE UNITED STATES

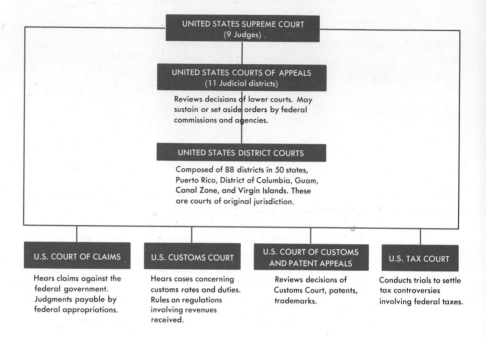

UNITED STATES SUPREME COURT
(9 Judges)

UNITED STATES COURTS OF APPEALS
(11 Judicial districts)

Reviews decisions of lower courts. May sustain or set aside orders by federal commissions and agencies.

UNITED STATES DISTRICT COURTS

Composed of 88 districts in 50 states, Puerto Rico, District of Columbia, Guam, Canal Zone, and Virgin Islands. These are courts of original jurisdiction.

U.S. COURT OF CLAIMS

Hears claims against the federal government. Judgments payable by federal appropriations.

U.S. CUSTOMS COURT

Hears cases concerning customs rates and duties. Rules on regulations involving revenues received.

U.S. COURT OF CUSTOMS AND PATENT APPEALS

Reviews decisions of Customs Court, patents, trademarks.

U.S. TAX COURT

Conducts trials to settle tax controversies involving federal taxes.

remedies obtained from the courts. One is known as *remedies at law* and the other as *remedies at equity.*

Equity, derived from the Latin *aequitas,* means "equality" or "justice." In general, remedies from courts of law provide only two forms of redress— namely, the restoring of real or personal property to one from whom it has been unjustly withheld, and the awarding of money damages. Since the remedies are limited, and because common law has not provided protective or preventive remedies, equity courts were developed to supplement the restricted remedies at law. Equity courts may issue an injunction, which is simply a court order directing a particular party to perform an act or to refrain from continuing a certain act. Thus, an order directing that a party carry out a contract provision is an example of equity remedy. A court of equity may order a written instrument changed if the evidence is clear and compelling that the instrument failed to reflect an agreement between the parties because of an error in preparing the contract.

In a court of law, either party has the right to have the issues of fact determined by a jury, which is the fact-finding body, although the judge decides the issues of law. But in a court of equity, the right to trial by jury does not exist. The judge makes the decision and therefore determines the fact as well as the law.

Discussion Questions

1. *How does statutory law differ from common law?*
2. *Which is the superior constitutional law, statutory law or common law?*
3. *Explain the purposes of the Uniform Commercial Code.*

MODERN BUSINESS LAW IN OPERATION

There are several areas of private law that relate directly to business. The following discussions pertain to these areas of business law.

Law of Contracts

Test

The law of contracts is the oldest and one of the most important laws affecting business. A *contract* is defined as an agreement between two or more competent parties in the form required by law, for a lawful purpose, and supported by consideration; and, if not performed by one party, it is enforceable by the other party. Notice the elements that must exist in an agreement for it to be enforceable: *mutual assent, competent parties, consideration, lawful purpose,* and, in some instances, *required form.*

Mutual Assent. When you make an offer and someone accepts it, both parties have freely and intentionally expressed assent on the same subject. For mutual assent to exist, one person, known as the offerer, must make a definite offer; the one to whom the offer is made, the offeree, must accept it exactly as it is made without any counteroffers. An advertisement to sell an article at a definite price is not a genuine offer; courts have ruled that advertisements only *invite* offers.

Test

Competent Parties. The law regards as a competent person one who has the capacity to incur a legal liability or to gain legal rights. Not all persons are considered competent to make a binding contract. According to common law, any person, male or female, under 21 is a minor, and is regarded as incompetent to make a binding contract.[4] Insane persons, aliens, convicts, and

Test

---

[4] Regarding the rights of minors, the constitutional amendment adopted in 1971 (Twenty-Sixth Amendment) giving full suffrage to persons at age 18 has created a new legal problem. This amendment does not give persons between ages 18 and 21 the right to contract and marry without parental consent. Each state must enact separate legislation to provide full legal status to those under 21. Vermont and Tennessee were the first two states to do this.

drunkards are also considered incompetent to make an enforceable contract. However, courts have ruled that contracts for necessaries made by minors can be enforced.

Consideration. Ordinarily, a promise is not binding unless it is supported by *consideration,* which is defined as the price that a person demands for his promise or performance. Consideration may consist of money, goods, services, or even another promise to do or not to do something you have a legal right to do. For example, Jones agrees to buy an automobile from Bailey for $600, provided Bailey will deliver it within 24 hours. The consideration is the money exchanged for the automobile.

Under the UCC, there are certain exceptions to the general rules of the Uniform Sales Act related to consideration. For example, under the Code, Section 2-304, the price can be made payable in money, goods, realty, or otherwise. The Code allows the parties to make a binding contract of sale even though the price is not stated specifically or settled upon as consideration. Promises or offers of subscriptions for charitable purposes are generally enforceable without consideration.

Lawful Purpose. Before you make a contract, you must be sure that the transaction is lawful as to its specific purpose. In states where gambling is illegal, promises to pay gambling debts, even when in written form, are not enforceable. A contract requiring payment of interest in excess of the legal rate (known as *usury*) is not enforceable, either. Agreements in restraint of trade are also unlawful.

Required Form. Generally, a contract is valid whether it is written or oral—although an important exception is that a written contract *is* required where there is a conveyance of land.

Some of the most common provisions pertaining to the form of contracts are contained in the Statute of Frauds, adopted in England in 1677, and subsequently incorporated in the Uniform Sales Act. Further changes have been made in the UCC version of the statute; for example, Section 2-201 of the Code provides a modification of the Statute of Frauds by which goods offered for sale by contract for the price of $500 or more require some written form sufficient to prove that a contract for sale has been made.

In business, a great many contracts are made so casually that they need not be in writing to be binding. This does not eliminate the importance of the need for businessmen to understand the many basic facts about contracts. The agreement shown on the next page exemplifies a contract containing the essential elements needed to make an agreement binding on both parties.

Remedies for Breach of Contract. Breach of contract occurs when there is failure of either party to perform according to the terms of the agreement. One remedy that is open to the injured party when a contract is breached is that he can avoid carrying out his part of the agreement, acting as though there had been no contract.

A G R E E M E N T

THIS AGREEMENT, made this fifth day of August, 19__, between Fred Herbert, hereinafter called "the employee," and Robert Lee, hereinafter called "the employer."

WITNESSETH:

In consideration of their mutual promises contained herein, the parties hereto agree as follows:

The employee agrees to perform his duties for the period of two (2) years from the date hereof as cashier in the store of the employer and agrees to serve faithfully the said employer in the best interest of said employer.

The employer agrees to pay the said employee the sum of one hundred dollars ($100.00) a week, payable weekly on the last working day of each week during the term of this agreement.

IN WITNESS WHEREOF, the said parties have hereunto set their hands on this, the date first above written in this agreement.

Witness: _____

_____   _____
(for both parties)

Date August 5, 19__

An agreement or contract

Or the injured party may bring an action for damages. Even if he has not sustained actual losses from the breach, he may still be entitled to a judgment for a nominal sum. This is known as *nominal damages.* It may be awarded to a plaintiff whose legal rights have been violated but where the loss sustained was not proved or does not entitle him to substantial compensation. On the other hand, if the injured party has sustained an actual loss, he is entitled to sue for *compensatory damages*—a sum that will, as far as possible, compensate him for the loss. As a rule, damages in excess of actual loss (for the purpose of punishing the defendant) cannot be recovered for breach of contract. Such damages are called *punitive* or *exemplary damages.*

Another action the injured party may take is to bring an action for "performance of the contract." If payment of damages would not actually compensate him for his real loss, the court may grant him special relief by ordering the defaulting party to perform the agreement. Ordinarily, a court does not compel performance if there is some other adequate remedy at law.

assign period in which you can bring action

Statute of Limitations. Each state provides that after a certain number of years have elapsed, a contract claim is barred. Under the statute of limitations, there is a time within which an action or suit at law may be instituted, but after this period, the claim is "outlawed." The period of limitation is computed from the time the right to sue arises, and the length of the period varies according to the nature of the claim. The statute of limitations does not discharge the contract; it merely supplies a defense to a claim for breach of contract, that defense being that no legal action was taken during the prescribed period. In any case, the defendant must plead the statute in defense in order to defeat any action brought against him. A new promise, in writing, to pay a debt (principal or interest) barred by the statute of limitations will revive the whole debt and start the period of limitation running again.

The Law of Agency

The Nature of Agency Relationship. One of the most common legal business relationships is between a principal and his agent. An agreement between two parties by which one is vested with authority to represent the other in business transactions with third parties is known as a *contract of agency*. The party who represents another is the *agent*. The *principal* is the party the agent represents.

Any person who has the right to act for himself may delegate his performance to an agent. Acts of a personal nature, however, such as voting, holding public office, or serving on juries, may not be delegated to others.

How Agency is Created. The usual way of creating an agency is by express authorization, either verbal or in writing. A formal written appointment is called a *power of attorney*, an example of which is shown in the form of a proxy in Chapter 5. The fourth section of the Statute of Frauds requires that a contract creating agency be in writing when the period of performance extends more than one year from the date of the contract.

Agency may also be created by the conduct of the principal. For example, if you knowingly and without objection permit another to act as your agent, the law will find this to be an expression of authorization to the agent, and you will not be allowed to deny that the agent was in fact authorized. This is sometimes known as *agency by implication*.

A third method of creating agency is by *estoppel*. This happens when a third party believes, because of the words and deeds of the principal, that another is his agent. If that person is not in fact authorized as an agent, but the principal has represented him to be one, the law will *estop* (stop) the principal from asserting this false information by creating an *agency by estoppel*.

A principal has the same obligations to his agent that an employer generally has to an employee. For example, the principal is obliged to reimburse the agent for legitimate expenses and to carry out the agreement that created the agency. If you appoint an agent for a year and then wrongfully discharge him in three months, he is entitled to damages for the loss of time. On the other hand, it is possible to terminate the relationship by mutual agreement on or before the completion of the task. Among other methods of terminating an ordinary agency are (1) the death of either party, (2) the insanity of either party, and (3) war involving the country of the principal and agent.

Discussion Questions

4. *Explain what is meant by the elements required to make a contract binding on the part of both parties.*
5. *What is the meaning of agency relationship, and what are the ways agency may be created and terminated?*

THE LAW AND YOUR PROPERTY

The term *property* has several meanings. It may be used to identify an object having a physical existence. It may mean "legal rights" that are attached to property with physical existence. It may mean a tract of land, known as *real property,* or it may be used to denote *personal property.* As used in this discussion, we are interested mainly in the two categories known as *real property* and *personal property,* and in the methods of acquiring and terminating property rights.

Classes of Property

The Constitution of the United States provides that no one can be deprived of his property rights without due process of law. In law, the word *property* is not restricted to the material object itself—property is both the right and the interest, whether real or personal.

In addition to the rights in land, buildings and fixtures, mineral deposits, and bodies of water on the land, real property is also anything that is attached to the soil (such as grass, trees, bushes, and fences) and must be conveyed by a formal instrument recorded in a public office. The Uniform Aeronautics Act, which has been adopted by 21 states, provides that the owner of land owns even the space above it, subject to the right of aircraft use that does not interfere with the use of the land below and does not make such use dangerous to persons or property lawfully on the land. But how far an owner's rights extend above the land is as yet undetermined by law.

Generally, all property that is not real is classed as personal property, which consists of things temporary and movable and not of a freehold nature (that is, not an estate of inheritance or an estate for life).

Forms of Real-Property Ownership. Real property held by a person in his own right, without any other person being joined with him, is known as an *estate in severalty*. Real property held by more than one person is said to be *co-owned*. The forms of co-ownership of property generally recognized in this country (although no single state recognizes them all) are *joint tenancy, tenancy in common, tenancy by entirety,* and *community property*. The basic distinguishing characteristic between joint tenancy and tenancy in common is right of survivorship.

A *joint tenancy* is ownership in real property held by two or more persons jointly, with equal rights to share in its enjoyment during their lives. In joint tenancy, after the death of one owner, his interest passes to the surviving joint tenant or tenants (owners), until only one joint tenant survives. Upon the death of the only remaining tenant, the estate passes to his heirs. The use of joint tenancy in some states has been abused because of the tendency to avoid probate proceedings upon the death of a joint tenant. A joint-tenancy relationship may be severed by sale or conveyance of the interest of any joint tenant, or by partition or agreement.

Tenancy in common is real-property ownership in which two or more persons have, or are entitled to have, undivided possession of a common property *without* right of survivorship. If one owner dies, his interest passes to his heirs rather than to the other owner or owners. During his lifetime, each tenant is entitled to possession and use of the entire property. In general, a tenancy in common can be terminated only by consent of the parties or by partition—a division of property held jointly. In some states, if a deed is made out to X and Y without any statement as to the nature of ownership, the presumption is that the parties are tenants in common.

Tenancy by entirety is property ownership that may be held only by husband and wife. In other words, it is dependent upon the marital status. This tenancy is endowed by the right of survivorship: Upon the death of one spouse, the entire property goes to the surviving spouse. Also, neither tenant alone can transfer his interest to a third party. Tenancy by entirety may be terminated only by joint agreement, and becomes a tenancy in common upon divorce.

Several western and southwestern states provide for a community system between husband and wife known as *community property*.[5] Under this law, all real and personal property acquired by the husband and wife during the marriage, except that acquired by will, gift, or descent, is jointly owned. Some statutes provide for the right of survivorship; others provide that the half of the property belonging to the deceased spouse shall descend to the heirs of

[5] States currently having community-property laws are Arizona, California, Idaho, Louisiana, Nevada, New Mexico, Texas, and Washington.

the decedent. In community-property states, husband and wife may each file a separate state income tax return, each reporting only half the community income. (The federal income tax law also permits the filing of separate returns.)

Forms of Personal-Property Ownership. Whereas real property consists of an interest in land and things attached to the soil, personal property is restricted to movable goods, such as furniture, stocks, bonds, automobiles, jewelry, and clothing. Intangible goods, such as monetary claims and debts, are personal property, too. *Chattels personal* consist of both tangible and intangible personal property. This is quite different from *chattels real,* which are interests in real estate limited to their duration. It is important to understand how these chattels differ, and the manner in which personal and real property differs, since the methods of acquiring or transferring ownership are different.

How Property May Be Acquired. You may acquire real and personal property in different ways. One common way is by gift; another is by inheritance (descent), or by *legacy,* which is by means of a will—a written instrument. Or you may acquire personal property by *accession*—that is, by an increase in something you already own. Crops grown on your land or animals born to your herd belong to you by *right of accession.* Then, too, you may acquire personal property by intellectual achievement. For example, as an author or inventor you may obtain exclusive rights to your production for a limited time by obtaining a copyright or a patent. Or you may acquire property by outright purchase, and if it is real property, the seller conveys a deed to you.

Deeds. A *deed* is an instrument, in writing and requiring a notary public's seal, by which an owner or *grantor* conveys or transfers his interest in land to the buyer, who is called the *grantee.* Unlike the case with a contract, no consideration is needed to make a deed valid. A deed is required for the transfer of title to land even when it is a gift and no money is exchanged.

In terms of the interest conveyed, there are two types of deeds: (1) the *quitclaim deed,* see the specimen on page 70, merely transfers whatever interest the grantor may have in the property; and (2) the *warranty deed,* which warrants or guarantees that the owner has the right to convey title to the land. A warranty deed also warrants the title, by guaranteeing that the property is free of debt unless otherwise stated. Actually, title to real property does not pass until the deed has been delivered. Since it is an instrument under seal, it must be recorded in the county where the property is located. The warranty deed shown on page 72 is ready to be recorded.

Apart from the protection provided him by recording the deed, a buyer may protect himself by requiring the seller to furnish an *abstract of title.* This is a summarized report, based on the county records, of all conveyances that affect said land, as well as a statement of all liens, charges, and encumbrances affecting the title to it. A purchaser of land should request that he be furnished an abstract of title brought up to date.

TO 402 CA (9-66)

Quitclaim Deed

AFFIX $_____ I. R. STAMPS ABOVE

FOR A VALUABLE CONSIDERATION, receipt of which is hereby acknowledged, We, JOHN PAUL JONES

and INA RENE JONES, his wife,

hereby REMISE(S), RELEASE(S) AND FOREVER QUITCLAIM(S) to WILLIAM H. GRAY and MARY GRAY,

his wife, as joint tenants,

the following described real property in the City of Sacramento   county of Sacramento
state of California:

Lot 25 as shown on the "Map of River Oaks Addition" recorded in the

office of the County Recorder of Sacramento County December 15, 1952,

in Book 19 of Map 21.

Dated ____December 6, 19_____

John Paul Jones

Ina Rene Jones

STATE OF CALIFORNIA
COUNTY OF__Sacramento_____ } SS.
On __December 8, 19_____ before me, the under-
signed, a Notary Public in and for said State, personally appeared
____JOHN PAUL JONES_____
____Ina Rene Jones_____

_____, known to me
to be the person S___whose name__S___ subscribed to the within
instrument and acknowledged that___they___executed the same.
WITNESS my hand and official seal.
Signature ____*Mary Smith*_____
____Mary Smith_____
Name (Typed or Printed)
*If executed by a Corporation the Corporation Form
of Acknowledgment must be used.*

(This area for official notarial seal)

Title Order No._____   Escrow or Loan No._____

MAIL TAX STATEMENTS AS DIRECTED ABOVE

A quitclaim deed is used to convey to the grantee only such interests in
the real property as the grantor may have without a warranty of title, the
grantee assuming responsibility for any claims brought against the property.

The State of Texas,
County of HARRIS

} Know All Men by These Presents:

That JAMES GREEN, a widower not since remarried

of the County of   HARRIS   State of TEXAS   for and in consideration

of the sum of   Ten Thousand ($10,000)---

-- DOLLARS

to be   paid, and secured to be paid, by the grantee

hereinafter named -- as follows:

The sum of one thousand ($1,000) dollars to be paid on the delivery of this instru-
ment, the receipt of which is hereby acknowledged, and the further sum of seventy-
five ($75.00) dollars the first day of each and every month thereafter until the
purchase price has been paid in full. All of said sums except the first payment of
one thousand ($1,000) dollars are to be represented by promissory notes in the amount
of seventy-five ($75.00) dollars and to bear interest at the rate of six (6) per cent
per annum from date until paid,

es
have Granted, Sold and Conveyed, and by these presents do/Grant, Sell and Convey, unto the said
WALTER H. JENSEN

of the County of   HARRIS   State of   TEXAS   all that certain
TRACE OR PARCEL OF LAND DESCRIBED AS FOLLOWS, TO-WIT:
   Lot Three (3) Block Six (6) in the OPAL Addition, City of South Houston,
   in the County of Harris and State of Texas.

TO HAVE AND TO HOLD the above described premises, together with all and singular the rights
and appurtenances thereto in anywise belonging unto the said Grantee, his

es
heirs and assigns forever and he   do/hereby bind
heirs, executors and administrators, to Warrant and Forever Defend, all and singular the said premises
unto the said   grantee, his

heirs and assigns, against every person whomsoever lawfully claiming, or to claim the same, or any
part thereof.
But it is expressly agreed and stipulated that the Vendor's Lien is retained against the above
described property, premises and improvements, until the above described note   , and all interest thereon
are fully paid according to   face and tenor, effect and reading, when this deed shall become
absolute.
WITNESS this   hand   at, South Houston
this 25th   day of November   19
Witness at request of Grantor:

Veedee Greenwood   *James Green*
Carol Griffin   *Walter H. Jensen*

A warranty deed used to convey title to real property. This type of deed
may also contain certain statements, usually by the grantor, that other
things will be done or are true.

Leases. When you start your own business, you may find it more practical to lease real property than own it. Your agreement with the landlord to use the property is a *lease.* You are the *lessee* and your landlord is the *lessor.* A lease for longer than a year must, according to the Statute of Frauds, be in writing to be enforceable. The ground on which Radio City is located in New York City is leased for 99 years. A lease is an example of chattels real.

The more formal types of leases, such as the one shown on page 73, usually contain the following information:

1. Date of agreement
2. Names of landlord and tenant
3. Description of property
4. Length of lease

5. Manner of payment of rent
6. Responsibility for repairs
7. Liability for injury to third party
8. Right to sublet or assign

Mortgages. Property may be pledged as security for a loan, in which case the owner gives the lender a claim against the property by offering a mortgage. Mortgages against real estate are known as *real estate mortgages.* Mortgages on tangible personal property are known as *chattel mortgages.* Mortgages must be in writing and executed under seal, and should be recorded in the county in which the property is located. The parties to a mortgage are the *mortgagor* (debtor)—the one who gives the property as security for the loan—and the *mortgagee* (creditor)—the person to whom property is given as security for the loan. In other words, the mortgagor is the borrower and the mortgagee is the lender. If the debt is not paid, the mortgagee has the right to foreclose and sell the property to pay off the debt.

The Law of Negotiable Instruments

No one knows for certain when negotiable instruments were first used, although it is common knowledge that "commercial paper" (legal documents used in making loans) appeared on the business scene at least as early as the Middle Ages. The law at that time, commonly known as "the law of merchant," was eventually assimilated by English common law, and finally became part of our legal structure when the colonies adopted the English system. In succeeding years, the several states enacted statutes pertaining to "commercial paper," which term eventually was changed to "negotiable instruments," and includes promissory notes, drafts, and checks.

The term *negotiable* comes from three Latin words, *neg-, otium,* and *habilis,* which when joined together mean "not able to be leisurely." The connotation is that if anything is not performed at leisure, it is done quickly. When applied to a legal instrument, this means that it has a ready or quick transferability from one person to another. Under early English common law, commercial paper was not easily transferable, mainly because the credit stand-

---

The State of Texas,
County of

} **Know All Men by These Presents:**

Made this   2nd   day of   MARCH   , A. D. 19   , by and between

Smithson R. Conway--, known herein as LESSOR,

and   Rollo J. Jenkins--

-- , known herein as LESSEE,

(The terms "Lessor" and "Lessee" shall be construed in the singular or plural number according as they respectively represent one or more than one person.)

WITNESSETH, That the said Lessor does by these presents Lease and Demise unto the said Lessee the following described property, to-wit: Lying and being situated in the County of   WALLER   , State of Texas, and being A single family dwelling located at 1301 First Street in the town of Hempstead, con- six (6) rooms and bath.

for the term of twelve (12) months   beginning the   2nd   day of   MARCH A. D. 196-   and ending the   1st   day of   MARCH, 19   , paying therefor the sum of   Twelve hundred ($1200)------------------------------------- DOLLARS, payable monthly installments the second day of each month in advance.

upon the conditions and covenants following:

First. That Lessee will well and PUNCTUALLY pay said rents in manner and form as hereinbefore specified, and quietly deliver up said premises on the day of the expiration of this lease, in as good condition as the same were in when received, reasonable wear and tear thereof excepted.

Second. That the said premises shall be used for Family residence by the lessee and his immediate family.

and for no other purpose.

Third. That Lessee will not sub-let said premises, or any part thereof, to any person or persons whatsoever, without the consent of said Lessor, IN WRITING, thereto first obtained.

Fourth. That on failure to pay the rent in advance, as aforesaid, or to comply with any of the foregoing obligations, or in violation of any of the foregoing covenants, the Lessor may declare this lease forfeited at Lessor's discretion and Lessor or Lessor's agent or attorney shall have the power to enter and hold, occupy and repossess the entire premises hereinbefore described, as before the execution of these presents.

IN TESTIMONY WHEREOF, The parties to this agreement have hereunto set their hands in duplicate, the day and year above written.

Smithson R. Conway , LESSOR

Rollo J. Jenkins , LESSEE

A lease for a period of one year

ing of the person desiring the transfer was often questionable. Further, even if that person possessed a good credit rating, it was risky for him to use commercial paper because the law permitted the maker of the document to take legal action against any transferees who did not meet its terms.

A *negotiable instrument* is a written contract evidencing rights to receive money, which rights by negotiation may be transferred from one party to another by indorsement. The instrument need not be on any particular kind of material to be legal, nor must it necessarily be written with a certain instrument. It may be in ink, pencil, crayon; it may be printed, hand-written, typewritten, or engraved.

In 1896, the Uniform Negotiable Instruments Act brought all the common laws and state laws together that dealt with negotiable instruments. This act was adopted *in toto* by most of the states. More recently, the UCC, in its sections dealing with commercial paper and negotiable instruments, has rapidly been replacing the Negotiable Instruments Act in most states.

The requirements to which a negotiable instrument must adhere are in the following sections of the UCC and may be summarized thus:

> *UCC Section 3-104: Form of Instrument.* A negotiable instrument must be in writing, must be payable in money, and must be signed by the person putting it into circulation (the maker or drawer); and the promise to pay must be unconditional.
>
> *UCC Section 3-105: When Promise or Order Unconditional.* This section provides that mere expressions of intention by a maker to pay his note, or a request of a drawee to pay a bill, are unconditional, and such intentions and wording will not create a negotiable instrument. A promise or order is not unconditional if the instrument states that it is subject to or governed by any other agreement.
>
> *UCC Section 3-106: Sum Certain.* The sum payable must be certain in amount, even if it is to be paid with stated interest, by stated install-ments, or with a stated discount.
>
> *UCC Section 3-107: Money.* An instrument is payable in money if the medium of exchange in which it is payable is money at the time the instrument is made.
>
> *UCC Section 3-108: Payable on Demand.* For an instrument to be payable on demand, it must be paid at sight or on presentation.
>
> *UCC Section 3-110: Payable to Order.* To be negotiable the instrument must be drawn payable to order or any person specified with reasonable certainty. Adding the words "or order" after the name of the payee makes the instrument negotiable because then the maker is willing to pay either the designated payee, or anyone to whom the payee orders that it be paid.

A distinction should be made between instruments payable "to bearer" and those payable "to order." Negotiable instruments (such as checks and drafts) marked payable to bearer on the face are freely transferred without indorsement, the same as money. Title passes by delivery. But an instrument payable "to order" requires the indorsement of the named payee before it may be negotiated. If it is lost or stolen before it is indorsed, title will not pass.

It should be evident from this discussion that such instruments as leases, wills, warranties, and sales tickets, for example, do not possess all the require-ments of a negotiable instrument and therefore are not negotiable. (Our more commonly used negotiable instruments—checks, drafts, promissory notes, and certificates of deposit—will be discussed again in Chapters 14 and 23, regarding their uses.)

Instruments Payable to Bearer. As we have seen, the payee of an order paper must be named with reasonable certainty. The same exactness is not required for negotiable instruments payable to bearer. Actually, a negotiable instrument may be made payable to bearer without naming him. For example, a check payable to the order of "cash" is negotiable although the payee is not named.

(handwritten margin note: payable to order named payee)

Instruments Payable to Two or More Payees. Sometimes negotiable papers are drawn to the order of two or more payees together or in the alternative. For instance, instruments payable to "A or B" are in the alternative. The instruments, therefore, may be negotiated by either A or B. But instruments payable to "A and B" together are not in the alternative and may be negotiated only by both of them. Both parties must indorse the instruments in order to negotiate them. As you can see, having an alternative as to which payee may indorse the order paper depends upon the way the instrument is drawn. The Code has incorporated most of the provisions of the Negotiable Instruments Law.

How Negotiable Instruments Are Transferred. Transfer of these commercial papers from one person to another is by the simple process of *indorsement,* by way of a signature that should appear on the back of the instrument. The person to whom the instrument is transferred is the *indorsee.* This person is also the *holder in due course,* which means that he must either be in possession of the instrument properly indorsed or be the bearer of the instrument, having been named as the payee. A holder in due course is one who acquires the instrument under the following conditions: (1) It must be complete and regular on its face; (2) the holder must have given consideration (value) for the paper; (3) it must be accepted in good faith; and (4) the instrument must be accepted without notice of defects in the title or defense against payment. If you accept a bank check by indorsement under these conditions, you are a holder in due course and the legal owner of the check.

Forms of Indorsement. Commercial law recognizes four principal kinds of indorsements that may be used to transfer ownership of a negotiable instrument. They are (1) blank, (2) special, (3) restrictive, and (4) qualified. Let us see how each of these forms of indorsement appears in everyday practice.

When the indorser merely signs his name, he is using a *blank indorsement.* This is the most common form used to indorse checks, drafts, and promissory notes. When you indorse a check in blank, you transfer ownership of the instrument, and you warrant that it is genuine and valid, that you had title to it, and that you accept a liability to pay the amount of the instrument if it is not honored by the drawee bank.

It is not wise business procedure to indorse a check in blank except at the time it is negotiated. If it is indorsed in blank and is lost or stolen, it may be negotiated by the finder or thief. By using an indorsement that restricts a check to certain purposes, or by indicating the name of the indorsee, you can avoid this danger.

A *special indorsement* consists of your signature and words specifying the person to whom you make the instrument payable. The language of this indorsement may read "Pay to order of Jack Johnson," followed by your own signature. This special indorsement is sometimes called an *indorsement in full.* As in the case of the blank indorsement, a special indorsement transfers title to the instrument and imposes a liability upon the indorser to pay the amount of the instrument.

BLANK INDORSEMENT	SPECIAL INDORSEMENT
Jim Right	*Pay to order of Jack Johnson Jim Right*

A *restrictive indorsement* prevents further negotiations of the instrument to any other person except for collection or deposit. If you hold several checks that you want to deposit in a bank to the credit of your account, you may indorse each check by writing "For deposit only," or "For collection only," or "For deposit to the account of James John." Actually, a restrictive indorsement restricts further negotiation of the instrument. It is an excellent safeguard.

A fourth way to indorse a check, although it is not commonly used, is by means of a *qualified indorsement,* which qualifies or limits the obligation that ordinarily exists when you indorse an instrument. It does not affect the passage of title, but it limits the indorser's liability to the extent of the qualification. In fact, it does not release you from all liability, but you are released if the drawee bank refuses to make payment. Thus, if you want to transfer a check or note by qualified indorsement, you indorse it by writing the words "Without recourse," followed by your signature. Qualified indorsements may be used by attorneys and trustees when representing another person but at the same time not wishing to accept the normal responsibility of an indorser. This form of indorsement is most often used when the qualified indorser is the one who admits to having no personal interest in the transactions, as in the case of an attorney who merely indorses to his principal a check made payable to him by a third party. Since the indorser is not a party to the transaction, he is not in a position where he should be required to guarantee payment of the instrument.

As we have already observed, the most common type of temporary transfer of the use of real property in business is by lease. Permitting others

RESTRICTIVE INDORSEMENT

For deposit only
Jim Right

QUALIFIED INDORSEMENT

Without recourse
Jim Right

to use or rent personal property, such as an automobile, without transferring title or ownership is known as a *bailment.* The person who owns the property is the *bailor,* and one to whom the owner delivers temporary possession is the *bailee.*

The law provides that ordinary and reasonable care must be exercised by the bailee. Failure by the bailee to return the property at termination of the bailment gives the bailor the right to seek recovery. Another example of a bailment relationship is the storage of goods in a warehouse.

Discussion Questions

6. *What are the basic differences between real and personal property, and what are some of the ways ownership in each may be transferred?*
7. *What requirements must an instrument fulfill to be negotiable, and how is negotiability accomplished?*
8. *What is the responsibility of the bailee to the bailor?*

THE LAW OF SALES

The buying and selling of tangible personal property (chattels) takes place at all levels of our marketing system. Ownership is legally represented by title, which in practice is symbolized by such documents as invoices, bills of sale, warehouse receipts, or bills of lading.

The sale of goods is in essence a contractual relationship whereby the seller, for consideration, agrees to transfer title and possession of the goods to the buyer. The seller is known as the *vendor* and the buyer as the *vendee.* A bill of sale is one way to transfer title to tangible personal property, and a deed, as we have said, is used to transfer title to real property. Our discussion here will deal primarily with two broad topics: *title transfers* and *warranties.*

When Does Title Pass?

Sale on Approval. A sales transaction may give the buyer the privilege of returning the goods. This is known as a *sale on approval.* Section 2-326 of the UCC provides that in the absence of a contrary agreement, title and risk of loss remain with the seller under a sale on approval. When there is approval by the buyer, then title transfers.

Title to Goods Sold f.o.b. When goods are sold f.o.b. (free on board) factory, it means that the title to the goods passes to the buyer at the point where he assumes the costs of shipping. As a general proposition, risk of loss is connected with the title, and if the goods are lost, stolen, or destroyed, the party who has title at that time will bear the loss.

Goods Sold at Auction. UCC Section 2-328 provides that when goods are sold at auction, title passes to the buyer when the auctioneer announces by the fall of his gavel or in any other customary manner that the auction is complete as to a particular lot.

Sale on Installment Plan. Under the UCC, possession of the goods is transferred to the buyer, but title remains with the seller as security until the full price is paid, at which time the title passes to the buyer.

Sale COD and for Cash. When goods are sold COD (cash on delivery), this generally implies that the seller has appointed the common carrier as his agent to collect the purchase price as part of the condition of delivery. Title passes to the buyer subject to delivery. Risk of loss of goods in transit is on the buyer who is not permitted to examine the goods upon receipt before he pays for them. In a cash sale, the title does not pass until the price is paid, which may mean until the buyer's check is cashed.

Warranties

A *warranty* may be defined as an affirmation of fact or promise, stated or implied by one party to another in a sale, that certain facts or conditions of the goods or services are as promised or implied. Often it is the warranty that induces the potential customer to buy. The law recognizes two kinds of warranties under the UCC: *express warranty* and *implied warranty.*[6]

Express Warranty. Any statement of fact made by the seller regarding the characteristics of the property sold, either orally or in writing, that becomes

---

[6] A product-warranty law recently enacted by the State of California, which is considered the first law of its kind at the state level, requires manufacturers in that state to designate service facilities that are available to fulfill promises in the warranty. This law does not require the manufacturer to provide any warranties, but if a warranty is made for the goods, it is the responsibility of the manufacturer to see that such services are available to the customer.

a part of the sales agreement is an *express warranty*. The following requisites must be fulfilled to constitute an express warranty: (1) conditions must be expressed orally or in writing in the sales agreement, (2) statements made by seller must affirm facts relating to the goods now or in the future, and (3) such affirmation of facts or promise must act as an inducement to the purchase of goods. For example, the seller may say, "This article is pure linen."

Implied Warranty. An implied warranty is one that was not made by the seller but that is implied by law. Fitness for a particular purpose is one kind of implied warranty. Another may be freedom from liens where the sale of the article involves title.

Discussion Questions

9. *What purposes do the following instruments serve? (a) bill of sale; (b) bill of lading; (c) warehouse receipt.*
10. *Explain the difference between an express warranty and an implied warranty.*

ETHICS AND MORALS
IN A CHANGING ENVIRONMENT

We already have rules (laws) to guide us that the vast majority of us are willing to use. What is sometimes missing in our behavior is the willingness to improve our conduct and police our ethical and moral standards.

Definition of Ethics and Morals

The term *ethics* comes from a Greek word meaning "custom." In a broader sense, ethics is more commonly regarded as pertaining to right and wrong behavior as defined by society. In other words, society has established positive guides regarding what ought to be done in certain circumstances, applied to one's personal behavior. And when ethics is applied to business, we call it *business ethics,* because these standards of behavior are supposed to be based on what is right and wrong.

Implicit in ethics is the concept of *equity,* a term that is often used in law as well. The Emperor Justinian said that equity means "to live honestly, to harm nobody, and to render every man his due." Equity is both the basis of ethics and a system of jurisprudence. As we have noted earlier in this chapter, in the courts equity implies fairness, justice, and honest dealings.

Morals comes from a Latin word, *mores,* referring to a code of conduct identified with religion. The fourth chapter of the first book of the Bible poses

Or Principles individual code

the question, "Am I my brother's keeper?"; and the Golden Rule, with its simple statement, "Do unto others as you would have them do unto you," has remained, over the centuries, basic in the moral code. Some persons are not willing to accept the full impact of social responsibilities that go with living under a moral code. They believe such a code may be for others but not for them. When this happens, personal standards become mixed, and individual responsibilities having to do with one's personal conduct are difficult to identify. This is the reason legal responsibilities turn into laws—in order to have explicit definitions of conformity.

Since personal standards among individuals vary according to the value placed upon truth, honesty, integrity, and responsibility, our ethics and our morals should be based on some kind of standards. The fact that these two terms are often used interchangeably makes the need for standards more important.

One basis of ethics and morals is the personal standard, having to do with concepts of mercy, fair play, social justice, and altruism. Business policies can be based primarily on this kind of standard.

A second basis is the theistic standard, founded on the belief that God, as the Creator, is the source of all that is good, and that the writings of the prophets reveal God's laws through the Holy Scriptures.

A third basis is the behavioristic standard, which represents the cumulative judgments of a large number of persons who have given sanction to the ways people conduct themselves based on a code. Pressures from our environment largely influence man's behavioristic standards. As these pressures change, our behavioristic standards change too.

The fourth basis is the legal standard. We all have personal rights under the laws, which are restrictive rather than permissive in determining our rights. When court decisions are rendered, as individuals we have a tendency to stay just inside the law in our behavior, yet this position is not entirely ethical or morally right.

Business should conduct itself ethically at all times. The extent to which this is possible relates to the question, Whose ethics should prevail? Some executives have one set of ethics for their personal lives and a different set, much less restrictive, for use in business.

Is Ethics Broader Than Law?

The concept of ethics includes more than the legal technicalities of punishing a person who commits an unlawful act. We take pride in the belief that civilization has advanced to the point where as mature individuals we know right from wrong. Yet the lack of ethical conduct on the part of some people makes you wonder what potential tragedy lies ahead. What has happened to some ancient civilizations could be a lesson to be remembered now.

A genuinely ethical man does not seek to justify his conduct by the plea that he has kept within the law, for an act may be lawful and yet highly unethical. Since ethics carries with it the broad idea of "what should be," it demands the existence of sound moral character.

Making Business More Professional

What has business done to make executives realize their responsibilities toward society?

Most businessmen recognize the need to raise the standards that govern their moral obligations. Local Better Business Bureaus, for example, seek to promote a better understanding of our economic system and to build public confidence in business by helping to establish codes of ethics for business groups. Trade associations are interested in promoting codes of ethics. Luther Hodges, former Secretary of Commerce, said at a conference on business ethics that "this matter of moral and ethical behavior in business or in government comes back, finally, to a personal situation."

There is a growing public demand for more practical moral guidelines in the form of concrete codes of ethics for business firms. For example, the American Management Association makes available over 400 examples of corporation codes of ethics. But despite these efforts, the pressures of competition and conflicting interests sometimes result in unethical practices.

Conflict of Interest. Today, one of the most talked-about ethical problems is the "conflict of interest" issue. A conflict of interest arises when an executive has an interest in a transaction about which he must make a decision so substantial that it might affect his personal judgment, thereby causing him to favor one company over another because of the personal gain he would receive. For example, the president of Company A approves, without investigating the price, the purchase of a large order from Firm B, a company in which he also owns shares. He is aware that this purchase will probably produce a substantial profit for both Firm B and him.

To avoid this conflict, many companies are now requesting that their executives who have assumed a financial or other outside business relationship that might ultimately involve a conflict of interest should inform the company of these circumstances. Then another executive, one who has no interest in the outside firm, can make these decisions.

Ethics in Advertising

Since the days of the patent-medicine show, the consumer has been plagued by persons who seek to sell their goods through the use of misleading facts in advertising. By the use of mass advertising media, quantities of goods are sold throughout the world by American producers. Because of the volume of advertising, it has become almost impossible to detect and apprehend all those who use deceptive practices, and detection has been made both costly and difficult for the advertising industry and for the federal and state governments.

There was a time when advertisers themselves were not in agreement as to what represented deception. One of the first concerted efforts to attack the problem of standards and dishonest advertising was made by *Printers' Ink,* a nationally known magazine devoted to advertising and marketing. This magazine developed a model statute that any state could adopt to regulate and control those who used false and deceptive statements in advertising. To date, 44 states and the District of Columbia have enacted legislation based on the *Printers' Ink* code, making it a misdemeanor to use in advertising an assertion or statement of fact that is untrue, deceptive, or misleading.

In 1917, when the leading advertising agencies formed the American Association of Advertising Agencies (the "4A's"), one of the first things this group did was to adopt a code of ethical obligations to the public, to advertisers, and to publishers who accept paid advertising. But despite the pressure from this code, advertising agencies sometimes still make exaggerated claims about their products. This may be due to a tendency of the agency to draw a thin line between what is regarded as ethical and what is not. On occasion, an agency may surrender to pressures from a client to make a statement or claim that is only a half-truth. Responsible advertising men know they must recognize these pressures and must be willing to accept their responsibility to tell the truth to the public, regardless of the advertising medium used. If they do not, the public will demand stronger government controls.

Another effective self-regulating procedure is the work done by those newspaper and magazine publishers whose policy is not to accept advertisements that do not meet the prevailing standards of accuracy and ethics. The *New York Times,* for example, has for years maintained a strong censorship by declining to take ads making questionable claims. And when Hadacol, a patent medicine, was popular, the *Milwaukee Journal* declined to take several thousands of dollars in advertising for it, presumably because it would have been in poor taste for the newspaper to publicize this product.

Ethics in the Accounting Profession

As with the practices of law and medicine, the history of accounting reaches back over the centuries. But as a profession with its own code of ethics, accounting is only about 75 years old. In 1896, New York state passed the first law establishing the Certified Public Accountant (CPA) designation. This was the beginning of professional public recognition and of a code of ethics for the accounting profession.

The code of ethics that the certified public accountant is expected to observe is strongly enforced by the members of his profession. The CPA serves both large and small enterprises. Each public-accounting engagement is a separate and distinct assignment. The work varies with the type and size of the business, the kind of record, and the amount of services required. Hence, the fee charged for the accountant's services is contingent upon the amount of work involved. Members of the profession are not permitted to advertise except by means of modest cards announcing the formation of a firm or the election of partners.

The CPA is forbidden to violate the confidential relations between himself and his client by revealing facts about his client's business. His professional judgment must not be influenced in any way by the personal interest of his client. Moreover, he must not allow his name to be associated with business forecasts in a manner suggesting that he guarantees the forecast. Few professions have taken their code of ethics more seriously than have the certified public accountants.

Discussion Questions

11. *Distinguish between a moral code and an ethical standard.*
12. *Why is conflict of interest considered a problem of ethics?*

SUMMARY

Over the years, our laws developed under a legal system that includes both civil law, derived from statutes, and common law, which consists of precedents based on court decisions. Laws concerned with the rights and liabilities of individuals, partnerships, corporations, and other organizations are called private laws. Under the Constitution, each state has the right to enact its own laws. The code that embraces the major areas of commercial law is the UCC.

A contract is a binding agreement between two or more competent parties in a form required by law, for a lawful purpose, supported by consideration, that may be enforced by either party. Some contracts are unenforceable because they lack the necessary contractual elements. Another common legal relationship is known as agency. This is the relationship between a principal and his agent. A principal is liable for all the acts of his agent, while an agent is bound to carry out the principal's instructions; but if he exceeds his authority, he becomes liable to his principal.

Real property is the term applied to an interest in land or other forms of real estate. Personal property is the right to moveable property, including stocks, books, furniture, and jewelry. If real property is used as security, the obligation created is a real estate mortgage.

A negotiable instrument, or commercial paper, is a form of contractual obligation that can be transferred by indorsement from one party to another. Examples of negotiable instruments are checks, notes, and drafts. To be negotiable (capable of being transferred by indorsement), an instrument must conform to the UCC or to the Uniform Negotiable Instruments Act. Among the requirements of negotiability are these: (1) the instrument must be in writing and signed by maker or drawer; (2) it must contain an unconditional promise or order to pay a sum certain in amount; (3) the sum must be payable on demand or at a definite future date; (4) *it must be payable to order or bearer; and (5) the drawee or payee must be named with reasonable certainty.*

Ethics and moral standards are important controls over business. An act may be lawful and yet unethical because it violates a moral standard involving the difference between right and wrong.

VOCABULARY REVIEW

Match the following vocabulary terms with the statements below:

a. Abstract of title
b. Adjective law
c. Compensatory damages
d. Contract
e. Deed
f. Ethics
g. Joint tenancy
h. Negotiable instrument
i. Quitclaim deed
j. Real property
k. Statutory law
l. Tenancy in common
m. Usury
n. Warranty deed

1. A written contract evidencing rights to receive money, which rights by negotiation may be transferred from one party to another by indorsement
2. A sum of money that will, as far as possible, compensate one for a loss
3. Anything that is attached to the soil, which must be conveyed by a formal instrument recorded in a public office
4. Law that has to do with procedural machinery required to enforce personal rights and duties
5. Real-property ownership in which two or more persons have, or are entitled to have, undivided possession of common property with right of survivorship
6. An instrument, in writing and requiring a notary public's seal, by which an owner or grantor conveys or transfers his interest in land to the buyer, called the grantee
7. Interest charged beyond the legal rate
8. The instrument that warrants or guarantees that the owner has the right to convey title to the land
9. Written law consisting of formal declarations or enactments (statutes) by government bodies and agencies
10. Ownership of real property held by two or more persons jointly with the right to share in its enjoyment during their lives
11. A rule of personal conduct that is accepted by society as being right and proper
12. A summary report, based on the county records, of all conveyances that affect real property, as well as a statement of all liens, charges, and encumbrances affecting title to said land
13. An agreement between two or more competent parties in the form required by law, for a legal purpose, supported by consideration, and enforceable by either party
14. The instrument that merely transfers to another whatever the grantor may have in the property

PROBLEMS AND PROJECTS

1. James held a note payable to himself. It was stolen from his office by Brown, who forged James's name in the indorsement and then sold the note to Williams,

who was not aware of the theft or forgery. Williams then indorsed the note to Gee for value received, but when the note became due, the maker (Ray) refused to pay it. If Gee sues Williams, can he recover? Discuss your reasons.

Mrs. Smith ordered a large unabridged English-language dictionary from a publishing company in San Francisco. She specifically requested that it be delivered COD parcel post to her home. Three months elapsed and she had not received it, so she wrote to the publisher. He replied that the book had been mailed to her seven weeks earlier but was not insured by the sender. Who is liable for this loss if the book cannot be found within a reasonable time? Explain your answer.

A BUSINESS CASE

Case 3-1   Loyd Grain Company *v.* Roller and Hiller

The Loyd Grain Company, plaintiff, brought an action against Jack Roller and Howard Hiller, defendants and partners, to recover the price of a truckload of grain purchased by the defendants as members of the partnership of Roller and Hiller. At the trial, the existence of a partnership was denied.

Sam Jones, owner of the Loyd Grain Company, a sole proprietorship, testified that he had known Howard Hiller for about five years and considered him to be an honest man. He testified that on July 29, 1972, Hiller brought Roller to the elevator and introduced him as his partner, saying that Roller was to provide the labor and Hiller the capital for the partnership. On that day, Hiller bought a load of grain and paid cash for it. On August 10, 1972, Roller called the grain company, asking to buy another load of grain for delivery on August 14. Roller signed the delivery ticket at the elevator and he gave the grain company a check in full. The check was honored by the bank.

On August 20, 1972, Roller asked Jones for another load of grain, which he picked up on August 21, giving the grain company a check in the amount of $1,595. Again Roller was the drawer of the check. The next day, the grain company was notified by the bank that this check was returned to the drawer because of insufficient funds. Jones then notified Roller that his check was refused for payment by the bank. Roller promised to send another check. But the following day, Hiller called Sam Jones to inform him that Roller was not his partner and that they had not been partners for about two months. He said he had no liability for this debt and that it was Roller's responsibility to make the check good.

During the next three months, Jones made repeated efforts to collect for the grain. Finally Roller told him he could not pay and that if he wanted his money he should sue Hiller. Suit was filed November 15, 1972.

1. Can the Loyd Grain Company recover the cost of the grain?

2. Who is liable for this debt? Why?

government
regulation
and
taxation

CHAPTER FOUR

Since the founding of this nation, the role of government in business has varied from a policy of *laissez faire* "to let alone" to control of business. During the early part of the nineteenth century, the phrase *caveat emptor* (let the buyer beware) prevailed between the seller and his customer. Today, the seller–customer affinity is *caveat venditor* (let the seller beware). Federal laws prohibit monopolies that restrain trade, regulate wages and working hours, control banking practices, set safety standards in mining, railroads, commercial aviation, approve communication channels and broadcasting station ownership, and enter into many other areas of business.

There are state laws covering intrastate transportation, public utilities, resource conservation, state banking operations, taxes, health codes, insurance operations, and natural-resource environment use.

Until late in the nineteenth century, businesses were largely unregulated at any level of government. This was the period in American industry noted for "rugged individualism," and it produced such business giants as Jim Fisk,

Jay Gould, James J. Hill, and Cornelius Vanderbilt, who with ruthless effort gained fortunes by controlling railroads, and J. P. Morgan and Andrew Carnegie, powers in the steel industry. The Mellons in coal, aluminum, and oil, and the du Ponts in chemicals were dominant in these industries. Oil baron John D. Rockefeller, Sr., finally lost his monopoly over oil as a result of a Supreme Court decision in 1911 that stemmed from the fact that judicial review is a constitutional right of business in its relations with the government; under the Fifth Amendment to the Constitution, "No person shall be . . . deprived of life, liberty, or property, without due process of law. . . ." Today's business methods, objectives, and organizations are a product of the past as well as the present.

Everyone agrees that labor, capital, natural resources, managerial skills, and technological know-how are indispensable in maintaining the high productive capacity needed to sustain this nation. But opinions differ widely as to the amount of government intervention required to provide these necessities for the overall good of society as well as for the benefit of a particular line of business. Students of government and well-informed businessmen alike give divided counsel on this subject. Meanwhile, government participation in and control of business and industry continue to increase (they have in fact reached a scale that could not even have been anticipated following World War II), and our taxes keep rising with no relief in sight.

The subject of taxation, like that of government regulation, is of exceptional interest to businessmen, for the increasing costs of government at all levels have imposed upon the business enterprise an increasingly heavy tax burden. There is no disputing the fact that in order for the government to finance its operations it must obtain vast sums of money by means of public taxes. The question is, What sort of taxes are most equitable, and who should pay them?

All in all, in this chapter we shall try to do five things: (1) explore the functions of our federal and state governments as related to our economy; (2) analyze the reasons for government controls over business; (3) discuss the nature of those controls, and of related laws; (4) analyze the various kinds of taxes that are levied on businesses and individuals; and (5) measure the effect of these taxes on our business system.

AUTHORITY AND FUNCTIONS OF GOVERNMENT

Businessmen are keenly interested in the present role of government in their field because they know they are much affected by it. And they are alert to signs of further governmental encroachment into their territory, aware that the regulation of business has increased steadily since the nation's founding. But the point of emphasis here is not that businessmen are alarmed by government regulations (true though that may be). It is that businessmen realize that in order to safeguard their interests, they must be familiar with the *overall* direction in which government is moving, and either move with it or try to change it.

Source of Government Authority

Our federal government derives its authority to pass legislation from the people. The basis of their authority is the Constitution of the United States. Article I, Section 8 of the U.S. Constitution gives Congress the power to make all laws "necessary and proper" to carry out its duties indispensible to the functioning of any business system, such as the power to coin money and punish counterfeiting.

Functions of Government

The functions performed by government may be classified as (1) political, and (2) economic. The main political functions, in summary form, are as follows:

Protection of Persons and Property. A political duty of government is to provide the people with personal security and protection for their property. This protection includes defense against unfriendly acts by foreign states.

Equitable System of Justice. The government is expected to establish and promote the administration of the legal code of the state, which includes both civil and public law. In an earlier chapter we studied many of the legal aspects of private contractual relations, property, and debts. The National Labor Relations Act is an illustration of public legislation, to be covered in a later chapter, dealing with the subject of labor legislation.

Guarantee and Promotion of Human Rights. Under the First Amendment to the Constitution, Congress shall enact no law "respecting the establishment of religion or prohibiting the free exercise thereof." Also, the right to vote shall not be denied on account of race, color, or previous condition of servitude.

Promotion of the General Welfare. Congress has the power to levy and collect taxes for the benefit of the "general welfare of the United States"; and the states have the "police power" to promote the health, safety, morals, and general welfare of all citizens.

The economic functions of government are these:

To Promote Production of Desired Goods. In performing this function, government is responsible for creating and maintaining competition, curbing monopolies, and promoting research and technology, and for the development and conservation of natural resources.

To Provide a System of Prices and Incomes. This function is concerned with the general principle of eliminating, as far as possible, economic discrimination, compulsion, coercion, monopoly, and fraud.

Discussion Questions

1. *Why was business largely unregulated until late in the nineteenth century?*
2. *What are the main functions of government at the federal level, and in what ways are these functions related to government regulation of business?*

GOVERNMENT'S INCREASED CONTROL OVER BUSINESS

In the kind of economy we live in, it is often asserted by some, government control over business and industry should be totally eliminated. Perhaps enough has been said thus far to indicate that this is unlikely, for there is no sacredness in private enterprise per se. Actually, the guiding principle should be as follows: *Whatever activity is needed in the best interest of the public should be performed by a government agency when (1) there is a strong expectation that it will be better performed by a government than by a private individual or agency, or (2) when private enterprise is not willing to or cannot perform such an activity.* In applying this guiding principle, there is no hard-and-fast line that determines when an activity should be performed by government and when it can be more satisfactorily provided by a private agency. The final choice is a matter of judgment, weighing all the facts, and not one of abstract theory.

Reasons

In light of the foregoing principle, here are some of the reasons that have been suggested for government regulation of business:

To protect the welfare of the individual and to promote higher standards of public health, safety, morals, and well-being. Most communities have established health and sanitary regulations that must be observed by restaurants, food stores, and other kinds of eating establishments. Without these regulations, some businesses might become careless and fail to apply proper precautions in the handling of food and equipment. Other laws have been enacted to protect the health of workers in offices and factories.

Local zoning laws help protect the value of residential property by restricting the areas in which industrial and other commercial enterprises may be established. Finally, traffic laws have been passed to safeguard human lives.

To prevent monopolies and combinations of business that tend to restrain trade or promote unfair practices. A monopoly exists when a firm exercises control over the supply of a commodity or service in such a manner as to give the organization either complete or dominant control over the price. If business interests were completely free of restraint, they would tend to take over competing firms in order to control selling prices or to dominate the sources of supply. The unrestrained monopoly that would inevitably grow out of such practices would undoubtedly prove detrimental to the public interest. (The subject of monopolies will be discussed at greater length in this chapter.)

To conserve our natural resources. The government is apparently the only agency in a position to protect our natural resources from willful destruction. Soil and water conservation, power-development projects, and reforestation programs are among the methods our federal government uses to conserve our natural resources.

To maintain an expanding and prosperous economy. Among the most common economic controls exercised by government are those over banks, building and loan societies, trust companies, investment companies, investment funds, and stock exchanges. Farm prices, wages, hours of employment, and personal credit are also subject to controls, on the ground that wise regulation will prevent recessions and depressions. Our government is dedicated to promoting and maintaining conditions that will help to sustain high employment, full production, and peak consumption.

To protect the public against abusive practices. Government control is needed to prohibit certain abusive business practices, such as usury, false advertising, and reduction in standards. At the state and local level, legislation in the form of sanitary codes and zoning laws helps to protect the health and welfare of the public.

To meet changing world conditions. A continued need for national defense has called for large government commitments for military efforts. This, when added to the goods required for technical aid to other nations, has required more domestic control to prevent inflation and help maintain sources of raw materials for defense use.

Competition and Monopoly

Traditionally, our economic system is characterized by the presence of *competition,* the pursuit of economic advantages in rivalry with others. Since competition supposedly assures efficiency and benefits consumers, it is encouraged. At the same time, our system sanctions certain enterprises in which competition is uneconomic. These are known as *natural monopolies* and are most common in the public utilities field. They are subject to direct government regulation.

Competition. Under capitalism, entrepreneurs in each line of business compete with each other, except in the case of selected public utilities, which enjoy a monopolistic situation and are subject to regulation by some government agency.

Early economists described the concept of *pure competition* as the presence of an indeterminate number of traders all dealing in the same product, with no individual buyer or seller able to influence price, which is determined by supply and demand. The perfectly competitive firm has no pricing problem, since market price is set by the market—perfect competition becomes another name for pure competition.

Oligopoly and Monopolistic Competition. The term *oligopoly* assumes a market situation in which comparatively few firms produce identical or similar goods and where sellers have the ability to influence price by changing the volume of goods produced. The steel, automobile, and cigarette industries are said to be oligopolistic. The tests to determine whether oligopoly exists are the size of each seller's production as it relates to the total supply and the number of competitors operating in the industry. While competition in many industries is keen, it is a fact that large firms sometimes account for 75 to 90 percent of the total output. *Monopolistic competition* is said to prevail in an industry when a firm is to some degree in the position of a monopoly but also competes with other firms. Through advertising campaigns and emphasis on brand loyalty, such firms are able to avoid the rigors of strictly price competition. Most firms are imperfectly competitive, since they are free to set the price at which they will sell their product.

Public Attitude Toward Controls

During the 1930's labor and business repeatedly objected to government legislation and regulations proposed by the federal government. Usually, such criticism was based on the contention that such legislation would destroy personal freedom and individual initiative. However, during World War II, all sectors of the public tended to cooperate fully. Practically all of the war-time rules were eliminated after peace was declared. Since then federal legislation pertaining to business has taken several forms. Most of the laws discussed in this chapter were designed to maintain a competitive business system.

A law that attracted only limited public attention at the time it was enacted by Congress was the Economic Stabilization Act of 1970. This act authorized stand-by-powers to the President to "issue such orders as he may deem appropriate to stabilize prices, rents, wages, and salaries." While the bill was being debated, the President said he was opposed to it and that he would not use it, although inflation was climbing, job rolls were shrinking, and unions were winning substantial wage increases that added to the inflation.

Unable to halt inflation by the process of shaping taxation and public expenditures—for which the general name is "fiscal policy"—the President on August 15, 1971, suddenly announced a 90-day freeze on wages, prices, and rents. Neither dividends nor interest rates were included, but voluntary restraint was urged. The purpose of the freeze was to shut off price increases and wage raises for a certain period thereby allowing the Administration time to prepare a more comprehensive program (Phase 2) of the Administration's control plan.

Rank-and-file union members generally supported the idea. Several labor leaders were skeptical that it would work; they wanted a freeze on profits as well. Businessmen in general were more cooperative than labor leaders, while the public indicated the action should have been taken sooner. Four university professors brought suit charging that the law was unconstitutional because Congress had delegated too much lawmaking power to the President.

Government and Public Policy

What Is Government? *Government* is a source of authority that is exercised in the name of society to maintain ordered relations in a community. This means that government is concentrated power that is supreme over other sectors of society in its power to command obedience. It is both a source of authority and the framework for exercising authority. It is used by those holding policy-making offices and having the responsibility for enacting legislative measures necessary to the maintenance of ordered relations.

As related to business in the United States, the functions of government are essentially twofold: (1) to encourage production of goods and services through private enterprise, and (2) to provide the means for determining prices and income in accord with public interest. To accomplish these functions, government works to devise and conduct social arrangements that include such relationships as freedom of choice, freedom of contract, right of private property, opportunity to compete, and maintenance of price structures and fiscal policies. At all levels governments have the right to express and adjust both public and private interests through the establishment of public policy.

What Is Public Policy? The term "public policy" lacks a precise definition because it is subject to varying interpretations. It may be either a restraining or an encouraging influence over business. As used here, *public policy* is a statement or an interpretation of an action carrying the weight of government authority that tends to influence business decision making. While enacting a law, Congress may make a statement of public policy for or against bigness in business that is based on investigation and debate.

It should be noted that not all public policy carries the full support of all citizens or all members of Congress. Instead, it is an assertion of government power having direct significance and application to a limited number of elected or appointed government officials and voters. In contrast, the term business policy, which is a guide in the decision process within a business organization, is designed to be used by all personnel in the organization who render decisions. Business policy is a subject of discussion in Chapter 8 in relation to the study of business organization.

3. *Compare the political and economic functions of government with functions of government specifically related to business.*
4. *Since competition is present in our economic system, which kinds of competition are deemed necessary to regulate and which are not so closely controlled?*

ANTITRUST LAWS AND COMPETITION

Up to the time of the Civil War—indeed, until the beginning of the twentieth century—most businesses were small. Only a few engaged in what might then be called "large factory" types of operation. Farming was the major occupation; the nation was predominantly rural. The kind of competitive system we have now involving big business was virtually nonexistent. A few railroads gave special rates to favored customers to secure their patronage. Companies involved in oil, coal, and steel were seeking new markets and were trying to expand. And in the 1880's, the "trust" agreement was introduced as a legal device to gain control over more companies. Using this type of trust, agreements were made with other companies to assign voting stock to a group of trustees in exchange for trust certificates. Thus, trustees acting for a single firm, were able to make unified pricing policies that would ultimately result in a monopoly. Subsequently, the trust device was copied by other companies to form such combinations as the sugar trust, the whiskey trust, and the cottonseed trust. Each trust became a monopoly working against the public policy interest to eliminate small competitors.

Antitrust Legislation

Sherman Antitrust Act. In 1890, Congress enacted the Sherman Antitrust Act, which became a milestone in government regulation. The basic purpose of this act and its subsequent provisions, including the antimerger law, is to maintain competition and free enterprise. As a part of this purpose, the laws forbid monopolization and practices that restrain trade. The main provisions of the act are Sections 1, 2, and 3, quoted as follows:

Section 1. Every contract, combination in the form of trust or otherwise, or conspiracy, in restraint of trade or commerce among the several states, or with foreign nations, is hereby declared to be illegal. . . .

Section 2. Every person who shall monopolize, or attempt to monopolize, or combine or conspire with any other person or persons, to monopolize any part of the trade or commerce among the several states, or with foreign nations, shall be deemed guilty of a misdemeanor. . . .

Section 3. Every contract, combination in the form of trust or otherwise, or conspiracy, in restraint of trade or commerce in any Territory of the United States or of the District of Columbia, or in restraint of trade or commerce between any such Territory and another, or between any such Territory or Territories and any State or States or the District of Columbia, or with foreign nations, or between the District of Columbia and any State or States or foreign nations, is hereby declared illegal. . . .

The fourth section provides that the several district courts of the United States shall be given jurisdiction to prevent and restrain violations of the act and shall have jurisdiction of the criminal and seizure sanctions.

In the many years since the enactment of the original Antitrust Act, the courts by their decisions have established the rule that the act applies not only to interstate trade, but also to *persons* who are shown to affect interstate commerce. This means that the act is broader than might originally have been interpreted. Retail stores locally owned but selling goods or liquor produced out of state, including in foreign countries, are subject to the act. Prior to 1955, violators of the Sherman Act could be fined $5,000 or sent to prison for one year, or both. In 1955, Congress raised the maximum fine to $50,000.

At this point you may ask why Congress passed antitrust legislation in the first place. Early English common law, from which our own legal system was derived, originally held that *all* restraints of trade were illegal. In the United States, common law during our early history distinguished between reasonable and unreasonable restraints, with only the latter being illegal. The courts even held that reasonable restraints of trade were valid where there was no intent to raise prices.

The *Addyston Pipe* case (1899) was one of the first tried under Section 1 of the Act.[1] This case involved six manufacturers who controlled about 30 percent of all cast-iron pipe production. These companies divided their sales territories and fixed prices on their pipe. The court ruled that this action was an effort to destroy competition. Evidence showed that the prices under the six-company agreements were one-third higher than they might have been under independent competition.

In 1911, the Supreme Court rendered decisions under the Sherman Act against two of the largest industrial companies in the nation at that time—

---

[1] *Addyston Pipe and Steel Co.* v. *U.S.*, 175 U.S. 211 (1899).

Standard Oil of New Jersey and the American Tobacco Company. The ruling against Standard Oil required that there be a breakup of the company into many smaller organizations. By this plan, each owner of one share of stock in Standard Oil received shares in some 33 separate corporations, in addition to his stock ownership in the parent company. Similarly, in the case of American Tobacco, the Court directed that the company, which controlled more than 95 percent of cigarette production, be broken up into three independent companies. Thus, in both cases the companies were ordered to dissolve their monopolistic mergers.

In 1903, a special Antitrust Division was created in the Department of Justice to investigate and prosecute alleged violations of the Sherman Act. Today the division has six field offices and a total of about 300 lawyers and 30 economists engaged full time. The division conducts investigations and secures evidence resulting from complaints, which number about 1,200 per year.

The Clayton Act and the Federal Trade Commission Act. During the period between 1890 and 1914, monopolies and trusts continued to flourish, until the Supreme Court established the so-called rule-of-reason principle in evaluating the legality of a combination. Applying this rule, the Court gave a very broad interpretation of the Sherman Act, resulting in many mergers being authorized that otherwise could not have been approved under a less liberal interpretation. (By merging, one corporation acquires controlling interest in or assets of another.[2]) Thus it was possible to create a monopoly by merger instead of by using a trust agreement.

The Clayton Act was passed in 1914 to bring within the antitrust laws abuses that previous experience had shown were not covered by the Sherman Act. For example, interlocking directorates among large banking corporations were prohibited, as were leases and sales in which the lessee or buyer must agree not to use goods of a competitor of the lessor or seller. It was declared unlawful for a company to acquire stock in a competing company in order to gain a monopoly. The act forbids persons engaging in interstate commerce to discriminate in price between different purchasers of commodities. Also, price-fixing to gain a monopoly is illegal.

The Federal Trade Commission Act, passed in 1914 shortly before the Clayton Act, declared unlawful such practices as the following:

1. Using false or misleading advertising to deceive the public
2. Offering bribes to customers' employees in return for their orders

[2]For example, Companies A, B, and C agree to merge. As a result, A and B are absorbed by C. When the merger is completed, A and B go out of business and C remains. *Amalgamation* is the proprietary union of two or more corporations into a new corporation, with the liquidation of the formerly existing corporations. *Acquisition* is the outright purchase of sufficient stock in another corporation to gain control. The corporation still continues to do business in its own name.

3. Misbranding of goods as to their composition, origin, or quality
4. Advertising rebuilt or reconditioned products as new

Subject to review by the Court of Appeals, the FTC acts as grand jury, prosecutor, and judge. The commission may initiate its own investigations or act on charges made by competitors or other outsiders. Sometimes the accused company admits its guilt and agrees to a voluntary settlement. In a contested case, the commission hears the evidence, and if the accused is found guilty, the commission issues a cease-and-desist order.

Although thousands of cases, involving many of the largest companies in America, have been heard under the Sherman and Clayton Acts, one of the most complex and far-reaching decisions involved the du Pont and General Motors corporations, decided by the Supreme Court against du Pont in 1961. The Court decided that du Pont engaged in restraint of trade by owning GM stock and ordered it to divest itself of 63 million shares of that stock. The company was allowed 34 months from May 1, 1962, to dispose of its stock to the public. The shares were carried on the du Pont books at a value of $1.2 billion but were later considered to be worth about $3.4 billion. Special tax legislation was passed by Congress, stipulating that any tax gains to the stockholders in this case be subject to capital gains, which carries a comparatively low rate of tax.

The Robinson-Patman Act. As we have seen, the Clayton Act was intended to prohibit price discrimination and exclusive agreements involving the sale of goods, including machinery, and other commodities for consumption. The act prohibited price discrimination against small firms where such discrimination substantially interfered with competition, except when price differentials were due to differences in quality, quantity, or grade. Many independent merchants, however, complained that this section of the Clayton Act gave chain stores an unfair advantage in getting quantity discounts from suppliers.

In 1936, the Robinson-Patman Act amended the Clayton Act, making it unlawful for any person to discriminate in price among purchasers if the effect of such discrimination might be to lessen competition, to create a monopoly, or to injure, prevent, or destroy competition. This law is actually designed to protect one buyer from another. For example, if a seller makes any allowance to one buyer, he must make the same concession to all other buyers. The offer or the accepting of a discount in excess of the permissible limit constitutes a criminal offense. As it turned out, the real targets of this act were the chain stores.

A special provision of the Robinson-Patman Act prohibits the payment of brokerage fees to a purchaser or his agent, except for services actually rendered. In 1947, the Great Atlantic & Pacific Tea Company was found guilty of violating this law.[3] The Atlantic Commission Co., a subsidary of A&P, obtained part of its income from brokerage fees on sales to independent wholesalers and retailers, as well as from distributing produce to the parent company. The court held that this practice strengthened the competitive price position of A&P against other independent stores who were also customers of the commission company but at the same time were competitors of A&P.[4]

Although Congress presumably intended the Robinson-Patman Act to prevent large organizations from receiving special discounts for big orders, this act in its final form does allow large-quantity buyers to receive increased discounts over those permitted to small firms. Such price differentials are permissible when the orders are based on actual differences in costs, including such factors as costs of selling, costs of manufacturing, and delivery expenses. The Federal Trade Commission, which is directed by the act to administer these provisions, has the difficult task of determining which cost differences are proper.

The Celler-Kefauver Antimerger Act. From the very beginning, the purpose of antitrust legistation was to preserve competition. But the vagueness of the laws, and some court inconsistencies in enforcing them, left businessmen in a quandary. In 1950, Congress amended Section 7 of the Clayton Act to eliminate a loophole. Under the Clayton Act of 1914, intercorporate stock purchases were prohibited where the effect might be to reduce competition between two or more corporations. But this provision had been so weakened by court decisions that it no longer prohibited acquisition of assets, although the same result accomplished by acquiring stock was forbidden. Thus, the purpose of the Celler-Kefauver Act was an attempt to tighten the stock-acquisition ban. It also prohibited the acquisition of assets of competitors where the effect was to substantially reduce competition. Consequently, companies who are major competitors cannot merge under *any* circumstances. If Company A is a giant, it cannot acquire Company B, no matter how small that company's share of the market is. Third, companies cannot merge if the consolidation would result in a control of 30 percent or more of the market.

The Antimerger Act also amended the Clayton Act by giving both the Federal Trade Commission and the Justice Department jurisdiction over merger cases. Businessmen are constantly asking for clarification of antitrust laws. Apparently, clarification should be even more widely sought; between 1950 and 1965, for instance, the number of suits initiated by the Justice Department

[3] *United States* v. *New York Great Atlantic & Pacific Tea Company,* 67 Fed. Sup. 626. Decision affirmed by Circuit Court of Appeals in 1948. This case has since established an important precedent in the matter of paying brokerage fees.

[4] The chief force pushing for passage of the Robinson-Patman Act was the United States Wholesale Grocers' Association. The original bill was written by the general counsel of that organization. Despite the bill's protective measures, the independents have continued to decline in numbers and the chain stores have gained in strength.

involving antitrust cases more than doubled. As the laws stand now, small companies find it difficult to grow and diversify in an industry dominated by giant corporations that may have taken the merger route.

Patents, Copyrights, and Trademarks

If you invent a mechanical device or develop a formula for a marketable product, federal statutes provide that you have the right to apply for a patent. Patents have an obvious importance to businessmen, since they provide the holder with a government-approved monopoly—at least for a limited time.

Patents. In the United States, a *patent* is in the nature of a contract between the inventor and the government, granting him the exclusive right to own, use, and dispose of his article for 17 years, after which this protection expires and cannot be renewed. The holder is also protected against infringements abroad, since the United States is a member of the International Convention for the Protection of Industrial Property, which is an agreement on patent regulations among the member nations.[5] The U.S. Patent Office in Washington, D.C., is the federal authority that grants patents. The first patent granted in the United States was under the Patent Law of 1790. Over the years it has been the feeling that even though patents take a good deal of time to acquire, they protect rather than discourage inventions.

The 1952 Patent Act established three requirements, or "tests," that every invention must meet (or pass) before a patent will be granted on it: (1) It has to be new, (2) it has to be useful, and (3) it has to be more than simply an improvement over previous inventions of a similar or related nature. Sometimes these points are difficult to prove—and, in fact, it is virtually impossible for the average layman to obtain a patent without the services of a patent attorney.

Copyrights. A *copyright* is a form of permission granted by the federal government to an author, artist, or publisher, giving him the exclusive authority to own, sell, or otherwise use his written works. Such items as books, songs, poems, plays, works of art, and even photographs may be copyrighted. (See the copyright in the front of this book, for an example.) A copyright may be obtained by sending a fee of $6 and a copyright form (obtainable through the U.S. Copyright Office), along with two true copies of the legitimate work, to the Copyright Office of the Library of Congress in Washington, D.C. A copyright is good for 28 years and may be renewed for 28 more.

---

[5] Prompted by a backlog of some 200,000 patent applications, President Johnson in 1965 appointed a commission to recommend changes in the patent law. Some of the proposed changes were (1) to make a patent valid for 20 years, instead of 17, after its earliest filing; (2) to hold a patent claim previously held invalid by a court from further royalty payments; (3) to provide that imports into the United States of unlicensed products made abroad by a patented process in the United States would be a patent infringement. As this book was being written, no legislative changes have been approved by Congress.

20 + 20

To ST

Trademarks. Most large businesses and some smaller ones use a *trademark*—a distinctive symbol, title, or mark readily identified with the product or the name of the business. By registering a trademark with the Patent Office, you are granted the exclusive right to use it for 20 years, and the registration may be renewed for another 20 years. (Applicants must submit a written application, five copies of specimens, and a fee of $35.) However, registration does not automatically protect the owner from involvement in law suits; once the trademark has been registered, the Patent Office is empowered to deny the registration of infringing trademarks, but the owner himself has to initiate legal action to restrain the use by another who has unlawfully adopted his trademark.

The major benefits derived from registering a trademark are as follows: (1) Registration is *prima facie* ("on first appearance") evidence of the registrant's exclusive right to use the mark; (2) it is a record that others can review before presenting their trademarks to be registered; (3) it provides federal-court jurisdiction in infringement cases; and (4) it allows the owner to secure an automatic embargo on foreign goods imported into this country that infringe on that trademark.

Licenses and Permits

Another method of regulating businesses and professions is by means of the licenses and permits issued by most towns, cities, and states. In principle, licenses and permits are intended as a means of protecting the life, health, and safety of the public. More recently, these devices have become important revenue-producers, and are often used chiefly for that purpose.

Discussion Questions

5. *What were the reasons for passing the Sherman Antitrust Act, and subsequently the Clayton Act and the Federal Trade Commission Act? Are these same reasons valid today or have conditions changed?*
6. *What is the chief purpose of the Federal Trade Commission? What are some examples of unfair business practices that the commission attempts to stop?*
7. *In recent years, the federal government has paid close attention to proposed business mergers or combinations. Why?*

TAXATION AND THE BUSINESS ENTERPRISE

People never cease to complain about taxes. But to get a reduction in taxes, many Americans would have to give up services they regard as essential.

Everyone tends to favor taxes that benefit him but regards as wasteful the taxes that may benefit others.

Taxes are an assessment levied by government to pay for services that citizens receive from government. By what authority does government levy taxes? Municipalities receive authority to tax from the city charter authorized by the state. State governments obtain their authority to tax from their state constitutions. The federal government receives its authority from Article 1, Section 8 of the Constitution. According to this article, Congress has the power to collect revenues, to pay debts, and to provide for the common defense and general welfare. Because this general-welfare clause has long been so broadly interpreted by Congress, the federal government consistently finds itself in need of more money to provide an increasing variety of miscellaneous services.

During the decade 1960–70 federal spending jumped 130 percent, the number of civilian government employees increased from one out of every eight U.S. workers in 1960 to one out of every six, and federal taxes went up 113 percent.

Purpose of Taxes

Taxes generally serve one or more of the following purposes: (1) to raise revenue, (2) to produce a restrictive effect on the market, (3) to regulate, and (4) to redistribute wealth. Every tax is in some measure regulatory. Most taxes are levied to raise revenue or to serve as some kind of restriction. Tariffs, which are special taxes on imports, restrict the quantity of goods that may enter from foreign markets. Income and sales taxes are typically revenue producing. The estate tax is a means of redistributing individual wealth.

Some Taxation Theories

Adam Smith, in his *Wealth of Nations,* offered four principles of taxation that today are still considered to have merit:

> *Principle of Equality: Everyone should be taxed in proportion to his income.*
> *Principle of Certainty: Each taxpayer should know exactly the amount of the taxes due and when.*
> *Principle of Economy: The cost of collecting the tax should be small in proportion to its yield.*
> *Principle of Convenience: The tax should be collected in a manner most convenient to the taxpayer.*

The *tax base* is the object being taxed: Corporate net profit is the base of the corporation income tax. The *tax rate* is the percentage of the base that is paid. Both the base and the rate may vary, depending upon the purpose of the tax. The *incidence* of a tax is its burden, which is borne by the individual or firm eventually paying the tax.

Enacting a suitable tax program is difficult. The total revenue produced should be sufficient to meet expenditures, and the tax burden should be distributed on an equitable basis. Because the government at the federal level expends a significant proportion of the national income, the most direct way to redistribute income is by a national taxation policy.

Classes of Taxes

Taxes are generally divided into three broad types: regressive, progressive, and proportional. The first two types are almost synonymous with the terms "unfair" and "fair" in relation to tax matters. Proportional represents the real dividing line between taxes that are regressive and those that are progressive.

Regressive Taxes. A *regressive tax,* such as a sales tax, is one that takes a larger proportion from people with low incomes than it does from those with high incomes. This is because the lower one's income, the more of it must be spent on the necessities of life. Most taxes on consumer goods (products for use by consumers or households) as contrasted with industrial goods (goods used in producing other goods) are in this class, since the tax rate is the same for rich and poor alike. Labor unions tend to dislike regressive taxes (general sales tax, for example) because persons with larger incomes pay a smaller percentage of their income than do persons with small incomes.

Progressive Taxes. A tax that falls more heavily on those with larger incomes is a *progressive tax.* This is the opposite of a regressive tax. The basis of the progressive tax is the ability to pay whereas the regressive tax takes from the low income person a larger percentage of his income than is taken from the high-income person. The personal income tax is the best illustration of a progressive tax because the tax rate increases as the base increases.

Proportional Taxes. A proportional tax is one in which the rate is the same, regardless of the base. For example, a tax rate of $10 for each $1,000 assessed valuation, regardless of the total amount of property owned, is a proportional tax. A retail sales tax is proportional in that the rate is always constant regardless of the size of the base. The regressive aspect of the sales tax is that low income persons are taxed upon a higher percentage of their income than are high-income persons.

The Best Tax System

The tax system that is best for most persons is a matter of personal opinion. But any sound tax system does contain certain elements, such as (1) simplicity—ease of understanding and collecting; (2) tax yield—provision of the largest return consistent with the number of taxpayers included; (3) convenience in paying—time and method convenient to both the government and the taxpayer (4) fairness—absence of discrimination; (5) directness—awareness by the taxpayer that he is paying taxes; (6) moderation—not an excessive amount of money extracted for each type of tax, and (7) absence of loopholes—no tax avoidance.

The Benefit Principle. Advocates of this principle contend that those who benefit from government services should pay for them. No one could argue very long that this is not a logical concept. The federal tax on gasoline, for example, is used to build highways, which in turn are used by those who drive automobiles. Thus, by the use of the excise tax on gasoline it is possible to apply the benefit principle. Of course, the application of this principle does have its limitations. Suppose public school taxes were levied only on parents, on the basis of the number of children they have in school. The local banker would probably experience no difficulty in paying his taxes, but how about the poor family with six school-age children? Obviously, the well-to-do could afford to pay the school taxes, whereas the poor could not. Generally speaking, however, there is considerable merit in the benefit principle when judging a tax.

The Ability-to-Pay Principle. Taxation based on this principle sounds even better to many people than that based on the benefit principle. But what measures one's ability to pay? Net money income received during a given year is probably the most widely accepted criterion. Others prefer gross income as the basis. But even after the measure of ability to pay has been agreed upon, there still remain the problems of determining the acceptable tax rate that correctly measures ability to pay, and whether the tax rate should be proportional or progressive.

Income taxes are broadly based and are set up on the basis of the government's estimates of the people's ability to pay what is asked of them. For example, a man with a $15,000 income may be asked to pay twice as much as one earning $7,500. Such a proportional tax considers the wealthy man's greater ability to pay more, and the dollar amount demanded in taxes is therefore adjusted to the size of the income. In the final analysis, tax-paying ability generally increases as income rises, and the best example of the ability-to-pay principle is the progressive income tax.

It is said that most tax systems combine regressive and progressive characteristics in an effort to extract as much revenue as possible. It has also been observed that the final "incidence" (or resting-place) of a tax may be far from the man who turns the money over to the government. Obviously it is this final incidence of the tax that is most important. The best system, then, becomes a matter of one's personal opinion, rather than of the application of scientific determination. On the other hand, it cannot be denied that taxes do nothing to increase demand for taxed commodities or businesses. Taxes tend to raise costs and thereby to reduce supply—and lower supply pushes up prices.

Discussion Questions

8. *Define the following terms and give an example of each: progressive tax, regressive tax, and proportional tax.*

9. *What effect does a progressive income tax have upon the redistribution of income?*

10. *Why is it difficult to determine if a specific tax is just?*

TAX SOURCES
AND TYPES OF TAXES

In light of the tax principles we have discussed, what are the main sources of tax revenue for the federal government and for the state and local governments? As you can readily see from the following illustration, the individual and corporate income taxes produce about 57 percent of all federal taxes combined. Income from excise taxes on beer, cigarettes, and gasoline produce about 8 percent, while Social Security taxes and contributions amount to 25 percent.

At the state and local levels, however, property taxes still account for almost half the total revenues of the state and local governments. A total of 39 states have general personal income taxes, with rates lower than those of the federal income tax, while 43 states have a corporate income tax. The general sales tax is on the books of 45 states, with rates ranging from 2 percent in Indiana and Oklahoma to 6 percent in Pennsylvania. Other state taxes include excise taxes on cigarettes, utilities, and boats. As shown by the graph on page 104, the total tax collections at the state and local levels has been increasing steadily since 1961. Schools and colleges get nearly half of all the state and

THE SOURCES OF THE U.S. TAX DOLLAR
(Fiscal Year 1972 Estimate)

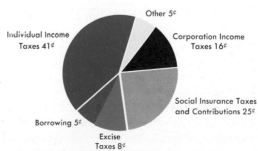

Other 5¢
Individual Income Taxes 41¢
Corporation Income Taxes 16¢
Social Insurance Taxes and Contributions 25¢
Borrowing 5¢
Excise Taxes 8¢

Sources: U.S. Bureau of the Budget; U.S. Treasury Department

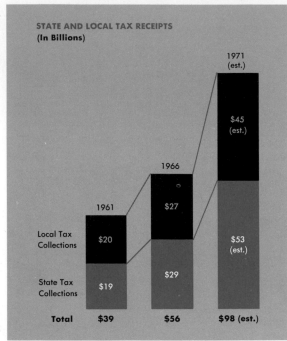

STATE AND LOCAL TAX RECEIPTS
(In Billions)

	1961	1966	1971 (est.)
Local Tax Collections	$20	$27	$45 (est.)
State Tax Collections	$19	$29	$53 (est.)
Total	**$39**	**$56**	**$98 (est.)**

Source: U.S. Department of Commerce; estimate by authors

local tax funds, and welfare costs during the last decade have tripled in total expenditures.

Particular Taxes

Personal Income Tax. This tax on individual income produces the largest amount of money collected as tax income. The present federal income tax was made possible by the Sixteenth Amendment to the Constitution in 1913. The income tax is progressive and broadly based. Every person residing in the United States, adult or minor, who has an annual gross income of a prescribed amount (for example, a single person with an annual income of $1,700 before deductions) must file a tax return. Probably the outstanding feature of the personal income tax is that it is based on the ability-to-pay principle. Of course, what seems fair to one person under this principle may be considered by another a gross injustice.

Corporation Income Tax. With the exception of the Social Security tax, which is in a separate category (see graph, page 103), the second most income-producing tax at the federal level is the corporation income tax. Like the personal income tax, it is popularly supposed to "soak the rich." This tax imposes no direct burden on the cost of doing business, and therefore it does not have the same direct deterrent effect on employment and production as do payroll and excise taxes. A tax that reduces profits does reflect the yield of investment and is bound to have some adverse effect by slowing down company growth. As in the case of the personal income tax, it is often argued that the corporation income tax discourages risk taking on the part of business and may stifle small-corporation growth. There may be some truth in this contention. The greatest virtue of the corporation income tax is the fact that it produces high revenues in good times. The personal income tax is based on the ability-to-pay principle, and the incidence is on the taxpayer; the tax cannot be shifted. The fact that corporation profits are subject to income taxes makes most of the stock dividends that are distributed subject to double taxation, which is a constant source of complaint to Congress.

Property Tax. Rapid population growth has put a great strain on public school funds and on other local government expenses, and the main source of income for many communities is the property tax. This tax is based on the assessed value of the property, but assessments and tax rates change slowly, and often the assessed value bears little relationship to the market value of the property.

Business-property taxes are not passed along to consumers as obviously as are sales taxes, but since they are included in the cost of doing business—like wages, salaries, and interest—the businessman or the landlord can shift at least part of his tax onto someone else, and homeowners complain that because of this, they pay more than their share of community costs.

Some localities also levy a tax on personal property, but people have been known to conceal their ownership of such items as jewelry and securities to avoid this tax.

Sales and Excise Taxes. A tax levied on the sales price of a product at the time of sale is called a *sales tax* or an *excise tax*. The difference between sales and excise taxes is simply that the former is a percentage of all prices subject to the tax, whereas the latter is a percentage based on prices of specific goods, but they are usually paid by retailers and then passed on to the customer. The manufacturer or the wholesaler may add the tax to his selling price.

Generally, sales and excise taxes are easy to administer, and they are justified on various grounds: (1) they are a reliable source of revenue; (2) incidence of the tax is sometimes difficult to shift completely; and (3) the benefit principle exists—as in the case of a federal excise tax on gasoline when the tax money is used for highways. Both of these taxes are regressive in nature; they tend to burden the poor. Some states have passed laws that exempt specific items, such as drugs and farm equipment, from a sales tax.

Estate, Inheritance, and Gift Taxes. An *estate tax* is a federal or state excise tax assessed against the net value of the estate of a deceased person, levied on a graduated basis on the right to transfer property from the dead to the living. A return must be filed if the gross estate exceeds $60,000 in value at the time of death. Estate taxes should not be confused with *inheritance taxes,* which are also excise taxes, levied by some states on the right of the living to receive property from the dead. Inheritance taxes are payable by the heirs and not by the estate of the deceased. A *gift tax* is levied on the transfer of money or property by gift from one person to another. At the federal level there is an exemption of $30,000 for each donor, which may be taken all at one time or spread over the years. Gifts that exceed certain amounts require payment of a tax. Tax rates and exemptions vary by states for gift, estate, and inheritance taxes, and not all the states levy them. The effect of these taxes is to make it almost impossible for large concentrations of wealth to remain in one family for several generations. This furnishes quite a contrast between the distribution of wealth in the United States and that in many European and South American countries where, under the doctrine of primogeniture, the eldest son inherits intact the whole of his father's estate.

The Corporation Franchise Tax. The annual fee levied on domestic corporations is known as the *corporation franchise tax.* In some states, it is based on the par value of the authorized capital stock. In others, it is calculated by adding to the value of issued capital stock the amount of the corporate surplus and undivided profits. If the corporation has issued only no-par-value stock instead of par-value stock, an arbitrary value is generally assigned to each share in assessing the tax. For foreign corporations, the term *privilege tax* is used.

Customs Duties. Taxes levied by the U.S. Treasury Department on the importation of certain foreign goods are called *customs duties.* During the early history of this nation, these customs duties were a major source of income to operate the federal government. At present, the receipts from customs duties are a small fraction of the total federal taxes collected. The subject of customs duties is discussed in Chapter 23, because of its relation to tariff policies and international trade.

Social Security Program

Since 1935, the Social Security Act has become an important part of American life in providing financial aid to the worker during unemployment and in meeting the financial and health problems that often accompany old age. Over 26 million people, about one person in eight, are receiving benefits. This program contains four parts, three of which involve a payroll deduction tax. Our purpose in studying the program is to explore its scope and significance as a social program and to note certain of its limitations. Since the benefits and rates are constantly being revised by Congress, no effort will be made to give detailed types of income benefits and tax rates. Such details are available from the Social Security Administration (a part of the Department of Health, Education and Welfare) through their more than 859 field offices, which also issue Social Security numbers.

Role and Scope of Program. The basic principle of Social Security is a simple one: During their working years, employees, their employers, and self-employed persons pay a payroll deduction tax, which is pooled as a special trust fund. (Technically, these tax payments should be regarded as insurance trust revenue for use at a later time for retirement benefits.) Social Security is not charity. When earnings stop on account of personal disability or when a worker reaches retirement age, monthly retirement benefits or disability payments are paid to replace his regular salary or income. Part of his tax also goes into a hospital trust fund to help pay for hospital care.

The program is nationwide and is compulsory for most classes of workers. Both employees and employers covered by the law must pay the Social Security tax, and employers are required to keep records and to deduct from his wages the amount paid by the employee. Benefit payments for old age retirement may begin at age 62.

The self-employed person makes a contribution based on his net annual earnings, paying this tax along with his personal income tax. When Social Security is added to the numerous other taxes businessmen must pay, we can see why some businessmen are asking for tax relief.

Major Parts of the Program. There are four parts to the program: (1) old-age, survivors, and disability insurance (OASDI); (2) unemployment compensation insurance, designed to pay weekly benefits to workers who are laid off and are unable to find suitable employment; (3) old-age assistance to the needy on public welfare and to dependent children and incapacitated persons; and (4) Medicare, a health insurance program for persons 65 and older, including hospital and nursing-home care, doctor bills, laboratory tests, and costs of equipment prescribed by a physician. The individual may choose his own physician.

Inequities of Social Security. The program does have some inequities, which only Congress has the authority to change by enacting an amendment.

Take the case of a wealthy woman, who qualified under the Social Security program and who has now retired and is receiving monthly retirement benefits. She can have outside income of $100,000 or more a year in dividends and not lose one cent in Social Security benefits each month. According to the law, dividends, interest, income from property, and annuities are not included in the test that determines who is entitled to retirement benefits. On the other hand, a chambermaid who has retired on Social Security and then decides to take a part-time job will lose part of her monthly benefits if she earns from outside employment over $1,680 a year.

Another inequity would occur in the case of an executive who retired early with a substantial company pension and also Social Security. He decides to work part time as a consultant, earning $20,000 a year. By working only in some months, he can still collect Social Security benefits for the months in which he does not work. Now compare him with a taxi driver who works until age 65, then retires on his Social Security and decides to work part time.

He will lose his Social Security benefits when his yearly income exceeds the current limit if he is employed in each month of the year.

Also the older worker retiring today may receive monthly benefits totaling many times the amount of taxes he paid into the system; his benefits are much greater in proportion to the taxes paid by him than today's young workers may expect to collect when they retire. (It is true, however, that the apparent inequity is somewhat decreased by the fact that most of the dollars the older worker paid in Social Security taxes were worth far more than the dollars he is receiving in benefits.)

And finally, a person earning $4,000 a year in wages pays 5.2 percent of his monthly pay to Social Security as a tax, but a person who earns $40,000 a year pays only 1 percent.

Social Security Trust Funds: How Safe Are They?

How safe are the Social Security trust funds that are paid into by people in the program?

There are four trust funds in the program. The oldest, the Federal Old-Age and Survivors Insurance Trust Fund, dates back to 1939 and is used to pay retirement and survivor benefits. The second fund, the Federal Disability Insurance Trust Fund, was established in 1956. It is used to pay disabled persons and their dependents. The two most recent funds, the Federal Hospital Insurance Trust Fund and the Federal Supplementary Medical Insurance Trust Fund, were organized in 1965 to finance Medicare.

By law, the money in all four funds can be used only for payment of benefits and operating expenses. Funds not required to pay current benefits or costs must be invested in interest-bearing U.S. government securities. Interest earned from these investments is added to the funds. In addition, federal legislation requires that costs and actuarial projections of the Supplementary Medical Insurance Trust Fund must be reviewed annually, and monthly premium rates adjusted when necessary. According to the 1970 Annual Report of the first and second trust funds, there is enough money in the funds plus projected taxes to pay all present and future benefits for the next 75 years.

The Value-Added Tax—A Proposed Tax

A relatively new concept in taxation, the value-added tax (VAT), is gaining in popularity in Europe and is now receiving attention in the United States. This is a tax at the manufacturers' level, based on the amount of value that is added to each stage of the product as it goes through the production or manufacturing process. In principle, it resembles a sales tax in that it can easily be passed on to the ultimate consumer. But in terms of what the consumer pays, the effect of a 5 percent value-added tax could be the same as a 5 percent sales tax. For this reason, the VAT is referred to as a national sales tax, although it can be adopted by a state and applied to manufacturing concerns operating in that state.

The main criticism of the VAT is that it is mildly regressive, falling more heavily on the poor than the rich. Its chief advantages are that it falls alike on the incorporated and unincorporated, on the efficient and inefficient, and that there is no easy tax shelter from it—except to spend less of one's income.

This tax has been adopted by France, West Germany, Belgium, the Netherlands, Luxembourg, Denmark, Sweden, Norway, and Italy. It was recommended by the Committee for Economic Development, and more recently, President Nixon said about it, "We may very well move toward it as a substitution for some of our other taxes."

Effects of Taxation on Business

The impact of taxes on decision making is a matter of increasing concern in business planning. Borrowing funds may well involve tax considerations. Borrowing results in interest charges, which are deductible for income tax purposes. In contrast, equity financing permits no deduction from income for the cost of the capital.

The form of ownership is often influenced by the prospective income tax burden, as is the decision to lease or buy property.

Growth of a business can be stimulated if tax laws permit a part of the expense of a new investment to reduce tax payments. This deduction has a tendency to induce more profitable firms owing high taxes to expand, in order to take advantage of the deductions. There are businessmen who are willing to incur deliberate tax losses because of the advantages that may accrue through tax loopholes.

Taxes can influence the choice of a business location: Several southern states have offered new industries special tax concessions, such as lower property taxes or reduced corporation fees, for a given number of years.

Taxation allowances for depletion of natural resources, such as oil and gas, play an important role in obtaining financing.

Are Taxes on Business Increasing?

Reports indicate a rapid growth in recent years of state–county–city–village taxes on business. Table 4.1 shows how nonfederal tax revenues have soared during the past five years.

At a recent meeting in Chicago sponsored by the Tax Institute of America, one corporate official said, "Every time we turn around, there's another city or county slapping us with a new tax." The general tax counsel for a large oil company reported his firm files about 12,000 tax returns annually all over the country.

TABLE
4.1
STATE AND LOCAL TAX REVENUES COLLECTED

Year Ending June 30	Total Tax Revenue (Billions)	Taxes per Person of Resident Population
1965	$51	$264
1969	77	380
1970 (est.)	87	427

Source: U.S. Bureau of the Census.

Growing Interest in Tax Reform

No tax is a pleasure for those who pay it. But since taxes seem inevitable, what would seem to be needed is a program of tax reform to remove the inequities and faults. Space does not permit a detailed discussion here of a total tax reform program, including expenditures. Our concern will be confined to relating reform to the needs of the businessman.

Types of Tax Reforms. Many businessmen are inclined to worry less about the amount of money involved in taxes than about the cost and red tape of the paperwork that is demanded of them by so many agencies, state and federal. The laws in business taxation are overlapping in jurisdiction and complex in nature. There is constant uncertainty as to what the rules really mean.

A total of 24 states authorize local units of government to enact their own sales taxes, and approximately 3,400 counties, cities, towns, and other subdivisions collect such taxes, mostly from business firms who collect from consumers. In addition, 43 state governments collect state corporate income taxes. Business firms must report much of the collection information to government agencies.

State legislatures, long opposed to granting local governments more autonomy, are now permitting more local taxing powers. This takes pressure off state officials to raise more taxes and puts the burden on local authorities. But state legislators never seem to eliminate any existing taxes; so businessmen face more taxes from both local and state levels.

Some businessmen favor strong congressional action to restrict the power of state and local governments to levy taxes on firms operating in more than one state or community. Some 20 states have formed a commission to study and encourage uniformity in tax laws.

Changing Unfair Tax Laws. One of the major problem areas is that of property taxes at the local level. Critics have observed that the property-tax system is a mess. Fiscal experts agree it is badly administered and unfair to millions of individual taxpayers. A Census Bureau study found that the typical homeowner can expect a tax bill for an amount 20 percent more or less than it should be; and some large property owners pay little or no taxes. Ralph Nader has added property taxes to his list of projected reforms.

In the area of state and federal income taxes, both the state and federal laws are often so complex and difficult to understand that they require the services of tax consultants. If these statutes were simplified, a greater number of taxpayers would be able to file their own returns.

Loopholes should be eliminated for those of the rich who avoid payment of income taxes. There is a saying in Congress that "one man's tax loophole is another man's sacred constitutional prerogative." If the loopholes are numerous enough, high tax rates do not really tax those with high incomes very much. As well over half of all federal revenue comes from personal and corporation income taxes, rates on all income levels could be cut without revenue loss, if existing loopholes were closed.

Taxpayers in the United States, like those in other industrial nations, see their tax load increasing with no end in sight. But the latest figures show that taxes in European nations are higher than those in the United States. As we see in Table 4.2, American tax levies look modest as compared with direct and indirect taxes and Social Security taxes abroad.

According to Table 4.2, Americans pay about 30 cents in taxes at the

TABLE
4.2

NATIONAL, STATE, AND LOCAL TAXES PAID IN THE UNITED STATES AS COMPARED WITH OTHER MAJOR NATIONS

(Levies based on cents per dollar of total national output)

Nations	Direct Taxes (On incomes, corporate profits, estates, and gifts)	Indirect Taxes (Sales, excise, and property)	Social Security Taxes	Total Taxes Collected
Sweden	20.2¢	13.9¢	8.2¢	42.3¢
Norway	13.8	15.2	9.2	38.2
Netherlands	13.2	11.2	13.4	37.8
France	6.5	15.9	14.5	36.9
Austria*	12.0	16.5	8.2	36.8
West Germany	10.4	13.7	10.6	34.7
Denmark	16.3	16.5	1.9	34.7
Great Britain	13.1	16.2	5.1	34.4
Belgium	10.2	13.3	9.5	33.0
Canada	12.7	15.1	3.4	31.2
Italy	6.8	12.6	11.1	30.5
UNITED STATES	15.5	9.1	5.3	29.9
Japan*	7.9	7.5	3.5	19.0

Source: *Organization for Economic Cooperation and Development, 1968.*
*Total for Austria and Japan are rounded.

national, state, and local levels combined for each dollar in national output—the gross national product—whereas in Sweden, for example, social-welfare programs have pushed taxes up to 42 cents for each dollar of national output. In direct taxes paid, the United States ranks third while in indirect taxes the United States is near the bottom of the list.

Discussion Questions

11. *What are some of the reasons for the increased use of the personal income tax and the sales tax as sources of revenue for states and the federal government?*

12. *Discuss some of the effects that taxes tend to have on business. Which kinds of taxes discussed in this chapter can be passed on with the least difficulty?*

13. *Why is tax reform important to businessmen, and what are some of the proposed reforms?*

SUMMARY

Until late in the nineteenth century, American businesses were largely unregulated by governments at the state and national level. Today there are a great many laws to regulate business. Our federal government derives its authority to legislate from the people. The basis of their authority is the Constitution of the United States. State constitutions provide authority for enacting laws at the state level. The political functions of the U.S. and state governments include (1) providing personal security for persons and their property, (2) establishing a fair system of justice through public laws, (3) protecting human rights, and (4) promoting the general welfare of the United States as it relates to the health, morals, safety, and general welfare of the citizens.

American public policy has long supported the principle that freedom to engage in a business of one's own should be guaranteed. As such, one purpose of public policy is to regulate unfair competition and prohibit illegal monopolies by such measures as the Sherman Antitrust Act, the Clayton Act, the Federal Trade Commission Act, and the Robinson-Patman Act. Authorized forms of monopoly such as public utilities are considered legal.

Another method of regulating business is the use of licenses and permits, authorized mainly at local and state levels. The federal government confers control of certain artistic productions and trade labels in the form of copyrights and trademarks.

The most direct way of redistributing income in the United States is through a tax policy. Most kinds of taxes are borne by individuals other than those who pay them directly to the government. A tax may be judged by four principles: (1) equality, (2) certainty, (3) economy, and (4) convenience. Not all taxes are actually based on all four of these principles.

Taxes serve various purposes—to raise revenue, to redistribute wealth, to regulate, and to restrict. For instance, tariffs tend to restrict the quantity of goods that may enter from foreign countries. The assumption of the excess-profits tax is that no business firm should extract high profits from war.

Taxes may be designed to apply the benefit principle, or they may be based on the ability-to-pay principle. The gasoline tax, which is earmarked for use in building public highways, is an example of the benefit principle, whereas the personal income tax illustrates the ability-to-pay principle. Sales and excise taxes are regressive in nature, because the tax falls more heavily on those with smaller incomes than on those with larger incomes.

The largest revenue producers at the state level are property, sales, and gasoline taxes. Local communities rely heavily on property taxes, with the sales tax ranking second. The individual income tax is the largest revenue producer at the federal level, with the Social Security tax ranking second. A new type of tax, known as the value-added tax, has been adopted by several European countries and is under consideration by our federal government. For each stage of production, a percentage of the value is added as a tax to the cost of the product. This tax resembles a sales tax because of its regressive characteristic.

The total tax system is in need of reform to eliminate inequities and to equalize the burden. Many state taxes on business are overlapping and expensive for business firms to collect. There is need for uniformity of taxes among the states. Taxes on real property are considered excessive and badly administered. At the federal level, loopholes exist, especially in the income tax.

VOCABULARY REVIEW

Match the following vocabulary terms with the statements that follow:

a. Acquisition
b. Amalgamation
c. Copyright
d. Estate tax

e. Monopolistic competition
f. Oligopoly
g. Patent
h. Public policy

i. Progressive tax
j. Pure competition
k. Regressive tax
l. Trademark

1. The situation that exists when a firm is to some degree in the position of a monopoly but also competes with other firms

2. The use of a statement carrying the weight of government authority that tends to influence business decision making

3. The proprietary union of two or more enterprises into a new corporation, with the liquidation of the formerly existing corporations

4. An outright purchase of sufficient interest in a business to gain control of it

5. A contract between an inventor and the government, granting him exclusive right to own, use, and dispose of his article for 17 years, after which this protection expires and cannot be renewed

6. An exclusive right granted by the federal government to an author or publisher, granting him the authority to own, sell, or otherwise use his written work

7. A distinctive symbol, title, or mark readily identified with a product or name of a business

8. A tax that takes a larger proportion from low incomes than it does from high incomes

9. A tax that tends to fall more heavily on those with large incomes or those who own great wealth

10. A tax assessed against the entire estate of the deceased

11. The presence of an indeterminate number of traders all dealing in the same product, with no individual buyer or seller able to influence price, which is determined by supply and demand

12. A situation in which comparatively few firms produce identical or similar goods and where sellers have the ability to influence price by changing the volume of goods produced

PROBLEMS AND PROJECTS

1. Using the library resources, including materials published by the Social Security Administration, prepare a written critique of the Social Security provisions, giving both the pros and cons, with emphasis on recent changes in the law to improve the benefits and increase the advantages of the program.

2. Robert and John Sydney, two brothers residing in your community, are giving serious consideration to the purchase of ten acres of land adjacent to the new interstate highway right-of-way near the city where you and they reside. They would like to construct a service station, a bowling alley, and a restaurant with adequate parking space. You have been asked by the two brothers to help them by furnishing a list of all the licenses and tax permits required by local and state laws. They also want to know what taxes are required to operate this business. You should discuss this problem with local officials in order to obtain accurate information.

A BUSINESS CASE

Case 4-1   Ennis Industries

Ennis Industries, a close corporation chartered under the laws of Arizona, operates a lightweight steel products manufacturing plant in Portland, Oregon, that serves a sixteen-state area west of the Mississippi River. Annual sales represent about 49 percent of the market for woven-wire fence, reinforcing rods, small seamless pipe, and galvanized sheets. The National Steel Company and Evans Products, Inc., also close corporations, are competitors, along with a Japanese company that imports some products. National Steel and Evans each furnish about 18 percent of the total demand for this area, with the Japanese company providing about 12 percent. Competition from eastern steel companies is very slight.

About three years ago, National Steel had a long labor strike that set the company back. Last year it was rumored that the company might close down. Two months ago, the directors of Ennis Industries discussed the matter of acquiring National, and they voted to make the company a tender offer to consolidate, with payment in cash and in Ennis common stock, details to be worked out between the two companies. What happened as a result of the proposal was not released to the public, but Evans Products requested that the Justice Department conduct a hearing by the Antitrust Division staff.

1. What factors must exist to support the fears expressed by Evans Products?

2. Do you agree with Evans? Why?

3. What advantages does the consolidation offer Ennis and National Steel?

organization and management of the enterprise

legal
forms
of business
ownership

CHAPTER FIVE

Whenever a new business is started, a key question, whose answer is vital to the continued success of the undertaking, is, "What is the most appropriate form of ownership for this venture?"

Just as there are different kinds of businesses—retail, wholesale, and manufacturing—there are also different forms of business ownership. The three most popular are the sole or individual proprietorship, with one person as owner; the partnership, or joint ownership; and the corporation, or stockholder form of ownership. In addition, there are others, including the joint-stock company, business trust, joint venture or syndicate, and cooperative, all of which exist in limited numbers but are also important. These various forms received their origin under statutory or code law or under common law.

The sole proprietorships and general partnerships have a common-law beginning. They are noncorporate, which means they are not required to have a charter (approval) from a government agency to do business.

In contrast, the corporation is of statute origin, which means that a corporation chartered in a given state must conform to the corporate laws of that state. Such a company is called a corporate enterprise to distinguish it from noncorporate forms.

Careful consideration to these types of companies at the time the business is formed is one way to avoid legal problems. So if you are planning to start a business, regardless of its size, here are some of the points of major consideration:

1. Total amount of capital needed and its availability
2. Means by which additional capital can be obtained
3. Legal status of the firm and its advantages and disadvantages
4. Ease of transferring ownership
5. Extent of owner's liability for the firm's debts
6. Ease or difficulty of starting
7. Extent of government regulation
8. Stability of existence
9. Tax advantages and disadvantages

OBJECTIVES OF A BUSINESS ORGANIZATION

The first objective of a business is to make and sell a product, or perform a service, at a profit. To do this, a firm must offer its customers what they want, when and where they want it, at a satisfactory price. A firm that does not do this will most likely fail.

In 1919, the Coca-Cola Company was a tiny business, unknown in almost all parts of the world. Today it is known worldwide and makes the largest-selling soft drink in the world. Certainly one of the reasons for Coca-Cola's growth is its policy of always thinking of the quality of the products and the best ways to service its customers. It has always stressed the need for maintaining the organizational objectives—quality and service at a profit.

Another organizational objective is growth and increase of position in the industry. Constant regard for a firm's position can create a corresponding improvement in the organization itself and a possible increase in its relative size.

The Essential Nature of the Firm

What is it that distinguishes a business firm from other economic and social groups? In the first place, whereas the firm usually has as its first objective to earn a profit, most other groups—such as the clan, the church, or the hospital—do not.

Aside from their personal responsibility, businessmen today face a moral dilemma in determining how much social responsibility should be assumed by their firms. The reason, of course, is that for at least the past two centuries, the community has not been of prime concern to the business firm. But the world is changing and business must change with it.

The Motivation of Business Firms

Motivation, from our present point of view, may be thought of as *the mental and emotional stimulation that creates the desire within persons in an organization to achieve certain results.* It is triggered by a maze of interacting factors that combine to create certain tensions and drives, which in turn develop into incentives. Different people are motivated by different incentives. Money, for example, is an effective incentive only in terms of how much it means to the individual. Some persons are to a large extent self-motivating. For example, a person working for himself provides his own variety of motivational stimuli, which may include—besides financial gain—the desire to be creative, to be respected, or to be recognized as an individual. But most persons are not self-motivating. Most employees (wage-earners and salaried persons), for instance, more often than not have to look to one or more "bosses" in the firm for direction—for motivation.

The usual answer to the question "What motivates firms to do what they do?" is "Profit." But although the profit motive is a powerful force in stimulating business activity, it is not the only one. The desire to render a vital and meaningful service can be very effective as a motive, too. Indeed, many more managerial decisions are based on the service objective than one might imagine. Or a firm may be motivated to achieve community prestige or favor. Every firm wants to have influence and a good image in the community in which it operates, and so certain business decisions are made to achieve this goal.

Communists believe in the inevitable collapse of capitalism. Moreover, the communist philosophy holds that no individual has the right to employ others to accumulate personal wealth for himself. While private ownership of personal goods, retail stores, and small-scale farms is permitted, it is unlawful for a proprietor to be motivated by the profit system. Nor is a businessman permitted to choose the exact legal form of a business he would like to organize. It is only recently that the USSR has permitted the amount of wages and the use of a bonus as incentives.

Discussion Questions

1. *What distinguishes the corporate from the noncorporate form of ownership?*
2. *Why is the selection of a form of ownership an important managerial decision? What are some of the more important factors to be considered?*
3. *Compare the kinds of motivation the business firm is subjected to in this country with those found in communist-dominated countries.*

SOLE PROPRIETORSHIPS

Sole proprietorship is the name given to a business owned and operated by one person. This form is as old as civilization itself, and it is the most common in the United States, as well as in many foreign countries whose economies depend upon the small shopkeeper. The proprietor performs both the managerial and the operative duties, and the responsibility for the success or failure of the firm rests entirely on him.

Legally, he owns all the assets of the firm and owes all its debts. The financial statement shown in Table 5.1 illustrates the nature of the proprietor's assets and the debts for which he is responsible, aside from his personal assets and debts, which are not part of his business.

Note that George W. Brown owns total assets worth $13,500; he owes debts amounting to $3,900, and his personal equity in the business is $9,600, which is his ownership claim against total assets worth $13,500. Such giants as S. S. Kresge, H. J. Heinz Company, and F. W. Woolworth started as very small businesses with this form of ownership.

Management Advantages and Disadvantages of the Sole Proprietorship

Among the management advantages of the sole proprietorship are these:

1. Ease of starting the firm
2. Return of all profits to owners
3. Freedom of owner to manage

4. Minimum of legal restrictions
5. Ease of dissolving firm
6. Taxation of owner, not business

TABLE
5.1

BALANCE SHEET OF A SOLE PROPRIETORSHIP

George W. Brown, TV Repair Shop

Assets (owns)		Debts (owes)	
Cash	$ 2,500	Accounts payable	$ 3,200
Parts inventory	1,200	Notes payable	400
Merchandise inventory	5,300	Mortgage on truck	300
Tools and equipment	1,500	Total debts	$ 3,900
Truck	3,000	Owner's equity	9,600
	$13,500		$13,500

On the other hand, the sole proprietorship also has some disadvantages:

1. Unlimited liability of owner for debts
2. Difficulty of raising capital
3. Possibility that overall direction may become a burden on owner when business grows
4. Limited opportunity for employees, since organization is not permanent
5. Uncertainty of duration: death, imprisonment, or insanity automatically terminate the firm

The individual owner is legally liable for all the debts of his firm; not only his original capital investment, but also his personal and real property may be attached by creditors. (In only a few states is a person's home exempt.) Moreover, he is limited almost entirely by the amount of money he possesses or the amount he is able to borrow from friends, banks, or relatives when starting the firm. And, unlike most other forms of ownership, this one ceases to exist when the owner dies; this limits the degree of permanence for the employees. Finally, the typical proprietor may have to be an expert in many phases of business, for his problems of management are numerous and he may have no responsible person to help him.

However, it is obvious that the small proprietorship is, by its nature, well suited to small-scale business, because of its common-law origin, its simple legal structure, and its ease of operation as compared with that of other forms. Indeed, its advantages so far outweigh its disadvantages that the majority of American businesses are sole proprietorships.

Discussion Questions

4. Why are so many small businesses organized as sole proprietorships?
5. What is meant by the term "unlimited liability of owner"?
6. To what extent is the individual owner liable for the debts of the business?

PARTNERSHIPS

The Uniform Partnership Act, which has been adopted by most states, defines a *partnership* as "an association of two or more persons to carry on as co-owners of a business for profit." Although most partnerships are operated for profit, a nonprofit organization established as a partnership is also legal. The partnership was actually devised to overcome certain weaknesses inherent in the proprietorship. It has distinct advantages and disadvantages that are not found in the proprietorship form. The authority for its creation rests in the common-law right of voluntary association. Consequently, there can be no partnership relation between individuals without an expressed intention on the part of both that a partnership is to exist.

Types of Partnerships

The law recognizes two distinct types of partnerships: general and limited. In a *general partnership,* all partners participate actively in the business, sharing all the responsibilities, including unlimited liability. The distinctive feature of the *limited partnership* is the limited liability of one or more partners. But there must always be at least one partner in a limited partnership who is subject to unlimited personal liability. The number of limited partners is not restricted by law, provided there is at least one general partner in the firm. The withdrawal of a limited partner does not necessarily dissolve the firm, but when a general partner withdraws, the partnership must be terminated.

A limited-partnership agreement must be drawn up in accordance with the laws of the state in which the firm is to operate, and a copy of the agreement must usually be filed with the appropriate state official. Limited partners exercise no voice in the active management of the business, but they do share in the profits according to the agreement. As a rule, they are prohibited from withdrawing their capital except under unusual circumstances. (In general, this point is covered in Section 16 of the Uniform Partnership Act.)

If no agreement is set up specifying that certain members of the firm are limited partners, all of them are considered to be general partners. Hence, when a partnership is formed and announced to the public, it is common practice to state in the announcement which members are general and which are limited partners.

Five states—Michigan, New Jersey, Ohio, Pennsylvania, and Virginia—have statutes permitting the formation of *limited-partnership associations,* an arrangement in which the liability of *all* partners is limited. This is more like a corporation than a partnership, however, because the partners elect a board of directors and authorize them to manage the association. The limited-partnership association is not widely used as a form of ownership.

Kinds of Partners

Common and statutory law recognize various types of partners. For example, an owner who takes an active role in the business but who does not want to reveal his identity to the public is known as a *secret partner.* A *silent partner,* on the other hand, takes no active part in the business even though he may be known to the public as a partner. A *dormant partner* is one who plays no active role and at the same time remains unknown to the public as a partner. A *nominal partner* is not actually one of the owners of the business, but he suggests to others by his words or actions that he is a partner. Under certain circumstances, the other partners may be obligated by the acts of a nominal partner and may become liable for his share of the debts.

A general partner who has been with the partnership for a long time and who owns a large share of the business is called a *senior partner.* *Junior partners* are those who have been with the business a relatively short time and who are not expected to assume great responsibility for major decisions.

Forming a Partnership

If you decide that a general partnership is the best form of ownership for the business you are planning to set up, you will find it fairly simple to organize. As with the individual proprietorship, few legal steps are necessary. The proposed business must be a lawful one, of course, and all that is required is an oral or written agreement between the partners. This agreement is known as the *Articles of Partnership* (sometimes referred to as *Copartnership Articles*).

As in any undertaking that involves more than one person, many questions are likely to arise after a partnership has been formed. Consequently, it is wise to have the partnership agreement drawn up in advance by an attorney who is familiar with partnership law. Although no two written agreements are absolutely identical, the following points are usually covered in the agreement:

1. Firm name
2. Names of partners
3. Addresses of partners
4. Location of business
5. General nature of business
6. Duration of the agreement
7. Amount of each partner's capital
8. Salaries or drawing accounts of partners
9. Distribution of profits or losses
10. Procedure for admitting new partners
11. Procedure for dissolving partnership
12. Each individual's duties and authority

Some states require that a written agreement be drawn up if the general partnership is to last more than one year. If it is organized to engage in the business of buying or selling real estate, the agreement need not be in writing. But if by the terms of the partnership agreement one partner is to receive an interest in real estate now owned by another partner, then the agreement must be in written form.

A general partnership is automatically dissolved if one partner dies, withdraws, or is declared insane, or if the firm claims bankruptcy. Because of these limitations, banks are often reluctant to extend long-term credit to general partnerships. Perhaps the most serious disadvantage is the joint and unlimited personal liability of each general partner for the debts of the firm. Unless limited by agreement, each partner is liable for the whole amount of the partnership debts, regardless of the size of his investment. If one partner lacks the personal wealth to assume his full share of the loss or debts, the other partners are required to make good on the deficit. In fact, all acts by partners in the name of the general partnership are binding on all other partners, even though the action may be unknown to them at the time.

Management Advantages and Disadvantages of the General Partnership

The advantages of the general partnership may be summarized as follows:

1. Ability to operate in any state
2. Better credit standing than sole proprietorship
3. Opportunity for specialization of managerial skills as well as pooling of partners' knowledge
4. Ease of dissolution
5. Freedom from tax on business income; partnership is taxed as an individual
6. Minimum of legal restrictions
7. Probability of larger capital resources than in sole proprietorship

While the partnership has many of the advantages of the sole proprietorship plus the advantage of pooling the resources and abilities of two or more persons, it also has certain disadvantages:

1. Restricted transfer of ownership
2. Difficulty in withdrawing investment
3. Possibility that partnership friction may terminate the agreement
4. Limitation of duration of partnership to lives of partners
5. Unlimited liability of partners for debts of business

Most general partnerships in this country are probably very informal organizations, operating on limited funds and without a formal written agreement. On the other hand, a formal agreement is required in the formation of a limited partnership. The agreement must be filed with an appropriate public official—often the county clerk—and must state who the general partners are and who are the limited partners. Interestingly, despite the apparent desirability of both the general and the limited partnership, neither is used as extensively as the corporation or the sole proprietorship.

Types of Business Adaptable to Partnerships

There seems to be no clear-cut method of deciding in advance which kinds of business are best adapted to the general or limited partnership. Any small or medium-sized firm could conceivably operate as a partnership. Some partnerships have as many as 100 partners.

There are, however, certain instances where partnerships seem to be advantageous. For example, in the professions of law, dentistry, medicine, and accountancy, partnerships work out particularly well. By sharing office and clerical expenses, the partners effect great savings. Stockbrokerage firms, investment banks, and consulting agencies can also operate efficiently as partnerships. The brokerage firm of Merrill Lynch, Pierce, Fenner & Smith once had more than 70 partners before it became a corporation in 1959. Cluett, Peabody & Co., Montgomery Ward, and Procter & Gamble all started as partnerships, too, and only eventually became corporations. Limited partnerships are commonly used for financing theatrical enterprises, in order to avoid the double taxation inherent in corporations.

Discussion Questions

7. *Explain the difference between a limited and a general partnership.*
8. *Why is it considered important in forming a partnership to have a written agreement? What are some of the important items in the agreement?*
9. *Under what conditions might it be better for a sole proprietorship to become a partnership? If you were invited to become a partner, would you be satisfied to be a limited partner?*

CORPORATIONS

The modern corporation has come to be the predominant form of economic organization in American life. It is the symbol of our capitalistic economy and of "big business." For many years it has been the principal means by which large sums of capital have been collected to operate thousands of industrial and business organizations. In fact, it is doubtful that American businesses could continue to expand were it not for the modern corporation.

Today it is almost impossible for one person to obtain sufficient capital to start an automobile factory, a steel plant, or an oil refinery. But by means of a business corporation, it is possible to obtain these funds from the sale of corporate stock or bonds, or both.

A corporation is created by state governments, through the enactment of legislation called *corporation laws.* These laws differ widely in stringency and interpretation among the various states; certain states have more lenient laws than others with respect to, say, incorporation requirements and taxation. (In this case, for instance, Delaware is considered a lenient state and New York a strict one.)

A definition often used to describe a corporation appeared originally in an opinion handed down in 1819 by Chief Justice Marshall, on the famous *Dartmouth College* case. According to Marshall's definition, a corporation is an "intangible reality"—an artificial but legal "person" that can, in spite of its Twilight Zone sort of semi-existence, be held responsible for many of the things a real person can. Fortunately, the term *corporation* has since been defined by the Supreme Court as "an association of individuals united for some common purpose, and permitted by law to use a common name, and to change its members without dissolution of the association." By abandoning the fictitious-person concept, the Court attempted to make the actual persons running the corporation more accountable for their acts. According to this view, a corporation consists of real people, rather than being a legal person separate from others in it. But regardless of which definition you use, a corporation has the right to buy, sell, own, manage, mortgage, and otherwise dispose of real and personal property that it possesses, and it may sue and be sued.

The corporation is a far more formal structure than either the proprietorship or the partnership. It becomes a legal entity when it receives its charter from a state agency. The owners are called *stockholders* or *shareholders*.

Classification of Corporations

Corporations may be classified in several ways:

1. Private and government
2. Profit and nonprofit
3. Stock and nonstock
4. Open and close
5. Domestic, foreign, and alien

Private and Government Corporations. A *private corporation* is one chartered, owned, and operated by individuals, either for profit, social, charitable, or educational purposes. Most corporations are private and are organized for making a profit. General Motors is a typical private, profit-making corporation, while the Harvard Corporation (University) is an example of a private, nonprofit corporation.

A *government corporation* is one organized by the nation, state, city, or some other political subdivision. Government corporations are also referred to as *public corporations*. The Federal Deposit Insurance Corporation, described in Chapter 14, is a typical government corporation. The Communications Satellite Corporation is a combination private and government corporation; private companies own stock in it, but the corporation was authorized by Congress.

Profit and Nonprofit Corporations. A *profit corporation* is one operated to make a profit for its shareholders. A large majority of all corporations in the United States and most foreign countries are of this type. A *nonprofit* *corporation* uses income that may result from its operation to promote the purposes for which it was organized. Religious and charitable organizations often incorporate as nonprofit enterprises.

Stock and Nonstock Corporations. A *stock corporation* issues stock certificates of ownership to the shareholders. *Nonstock corporations*—also private corporations, but not chartered to make any profit for their members—do not issue stock certificates.

Open and Close Corporations. An *open corporation* is one that offers its stock to the public. Conversely, an incorporated business that does not offer its shares to the public is a *close corporation*—the shares are owned by the incorporators, who may be members of a single family.

Many businesses start on a small scale and find it advantageous to restrict the sale of their shares to a few persons. This enables the company to withhold as private information various financial facts about the condition of the corporation. And as a business expands, requiring more capital, the corporation directors often decide to "go public" by selling shares to others. The close corporation gives more latitude to its owners as to how they can spend their profits. "You don't have outsiders looking over your shoulder and second-guessing you," says Edmund F. Ball, chairman of the board of directors of Ball Brothers, Muncie, Indiana.

Domestic, Foreign, and Alien Corporations. A business chartered under the corporate laws of one state is regarded as a *domestic corporation* of that state; but in every other state, it is a *foreign corporation*. For example, the Stewart-Warner Corporation, which has a charter from Virginia, is a domestic corporation in Virginia, but if it operates in California, that state regards it as a foreign corporation. A company doing business in the United States but chartered by a foreign government is known (in the United States) as an alien corporation.

Organizing a Corporation

Let's assume you have decided on the kind of business you want to start, and that you have determined to incorporate. What is your next step?

First, you apply for a charter from one of the 50 states. Here are the actual steps that must be followed:

1. Secure the necessary application forms from the appropriate official of the state in which your concern plans to do business.
2. Complete the papers and file them with the state official.
3. Pay the required fees to the state authority.

The application must bear the signatures of at least three petitioners of adult age who desire to form the corporation—these are known as the *incorpo-*

rators. The application must be notarized and accompanied by the required financial information. In general, an application must furnish the following facts about the proposed business:

1. Name and address of the proposed corporation.
2. Names and addresses of the incorporators.
3. Proposed duration of the organization, which may be either perpetual or for a limited number of years.
4. Kind of business in which corporation is to engage.
5. Names and addresses of the officers and directors.
6. Address of the principal business office.
7. Amount of capital to be authorized. The amount of capital is officially known as the *authorized capital stock,* and it is divided into shares of ownership ranging in value from $1 to $1,000. Some states require a minimum of $1,000 in capital stock; all require at least $500.
8. Maximum number of shares, called *authorized stock,* to be issued, and whether these shares are to be par or no-par value, and with or without voting rights.[1] Shares are in the form of stock certificates, which are numbered serially and recorded when issued on the books of the company. To be valid, they must bear the officers' signatures.
9. Name and address of each subscriber to certificates, and statement showing the total number of shares paid for by each subscriber.

The information entered on the application should be carefully worded, in order to permit as much freedom as possible in determining the future activities and objectives of the company.

It is easier and less expensive to set up a corporation in some states than in others. Delaware, Maryland, New Jersey, Arizona, Nevada, South Dakota, Maine, Florida, and Texas are popular states in which to incorporate. They demand smaller incorporation fees, impose lower taxes, and offer more liberal provisions in their corporation laws.

The Corporation Charter

After you have paid your filing fees and organization taxes and have fulfilled any other necessary conditions, your application is, let us say, approved. Now the secretary of state issues your corporation charter and mails a copy to the county clerk of the county in which the principal office of the newly formed corporation is to be located. (This procedure varies slightly in different states.) The following items illustrate what a typical charter might contain:

1. Title of corporation
2. Name of state granting corporation charter

---

[1] The terms *par* and *no-par value* are explained in Chapter 13.

3. Descriptive statement of purpose of corporation
4. Location of corporation's general office
5. Term of years for which corporation is incorporated
6. Number of directors, including minimum and maximum
7. Names of directors and their addresses
8. Amount of capital stock fully subscribed and paid up
9. Notarization by notary public in the county in which corporation is to maintain its general office

The Corporate Structure

The structure of a corporation stems from its charter. According to the charter, the shareholders are the owners. It is their responsibility to meet and elect a board of directors, which in turn meets and elects the necessary officers as prescribed in the charter. In most states, the full board is required to meet at least once each year, but it may meet as often as deemed necessary to conduct the corporation's business. The shareholders must vote on the proposed by-laws, which serve as the general rules for operating the business and list the duties of the officers. The amount of stock represented at a stockholder's meeting must be sufficient to constitute a quorum.

The accompanying chart shows the actual structure of the corporation and the relationship of stockholders to the directors and officers.

Corporation Officers. The officers of the corporation carry on the active management of the company. The by-laws usually specify that they are to be chosen by the board of directors. The president is normally the highest-ranking officer, although some firms regard the chairman of the board as top man. Other officers are vice-president, secretary, treasurer, and sometimes a controller. It is the practice in some companies to name several vice-presidents, each responsible for a specific operation, such as production, sales, or personnel.

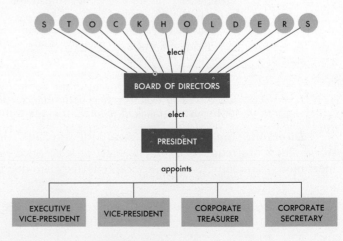

TOP-MANAGEMENT STRUCTURE OF A CORPORATION

The corporate secretary keeps the corporation seal, signs all corporation documents, and records the minutes of meetings held by the directors and stockholders. The treasurer is the chief financial officer and often is responsible for the entire accounting operation. In a very large company, the controller may be authorized to take over some of the accounting and finance duties from the treasurer.

Legal Responsibilities of Directors.   The boards of directors of American business corporations vary greatly in their methods of functioning. (As you might expect, in family-owned corporations the board of directors is an often-ignored formality.) In many corporations whose stock is listed on an exchange, with hundreds of thousands (sometimes millions) of shares outstanding, the boards of directors are complete strangers to most of the shareholders. Very often these directors have leading positions in other companies, professions, or public service. They are chosen because it is believed they can bring business or add prestige to the organization. Some boards meet often and deal with many and detailed topics. Others meet infrequently and concern themselves with establishing only broad policies to guide the business.

Professor Myles L. Mace, Harvard University Graduate School of Business, in recent interviews with 75 executives and corporate directors, noted a gap between what consultants and professors say directors should do and what they actually do. According to Mace, directors are not the decision makers who really originate corporate policies and objectives. "Too many directors," says Martin Stone, chairman and chief executive officer of Monogram Industries, Inc., "are not in a position to learn enough about a company to serve responsibly."[2] More critics inside and outside business are saying that directors must do a better job or resign.

The legal responsibilities of the board of directors may be summarized as follows:

1. The directors should manage the company in the interests of the shareholders. To do this legally, the board must be entrusted by law with the necessary powers of business management.
2. As company management, board members must exercise reasonable business judgment—at least the same degree of prudence that reasonable men would exercise in conducting their own affairs.
3. The board may delegate extensive decision-making authority to officers and other employees of the company, but the board must supervise and evaluate their performance. Directors are not liable for honest mistakes of judgment, made without carelessness.

Directors' Meetings.   The board of directors, the officers, and the stockholders are required by law to meet at least once each year. They may meet more frequently if the by-laws specify they should. The corporate secre-

---

[2] "The Board: It's Obsolete Unless Overhauled," *Business Week,* May 22, 1971, p. 50.

tary notifies the stockholders by mail of the time, date, place of meeting, and any specific resolutions to be voted on. If there are several thousand stockholders, it is unlikely that all of them will be present at any one meeting. In fact, it is common practice to enclose a proxy form (see sample below) with the notice of the meeting. By signing and returning the form, the stockholder can submit his vote in lieu of attending the meeting in person.

Legally, a *proxy* is a power of attorney that transfers to a third party the stockholder's right to vote; it does not, however, transfer his legal title of ownership of his shares. The proxy is usually valid only for a given meeting; it does not transfer the voting right indefinitely. A stockholder who cannot attend the meeting is not obliged to return the proxy, but he loses his vote (for that occasion) if he does not. When the stockholder returns his proxy, he

---

PRENTICE-HALL, INC.

PROXY SOLICITED ON BEHALF OF THE MANAGEMENT

The undersigned stockholder of PRENTICE-HALL, INC. hereby appoints WILLIAM J. DALY, JR., FRANK J. DUNNIGAN and Z. A. POOL, III, and each of them, to act as agents and proxies of the undersigned with power of substitution and revocation, at the Annual Meeting of Stockholders of such Company to be held at its office, 229 South State Street, Dover, Delaware, on May 7, 1971 at 10:00 A.M., Eastern Daylight Time, or at any adjournment thereof, with authority to vote all shares of stock registered in the name of the undersigned:

1. For the election of Directors.   FOR ☐ WITHHOLD VOTE ☐

2. To ratify the appointment of Haskins & Sells as auditors   FOR ☐ AGAINST ☐
   for the Corporation for the year 1971.

and at their discretion upon such other matters as may come before the meeting.

Management favors a vote "FOR" proposals 1 and 2.

Unless a contrary choice is specified above, this proxy will be voted "FOR" proposals 1 and 2.

(Continued, and to be SIGNED, on other side)

The undersigned hereby acknowledges receipt of the Notice of Annual Meeting of Stockholders and the Proxy Statement relating to such Annual Meeting, both dated April 2, 1971.

Dated ...., 1971   ....

.... (Seal)
Signature

IMPORTANT: In signing this proxy please sign your name in the same way as it appears on this Proxy. When signing as attorney, executor, administrator, trustee or guardian, please give your full title as such.

Courtesy Prentice-Hall, Inc.

Most stockholders vote by proxy using a form similar to the one above.

may simply sign it and give no specific instructions on how his vote is to be cast. In this case, management simply assumes that he is willing to have his vote cast in the affirmative on all the issues stated on the proxy. The Securities and Exchange Commission regulates the solicitation of proxies in respect to registered securities.

The Board's Relationship to Company Officers.   Many companies point out that it is difficult, if not impossible, to distinguish the boundaries between the functions of the board and those of the corporate officers. Nevertheless, it is a widely accepted principle that boards of directors concern themselves with basic policy (as opposed to operating policy), with matters of importance (as opposed to routine matters), and with planning (rather than with how to implement a decision that has already been made).[3]

The relationship of trust and confidence between directors and officers is called a *fiduciary relationship.* The significance of a fiduciary relationship is that neither party is allowed to take advantage of the other for personal gain. If he does, he is legally liable and accountable to the corporation for whatever profit he has made or caused the corporation to lose.

Classes of Corporate Stock

Several kinds of stock are issued by modern corporations, but almost all of them may be classified as either *common* or *preferred stock.* In Chapter 13 we shall look closely at both these classes of stock; here we shall simply note their general characteristics as they relate to the ownership and control of the corporation.

Common Stock.   Common stock is the least complicated and most frequently issued corporation stock. Holders of common stock are in much the same position as the partners in a partnership. They participate in the management of the business and share in the profits or losses. Their liability is limited to the value of their stock; consequently, the most any common stockholder can lose is the value or amount of his investment. Dividends may be paid from profits after all interest on funded obligations, including mortgages, has been paid, and after dividend payments to preferred stockholders have been made. Likewise, common stockholders share in the liquidation of the corporation after bondholders and creditors have been paid.

Preferred Stock.   As the name implies, this class of stock guarantees to its owners certain priorities or preferences not available to common stock-

---

[3] In some Common Market countries, employees are given membership on boards of directors. The two-tier system, used mostly in Germany, consists of a supervisory board of directors of outsiders and employees, directing a lower-tier board composed of executives from management. Corporation management in the United States generally regards this system as cumbersome and ineffective.

A stock certificate typical of the kind issued to stockholders of an open corporation. On the following page is an illustration of the reverse side of the certificate. When a person sells his shares, he fills out this assignment form and transfers ownership to another person by indorsement.

Courtesy Tenneco Inc.

TENNECO INC.

The following abbreviations, when used in the inscription on the face of this certificate, shall be construed as though they were written out in full according to applicable laws or regulations:

TEN COM   — as tenants in common

TEN ENT   — as tenants by the entireties

JT TEN   — as joint tenants with right of survivorship and not as tenants in common

UNIF GIFT MIN ACT — ....Custodian............
                                (Cust)   (Minor)
                     under Uniform Gifts to Minors

Act............
         (State)

Additional abbreviations may also be used though not in the above list.

THE CORPORATION WILL FURNISH WITHOUT CHARGE TO EACH STOCKHOLDER WHO SO REQUESTS THE DESIGNATIONS, PREFERENCES AND RELATIVE, PARTICIPATING, OPTIONAL OR OTHER SPECIAL RIGHTS OF EACH CLASS OF STOCK OR SERIES THEREOF OF THE CORPORATION, AND THE QUALIFICATIONS, LIMITATIONS OR RESTRICTIONS OF SUCH PREFERENCES AND/OR RIGHTS. SUCH REQUEST MAY BE MADE TO THE CORPORATION OR THE TRANSFER AGENT.

*For value received,*_____ *hereby sell, assign and transfer unto*

PLEASE INSERT SOCIAL SECURITY OR OTHER
IDENTIFYING NUMBER OF ASSIGNEE

PLEASE PRINT OR TYPEWRITE NAME AND ADDRESS OF ASSIGNEE

Shares

*of the capital stock represented by the within Certificate, and do hereby irrevocably constitute and appoint*_____

Attorney to transfer the said stock on the books of the within named Corporation with full power of substitution in the premises.

*Dated*_____

NOTICE: THE SIGNATURE TO THIS ASSIGNMENT MUST CORRESPOND WITH THE NAME AS WRITTEN UPON THE FACE OF THE CERTIFICATE, IN EVERY PARTICULAR, WITHOUT ALTERATION OR ENLARGEMENT OR ANY CHANGE WHATEVER.

THIS SPACE MUST NOT BE COVERED IN ANY WAY

Courtesy Tenneco Inc.

holders. These preferences may pertain to the granting of dividends, to the distribution of the assets after dissolution, or to voting rights.

The dividend rate, expressed either as a percentage or in dollars and cents, is printed on the face of the preferred-stock certificate. A $5 preferred stock is one on which the company is to pay $5 a year. Nevertheless, there is no guarantee that the dividend will be paid unless it is earned and declared by the board of directors. As a rule, preferred stock does not provide the right to vote, whereas common stock usually does provide that right.

Are Stock Certificates to Become Obsolete?   While it is still some time off, the day is probably coming when stock certificates will no longer be used in securities-market transactions. Among the compelling forces that may cause certificates to disappear are the ever-rising mountains of paperwork in broker-age houses, the appalling increase in stock-certificate thefts, and the possibility of higher costs for more computerization equipment to cut paperwork. Possible impacts that this change may have on securities-market transactions are dis-cussed in Chapter 13.

The Stockholder's Ledger.   Immediately after a stock certificate is issued to a stockholder, the company opens an account for him known as the *stockholder's ledger*. These ledgers differ in form from one company to another, but they usually contain the following information: (1) name and address of stockholder, (2) number of shares of stock issued, (3) date shares were acquired or sold, and (4) the stock certificate number shown on the certificate. The facts recorded in this ledger determine if the stockholder is entitled to the dividend paid to those who owned stock prior to a certain date. Usually the corporation secretary is responsible for maintaining this record, but in large corporations with thousands of stockholders, this and other records are maintained by a transfer agent, which is usually a bank employed for this purpose.

Corporation Bonds.   If a corporation needs additional funds and does not wish to issue more stock, it may sell bonds. A *bond* is a certificate of indebtedness given as evidence of debt to the bondholder. In some respects, a bond is a kind of promissory note, except that it ordinarily extends over a longer period of time than the usual promissory note. (Since financing by bonds is a method of borrowing, this subject is dealt with more fully in Chapter 13.)

Discussion Questions

10. *Explain the popularity of the corporation as a form of ownership.*

11. *What is the essential difference between a corporation and a general partnership?*

12. *In a corporation, who (a) makes broad policies, (b) elects the board of directors and officers, (c) carries out administrative policies?*

Corporate Ownership and Management

Corporations whose stock is held by the public impose pressures on managers that are different from the ones proprietorships and partnerships must face, because corporation owners and managers are two separate and distinct groups, possessing different responsibilities. For this reason, it is important to note the differences between the two groups.

Who Are the Stockholders? Every firm has an owner or owners. In individual proprietorships and partnerships, with some exceptions in the case of large partnerships, the owners are the managers. But in large corporations—and in most small ones—the owners, who are the stockholders, are seldom the managers. Hence, there is a separation between ownership and management in most corporations.

It is estimated that today there are over 30 million people who, as stockholders, have direct ownership in one or more corporations. These people come from every walk of life. Other millions of people have an indirect ownership in corporations, through insurance policies, banks, pension funds, profit-sharing funds, and mutual funds. (Banks, insurance companies, and savings-and-loan firms generally choose to hold preferred stocks or bonds; mutual funds, private pension funds, and profit-sharing funds favor owning large blocks of common stock.)

Most shareholders are not active participants in the business they have invested in, but have turned this responsibility over to professional managers of one kind or another. But even when these managers gain virtual managerial control over the corporation, they must still be concerned with what the stockholders want, since angry owners may take retaliative action that could prove most embarrassing to the managers.

What Do the Stockholders Own? It is commonly accepted that stockholders are the owners of the company in which they hold stock. But what do they actually own? Are these stockholders really the owners of corporate property? Or do they simply own pieces of paper, in the form of stock certificates, whose value is determined day by day in the stock markets?

From a purely legal standpoint, stockholders do not own property in the sense in which we normally think of property ownership. For one thing, they do not possess title to the company property, and therefore cannot control its use, as can the single proprietor. Property is owned by the corporation, and not by the individual stockholders. Although it is true that, in the case of business failure and liquidation, stockholders have a direct claim on corporate property, their claims are subordinate to those of creditors, preferred stockholders, and bondholders.

Looking at it realistically, "owning a share of stock" is just what the phrase implies: having a fractional interest in the total entity called the corporation. But this claim is not for a fixed amount payable at any time, because its value does indeed fluctuate. From this viewpoint, then, on any given date, a stockholder owns merely an unapportioned share of the corporation's net worth on that day.

Rights of the Stockholders.   Stockholders have certain legal rights, which for discussion purposes may be classified as group rights and individual rights. *Group rights* are those rights that stockholders have when assembled at regular and special meetings. *Individual rights* are those that each stockholder has without any reference to other stockholders. Stockholder common-law group rights are:

1. To elect directors
2. To adopt and amend the by-laws
3. To change the charter with the consent of the state
4. To sell or otherwise dispose of corporation assets
5. To dissolve the corporation

In the absence of any restrictions by state law or the corporate charter, each holder of stock has, among others, these individual rights:

1. To buy and sell stock registered in his name
2. To receive dividends in proportion to the number of shares owned, provided each dividend has been duly declared by the board of directors

Courtesy General Motors Corp.

An annual meeting of stockholders, at which the corporate officers give an oral report on the corporation's achievements and future plans. Stockholders may ask questions about the affairs of the corporation.

3. To share in the distribution of assets on a pro rata (proportional) basis if the directors decide to dissolve the firm
4. To subscribe to additional stock before shares are offered to the public, unless this right is waived[4]
5. To review and inspect company records
6. To vote at regular stockholders' meetings
7. To receive stock certificates
8. To sue officers and directors for misuse of power or for fraud

Management Advantages and Disadvantages of the Corporation

From the viewpoint of business management, with its concern for operating costs, income, profits, and efficiency, the major advantages of the corporation are as follows:

1. Life of corporation is almost perpetual
2. Limited stockholders' liability
3. Ease of transferring ownership
4. Ease of expansion
5. Greater permanence
6. Lack of necessity for investors to manage
7. Adaptability to both small and large businesses
8. Opportunity for use of management specialists
9. Allows for concentration of large amounts of capital

In contrast with these advantages, there are certain disadvantages of the corporate form of ownership. One of the more serious is the heavy tax burden imposed upon corporations. For example, the federal government taxes their profits; then, when these profits are distributed as dividends, another tax must be paid by the stockholder as part of his personal income tax.[5] State taxes are not generally levied on the sole proprietor or partnership but paid by corporations are a filing fee, payable to the state on application for a charter, and a special corporate franchise tax paid to the state for privilege of doing business there. Some states also tax corporations on the amount of their capital stock.

These and other disadvantages may be summarized as follows:

1. More kinds of taxation
2. Greater difficulty and expense of organizing than other forms
3. Possible limitation of activities by charter restrictions
4. State and federal controls

---

[4] The right of additional shares, called the *preemptive right,* has frequently been limited by state law and by charter provisions.

[5] Under the Technical Amendments Act of 1958, a corporation can be taxed as a partnership if only one class of stock is issued, and if there are no more than ten stockholders, who must consent to this method of taxation by an election. The effect of such tax treatment is to levy income taxes on the stockholders as partners, with no income tax payable by the corporation.

5. Tendency for more impersonal relationships between management and employees, and management and customers, in large corporations

6. Higher tax on business income

7. Requirement of special permission to transact business outside state of incorporation

Corporate Mergers and Combinations

There are many reasons why firms may combine. A corporation manufacturing one product may find that it is not only more profitable to make others, but that diversification adds "safety." Or the owners may find that their business must expand or die—it cannot remain static and continue to be competitive. Also, when a small company and a large one combine, much-needed capital can be obtained through the substitution of the credit rating of the larger for that of the smaller. And operating costs can be reduced by eliminating duplicate facilities. In short, then, the economic and other advantages of stepping up to a larger-scale operation may be very significant.

Merger. More corporations are resorting to the use of a merger as a means of achieving expansion. When two firms merge, one firm acquires sufficient stock in the other for purposes of control. Usually, the larger company absorbs the smaller one. The stockholders of each corporation must approve the merger, very often by a two-thirds-majority vote. Preparing the merger details may take many months of negotiation. There is always the possibility that the merger may require sanction of the U.S. Attorney General to make certain there is no violation of the antitrust laws.

The stock price proposed by the offering corporation to the shareholders of the other company is the *tender price offer.* The stockholder has the right to agree or refuse to tender his shares at the proposed price. The tender offer is growing in popularity, partly because it is far cheaper than a proxy fight and less time-consuming for all parties involved. The costs of it are limited to advertising expenses, legal fees, and interest charges on standby financing, where it is necessary. A proxy contest, by contrast, can require tremendous outlays for publicity, mailing charges, and presenting arguments before the Securities and Exchange Commission.

A merger designed to consolidate several firms producing the same product or engaged in the same type of business is called a *horizontal merger.* Should two motel chains merge, for instance, this would be a horizontal merger or *combination.* A *vertical merger,* on the other hand, brings under one corporate ownership a control over unlike plants, engaged in various stages of production from raw materials to the end product.

A third type of merger is the *conglomerate.* The conglomerate is a collection of unrelated companies producing diverse products, merged by the exchange of corporate stock. The basic purpose of the conglomerate is to achieve quick growth and thereby increase the earnings per share via successive acquisitions. Litton Industries, an example of a conglomerate, has merged with over 50 companies since 1954. Gulf & Western Industries has participated in over 90 conglomerate mergers in the past nine years. The usual technique is for the larger company to trade its own high-priced stock for the lower-priced stock of the acquired company. Antitrust enforcement has in many instances encouraged the conglomerate trend; since the companies acquired are in unrelated fields of business, this type of merger is not usually considered to promote restraint of trade. The conglomerate differs from a holding company in that the latter usually owns little more than 50 percent of the subsidiary and very often controls several firms in the same industry. In some cases, the one reason for conglomerate growth is to become more efficient, so as to compete with other large companies. The trend in number of mergers is down. More companies are selling entire divisions and product lines seeking to streamline their operations, cut costs, or raise cash.

The Holding Company.   Another means of achieving a combination of business units is the *holding company.* In principle, any corporation holding stock in other corporations is a holding company. However, in a strictly legal sense, the term is usually limited to a corporation that owns stock in one or more other corporations, called subsidiaries, for the purpose of exercising control over those companies. Through this control over the officers, the policies of the various companies are effectively determined by the holding company. A typical holding company is the American Telephone and Telegraph Company, which owns controlling interest in some 22 companies, most of which are regional telephone companies that also are corporations.

Present antitrust laws prohibit mergers that "may tend to substantially lessen competition or tend to create a monopoly." Mergers or combinations such as a holding company may be stopped by the U.S. Department of Justice, which has the power to request an injunction (an order by a court designed to stop or delay action) when it is obvious that the intent is to conspire to monopolize or restrain trade.

To curtail the growth of holding companies and eliminate the many abuses that existed in the operation of public-utility holding companies, Congress in 1935 enacted the Public Utility Holding Company Act. This legislation has been called "a specialized antitrust act," because its purpose is to prevent economic concentration of power in the public-utilities field. One important provision of the act requires holding companies to register with the Securities and Exchange Commission, to file with the commission certain basic data, and to submit annually such information as the commission may request. Interlocking directorates with banking companies are prohibited, and intercompany borrowing is illegal. Since this act was passed, many utility companies have gradually emerged from the layers of pyramided holding-company organizations.

13. *Explain why the corporation is so popular with large businesses as a form of business ownership.*

14. *What do stockholders own in a corporation, and what are their rights?*

15. *What are the steps to be followed in organizing a corporation?*

OTHER FORMS OF LEGAL OWNERSHIP

While the forms of ownership discussed thus far represent the major ones in the United States, there are several other types that warrant mention. Among these are joint-stock companies, business trusts, joint ventures, and cooperatives.

Joint-Stock Companies

Joint-stock companies were first organized by the English and Dutch to meet the need for large concentrations of capital during the establishment of their colonies in America and in other parts of the world. The East India Company, chartered in 1600, was the first large-scale English joint-stock company.

The *joint-stock company* is a voluntary association of persons operating under the articles of agreement and with the capital divided into transferable shares. These shares may be readily bought and sold, with almost no restrictions by the states. Owners of shares take no part in the management; they elect directors who have the authority and responsibility for the directing of the business. It is similar to a corporation in that it has transferable shares and continues for a fixed term. For purposes of income tax, it is considered the same in many states.

The joint-stock company has several advantages, including the following: (1) It is inexpensive to start, (2) the death of a shareholder does not terminate the agreement, and (3) ownership certificates are transferable.

The main disadvantage, the unlimited liability of its members, has been known to discourage prospective investors. This form of ownership is not popular in this country.

Business Trusts

Sometimes called *common-law trust* or *Massachusetts trust,* the *business trust* offers the advantages of a corporation and eliminates the disadvantages of a partnership.

The owners of real property deed it to trustees for purposes of management, receiving in return a proportionate share in the income. The trustee (or board of trustees) manages the enterprise under whatever authority is granted by the trust agreement. Profits are distributed on the basis of trust shares held by investors. Shares are transferable, and liability is limited to the amount invested. Among its advantages are (1) simplicity of formation, (2) inexpensiveness to start, (3) relative freedom from government control, and (4) freedom of the investors from personal liability. The disadvantages include these: (1) It is taxed as though it were a corporation; (2) its securities are not as easy to market as those of a corporation, mainly because most people do not understand this type of organization; and (3) it is possible to place specific limitations on the life of a trust.

Recently, the real estate investment trust (REIT) has become popular as an investment to serve as a hedge against inflation. Approximately 175 REIT funds have been organized since the early 1960's, representing a total of $5,500 million in assets today as compared with $288 million in 1962.

Cooperatives

Cooperatives, or *co-ops,* as they are often called, are incorporated under the laws of a state. However, they differ from corporations in the following respects:

1. Each shareholder is a user–member of the co-op group.
2. Each co-op member has only one vote, regardless of the number of shares of stock he owns.
3. The number of shares each member may buy is limited, and dividends are paid on a patronage basis. These are known as *patronage dividends.*
4. Capital to form the co-op is subscribed only by the members.
5. Any interest paid the members is based on the investment of each shareholder.

Like other forms of business ownership, cooperatives have certain disadvantages. For example, the producer members are not free to sell their produce at any time they desire. Cooperatives lack the profit-making incentives common to other forms of ownership. Finally, members of the board of directors usually receive no pay for their services, and salaries paid to regular employees are often low, resulting in a high turnover among a cooperative staff.

There are cooperatives in many areas of business, including retailing, telephone service, and money lending, but the most extensive use is in agriculture. Farm products commonly marketed through farmer cooperatives include citrus fruits, milk, potatoes, livestock, rice, and poultry. The Sunkist Growers, Inc., for example, markets oranges and lemons, and Land-O-Lakes Creameries, Inc., markets dairy and poultry products. These organizations are known as *agricultural marketing cooperatives.* A second type that serves farmers is the *agricultural purchasing cooperative.* These associations buy and resell to both members and nonmembers such commodities as seeds, feeds, gasoline, tires, fertilizer, and farm machinery. Dividends, in cash or stock, are distributed on the basis of the patronage of members.

The *consumer cooperative* is a retail store established by a group of consumers who seek to buy goods at the wholesale cost. In other words, the objective is to eliminate the profit made by the regular retailer. Such stores are not common in the United States but are often found in Scandinavian countries. In fact, it is interesting to note that in one region of the United States where cooperatives have thrived, the North Central states, there are concentrations of people of Scandinavian descent.

Joint Ventures and Underwriting Syndicates

The joint-venture type of ownership used in modern business is very similar to that found in foreign countries during the seventeenth and eighteenth centuries, when European traders sponsored trading missions to China, India, and other countries. In this country, a *joint venture* is an association of two or more persons for a limited purpose, without the usual rights, powers, and responsibilities that accompany a partnership. Thus, if two people buy real estate now for resale later, they may form a joint venture. But if they make a formal agreement whereby each contributes money and services to carry on a real-estate business, they become partners, subject to a partnership agreement. The joint-venture type of ownership is often used in such undertakings as real-estate developments and large-scale construction jobs.

When used for the sale of stocks and bonds, the joint venture is often called an *underwriting syndicate,* and is a group of investment banks or securities dealers who join together temporarily to sell a new issue of securities. Upon completion of the sale of these securities, the syndicate is dissolved. *Syndicate* is the term used in general for temporary associations or firms that terminate automatically when their purposes have been accomplished.

Discussion Questions

16. *Discuss the similarities and differences between a joint-stock company and a corporation.*

17. *What are the advantages that a business trust has over a corporation?*

18. *How does an underwriting syndicate work?*

19. *Does the joint venture offer more or less restrictions to the persons involved than does a business trust?*

SUMMARY

Business is based on rights associated with the ownership of property. In order to have legal status, a business firm must adopt a form of ownership that is recognized in the eyes of the law. In all states, the law recognizes the sole proprietorship, partnership, and corporation as acceptable forms of ownership. Since there are advantages and disadvantages to each of these forms, business owners must decide which form to adopt. Other forms of ownership, not recognized alike in all states, are the joint-stock company, the business trust, the joint venture, and the cooperative association.

In general, sole proprietorships and partnerships are relatively easy to organize and are permitted considerable freedom of operation. On the other hand, both forms necessarily subject the owners to substantial amounts of risk; both have the inherent disadvantages of unlimited liability and limited life.

Proprietorships and partnerships predominate in small-scale businesses. Although both forms appear in all businesses, except where excluded by law in the case of commercial banks and public utilities, they are more common to retail and service enterprises. As a business increases in size, the most common transition is to corporate form.

The corporation grew from the need for a form of ownership that would combine flexibility of operation with capital-raising advantages. Among the characteristics of the corporation are these: (1) The corporation is a legal entity, separate and distinct from its owners, the stockholders; (2) it can own, buy, and sell property, and be sued; (3) it exists for many purposes, but its powers are derived from and limited by its charter, which is granted by the state; (4) it may be established for profit or nonprofit purposes, and the sale of its stock may be open to the public or restricted.

There are, however, disadvantages to the corporate form. For one thing, it is more difficult to start because of legal requirements. Also, a heavier tax burden is imposed on corporations than on other forms of ownership. And it is subject to more government control than other forms. But despite these disadvantages, the corporation has become a symbol of "big" business, and the fact that ownership can be divided into small fractional amounts has proved attractive to investors. Hence, it is easy to understand why the corporation has become the dominant legal form.

The joint-stock company is comparable in many respects to the corporation. For example, the shares are transferable and the life of the company does not terminate upon the death of a member. For income tax purposes, it is considered the same in many states. The board of directors, elected by the members, manages the business of the joint-stock company.

VOCABULARY REVIEW

Match the following vocabulary terms with the statements on the next page.

a. Articles of partnership
b. Close corporation
c. Corporation

d. Corporation bond
e. Conglomerate
f. Consumer cooperatives

g. Fiduciary relationship
h. General partnership
 i. Government corporation
 j. Joint-stock company
k. Limited-partnership association
 l. Open corporation
m. Partnership

n. Private corporation
o. Proxy
p. Preemptive rights
q. Secret partner
r. Silent partner
s. Stock corporation

1. An association of two or more persons to carry on as co-owners for profit
2. An arrangement in which all partners participate actively in the business, sharing all the responsibilities, including unlimited liability
3. An arrangement in which the liability of all partners is limited
4. A partner who takes an active role in the business but who does not want to reveal his identity
5. A partner who takes no active part in the business even though he is known to the public as a partner
6. An association of individuals united for a common purpose
7. A written agreement among the partners
8. A type of corporation chartered, owned, and operated by individuals either for profit, social, charitable, or educational purposes
9. A corporation organized by the federal, state, city or other political subdivision
10. A power of attorney that transfers to a third party the stockholder's right to vote
11. A corporation that offers its stock to the public
12. The relationship of trust and confidence between directors and officers
13. A corporation that does not offer its shares to the public
14. A corporation that issues its stock certificates of ownership to the shareholders
15. A certificate of indebtedness given to the holder as evidence of debt
16. The right of a stockholder to buy additional shares
17. A collection of unrelated companies producing diverse products, merged by the exchange of stock
18. A voluntary association of persons operating under articles of agreement and with capital divided into transferable shares
19. Retail stores established by a group of consumers who seek to buy goods at the wholesale cost

PROBLEMS AND PROJECTS

1. Three young college friends have heard about making fortunes in real-estate development. They have an option to buy 200 acres of undeveloped land on the edge of the city at $500 per acre. They believe the city will soon grow out to this acreage, and therefore it is urgent that they develop the property for residential homes. Their idea is to sell lots 100 by 150 feet. A local engineering firm has informed them that the cost of installing sewer lines and paved streets with gutters is approximately $100,000, which can be recovered by adjusting the price of each lot. Advise them as to the form of organization to use to establish this business. Give your reasons for the recommendations you make.
2. Tom Fry owns and operates a small modern dairy farm fifteen miles from a city

of 400,000 population. He sells to retail stores and also delivers to homes, using three driver–salesmen. He has two competitors, each a large corporation, that market almost a full line of national-brand dairy products. As a sole proprietor, Tom has tough competition. He would like to know what action he should take to reduce, as much as possible, his personal liability. In your opinion, which form of ownership would be the most appropriate for him? Give your reasons.

3. A, B, and C have decided to form a general partnership to construct and sell homes. All three are experienced businessmen as sole proprietors, but they have never owned a partnership and are not too familiar with the details involved. Each has agreed to invest $25,000 and each will work full time in the business. List the main points they should include in the general-partnership agreement.

A BUSINESS CASE

Case 5-1 An Inventor's Dilemma

Charles Bell, a former Air Force pilot, became a civilian in 1970 and took a position with an aircraft manufacturer. After working for a year, he invented a device that can be attached to the carburetor of a gasoline engine and is designed to reduce the percentage of carbon monoxide and hydrocarbons more efficiently than any product now on the market. Tests made by Bell on his own eight-cylinder car showed a reduction of 90 percent in emissions. He recently obtained a patent, and he would like to form an organization to manufacture this product, which is to be sold through auto-parts stores or bought by the four major car manufacturers in the United States. He would also like to explore the possibilities of selling the product to foreign automobile companies marketing in the United States, or of selling the product outright to a car manufacturer, although this would not offer the inventor the personal challenge he would like.

Preliminary estimates by Bell indicate that the product can be mass-produced at a cost of $60 per unit. This would probably add $90 to the price of the new car or $100 to a used car. However, Bell believes that there are ways to cut these costs.

Bell has $25,000 to invest. His banker advised him that the bank would consider making him a five-year loan of $50,000 at 8 percent if he would assign the patent to the bank. Bell believes he might be able to borrow as much as $35,000 from his close friends, and if he formed a corporation there would be possibilities of selling a million shares with a par value of $1. Bell readily admits he has no business experience in financing a company. His knowledge is mainly in engineering and production methods.

1. What is Bell's main problem?
2. What are the factors that would determine his best course of action?

the small business enterprise

CHAPTER SIX

To become an independent proprietor is a dream of many young men and women. This desire is a natural one, because people like the freedom of being their own bosses. Such motivation is the backbone of modern American business; every year, thousands of enterprising persons venture forth into careers as owners of small firms.

Oddly enough, many of today's giant enterprises began as one-man ventures, including steamship lines, mail-order houses, automobile manufacturing companies, and chain stores. Fortunately, the United States offers the kind of business climate that makes it possible for a person with a simple idea, a will to work, and a few hundred dollars to start his own business. History is replete with such business successes as those achieved by J. C. Penney, R. H. Macy, King Gillette, and Milton S. Hershey. And because business history continues to repeat itself, today firms like the Polaroid Corporation, Kentucky Fried Chicken franchises, the Howard Johnson chain are part of the newer assortment of nationwide companies that were each launched with a humble beginning by one man.

The fact that thousands of men and women who hold good positions in well-established companies annually venture forth to become their own bosses proves that rugged individualism is not dead. As you might expect, some of these ventures fail, but knowing this does not discourage others from joining the ranks of new entrepreneurs.

This chapter will give you a look at the myriad problems associated with small enterprises. It will also give you some idea of what is needed for success as the proprietor of your own business.

THE PLACE OF SMALL BUSINESS IN OUR ENVIRONMENT

Today there are at least two ways to have a career in business. One is to hitch your star to an established company and work your way up the managerial ladder. The other way, which we shall treat in this chapter, is to start your own company. To the hard-driving, ambitious individualist, owning a business provides the kind of freedom and independence that employees do not have.

What is Small Business?

As a rule, most people apply the term small business to the local corner drugstore, service station, or barbershop. This concept may be accurate enough

In 1861 Gilbert Van Camp produced the first factory canned pork and beans at this site in Indianapolis. Today the Stokely-Van Camp Corporation is international in its operations with a wide assortment of canned foods—all beginning with a one-man venture.

Courtesy Stokely-Van Camp, Inc., Indianapolis, Indiana

for general use, for most small firms operate on this scale, yet it is not the complete meaning of the term. Public Law 85-536, which was enacted on July 16, 1958, as an amendment to the Small Business Administration Act, states that "a *small business* concern shall be deemed to be one which is independently owned and operated and which is not dominant in its field of operation." In addition, for purposes of making loans, the SBA defines a small business as one that meets the following standards:

> *Wholesale*—Annual sales from $5 million to $15 million, depending on the industry
>
> *Retail* or *Service*—Annual sales or receipts from $1 million to $5 million, depending on the industry
>
> *Construction*—Annual sales or receipts of not more than $5 million, average on a three-year period
>
> *Manufacturing*—From 250 to 1,500 employees, depending on the industry[1]

The Committee for Economic Development (CED) offers a slightly different concept for defining small business, by advancing qualitative rather than quantitative criteria that distinguish small firms from large ones. The CED considers a company a small business when at least two of the following characteristics prevail:

> **1.** *Management is independent.* Generally, the managers are the owners.
> **2.** *Capital is furnished by an individual owner or small group.*
> **3.** *The area of operation is local.* Employees and owners reside in one home community. (Markets served need not be local.)
> **4.** *Size within the industry is relatively small.* The business is small when compared to the biggest units *in its field.* (The size of the top bracket varies widely, so that what might seem large in one field would be small in another.)[2]

As you can see from this definition, the CED regards small business as an institution that is highly self-initiated, largely self-financed, and closely self-managed with relatively small size when considered as part of the industry. To the authors, it makes little difference which standards are used to define or describe small business. What is important is the fact that most small businesses operate on a small scale with limited capital and few workers. Service is their most important contribution to society and to the economy. At the same time, it must be remembered that small business facilitates big business.

[1] *Small Business Administration, What It is—What It Does* (Washington, D.C.: Government Printing Office, February 1970), p. 3. (Distributed free by SBA.)
[2] The Research and Policy Committee of the Committee for Economic Development, *Meeting the Special Problems of Small Business,* policy report of the Committee for Economic Development, New York, June, 1947, p. 14.

Hundreds of mass-produced consumer goods, although produced by large corporations, are distributed and serviced largely by thousands of small stores.

Characteristics of Small Business

Apart from the matter of size, small businesses usually differ from large ones in three distinguishing characteristics: *management, capital requirements,* and *local operation.*

Management.[3] The management is generally independent. Since the manager is the owner, he is in a position to make his own decisions. As a small operator, the owner is both investor and employer, giving him far more freedom to act than if he were merely an employee. Most small businesses are either sole proprietorships or partnerships. Absentee ownership is rare.

Capital Requirements. The amount of capital required is relatively small as compared with most corporations. The source is often the owner's savings, or funds from friends and relatives.

Local Operation. For most small firms, the area of operation is local, owing mainly to the fact that both the employer and the employees live in the community in which the business is located. This does not necessarily mean that all small firms serve only local markets. Small importing and exporting firms and canning and packing plants sometimes operate nationwide.

The main characteristics of the small business and the big business are compared below.

Small Business	Big Business
Generally owner-managed	Usually non-owner-managed
Simple organizational structure	Complex organizational structure
Owner knows his employees	Owners seldom know many employees
High percentage of business failures	Low percentage of business failures
Lacks specialized managers	Management specialists commonly used
Long-term capital difficult to secure	Long-term capital usually relatively easy to obtain

Scope of Operation. According to the SBA, approximately 5.2 million firms, excluding farm units, are classified as small business establishments. The economic importance of these small concerns is indicated by the accompanying

[3] The term "management" as used here refers to the person who owns and operates the business. This term has other meanings, which will be discussed in later chapters.

**ROLE AND SCOPE OF SMALL BUSINESS
IN THE U.S. ECONOMY**

As defined by the federal government, small businesses
account for.....

... a large majority of total business firms in the
country— 5.2 million, which is 95 percent of the total.

95%	5%

... production of about 37 percent of the nation's total
goods and services.

37%	63%

... employment of four out of every ten civilian workers.

4 civilians	6 civilians

Source: Small Business Administration, 1970 Annual Report

chart, which shows that four out of every ten civilian jobs are in small business
and that these firms produce about 37 percent of the nation's total goods and
services.

One-fifth of all the small firms in the United States are concentrated in
New York and California, and about 30 percent are in Pennsylvania, Illinois,
Texas, Ohio, Michigan, and New Jersey combined. The largest single group
of small firms deals in service types of operations that include the services in
the following list.

1. *Bank services*—including commercial, trust, and savings banks
2. *Communication services*— such as telephone companies and broadcasting stations
3. *Entertainment*—night clubs, theaters, and casinos
4. *Household-appliance sales and warranty maintenance*— television sets, washers, dryers, refrigerators, and other kitchen appliances
5. *Lodging services*—mainly small motels and hotels
6. *Personal services*—mostly barber and beauty shops, dry cleaners, photography studios, and laundries
7. *Real estate and insurance*— firms that sell property, others that rent and manage it
8. *Repair stores*—clocks, watches, radio and television, and automobile repairs
9. *Transportation*—automobile agencies, taxicab companies, household movers, and storage operators
10. *Restaurants*—including cafeterias, coffee shops, and hotel dining rooms

Approximately one out of every two persons gainfully employed in this country either owns, manages, or is employed in a small establishment, mostly in the service-type industries. The majority of these are retail stores, including food, eating, and drinking establishments. About 75 percent of all small firms have three or fewer employees. Only 1 percent employ as many as 50 to 100 persons.

Discussion Questions

1. *Discuss some of the ways in which small firms differ from large ones.*
2. *Compare the definition of a small business used by the CED with one accepted by the SBA.*
3. *How do you account for the fact that most small businesses are in service-type establishments?*

AN ESTABLISHED FIRM OR A NEW ONE?

One of the most important questions that persons interested in owning a small business must answer is, Which road to business ownership is better: buying an established firm or starting a new one?

Statistics would indicate that most people find it difficult to decide which is best suited to them. This decision becomes less difficult after a comparison of the relative advantages of the two roads.

Buying an Established Business

One of the major advantages of buying a going concern in a good location is that the choice of location has been proved. With a new business, research must first be conducted to measure traffic at the location.

A second advantage to buying a going operation is that, to some extent at least, the uncertainty of its success in the future is reduced. The actual operating record of an existing business is far superior to an evaluation of a firm not yet in existence.

Third, the business may be available at a bargain price. The owner may wish to retire and, in order to make a quick sale, may sacrifice it by lowering the price. Or the price may be reduced to settle an estate. Of course, in any case the value of the business must be carefully verified to make certain it is a bargain.

A fourth advantage is the elimination of much of the time, effort, and costs related to the starting of a new firm. The seller has already accumulated an inventory of stock and has assembled the needed personnel (who, if competent, can be an asset to the new owner).

Starting a New Business

For various reasons, some persons prefer to start a completely new enterprise rather than to buy one already established. Some of the advantages of doing this should be noted.

First, starting from scratch allows the owner to choose his own location, employees, brand of merchandise, and kind of equipment. Furthermore, a loyal clientele can be cultivated without assuming any ill will that an existing business may have.

Second, one may find upon examination that because of the inefficient management of existing concerns that are for sale, the market is not adequately served by them, and that there is a need for a new, aggressive, and efficient firm.

Third, often it is possible to start on quite a small scale, with little capital. It is a mistake to assume that all new enterprises must start on a large scale; the facts show that many do not.

The arguments on this subject may be summarized as follows:

Established Firm	New Firm
Less time needed to begin operations	Can build to meet needs of new business
Old location may be better than new one	New location may be better than old
Maintaining old equipment may cost less	Can start with new stock and equipment
Can begin with a nucleus of customers	Possible to select customers
No delay in waiting for stock or equipment to operate	New firm gives greater freedom to organize
May take advantage of reputation	Not bound by old firm's policies and practices

Discussion Questions

4. *Compare the advantages of buying an established firm with those of starting a new one.*
5. *What are some of the difficulties in starting a new business?*

THE MORTALITY OF SMALL BUSINESS

In every kind of business—small, medium, or large—there is an element of risk for the owners. Unfortunately, too many persons are unwilling to accept risk as a factor in small business because they overestimate their own qualifications and therefore believe they will succeed where others fail. Small firms seem to be particularly vulnerable to such factors as general economic conditions, store location, and competition. Studies show that the failure rate is higher for these small firms than for big business and that failures usually occur for certain specific reasons.

Causes of Business Failures

Nationwide statistics dealing with business failures, gathered by Dun and Bradstreet, a credit-reporting firm, reveal that managerial inexperience and incompetence account for almost 90 percent of small-business failures. These weaknesses of management manifest themselves in several ways:

1. Lack of ability to supervise and direct others
2. Lack of capital, an indication of poor financial management
3. Lack of ability in sales promotion and sales management techniques
4. Lack of ability to collect bad debts and to curtail unwise credit policies

How can a proprietor determine that his business is failing? As a rule, there are five indicators of impending business failure:

1. Declining sales record over several fiscal periods
2. Progressively higher debt ratios
3. Increased operating costs
4. Deterioration of working-capital ratio
5. Reduction in profits (or increasing losses)

These are the danger signals, and not all of them appear at the same time. When one or more of these signals first appear, it is time for the owner to take action. Some of the possible steps may include (1) cutting operating expenses by eliminating all expense items that cannot be justified; (2) striving to improve sales promotion and sales effectiveness; (3) reviewing credit policies to make certain that poor credit risks are not extended credit; and (4) re-examining stock inventories to see that they are not excessive or that the business does not have too much idle cash on hand.

Maintaining liquidity of working capital is essential to a satisfactory working-capital position. One way to measure working-capital liquidity is to ascertain the average number of days that accounts are outstanding. Both the current ratio and the operating-expense ratio, which are discussed later in this chapter, are measures of working-capital adequacy.

Number and Rate of Failures

The fact that a business is small suggests that its chances of failing may be significantly greater than those of a big business. It is a fact that as a group, small businesses are more subject to business failures than are larger ones. "Business failures" include only those discontinuances that involve court proceedings or voluntary actions that result in loss to creditors. This relates to voluntary and involuntary petition in bankruptcy which we will discuss later in this chapter.

The Number of Business Failures. The number of business failures, as shown by the accompanying chart prepared by the Small Business Administration, closely parallels fluctuations in our economic condition. Since 1925 the

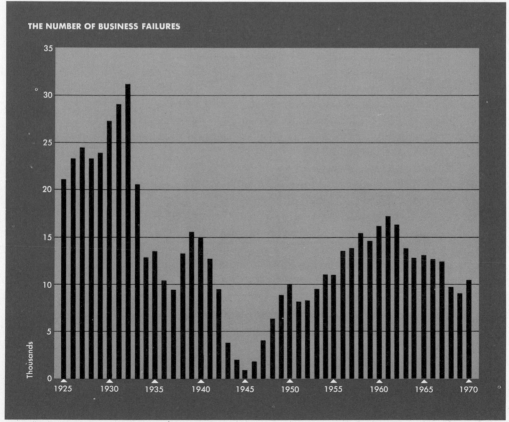

THE NUMBER OF BUSINESS FAILURES

Source: Small Business Administration, 1970 Annual Report

TABLE
6.1
TOTAL ANNUAL U.S. BUSINESS FAILURES BY FIELDS FOR SELECTED YEARS

Business Fields	1970	1969	1968	1967
Commercial Service	1,392	1,159	1,106	1,329
Construction	1,687	1,590	1,670	2,261
Mining and Manufacturing	2,035	1,493	1,513	1,832
Retail Trade	4,650	4,070	4,366	5,696
Wholesale Trade	984	842	981	1,246
	10,748	9,154	9,636	12,364

Sources: Dun & Bradstreet, Inc., The Failure Record Through 1969, *p. 11; "Business Failures,"* Dun's Review and Modern Industry, *Vol. 95 (February 1970), 99; op. cit., Vol. 97 (February 1971), 91.*

peak in business failures was during the early 1930s. The lowest number of failures occurred in 1945 which was the end of World War II. Failure rates have increased since then reaching a peak in 1961 to be followed by a low point in 1969.

Another index of business failures, covering classes of business, is shown in Table 6.1. According to these data, the trend in total number of business failures since 1967 has declined with business mortality highest among establishments in the retail trade and lowest in wholesale businesses in 1970. As sales and profits of firms slipped, the total number of businesses which went into bankruptcy or otherwise failed with loss to creditors rose 17 percent from 9,154 in 1969 to 10,748. Failures increased in mining and manufacturing, which is an area of relatively heavy capital investment. Continuing inflation also increased the level of bankruptcy liabilities.

Still another picture of business mortality is given in the accompanying pie graph, which shows that the majority of firms that fail do so during their first five years. In 1970, for 54 percent of those that failed, it was during their first five years of existence. This would seem to indicate that if a small firm can survive its first five years, it has a better-than-average chance of continuing until at least its tenth anniversary.

Certain kinds of businesses are more vulnerable to the causes of failure than others. In manufacturing industries (for example, see the related statistics on page 157), the failure rate per 10,000 concerns is highest in furniture, with a rate of 116, and lowest in machinery manufacturing with a rate of 50.

Insolvency and Bankruptcy

Since business failure is the fate of many small concerns as well as some large ones, the legal aspects of insolvency and bankruptcy are pertinent to the owners of small firms. These terms are not synonymous. A proprietorship may be insolvent—in other words, with liabilities larger than its assets—and still

BUSINESS FAILURES BY AGE OF FIRM, 1970
(Data Based on 10,748 Failures)

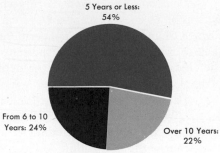

5 Years or Less:
54%

From 6 to 10
Years: 24%

Over 10 Years:
22%

Courtesy Dun and Bradstreet, Inc.

not be bankrupt. *Bankruptcy* is a means of liquidation for a debtor hopelessly in debt or for a person or business seeking liquidation for some reason. Bankruptcy requires a court proceeding initiated either voluntarily by the debtor or by unpaid creditors. This act is performed under the jurisdiction of the courts as prescribed by the National Bankruptcy Act. *Insolvency* is defined as the financial condition of a person or business when all the assets are not sufficient to pay the debts. There are three possible methods for salvaging an insolvent business: (1) creditor agreements, (2) equity receivership, and (3) bankruptcy.

If the creditors agree that the business can be operated at a profit in the future, they may be willing to postpone the due date for the debts. In an equity receivership, the court appoints a receiver, who runs or liquidates the company in the interest of all the creditors. Equity receivership is under the jurisdiction of either a state court or a federal court, depending upon whether the business is local or interstate.

Bankruptcy may be either voluntary or involuntary. It is always under *important* the direction of a federal court, because the Constitution of the U.S. provides for a national uniform bankruptcy law. The judge appoints a referee to act for him. *Voluntary bankruptcy,* which is more common under present laws, occurs when a debtor files a petition with the court asking to be adjudged bankrupt and asserting that he is willing to make his assets available for

Kinds of Businesses in Manufacturing Industries	Failure Rate per 10,000 Concerns
Furniture	116
Transportation Equipment	107
Textiles	80
Apparel	64
Electrical Machinery	59
Leather and Shoes	52
Machinery	50

equitable distribution among his creditors under the supervision of the court. If this is approved, he is discharged from his debts and is free to begin anew.

Involuntary bankruptcy occurs when one or more creditors of an insolvent person or business (except a wage earner receiving less that $1,500 yearly, a farmer, or any corporation not permitted to declare itself a voluntary bankrupt) seek to have that business or person declared bankrupt. To accomplish this, the creditors must prove that the debtor committed one or more of the acts of bankruptcy as defined in the law.

The acts may be summarized as follows: (1) removing or concealing assets; (2) transferring, while insolvent, a portion of his property to one or more creditors; (3) allowing any creditor to obtain a lien upon his property and failing to discharge the lien within 30 days; (4) admitting in writing his inability to pay his debts; (5) making a general assignment of his property for the benefit of creditors; and (6) while insolvent, accepting or permitting the appointment of a receiver or trustee to take charge of the property.

When a petition of involuntary bankruptcy is filed in the federal court, the judge appoints a receiver. An investigation is conducted by the court to determine if the debtor is actually insolvent and if he is guilty of violating one of the acts of bankruptcy. If there has been a violation, the court takes over the supervision of the assets by appointing a referee in bankruptcy, who notifies the creditors to file and prove their claims. The creditors then meet and elect a trustee in bankruptcy, who is charged with the task of liquidating the business or estate. This same procedure applies to both voluntary and involuntary bankruptcy, after the court has declared the defendant bankrupt.

The Bankruptcy Act permits payment to creditors under the following priority: (1) administrative costs, including certain expenses of creditors, fees, trustee's expenses, etc.; (2) wages due to employees, not to exceed $600 earned within three months before the date of commencement of proceedings; (3) reasonable expenses incurred by creditors who oppose approval of a settlement plan on behalf of the parties or who object to a settlement plan involving a wage-earner of the company who also seeks relief or through whose efforts a conviction is obtained under the act for an offense; (4) taxes due to the municipality, state, county, or the federal government; (5) debts due anyone according to the priority under state and federal laws.

Discussion Questions

6. *Explain the statement that most business failures are caused by managerial inexperience.*

7. *What are some of the symptoms of impending business failure?*

SOME PROBLEMS OF OWNING
YOUR OWN BUSINESS

By this time you must be aware that starting your own business can be both challenging and risky. However, neither challenge nor risk is apt to hold back a really ambitious person, because the ambitious invariably believe that challenges should be met. Whatever may be your attitude toward risk, before you decide to start your own business, you should be able to answer satisfactorily the following questions about your plans:

1. Have I selected the right kind of business? Am I qualified to operate it?
2. Is the type of business I propose to start already crowded with strong competition?
3. Do I have sufficient capital to carry me through early unforeseen difficulties?
4. Have I made the right choice of legal form of ownership?

Choosing the Right Business

The choice of a business is often the most difficult decision to make when you are thinking about starting your own business, for the fact is that you cannot be sure whether you have made the right choice until you have actually had some experience in the business you have chosen. At the very least, however, you should have some liking for the kind of activity in which you will be spending your time. And the qualifications required by the business should be in line with your own qualifications and your likes and dislikes.

Probably the best procedure at the outset is to prepare a list of different kinds of businesses. Then select several from the list and make a careful examination of the important factors involved in each. Regardless of how extensive your analysis is, you must ultimately come to some specific conclusions concerning such factors as the amount of capital the business will require, the amount of risk involved, the kind of personal qualifications needed, how well your own qualifications meet these requirements, and finally, your own ability to manage. A natural tendency of some persons who want to go into business for themselves is to be overoptimistic about their own ability and the opportunities the venture offers them.

Determining Your Capital Needs

Records show that most small firms start with inadequate capital. And as we mentioned earlier in this chapter, lack of sufficient capital is a prime cause of business failure.

Speaking very broadly, *capital* means purchasing power. It includes not only the funds invested by the owner but also funds made available by creditors. Thus, for a business requiring initial capital of $12,000, the owner may have $7,000 of his own, plus a bank loan of $3,000 and credit amounting to $2,000 from one or more wholesalers or manufacturers.

Capital invested in machinery, buildings, land, and fixtures is classified as *fixed capital. Working capital* represents funds spent for such items as supplies, materials, rent, and wages. Good planning requires that the owner be able to distinguish between these kinds of capital in estimating capital needs. It is also important for the small businessman to realize that a reasonable period, usually a minimum of six months, will normally be required before his income will be sufficient to cover his expenses. Thus he must include in his estimated needs a minimum salary to provide for his living during this period.

Capital requirements for one kind of business may easily differ from those of another. For example, according to Dun and Bradstreet estimates, the minimum capital needed to start a small retail furniture store is from $20,000 to $25,000; for a drugstore, from $25,000 to $40,000. A retail store's largest single investment is probably in merchandise. Trade credit extended by suppliers can help to reduce capital needs. Service-type firms, such as radio and television repair shops, do not need large stock inventories because they are primarily engaged in selling repair service. It is true that firms selling on credit need more initial capital than noncredit businesses.

Choosing the Form of Ownership

In Chapter 5 we discovered several different forms of business ownership developed to meet the needs of all kinds of business enterprises, both large and small. The problem is to select the one that is best adapted to the situation.

The simplicity of the sole proprietorship makes this form well adapted to small enterprises, but under certain conditions the partnership and corporate organizations are also satisfactory forms of operation for small-scale ventures. You will have to decide as early as you can which form to use. Here are some helpful questions to ask yourself:

> *How large is my business going to be?* Your answer should help you determine how much working capital you will need. Should you take in a partner to obtain the required initial capital? If you need more than one partner, would it be better to form a corporation?
>
> *How much business risk am I, as owner, willing to assume in starting the venture?* You know from the preceding chapter that the sole proprietorship and partnership forms of ownership involve unlimited liability. This is the reason so many small businesses incorporate.
>
> *What about my tax position?* The sole proprietorship and partnership offers you a favorable tax position. They avoid the double tax on

business profits of corporations and the stockholders' tax levied on dividends. The proprietorship and partnership pay no annual franchise tax nor any stock-transfer taxes. The proprietor and the partners pay a personal income tax on taxable income, including net business profits at individual tax rates, which are generally lower than for corporations.

Factors in Determining Small-Business Corporations

For the owner of a small business to be informed about changing conditions within the business is as important as it is for the owners of large enterprises. Assuming that the owner keeps complete and adequate records from which his financial statements are to be prepared, it is possible to observe what is happening to the financial condition of the firm by using acceptable accounting records and statements. One method for doing this is known as *ratio analysis,* a technique for analyzing financial statements to determine trends and changes in the company and to compare their differences with those of other companies in a similar kind of business.

A *ratio* is a mathematical means of expressing a relationship between two items. It is the quotient that shows the relationship between two or more relevant items—in this case, two items taken from a financial statement. Three of these ratios and their uses will be mentioned here.

The Current Ratio. The *current ratio,* which is discussed in more detail in Chapter 16 because it is related to accounting, is found by dividing the total current assets by the total current liabilities. The small-business owner often uses this ratio to test the adequacy of his working capital; however, this is not what the current ratio really shows. Instead, it indicates the extent to which the value of current assets may decline and still be sufficient to pay the current liabilities. A concern that has a rapid turnover of its current assets will usually require a smaller excess of current assets over current liabilities than one with a slower turnover of current assets.

The Sales-to-Net-Worth Ratio. To produce this ratio, divide the net sales by the net worth. By the resultant figure it is possible to determine the dollars of sales for every dollar of owner's equity.

The Operating-Expense Ratio. To find this ratio, divide net sales or gross income by total operating expenses. For example, if the net sales are $300,000 and the operating expenses $60,000, the operating ratio may be shown as 5:1. This means it costs an average of $1 to sell $5 worth of goods. Stated another way, the cost of doing business is 20 percent of sales.

Franchising and Small Business

One way to start your own business is to obtain a franchise. Although franchising is not new, the widespread use of it that has occurred since 1960 is attracting great attention.

What Is Franchising? According to the Small Business Administration, *franchising* is a system of distribution under which an individually owned business is operated as though it were part of a large chain, complete with product name, trademark, and standardized procedures. The key to franchising is the franchise contract. The parties to a franchise agreement are the *franchisee,* an independent businessman, and the *franchisor,* sometimes called the licenser. In effect, a franchise contract is an investment between the franchisor—sometimes known as the parent company—and the franchisee, the investor. There is no standard franchise agreement, any more than there is a uniform code of business practices. But in a typical contract, the parties usually agree to perform as suggested by the boxed list at the bottom of this page.

Contracts also often provide terms under which the agreement may be cancelled and terms under which the franchisee may sell the business to another party. Liabilities of the parties are also specified.

Franchising is popular in many fields, especially in retailing and service businesses. For many years, the Walgreen and Rexall drug products were sold as franchises to independent druggists, principally in small communities. Automobile dealerships were among the early franchises. In the soft-drink field, Coca-Cola, Pepsi-Cola, and Dr. Pepper have been popular franchises. More recently, Shakey's Pizza, Howard Johnson restaurants, and H. & R. Block have become popular franchising operations. One of the fastest-growing franchise

The Franchisor Agrees To:	The Franchisee Agrees To:
1. Assign an exclusive sales territory to the franchisee	1. Operate the business according to the rules and procedures offered by franchisor
2. Provide a stipulated amount of management training and assistance	2. Invest a minimum amount in the business
3. Furnish merchandise to the franchisee at a price competitive with the market	3. Pay the franchisor a certain amount (usually as a royalty on a fixed percentage)
4. Advise the franchisee on location of business and design of building	4. Construct or otherwise provide a business facility as approved by the franchisor
5. Participate in furnishing a certain amount of money (usually as a royalty on a fixed percentage)	5. Buy supplies and other standard materials from franchisor
6. Offer certain financial assistance to franchisee	

motels is Holiday Inns of America. Its approximately 1,250 inns, with well over 100,000 rooms make it larger than Hilton Hotels, the Hilton International chain, and the Sheraton Hotel chain combined. Other franchising operations that have expanded significantly in recent years are the car-washing stations, dance studios, slenderizing salons, ice cream stores, and coin-operated laundries.

Franchising offers small companies a way to accelerate their growth by increasing sales. Many other franchisees invest their money because they want to work for themselves. Or they want to join with a going concern that makes profitable products, rather than taking the risk of starting from scratch themselves.

How much capital is required? In a few instances, only about $2,000; however, most franchises require amounts ranging from $10,000 to $100,000 to start, although part of this can be borrowed from the franchisor.

The SBA gives this advice regarding the matter of selecting the right franchise: "In looking for a franchise that is right for you, you should watch for the 'fast buck' operator. The rapid growth of franchising has attracted an unsavory group of these operators who will take you if they can."[4]

Discussion Questions

8. Explain ratio analysis. What is the difference between the sales-to-net-worth ratio and the operating-expense ratio?

9. What are some of the problems involved in choosing the right form of ownership?

10. Define a franchise. What is there about franchising that has made it so popular?

What's Worrying Small Business Owners

Small firms have difficulty in effecting the savings in operating costs that can often result from large-scale operations. High taxes, increased wages, and other costs often take more of the firm's capital than anticipated. Large firms can borrow funds at lower interest rates than small firms.

Large firms, in an effort to reduce taxes, frequently find it more economical to build a building and then sell it to an investor and lease it back over a long period. Small firms generally do not have sufficient capital to make deals of this kind. One small-business owner reports that in his opinion big business gets tax advantages, because these firms can afford to employ full-time tax experts whereas the small firm finds this practice too expensive.

Changes in minority-hiring regulations present a problem, in that many

---

[4] A. L. Tunick, *Are You Ready for Franchising?* Small Marketers Aids No. 115 (Washington, D.C.: Small Business Administration, February 1970).

TABLE
6.2
CAPITAL REQUIRED TO START YOUR OWN BUSINESS

Amounts are estimates obtained from various associations.

Type of Business	Capital Range	Nature of Expenditures	Source of Information
Beauty Salon	$10,000 to $20,000	Plumbing, electrical costs, furniture, equipment	National Hairdressers and Cosmetologists Assn., 3510 Olive St., St. Louis, Mo. 63103
Coffee Shop	$20,000 to $45,000	Equipment and seats for 25-seat shop, dishes and cutlery	National Restaurant Association, 1530 N. Lake Shore Dr., Chicago, Ill. 60610
Self-Service Car Wash, Coin-Operated	$23,000 to $30,000	Site preparation, equipment, installation for four-bay operation. Real-property costs not included	National Carwash Council, Seven S. Dearborn St., Chicago, Ill. 60603
Laundry/Dry Cleaner Combination, Coin-Operated	$55,000 to $75,000	Equipment, installation, supplies, promotional costs, and reserve for store with six units	National Automatic Laundry and Cleaning Council, Seven S. Dearborn St., Chicago, Ill. 60603
Gasoline Service Station	$12,000 to $18,000	Lease cost, accessories, gasoline and oil inventory, tools	National Congress of Petroleum Retailers, 2945 Banksville Rd., Pittsburgh, Pa. 15216
Retail Nursery	$40,000 to $65,000	Building cost, equipment, rent, inventory, cash reserve	American Assn. of Nurserymen, Inc., 835 Southern Bldg., Washington, D.C. 20005

small firms are required to employ minority workers. Some have the necessary skills, while others must be trained. The cost to train these workers then becomes a burden for the owner. Small firms are less able to underwrite these costs or absorb them than are large companies.

Some firms experience difficulties not entirely common to large companies. The owner of a small firm must be a self-starter. Everything depends upon him, and if he fails to give leadership or imagination, the firm has difficulty starting and growing.

Small firms sometimes are unable to accommodate the changing desires of shoppers. For example, a small dress shop would have more difficulty than a large one in keeping a wide range of styles in stock at a time when fashions were undergoing a change.

THE SMALL BUSINESS ADMINISTRATION

The general aims of the Small Business Administration are as follows:

1. To help small-business owners gain access to capital and credit
2. To help small businesses obtain a fair share of government contracts
3. To make available to small-business owners managerial, production, and technical counsel
4. To make disaster loans to persons whose homes or businesses have been damaged or destroyed by various kinds of disasters, and to make available to minority individuals loans and other services so they can become more successful business operators

Management and Technical Publications

The SBA distributes a wide range of management and technical publications to established or prospective owners of small businesses. These publications include several series available without charge from SBA offices and several obtainable from the Superintendent of Documents, Washington, D.C.

Free Series of Publications.

1. *Management Aids for Small Manufacturers*—discussions of the various phases of managing a small manufacturing business, including accounting, financial management, personnel management, purchasing, and market research.
2. *Technical Aids for Small Manufacturers*—facts on significant development in fields such as materials, processes, equipment, and maintenance.
3. *Small Business Bibliographies*—reference sources for business owners and managers and prospective small businessmen.
4. *Small Marketers Aids*—discussions of various phases of managing a small retail, service, or wholesale business including advertising, competitive strategy, controlling, and selling.

Financial Assistance

Business and disaster loans, the backbone of the SBA assistance program, consisted in 1970 of 49,179 loans of all types for $1.1 billion. A record number of these loans were made to victims of natural disasters. The SBA ended the year 1970 with a portfolio of 126,073 loans, valued at $2,464,009,000. The number of loans made to small businesses, excluding disaster loans, in 1970 reached a record total of 17,425 for a total of $864 million. Some 89 percent of the funds for business loans were furnished by banks under a participation plan whereby banks and the SBA share in the loan, or under the guaranty plan in which the banks fund the entire loan with a guarantee of SBA. Interest rates ranged from 7.7 to 9.15 percent depending upon the size of the loan.

A CAREER IN SMALL BUSINESS

Few persons eventually succeed in owning a substantial number of shares of the business in which they are employed. Many people, however, at some time or another consider working for themselves. As you have seen, the attrition rate of small businesses is high, owing mainly to a number of risks that are involved; but there are rewards, too, as many can testify. What is the best preparation for personal ownership? What kind of person is most likely to be successful as an entrepreneur?

The College Graduate and Small Business

Small business does provide an opportunity to have your own business. It offers young men and women the satisfaction of being their own bosses, but one should be the "self-starter" type with a capacity for imagination and a willingness to take chances. One way to evaluate yourself is to work for a time in an establishment of the kind you want to own eventually.

While in college, the student who plans to own his own establishment after graduation should give consideration to the courses he should study. Accounting and finance are important, as well as such subjects as economics, business writing, marketing, and an introductory course in business administration.

The long-time trend in America has demonstrated that this nation needs the small enterprise. In many instances, small firms are suppliers of large companies, another reason to conclude that small firms have made a contribution to the total economic development. Small business helps link big business with the consumer. Literally hundreds of articles produced by giant companies are distributed and serviced by thousands of small enterprises. Small business encourages competition.

Discussion Questions

11. *What are the main purposes of the Small Business Administration, and what are some of the ways it fulfills its purposes?*

12. *How can you determine whether you would be interested in becoming an owner of a small business?*

13. *What contributions do small firms make to the economy?*

SUMMARY

The prevailing notion that owning your own business is easy and profitable has caused some persons to start a business without having adequate background and financing. Consequently, the rate of failure is high. Some of the causes for failure are lack of managerial experience, insufficient capital, poor location, excessive spending, and inventory difficulties.

The characteristics of the small firm differ from those of the large concerns. In a small business, management and ownership are generally the same. Most small firms serve only a small location, leaving national markets to larger companies. Capital requirements are far less for large companies. Then, too, the small firm seldom sells stock to raise its capital; instead, its capital comes from the owners, their friends, and banks.

The small business typically uses a simple organization structure. Most are proprietorships or partnerships; only a few begin as corporations. There is an increasing interest on the part of the federal government in making small firms more substantial through the help of the SBA.

VOCABULARY REVIEW

Match the following vocabulary terms with the statements below.

a. Current ratio
b. Fixed capital
c. Franchising
d. Insolvency

e. Involuntary bankruptcy
f. Ratio
g. Ratio analysis

h. Small business
i. Voluntary bankruptcy
j. Working capital

1. A business that is independently owned and operated and that is not dominant in its field of operation
2. The financial condition of a person when all his assets are not enough to pay his debts
3. The filing of a petition by a debtor with the court, asking to be adjudged a bankrupt and asserting willingness to make his assets available for equitable distribution among his creditors under the supervision of the court
4. When one or more creditors of an insolvent person or business seek to have a business or person declared bankrupt
5. Capital invested in machinery, buildings, land, and fixtures
6. Funds spent for such items as supplies, materials, rent, and wages
7. A mathematical means of expressing a relationship between two items
8. A technique for analyzing financial statements to determine trends and changes in the company and to compare their differences with those of other companies in similar kinds of businesses.
9. A ratio found by dividing the total of current assets by the total of current liabilities
10. A distribution system under which an individually owned business is operated as though it were part of a large chain, complete with product name, trademark, and standardized procedures.

PROBLEMS AND PROJECTS

1. Select a local businessman who owns and operates a small business in your community—other than a franchise business, such as an automobile agency, franchise motel or food store. Using the interview technique, gather material about the problems of starting and operating a small business. Following are some of

the questions you may want to ask during the interview in order to obtain enough material for your report.

    a. What were the reasons the owner wanted to own his own business?
    b. Why did he prefer working for himself in preference to working for someone else?
    c. How did he go about making the decision as to his choice of business?
    d. Did the owner determine his qualifications to own a business in the beginning?
    e. What personal qualifications did the owner determine that he had as being pertinent to his choice of small business?
    f. Where did the owner obtain his starting capital?
    g. Was it difficult to raise?
    h. Did the owner investigate the matter of buying an established business rather than starting a new one?
    i. What are his plans for expansion?

2. Examine three or four recent issues of any one of the following business management magazines: *Dun's Review & Modern Industry, Nation's Business,* or *Forbes.* Look for articles you consider to be helpful to anyone interested in starting a business of his own. On the basis of your information, write a report explaining what you found from your reading that would help any person planning to become his own boss. Include in your report special comments and quotations from these sources.

3. Choose a local owner of a franchise business in your community and conduct an interview about how he selected the franchise organization, the kind of help the franchiser gave him in getting started, the amount of money that was needed, and how long the owner was asked to attend a training program. The purpose is to gather materials to give a talk before your class on this subject. Write a summary of your findings, to be presented to your instructor prior to your oral report.

A BUSINESS CASE

Case 6-1   The Case of Sam Fong

Sam Fong and his wife own and operate the S & M Flower Shop in a community near Chicago. A specialty of the business is manufacturing artificial flowers, using imported raw materials from Japan. This business has become widely known for its beautiful artificial orchids, roses, carnations, and gardenias.

Until recently, Sam's store was the only one in his community with artificial flowers for sale, but now a local department store has started advertising a line of wax flowers imported from West Germany. Even though Sam's prices are about 10 percent higher than those of his local competitor, his sales volume has been maintained. But Sam is in constant fear that one or more of the four young women who make these flowers for him will resign and open their own store. They were trained by Sam, who says it takes about one year to qualify a trainee to produce a lifelike flower at the maximum production rate.

Recently, a buyer from a national discount chain visited Sam's store and offered to sign a contract to buy from him annually up to 15,000 artificial orchids, 5,000 roses, and 10,000 gardenias. The price offered Sam was a few cents per flower above his present production cost. However, Sam believes he could reduce his present unit cost about 10 percent by adding four more employees to make the flowers. These workers would be carried for six months at a trainee wage, and in about six months more they would be capable of producing a limited number of flowers, reaching peak production by the end of the second year. Although it could be difficult, Sam is of the opinion that he can find four young women for this kind of work.

Sam is not certain whether this is the appropriate time to expand. This is an inflationary period, and prices are climbing. On the other hand, this may be a type of offer that will not be repeated to Sam. He knows there are some problems facing him. He would need more capital at a high rate of interest. He might not be able to find a sufficient number of trainees. Then there is a possibility of more competition from foreign sources. Is this the time to expand the business?

1. Prepare a recommendation for Sam regarding the issue before him.
2. Does Sam have any alternatives open to him?

business management

CHAPTER SEVEN

Probably no business executive understood better the meaning of the word "management" than did James Michael Roche who, until his retirement, was chairman of the board of directors of the General Motors Corporation, the world's largest manufacturer of motor vehicles. As the chief executive officer, he was involved in decision making affecting millions of people and billions of dollars of assets. He also had an interest in the welfare of 1.3 million stockholders, 749,000 employees, 16,000 independent auto and appliance dealers, and 7 million customers. In addition he kept an eye on the health of the economy and the changing ecological environment.

It is managers like James Michael Roche who are responsible for seeing that society receives the firm's goods and services at the right time, in the desired amounts, and at a price the customers are willing to pay. In carrying out these responsibilities, management performs certain basic administrative activities commonly referred to as "management functions" that are performed by managers. In this chapter we are concerned with the role of management and the nature and responsibilities of management in today's complex and rapidly changing environment. Business management is the main link between business and its environment.

MANAGEMENT:
WHAT IT IS AND WHAT IT DOES

Since the beginning of the managerial movement that began as an outgrowth of the factory system during the last half of the nineteenth century, the term *management* has been identified by various meanings. Some writers describe it rather than define it. Economists in the eighteenth and nineteenth centuries seldom used the term without relating it to such words as "proprietor," "entrepreneur," or "capitalist."

Peter F. Drucker sees management as "the specific organ of the business enterprise"—a broad definition.[1] Professors Hersey and Blanchard define management as "working with and through individuals and groups to accomplish organizational goals."[2] George L. Morrisey, a management executive, considers management "any work that must be performed by the manager himself because it cannot be performed as well or better by subordinates or staff groups."[3]

For the purposes of our discussion, we define management as the process whereby resources are combined into an integrated system in order to accomplish the objectives of the system. This definition specifically treats management as a process within a total system, with managers who get things done by working with people and other resources. To structure a business according to the systems concept, it is necessary to organize it by functional areas concerned with such divisions as sales, finance, and production. Managers of these organizational divisions perform their duties by engaging in certain functions of management that, if properly applied, can result in effective use of men, money, machines, materials, methods, and markets. All management functions stem from this responsibility.

Management as an Art and a Science

Management is often referred to as an art because it deals with the application of both knowledge and skill to achieve an objective. And since it involves the use of certain management-technique principles, it is also called

---

[1] Peter F. Drucker, *The Practice of Management* (New York: Harper & Row, Publishers, 1954), p. 7.
[2] Paul Hersey and Kenneth H. Blanchard, *Management of Organizational Behavior* (Englewood Cliffs, N.J.: Prentice-Hall, Inc., 1969), p. 3.
[3] George L. Morrisey, *Management by Objectives and Results* (Reading, Mass.: Addison-Wesley Publishing Co., Inc., 1970), p. 4.

a science. As a science, then, management includes the orderly application of pertinent facts to specific management problems. Some examples of the types of problems in which scientific methods may be used include employee testing, production cost analysis, market analysis, and systems of inventory control.

It is also important to note that, as an art, management has played a significant role in the programs of modern business. There are many decisions to be made in business concerning which not all the facts are available and whose effectiveness often depends on extemporaneous value judgments. The art of management involves the ability of the manager to make these important decisions and to take action *even though* all the facts are not present (and indeed perhaps cannot be obtained). Thus, management as an art has become very much a matter of knowing when and to what extent one should exercise his powers of leadership. It goes without saying, perhaps, that although it is much more difficult to practice management as an art than as a science, there is no doubt that management will always be—to the wonderment of those involved in decision making—a mixture of both art and science.

Areas of Managerial Authority

In our study of what management is and does, it is important to understand that managerial authority and responsibility break down into two broad areas: *administration* and *execution.* The distinction between these two areas may be clearly seen in the accompanying diagram. The board of directors, company president, and vice-presidents are members of *administration,* or *administrative, general,* or *top management,* as it is sometimes called. These are the officers concerned chiefly with the activities so vital to the success of any business venture—planning, organizing, staffing, and controlling.

Executive management, or *execution,* is concerned with carrying out

AREAS OF MANAGEMENT AUTHORITY AND EXECUTION

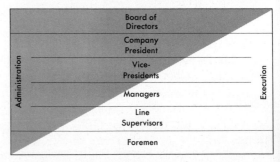

Areas of management authority and execution

FLOW OF COMMUNICATIONS IN A BUSINESS ORGANIZATION

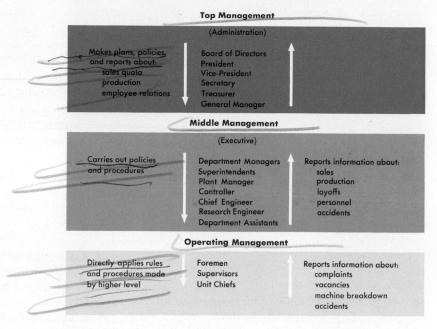

Top Management

(Administration)

Makes plans, policies, and reports about:
- sales quota
- production
- employee relations

Board of Directors
President
Vice-President
Secretary
Treasurer
General Manager

Middle Management

(Executive)

Carries out policies and procedures

Department Managers
Superintendents
Plant Manager
Controller
Chief Engineer
Research Engineer
Department Assistants

Reports information about:
- sales
- production
- layoffs
- personnel
- accidents

Operating Management

Directly applies rules and procedures made by higher level

Foremen
Supervisors
Unit Chiefs

Reports information about:
- complaints
- vacancies
- machine breakdown
- accidents

Levels of management authority and execution (arrows show flow of communications)

specific projects. In this area are departmental executives, such as the sales manager, office manager, and traffic manager, who have the responsibility of carrying out plans established by administration. The principal function of executive management is that of control.

Some companies use the term "executive" to identify top management. They tell their first-line supervisors that they are members of the management team, which is true. Such a distinction, however, is not logical, because management is the function of executive leadership throughout the organization.

Perhaps a fuller understanding of the areas of management authority and execution may be attained by envisioning *levels* of management—even though in some organizations it is admittedly difficult to identify more than one level. In large firms there are usually three levels: (1) top management, (2) middle management, and (3) operating management. The chart above illustrates the manager's role for each of these levels of management. The arrows show the flow of communications from one level to another. Managerial authority and responsibility decrease as administration moves closer to the lowest level. Notice that stockholders are not shown at any level of management.

---

1. *Distinguish between management as a science and as an art.*
2. *What is the difference between the administrative area and the executive area in a business?*

HISTORICAL BACKGROUND
OF MODERN MANAGEMENT

Before going into details on the subject of management, let us look at the historical background that helped to develop our modern managerial techniques for American business.

The Rise of a Managerial Class

The Industrial Revolution in the United States greatly accelerated factory production, and at the same time helped create a managerial class. The change from the sole proprietorship to the corporation imposed certain limitations on the personal liabilities of stockholders. Not only did the corporation offer industry a means of raising more capital for expansion, but the size of corporations created a need for qualified managers.

The number of managers in the United States has increased fourfold since 1900. At that time there were 1.6 million managers in the total work force. By 1960, the total reached 7 million, and it is anticipated that by 1975 it will exceed 9 million. Despite the increase, competent managers continue to be scarce.

Although most businesses have managers, or at least a managerial job to be performed, there is no standardized managerial position common to all firms. The president of one company may devote most of his time to engineering, the field he knows best; another may spend much of his time in finance or marketing. The widespread use of such titles as sales manager, general manager, and production manager implies that these are standardized positions; and yet, when we consider the total picture, the functions within such classifications may be quite dissimilar in different companies.

Over the years, as businesses have expanded in size and scope, the manager's responsibilities have grown. Today's managers see themselves not only as specialists, but as generalists, in that they can be moved throughout the organization from one job to another as part of their preparation for an eventual top-level assignment. This would seem sufficient reason for placing as much stress on the selection and education of managers as of persons preparing for other professional careers.

The Scientific Management Movement

Although people had talked about how to improve their work for hundreds of years, few had ever really examined human work systematically until Frederick W. Taylor began his studies, about 1885. It is quite true that Henri Fayol (a Frenchman who managed a coal mine a few years before Taylor became interested in managers) analyzed the process of management and is generally credited with giving us the basic principles upon which Taylor developed his theories of scientific management. However, in the United States, Taylor is generally given credit for being the father of scientific management. The fact that he did most of his work in shops probably accounts for the concentration of scientific management in industrial plants.

Contributions of Taylor. Taylor recognized that labor-saving machinery, job specialization, mass production, and large-scale distribution were all worthless unless those who managed were able to keep pace with technical improvements. He recognized too the need to systematize management, to assign parts of a job to those best placed in the organization to perform them, and to analyze the work to be done. Managers, Taylor declared, should concern themselves with such work as setting up and enforcing standards and finding ways to improve methods and promote cooperation. Today, his conclusions seem rather commonplace.

Born in Philadelphia in 1856 of a fairly well-to-do family, Taylor was urged by his parents to study law, but because poor eyesight forced him to give up this objective, he took a job as a laborer with the Midvale Steel Company. In a short time he was promoted to clerk, then to machinist, gang boss, and finally, chief engineer. During this same period, he became interested in experiments involving work accomplishment, including the "science of shoveling." During the next several years, he conducted experiments involving the analysis of pig-iron handling. Out of this research came recommendations that increased productivity in steel mills from $12\frac{1}{2}$ to $47\frac{1}{2}$ tons per man per day, and raised average daily earnings from $1.15 to $1.85 per man.

After leaving Midvale Steel, Taylor joined Bethlehem Steel, where he spent a great deal of time testing many of the scientific methods he had written about previously. His philosophy was that by increasing productivity through the application of scientific principles to managerial tasks, it would be possible to pay higher wages to workers and higher profits to owners while decreasing the individual employee's workload.

Among the principles of scientific management advocated by Taylor are these:

1. All managers must be trained to use scientific principles, replacing the rule-of-thumb methods, to solve problems.
2. Managers should select and then train and develop their workmen rather than let them choose their own work habits.

3. There must be an almost equal division of work responsibility between management and workmen.[4]

Taylor was not the only person to contribute to scientific methods in management. Among his associates who made significant contributions were Frank C. Gilbreth and his wife, Dr. Lillian M. Gilbreth; Henry L. Gantt; and Carl Barth. The Gilbreths initiated early studies in the field of motion-and-time analysis, using motion pictures. Both Gantt and Barth were associates of Taylor and worked with him on several of his experiments. Gantt's major contribution was the promotion of graphic techniques for analyzing data for managerial control. The Gantt charts, used widely in the United States and Europe, have probably done more than anything else to make him famous. Gantt charts plot activities and time along a horizontal scale; then planned activities can be compared with the time schedule along the scale to determine whether the actual performance is according to the schedule. This system can be used to control production for single machines, groups of machines, or even entire departments. The chart can also be used for other activities, such as personnel recruiting, purchasing, and transportation facilities.

In spite of the many contributions that Taylor and his associates made, they did not develop a systematic body of knowledge to qualify management as a science. A probable reason is that they lacked an adequate conceptual framework, since various concepts of management had not yet been perfected to formulate specific management processes.

Systems-Analysis Approach in Management

Over the past decade, there has been emerging a useful concept known as "systems analysis," by which managers can facilitate decision making with the help of computers. As applied to the business firm, systems analysis involves the flow of information and materials. Information flows may be both internal and external and may include directives, purchases, and orders that flow along vertical and horizontal lines of authority. Material flows represent the movement of physical goods inside the firm and outside to the customers. It is the purpose of systems analysis to integrate the movements of information for decision-making purposes. However, the physical distribution of finished goods is more difficult to systematize.

A liaison person, called a "systems analyst," is expected to bridge the communications gap between the programmer and the manager who requests the information. This person is an expert first on business operations, and second on the computer; before a programmer writes the computer program, the systems analyst tells the programmer what is required. In Chapter 12, you will observe how systems analysis may be applied to the function of production.

[4] Frederick Winslow Taylor, *The Principles of Scientific Management* (New York: Harper & Row, Publishers, 1911), pp. 36–37.

Is Management a Profession?

The scientific-management movement caused executives in larger businesses to think of themselves as separate and apart from labor within the organization. As a group, they began to seek scientific methods to apply to their work, and to encourage the preparation of managers through various courses in schools of business at the collegiate level. Of course, not all businessmen believe in the value of using scientific methods to solve their problems; nevertheless, the application of science to the field of management is a common practice.

Is management therefore a profession? The answer is that it is not, although it may be considered semiprofessionalized. To date no attempt has been made by either the management group or by institutions to professionalize management by licensing prospective managers or by requiring people to have special academic degrees for management positions. Managers have not developed a well-formulated body of defensible principles to guide them in making decisions, despite the fact that more managers are using techniques in quantitative analysis, behaviorial science, and modern mathematical theories than was formerly the case. In fact, management draws from several fields, including mathematics, economics, psychology, sociology, and statistical theory. Finally, management deals with people and can never be controlled by exact scientific principles. Where management falls short of a profession is in the application of professional standards, including the licensing of those entering the field, a practice that would require them to subscribe to an accepted code of ethics. Many people in business still regard management as a practical art.

Discussion Questions

3. *What principles did Taylor propose that are related to management practices today?*

4. *Explain how the Industrial Revolution accelerated the need for a managerial class.*

MANAGEMENT FUNCTIONS

As we have already noted, the managers of a business are responsible for seeing that the firm is operated as efficiently as possible within the plans and goals of the organization. Every manager, therefore, must function (act) in such a way that his subordinates work effectively. This he does by planning, organizing, directing, and controlling. These activities are called *management functions,* because they identify broadly what managers do. These management

**THE FUNCTIONAL PROCESSES OF
BUSINESS MANAGEMENT**

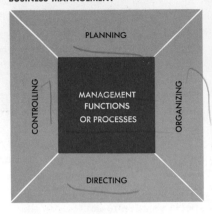

functions are sometimes termed the *management processes,* and as such they are interrelated as illustrated in the accompanying chart. In most instances, these functions occur simultaneously, although at any one time, one or more may be of primary importance.

Planning

Planning is the executive function that involves determining in advance the line of action by which desired results are to be achieved. It is essential to all activities and performed by all levels of management. Performing this function involves the following activities:

1. Determining the firm's overall objectives—both short- and long-range
2. Formulating business policies, procedures, and programs
3. Preparing budgets and allocating resources that may be required

Planning is equally important in day-to-day activities, such as that done by departmental and operating personnel for the purpose of achieving objectives already determined. The chart on page 179 shows how planning is related to all the various activities as a means of promoting maximum benefits to stockholders, employees, and the general public. Planning is a continuous process and must take into account changing conditions.

Organizing

The preparation required for implementing plans into action is called *organizing*. This management function involves classifying and dividing work activities into manageable units, processes that include the following:

1. Grouping work activities according to their relationships, to assure more effective teamwork and individual efficiency
2. Defining and delegating individual authority and responsibility for those working in the organization
3. Developing organizational relationships, in order to achieve coordination of effort at different levels of the organization

Managers sometimes have a tendency, during periods of increasing profits, to add more employees without first determining if they are needed. Eventually, it becomes necessary to reexamine the organization to see which positions are now unnecessary. Like planning, the organizing function should be performed continuously, because conditions change constantly.

Directing

Directing is a function that involves guiding and supervising subordinates to make certain they have an understanding of what is expected of them as

DETERMINING COMPANY OBJECTIVES BY OPERATIONAL PLANNING

Planning is a management function that, if properly used, affects the entire organization and brings maximum benefits to shareholders, employees, customers, and the public.

employees. It is performed at all levels of authority, but it is particularly important at the operative level, where much of the work is concerned with routine operating duties. In practice, the functions of planning, organizing, and directing are carried on simultaneously, because of their close interrelationships.

Controlling

Controlling is the management function which attempts to maintain conformity between goals and results. This requires that management must know what is occurring in order to change operations when the goals are not being achieved. Controls are intended to provide a continuing check of actual activities against planned results. You can see this is not the same as giving commands, which is the meaning often attributed to this function.

The control functions are: performing routine planning, scheduling work, establishing standards, reviewing costs, exercising supervision, and taking corrective action.

Essentially, the procedure for comparing performance with standards requires a system that checks key procedures and operations. By using this procedure it is possible to detect mistakes.

Another procedure is to compare performance with standards by using a control device. Often budgets serve as control devices. The statistical control chart is used to control production processes. Quality control involves a periodic sampling of the product being produced to make certain that it conforms to the specifications set up for this product.

When adopting control procedures and control systems (such as for office procedures or product quality), one must assume that authority has been granted to use these techniques; otherwise it is unreasonable to assign responsibility for the outcome.

We have covered the four general management functions, which may be used regardless of the size of the business. As can be seen from the chart on page 181, these management functions are performed at all levels, but the proportion of management effort devoted to them varies. Top management performs more planning than operating management. On the other hand, top managers are responsible for less directing and controlling than are operating managers.

Discussion Questions

5. *Explain why management functions are important to a business organization.*
6. *How does the planning function differ from the organizing function?*
7. *Distinguish between the control function and the directing function.*

MANAGEMENT FUNCTIONS PERFORMED AT DIFFERENT LEVELS OF MANAGEMENT

Planning	Organizing	Directing	Controlling	**Top Management**
Planning	Organizing	Directing	Controlling	**Middle Management**
Planning	Organizing	Directing	Controlling	**Operating Management**

A chart showing the approximate distribution of management effort expended in performing managerial functions in a medium-sized manufacturing business

QUALITIES OF EXECUTIVE LEADERSHIP

It has been said that most contemporary executives regard themselves as members of a semiprofessional hierarchy called "management," which has the responsibility for what takes place in the company's operations. Although many of these executives are shareholders in the companies in which they work, few own enough stock to exercise complete control. In the sole proprietorship and partnership, the managerial functions are concentrated in the hands of a few persons. In most other businesses, the functions are apt to be widely distributed, because of the size of the organization. As a prototype, what is an executive like; what kind of qualities make him an executive?

What Is an Executive?

An executive is a person who is responsible for the work performed by others under his supervision; he is the medium through which orders flow from administration to workers. The manager's job of getting things done is made easier when he is a skillful leader.

An executive must have a capacity for analyzing problems and making the right decisions. As a decision maker, he must have three basic kinds of skills, which we will call *technical, human,* and *conceptual skills.*

Technical Skills. Technical skills comprise the ability to use the methods, equipment, and techniques involved in the procedures and processes of performing specific tasks. These skills are developed from both experience and education. The accountant and the engineer are examples of professional people who require technical skills.

The appropriate mix of technical skills tends to differ at various levels of management, as is illustrated in the chart on page 182. For example, the

**MANAGERIAL SKILLS NEEDED AT
DIFFERENT MANAGEMENT LEVELS**

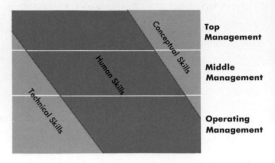

A chart reflecting the varying amounts of management skills required at different levels of an organization structure, as a manager advances from
one level of management to another.

chart shows that supervisors at lower levels tend to need more technical skills
in their work than do people in middle or top management. This is because
they are often required to train technicians and other employees who work
in operative-type jobs.

Human Skills. Human skills are those that help managers develop a
sense of fellow-feeling toward others and an appreciation of others' rights.
These skills apply to the way the executive recognizes his subordinates, his
equals, and his superiors, and to his relations with them in planning and
carrying out the objectives of the firm. The human skills are the crucial common
denominator at all levels of management, and according to a report by the
American Management Association, the most important of all skills. As is
obvious from the chart, human skills are used at all levels in similar proportions.

Conceptual Skills. Conceptual skills involve the executive's ability to
see the whole enterprise, including how the parts of the organization are
dependent on one another. These skills are most useful in decision making,
where one must be able to conceive the nature of the problem before deciding
on its solution.

Managerial Leadership

A business without a leader is like a team without a captain; the team
tends to lose its direction. In business, a good leader plans the work, organizes
the group, makes decisions, and directs and controls his subordinates. It is
through the quality of leadership that the firm's potential is eventually realized.

Definition of Leadership. Leadership is the process of influencing an
individual or group to strive for achievement in a given situation. In essence,
leadership involves the accomplishment of certain goals through people. Con-

sequently, the leader is concerned about activities and human relationships. Leadership is useful in any kind of group or organization.

Importance of Leadership to Management. The value of leadership behavior to business management can be seen by noting some of the human-relations problems with which management is involved.

1. What can managers do to create more interest in workers toward their jobs?
2. How can managers motivate others in the organization to accept change?
3. How far should management decentralize authority within the organization?
4. What is the most effective way to encourage employees to improve their personal growth and individual development?
5. What causes morale problems among employees?
6. How can management communicate more effectively with persons within the organization?

Types of Leadership Behavior. Leaders are known to exercise certain types of behavior when dealing with others. Writers generally agree that the three types of leadership behavior are autocratic, free-rein, and participating. (See the chart below.)

Autocratic leadership is the type of human behavior that centralizes authority and decision-making processes in the leader. There is little if any participation by subordinates, because the leader tells them what to do. Leaders whose behavior is considered to be autocratic tend to be more task-oriented than relationship-oriented, and as a result, they put more emphasis on the tasks to be performed than on how to understand better human relations. *Free-rein leadership* behavior is the kind that allows the group to establish its own goals and work out the solutions to problems. Any leadership that exists is used mainly for contact with others outside the group organization. *Participating leadership* behavior recognizes decentralized managerial authority, with deci-

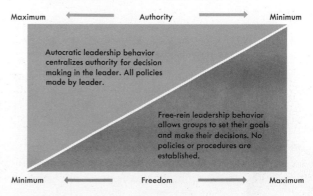

EXTREMES IN PATTERNS OF LEADERSHIP BEHAVIOR

Maximum ←——— Authority ———→ Minimum

Autocratic leadership behavior centralizes authority for decision making in the leader. All policies made by leader.

Free-rein leadership behavior allows groups to set their goals and make their decisions. No policies or procedures are established.

Minimum ←——— Freedom ———→ Maximum

sions an outgrowth of consultation with other group members. This means that followers are informed of the problems affecting their group and are encouraged to make suggestions and transmit ideas for solving the problem.

All three types of leadership behavior exist in business. A weakness in the free-rein behavior is that the manager rarely uses his leadership abilities to give direction, but relies on others—group members must provide their own motivation. Autocratic behavior is often criticized for placing more importance on direct orders than on freedom of choice. On the other hand, it permits quick decision making, because only one person is involved. Participating leadership is intended to make complete use of group members, since it allows them some freedom of action; however, its main disadvantage is that it requires more communication and understanding between the leader and the group than do the other types.

The question of whether leaders are born or developed has long been controversial. Some argue that inherited qualities are more important to the achievement of leadership positions than are acquired qualifications. Others contend that it is possible to develop leadership abilities through environmental and educational experiences. Certainly, executive skill is an attribute that some people have in abundance while others seem to have little. But between these two extremes there are a greater number of people who are gifted to a moderate degree, and for them education and self-development provide opportunities for developing leadership qualities.

Some studies of leadership stress that the attainment of desired goals requires the use of power and influence on the part of the leader to achieve collaboration between workers and management. In contrast are other explanations of leadership that stress a less power-motivated approach to harmonious group relations. In these, emphasis is on minimizing personal conflicts and on the creation of mutual confidence between leaders and followers. Studies of this subject will continue to be made, and our knowledge of the topic undoubtedly will expand, but the theories we have mentioned here will suffice for our present purposes.

Discussion Questions

8. *Explain how the three basic management skills are used in a business organization.*

9. *Define the term* leadership, *and explain some of the characteristics of the three kinds of leadership discussed in this chapter.*

THE EDUCATION OF AMERICAN EXECUTIVES

Some useful insights about the education of practicing executives are provided by several surveys. A study by Dr. Mabel Newcomer, of 1,000 top officers of the 600 largest nonfinancial corporations in the United States, dealt with the social, educational, and cultural backgrounds of these persons.[5] She found in her survey that, whereas in 1900, 71 percent of all executives had no more than an elementary school education, by 1964 only about 12 percent were in that category. The percentage of executives with degrees in science and engineering had increased nearly five times—from 7 percent in 1900 to 33 percent in 1964. In addition, 91 percent of the executives studied had some college education. Engineering, the natural sciences, economics, business administration, law, and accounting are the most common educational fields in which these big-business executives had majored while in college.

A conclusion reached from the Newcomer study is that executives tend to be better educated than is the population in general. Moreover, a college education has come to be more important than ever as a basic qualification for initial employment in business and industry.

What Education Is Appropriate for Executives?

Writers on the subject of executive education have frequently lauded a broad liberal-arts education as the ideal preparation for executive positions. An increasing number of lawyers have been selected for top-executive positions, most of them without business experience in lower management levels. On the other hand, recruiters from industry visit college placement offices in search of young graduates who have one or more specialties, such as a major in accounting, marketing, finance, advertising, or management.

The trend in collegiate business education is to stress as much broad preparation in the basic liberal arts (science, economics, mathematics, English, etc.) as possible, without neglecting the study of business subjects in the functional areas, including accounting, finance, management, marketing, and transportation. Other essential courses include business communications, business law, quantitative analysis, systems analysis, and computer science.

Lawrence A. Appley, former president of the American Management Association, predicts that within 15 years, those who aspire to top-management positions will be at a serious disadvantage without an M.B.A. (master of business administration) degree.

Collegiate Management Courses. College-level courses in business management are relatively new. Most of the specialized courses in this field have developed during the past two decades. Among them are those in principles of personnel management, business organization, labor relations, labor law, business policies, and managerial decision making.

Opportunities for Executives in Management

In America we have the only system that utilizes a large number of college- and university-trained graduates as managers. Business management

---

[5] Mabel Newcomer, *The Big Business Executive 1964* (New York: Scientific American, 1964), pp. 2–10.

has become one of the largest fields of employment. Above the foreman or supervisory level, there are substantial numbers of positions in middle management, such as those of office manager, personnel manager, sales manager, district manager, department manager, traffic manager, risk manager, and financial manager.

There is also a field of managerial occupations generally described as industrial management, which includes plant managers, industrial-relations supervisors, training directors, and safety supervisors. Outside of business, tremendous expansion of the federal government has opened up opportunities in managerial positions at almost every level of government. Many of these are civil service appointments and require advanced educational preparation. There are opportunities for managers in hospitals, trade associations, chambers of commerce, and educational nonprofit foundations. In all these fields there is a scarcity of trained candidates.

Discussion Questions

10. *What has brought about the increased emphasis on college education of business managers?*

11. *What other areas of employment are also open to managers?*

SUMMARY

The strength of every organization is in its managers. Business managers bear a heavy responsibility in satisfying the needs of customers, employers, and employees.

Since 1900, the number of managers has increased about fourfold, largely owing to the increase in production by American business and industry. Frederick W. Taylor and his associates were among the first Americans to approach management problems more or less scientifically. Taylor experimented with techniques in an effort to eliminate waste motions, thereby increasing unit output. He advocated the principle of planning for production in advance.

A manager is a person who gets things done by working with people and other resources. In order to reach the desired objectives, he performs certain managerial functions, including (1) planning, (2) organizing, (3) directing, and (4) controlling. A key activity of all managers is planning. This requires both imagination and analytical ability. The purpose of planning is to develop a blueprint for future action and decision making. Organizing involves the assigning of tasks to the proper persons. In organizing, the manager must find ways of getting the necessary work done and at the same time make certain that it follows a plan. Directing involves guiding and supervising subordinates to make certain they have an understanding of what is expected of them. The control function is the process of ensuring that performance corresponds with plans and procedures.

Aside from having a dedication toward his company, a good executive has leadership qualities. He uses three basic skills: technical, human, and conceptual.

Technical skills involve the use of methods, equipment, and techniques to perform specific tasks. Human skills help managers to develop a sense of feeling toward others. This skill is important at all management levels. Conceptual skills involve the executive's ability to see the whole enterprise rather than a few parts. These skills are especially useful in decision making, where one must be able to conceive the nature of the problem before making a decision to reach the solution.

VOCABULARY REVIEW

Match the following vocabulary terms with the statements below.

a. Autocratic leadership behavior
b. Controlling
c. Conceptual skills
d. Directing
e. Free-rein leadership
f. Human skills

g. Leadership
h. Management
i. Organizing
j. Planning
k. Technical skills

1. The process of influencing an individual or group to strive for achievement in a given situation
2. A management function that attempts to maintain conformity between goals and results
3. The executive function that involves determining in advance the line of action by which desired results are to be achieved
4. A process whereby resources are combined into an integrated system in order to accomplish the objectives of the system
5. A type of leadership behavior that allows the group to establish its own goals and work out the solutions to its problems
6. Those skills that help managers develop a sense of feeling toward others and an appreciation of their individual rights
7. The preparation required for implementing plans into action
8. The executive's ability to see the whole enterprise, including how parts of an organization are dependent on one another
9. A type of leadership behavior that centralizes authority and decision making in the leader
10. A management function involving guiding and supervising subordinates to make certain they have an understanding of what is expected of them as employees
11. The ability to use methods, equipment, and techniques involved in procedures and processes in performing specific tasks

PROBLEMS AND PROJECTS

1. Using available library references, write a 400-word report on the history of scientific management and the contributions that were made to the field by Frederick W. Taylor.

2. Select three executives from local businesses or industries who occupy positions that involve leadership responsibilities of the kind discussed in this chapter. Arrange for an interview with each for the purpose of finding out what he believes to be the most important methods and means of developing qualities of leadership, and how his firm does this. Write a report explaining what each interview revealed. Your instructor may wish to advise you about the length of the report.

3. Assume that the top management of a business consists of the board of directors, chairman of the board, president, and two vice-presidents. Also assume that middle management consists of credit manager, production manager, and heads of the following functional departments: purchasing, sales, advertising, accounting, and maintenance. Operating management consists of shop foreman, unit supervisors, and crew chiefs.

Match the following managerial activities with the appropriate level of management at which this activity is likely to be performed:

Nature of Activity	Top Management	Middle Management	Operating Management
a. Decision to close a plant			
b. Decision to hire a salesman			
c. Decision to change location of a shop toolroom			
d. Decision to omit a dividend			
e. Decision to deny a shop grievance			
f. Decision to pay an entire crew overtime			
g. Decision to use direct-mail advertising			
h. Decision to sell a new stock issue			

A BUSINESS CASE

Case 7-1   The Becker Corporation

The Becker Corporation is an established company that manufactures a line of men's sports clothes, shirts, pajamas, and underwear. Plants are located in South Carolina and Virginia. The company is the second largest and one of the oldest in this line of business. It was founded by Henry and James Becker in 1936, and upon the death of James, the business was incorporated, with all but 1000 shares of the stock retained by Henry Becker and his son Alvin.

Four years ago, Henry moved up to the position of chairman of the board, and Alvin became president. In addition, there are 15 middle-management executives in the home office, located in Atlanta, Georgia. There is a plant manager in charge of the two plants.

Henry Becker makes most of the decisions. He has positive ideas and is not often inclined to discuss matters with his son or with any of the executives. Executive morale is low, and Alvin frequently complains to his father when his suggestions are turned down.

The company markets its line through department stores, men's clothing stores, and discount stores. Competition from other manufacturers is strong, and new ideas are constantly being tried out by the competitors. Three years ago when profits started to drop, the sales manager proposed to set up branch offices in order to provide more service like the competing companies, but Henry Becker turned down the idea and nothing was done. The advertising manager proposed that television time be bought, but this idea was not approved by Henry either. When the advertising manager resigned, Henry took over this operation.

Last year profits dropped again, and this time Alvin called a conference of all the executives to study the situation, while his father was on a vacation. It was decided to call in an outside management-consulting firm to review the situation and make recommendations. This was done, and the proposal was made to modernize both the plants at a cost of $600,000. This could be done without borrowing any funds or selling any stock. The consulting firm projected a possible reduction of operating costs by as much as 35 percent through this program. When Henry returned, Alvin presented this idea; but the whole matter was turned down by his father, who claimed the machinery was only 20 years old and was not worn out. First-quarter profits this year were again lower than they were last year and the year before. The company's production costs still continue to be a matter of concern because two competing firms announced price reductions well below several prices in the Becker line of merchandise.

While on a recent business trip to New York, Henry Becker died of a heart attack; a week later, the directors announced that Alvin Becker had been appointed chief executive officer.

1. What are some of the more important problems facing Alvin Becker?
2. What do you believe Alvin should do as the chief executive officer?

internal
organization
structure

CHAPTER EIGHT

Much of the success of a business depends on its internal organization structure. In observing people at work in business, you may wonder how they work together as a team. The answer is, of course, that there are two integrating forces operating in a business if it is well organized. First, there is an organization structure, which serves to relate subordinates and superiors into an efficient combination. Second, there is a series of procedures which identify the sequence in which work is performed. Our main interest in this chapter is the subject of organization structure.

As we noted in earlier chapters, there has been a trend toward the separation of business ownership from business management, especially in medium-size and large concerns. This trend puts even more emphasis on the importance of organization in a business.

In the creation of the framework of the organization, various requirements should be met. For example, the structure must be sufficiently flexible to cope with new and varying business conditions. There must be ease of communication, because communication bottlenecks delay action. Provision must be made for a means of supervising tasks, so that assignments will be carried out as planned.

Our purpose is to explore and analyze the various types of plans that a business may use to develop and perfect its internal organization. As we analyze these plans, we shall note some of the advantages and disadvantages they have, regardless of whether the business is organized around product lines, geographical regions, operating divisions such as in some conglomerates, or business functions such as production, finance, and marketing.

DYNAMICS OF BUSINESS ORGANIZATION

When a chemist mixes known chemicals in the test tube, he can usually predict with reasonable accuracy that the reaction will be in accordance with unchanging physical laws. But when a business executive proposes drastic changes in his company's internal organization, he cannot always predict the outcome. The only thing he is sure of is that our business environment changes constantly, with the frequent result that behavioral conflicts arise within the organization.

WHAT IS ORGANIZATION?

The term *organization,* as applied to business, has several definitions. Webster's is "the executive structure of a business." This definition indicates that organization is the framework by means of which the work of a business, managerial and otherwise, is performed; that it provides the required channels, points of origin, and flow of management direction and controls. Organization also denotes a creative process. All the parts of a business do not come into existence spontaneously; they are the result of managerial efforts to carry out a predetermined course of action—and thus, of organization. (You can see from these two definitions that there is a distinct relationship between organization and management.) *Organization* is often used also to refer to the total business enterprise, including facilities, materials, money, and manpower. This final definition implies the "team" concept, according to which each member is assigned specific duties, and under the terms of which all members work effectively together within a framework of superior and subordinate relationships.

All these things considered, it should go without saying that modern business cannot function long without organization.

How Is Organization Developed?

In the small business operated entirely by one person, the owner has no real need for a complicated organization. Since he does everything himself, there is no one to whom he can delegate any authority or responsibility. As owner, manager, and chief executive, he is the sum total of the organization. But with the addition of employees, a greater organization becomes necessary. Working relationships among employees need to be established, as well as arrangements for coordinating decisions and for assigning the work load. Naturally, the larger the firm, the more complex its organizational setup tends to become; the limited capacity of each executive is but one factor that makes the need for better organization imperative.

To help improve organizational efficiency, an executive can reduce his work load by delegating certain of his lesser tasks to the next lower level. But this may itself cause complications, for each time new employees are added, another level of executive personnel may eventually be needed.

As the firm continues to grow, it becomes necessary to separate operations into divisions, departments, or sections (these terms are often used interchangeably), each under the supervision of a person with administrative authority and responsibility. It is not enough in most situations simply to divide the work and to establish an authority hierarchy; ultimately, some kind of overall organization plan or pattern is needed. Although some companies begin without a clearly defined plan, they eventually see the need for one of a specific type.

Later in this chapter we shall discuss in detail four of the most widely used organizational plans: line, functional, line-and-staff, and committee. As we analyze them, you will see the advantages and disadvantages of each.

Human Behavior and the Organization

Because people are a primary resource of business firms, a knowledge of how people behave is important to the solution of many types of management problems. To be an effective manager requires an understanding of the interactions between members of subgroups and those on higher levels of the organization, and also between them and the organization as a whole. As an organizer and supervisor, the manager must be able to accurately predict employee behavior. (The term "employee" is broadly used to mean anyone working in the firm, regardless of his task.) All types of factors must be taken into consideration in making business decisions involving the behavior of people in an organization.

If you have ever participated in the activities of a student group—a club, fraternity, or sorority—you may have observed some problem situation that developed as a result of personal conflicts within the group. The group leader who understands human behavior can usually prevent the development of such situations. For obvious reasons, the business manager also needs to understand the behavior of people—both as individuals and as members of groups.

The study of individual behavior is generally considered to be the province of the psychologist, and group behavior of the sociologist and cultural anthropologist, although there is some overlap among these disciplines. Very often we use the term "behavioral sciences" in referring to these areas of study. It is the role of the behavioral scientist to study how people behave and why, and the relationship between human behavior and the total environment. Many firms either sponsor or run programs by which their employees can study human behavior. Some of these programs include college courses in the behavioral sciences—an area that has been gaining new emphasis in business administration courses, too.

Discussion Questions

1. *Define the term* organization structure *as applied to business.*
2. *What meaning would the behavioral scientist give to the term* organization?
3. *As a firm grows larger, what usually happens to its organization structure?*

CONCEPTS OF ORGANIZATION PLANNING

When you are trying to organize a new business or to improve the structure of an existing one, it is not enough in most instances merely to divide the work by creating divisions or departments. The matter of who is to make major decisions and to whom these decisions are to be referred must also be clarified. Generally, this issue is resolved by a choice between two distinct types of organizational policies: centralized or decentralized managerial control. In making this choice, it is necessary to take into consideration a number of factors.

Centralized Management vs. Decentralized Management

What does the term "centralized management organization" mean? A business that adopts a policy of placing all major decision-making authority and control in the hands of a few top-level executives subscribes to a centralized management organization structure. Thus, a *centralized management organization* is a system that delegates authority and control to a central area within the organization, usually at the top.

In a centralized management organization, as shown in the chart at the top of page 194, subordinate executives make relatively few important decisions. Since this type of organization is common to large companies, size is a factor.

Advocates of this plan contend it provides more effective control over operations and tends to reduce the decision-making time. Centralization makes for uniformity of action regarding such matters as hours of work, salary ranges, promotion standards, and grievance handling. Orders are generally issued to

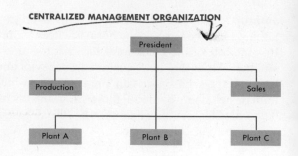

CENTRALIZED MANAGEMENT ORGANIZATION

spell out what subordinate executives can do, and any deviation from routine practice must be referred to headquarters for approval. Even where there are multiple plants, under this system most decisions are made at headquarters rather than at the local factory. Chain department and grocery stores often adopt a centralized management organization. At a central office, responsibility for buying, advertising, accounting, marketing, and other functions are made for all the branch stores. This plan allows the central office close controls. However, a company president who delegates little or no authority not only limits the number of managers in his organization but provides little experience for them to grow in ability to make decisions.

A *decentralized management organization* represents a systematic effort to delegate to lower levels all authority except that which can be exercised only at the highest level. Decentralization of responsibility is not a matter of primary concern simply because work must be assigned to the levels where it is to be performed. The key question is, How *much* authority should be given to those who do the work? The answer is, Give them as much authority as they are capable of carrying, within the broad policies made at a higher level. In general, this is the concept practiced by such companies as General Motors, Ford, General Electric, Prudential Life, American Brake Shoe, and J. C. Penney. Notice in the chart following, which shows the structure of authority of a decentralized organization, that the president delegates to each plant manager the responsibility for making decisions concerning production and sales in his own area of authority.

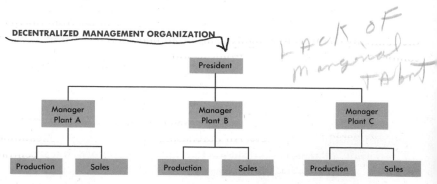

DECENTRALIZED MANAGEMENT ORGANIZATION

Decentralization takes place in different companies at different rates, in different levels, and for different reasons. For example, some firms decentralize their managerial functions because they know that conditions vary from plant to plant, and that the officials at each plant know their own operation better than other officials and are thus prepared to make the best decisions affecting that operation. Then again, when a company has a strong management team at the local level, top management may decide to decentralize by giving that team as much authority as possible in order to allow headquarters personnel more time to devote to long-range planning. Although decentralization generally works best in those firms having extensive decentralized operations on a product-division basis, even under such favorable circumstances some companies find lack of managerial talent a limiting factor in their plans for the decentralization of management.

Let us summarize what we have said about decentralization and add a further observation. Decentralization places responsibility and authority in field offices where the action occurs, allowing top-management functions of planning and financing to be performed where they should be—in the central office—and lesser managerial functions to be delegated to lower levels of management. Decentralization also tends to give local managers greater incentive (they virtually hold full sway over their own activities) and thus serves as a boon to greater product and market emphasis.

The Size of the Enterprise

Both the scope and the detail of planning increase with the size of the operation. And an expanding business may even be faced with planning for a form of organization radically different from its present one—with the peculiar problems of the new form best taken into account well in advance. A growing business invariably needs to include in its plans a possible change in its policies in more than one direction, in order to meet changing conditions. For example, the American Can Company's reorganization of its top-level internal management structure is shown in the chart on page 196.

Prior to its reorganization, American Can was considered a fragmented federation of almost autonomous divisions that had found it difficult to keep pace with changes in the packaging industry. As you can see from the diagram, the company changed to a highly centralized managerial structure with almost complete control vested in a strong headquarters group. Headquarters staffs were enlarged to do more of the work formerly handled by divisional staffs in areas such as accounting, advertising, taxes, and law. Under the new plan, interlocking committees keep key officers in close touch with all departmental decisions. A company-wide accounting system replaced divisional systems that were considered incompatible. All purchasing was transferred to headquarters. And finally, marketing and product-planning operations were centralized, allowing headquarters to take a broader look at the total enterprise.

**HOW THE AMERICAN CAN COMPANY CHANGED ITS STRUCTURE
BY RECENTRALIZING MANAGEMENT CONTROLS**

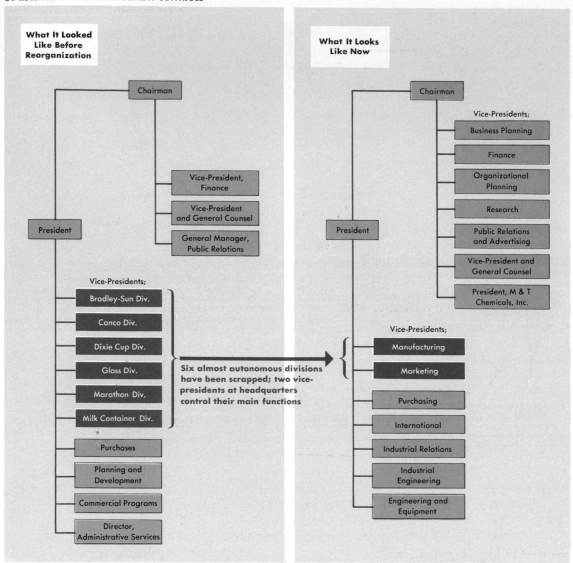

Courtesy Business Week Magazine (© *1966, McGraw-Hill, Inc.*)

A chart indicating how the organization structure of a large corporation may
be changed by the process of shifting from a decentralized to a centralized
operation involving the company president and chairman of the board of
directors

4. *Explain the difference in the assignment of authority and control under a centralized and a decentralized management organization.*
5. *Describe the situation in the American Can Company as shown by the chart before and after the reorganization.*

UNDERSTANDING FORMAL AND INFORMAL ORGANIZATION

Organizations are either formal or informal in their structure of group relationships. People use organization to accomplish goals. In addition to centralizing or decentralizing management authority, organizing is a means of dividing work and the accompanying delegation of duties. The need to understand human behavior becomes even more important. Taking a note from social psychologists, who have long recognized that group behavioral patterns differ under the formal and the informal organization structure, management now tends to give more consideration to the advantages and disadvantages of formal and informal organization. Since the formal type of organization usually serves as a starting point in organization planning, we should look first at formal organization.

What Is Formal Organization?

In business parlance, *formal organization* is a system of well-defined jobs, each requiring a measure of authority, responsibility, and accountability. This type of structure is created to deal with both routine and recurring activities, and thus it provides a framework for applying such human-relations phenomena as leadership, job incentives, and job status. At the same time, however, the work each individual does is part of a larger pattern. Except in the case of a few top executives, no one person can see both the starting and ending point of work because of so many departmental separations. This is especially the case in large organizations.

What Is Informal Organization?

The informal organization is largely concerned with human personalities, individual attitudes, and emotions toward others in the organization. *Informal organization* is the grouping of people into a unit of organization in the absence of written formal rules or established procedures. Since there is no organized effort to control behavior, employees are free to express their attitudes and emotions. It is often easy to detect the existence of an informal organization structure by the presence of the "communications grapevine." Sometimes called the "rumor factory," the grapevine is one of the most common expressions of informal relations within an organization.

Informal organization is more common to small- and even medium-size firms than to large ones. Often the small firm proceeds on an informal basis because it has few people to organize, few activities to coordinate, and just one group, rather than several departments, to control.

Organizational Relationships

Before any business organization plan involving formal relationships can be made to work effectively, its activities must be grouped into proper units of responsibility, and the relations between these units must be determined. Certain fundamentals of organization must be taken into consideration, including an understanding of the following terms: (1) policy, (2) authority, (3) responsibility, (4) accountability, (5) delegation, and (6) principles.

Policy. The term *policy* has several meanings. It is often used to indicate an ethical connotation, such as "Honesty is the best policy." In its business sense, policy means an oral or written statement that serves as a guide for management decisions. Although policies are issued only by top management, it is the people at lower levels who make policies work. Some policies are referred to as "working policies," since they relate to rules governing such specific operations as employment, sick leaves, and retirement.

Authority. The term *authority* has a twofold meaning. First, it denotes the right to make decisions as part of the executive function of planning; and second, it represents the power to direct subordinates, requiring their obedience, to perform certain duties. (Authority also implies the right *not* to act or decide.) Some people have authority because of their knowledge of a subject. In a corporation, authority is passed from its source, the stockholders, to a board of directors. They in turn delegate authority to the topmost company officers, starting with the president or chairman of the board. Ultimately, all rights and powers of management rest with ownership. But ownership must necessarily delegate its authority to those in managerial positions.

Responsibility. *Responsibility* may be defined as the individual's obligation to carry out duties assigned to him. Embodied in this definition are three characteristics: *obedience, dependability,* and *compliance.*

Responsibility and authority can never exist in isolation; they must inevitably go hand in hand. Imagine what would happen if an executive were given the responsibility to plan the manufacture of a new product without being given the authority to select the materials, obtain the equipment, and employ the people to produce the product. (The relationship between authority and responsibility will be covered more fully later in this chapter, in our discussion of organization charts.)

Accountability. By *accountability* is meant the liability of a subordinate, for the proper discharge of his duties. In substance, to be accountable is to be answerable for one's conduct in satisfactorily fulfilling an assignment. Accountability is always *upward,* because a person is always accountable to the superior who has delegated responsibility and authority to him; the flow of authority and responsibility is *downward,* because both are delegated to subordinates by a higher authority.

passing on power to act for another

Delegation. We noted previously that authority and power go hand in hand. Like authority, power (in the business world, at least) is not assumed—that is, unilaterally claimed as an inherent right or by virtue of seizure. It is delegated. *Delegation* is the investment of one person with the power to act for another. The primary purpose of delegation is to make organization possible. Since no one person in an organization can do all the tasks, authority must be delegated to subordinates who will make decisions within the area of their assigned duties. Delegation is considered an art of management that is generally not well practiced; studies show that a principal reason for failure by managers is their inability to delegate authority.

Principles. The successful manager usually has the ability, based on experience, to apply general ideas or concepts to his work. He often states these in the form of "laws" or "principles." A *principle,* according to Webster, is "a settled rule of action; a governing law of conduct." A principle emphasizes the idea of a basic truth, unvarying and general in its application to a given consideration. In the study of business, there are certain truths that are accepted or professed as fundamental and are used as guides. For example, we refer to principles of accounting, or principles of economics. In this chapter we are concerned with principles of organization—and this requires that you understand the meaning of the term "principle."

Discussion Questions

6. *What are the main differences between a formal and an informal organization?*
7. *What is the significance of formal organization to human relations?*
8. *Distinguish between authority and responsibility and accountability and delegation.*

PRINCIPLES OF ORGANIZATION

Before turning our attention to an analysis of the various types of formal organization plans, we should consider some of the principles that underlie all types of organization structure. It is widely assumed that the designing of a company organization structure requires little more than the balancing of an assortment of rectangles on an organization chart. This is a serious and naïve fallacy. There are certain accepted principles of organization to be observed, chief among which are the following:

Every organization should have an objective. The performance of all parts of the organization should be directed toward the achievement of the same objective. This is known as *unity of objective;* it is necessary in order to develop effective teamwork within an organization. A distinction should be made, however, between the organization's objectives and the individual goals of the people (executives, supervisors, and workers) who make up the organization. The individual worker's goal is not the same as the organization's objective. For example, the objective of raising additional operating funds may be assigned to the chief finance officer. The employees, through their local union, may vote to have as their objective a 10 percent hourly wage increase. The two goals are different and would be achieved differently.

There must be clear lines of authority and accompanying responsibility, beginning at the top and descending to the lowest level. A good organizational structure provides for delegation of authority from, let us say, the president to the vice-president, to the general manager, to the supervisor or foreman, and finally to the workers. Thus, authority stems from the highest executive level and is progressively delegated downward. The president of the firm may, for example, assign to his manufacturing vice-president the responsibility of buying raw materials and new equipment, and of hiring new employees. At the same time, the vice-president must have the authority to determine what prices he will pay for these items.

The number of levels of authority should be held to a minimum. Each time a new management level is created, another link is introduced into the chain of command. And the longer the chain, the more time it takes for instructions to pass down to the lower levels and for information to travel up to the top level. The number of levels depends upon whether the firm is to be centralized or decentralized. Where there are too many levels, authority is splintered. In such a case, a problem cannot be solved or a decision made without pooling the authority delegations of two or more managers. In many day-to-day operations there are cases of splintered authority, and probably most managerial conferences are held because of the need to pool authority before making a decision.

No one in the organization should have more than one supervisor. This is known as the *unity of command* principle of organization, a principle based on the theory that each subordinate should report to only one superior. This principle is useful in the clarification of authority-responsibility relationships, because whenever a manager lacks total control to hold his subordinates responsible, his position becomes one of confusion and frustration, and in fact it eventually may be undermined.

There is a limit to the number of positions one person should supervise directly. This is called the *span of control* principle. Application of this concept in developing the organization structure is important, in that it places some kind of limit on the number of subordinate persons who can be satisfactorily managed by a single executive. While the span of control is rarely uniform throughout an organization, authorities generally agree that from six to eight persons should be the maximum permissible limit. Where the operations of a concern have been de-centralized, however, with operating units that are nearly autonomous, it is possible for top-level executives to supervise as many as 12 positions.

The organization structure should be flexible enough to permit changes with a minimum of disruption. Since change is inevitable in any business, the ideal organization structure is one that permits an executive to make changes without destroying the continuity of the business or the efficiency of the employees. Good organization structure must not be a straitjacket.

Line, Staff, and Functional Relationships

In addition to being classified as either formal or informal in structure, business organizations are also classified according to the nature of authority relationships within their internal structures. These relationships are identified as *line, staff,* or *functional,* according to the division of definite functions and assignments for executives and groups of employees within the formal or informal structural plan.

Some writers identify "line" and "staff" in terms of the kind of work to be performed. Others add to this concept the nature of the authority relationships among persons in the organization. Since there is a distinction, it is important that both the superior and the subordinate know whether they are acting in a staff or a line capacity. Suppose we approach this subject by examining first the nature of and the differences among these authority relationships.

Definitions

Line Relations. When there is a recognized chain of command between the superior and the subordinate, a line relationship is said to exist. (See the chart on page 202.) In this situation, the subordinate accepts responsibility for carrying out the orders he receives from his superior. You can see by the chart showing the line or scalar principle that this is a direct relationship between superior and subordinate. The concept of "line" as it pertains to an organization is simply a matter of relationships. Hence, the phrase *line relations,* which denotes the existence of authority found in all formal organizations in business, expressed as an uninterrupted scale or series of steps. This hierarchical arrangement of line authority is frequently referred to as the scalar principle in organization. When one looks at an organization as a whole, *line relations* may be defined as a recognized chain of command that exists between the superior and the subordinate. Generally, it can be said that in a business

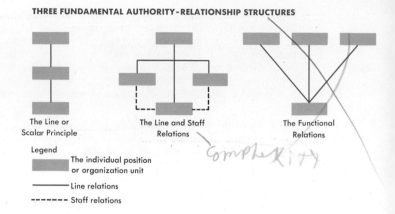

THREE FUNDAMENTAL AUTHORITY-RELATIONSHIP STRUCTURES

The Line or Scalar Principle

The Line and Staff Relations

The Functional Relations

Legend

The individual position or organization unit

—— Line relations

----- Staff relations

Complexity

organization, no one can give direct orders to another and expect to be obeyed unless he is a direct line superior.

Staff Relations.   The nature of the staff relationship is advisory. A legal counsel or public relations counsel performs in a staff capacity by advising a line executive. (See the above chart.) Thus, *staff* refers to those organizational components that exist mainly to provide technical and special advice and service to other units.

The distinction between line and staff employees in terms of their assignment of management duties may be in part due to the efforts of Frederick W. Taylor, who, at the turn of the century, conducted research studies in an effort to separate certain managerial-level functions from the purely routine, work-performance tasks. From his research, Taylor concluded that the use of staff personnel to help line executives would make the business more efficient. Today, the line–staff distinction is common to all large companies.

Functional Relations.   Some businesses use a third type of managerial relationship, known as *functional relations,* which is not restricted to managers or departments. Where functional relations exist, a staff specialist has authority over his particular function (consequently, the term "functional"), no matter where in the organization it is performed. For example, a personnel manager exercises functional authority when he is assigned full responsibility for all matters pertaining to personnel problems in the business. Banks, industrial plants, and department stores often assign functional authority to staff specialists in personnel problems. The chart shown above illustrates this functional structure. Notice also that each employee has more than one supervisor, with each representing a different functional area.

You are likely to find more staff positions in a big business than in a small one, because size inevitably brings a need for more specialized information. However, line positions are common in both large and small organizations.

We will have more to say about the line, line-and-staff, and functional plans as we continue our study of various kinds of formal organization plans, and we will show an organization chart for each plan.

Discussion Questions

9. *Distinguish between the principles of* unity of command *and* unity of objective. *Explain how each principle may be applied when starting a new business.*
10. *What is meant by the principle of* span of control? *What factor is most important in determining how large the span should be?*
11. *Explain the difference between the duties of a* line *and a* staff *executive.*

FORMAL TYPES OF ORGANIZATION STRUCTURE

After giving consideration to the basic principles of business organization and the factors that influence the design of company organization structure, our next step is to analyze the several types to determine which is best suited to a particular situation. Basically, there are four identifiable formal organization types. Only two of these are in common use today, the line and the line-and-staff. A third form, called the "functional organization" by its originator, Frederick W. Taylor, is used by business to make the transition between the line and the line-and-staff. The fourth form, the committee organization, has limited use by itself, but it is sometimes used as a suborganization—as part of either the line or the line-and-staff scheme. No one plan is practical to use in its pure form; the realities of business life always seem to dictate that certain modifications be made to enable the organization to adapt to its environment.

Line Organization

The oldest and simplest of the formal organizations used in business is the line organization. A line organization used by a bank is shown on page 204. Authority passes from the president directly to department heads and then down to the employees. Each department head performs all supervisory functions within his own department. Notice that the employees within each functional department are responsible to only one boss, and each department head or manager is responsible to only one boss. This line relationship that exists between the supervisor and subordinate is based on the scalar principle, which is the relationship between superior and subordinate, and occurs when areas of work are divided into different levels of authority and responsibility.

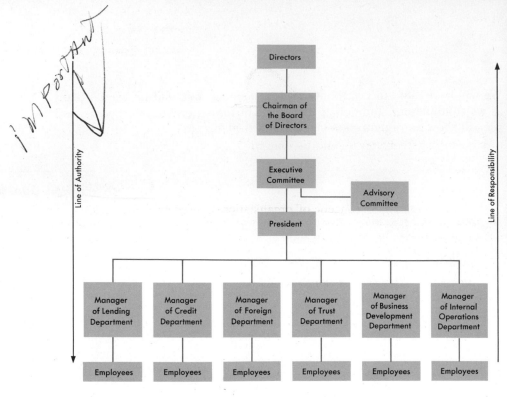

A line organization plan of a medium-size bank. In this plan, the department head must perform highly specialized functions and at the same time direct or supervise his subordinates.

As a formal organization, the line plan has certain advantages and disadvantages which may be summarized as follows:

ADVANTAGES OF THE LINE ORGANIZATION

1. The plan is simple and easy for employees and management to understand.
2. It allows for definite designation of authority and responsibility for each position.
3. Each worker is responsible only to one boss, who is the immediate source of authority.
4. The plan makes for direct communication upward and downward along the chain of authority.

DISADVANTAGES OF THE LINE ORGANIZATION

1. Each supervisor has responsibility for several duties and cannot become an expert in all of them.
2. The plan overburdens top executives with day-to-day administrative details, to the point where they have little time to devote to planning.
3. The plan fails to provide a specialized staff for more highly specialized management activities.
4. As a business grows and the chain of command increases, more and more time is needed to execute orders.

The line organization plan is more likely to be used in medium-sized or smaller businesses where there is desired a high degree of centralized control for quick decision making. Certainly, there can be no quibbling as to who gives orders and whether they should be obeyed.

Line-and-Staff Organization

The line-and-staff concept of organization is used in some form by a majority of the larger business organizations. Its purpose is to combine the best features of the line organization, which provides direct control and specialization, and at the same time to use staff personnel as technical advisers to line executives. For example, a line executive who is confronted with a legal problem may call on the services of counsel from the legal department for advice.

In the accompanying chart, the lines of authority are indicated by solid lines; staff relationships are marked by broken lines. Notice how the lines of authority flow from the top down to the three vice-presidents; then to the plant

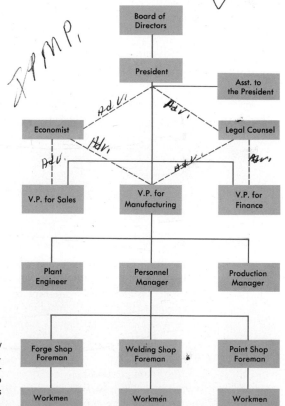

A line-and-staff organization plan. Solid lines show line of authority; broken lines show staff functions. The positions of Assistant to the President, Economist, and Legal Counsel are filled by staff officers who serve in an advisory capacity to the top-ranking officers of the firm.

engineer, personnel manager, and production manager; then to each foreman; and finally, to the workmen supervised by each foreman. This illustration demonstrates the "unity of command" previously discussed. Both the president and the three operating vice-presidents are at liberty to call on the company economist and legal counsel for advice. In both the line and functional plans, this consulting service is not available as such.

Examples of staff executives and the corresponding line executives they generally advise are shown in the chart below.

Staff Executives	Line Executive Being Advised
Research Director	Advises president, vice-president, general manager, and perhaps the production manager
Legal Counsel	Advises president and other top-ranking officers
Economist	Makes studies for and advises president and other high-level line officers
Controller	Makes analyses and furnishes advice and recommendations to high-level line officers
Advertising Manager	Furnishes top-line officers with information and advice regarding advertising and marketing problems
Chief Engineer	Advises high-level line officers on matters of a technical and engineering nature

Among the advantages and disadvantages of the line-and-staff organization plan are these:

ADVANTAGES OF THE LINE-AND-STAFF ORGANIZATION

1. It provides for line authority with flexibility to use staff specialists who can operate across various department lines.
2. It allows for highly qualified technical specialists to advise line executives.
3. No matter where an employee works in a service, staff, research, or production department, he rarely reports to more than one person.

DISADVANTAGES OF THE LINE-AND-STAFF ORGANIZATION

1. Decisions may be slowed up by line executives who are waiting for staff personnel to furnish technical information.
2. Staff personnel may attempt to become line officers and assert administrative control, resulting in confusion and misunderstanding.
3. The use of staff specialists increases company overhead costs.

Functional Organization

As we indicated earlier in this chapter (in the discussion of functional relations), it is possible to assign authority and responsibility in a different

A FUNCTIONAL ORGANIZATION PLAN OF A MANUFACTURING BUSINESS

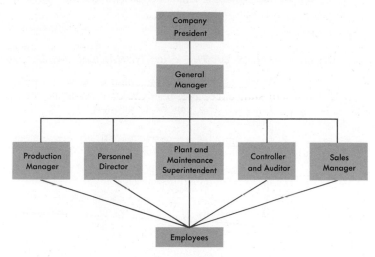

pattern from that of the line-and-staff structure. This may be accomplished by giving a manager power over specified processes or functions. He will thus supervise employees in several different departments, but only on matters concerning a specific functional area. In the organization chart of the functional organization plan shown above, you will observe that each employee has five different supervisors, each representing a functional area of the total organization. Although the practice of having more than one boss for each employee is at variance with the important organizational principle of "unity of command" discussed earlier in this chapter, many firms do not hesitate to follow it.

In this plan every person, except for those at the top levels, reports to several different supervisors. Each supervisor is a specialist in his field, with authority to supervise his particular function in the entire organization.

How well does the functional plan work? It works well for some businesses that can be organized into functional departments. But as a business grows, the tendency is to change over to a line-and-staff plan of organization in order to have the advantage of staff specialists. In the following illustration you will see that the employees are responsible to several immediate supervisors, each of whom is expert in a highly specialized kind of management work in his own department.

Here are some of the plan's advantages and disadvantages:

ADVANTAGES OF THE FUNCTIONAL ORGANIZATION

1. Each supervisor works exclusively in his specialty. This means he can grow with the firm.
2. Activities of the business are divided into functions and assigned

to specialists. Each specialist spends his time performing only one type of duty.

3. Expert advice is available to each individual worker.

DISADVANTAGES OF THE FUNCTIONAL ORGANIZATION

1. Workers have more than one boss, because separation of functions results in each supervisor's having authority over his particular function. This can be in conflict with the "unity of command" principle.

2. Since employees report to more than one supervisor, discipline tends to break down—there are just too many bosses.

3. Overlapping of authority among supervisors often promotes conflict and encourages buck-passing.

4. With so much emphasis on specialization, a supervisor seldom has an opportunity to become broadly trained outside his field.

Committee Organization

A committee organization is one in which a formally constituted committee drawn from the managerial ranks replaces an individual at one or more managerial levels. Most often this plan becomes integrated into a line-and-staff organization, with the committee replacing staff officers as committee members undertake managerial functions. This form of formal organization does not conflict with the use of other committees to make research studies and issue separate recommendations.

The advantages and disadvantages of this plan are as follows:

ADVANTAGES OF THE COMMITTEE ORGANIZATION

1. It combines the judgments of several officials when decisions are being made.

2. Committees act in a less personal way than do individuals when discussing the pros and cons of an issue.

3. Committees are usually composed of specialists who can devote more time to important problems than can most line officers.

DISADVANTAGES OF THE COMMITTEE ORGANIZATION

1. Committees often take longer to reach a decision than does a single individual.

2. An original idea often has to be compromised and modified before committee approval can be won.

3. If an aggressive person dominates the committee, the other members may be unduly influenced by him in rendering their final decisions.

4. Final decisions of the committee may not be entirely acceptable to everyone on the committee.

12. *Discuss the major differences between line and line-and-staff organizations.*

13. *Explain some of the advantages and disadvantages of the functional organization. How do you account for the fact that this organization plan is not more widely used?*

14. *What is the difference between a line and a staff authority relationship?*

ORGANIZATION CHARTS

As we discussed each of the formal organization plans in the preceding pages, we used a diagram as part of our analysis of the relationship of one part of the plan to another. A graphic means of showing the organization structure is called an *organization chart*. Every organization can be charted, for a chart merely depicts how departments or units are tied together along the lines of authority. As a blueprint, an organization chart not only indicates the lines of authority; it also identifies job titles for those persons who occupy positions of responsibility. Because charts are so effective in developing coordination among departments, many executives display them prominently in their offices and work areas. Too, as a business grows, the use of charts can become progressively more important. For instance, a chart can perform a valuable service merely by allowing an executive to see the entire organization in a simple perspective as it changes. And since a chart maps lines of authority, sometimes it may show inconsistencies and complexities that will lead to their correction.

In a recent survey of organization charting made by the American Management Association, 67 of the 118 companies studied stated that major purposes of organization charting are to fix responsibility and authority and to establish the chain of command. Twenty firms stated that charting helped to improve communications.

Making Organization Charts

Organization charts may take one of several forms. Most companies use a pyramid-type chart with rectangular boxes connected by lines. The boxes may be linked together with solid lines to show line relationships. Sometimes lines of different colors may also be used to show positions. Broken lines are often used to indicate staff relationships. The lines connecting the boxes represent the flow of responsibility from the bottom upward and the flow of authority from the top downward.

Limitations of Charts

Although charts are revealing and useful to company management, they are subject to serious limitations. For one thing, a chart does not reflect the many informal and informational relationships. It fails to depict (with the possible exception of the top position) how much authority actually exists at any point in the organization. Finally, charts easily become outdated, because from time to time company executives are transferred, promoted, or retired, or die.

One form of organization chart follows. (The type of chart shown on page 204 is more common than this one.)

STAFF EXECUTIVES

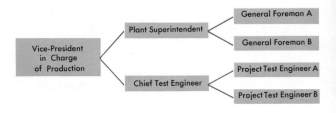

Discussion Questions

15. *What is the purpose of an organization chart, and what kind of information does the chart give?*

16. *Discuss some of the more serious limitations of organization charts.*

SUMMARY

Every business—small or large—needs organization planning. Internal organization makes it possible to bring together a group of people to work effectively under a central authority.

An effective and efficient organization is based on certain fundamental principles, such as unity of command, span of control, organization balance, and flexibility. For example, in a good organization no one should have more than one immediate supervisor, the levels of authority should be held to a minimum, and the organization should provide for top-executive planning.

In organization planning, it is essential to provide for the delegation of authority and responsibility. Each employee has a certain amount of responsibility, which increases with his rise in rank and work assignment. Authority commonly originates at the top and flows downward to the lower levels of command. If we assign a person to perform certain responsibilities, we must also give him the authority to carry these tasks out.

There are four basic organization plans. In the line plan, authority passes in a direct line from the top downward. Employees are responsible to only one boss. Throughout the organization, each supervisor or executive is in complete charge of the specific activities assigned him. A characteristic of the line plan is the manner in which authority is delegated along the straightforward chain of command.

The functional plan differs from the line plan. For one thing, it allows for the use of specialists. And, since workmen are responsible to various specialists, each workman reports to more than one foreman in a completely functionalized structure. It is probable that no completely functionalized organization has ever been developed.

The line-and-staff plan combines the various features of the line plan and the functional plan of organization. In the line-and-staff plan, the line officers are supplemented by experts or staff assistants, who serve in an advisory capacity. In the functional plan, the distinction between line and staff tends to disappear, because the executives exercise direct authority over line personnel in respective areas of specialization.

In the committee plan, groups of officers are provided to assist the line executives in making decisions.

Organization charts provide a valuable means of communication within the firm and enable both employees and executives to recognize lines of authority, responsibilities, and duties.

VOCABULARY REVIEW

Match the following vocabulary terms with the statements below.

a. Accountability
b. Authority
c. Centralized management organization
d. Decentralized management organization
e. Delegation
f. Formal organization
g. Informal organization
h. Line relations
i. Organization
j. Organization chart
k. Policy
l. Responsibility
m. Span-of-control principle

1. A system of well-defined jobs, each bearing a measure of authority, responsibility, and accountability
2. The total business enterprise, including facilities, materials, money, and manpower
3. The investment of one person with the power to act for another
4. A system that delegates authority and control to a central area within the organization, usually at the top
5. A graphic means of showing organization structure
6. The power to direct subordinates, requiring their obedience, to perform certain duties
7. A systematic effort to delegate to lower levels all authority except that which can be exercised only at the highest level
8. To be answerable for one's conduct in satisfactorily fulfilling an assignment
9. An oral or written statement that serves as a guide for management decisions
10. The grouping of people in an organizational unit in the absence of written formal rules or established procedures
11. A recognized chain of command that exists between the superior and subordinate

12. The individual's obligation to carry out duties assigned to him
13. A limit to the number of positions one person should supervise directly

PROBLEMS AND PROJECTS

1. Using a library and other outside sources, prepare a definition and give an illustration for each of the following terms: managerial responsibilities, first-line supervisor, informal organization, committee organization plan, and staff executive.

2. Construct an organization chart that fits the internal organization plan at your college. Show the positions for both academic and nonacademic personnel, using departmental titles or some other appropriate titles used by the college. It is not necessary to write in the names of all college administrators; instead use only their position titles in the chart. On the basis of what you have studied in this chapter, prepare changes in the chart that, according to your sources of information, would make the college organization more responsive and the duties of the faculty more relevant.

3. The White Cross Supply Corporation operates a manufacturing plant in Palo Alto, California, producing mainly hospital supplies such as operating equipment, bandages, and adhesive tapes. The introduction two years ago of a new line of hospital operating-room equipment has greatly expanded sales and plant-production facilities. The company officials, aware that action is necessary to correct the space problem, constructed two branch plants, one in Texas and the other in Utah. (The company sales are limited to an area west of Chicago.) The present organization structure is best described as a centralized line-and-staff type. The corporation president feels that the entire corporation should be reorganized to provide more effective supervision of the two branch plants, as well as the home office in Palo Alto. At present, the structure seems to be top-heavy, with too many decisions being made at the home office. The only purely staff operation is the work of a legal department to defend the company from public-liability suits. You are asked to make recommendations about improving efficiency. In what ways could the organization structure be improved?

A BUSINESS CASE

Case 8-1   Wyat Metal Work Company

The vice-president for plant production for the Wyat Metal Works Company has consulted you for advice in solving a conflict that seems to exist between him and the chief engineer. After several conferences with different persons, including these two, you determine that the relationship of personnel directly responsible to the vice-president for production appears to be as shown in the accompanying chart—see bottom of page, opposite.

The solid lines on the organization chart indicate lines of authority, and the dotted lines express frequent contact relationships, which you detected were caused by the following situations:

1. The die-shop engineer consults with the chief engineer informally, partly because he likes him but mostly because he thinks the chief engineer will probably be the next vice-president for production.
2. The tool-shop foreman and the die-shop engineer cannot get along well, so the foreman refers his problems to the chief engineer too, bypassing the die-shop engineer, to whom he is supposed to report. When this happens, the die-shop engineer is furious.
3. Shift operators #1 and #2 are personal friends of the tool-and-die designer. Shift operator #3 has decided he can get a promotion quicker by going directly to the production engineer when he has a problem.
4. Everyone in the whole organization under the vice-president for production has been allowed to report to anyone in the department who is willing to help him. This situation probably started because the vice-president is not an easy person to see during the course of the day.

As a troubleshooter, you are assigned the task of making an investigation. You have discovered that the organization chart pretty well reflects what has happened in the company: Employees have altered the channels of authority to satisfy themselves. While the production vice-president is aware of what has happened, he does not regard the situation as serious. When he discovers you have been assigned the task of making recommendations, he is obviously upset. He has not, however, refused to cooperate with you.

1. In your judgment, what is the cause of the problem?
2. Who is responsible for what has been allowed to happen?
3. What recommendations are you going to make?

BUSINESS CASE ORGANIZATION CHART

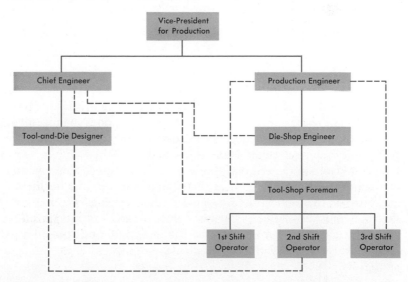

human
resources
administration

CHAPTER NINE

We have already seen that the economics of today's society has become increasingly complex, and that it is far more comprehensive than comprising just the scientific and technological factors. There are the human resources with their psychological and sociological natures. How does management go about putting together a production family, directing its activities toward economic goals, and keeping its members satisfied on the job? In addition, how are people matched to jobs in the first place, and how are they motivated toward maximum effort and the full utilization of their potentialities? If a business is to grow and prosper, the total work force must work together as a team; and to achieve this, they must all share satisfactorily in the fruits of production. The management of personnel is concerned with all these varied human motivational, sociological, and psychological elements.

THE IMPORTANCE OF
PERSONNEL MANAGEMENT

In order for workers to contribute most effectively to the operation of their company, certain basic conditions must be fulfilled. In the first place, employees must be placed in positions for which they possess the knowledge and skill they need to perform satisfactorily. But proficiency on the job goes beyond these basic essentials; it requires some form of self-satisfaction that spurs workers toward their maximum potential because they have the desire to achieve something. The really effective employee is the interested one, who has a genuine desire to do the best possible job and strives constantly to improve his performance. And—hardly less important—he must be able to work well with others as well as alone. Thus one of the major concerns of management is that of providing the kind of environment in which people can function collectively as well as individually.

People like to be rewarded for their achievements. Just as the teenager strives for scholastic honors, high marks, medals, and so on, workers strive for higher earnings, promotions, and other recognitions, as well as the satisfaction that comes from doing a job well. So the maintenance of high morale and the spirit of teamwork and cooperation are other major concerns in the realm of managing the human resources of a business.

What Is Personnel Management?

Personnel management has the responsibility of planning, organizing, directing, coordinating, and controlling all activities that concern employees: selecting, developing, and compensating them, and meeting their needs in a number of other respects. It is the goal of personnel management to utilize effectively each employee's talents so that company objectives are attained efficiently and economically. This implies that each employee is enabled to use his competencies, interests, and opportunities to his and the company's best advantage. The chart at the top of page 216 outlines the various aspects that distinguish one worker from another.

Because manpower is the most important asset of business and industry, the full and effective utilization of this wellspring of employee talent is a major responsibility of management. Improved working conditions, rising wages, and increasing benefits make employees better satisfied, more loyal, and more productive. Management and proprietor enjoy the resultant benefits if increased production, reduced labor turnover, and decreased labor–management conflict.

The management of a small business is just as much concerned with personnel policies and direction as is that of a large business. The difference is that in a large business the typical organization pattern provides for the establishment of a personnel department to plan, coordinate, and direct employee activities and to meet their personal concerns.

A USEFUL CONCEPT FOR LEARNING ABOUT INDIVIDUAL DIFFERENCES

Courtesy Shepherd Associates, Fort Worth, Texas (by B. E. Lindberg)

The Role of the Personnel Manager

The work of the personnel department is so extensive and varied that no one person can perform in all the respective areas. In medium-size and large companies, a vice-president is usually responsible for coordinating and directing the operations of the personnel department.

You will recall from an earlier discussion of the internal organization of businesses that the personnel department usually operates as a staff function. In other words, its task is to serve and advise other staff personnel as well as all line personnel, thus including both line and staff functional areas. In a staff capacity, the personnel department assists other departments in the hiring and training of employees and in serving the needs of those employees. But final decisions concerning personnel matters are made by the department heads.

Sometimes the personnel department is given functional authority. In this capacity it does not just assist or serve other departments but actually makes the final decision in hiring, conducts specialized training, decides who is to be promoted, and so on. The important thing to remember is that the function of the personnel department is determined by the authority granted to it by top management. If this authority is staff, it serves and advises other departments. If it is functional, the personnel department has the power to command and to carry out programs it has designed for other departments.

Discussion Question

1. *Explain why manpower is considered to be the most important asset of any business.*

FUNCTIONS PERFORMED BY THE PERSONNEL DEPARTMENT

The various activities carried on in the personnel department can be grouped into five major areas, as the boxed list shows.

1. The selection of the best workers available to fill specific positions

2. The development of selected workers to ensure that they are well prepared for their assignments

3. The creation and maintenance of working conditions that are conducive to high morale and high production

4. The development and operation of a fair and adequate program of monetary reward

5. An honest concern with the wants, motivations, attitudes, morale, safety, and health needs of employees

Recruitment

A primary task of any personnel department is to find new workers. As a general rule, the best workers are those who are recruited by present employees. Employees will not recommend their firms to persons who are seeking work unless they themselves are satisfied on the job. Their enthusiasm and satisfaction rub off on those they recruit. But it is rare that a business firm can fill all its openings from people recruited by its employees.

In addition to those who are recruited by the business firms' present employees, new workers are secured through direct applications on the initiative of job seekers, advertising of job vacancies, school placement services, employment agencies, and referrals from business associates.

The recruitment of the right kind, quality, and quantity of workers is a continuous task. The various operational departments of a business look to the personnel department to obtain these new employees.

Job Analysis

Long before the personnel department seeks out, interviews, tests, and evaluates prospective employees in its efforts to fill every available position with the most qualified person it can secure, it must be thoroughly acquainted with those positions. Experience has proved that familiarity of this sort comes only through job analysis, which involves the preparation of job descriptions and job classifications.

The U.S. Employment Service defines the term *job analysis* as the process of determining by observation and study, and of reporting, pertinent information relating to the nature of a specific job. It is the determination of the tasks that comprise the job, and of the skills, knowledge, abilities, and responsibilities that are required of the worker for successful performance and that differentiate the job from all others. Job analysis includes not only a study of the job but also an analysis of the conditions and environment in which the job is performed.

From the standpoint of the personnel department, job analyses are made in order to:

1. Provide facts for evaluating the work station to see how it relates to other positions
2. Supply information about the activities to be performed
3. Determine the requirements for measuring employee performance
4. Identify potential safety hazards
5. Identify basic information on operational procedures
6. Clarify lines of authority and responsibility
7. Provide the data needed for developing a job classification system
8. Make sure that there is compliance with such legal regulations as those of the Fair Labor Standards Act

Data for making job analyses are obtained by interview and by observation. Certain questions must be answered in order to give a true picture of the degree of skill and the other qualifications needed for the worker to perform effectively in the task under consideration. These questions are listed in the box at the top of the next page.

Job Description. The *job description* is a written report based on the analysis of a particular job. It should include or describe (1) the job title; (2) a statement of where the work is to be performed; (3) the job's relation to other jobs, as well as its importance to the operation of the business; (4) the

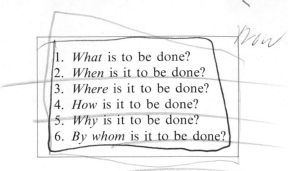

1. *What* is to be done?
2. *When* is it to be done?
3. *Where* is it to be done?
4. *How* is it to be done?
5. *Why* is it to be done?
6. *By whom* is it to be done?

tools, machines, and equipment to be used, and the ways in which they are to be used; (5) the materials and supplies to be used, and the ways in which they are to be used; (6) the physical and mental skills required; (7) the working conditions; and (8) the duties and responsibilities assigned to the job. The importance of the job description becomes clear when we realize that management uses it as the basis for selecting and training workers and for promoting and transferring employees.

Job Classification. In a large organization, there are usually hundreds of different jobs. Rather than having a different wage-scale assigned to each job, the problem of wage administration is simplified by assigning specified rates to a group of jobs that fall within a certain range of values. A job classification, therefore, is the grouping together of several positions into a single bracket or class. The "GS" ratings employed by the Federal Civil Service Commission are examples of job classification. The technique of classifying is useful for determining wages and in the transferring and promoting of employees. Job classification, therefore, serves as a guide to the selection of the right person for each position.

Employee Selection and Job Placement

We have seen that job analysis is the first step in the wise selection of workers. Making use of information obtained during the analysis, the personnel department can then carry out the important task of selecting new workers and placing them in the jobs for which they are best qualified. So the next step in the selection process might be called *applicant analysis.*

Application Forms. Almost every business uses some type of application form to obtain information that will be needed for the applicant's personal file. Such personal information as name, education, age, address, and telephone number is always included.

The would-be employee's history of work experience is probably the most important information provided by the application form. This record indicates more than the type and extent of his experience; it indicates whether he sticks with an assignment or changes jobs frequently. In the application form, emphasis is given to the applicant's work history.

Job Application Form

File No. _____

Date _____

Form B published by Shepherd Associates, Personnel Consultants, P. O. Box 846, Fort Worth, Texas

PERSONAL DATA

PRINT NAME

NAME _____ (MAIDEN NAME) _____

         First   Middle   Last

FULL NAME OF SPOUSE _____ PERSON TO NOTIFY IN CASE OF ACCIDENT? _____

                                                                     TEL. NO.

APPLYING FOR POSITION AS _____ WHEN AVAILABLE? _____

PHONE NO. _____ SOCIAL SECURITY NO. _____ SALARY OR WAGES EXPECTED _____

PRESENT ADDRESS _____

               Street   City   State   Period of Residence

LAST PREVIOUS ADDRESS _____

                                                                            Period of Residence

BIRTHDATE _____ AGE* _____ SEX* _____ PRESENT EMPLOYMENT STATUS _____

*Note: This information may be asked for but discrimination because of sex prohibited by Federal law. Also, discrimination by age prohibited by law in states with Fair Employment Practices.

☐ SINGLE   ☐ ENGAGED   ☐ DIVORCED

HOW MANY DEPENDENTS? _____ NUMBER, AGES, SEX OF CHILDREN _____

☐ WIDOW(ER)   ☐ MARRIED _____ YEARS

REFERENCES

NAMES OF THREE PERSONS, NOT RELATIVES, FORMER EMPLOYERS, OR PERSONNEL OF THIS COMPANY WHO HAVE KNOWN YOU FOR AT LEAST TWO YEARS, ALSO NAME OF BANK WITH WHICH YOU DO BUSINESS

NAME	ADDRESS	BUSINESS AND POSITION	TELEPHONE (If known)

U. S. MILITARY SERVICE

VETERAN OF U.S. ARMED FORCES? ☐ YES ☐ NO   RESERVE STATUS _____   DRAFT STATUS _____

BRANCH _____ SERIAL NO. _____ DATE ENTERED _____ RANK ON ENTERING _____

DATE OF DISCHARGE _____ RANK AT DISCHARGE _____ TYPE OF DISCHARGE _____

IN WHAT THEATERS DID YOU SERVE? _____

MAJOR DUTIES _____

SERVICE SCHOOLS AND OTHER SPECIAL TRAINING _____

EDUCATIONAL DATA

SCHOOLS	NAME AND ADDRESS OF INSTITUTION	DATES FROM — TO Mo.-Yr. Mo.-Yr.	GRADUATED Yes — No	DEGREE RECEIVED	AVERAGE GRADES	AREAS OF SPECIALIZATION
GRADE SCHOOL				—		
HIGH SCHOOL				—		
COLLEGE						
GRADUATE SCHOOL						
TRADE, BUS., NIGHT OR CORRESPONDENCE						
APPRENTICE SHIPS				—	—	
OTHER						

Courtesy Shepherd Associates, Fort Worth, Texas

Space for listing the names and addresses of people for whom the applicant has worked is provided on the application form, too. Letters and telephone calls to former employers are frequently useful in securing information about an applicant's attitudes and personal qualities.

The accuracy, care, and precision with which an applicant completes this form may give the company a valuable clue concerning his work habits. One who is careless in the preparation of an employment application may well prove to be careless in his work habits, too.

The Employment Interview. Very often, the next step in the selection process is an interview of the applicant by a member of the personnel department. The chief purpose of the interview is to gather additional information about the applicant. It also gives the interviewer a chance to have the applicant validate his answers to any or all questions on the application form. Through carefully phrased questions, the interviewer attempts to discover how the applicant might fit into the organization and what his attitude probably would be toward his associates on the job. The interviewer also explores the applicant's attitude toward his work in former jobs, his ability to express himself clearly, and his personal traits and characteristics. Many business firms have had great success with interviews, because they have seen to it that interviewers were trained and unbiased and that interviews were carefully planned to bring forth specific information.

But interviews are not always completely reliable as a means of selecting employees. Indeed, they are sometimes very unreliable. One reason is that the interviewer is seldom entirely free from prejudice, and prejudices make it hard to conduct an interview with scientific objectivity. Another reason is that the (in some way) "weak" applicant may just happen to be having one of his rare and lucky "strong" days, and may fairly mesmerize the interviewer (who may be having a "weak" day).

Approximately three-fourths of the employees who lose their jobs do so because of personal reasons. But not all these people are misfits with undesirable or unacceptable personalities; some are doomed from the start merely because they are placed in jobs for which they are not suited. In trying to prevent matching the right man with the wrong job, the interviewer who knows his business tries to determine what sort of job will suit the personality and talents of each applicant. And he can do this only by taking all relevant facts and factors into consideration. The knowledgeable interviewer realizes as do few others that when the qualified employee is properly placed, when he is given the necessary training, and when he associates with people he enjoys working with, the chances are that he will succeed—on behalf of his employer.

The interview is intended to achieve yet another important function—that of supplying the applicant with information about the firm, including its policy on salaries and promotions, working hours and conditions, and skills required. The usual practice is to hold a preliminary interview and later a follow-up interview. The purpose of the preliminary interview is to size up the applicants in a general way and to eliminate those who obviously would not fit into the company organization. This interview may be held even before the application form is completed. The follow-up interview may be held at the time the worker is finally accepted or rejected. For this interview, a prescribed form may be followed to assure that critical questions are not overlooked.

Here are ten questions that help employing officials in organizing their thinking and that reinforce their decisions when hiring new workers.

The Use of Tests. In addition to interviewing the applicant and investigating his record, many companies make use of tests. Among the various types of tests that have found wide acceptance and use in recent years are interest tests, knowledge tests, tests for special aptitudes and abilities, and skill or performance tests.

The most widely used are the *aptitude tests.* If a person is being considered for a clerical position, let us say, he will be tested for potential talents (aptitude) in that area of work. A wide variety of aptitude tests is available, and some industries have developed specialized tests of this sort to serve their particular needs. Most people will respond to training if they have ability (or at least potential ability) in the area for which they are being trained. But if a person is weak in the special aptitudes needed to perform successfully in a particular type of work, no amount of training or experience will make a master workman

1. What is the applicants real reason for changing jobs?— not necessarily his stated reason.

2. Are you satisfied with the stability of his work record?

3. Is his ambition level compatible with your job requirements?

4. What has he accomplished on his own—what has he started and finished?

5. How does the applicant feel about his former employers?

6. Is the trend of his experience favorable for your job?

7. Back off, close your eyes; think about the applicant; how does he impress you? (Check your delay or reluctance to reach a quick decision, positive or negative.)

8. Any outward signs of physical limitations—size, weight, nervousness, excessive smoking, alcoholic scars?

9. How much does the applicant really know about his abilities?

10. Are interview impressions consistent with the work-history record?

SELECTION AND EMPLOYMENT PROCEDURE

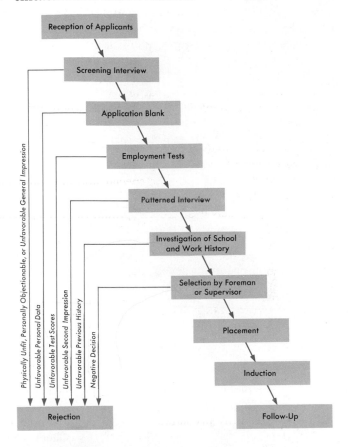

of him. Aptitude is what separates the gifted artist from the well-meaning, hard-working, but at best merely adequate artisan.

Performance tests are designed to indicate the degree of skill an applicant has for a specific type of work. Such tests show whether the worker is qualified to perform the tasks required or needs further training.

It is important to note that aptitude and performance tests require a skilled person to administer them. A poorly administered and poorly evaluated test is worse than no test at all.

The Physical Examination. Almost every modern firm now requires an applicant to submit evidence of physical health. He may have to produce a certificate from his family physician or undergo a check-up by the company doctor. More and more firms are following the latter procedure.

The company must know whether the applicant is physically able to perform the work that his job assignment calls for. It might require constant standing, manipulative skill, extremely good eyesight. The physical test, then, is designed to discover any impairments that might prevent satisfactory performance on the job. It is also for the purpose of ascertaining whether the would-be employee has any trouble that might serve as the basis for a future claim against the company for physical disability.

Discussion Questions

2. *What are the most-accepted procedures in the selection of new employees?*
3. *Which of the steps in the employment procedure do your consider more important than others?*

EMPLOYEE DEVELOPMENT

Most persons, at the time they are employed, are prepared for some type of work at only a beginning level. After that, they are trained for specific tasks for which they lack the necessary skill. However, before they actually begin their work, most new employees are given some type of orientation to the company and to their departmental relationships, as well as to their specific

Department heads confer about a staff decision.

work assignments. Each new worker must learn basic company policies as early as possible; the orientation session acquaints him with these, and in addition, suggests procedures for following through in the days ahead.

Orientation and Training

In all probability, the orientation period will include a tour of the physical plant, a visit with the department head and one's immediate supervisor, and an acquaintanceship with the employee manual. Information in which new employees are particularly interested includes the times for rest periods, the location of lunch facilities, locker rooms, recreational facilities, the infirmary, and first-aid stations, and the safety rules that must be observed. In addition, they want information on company policy regarding sick leave, medical benefits, vacation, pay periods, and employees' organizations.

Training Patterns. Orientation training often begins the first day a new employee reports for work and may continue periodically as long as he is with the company. As a part of his orientation, he is trained to perform the basic operations essential to his work. Periodically he may study in formal classes as a means of upgrading skills needed on the job.

Some companies hold short-term formal classes at the various job levels— including middle-management positions—right on the premises. In some cases, employees are given time off during the workday to attend such classes. Many corporations will pay the tuition and textbook costs for those of their employees who attend college or university classes.

Trade associations provide training and educational opportunities for employees, managers, and top executives of business firms. Many businesses send their executives to special workshops in executive training conducted by universities or business and professional societies.

Companies frequently pay for their employees' training even though they themselves have no such formal programs. Learning through experience—trial and error—can be the most expensive way to receive one's training.

There are five approaches to the development of company personnel:

1. *On-the-job training* provides the worker with specific training for one job while under supervision. This at present the most commonly used type of training, for it is simple, easy to administer, and interesting to the trainee. The primary burden for training is on the trainee's immediate supervisor.

2. *Apprenticeship training* is similar to on-the-job training, except that here the worker is learning a craft that involves many related tasks, rather than just one job. Apprenticeship programs give more emphasis to education that do job training programs. They combine on-the-job training and experience with formal classroom instruction.

3. *Vestibule training* is conducted away from the job, but in a simulated job situation. In this program, skilled instructors from the training

department strive to develop techniques and working processes that are identical to those needed on the job. The advantage of the vestibule school is the high degree of specialization provided through the instructors. They are skilled both in technical knowledge and in the teaching process. The vestibule school also frees the trainee from the pressure of the production line and permits him to concentrate on the learning process.

4. *Supervisory training* is basically leadership training in orientation, administration, human relations, technical knowledge, and instruction. Employees who rank high in desirable personal qualities, get along well with others, and exert leadership in group situations are those most often promoted to supervisory positions. Frequently they enroll in formal classes for instruction provided or arranged by company executives.

5. *Executive training,* the highest level of training, is designed to build the highest quality of administrative leadership. This preparation is usually provided through experience in junior-executive positions, supplemented by formal courses of study. The latter may be given by the company or supplied by staff members of a nearby college or university.

Management Appraisal

A practice that has become popular among large companies is the periodic appraisal of workers. The purpose of such evaluations is to determine if the workers are happy and successful in their positions. The first follow-up is usually scheduled several days after a new employee has joined the company's work force, and subsequent checks are made at regular intervals thereafter, at least once or twice a year.

Should the first follow-up reveal that a worker does not seem to fit into the job to which he has been assigned, he may be given special training or transferred to another type of work. Later appraisals serve as the basis for retraining, transfer, promotion, or dismissal.

The most extensive use of such evaluation is for the appraisal of supervisory personnel and persons in management positions.

Multiple Ratings. There is a good deal of evidence that ratings made by one's peers differ greatly from those made by his superiors. Similarly, there are differences between self-ratings and those made by superiors. Self-ratings seem to overrate ability to get along well with others, while ratings by superiors give more weight to such qualities as initiative, loyalty, and knowledge of one's work.

Self-ratings do seem to lead to improved performance in one's assignment, and peer appraisal aids in identifying people with leadership ability. The current trend is toward using a combination of self-ratings, peer judgment, and appraisal by superiors, thereby providing balance in appraisal. The knowledge that superiors are also making appraisals tends to reduce bias and increase objectivity in the ratings by one's self and one's colleagues. Perhaps the chief value of the three-rating procedure is that it provides much more information about the person being evaluated than could be obtained through appraisal by superiors only.

Research shows clearly that there are advantages to using more than a single rater. Averaging together the ratings of several persons (even though they are superiors or peers) reduces the effect of a particular rating that may have been prejudiced. A high rating given by a manager who is unusually kind and considerate of his workers might be counterbalanced by that of a manager who emphasizes production success. People who have a wide knowledge and observation of the work and behavior of the person being rated make the best and most reliable evaluations.

Discussion Questions

4. *What three things above all others would you include in an orientation program for new workers?*
5. *What are the relative advantages and disadvantages of vestibule training and apprenticeship training when compared with each other?*
6. *Why are self-ratings usually higher than ratings of superiors?*

EMPLOYEE COMPENSATION PLANS

The development and operation of a fair and equitable wage-and-salary system is perhaps the most difficult function of personnel management. Since the amount of money a person earns determines the quantity and quality of goods and services he can purchase, the compensation function is very important to each employee. Of course, the function is important to the company, too. When employees are overpaid, a company's products may be overpriced in a competitive market. When employees are underpaid, turnover is high, morale is low, and production is inefficient. In an effort to determine the amount of compensation a worker should receive, scores of plans have been advanced. Most workers in the United States today are paid either time wages or piece wages. *Time wages* are based on the amount of time spent on the job. *Piece wages* are based on the number of units produced.

Time Wages

In many types of work, it is more practicable to base wages on the employee's responsibilities than on his productivity; in fact, in many instances it is impossible to measure output objectively. When quality rather than quantity is important, or where the employee is continually interrupted in his work, time wages are usually more appropriate.

However, time wages do have one serious disadvantage. They fail to encourage some employees to make their maximum effort. Because there is no immediate recognition of a worker's superior performance, he may become discouraged and put less than his best into the work.

Piece Wages

Under the piece-rate payment plan, a certain sum is paid for each unit a worker produces. (Of course, this plan can be used only when the output can be counted or objectively measured in some way.) The unit payment may be based on the output of an individual worker, or it may apply to the work of a group or even an entire department. The system is particularly valuable when applied to work wherein loitering is difficult to detect. By encouraging the workers to "supervise" themselves, it decreases supervisory costs.

When great emphasis is put on quantity, there is always a tendency among workers to sacrifice quality—so management must keep under careful control the quality of the units produced. It is also good practice, management finds, to reward workers for maintaining a low level of material waste and spoilage. Sociologists have proved what management has long suspected of piece-rate workers: that they often hesitate to increase their production too greatly for fear that the employer will decrease the price paid per unit produced. The fear is not without grounds, because all too often employers *have* cut unit wages following an increase in production. You can see that such a move on the employer's part might well destroy any incentive that had been gained through using the piece-rate system.

Wage-Incentive Plans

Some manufacturing firms have set up wage-payment plans designed to reward the worker with added compensation for exceptional performance. Known as *wage-incentive plans*, they are based on the piece-rate method of making wage payments.

In 1895, Frederick W. Taylor developed the first wage-incentive plan, the *Taylor Differential Piece-Rate Plan*. Here is how it works: First, a careful scientific study is made of each worker's operations. Then a standard rate of output is established that is within the reach of the average worker. Two rates prevail—one for the worker who fails to reach the standard, and a higher rate for the worker who exceeds it. For example, if the standard output is 100 units per day, a worker who produces fewer than 100 pieces might receive 25 cents per piece. On the other hand, a worker who exceeds 100 units might receive 27 cents per piece. The worker who produced 98 units would receive $24.50 for his day's work, whereas the worker who produced 105 units would earn $28.35.

A second wage-incentive plan is the *Gantt Task and Bonus System.* Under this plan, if an employee exceeds the set standards by completing the work in less time, he receives as a bonus a percentage of the base rate. The bonus is usually figured on a sliding scale, varying from 15 to 35 percent of the base rate. A worker who fails to complete the task in the time allotted for it receives the regular hourly rate but no bonus. There are two special features of this plan: (1) The bonus rate usually begins when the worker does three-fourths as much as the standard. This serves to encourage those who are striving to reach the standard, as well as those who have already passed it. (2) The foreman is usually given a bonus also, depending upon the amount or number of bonuses paid to the workmen he supervises.

There are many other wage-incentive plans, such as the Rowan, Emerson, Bedaux, and Halsey plans, and the 100 Percent Time-Saving Plan. The ones we have discussed have been given to illustrate the manner in which such plans operate. Detailed study of the other plans is reserved for courses in personnel management and industrial relations.

A well-conceived wage-incentive plan will include the following objectives:

For management:
1. Lowered costs resulting from increased productivity
2. Improved cost control, leading to production that is more consistent, more uniform, and less variable in actual cost
3. Improved facility utilization
4. Improved worker morale as earnings become proportionate to individual effort

For employees:
1. An opportunity to earn money in excess of base rate and in proportion to individual effort
2. An opportunity for individual recognition
3. An opportunity for a healthful competitive spirit among employees
4. An opportunity for an employee to control (at least partially) the level of his standard of living by his own initiative

Any wage incentive must recognize this dual direction of benefits.

Employee Profit Sharing

The term *profit sharing* is used to refer to wage-payment plans that provide remuneration beyond basic pay schedules. These extra payments go to all employees; their amounts are tied directly to the profits earned. The Council of Profit Sharing Industries has defined profit sharing as "any procedure under which an employer pays or makes available to all regular employees, in addition to regular rates of pay, special current or deferred sums based on the profits of the business."

The basic philosophy of profit sharing is that it creates a "partnership relationship" on the part of employees. It draws labor and management closer together and develops a working relationship and atmosphere favorable to efficient workmanship. Those who advocate profit sharing claim that it makes for high employee morale, reduces the number and extent of employee grievances, reduces labor turnover, provides greater security for workers, and improves public relations.

There is, of course, a wide variety of practices in profit-sharing programs. Some plans provide for cash payments; others provide for deferred payments, which are frequently tied to the issuance of stock. Some of the factors entering into the structure of a profit-sharing plan are whether the percentage to be paid is to be a fixed or sliding rate, whether the percentage is to be applied to profits before or after taxes, and the amount of the profits to be shared.

Eastman Kodak's profit-sharing plan is determined by the amount of the cash dividend paid on the common stock. Employee bonuses are paid on the basis of individual total yearly earnings.

One of the best-known plans is that of the Lincoln Electric Company, of Cleveland, Ohio. Under this system, each job is evaluated to establish its importance to the company's operations, and a pay rate is established for it. The workers are rated twice a year; they are graded on the quality and quantity of their work, their skill, and their attitudes. These ratings determine the amount of bonus each worker is to receive in relation to his base salary. The company experiences an annual productivity increase five times that of the average for all industries and has a labor turnover rate approximately one-third that of other manufacturing plants.

Organized labor looks with disfavor on wage-payment plans that sponsor competition among the workers, setting one against another. It prefers plans that are universal throughout the plant and that apply to all the workers. Labor leaders also oppose plans that reward only increased productivity that results directly from increased personal effort. They feel that wage-incentive plans should reward workers for increased output that results from other factors, as well as from workers' personal skill and effort.

Production-Sharing Plans

Production sharing is similar to profit sharing, in that such programs utilize the cooperative efforts of both management and labor. Rather than shared profits, they represent a sharing of savings that result from reducing production costs. Since savings from production are much narrower in scope than are company profits, it is easier to relate an individual's efforts to the results of a small group.

One of the best-known production-sharing plans is the *Scanlon Plan*. This plan was first used in the Lapointe Machine Tool Company in Hudson, Massachusetts, by Joseph Scanlon, an official of the United Steel Workers. Scanlon claimed that individual incentive plans lead to cutthroat competition among workers, at the expense of the best welfare of the group as a whole.

The Scanlon Plan emphasizes the sharing of savings in production with all workers. Under the operation of this technique, a normal labor cost is computed per unit of production. Then if, through the cooperative efforts of the group as a whole, the improved efficiency results in lower unit labor costs, the amount of such savings is passed along to all workers as a bonus. In some cases the efficiency is measured in terms of productivity: If there is a 5 percent increase in productivity, wages are increased by the same percentage.

Under the *Rucker Share-of-Production Plan,* both company and workers share the increased value of goods produced, which results from the joint efforts of management and workers. This plan includes all hourly employees, not just those whose work can be measured. The standards employed are not based on the number of physical units produced, but on the ratio of sales income to the cost of labor input. It also shows a worker the relationship between the dollars he earns and the economic value of the goods he helps produce.

The *Kaiser Long-Range Sharing Plan* has received much attention in recent years, because it has several unique characteristics. In order to discourage worker resistance to the use of modern equipment, the plan provides protection against layoffs resulting from increased mechanization. It also encourages waste reduction in materials and supplies as a factor in reducing the cost of production.

Actually, production sharing is more than a way of paying monetary compensation to workers. It represents labor–management cooperation. In some cases, such as under the Scanlon Plan, the awards for suggestions that improve production efficiency are paid to the group rather than to the individuals who submit the suggestions. The emphasis is on teamwork for the benefit of all. With teamwork, production increases of as much as 50 percent have been achieved.

Management Compensation

Whereas wage-incentive plans are less popular today for workers than they were two decades ago, they are significantly more important for managers. Research supports the view that for managers, pay is a strong incentive for exceptional service when it is tied to job performance in such a way that it serves as a reward for effective performance. A study of 500 managers at all levels, covering a wide variety of organizations, showed that the majority of them are concerned with how their salary is divided between cash and fringe benefits.

The *stock-option plan* is very popular today as a scheme for rewarding top management. Under this plan, top management is permitted to buy company stock at some future time at the market price of the stock on the date the option to purchase was granted. This scheme is viewed as a means by which a company can induce valuable officers to remain with the company.

The same type of benefit does not always suit all persons in top-management positions with a given company. To meet the needs of a group of managers, the so-called *cafeteria wage-payment plan* is sometimes used. Under this system, several different types of benefits are made available, and each manager is allowed to select the type of benefits that would be of the most value to him.

Discussion Questions

7. *Why do we say that a wage-incentive plan must have a dual objective?*

8. *What is the distinction between profit sharing and production sharing?*

9. *How do you feel about letting corporation officers exercise stock-purchase options but denying this privilege to ''workers''?*

EMPLOYEE BENEFITS
AND SERVICES

We have seen that compensating employees for their services is an important function of the personnel department. Today most managers agree that compensation programs should include certain benefits beyond direct wage or salary payments. Since World War II, organized labor and management have been increasingly concerned with employee benefits and services. Indeed, such benefits and services are frequently given greater consideration than are wages during the negotiation of a collective-bargaining agreement. Although benefits and services may not involve direct monetary payment to employees, they are costs to business; they frequently exceed the costs incurred by granting wage increases.

One of the earliest benefits to be provided was payment for holidays and vacation periods. Today it is common practice for businesses to pay their employees for one or more weeks of vacation time and for six to eight holidays each year. Some companies, in the metals industry for example, provide vacations of several weeks' duration every five years or so for employees who have been on the payroll for a specified number of years. Other benefits that were among the first to be included in collective-bargaining agreements are hospitalization and life insurance. It is now common practice for companies to pay a good portion of such insurance premiums, if not the full amount.

The benefits and services that we have been discussing are called *fringe benefits.* Others that may be found include employee discounts on purchases of company products, credit unions, retirement-income provisions, and loans during layoff periods. An increasing number of companies also offer legal-aid counseling, income tax counseling, low-cost cafeteria facilities, libraries, and educational opportunities.

EMPLOYEE BENEFITS IN PRIVATE INDUSTRY

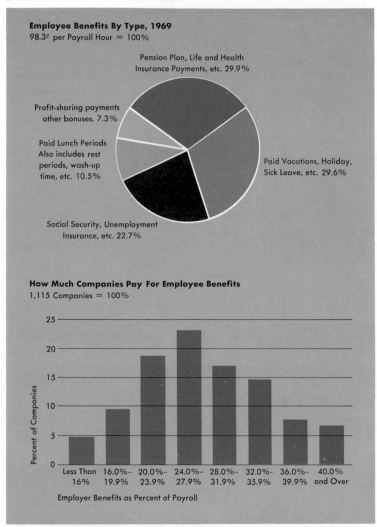

Employee Benefits By Type, 1969
98.3¢ per Payroll Hour = 100%

Pension Plan, Life and Health Insurance Payments, etc. 29.9%

Profit-sharing payments other bonuses. 7.3%

Paid Lunch Periods Also includes rest periods, wash-up time, etc. 10.5%

Paid Vacations, Holiday, Sick Leave, etc. 29.6%

Social Security, Unemployment Insurance, etc. 22.7%

How Much Companies Pay For Employee Benefits
1,115 Companies = 100%

Percent of Companies

| Less Than 16% | 16.0%–19.9% | 20.0%–23.9% | 24.0%–27.9% | 28.0%–31.9% | 32.0%–35.9% | 36.0%–39.9% | 40.0% and Over |

Employer Benefits as Percent of Payroll

Sources: U.S. Department of Commerce; U.S. Chamber of Commerce; The National Industrial Conference Board, No. 1674, September 15, 1971

The U.S. Chamber of Commerce survey of 1,115 companies revealed that employee benefits cost an average of 27.9 percent of payroll in 1969, up moderately from the 22.8 percent average recorded in 1959. The proportion of firms incurring employee benefit costs of more than 30 percent of payroll, however, jumped from 14.7 percent in 1959 to 37.7 percent in 1969.

Fringe benefits are important to the health and well-being of employees during their working years, and they provide security in retirement. You will see that they are also important in the development and maintenance of high morale among the work force; a discussion of morale and its importance is included later in this chapter.

TRANSFER, PROMOTION, AND SEPARATION

Since transfer and promotion are such important phases of the personnel function, a definite and clearly understood policy regarding them must be established. A company that does not establish such a policy risks poor employee morale and high labor turnover.

Transfer

The term *transfer* refers to the shifting of an employee from one position to another without increasing his duties, responsibilities, or pay. Every business finds it necessary to transfer workers to different positions. There may come a time when older workers must be given assignments that require lighter work. Or if a worker has been assigned to a job on which he is not doing satisfactory work, he may be shifted to another job. There are times, too, when the work load is heavier in some departments than in others, or when it is desirable to rotate workers into and out of dangerous positions. Occasionally a transfer is necessary because of personal differences among employees, or because of personality conflicts between workers and supervisors. Also, employees are often rotated from position to position as a training device.

When a transfer has to be made, management must double-check to make sure that there are valid reasons for it and that the employee will not suffer hardship as a result of it. And it is important for management to tell employees their reasons for moving them—to make them feel that they are being treated fairly, and are not being shifted merely for the convenience of someone else. Management should also tell people it shifts around whether the transfer is permanent or temporary, and, if it is only temporary, how long they will be working in the new job.

Promotion

The term *promotion* refers to the shifting of an employee to a new position in which both his status and his responsibilities are increased. (Higher pay does not always accompany a promotion, although it usually does—or at least follows soon after.) Promotions are advantageous to the firm as well as to the employee. Management knows that deserving employees have been taken care of, that workers are situated where they can produce the most, and that the cost of orienting and training new people has been reduced. When a promotion is made, however, it should be deserved. An employee should not be given a promotion when he has not earned it or when others are better qualified or more deserving. Length of service must also be considered. When two employees are equally deserving of being promoted as far as ability and performance are concerned, the promotion usually goes to the person who has been either with the company or on the job the longest. This person is said to have seniority.

An advancement in pay that does not involve a move into a new job classification is called a *horizontal promotion.* An advancement that moves an employee into a job with a higher rank or classification is called a *vertical promotion.*

If management is to avoid increased labor unrest and labor turnover, it must develop a systematic plan for promotions. The best-qualified employees of a company become dissatisfied and leave if few opportunities for advancement exist or if promotions are made only infrequently. Employees should know all the factors included in the company's promotion policy and the relative importance of each

Separation

Separations from the employ of a company may be either temporary or permanent, voluntary or involuntary. A layoff is temporary and involuntary, usually traceable to a lull in business. It is customarily assumed that those who are laid off will be reemployed as soon as business returns to normal. The usual procedure is to lay off first those workers with the least seniority.

A discharge is a permanent separation of an employee at the will of the employer. A person may be discharged if he is not competent in his job even after (as often happens, though not always) an honest effort has been made, through transfers, to find a suitable job for him. A worker who is guilty of breaking company rules may also be subject to discharge if the seriousness of the infraction merits such action, or if the worker has a history of ignoring and breaking certain rules. Insubordination is also just cause for discharge. (Where the workers of a company are members of a union, the conditions that govern discharge are included in the labor agreement reached by the company and the union. This situation is discussed more fully in the following chapter, on labor–management relations.)

When employees leave the company of their own free will, management should make a sincere attempt to find out the reason for their departure, for it can use this information to improve conditions and thus decrease labor turnover.

10. *What type of fringe benefit do you consider to be the most important to workers today?*

11. *What is the distinction between a horizontal promotion and a transfer?*

12. *Why should management be interested in interviewing persons who have decided to leave the business to accept employment elsewhere?*

EMPLOYEE MORALE

Employee morale is the attitude or feeling of individuals or groups toward their jobs, their associates, and the company. It is affected by all the varied factors that make up the employee's environment, including the extent to which his needs and wants are satisfied by working in a particular job or for a certain company.

If the employee feels that he is treated fairly by management, that his salary is adequate, and that working conditions are good, he is likely to have high morale. When employees have high morale they are enthusiastic and are inclined to cooperate with management. Employees with low morale are easily discouraged, tend to be uncooperative, and generally reveal negative feelings. Morale affects efficiency of operation and is therefore of great importance to management, especially to those involved in the personnel function. Many authorities believe that rates of production are more sharply influenced by a work force's morale than by any other environmental factor.

Morale Factors

Many factors combine to determine the level of employee morale. Unhealthful working conditions, including the prevalence of communicable diseases, the lax enforcement of rules, poor communications, and a feeling among employees that no one is interested in listening to sincere complaints or in improving the conditions that give rise to them—all are contributors to low morale.

Let us take a look at some of the specific facets of business life that (1) affect morale, or (2) are affected by the level of morale that exists in an organization.

Employee Needs and Wants. Management must remember that an employee's needs and wants are extremely important to him and that he will not continue working in a company where they are not satisfied. *Basic human needs* such as food, clothing, and shelter; *social needs* such as friendly contact with people and acceptance by others; *egoistic needs* such as independence, recognition, and achievement—all these are "translated" into specific employee *wants* on the job. Examples of such translated wants include, among others, adequate pay, friendly co-workers and supervisors, a job with opportunities for promotion, and sincere compliments for a job well done. In the early days of business operation, little attention was given to employee needs and wants. Today the effective manager is aware that they must be determined and that steps must be taken to ensure their satisfaction. He knows that employee satisfaction is absolutely essential if morale is to be maintained at high levels and if the worker is thereby to be motivated to do a good job.

Health Programs. Because an employee who does not feel well is an unproductive worker, larger companies today maintain extensive on-the-premises health services. Besides working physically, this works psychologically to keep a healthy work force on the job. Employees come to feel that management is interested in their physical well-being and is making a genuine attempt to provide needed health services—and thus they are happier and more productive.

We have already noticed that the physical examination is an important consideration at the time of employment. But the physical is only the beginning of the ideal continuing health program. A complete health program (usually found only in the larger companies) provides for first aid, dental services, optical needs, mass X-rays and inoculations, periodic physical examinations, and even psychological and psychiatric counseling. Attention is also given to proper sanitation and lighting, adequate heat and ventilation, safety, and industrial hygiene. Since approximately 2 percent of a worker's productive time is lost because of illness, and since illness is responsible for about 8 percent of all permanent separations from the labor force, the need for an adequate health program can easily be seen.

Safety. A poor safety record in any organization is extremely bad for employee morale. It results in increased costs of operation and in substantially reduced efficiency. Accidents may result in physical injury to employees, or in damage to machines and supplies, to the physical plant, or to raw materials and products of the plant. Injuries on the job cause lost time not only by the injured but also by other employees, who invariably gather to discuss the details. And an on-the-job accident that results in the death of an associate, needless to say, lowers employee morale greatly.

Accurate figures on the frequency of industrial accidents are difficult to obtain, owing to the lack of uniformity in reporting accidents to state authorities. Usually, the only accidents that are reported are those that result in a loss of time greater than the shift during which they occur, and in some states only accidents for which compensation is paid are reported. Figures on costs of accidents are sometimes meaningless because of the lack of uniformity in computing such costs. It has been said that the true costs of an accident are like an iceberg; most of them are hidden below the surface and are discovered and measured only through extensive study. Examples of such hidden costs are time spent by management in compiling information and reporting the accident, loss of productive efficiency, work that spoils owing to loss of production time, and costs of training new workers. In spite of the difficulty in obtaining accurate figures concerning industrial accidents, we do know that approximately 2 million work injuries occur every year, of which one in 20 results in permanent total disability, and one in 23 in permanent partial disability. We also know that the annual cost of industrial accidents is probably in excess of $5 billion. Accidents represent a tremendous loss of time and money that must be either absorbed by the company or passed on to the consumer as part of the cost of the article manufactured. In either event, it can be seen that it is to the advantage of both the business and the public to prevent industrial accidents.

For the purpose of working out preventive techniques and procedures, many investigators have undertaken research studies to determine the causes of industrial accidents. They have classified into two distinct types the many factors that contribute to industrial accidents: first, the personal characteristics and attitudes of workers; and second, the impersonal factors—technical deficiencies in the work environment. Personal deficiencies include lack of knowledge on the part of the worker, improper attitudes, physical defects, reckless indifference to danger, and so forth. Technical deficiencies include inadequate lighting and ventilation, poor design of equipment, improper material-handling techniques, ineffective safeguards on machinery, and others. However, it is significant to personnel management that four out of every five accidents are caused by personal rather than technical deficiencies.

An effective safety program involves establishing safety standards and policies, conducting safety inspections, utilizing up-to-date engineering techniques to assure that equipment and working conditions are satisfactory, educating the workers to become safety-conscious, and enforcing safety rules and regulations. Some of the techniques used by modern firms in safety education and enforcement are records of injuries, posters, the plant magazine, individual and group conferences, films, training in the use of fire equipment, and manuals that include safety rules and penalties for infractions. Some companies conduct safety contests, rewarding workers whose records indicate that they are observing safety rules and regulations.

Workmen's compensation laws give a company a financial incentive to maintain safe working conditions. A company with a high accident rate or a poorly run safety program must pay higher premiums for its workmen's compensation insurance coverage than one with a good safety program or a good record.

Absenteeism. The term *absenteeism* refers to the failure (whether voluntary or involuntary) of a worker to be present at his assigned place of work as scheduled. It should be remembered that according to this widely accepted definition, tardiness is also a form of absenteeism. Studies show that there is a close relationship between absenteeism and unrest; excessive absenteeism is an indication of low morale, whereas high morale results in a lower rate of absenteeism.

Management sometimes uses the rate of absenteeism as an indication of the level of morale. If an employee who is eligible to work 25 days during a month fails to work on three of these days, his absentee rate would be 3 ÷ 25, or a rate of 12 percent. By utilizing this same method, the rate of absenteeism for a department or an entire firm could be computed. Rates are sometimes computed for various groups of employees according to age, sex, level of job, and so on. Such analyses make it much easier to determine causes for absenteeism.

The rate of absenteeism varies from one industry to another and from peacetime to wartime. It also varies with age, length of service, status of health, and sex. There are several significant factors that contribute to absenteeism. Illness and personal injury account for approximately 50 percent of all justifiable absenteeism. The search for other employment, home-related duties, poor job attitudes, poor working conditions, poor housing, the lack of adequate transportation and child-care facilities, and other factors contribute significantly to a high absenteeism rate.

Excessive absenteeism frequently indicates that an employee has been improperly selected or placed, instead of being in a job he can perform well. And from the high frequency of illness and personal injury as causes for absenteeism, it can be seen that effective measures to improve the health and safety of workers tend to reduce absenteeism. Management has only recently discovered that attempts to get at the causes of absenteeism are far more effective in reducing the rate than are penalties imposed on "absence-prone" employees.

Labor Turnover. The phrase *labor turnover* refers to the movement of employees into and out of employment in an organization. The most commonly used measure is the *net labor turnover rate,* which represents the number of replacements per hundred workers—that is, the number of employees who are hired to fill positions left vacant by separations. A firm that has an average work force of 100 and has to replace five men who have quit and five who have been discharged would have a net labor turnover of (5 + 5/100), or 10 percent.

Naturally, an excessive labor turnover is to be avoided. It is undesirable for a variety of reasons; the fact that it is very expensive is but one. It must be analyzed carefully and its causes corrected. Several of the more important causes of turnover are marriage, transfer of spouse to another community, "raiding" by a competitor, retirement, poor working conditions, inadequate supervision, poor pay and promotional opportunities, and poor selection and placement procedures. Turnover rates vary with the workers' degree of skill—unskilled workers show higher turnover rates than semiskilled and skilled workers.

Grievances. *Grievances* are the complaints, discontents, or dissatisfactions existing when workers feel they have been done an injustice. Even though the company management may not be at fault, adequate consideration must be given to employee grievances. A grievance may involve a single individual, a group of workers, or all the workers in the plant. The grievance procedure established in the contract between management and labor spells out the steps to be taken in settling an employee grievance. This topic and its place in the labor agreement are discussed in detail in Chapter 11, Labor–Management Relations.

Discussion Question

13. *Why is a high absenteeism rate considered to be an indication of low morale?*

SUMMARY

Personnel is generally considered to be the most important and most valuable asset of any business, and the directing and coordinating of employees is a most important function. It costs time and money to interview, hire, and train new workers, and the most costly training is that of ''learning on the job through trial and error.'' The personnel department is concerned with all the different aspects of workers—health and physical safety, mental attitude, relations with others, employee morale, and welfare.

Employee compensation is also the concern of the personnel department. Production sharing differs from profit sharing in that it represents a sharing of savings that result from lower product costs. The personnel department must see that workers' potential is developed fully, for their own benefit as well as that of the company. When a transfer is needed it should be arranged. When a promotion is deserved it should be forthcoming. In fact, employee benefits and services are probably more in the limelight today than ever before.

VOCABULARY REVIEW

Match the following vocabulary terms with the statements below.

a. Absenteeism	f. Job analysis	k. Profit sharing
b. Apprenticeship training	g. Job description	l. Promotion
c. Aptitude test	h. Morale	m. Transfer
d. Discharge	i. Piece wages	n. Turnover
e. Fringe benefits	j. Production sharing	o. Vestibule training

1. Studying a work position to see what types of work activities are involved
2. A written statement of the various components that constitute the chief activities performed at a given work station
3. A type of test that assesses a person's special talents or ability to perform acceptably in a specific area
4. A formal training program that combines classroom instruction and experience on the job
5. A scheme of formal training in a situation that resembles one's performance role in the actual work situation
6. A compensation formula that is based on the quantity of a given commodity one produces
7. A compensation plan that provides extra remuneration for workers beyond their basic pay schedules
8. A wage-payment scheme closely tied to increased earnings that apparently result directly from savings in production expenses
9. A group of employee values or services other than direct monetary payments
10. Increasing one's responsibility and the importance of his position
11. Shifting an employee to a new and different type of work station without a significant change in the level of his work
12. A permanent separation from the work force, initiated by the employer
13. The attitudes and feelings of workers toward their company and their work situations
14. Failure on the part of employees to report for work
15. The rate of change of employees in an organization

PROBLEMS AND PROJECTS

1. Assume that you are to interview five young women who are applying for two openings in secretarial positions with your company. (a) What types of questions would you ask them during the interview? (b) What types of information would you want to give them?
2. If you were developing a suggestion-awards plan for a factory that manufactures electrical appliances, what aspects or factors would you include in your plan?
3. Assume that the number of persons voluntarily leaving your company has increased greatly in recent weeks. Your company is competitive salary-wise in your community, so what might be the various causes of this turnover, other than wage rates?

BUSINESS CASES

Case 9-1 Merit Ratings

The management of the Walton Corporation has decided to institute a formal merit-rating scheme for all factory workers, all office employees, all supervisors, and all those in the lower echelons of management.

1. In which of these categories would you recommend the use of each of the following?

   a. Self-ratings
   b. Peer ratings
   c. Superiors' ratings

2. Prepare a list of criteria that might be used in evaluating the factory workers' attitudes and performance.

Case 9-2 Management Incentives

The Gilmore Corporation has been unable to retain its top-management personnel because there are no extra incentives in their compensation plan. The top managers are paid good salaries but complain that too much of it is taxed away from them. Under consideration by the board of directors is the idea of introducing a stock-option purchase plan.

1. How do stock-option plans work?

2. What is the tax-saving feature in such plans?

3. Why should this benefit not be extended to the entire work force?

4. As a stockholder, how do you feel about such plans?

PART THREE

*operating
problems
of the enterprise*

organized
labor

CHAPTER TEN

Almost everybody ultimately becomes part of the total labor force in this country, and many persons join labor unions. The fact that most of us spend about half our waking hours at work makes the subject of labor more meaningful. Labor unions are definitely a part of American capitalism, and what happens to union members affects the economic stability and efficient use of our resources.

Some observers feel that labor unions are now approaching the most critical period of their existence—that having largely achieved the social objectives of improving wages, working conditions, and hours of work, unions should direct more of their efforts to improving the broad areas of social problems, working in partnership with business and government.

In this chapter we shall discuss the labor movement and how it has altered the economy and the business climate. In order to do this, we must understand something of the history of labor unions, their objectives, and the methods they have employed to achieve these objectives.

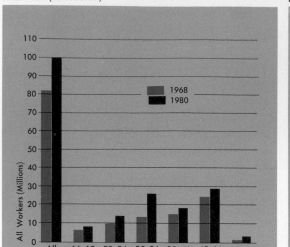

SHAPE OF THE LABOR FORCE, 1968 (ACTUAL) AND 1980 (PROJECTED)

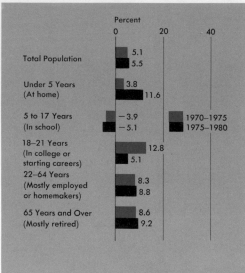

PROJECTED RATES OF CHANGE IN POPULATION, BY AGE GROUPS

Sources: Bureau of Labor Statistics; Bureau of the Census; National Consumer Finance Association

THE LABOR FORCE

By the end of 1972, there were slightly more than 88 million people of working age in the United States, and this number was expected to exceed 100 million by 1980, owing largely to population growth.

Although the rate of increase between 1970 and 1980 will be close to that of the 1960 decade, when 14 million were added to the labor force, the proportion of the different age groups within the labor force will differ sharply from that in the sixties.

In the first place, during the coming decade the teen-age labor force will grow much more slowly. Instead of a yearly gain of almost a quarter of a million, there might be an average annual gain of only 100,000. The group 20 to 24 years old will also increase at a lesser rate than in the 1960's, so that the workers under 25 will no longer be the group with the most rapid growth rate.

Second, the number of persons aged 25 to 34 will increase at a dramatic rate during the next ten years, growing by 800,000 a year, compared with an average of 175,000 in the 1960's.

Third, another sharp change in the population pattern will appear in the group 45 to 54 years old. Here the rapid growth experienced in the 1960's will disappear entirely, and the number of workers may even decline slightly. For the broader age group 45 to 64, the average annual growth will be 150,000, about one-third as large as the average annual change between 1960 and 1970.

The changing pattern of population growth is the principal reason for these variations in labor-force growth from one decade to the next. For example, the sharp shift of greatest growth rate from those under age 25 to the group between 25 and 34 reflects the upward movement along the age scale

246

for the very large number of people born during the first ten years following World War II. Similarly, the lack of further increase during the 1970's in those aged 45 to 54 will occur primarily because of the low birthrate in the early 1930's. The growth in the labor force and distribution by age groups are shown in the two graphs at the top of page 246, opposite.

Approximately one-third of the total labor force are women. During the decade of the 1960's, the increase in the number of women workers exceeded the increase in the number of men workers. This may not be the trend, however, during the 1970's, for the big population increase will occur in ages 25 to 34, where—because of married women's family responsibilities—their labor-force participation rates are low compared with other ages.

The participation of married women in the labor force is shown in the accompanying graph.

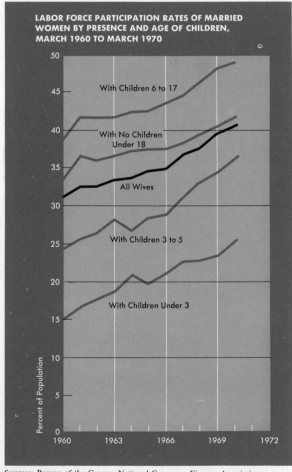

Sources: Bureau of the Census; National Consumer Finance Association

The Job Prospects for the Next Decade

White-collar workers, including office employees and those engaged in the professions, outnumbered the so-called blue-collar workers—those in the factories and on the farms—for the first time in 1956. Over the next decade, expectations are of a continuation of rapid growth in white-collar occupations, a slower growth in blue-collar occupations, a faster-than-average growth among service workers, and a further decline among farm workers.

The greater growth expectation for the number of white-collar jobs reflects the continued expansion anticipated for the service-producing industries; the growing demand for personnel capable of performing research in industry; the increasing needs for educational and health services; and a continuing growth in the amount of paperwork necessary in all types of enterprises. Although the number of blue-collar workers as a group will increase at a much slower rate than that of white-collar workers, the number of craftsmen will grow at about the same rate as total employment. Employment by major occupation groups is shown for selected years in Table 10.1 on facing page.

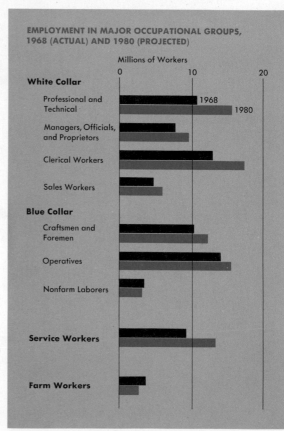

EMPLOYMENT IN MAJOR OCCUPATIONAL GROUPS, 1968 (ACTUAL) AND 1980 (PROJECTED)

Source: *American Vocational Journal*

TABLE
10.1
**EMPLOYED PERSONS BY OCCUPATION GROUPS,
SELECTED YEARS, 1960–1975**

In millions

Workers	1960	1966	1968	1969	1970	Projected 1975*
White-collar	28.5	33.1	35.5	36.9	38.0	42.8
Professional and technical	7.5	9.3	10.3	10.8	11.1	13.2
Managers, officials, and proprietors	7.1	7.4	7.8	8.0	8.3	9.2
Clerical workers	9.7	11.8	12.8	13.4	13.7	14.6
Sales workers	4.2	4.6	4.6	4.7	4.9	5.8
Blue-collar	24.1	26.9	27.5	28.2	27.8	29.9
Craftsmen and foremen	8.6	9.6	10.0	10.2	10.2	11.4
Operatives	12.0	13.8	14.0	14.4	13.9	14.8
Nonfarm laborers	3.5	3.5	3.5	3.6	3.7	3.7
Service	8.0	9.2	9.4	9.5	9.7	12.3
Private household workers	2.0	1.9	1.7	1.6	1.5	—
Other	6.0	7.3	7.7	7.9	8.2	—
Farm	5.2	3.7	3.5	3.3	3.1	3.0
Total employed	65.8	72.9	75.9	77.9	78.6	88.0

Source: Bureau of Labor Statistics.
Note: Parts may not add to totals due to rounding.
* Projected requirements.

Discussion Questions

1. *As you study the population shift by age groups now taking place, what types of consumer products do you think will be in greatest demand in the next decade?*
2. *How do you account for higher employment growth rates in clerical and service occupations than in numbers of factory workers?*

TYPES OF LABOR ORGANIZATIONS

There are two basic types of unions in the United States: craft unions and industrial unions. *Craft unions* are organizations of skilled workers engaged in various crafts or trades. All the members of a given craft union do the same kind of work. For example, there are craft unions for machinists, carpenters, painters, and plumbers.

Industrial unions are those that enroll all the workers in a given industry, rather than those in some special skill. They are not restricted to skilled workers; they also include semiskilled and unskilled workers. For example, workers in the automobile industry are represented by the United Auto Workers, in the clothing industry by the Amalgamated Clothing Workers Union, and in the mining industry by the United Mine Workers of America.

Local Union Organization

Each local union elects officers who manage the affairs of the local. Generally, there is a president, a vice-president, a secretary-treasurer, and perhaps an executive board. In addition, a shop steward is elected by the membership in a given shop or department of a plant. His chief union function is to settle grievances that arise between the union membership of that department and the foreman. The shop steward, as a rule, is paid by the company for his time spent in the plant. The business agent of the local union is a full-time paid member, employed by the local to serve as a walking delegate. He may not only perform the role of shop steward but participate in negotiation of new contracts. In most local unions, the two most important committees are the grievance committee, which works with management to settle complaints, and the negotiating committee, which is concerned with the terms of the contract.

HISTORY OF AMERICAN LABOR UNIONISM

The history of the American labor movement, which dates from the beginning of this country, is colorful and at times marked by violence. Even before the Declaration of Independence, skilled artisans in handicraft industries joined together in benevolent societies. Their primary purpose was to provide members and their families with financial assistance in the event of serious illness, debt, or the death of the wage earner. Although these early associations had little resemblance to present-day labor unions, they did bring workers together to consider problems of mutual concern and their solutions.

As early as 1790, there were small groups of craftsmen, such as printers, carpenters, and shoemakers, who banded together and formed unions they hoped would be permanent. These unions were largely confined to local areas and often proved to be poorly organized and lacking in financial strength.

Two factors accounted for their lack of stability. One was the reluctance of businessmen to recognize them as bargaining agents, and the other was the hostility and reluctance of the courts to give them legal status. Much of this resistance continued to exist until the 1930's, at which time federal legislation was enacted that gave the unions recognition.

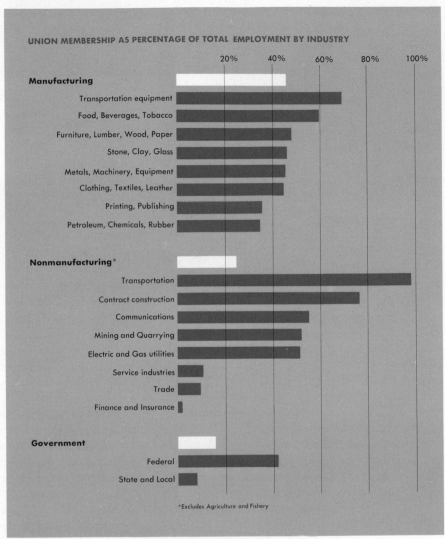

UNION MEMBERSHIP AS PERCENTAGE OF TOTAL EMPLOYMENT BY INDUSTRY

Manufacturing
- Transportation equipment
- Food, Beverages, Tobacco
- Furniture, Lumber, Wood, Paper
- Stone, Clay, Glass
- Metals, Machinery, Equipment
- Clothing, Textiles, Leather
- Printing, Publishing
- Petroleum, Chemicals, Rubber

Nonmanufacturing*
- Transportation
- Contract construction
- Communications
- Mining and Quarrying
- Electric and Gas utilities
- Service industries
- Trade
- Finance and Insurance

Government
- Federal
- State and Local

*Excludes Agriculture and Fishery

Sources: Bureau of Labor Statistics; The National Industrial Conference Board, Inc.

During the decade of the 1820's, despite several economic slumps, the unions continued to grow. Most unions were small locals, since progress in rapid communication had not yet been achieved. But the isolated locals soon learned that by pooling their resources and cooperating with one another, they could more effectively deal with employers and at the same time give help and support to locals in distress. In 1859, the machinists and blacksmiths formed locals as a part of a permanent national organization. Molders and printers also organized unions. By the end of the Civil War, a total of at least 32 national unions had been formed. Some of them still exist today, such as those of the carpenters, bricklayers, and painters. The purpose of these unions was always the same: to influence wages, obtain better working conditions, and achieve more satisfactory work rules throughout their trade.

The Knights of Labor

The first national union was actually the Noble Order of the Knights of Labor, which was founded as a local union of garment workers in Philadelphia in 1869. Seventeen years later, this union claimed more than 700,000 members throughout the United States. Internal conflict between those who favored employing the process of collective bargaining and those committed to political action and social change, together with a conflict of interests between skilled and unskilled workers, led to the weakening and dissipation of the Knights of Labor and thence to the formation of the American Federation of Labor.

The American Federation of Labor

The Federation of Organized Trades and Labor Unions was established in 1881 through the coming together of a number of craft unions. In 1886 another group of unions, which had previously been affiliated with the Knights of Labor, broke away from that group and joined with the unions in the federation. At that time, the organization adopted the name, American Federation of Labor (A.F. of L.). It was in truth a federation of affiliated autonomous groups. As an organization, it had little power over its sovereign units, but it did have the power to expel a union or a group of unions from membership. Historically, the A.F. of L. was predominantly a craft union, although some industrial unions were affiliated with it. Perhaps its most notable and powerful industrial union affiliate was the International Ladies' Garment Workers' Union. The affiliated unions found that by joining together into one organization, they commanded greater strength in securing favorable congressional legislation than by working separately.

Under the able leadership of its first president, Samuel Gompers, the A.F. of L. grew and prospered. Much of its appeal lay in its radical departure from the traditional philosophy of unionism. Previously, unions had been chiefly concerned with social objectives. Samuel Gompers led the A.F. of L. to emphasize the economic aspects of unions—what is known as *business unionism,* or "bread-and-butter unionism." The A.F. of L. can truly be said to have constituted the cornerstone of the organized labor movement in America.

For many years, the A.F. of L. followed a policy of neutrality in political activity. In addition to business unionism and nonparticipation in politics, Gompers strongly advocated the principle of the autonomy of each craft. He felt that this principle was inherent in forming a strong foundation for successful union growth and influence.

The Congress of Industrial Organizations

The A.F. of L.'s adherence to a policy of a single union for each craft led to the formation of a new labor organization, the Congress of Industrial Organization (C.I.O.). As American industry became more mechanized, there were increasing numbers of workers operating machines rather than following a trade or craft. Understandably, these men could not qualify for membership in the "trade" unions. So in 1935, the presidents of eight of the A.F. of L. unions formed what was called the Committee for Industrial Organization. Opposing the A.F. of L.'s emphasis on craft unionism, this new group wanted to organize large industries (such as rubber, steel, and automobiles) along the lines of industrial unionism. The feeling became so intense that in 1936, the unions that had associated themselves with the Committee for Industrial Organization were suspended from membership in the A.F. of L. This move resulted in the group's formation as a rival labor organization, which in 1938 adopted a name very much like their original one: the Congress of Industrial Organizations. During the following decade, by pushing the organization of workers in many fields that had not previously been organized, the burgeoning C.I.O. grew in power to the extent that it came to seriously compete with the A.F. of L.

Merger of A.F. of L. and C.I.O.

In the early 1950's, the leaders of these two rival organizations realized that the cause of organized labor would be greatly strengthened if they could join forces. So in December, 1955, the A.F. of L. and the C.I.O. unified the two federations into the AFL-CIO. Since that time, separate labor groups in particular areas—such as individual states—have come together into one group with one set of officers. Now four out of five labor unions are affiliated with the AFL-CIO.

The AFL-CIO is a voluntary federation of 121 national and international labor unions, which are in turn made up of 60,000 local unions. The AFL-CIO itself does no bargaining; it is not a union, but a federation of unions. The bargaining is done by representatives of individual unions or a collaboration of several unions. The AFL-CIO serves its constituent unions by:

1. Speaking for the whole labor movement before Congress and other branches of government
2. Representing American labor in world affairs through its participation in the International Labor Organization, a United Nations specialized agency, and through direct contact with the central labor organizations of free nations throughout the world
3. Helping to organize workers
4. Coordinating such activities as community services, political action, and voter registration

The preamble to the AFL-CIO constitution reads as follows:

The establishment of this Federation through the merger of the American Federation of Labor and the Congress of Industrial Organizations is an expression of the hopes and aspirations of the working people of America.

We seek the fulfillment of these hopes and aspirations through democratic processes within the framework of our constitutional government and consistent with our institutions and traditions.

At the collective bargaining table, in the community, in the exercise of the rights and responsibilities of citizenship, we shall responsibly serve the interests of all the American people.

We pledge ourselves to the more effective organization of working men and women; to the securing to them of full recognition and enjoyment of the rights to which they are justly entitled; to the achievement of ever higher standards of living and working conditions; to the attainment of security for all the people; to the enjoyment of the leisure which their skills make possible; and to the strengthening and extension of our way of life and the fundamental freedoms which are the basis of our democratic society.

We shall combat resolutely the forces which seek to undermine the democratic institutions of our nation and to enslave the human soul. We shall strive always to win full respect for the dignity of the human individual whom our unions serve.

With Divine guidance, grateful for the fine traditions of our past, confident of meeting the challenge of the future, we proclaim this Constitution.

Each member union affiliated with the AFL-CIO remains autonomous, conducting its own affairs, with its own officers and its own headquarters. It is free to withdraw at any time, but as long as it is affiliated it must observe the items stipulated in the AFL-CIO constitution.

The Independent Unions

Unions not affiliated with a labor federation are known as *independent unions*. Among the large and well-established unions that have not affiliated with the AFL-CIO is the United Federation of Electrical, Radio, and Machinists Workers of America. And the United Mine Workers of America, which is an industrial union, is not now affiliated with the AFL-CIO, although at one time or another it was associated with both the A.F. of L. and the C.I.O.

One of the large, powerful, and well-known independent unions is the International Brotherhood of Teamsters, commonly referred to as the Teamsters Union, which was formerly affiliated with the C.I.O. It was expelled from membership in the AFL-CIO in 1957 and is currently an independent union.

The United Automobile Workers Union, also independent now, was expelled from the AFL-CIO in the spring of 1968 for failure to pay dues to the federation.

There is currently speculation that both the Teamsters and the United Auto Workers may soon rejoin the AFL-CIO. Should this happen, it would, of course, greatly strengthen the position of organized labor in the United States.

The railroad brotherhoods—the Locomotive Engineers, the Locomotive Firemen and Enginemen, the Railroad Trainmen, and the Order of Railway Conductors—were organized shortly after the Civil War. They are recognized as among the most efficiently functioning unions in the country, and their conservative practices and strong discipline over their members have gained them great importance and prestige.

Union Membership

The economic prosperity that followed World War I, together with protective pro-union legislation during the 1920's and 1930's, brought about rapid growth in union membership. The greatest impetus to union growth was the passage of the Wagner Act in 1935. (See page 286.) During the ten-year period from 1935 to 1945, union membership increased fourfold, from fewer than 4 million to almost 15 million, and by 1956, had exceeded 18 million. The growth trend in union membership is shown in Table 10.2.

The degree to which workers in specific industries are organized varies greatly throughout the different regions and industrial groups in the United States. The most highly organized unions are those in the long-established industries such as transportation, in which are included the Teamsters, the railway unions, and the public transit unions. Contract construction, wherein the workers are organized on a craft basis, has signed up as union members almost all those who follow the construction trades.

The largest single union in the United States today is the International Brotherhood of Teamsters, which has more than 1.6 million members; the second largest is the United Automobile Workers, with 1.4 million members. The relative size of the ten largest unions in this country is shown in the accompanying bar graph.

When discussing union membership, we must remember that the hours, wages, and working conditions of many workers who are not union members are often shaped by the bargaining successes of the unions themselves. Whereas only slightly more than one-third of all "organizable" workers are actually union members, about half of all such workers are now covered by *collective* agreements.[1]

---

[1] A *collective* agreement is a written contract between the management of a firm and its workers as a group. Such agreements are discussed in the next chapter.

TABLE
10.2

LABOR UNION MEMBERSHIP, SELECTED YEARS, 1897–1968[a]

(In thousands)

Year	Total, all Unions	American Federation of Labor	Congress of Industrial Organizations[b]	Unaffiliated
1897	440	265		175
1900	791	548		243
1905	1,918	1,494		424
1910	2,116	1,562		554
1915	2,560	1,946		614
1920	5,034	4,079		955
1925	3,566	2,877		689
1930	3,632	2,961		671
1933	2,857	2,127		730
1935	3,728	3,045		683
1940	8,944	4,247	3,625	1,072
1945	14,796	6,931	6,000	1,865
1947	15,414	7,578	6,000	1,836
1953	17,860	10,778	5,252	1,830
1954	17,955	10,929	5,200	1,826
1955	17,749	16,062		1,688
1956	18,477	16,904		1,573
1957	18,431	16,954		1,476
1958	18,081	14,993		3,088
1959	18,169	15,124		3,044
1960	18,117	15,072		3,045
1961	17,328	14,572		2,756
1962	17,630	14,835		2,794
1963	17,586	14,818		2,768
1964	17,976	15,150		2,825
1965	18,519	15,604		2,915
1966	19,181	16,198		2,983
1967	19,712	16,638		3,074
1968	20,258	15,608		4,650

[a] Includes members outside the United States, primarily in Canada.
[b] Organized in 1938.
Source: AFL, 1897–1947, Proceedings *of conventions; 1953–60, Bureau of Labor Statistics,* Directories *of national and international labor unions in the United States. CIO, 1940–47, statements at conventions; 1953–60, BLS* Directories. *Unaffiliated unions, 1897–33,* Ebb and Flow in Trade Unionism, *by Leo Wolman, with 1930–33 adjusted to include membership in the Trade Union Unity League; 1935–47, BLS estimates; 1953–60, BLS* Directories. *Figures for 1955–68 reflect the merger of the AFL and CIO into a single federation.*

Discussion Questions

3. *How would you summarize in one sentence the contents of the preamble to the constitution of the AFL-CIO?*

4. *What would be the chief values of the return of the Teamsters Union and the United Auto Workers to the AFL-CIO?*

5. *What were some of the factors that caused the rapid growth in union membership between 1935 and 1945, and the leveling-off since 1960?*

FORCES THAT LEAD TO
UNIONIZATION

There are several factors that prompt members of the labor force to band together. Perhaps the most important ones, in our country at least, are the added strength that comes from an effective organization of large numbers working together and the advantages of having qualified negotiators in bargaining with employers.

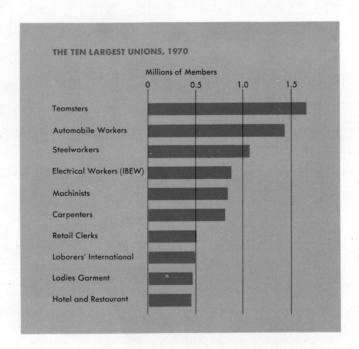

THE TEN LARGEST UNIONS, 1970

Strength of Numbers

An individual worker is at a decided disadvantage when he is dealing with the management of a large corporation. If his requests for better working conditions, shorter working hours, or higher pay are refused or only partially granted, there is little he can do. But when he unites with other workers like himself, the bargaining position of each of the members of the group is greatly strengthened. Whereas an employer might ignore the demands of an individual worker, he must take notice of those of his entire labor force.

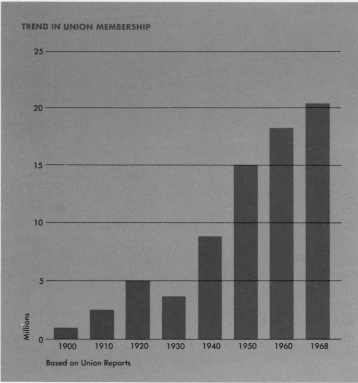

TREND IN UNION MEMBERSHIP

Millions

Based on Union Reports

Source: Bureau of Labor Statistics

Representation by Qualified Negotiators

Organization makes it possible for workers to select their own representatives. An individual worker may not feel qualified to argue his own case, but once he has joined with his fellow workers, he has the advantage of being represented by the most able persons in the group. In fact, local labor groups often make use of the services of experienced negotiators who are members or employees of the parent union but who are not members of the local group. These men have access also to legal counsel, research assistants, and other full-time staff members with expertise in labor negotiations.

Discussion Question

6. *What are the factors that cause workers to form labor unions?*

PRESENT OBJECTIVES
OF LABOR UNIONS

The greater benefits and advantages for their members that comprise the overall purpose of labor organizations include higher wages, shorter hours, better working conditions, and greater security. As the result of continued union pressure over the years, these objectives have been achieved with great consistency.

The Four-Day Workweek

The 40-hour workweek has been the accepted standard for many years now, with time and a half or even double pay for work time beyond the 40 hours. The further shortening of the workweek (without a corresponding decrease in pay) appears to be one of organized labor's chief long-term objectives. Recent talk by labor leaders suggests that a shorter workweek will rank high in future contract negotiations.

A good many manufacturing companies and service institutions, including textile companies, foundries, banks, hospitals, and police groups, have recently adopted a four-day workweek. Employees still work 40 hours, but they man a ten-hour shift for only four days. The management in several of these companies reports that output has been increased as a result. And the workers feel that the extra day off enables them to stand the pressures on the job better and make them more eager to get back to work at the beginning of the new week. This may become a popular work pattern in the immediate future.

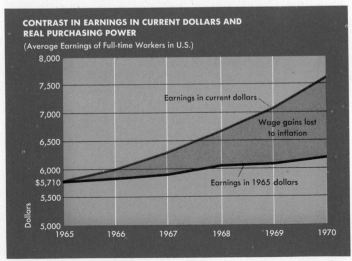

Source: U.S. Department of Commerce

TABLE
10.3
COST OF WEEKLY EMPLOYEE BENEFITS

Industry	Per Employee Per Week
All Industries	$39.46
Manufacturers:	
Petroleum industry	56.50
Chemicals and allied products	47.00
Primary metal industries	44.19
Transportation equipment	41.27
Food, beverages, and tobacco	41.21
Machinery (excluding electrical)	39.48
Printing and publishing	38.38
Stone, clay, and glass products	36.94
Electrical machinery, equipment, and supplies	36.13
Instruments and miscellaneous industries	34.84
Rubber, leather, and plastic products	34.58
Fabricated metal products (excluding machinery and transportation equipment)	34.31
Pulp, paper, lumber, and furniture	31.77
Textile products and apparel	23.04
Nonmanufacturing:	
Public utilities	$49.06
Miscellaneous nonmanufacturing industries (mining, transportation, research, warehousing, etc.)	42.67
Banks, finance and trust companies	41.75
Insurance companies	39.81
Wholesale and retail trade	24.96
Department stores	21.69

Fringe Benefits and Working Conditions

A second major consideration lies in the area of the continued improvement of working conditions within the plant. It is quite common to have local unions in individual plants continue on strike after a national settlement is reached in a major industry, such as automotive or electrical equipment manufacturing. The industry-wide bargaining brings about agreement on the major issues of wage rates, seniority recognition, pensions, paid holidays, and other fringe benefits. But specific provisions regarding sanitary conditions, rest periods, and other similar grievances vary considerably from plant to plant within a given industry. These are usually hammered out at the local level.

Nation's Business reported the cost of fringe benefits for selected industries as shown in Table 10.3 above.[2]

Union Strength and Political Activity

A third major objective of organized labor, and one that has become increasingly important in recent years, is the strengthening of the unions themselves. Unions have fought to gain recognition as the official representatives of all workers, and they have taken an active role in politics in order

[2] *Nation's Business,* September 1970, p. 85.

to win a more favorable position in the eyes of the government, the public, and business management. They are dedicated to unity and equality regardless of one's race, religion, color, creed, or political party.

A fourth major objective is a general membership concern with legislative, political, social, and civic matters. Union members are urged toward active participation, both directly and indirectly, in all such activities that concern their best interests as union members and as citizens.

Perhaps one good way to get a picture of the full scope of union objectives is to list the aims and purposes of the AFL-CIO as spelled out in its constitution. In summary, they are:

> To improve wages, hours, and working conditions for workers
>
> To bring the benefits of free collective bargaining to all workers
>
> To achieve equality of opportunity for all workers, regardless of race, creed, color, or national origin
>
> To support legislation that will aid workers and to oppose harmful legislation
>
> To protect and strengthen democratic institutions and to preserve America's democratic traditions
>
> To aid in promoting the cause of peace and freedom in the world
>
> To protect the labor movement against corruption and racketeers
>
> To safeguard the labor movement from Communists, fascists, and other totalitarians
>
> To encourage workers to register and vote and to exercise fully their responsibilities as citizens
>
> To encourage the sale of union-made goods through the use of the union label

Early Retirement and Sabbatical Leave

Among the newest benefits achieved by labor are early retirement and extended vacation leave. Employees in many companies may now retire at 60 or 62 and qualify at that time for their company pensions. Earlier retirement under Social Security has helped bring this about. Another benefit of a similar nature is the sabbatical leave. After a worker has been with a company a stated number of years, he is granted an extended vacation with pay for a period of from three to six months.

Discussion Questions

7. *What are the leading objectives of organized labor?*

8. *Which single goal of organized labor do you see as being of the greatest importance today? Why?*

9. *Do you think labor unions have much influence in government? Explain.*

THE POWER AND INFLUENCE
OF ORGANIZED LABOR

The labor movement in this nation has gained strength and momentum with the overall economic development of the country. In the early days of our business history, the labor force was entirely unorganized. The individual worker had little authority and was without any effective way to promote his own interest. During most of the century from 1785 to 1885 there was no real labor movement in the United States; large-scale organization of production was still in the future.

The trade-union boom of the early 1920's continued through the brief post-war prosperity period that followed. Contrary to what might be expected, however, the power and influence of labor as an organized group steadily declined during the period from 1930 to 1936. It was not until the second Roosevelt administration that American trade unions began to respond to the series of stimulants advanced by that administration. One of these stimulants was the passage of the National Labor Relations Act of 1935, better known as the Wagner Act.[3] The principal aim of this law was to strengthen organized labor's power to deal with employers. In 1938, the Fair Labor Standards Act was passed, establishing a minimum hourly wage for employees in certain industries.

Today the unions have vast power. And the right to strike has been one of organized labor's strongest weapons in achieving that power. Once a union wins a bona fide election, the recognition of that union as a bargaining agent for the workers is guaranteed by law.

The chart shown on page 257 reveals the relative size of some of our major unions. The Teamsters Union is far and away the largest and most powerful. Should the Teamsters call a nationwide strike, they would bring commerce to a standstill. The organization of all forms of transportation on a national basis has given this one union the awesome power to cripple the mightiest nation in history.

Now that big unions have grown into economic giants, with monetary powers equal to those of many large corporations, many people are asking this question: Have labor unions become monopolies, and should they be regulated in the same manner as business monopolies are?

Many serious observers think there is a need for firm governmental control over unions. They argue that making labor unions subject to the authority of federal antitrust and antimonopoly laws would be neither discriminatory nor punitive.

Legislative correction is not a simple matter of applying the antitrust laws to unions. Rather, it should involve the application of American principles of power dispersion to unions in a way that would safeguard the full benefits

[3] This act is discussed in Chapter 11, in the section dealing with labor legislation.

of collective bargaining and prevent any new form of bargaining inequality. The ultimate objective of any legislation of this kind would be to prevent either combinations of employers or combinations of unions from destroying our competitive system.

Since union negotiators bargain for whole groups of workers, thousands of individuals and their families have a vital interest in the results of labor–management negotiations. Everyone has a stake in these bargaining sessions: workers, management, and, indirectly, you as a consumer, because the price you pay for the finished product is affected by the cost of producing it. Our government is responsible for representing the American public and for achieving a peaceful and fair settlement of labor–management differences.

Idleness due to strikes in industry and business is costly to labor, management, and the public. Thus, it is to the advantage of everyone to settle labor–management controversies in order to avoid a work stoppage.

Discussion Question

10. *How did labor unions attain the great power they now seem to have?*

TYPES OF UNION SECURITY

Among the chief objectives of organized labor are the maintenance of unions' existence, their protection, and their security. Of course, laws have been passed to guarantee their right to exist, but they had to work hard to secure this protective legislation. Unions utilize various types of recognition in the form of different shop agreements to provide their security.

The Open Shop

An open-shop situation exists when there is no union and no effort on the part of management either to promote or to prevent the organization of one. Employees enjoy freedom of choice as to whether or not they wish to organize. In many such situations, there are some employees who are members of unions, and this makes the open shop an attractive target for union organizers.

The Simple-Recognition Shop

Under this type of agreement, some designated union has been recognized by the management as the rightful and exclusive bargaining agent of its employees. If more than 50 percent of the workers vote in favor of a specific union as their official bargaining agent, a simple-recognition shop exists. This union is recognized as the workers' bargaining agent for all employees for a period of at least twelve months, since the National Labor Relations Board will not hold recognition elections more often than once a year. Under this type of shop, all employees enjoy the benefits that result from the union–management negotiations.

The Agency Shop

A modification of the simple-recognition shop is the agency shop. Under this agreement, the nonunion employees as well as the union members pay union dues. The nonunion workers, however, do not participate in determining union policies, are not subject to disciplinary action by the union, and do not attend union meetings. Their payment of dues to the union is in return for the benefits they receive because of union negotiation with management.

The Preferential Shop

In the preferential shop, not only is the union recognized as the bargaining agent for all employees, but union members are given some preferences over nonmembers in certain areas of employment, and when new workers are employed, union members are given preference over nonmembers. In fact, when new workers are needed, the employer asks the union to supply them before he seeks to fill the positions in other ways. In some preferential shops, union members enjoy preferences over nonmembers in transfers and promotions, and are the last to be laid off. Because excessive preference for union members could, in reality, constitute a closed shop, which is forbidden by the Taft-Hartley Act, this type of shop setup is subject to close governmental scrutiny.

The Union Shop

The union shop is the type of union security most commonly found. It recognizes compulsory union membership on the part of all employees. The management of a business may employ anyone it desires, but he will be required to join the union within a stated period of time after he is employed. The Taft-Hartley Act provides a minimum of 30 days as the grace period prior to compulsory membership, but the Landrum-Griffin Act permits a minimum period of only seven days for workers engaged in the construction industry. The Bureau of Labor Statistics reports that of the contracts it has surveyed in recent years, almost three-fourths provide for the union shop.

The Closed Shop

Under this agreement, any new employee had to be a member of the union before being hired. In this way, the union was the only source of employment available to the employer. But the closed shop was declared illegal by the Labor Management Relations Act, passed in 1947, and no longer exists.

Discussion Question

11. *How do you feel toward the union shop? the closed shop? Do you favor them or not, and why?*

THE FUTURE OF ORGANIZED LABOR

The early 1960's brought a decline in union election victories. During the 1960's in the elections to determine whether unions would represent workers, the unions were selected as the bargaining agent less frequently than was true before 1950. Also, the size of the new worker groups that unions have been able to organize has been smaller.

The changing occupational and industrial pattern is unfavorable to employment in the older industries, in which unions have their most substantial foothold. As technology, competition of products and services, changing consumer demands, and rising labor productivity take their toll of employment, unions in older economic areas necessarily decline in size. Many unions have sought to offset the shrinkage by broadening their industrial coverage.

The Effects of Geographical Industrial Movement

Another disturbing trend has been the shift in industrial location from the East and Midwest, where unions have been strong, to the South and to smaller communities where unions still have only limited influence. Bargaining rights do not move with the plant. Unions have to start organizing drives at the sites of the new plants, and frequently find their task most difficult because of unfriendly local attitudes. Even where the national employment figure is maintained in a union's jurisdiction, the shift to unorganized areas represents a serious setback in immediate membership potential, and in cases where a decline in the size of the industry is combined with a change in its location, the impact can be severe.

Future expansion of union membership must come from organizing efforts outside existing frontiers. And the area that seems to offer the most substantial potential growth is the southern geographic region. If each of the industries that exist in the southern region were to be unionized to the same degree that they are in other regions, union membership would increase by more than 1.5 million. And this potential membership will be even greater as the South becomes more industrialized.

But the South is a region where there is a surplus of labor. Also, in some communities where significant efforts have been made to attract industry, the public attitude is not especially warm toward strong unionization of workers. Many of the industries in the South are relatively small in size, and the scope of their operations gives them a strong local flavor. In addition, many of the southern industrial operations are highly competitive. And the people of the South are traditionally resistant to change. All these factors combine to make the southern region one that is difficult to organize easily and rapidly.

White-Collar Unions

Because the ratio of blue-collar workers to white-collar workers has been declining, unions have put their major efforts toward organizing groups of white-collar workers. The teamsters and the auto workers unions have had good success in organizing workers in government, insurance, communications, and finance.

By 1970 almost 3 million office and professional workers were members of unions that were affiliated with the AFL-CIO. Almost one-tenth of the white-collar workers had become union members. Union membership among government employees increased 18 percent between 1964 and 1966.[4] And the number of public school teachers who are union members is increasing.

Criticisms of Labor Unions

Despite the ability of labor leaders to gain improvements for the plight of workers through shorter hours, higher wages, more fringe benefits, added collective-bargaining legislation, and so on, unions are constantly being criticized. Critics of labor contend they are a monopoly and should be subject to antitrust laws because of their tight regulations of union policies. They envision unions as uncontrollable, and periodically, persons who hold leadership positions in Congress and in industry speak out for legislation that would subject unions to more stringent regulation.

One of the strongest criticisms is that unions impair the operation of the price mechanism in labor markets to the detriment of the rest of the

---

[4]Dale Yoder, *Personnel Management and Industrial Relations,* 6th ed. Englewood Cliffs, N.J.: Prentice-Hall, Inc. 1970, p. 427.

economy. In addition, some unions, such as the Teamsters, have the capacity to affect adversely the lives of all our citizens by a work stoppage. And it has happened that certain industries have been permanently damaged by organized labor—as in the case of newspapers, which have greatly decreased in number, and in the number of people they employ, in recent years, largely because of the owners' alleged inability to meet union demands. All the unfavorable publicity in these areas has hurt the image of organized labor in the eyes of the public at large, and is undoubtedly an important deterrent to union growth.

The AFL-CIO and the Future

The AFL-CIO has this to say about organized labor and the future:[5] "The fundamental reason for the very existence of unions is in fact to help workers achieve a better life. That purpose will remain valid as long as there remain unachieved goals on the horizon, and as long as a single worker remains subject to unfair treatment.

"The AFL-CIO is committed just as firmly to the belief that union members can gain nothing of value at the expense of their fellow citizens, that 'what is good for America is good for labor.'

"The unachieved goals of labor and the nation are many—the complete eradication of the poverty that grips millions of people; a job at fair wages and a decent place to live for every American; fulfillment of democracy's promise of equal rights and equal opportunity for persons of every race and creed; full education for every youngster, with no ceiling except his own ability; adequate security against the hazards of illness and old age; and above all, the opportunity to live in a world where peace and freedom prevail.

"These are just the high-priority objectives, the immediate 'more' that labor is seeking. The AFL-CIO states that it will pursue them with the same determination, the same dedication to democratic principles that in the past have produced such gains as the basic Social Security program, the federal minimum wage, the elimination of child labor, and the highest living standard in the world for the American worker.

"Critics and enemies of organized labor have predicted its demise time and again over the past century, frequently claiming that collective bargaining was 'obsolete' or had 'outlived its usefulness.' These critics were proved wrong, and labor and the bargaining process not only survived but grew more vigorous.

"Today, organized labor faces new challenges in an increasingly complex industrial society. The AFL-CIO has stated its determination to meet these challenges with confidence in its ability to adjust to change, to respond to the needs and opportunities of the times, and to apply the pragmatic lessons of its history."

[5] *This is the AFL-CIO,* Publication No. 20, published by the American Federation of Labor and Congress of Industrial Organizations, November, 1969 revision, pp. 23 & 24.

SUMMARY

The labor force is made up of all persons over 16 years of age who are working or seeking work. It includes persons employed on farms, in the factories, and in the professions, and members of the armed forces. It is currently increasing at the rate of about 1.5 million persons per year.

The most rapid growth rates among various employed groups occur in the professions, technician jobs, service occupations, and clerical work.

Early attempts at organizing the labor force were largely ineffective, with social objectives as their motivational impetus. However, with the formation of the American Federation of Labor in 1886, a definite shift occurred, both in purpose and growth. Under the able leadership of A.F. of L. president Samuel Gompers, business unionism was the order of the day, with economic benefits for union members the chief objective.

The era of most rapid union growth occurred during the ten-year period following the passage of the Wagner Act in 1935, when union membership increased fourfold. Then in the early 1950's, the A.F. of L. and the C.I.O. merged. This strengthened labor considerably, and union membership jumped to 18 million by 1956.

The chief objectives of organized labor are increased pay—including additional economic fringe benefits—improved working conditions, and strengthening of the unions themselves.

Organized labor has become a way of life in America, and as a political force, labor has greater influence than ever before. As long as the principles of democracy flourish, and as long as there are persons earning less than the minimum income needed to escape the ''poverty level,'' labor unions will continue to thrive and be a potent influence on the many facets of American life.

VOCABULARY REVIEW

Match the following terms with the statements below.

a. Agency shop
b. Business unionism
c. Craft union

d. Independent union
e. Industrial union
f. Labor force

g. Open shop
h. Preferential shop
i. Union shop

1. The total of all persons employed and those looking for work, including members of the armed forces
2. A union whose members follow a particular trade
3. A union whose membership is open to all workers in a particular industry
4. Unionism that is concerned about the economic aspects of its members
5. A union that is not affiliated with a labor federation
6. A working situation in which there is no union but also no attempt being made to promote or prohibit the formation of a union
7. An arrangement whereby both the union and nonunion members of a given company's work force pay dues to the union
8. A situation in which union members are given preference over nonmembers when new workers are employed

9. A shop where all employees are union members—where nonmember workers may be employed but must join the union within 30 days

PROBLEMS AND PROJECTS

1. Study Table 10.1 which shows the employment trends for four groups. What implications does this have for counseling young people interested in making job choices?

2. The statistics regarding the current shifts in the labor force for different age brackets are supplied on page 246 of this chapter. What is their significance in terms of availability of manpower for middle-management positions, women in the labor force, and job opportunities for youth seeking employment?

3. The graph on page 259 shows the current trend in factory wages and the purchasing power of those wages. Does this show that the typical factory worker is relatively better off financially than he was a decade ago, or that he is not doing as well? Have the changes in cost of living been accounted for in this figure?

4. Name the various ways that nonunion labor benefits from the union membership of many other workers in any given industrial community.

BUSINESS CASES

Case 10-1 Prospects for Union Membership

Assume that you have been chosen by organized labor to launch a new campaign to gain union members in areas not yet highly organized. It has been suggested that office workers, farm laborers, municipal employees, and public school teachers are likely prospects.

1. Rank these groups in the order that you feel would be the easiest to organize. Give your reasons for thinking as you do.

2. Select one of these groups and explain what steps you would take to influence them to join a union.

Case 10-2 Union Growth and Expansion

It has been decided by union officials to make a push for new members in industries where unions already have a foothold but where one-third or more of the workers do not now hold union membership.

1. What fields of employment should be considered for this drive?

2. For each of the groups you mention in part 1, indicate how strongly your geographic region (include eight to twelve states) is organized: less than one-third of the possibilities, from one- to two-thirds organized, or more than two-thirds organized.

labor-
management
relations

CHAPTER ELEVEN

The working relationship between the management team and the workers in a business organization is very different today from what it was three decades ago. Labor unions have become strong by virtue of their large numbers, their able leadership, and their collective action. Workers today participate in company policy formulation to a much greater degree than most people realize.

Management and labor have strong common interests. The fruits of production are lost by both when there is a work stoppage. Both have a strong stake in the profits earned by the business and both insist that their contributions to the common cause be adequately recognized.

Employer and employees must work together to achieve their common goals and satisfy their mutual interests. Their efficiency and output, and consequently their standard of living and other rewards, are significantly determined by the degree to which they work in an atmosphere of mutual cooperation, confidence, and respect. Both management and labor agree that they are mutually dependent on each other. The differences between them, however, arise over appraising the comparative value of their efforts in the operation of the business, and therefore the extent to which each should be rewarded financially.

The public and its representatives, governments, benefit from peaceful cooperative working relations in industry. Increased productivity means lower unit costs and more benefits for consumers. And the more a business earns, the more income the government receives from the taxes it pays. When productive endeavor comes to a halt, everyone loses. It is when the issues between management and labor can be resolved cooperatively that the nation's resources are utilized most economically.

In this chapter we shall look at some of the ways in which labor and management work together and some of the ways they combat each other. We shall examine the techniques used by labor to gain concessions and the countermeasures used by management. We shall consider the bargaining process and the important elements of formal agreements between labor and management. We shall also look at the role of the government in helping to settle disputes between labor and management, and at some of the key legislation that has been enacted by Congress and the states.

COLLECTIVE BARGAINING

One of the most important functions of labor organizations is *collective bargaining,* a process by which labor representatives bargain with management over the terms and conditions of labor contracts, or agreements. It is called collective bargaining because labor acts collectively—that is, as a group. (Employers also may act collectively.)

Collective bargaining was developed over a period of time as a method of utilizing democratic procedures in employer–employee relationships. The individual exercises his voice in the bargaining process through his union representatives. He shares with his fellow workers and with his employer the responsibility for agreeing on orderly, established bargaining procedures—procedures for determining working conditions, practices to be used in promotions and layoffs, and penalties for violation of the work rules.

How the Process Functions

A union becomes the bargaining agent for a group of workers when the employer agrees that it represents the majority of them. Most commonly, this is determined by a secret vote conducted by the National Labor Relations Board. If a clear majority of the workers involved indicate a desire to be represented by the union, then that union is "certified" as the collective-bargaining agent for the employees.

Representatives of the union and of management then meet together at the bargaining table and try to reach agreement on a contract. Rarely are the two sides in agreement when they begin their meetings, and rarely is the final product of their deliberations precisely what either side wanted when they started. The first meeting between labor and management negotiation teams usually establishes rules, policies, and schedules for future meetings. Sometimes at this first meeting the representatives of labor formally present their specific proposals for changes in the existing labor agreement. At succeeding meetings, management submits counterproposals. Both groups seek opportunities to suggest compromise solutions in their favor until an agreement is reached.

Collective bargaining is a matter of give and take, with labor and management gradually moving closer together. When union and management representatives have finally agreed on a contract, the union representatives take the contract back to their members. If it does not satisfy the members, they may send their representatives back to continue the bargaining process or they may decide to reinforce their demands by going on strike.

If labor and management find it impossible to come to an agreement, a third party may be brought in from the outside. This might be a governmental or a private mediator, or a mediation team.

Once the contract has been ratified by the union and by the management, it becomes the guiding principle of labor-management relations for the duration of the agreement. All collective agreements run for a specific period of time, usually from one to three years. Months before an agreement is to terminate, representatives of both management and labor sit down together to negotiate terms for a new contract.

Generally, collective agreements cover the workers in a single plant or the workers of a single company that has several plants. The idea of collective bargaining is an accepted procedure in American industry today. In fact, many employers prefer to bargain with labor collectively rather than as individuals.

There are more than 150,000 collective agreements in force in the United States today. On the average, 300 such agreements are concluded every day.

Variety of Patterns

The precise form of collective bargaining varies considerably from one industry to another, depending largely upon the nature of the industry.

Local-Market Bargaining.   One pattern of bargaining occurs mainly in the local market. The building construction industry is an example of this type of bargaining, for building contractors operate essentially in a local market. The work must be done where it is needed, unlike the kinds of manufacturing that can easily be moved from one city to another. Since their product is not transportable, building contractors are competitive in the local market area only. Bargaining takes place between various local unions of construction workers and the local trade association of contractors. These local unions have a great deal of autonomy in bargaining, and no attempt is made by their international unions to impose a uniform pattern of wages or working conditions.

Retail food stores and newspaper publishers are similarly competitive on a local market only, and therefore collective bargaining is customarily done at the local level.

Industry-wide Bargaining. The women's apparel industry is a good example of one in which manufacturers compete over a nationwide market. Most of the companies are small-scale producers requiring relatively little capital investment, and labor accounts for a major part of the cost of the finished product. An increase of just a few cents in labor costs may well make the difference between financial success and bankruptcy for an employer.

For this reason, the union and the employers found out long ago that effective collective bargaining in this industry requires the negotiation of collective agreements between the union and an association of competing employers. In this way, the individual garment manufacturer knows that granting new benefits to his workers will not prove financially ruinous to him, because his competitors will be granting the same benefits.

Bargaining with the Corporate Giants. Other industries that operate throughout the country are dominated by huge enterprises with capital assets running into the billions of dollars. The automobile industry is an example of this type. The pattern of collective bargaining employed here is completely different from that used in the textile trade. Let us use the General Motors Corporation as our illustration.

Workers in each General Motors plant belong to their own local union of the United Automobile Workers. Each of these locals is part of the UAW's General Motors Council, and it is this council that negotiates a collective-bargaining agreement with General Motors. Purely local issues are left to be settled in separate negotiations between the local unions and the local plant managers, but the basic structure of collective bargaining is determined nationally. What is more, having reached agreement with General Motors, the union must then press for similar benefits from Ford and Chrysler; otherwise General Motors would be at a competitive disadvantage because of the benefits to which it had agreed in collective bargaining with the union.

Coalition Bargaining. Organized labor favors coalition bargaining because it tends to strengthen bargaining lines where they are weakest—among small and weak unions. In *coalition bargaining,* several different unions within a given industry will collaborate in bargaining with an employer.

An outstanding example of union success in coalition bargaining occurred in 1966. The General Electric Company had historically insisted on bargaining separately with each individual union. However, in the summer of 1966, eleven different electrical unions—all affiliated with the AFL-CIO—formed an alliance, cutting across union jurisdictions to bargain as a group with General Electric. The largest and strongest of the eleven unions, the International Union of Electric Workers, took the lead in the negotiations. The AFL-CIO backed the negotiation team by pledging a sum of $8 million to carry out the negotiation effort. It employed a nationwide network of teletype stations in strategic cities to keep union members informed and in line. Although the General Electric management at first resisted the idea of coalition bargaining, in the end it settled with the coalition group.

Discussion Questions

1. *What are some of the common interests and concerns of employers and employees?*
2. *Describe the procedure normally followed in collective bargaining.*
3. *What are the advantages to employers in bargaining with workers collectively?*
4. *How does coalition bargaining strengthen labor's position in contract negotiations?*

THE BARGAINING AGREEMENT

The written labor agreement as we know it today is a peculiarly American phenomenon. It first appeared in the late 1930's, during the time when unions in such industries as rubber, steel, and automobile manufacturing were organized. Before then, labor agreements, which existed principally in the railroad and printing industries, were abbreviated, generalized agreements that left working rules to informal arrangements. Under such generalized agreements, neither party was inclined to curtail its flexibility by agreeing to detailed clauses. Management wanted most to have the freedom to manage and operate without hindrance from the union, while the union wanted to be free to seize any opportunity to make gains for its members.

Today, the trend is for both parties to spell out every possible detail, so that any dispute that may arise is covered by the contract. Negotiating an agreement now often takes many months of give-and-take negotiation, reflecting union demands and employer resistance. Since agreements are all-inclusive contracts, they generally cover a wide range of topics and conditions, and range from a few pages in length to a hundred or more. Labor agreements are expected to:

1. Indicate clearly the classification of workers to be included and those to be excluded under the terms
2. Spell out detailed rights and duties of the parties concerning working hours, wage rates, overtime, promotions, layoffs, transfers, management prerogatives, and work scheduling

3. Provide machinery for settling grievances and arbitration

4. Define procedures for renewing the agreement

Most contracts stipulate work assignments, in order to avoid jurisdictional disputes that occur when there is a question about whether certain work should be performed by employees in one bargaining unit or by those in another. Such issues as the subcontracting of work outside the union and the automation of mechanical processes are highly controversial subjects that require lengthy negotiations leading up to a collective bargaining agreement. Wage increases are a complex issue, often resolved only after a strike. And there are always many questions apart from wages, such as these:

1. Should the employer contribute toward the health plan, or should he put the money into improving the retirement plan?

2. Should seniority lists be made up by departments or by job classifications, or should they be plant-wide?

The factors that are generally included in labor agreements are summarized in the following boxed list.

Wage rates and wage payment policies	Selection, promotion, and layoff procedures
Normal workday or workweek	Production standards
How overtime is to be calculated	Seniority—the degree it is to be recognized and how it is to be determined
Time to be taken for meals, regulations for making up lost time, working on holidays	Transfer of workers to new job assignments
Working conditions—rest periods, restroom facilities, safety rules and devices, medical care to be furnished	Employment practices for using temporary workers
Vacations, leaves of absence, holidays, paid holidays; when vacations are to be taken; how the length of vacations varies with length of service	Welfare payments
	Grievance procedures
	Strikes and lockouts
	Length of the agreement and when it is to terminate

In European countries, labor agreements place fewer limitations on the rights of management; therefore, many subjects covered in the American labor-union bargaining agreement are not contained in European labor contracts. In France there is little sharing of values between management and workers. Management is seldom challenged by French union leaders over such matters as automation, transfers, or contracting work to outside parties who are not members of the union. In England, France, and West Germany, labor supports a political party that aspires to widespread economic and social goals through legislation rather than by collective bargaining. This is one reason why some European countries provide a broader program of health care to all workers than we have at present in the United States. In Japan, unions function more like American than like European unions.

Grievance Procedures

One of the essential provisions of any collective agreement is that of the grievance procedures through which disputes can be adjudicated. Grievance procedures vary considerably, depending upon the nature of the industry involved, but they always involve a method by which the individual worker can process a complaint through his union. Usually there are three steps. The first step involves the local union steward and the union foreman or supervisor; if they cannot agree, the next step involves the union grievance committee and the next higher supervisor; and the third step is to appeal to the plant manager for his decision. If the grievance is not settled to the satisfaction of both parties, it goes to arbitration. Sometimes there are four steps in the grievance procedure, for the shop steward is nearly always involved in a grievance. The final appeal in most contracts today is by the company and the union to an impartial arbitrator who, after hearing the evidence from both sides, issues a decision that is binding and legally enforceable for both sides. His decision is based not upon what he thinks may be wise and just, but upon how he understands the language of the contract to apply to the case at hand. He relates the case to the contract, just as a judge relates a case to the law. This is voluntary arbitration, a procedure written into the contract.

Discussion Questions

5. *Enumerate the items that are normally covered in a labor contract.*
6. *How are workers' complaints handled before they reach the arbitration stage?*

RELATIONSHIPS BETWEEN MANAGEMENT AND UNIONS

As unions gained the legal support necessary to allow them to organize and bargain, employers began to react in different ways. For example, some firms took militant stands and evoked militant union leadership in response. In other cases, militant union leadership prompted militant employer leadership in response. Where firms took a moderate view of the unions, not infrequently moderate union leadership emerged.

Labor as Cost or Partnership in Production?

How should we classify labor? Is labor one of the costs of production, or are workers partners in production? At one time, labor was regarded as a commodity, to be bought as cheaply as possible and paid for in economic terms only. Traditionally, labor is considered to be one of the economic resources necessary for production.

Here is a basic difference of opinion between labor and employer. After the materials have been purchased, the workers must be paid; but the higher the labor costs, the less there is left as profit for owners. Naturally, management is interested in hiring workers at the lowest figure. So there is a tendency for management to regard labor as a cost of doing business, a cost that should be kept as low as possible, just like other costs. On the other hand, in a quasi-partnership role. Management argues that unions tend to ignore the principle that wage rates cannot be higher than the value of the job's contribution to the business and wages cannot drop below the amount competing firms pay. The bargaining, therefore, takes place between these two limits.

Risk and the Return on Investment

There is little argument in the matter of risk. Labor seldom has capital funds invested in the business enterprise. If the business fails, the owners stand the loss. So owners are entitled to a payment representing an interest return on their investment. In addition, ownership is entitled to payment for the risk taken—the original investment might be lost. But no one seems to know what represents a fair return for risk and investment. Labor philosophy of the more abstract variety has expressed the idea that the employees of a company invest a good amount of their lives in it, and that human life is at least as valuable as money.

Labor holds the point of view that after fees for management have been paid and the owners have received a "reasonable return" on their investment, the workers should share in any excess profits. Management, however, sees these profits as rewards for risk and for initiative and ideas in administration. In general, management does not see any percentage figure as constituting a "fair return" for risk and investment. Rather, the accepted view is that one is entitled to as much profit as the traffic will bear—as much profit as the competition will allow.

One of the basic problems here is that it is difficult to determine the degree to which profits are the direct result of labor and the extent to which they result from the contributions of management.

Participation in Decision Making

The prevalent view among owner–managers is that decision making regarding the running of a business is an inherent right of ownership. They agree that workers should be paid reasonable wages and provided with good working conditions. However, they hold that the right to hire and supervise workers and otherwise manage business operations is the right of management.

In contrast, organized labor feels that the workers should be represented in at least certain types of decision making. One point on which labor maintains a strong position has to do with modernization techniques, especially those that automate mechanical operations. These usually reduce the number of workers needed to perform routine tasks and operate the machines. Labor also feels it has a legitimate stake in decisions pertaining to employment, transfer, promotion, seniority rights, and the discharge of workers. There is increasing evidence that more and more unions want authority to participate in management decisions, planning, scheduling, and operating the business. Managers are resisting this pressure from unions.

These basic differences in attitudes on the part of management and organized labor sometimes lead to serious conflicts. When negotiation breaks down, labor may go out on strike in order to reinforce its bargaining position.

There has emerged in this country a public policy toward the unionization of workers that protects them against many forms of coercion, by either employers or union officials, as they choose the unions that are to serve as their representatives. This policy has been established through laws passed by the federal government. The Labor Study Group appointed by the Committee for Economic Development gave its support to this principle of self-determination because it extends into employer–employee relationships a procedure that is basic to democratic values. It helps avoid an undesirable alternative: a decision for or against collective bargaining based solely on an employer's or union's power to coerce.

Bargaining Pressures Used by Labor

In collective bargaining, union negotiators try to secure the highest possible price in terms of wages, fringe benefits, and working conditions, in return for the services of their union members. Unions have developed several devices to help win their objectives. The principal weapons used by them are *picketing,* the *boycott,* and the *strike.* In the following paragraphs we shall look at these techniques.

Picketing. Picketing has proved to be one of labor's most effective techniques in winning concessions from management. Union members carrying banners and placards that announce their complaints against the management are stationed at each entrance to a business or industrial establishment. The purpose is to inform the public of their case and to enlist sympathy and support. Picketing's greatest effectiveness is in cutting down the available labor supply by preventing union men from reporting for work. In addition to members of the union directly concerned, members of closely allied unions may respect the picket line and also refuse to report for work. If the employer hires non-union workers to do the work of the striking union men, associated unions will sometimes refuse to work even if they did not respect the picket line originally.

Boycott.   The boycott is an attempt on the part of a union to restrict the patronage of a business firm by influencing people not to do business with the firm. In the *primary boycott,* employees of the firm refuse to buy from their employer. Obviously, this is effective only when the amount of their patronage is significant.

A *secondary boycott* occurs when a union that is seeking concessions from the employer (Company A) places pressure on another firm (Company B) in an effort to get the second firm to influence the worker's employer, or tries to get the public to avoid Company A's product. The idea here is to influence customers of Company A to refuse to do business with the company unless the union's demands are met. The purpose is to threaten Company A with the possible loss of business from one or more of its best customers. In some instances, the pressure by the union takes the form of a strike, or the threat of a strike, against Company B. This tactic is usually used where the union is already recognized by Company B and it is attempting to organize the workers of Company A.

The secondary boycott is defined as an unfair labor practice by one of the provisions of the Taft-Hartley Act. However, it is often difficult to determine whether a threatened strike is truly a secondary boycott. Therefore, it continues to be one of the weapons used by labor.

Strike.   When all other devices fail, a union may decide to go out on strike. Although there are many different kinds of strikes, the net effect is always the same: The workers refuse to work until their demands are met or a compromise is reached. Either a partial or a complete work stoppage results. Most strikes are called by unions to back up their demands for increases in wages, shorter hours, recognition of the union as the bargaining agent, improved working conditions, and job security. Whatever the ultimate outcome of a strike, the workers lose their weekly pay and business costs are increased. Both business and the public suffer. But without the possibility of a strike there can be no true collective bargaining.

The chief purpose of the strike is to injure the business by halting production. A strike is most effective at a time when it is most damaging to the business. Thus, the ideal time to call a strike is when production is high and inventory accumulations are low, or when the employer is in a strong competitive battle with a rival business.

There are various kinds of strikes. The *recognition strike* is an attempt to force the employer to recognize the union as the legal bargaining agent of the workers. This type of strike has been largely replaced by elections conducted by the National Labor Relations Board. The *jurisdictional strike* develops when two unions disagree as to which one should perform certain types of work. For example, the labor contract may specify that certain types of operations are to be performed by iron workers and that other types are to be done by sheet-metal workers. Sometimes it is difficult to determine just which group is responsible for a given task, and a jurisdictional dispute arises. When the dispute develops to the point of a walkout by one of the unions, a strike is in progress. The *sympathetic strike* results when a union that is not a party to the original walkout refuses to cross the picket line and agrees to strike in sympathy with the original union that is on strike. Sometimes workers just slow down or call in sick as a means short of striking.

Strikes make news, and sometimes they get out of control. However, to repeat, they are a necessary complement to the collective-bargaining process. The general impression given the public by the news stories about strikes seems to be out of proportion to the strike record in recent years. There are more than 150,000 collective-bargaining contracts in force in this country, covering more than one-third of all the workers employed in nonfarm labor. The man-days lost through strikes during a recent year, for example, amounted to only four hours per worker (for all persons working), or 0.17 percent of the total man-days worked during the year.

Techniques Used by Management

Management counters the pressure of labor by group action through *employers' associations,* by the *court injunction,* by the *lockout,* by *lobbying,* and by *direct appeals to the public.*

Employers' Associations. Employers' associations have been in existence for many years, rendering such services as advertising, research, and lobbying. In addition, they sometimes function in labor–management negotiations. These associations may be formed on a city, regional, or national basis. Some of the best known are the National Association of Manufacturers, the Chamber of Commerce of the United States, and the Appalachian Coal Association. The formation of an association for labor-negotiation purposes usually takes place when there are many small employers and a single large union that represents all the employees of the many small businesses. Representatives from the association and the union come together to negotiate the terms of the labor contract.

The Court Injunction. Court injunctions make it possible for employers to prevent certain specified undesirable acts on the part of labor groups—acts such as coercive practices and destruction of a firm's property. Violating an injunction places the union in contempt of court and makes it subject to punishment by fine or imprisonment, or both. Perhaps the most notable examples of the use of this weapon—although it was employed in this case not by an employer but by the federal government—were the rulings of Judge

Goldsborough against John L. Lewis and the United Mine Workers of America in 1946 and 1948.

The Lockout.   A lockout exists when management closes its factory and refuses to permit the workers to enter the plant. The lockout is seldom used today, because it is the employer who establishes the working environment in the first place. Most employers prefer to have the workers strike rather than to employ the lockout, because in the eyes of the public the strike makes the employer appear to be the injured party.

Lobbies.   Big business exerts a strong influence on federal and state legislative bodies in an effort to persuade lawmakers to enact laws favorable to management. This pressure is greatest when Congress or a state legislature has before it important labor legislation. Personal visits to key senators or representatives, telegrams, letters, and advertisements in newspapers and magazines are all employed in industry's lobbying activities.[1]

Appeal to Public Opinion.   You sometimes see full-page newspaper or magazine advertisements used by a company or industry when it is being struck by labor. This is an attempt on the part of management to explain its side of the issue directly to the general public. The purpose of this direct appeal is to counteract the pressure of the union by giving the public information in the hope of winning support to the cause of management rather than that of labor.

Perhaps it should be stated here that not all business enterprises are opposed to collective bargaining with labor organizations. Many businessmen feel that collective bargaining is advantageous to management as well as to labor. They realize that a collective labor agreement makes it unnecessary for management to deal with individuals on matters of wages, overtime, and working conditions. Then, too, since collective bargaining tends to promote uniform labor policies and practices within a given industry, management knows that competitors are not gaining an advantage by hiring cheaper labor or by maintaining inferior working conditions.

Discussion Questions

7. *What are some of the matters over which labor and management frequently develop conflicts?*
8. *How do labor unions bring pressure to bear upon employers?*
9. *What techniques does management use to resist union demands?*
10. *What are some of the factors that decide whether a strike was successful?*

---

[1] Lobbying activities are also engaged in by organized labor groups to try to influence legislation favorable to labor.

SETTLEMENT OF LABOR DISPUTES

As we have seen, a labor agreement outlines a grievance procedure that will guarantee employees a hearing when they feel they are being treated unfairly. It also indicates the procedure to be followed when differences arise that are not covered by the agreement or when a difference of opinion develops on the interpretation of certain agreement provisions. The methods most commonly used in settling labor–management differences are *conciliation, mediation,* and *arbitration.*

Most grievances are settled at the first level in the grievance procedure (company supervisor, union steward, and worker). Only a relatively small percentage of the grievance cases ever pass unsuccessfully through all management–labor procedural levels and finally require the use of a third party to settle the dispute.

Methods of Settlement

In *conciliation,* a go-between makes every effort to bring the two groups in a dispute together. The conciliator encourages them to continue negotiations, trying to get each group to see the other's point of view, and helping them settle their differences themselves. In one sense, conciliation is an effort to correct unforeseen weaknesses in the labor agreement.

Mediation goes further than conciliation by offering specific suggestions in addition to those proposed by management and labor. The mediator does not act as a judge who holds hearings and renders decisions. Rather, his task is to influence each group to make concessions, helping them to narrow the gap between their demands and aiding in bringing about a compromise that is acceptable to both groups.

There is nothing compulsory about conciliation or mediation. They simply represent the efforts of unbiased outsiders to help the disputants to reach an agreement. They are both constructive processes, since they offer the disputants no escape from the responsibility of making their own decisions and attempting to understand and evaluate each other's position.

Arbitration is similar to mediation, but there is one important difference. The mediator can only recommend a solution to a dispute between management and labor, but the arbitrator is authorized to determine the solution. This means that the arbitrator serves in the role of a judge who hears both sides of the case as an impartial authority. When arbitration is used, both sides agree in advance to abide by the arbitrator's decision. Sometimes a panel of several (usually three) people serve, rather than one person. In this case, one member of the panel is nominated by the company, one by the union, and the third is an impartial outsider who is experienced as an arbitrator. When both parties to the dispute agree to arbitration, the process is known as *voluntary arbitration.* If the union and the company are required by law to submit their dispute to a third party for a decision, the process is known as *compulsory arbitration.* Arbitration is commonly used in labor and industrial disputes when it is provided for in the contract.[2]

Most collective-bargaining agreements provide that specific disputes that cannot be resolved by any of the other procedures established by the agreement must be submitted to voluntary arbitration for a final decision. The prevailing procedure in collective bargaining is to designate the type of arbitration procedure to be used when grievances cannot be settled by management and labor themselves without third-party assistance.

According to a study made by the Bureau of Labor Statistics of 1,254 labor agreements in 14 industries, three out of four union agreements, covering about 83 percent of the workers under the agreements analyzed, provide for arbitration as the terminal point in the grievance machinery. Of the 1,254 agreements, that is, 915 provided for arbitration. Of the total number of workers covered by agreements containing the arbitration provision, 28 percent were subject to permanently established arbitration machinery. The remaining 72 percent were subject to procedures calling for the selection of arbitrators whenever the need arose.

Of all the arbitration agreements, 93 percent (covering 91 percent of the workers) provided for *automatic* arbitration, or arbitration at the request of either party. Under this procedure, arbitration must be carried out if either party requests it, and both parties agree in advance to accept the decision as final and binding.

Several private organizations have been established to serve management and labor in settling industrial disputes. The Council on Industrial Relations for the Electrical Contracting Industry, for example, was established in 1920 for the purpose of serving the entire industry. Any segment of the electrical industry in which contractual relations exist between employers and the International Brotherhood of Electrical Workers may make use of the council's arbitration machinery. The American Arbitration Association serves management and labor by helping to select permanent arbitrators, by appointing fact finders, and by conducting polls to determine whether the members of a union approve a collective-bargaining agreement and which union they prefer to have represent them in negotiations with management.

The Government's Role in Settling Disputes

Industrial disputes have long been the concern of the federal government. Whenever a strike jeopardizes the public welfare, the government usually steps

---

[2] In all, 30 states have enacted arbitration statutes modeled more or less along the lines of the Uniform Arbitration Act. Naturally, the statutes in some states are more comprehensive than those in others, but they usually cover at least two of the three primary forms of arbitration practice in the United States—commercial, labor–management, and accident claims.

in and works for an immediate settlement of the controversy. Two of the most important government agents in labor–management negotiations are the National Mediation Board and the National Labor Relations Board.

The Federal Mediation Service. The Federal Mediation and Conciliation Service helps to formulate new labor agreements and interpret existing ones. It helps to settle labor–management disputes by furnishing a panel of arbitrators. The Service also makes available to industry a roster of arbitrators and otherwise aids employers and unions in handling labor-relations problems. Requests for such assistance are usually made by one or both parties to a labor dispute, although the Service can enter cases on its own initiative where the public interest requires it. Cases handled by the Service fall into these categories:

> *Work stoppage.* A strike or lockout.
>
> *Threatened stoppage.* A situation where a definite strike date has been announced or a 30-day strike notice has been filed.
>
> *Controversy.* A dispute that has not reached the stage of a work stoppage or a threatened stoppage.
>
> *Arbitration.* Upon the request of both parties to a dispute, arbitrators nominated by the Conciliation Service render final and binding awards that the parties agree in advance to accept.
>
> *Technical activities.* Upon the joint request of both parties to a dispute, the Service will offer advice on such technical matters as wage-incentive plans, time studies, and job evaluations.
>
> *Special services.* Upon request, the Service will furnish labor-relations information, consult with labor and management on specific problems, and provide speakers for groups who are interested in the Conciliation Service, labor problems, and related subjects.

The National Labor Relations Board. Another government organization that aids in the settlement of labor disputes is the National Labor Relations Board, which was created by Congress in 1935 to guarantee labor the right to organize and bargain collectively. The board consists of five members appointed by the President of the United States; each member serves for five years.

There are two types of labor hearings. The first type pertains to the investigation of employers who are accused of unfair labor practices. The Labor Management Relations Act of 1947 assigned responsibility for this type of case to a general counsel. If the employer is found guilty, he is ordered to stop interfering with the workers' right to organize; if necessary, the federal courts may be called on to enforce the counsel's rulings.

The second type of case pertains to representation. This type comes under the direct jurisdiction of the Labor Board. The board provides election machinery to determine the workers' preferences on how they want to be represented in collective bargaining. According to the policy of the board, the workers have the exclusive right, without any interference from the employer, to decide whether they want to be represented by any union, and if so, which union they want. The union that receives a majority of the votes cast is selected as the workers' official representative. The board also initiates procedures for orderly collective bargaining between the union that is chosen and the employer.

Many cities have mediation boards—New York, Newark, and Toledo are noted for their leadership in this service. Several states have conciliation boards to serve in disputes that do not fall under the jurisdiction of the National Labor Relations Board.

Discussion Questions

11. *How do conciliation, mediation, and arbitration differ?*

12. *What are the chief functions of the Federal Mediation and Conciliation Service and the National Labor Relations Board?*

13. *Why does the federal government take such an active role in settling labor disputes?*

LABOR LEGISLATION

The subject of labor legislation has long been a sensitive topic among politicians. Over the years, both labor and management have struggled for power, security, and status.

Two distinct types of legislation affecting labor and employers have been enacted. The first pertains to working hours, wages, safety regulations, and health; the second concerns the rights and responsibilities of labor unions and employers.

The earliest control over working hours applied specifically to women and children. In 1924, Congress proposed a constitutional amendment granting itself power to limit, regulate, and prohibit the labor of persons under 18 years of age, but an insufficient number of states approved it. All the individual states, however, have laws of one kind or another governing the length of the working day and the use of child labor. Many states have legislation restricting the hours women can work in specified employment, but only a few states have attempted to regulate the minimum wages paid to male workers. The federal government is, of course, concerned only with the regulation of businesses engaged in interstate commerce. Those firms whose activities and operations are within a single state are regulated by state labor laws.

The Norris-LaGuardia Act of 1932 contained the first statement of general policy toward unionization of labor ever adopted by the U.S. government. This policy said that workers should have the right to organize into unions if they choose to do so. The act outlawed the "yellow dog" contract, whereby workers, as a condition of employment, would agree not to join a union, and it restricted somewhat employers' utilization of the labor injunction to halt work stoppages. The following year, the right to organize was incorporated into the National Industrial Recovery Act, but that act was declared unconstitutional in 1935.

The National Labor Relations Act of 1935

The labor provisions of the NIRA were incorporated into a separate law passed in 1935—the National Labor Relations Act, otherwise known as the Wagner Act. This statute is clearly a workers' law, for its regulations are designed to control the actions of employers. In fact it has sometimes been referred to as "labor's Magna Carta." In general, it guaranteed workers the right to organize. This was accomplished by making it unlawful for employers to:

1. Refuse to bargain collectively with representatives chosen by employees
2. Interfere with the employees' right to bargain collectively
3. Dictate in any way to labor officials about their administrative procedures
4. Discriminate against union members in either hiring or firing
5. Discriminate against employees who take advantage of their rights under the law

The law established the National Labor Relations Board to administer the provisions of this act in settling disputes, and also to serve as a quasi court in protecting workers against unfair practices. Its chief functions were to prevent or correct any violations of the five practices enumerated above, and to establish proper bargaining units and organizations to represent the workers. In substance, what the Wagner Act did was to set up an orderly process of democratic elections by the workers to replace the former tactic of striking in order to force the employer to recognize the union as the employees' rightful bargaining agent.

The Fair Labor Standards Act of 1938

In 1938, Congress passed the Fair Labor Standards Act, which contained provisions related to both wages and hours in industries that engaged in interstate commerce. This act stated that beginning on October 24, 1940, workers should be compensated at a rate of one and one-half times their standard rate of pay for any hours they worked over 40 hours during any given week.

This act also set a floor under minimum wages that could be paid. The first minimum wage was set at 25 cents an hour, and it was to increase to 40 cents on October 24, 1945. This "floor" or minimum was and has repeatedly been raised—to 75 cents an hour in 1949, to $1 in 1955, and to $1.25 in 1961.

The act was amended in 1966, raising the minimum wage to $1.60 effective February 1, 1968. The law specifies that any time an employee is "suffered or permitted to work" is to be counted as working time. All time spent by an employee in physical or mental exertion, whether burdensome or not, that is "controlled or required" by the employer, and pursued necessarily and primarily for the benefit of the employer, is to be counted as working time. Thus, work not requested, but suffered or permitted, is working time. If work is permitted away from the premises or even at the employee's home, it is counted as working time.

The law stipulates that an employer may not discriminate on the basis of sex by paying employees of one sex at rates lower than he pays employees of the opposite sex for doing equal work on jobs requiring equal skill, effort, and responsibility and performed under similar working conditions.

The Labor Management Relations Act of 1947

There were many causes of industrial unrest and work stoppages in 1945 and 1946. Collective bargaining was still comparatively new in many situations; a considerable measure of employer opposition to unions existed. Some of the newly formed or rapidly growing unions could not maintain union discipline under the accumulation of wartime grievances or accustom themselves to the less militant methods of collective bargaining after winning recognition. Neither group adjustment nor individual self-discipline was aided by the wholesale shifting of workers to war industries and new industrial centers and then to other jobs and locations during reconversion. The quick withdrawal of wartime public controls over labor–management relations and also over production, prices, and wages placed additional responsibilities on both unions and employers at a time when the cost of living was rising rapidly.

The series of postwar work stoppages symbolized serious industrial unrest in the public mind. Strike idleness as a percentage of total working time (perhaps the best measure for comparison over a period of years) began to rise soon after the war from the unusually low wartime levels. Even in 1937, a prewar year of above-average strike activity, strike idleness had been less than 0.05 percent of total working time; in 1946, it was 1.43 percent—the highest ever recorded.

The unsettled labor–management situation after the war revived and greatly strengthened opposition to the Wagner Act. Senator Robert A. Taft, one of the leaders in the demand for change, argued that although the act had been passed to aid unions in maintaining an appropriate balance of rights and responsibilities between workers and employers, it had gone far beyond such a balance in its actual administration. He and Congressman Fred A. Hartley sponsored a rewriting of the act. The resulting measure, the Labor Management Relations (Taft-Hartley) Act, gained such widespread support that despite strong objections by organized labor and a presidential veto, it became law on June 23, 1947.

Some provisions of collective agreements that many unions had obtained or sought were banned or limited under the revised law. Provision for the so-called closed shop can no longer be included in agreements. Other widely adopted provisions of agreements, such as the union shop, checkoff of union dues, welfare funds, and contract termination arrangements, are regulated.

The concept of striking a balance between unions and employers led to the inclusion of a list of unfair labor practices applying to unions, along with the list applying to employers. Among various other practices, refusal to bargain in good faith, engaging in secondary boycotts, stopping work over a juris-dictional or interunion dispute, and charging excessive initiation fees to keep new members out of the union are considered by the law to be unfair. Em-ployers as well as workers are permitted to appeal to the National Labor Relations Board against unions in connection with such practices. Certain practices may be penalized by court action and lawsuits for damages. Restric-tions on the use of injunctions are eased.

Special rules were written into the Taft-Hartley Act for handling contro-versies or strikes that, in the judgment of the president, create or threaten emergencies by imperiling the national health or safety. In any such dispute or strike, the president is authorized to appoint a board of inquiry to investigate the facts. Thereafter, a court injunction can be obtained forbidding the occur-rence or continuance of a stoppage for a period of 80 days. During this "cooling-off" or waiting period, further efforts are to be made to settle the dispute. If no voluntary agreement can be arranged within 60 days, the em-ployees are to be polled by secret ballot as to whether they will accept the final offer of the employer. After all these steps are taken, however, the injunc-tion must be dissolved whether or not the dispute is settled. This procedure— government attempts to force the settlement of labor–management disputes— has been used sparingly in recent years.

Union opposition to the Taft-Hartley Act was intense in the first few years after its passage. The act was denounced as a slave-labor law and its repeal became a major goal of the labor movement. Many proposals were made for changes in the new law by its critics and also by its sponsors—changes that, for the most part, would ease the restrictions on unions. Revision proved to be difficult, partly because of the problem of reconciling the views of those who were fearful of going too far in modifying the law with the views of those who felt that any obtainable amendments would not satisfy their objections. By 1951, practical circumstances had brought about general agreement to repeal the requirement that elections be held to validate union-shop agreements. Experience had shown that in nearly all cases, large majorities of workers voted for the union shop. Accordingly, the law was amended to eliminate this requirement.

The Labor Management Reporting and Disclosure Act of 1959

Working under some of the most intense public pressure in years, Congress passed, on September 4, 1959, the first major labor-reform amendments to the Taft-Hartley Act. This act was the Labor Management Reporting and Disclosure Act, commonly called the Landrum-Griffin Act. It is quite correctly titled, because the major portion of the law requires a series of reports to be made to the Secretary of Labor by both labor unions and business management. Among the reports required are:

1. Reports of the constitution and bylaws of union organizations
2. Reports of union administrative policies pertaining to initiation fees, union dues, and other financial assessments; calling of union meetings; qualifications for membership in the union; and the ratification of contracts
3. Annual financial reports by the unions, showing the amounts of assets, liabilities, and cash receipts; salaries of officers; and loans to members, union officials, or businesses
4. Reports of personal financial transactions on the part of union officials that might in any way conflict with the best interests of the union
5. Reports by employers of any expenditures made in order to prevent their employees from organizing

This law gives to employers new protection from union racketeers and unscrupulous labor leaders. Members have more voice in their local union affairs. Elections must be held by secret ballot. Local officers must be elected at least once every three years, and national officers every five years. Union members can sue in federal courts if justice is not provided. The law prohibits communists or anyone convicted of a felony within the previous five years from holding union office. A union official permitting a felon to hold office is subject to a year in jail and a $10,000 fine.

State "Right-to-Work" Laws

You will recall that one of the major objectives of organized labor is the strengthening of the labor unions themselves. But labor has been unsuccessful in getting Congress to repeal Section 14-b of the Taft-Hartley Act. This provision permits the states to enact laws prohibiting the union shop; it has been a strong influence in preventing continued union growth, and its repeal is currently one of the primary goals of organized labor.

Under the Taft-Hartley Act, Section 14-b, states are permitted to outlaw any form of compulsory unionism, including the union shop. This was a change from the original interpretation of the National Labor Relations Act of 1935 (Wagner Act), which not only allowed the unions the right to negotiate compulsory union-membership agreements but also prevented a state or municipality from nullifying the unions' right in this respect. The right of the states to restrict union security is clearly provided for in Section 14-b of the Taft-Hartley Act, which states:

> Nothing in this Act shall be construed as authorizing the execution of application of agreements requiring membership in a labor organization in any State or Territory in which such execution or application is prohibited by State or Territorial Law.

Florida enacted the first right-to-work law by constitutional amendment in 1944. In 1956, Louisiana repealed a general right-to-work law but substituted a new law banning union-shop agreements involving workers in agriculture and in certain agricultural processing operations. Right-to-work laws have been passed by other states, mostly in agricultural areas, including Alabama, Arizona, Arkansas, Georgia, Iowa, Kansas, Mississippi, Nebraska, Nevada, North Carolina, North Dakota, South Carolina, South Dakota, Tennessee, Texas, Utah, Virginia, and Wyoming. This makes a total of 19 states that currently have such laws in effect. In all, 24 states have enacted such legislation, but five of them have subsequently repealed it.

There are two sides to the argument over right-to-work laws. One, shared by many employers, is that it is morally improper to require workers to join a union in order to obtain or hold a job, and that union-shop agreements are actually intended to perpetuate the bargaining power of unions. On the other side, the unions argue that right-to-work laws are actually designed to wreck labor organizations, and that any worker who benefits from union activities should be obliged to share in the cost by paying union dues.

Unquestionably, right-to-work laws hinder union growth in those states where such laws exist. Therefore, the repeal of Section 14-b of the Taft-Hartley law is high on organized labor's list of priorities. In fact, following the 1964 general elections, a well-organized campaign was launched to influence members of Congress to repeal the section. The drive had the indorsement and support of President Johnson, and the House of Representatives passed the needed legislation, but the bill was defeated in the Senate in the spring of 1966. But organized labor has not given up on this objective and will be heard from again.

Discussion Questions

14. *How did the Wagner Act of 1935 give union membership a strong growth impetus?*

15. *Take a position favoring or opposing the idea of permitting state legislatures to make the union shop illegal. Support your position.*

SUMMARY

Labor and management are bound together by a strong common interest and a common goal. They are in the business of meeting people's economic needs and wants as a joint venture. When they are able to work together to prevent a work stoppage, everyone gains—management, labor, the public, and governments.

Bargaining today is done collectively, with labor acting as a unit through its representatives. Sometimes employers also bargain collectively, through their employers' association. Some bargaining is done at the local level, but more often it is done on an industry-wide or national level.

The labor agreement covers a wide variety of factors: wage rates, methods of wage payments, working conditions, seniority rights, vacations and holidays, dismissal policies, and how grievances are to be handled.

Most of the issues between management and labor are basically economic or jurisdictional. Historically, management has looked upon labor as a cost of production, whereas persons who make up the labor force see themselves more as partners in production. Other issues revolve around the questions of who should share in the excess profits, and the degree to which representatives of labor might share in policy formation and decision making at the operational level.

The principal techniques used by labor in attempting to secure benefits for workers are, jurisdictional limitations, limitation of output, the union shop, picketing, the boycott, and the strike. Employers may use appeals to the public, the court injunction, or the lockout.

When labor and management are not able to reach an agreement, they may call in outside help. This help may take the form of conciliation, mediation, or arbitration. There are private organizations whose sole function is to help management and labor reach agreement. The federal government is also very active in this field. The Federal Mediation and Conciliation Service and the National Labor Relations Board are the chief agencies of the federal government for assisting labor and management in settling their disputes. When it is possible for disputes to be settled without a strike, not only do management and labor gain, but the general public benefits as well.

The public, acting through the federal government, has established the policy of self-determination by workers in deciding who their representatives should be in negotiations with their employers. The right to organize has been guaranteed through the enactment of the Wagner Act. The Taft-Hartley Act prohibits certain unfair practices of labor unions, and the Landrum-Griffin Act provides protection to workers from certain types of abuse by both their employers and their union officials.

VOCABULARY REVIEW

Match the following vocabulary terms with the statements below.

a. Arbitrator
b. Boycott
c. Coalition bargaining
d. Conciliation
e. Controversy

f. Grievance procedure
g. Injunction
h. Jurisdictional dispute
i. Lockout
j. Mediator

k. Picketing
l. Secondary boycott
m. Strike
n. Work stoppage

1. The collaboration of several different unions within an industry, in bargaining as a group with an employer
2. A provision in a labor contract that explains how employees may ask for a hearing when they feel an injustice has been experienced by them
3. The stationing of banner- and placard-carrying workers at the entrance of a business
4. A refusal on the part of employees to patronize their employer's business
5. The situation when workers walk off the job and refuse to work until their demands are met (or a compromise is reached)
6. An attempt by the employees of a business to influence the public not to transact business with the firm
7. A dispute between two groups of workers over the right to perform certain types of tasks
8. A court order preventing labor or management from carrying out an announced course of action
9. Refusal by an employer to permit his employees to work until they agree to his stipulation
10. A go-between in a labor dispute who attempts to bring the two parties to the controversy together to continue negotiations
11. An outside party attempting to get labor and management to agree, who offers suggestions as to a possible compromise
12. An outside party in labor-management negotiations who serves as a judge in the dispute and renders a decision
13. A labor dispute that has not yet reached the stage of a threatened work stoppage
14. A cessation of business operations caused by a strike or a lockout

PROBLEMS AND PROJECTS

1. Through the years, there has been much discussion of the "guaranteed annual wage."

   a. What is usually meant when this term is used?
   b. What is labor's justification in asking for a guaranteed annual wage?
   c. What is management's justification in granting such a guarantee?
   d. What type of manufacturing enterprise can give a guaranteed annual wage with the least risk?

2. Assume a wage scale of $3.10 per hour and a work week of 36 hours. The employees strike for 12 weeks in an attempt to secure a new wage rate of $3.80 per hour, but in a compromise settlement they agree to accept $3.50 an hour.

    a. How much in wages did an individual worker lose during the 12-week period?

    b. Assume that he received one-third of his regular wages as strike benefits from the union. How long would he have to work at the new wage of $3.50 in order to make up for the monetary loss he suffered while on strike?

    c. Assuming a work force of 800 employees, how much did the union pay out as strike benefits?

3. Many unions are now bargaining for the right to retire early (before the age of 65) and still receive a company pension.

    a. What factors might justify early retirement for any particular worker?

    b. How do Social Security retirement benefits relate to early retirement?

    c. Why must the amount of company pension payments be reduced somewhat when a worker retires early?

BUSINESS CASES

Case 11-1 Was This Strike Justified?

A factory located in one of our southeastern states was struck when 5,000 workers walked off the job. After five days, the company had to lay off an additional 8,000 workers because normal operations could no longer be carried on. After an additional three days, the company agreed to settle the claim, and all workers returned to their jobs.

The issue was $35 that a former employee, who had left the company a year earlier, claimed he was due in back pay. The former worker filed his grievance three months after he quit the company, but no action had yet been taken at the time of the strike.

1. Why do you suppose it took so long for the company to settle this claim?

2. Using an eight-hour day and an average wage rate of $3.05 per hour, how much in wages did the work force lose during this strike?

3. How much did an individual worker lose who struck for the full eight days?

4. How much did one of the workers who was laid off lose?

5. Assuming that this was an isolated instance, do you consider this issue worthy of a strike by 13,000 workers?

Case 11-2   Let's Form a Union!

The Standard Products Corporation stamps out parts that are used in assembling refrigerator cabinets and electric stoves. None of its employees are members of a union. Its wages are equal to those currently being paid by other manufacturers in the community. The fringe-benefits package includes $3,000 of life insurance coverage, with half the premium being paid by the company; free hospitalization benefits; and five paid holidays a year.

Assume that one of your worker colleagues is pushing for the formation of an industrial union with membership open to all employees, including those who work in the office. He has urged you to help him work in organizing the union.

1. What factors would influence you in deciding whether to work for organizing a union?
2. What immediate (short-term) advantages to the workers do you see in forming such a union?
3. What long-term advantages would there be in having a union for all workers?
4. What might be some disadvantages *to you,* as an individual employee, in working for the formation of a union if the effort did not prove successful?

production management

CHAPTER TWELVE

The United States is an affluent nation with a high standard of living, but it has not always been this way. Our present standard of living came about because we learned how to produce more goods in less time and at increasingly lower unit costs, and it has taken more than a hundred years to achieve our present status of affluence. Two of the reasons for our success in production have been our ability to develop and improve machines and our emphasis on specialization in manufacturing operations.

Many of the things consumers take for granted now have not been available very long, and a great deal of energy, time, and ingenuity have been invested in order to bring them into existence. Most of the items consumers buy today are produced by blending together raw materials from our farms, mines, forests, and oceans. These raw materials must be extracted from the earth, then changed in form, and finally shaped and polished into finished products. Large numbers of workers, performing a wide variety of tasks, collaborate in the production process. Those who understand how our system works know that the production achievements of the nation are no accident, but the result of applying modern scientific principles in our manufacturing operations.

The lessons on how to produce goods on a large scale came to us from England, where, in the middle of the eighteenth century, the Industrial Revolution introduced a completely new concept—the substitution of machines for manpower. Our own Industrial Revolution did not flower until after the Civil War. From our start as a struggling young nation, we have reached our present peak of consuming nearly half the free world's output. In addition, we have made loans, gifts, and grants to other nations amounting to billions of dollars.

The focal point of our business system is production—the subject of our study in this chapter.

THE IMPORTANCE OF PRODUCTION

At first, manufacturing in this country was largely concentrated in New England and the Middle Atlantic states; then it expanded into the eastern North Central region, north of the Ohio River. Since World War II, all sections of the country have become industry-conscious, and many small communities have sought and found industries suited to their localities. Even the southern region, once almost wholly agricultural, is becoming important in manufacturing.

Modern factories give employment to millions of workers. In fact, more people are employed in production than in any other major segment of our business system. Manufacturing offers jobs to many different kinds of workers—the unskilled laborer, the semiskilled machine operator, the machinist, the engineer, the stenographer, the production manager. It directly supports approximately one-fourth of all the people who are gainfully employed in the United States.

Not only does manufacturing employ millions of workers directly, but it also supports additional workers in other fields of employment. The Industrial Bureau of the Atlanta Chamber of Commerce reports that the payroll of one factory employing 150 men supports, on an average, 383 occupied homes, 24 professional men, 6,000 acres of farm products, 18 teachers, and 33 retail stores. All this accounts for $500,000 in retail sales annually, 320 automobiles and the services needed for them, and $2.5 million in tax valuation.

Manufacturing can truly be called the cornerstone of our American business system. Its economic contribution lies in three areas: the employment of many people (approximately 20 million); the changing of the form of raw materials into useful products; and the adding of value to the raw materials.

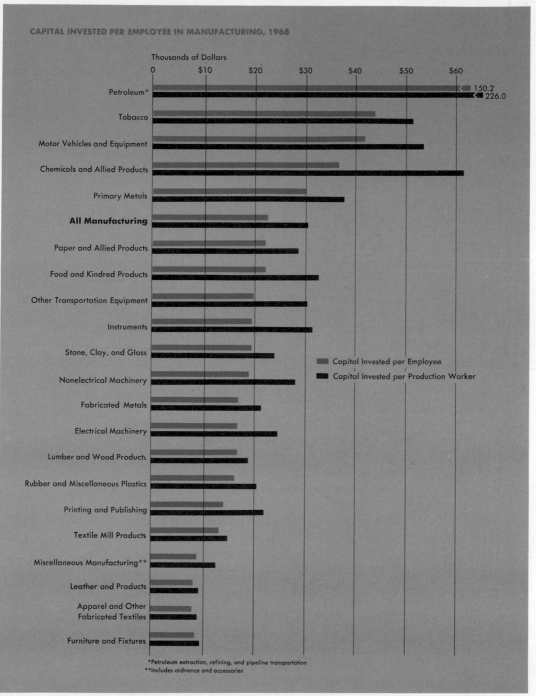

CAPITAL INVESTED PER EMPLOYEE IN MANUFACTURING, 1968

Thousands of Dollars

Petroleum*	150.2 / 226.0
Tobacco	
Motor Vehicles and Equipment	
Chemicals and Allied Products	
Primary Metals	
All Manufacturing	
Paper and Allied Products	
Food and Kindred Products	
Other Transportation Equipment	
Instruments	
Stone, Clay, and Glass	
Nonelectrical Machinery	
Fabricated Metals	
Electrical Machinery	
Lumber and Wood Products	
Rubber and Miscellaneous Plastics	
Printing and Publishing	
Textile Mill Products	
Miscellaneous Manufacturing**	
Leather and Products	
Apparel and Other Fabricated Textiles	
Furniture and Fixtures	

Capital Invested per Employee
Capital Invested per Production Worker

*Petroleum extraction, refining, and pipeline transportation
**Includes ordnance and accessories

Sources: Bureau of Labor Statistics; U.S. Department of Commerce; Internal Revenue Service; the National Industrial Conference Board, Inc.

1. *Explain how manufacturing supports employment in other segments of a nation's economy.*

THE CHARACTERISTICS OF PRODUCTION

As production progressed from the handicraft to the machine stage, businesses became large and complex structures. Today, they apply scientific principles to work processes, and present-day manufacturing industries require well-trained and experienced executives in industrial management. As industrial production grew, there developed certain characteristics; namely, mechanization, large-scale operation, standardization, specialization, automation, and research and development.

Mechanization

Today a manufacturing concern cannot meet its competition and stay in business by employing hand labor and handicraft techniques. Machines have been substituted for hand labor to such a degree that we even have machines directing and controlling other machines.

This mechanization of industry not only yields greater overall production but also increases the productivity of each worker. Productivity has increased by the average of approximately 3 percent per year. During the past 100 years, the employed labor force has increased tenfold, and the gross national product more than thirtyfold. Mechanization leads to a higher quality and an increased uniformity of the product, with a greater degree of accuracy in the manufacturing of it.

Large-Scale Operations

The use of machines makes it possible to manufacture goods by mass production. Because overhead charges do not increase greatly as production volume is enlarged, the trend has been toward mass production, which has thus brought about lower unit costs. Lower prices for raw materials, resulting from the purchase of larger quantities, and lower unit costs for labor have further helped to bring about lower selling prices for manufactured articles. Mass production has also made it profitable to manufacture useful by-products from substances that were formerly waste materials.

Standardization

Standardization in industry simply means setting up uniform methods for the performance of each task, and then seeing to it that these methods are always followed. Standardization may include more than method, however; equipment, machine parts, products, procedures, and processes are all made to conform to uniform patterns. Standardization makes it possible to specialize the handling of each step in a process, and to reduce costs through quantity purchases of raw materials.

One of our earliest records of standardization in manufacturing is from the area of the production of firearms. Eli Whitney established a gun factory in 1789 and began to produce firearms by a new principle. He standardized all parts so that replacements could be used in different models. Formerly, guns for which no spare parts were available had simply been thrown away.

Frederick W. Taylor, whose contributions to scientific management are discussed in Chapter 9, suggested that raw materials, tools, machinery, and supplies must be standardized before work methods can be standardized.

Standardization brings about cost reductions because once a machine is set up, it can run for an extended period of time, producing the same item repeatedly. It reduces tooling costs because fewer dies, casts, and molds are required. Labor cost is also reduced, because workers do not have to alter their routines or adjust their machines to accommodate different types of operations.

Specialization of Labor

When this country was first settled, the family was an almost self-sufficient unit. Each family grew and raised its own food, made its own clothing, built its own home. Today, the family calls in a contractor to build a new home. The contractor then hires plumbers, carpenters, painters, and unskilled laborers, each to do a specific type of work. This same principle of specialization is very apparent in modern industry. Not only does a worker restrict his activities to operating a lathe, for example, but he machines only specified parts on it. One factory worker inserts bolts in a machine casing and starts the nuts on the bolts; another worker takes over and tightens them.

Not only does the individual worker specialize by narrowing the scope of his work, but businesses also specialize. A particular plant restricts its manufacturing activities to a narrow line of products. Even large corporations that are diversifying their manufacturing operations will build a new plant for a complete new line of products. For example, the International Business Machines Corporation will produce its typewriters in one plant but build its computers in a different location. And Procter & Gamble manufactures soaps and detergents in one factory but its perfumes and related products in another.

The location of certain types of manufacturing enterprises near the sources of raw materials creates to some degree a geographical specialization:

the production of automobiles in the Detroit area, furniture in Michigan and North Carolina, petroleum refining in Oklahoma and Texas, and so on.

Although specialization goes hand in hand with mass production and makes for efficiency in manufacturing, it has some shortcomings as well. Many a worker's activities are narrowed to such an extent that his work lacks motivation. Specialization also makes the operations of any given plant dependent upon many others. A strike in a company that produces parts may shut down assembly lines in several other factories. Likewise, a strike in an assembly plant may close down several factories where parts are made by its suppliers.

Automation

The newest development in manufacturing is automation. This means that both the handling of materials and the control of production processes is done automatically—without the utilization of human labor. It includes not only the moving of parts and materials from one work station to another, but also automatic positioning and machining throughout the production cycle.

Automation has been in operation for some time in such industries as bottling plants and canneries, and it is currently being extended to many other types of production processes. The automotive industry, for example, has developed electronically operated equipment for the production of engine blocks. Each block is moved from station to station, positioned, and drilled, and comes from the production line ready for assembly. It is estimated that this automatic process saves from two-thirds to three-fourths of the time and labor cost formerly required.

Several factors combine to increase the utilization of automation in industry. Automated machines handle many jobs too complicated to be done efficiently by hand, and performs numerous mechanical operations so rapid that the human eye and hand cannot stay with them. Also, automated machines are more accurate than human beings, and they are invaluable in their ability to execute hazardous operations in such industries as munitions, chemicals, and atomic energy.

Research and Development

Research and development is an important part of modern manufacturing. Most company executives will tell you that they could not remain competitive except for the new products and processes that come from their research laboratories.

The leading function of research is product improvement. No product ever made is perfect, and unless it is improved, competition from other products drive it from the market.

Basically, research in industry is concerned with future development. It helps management in planning for tomorrow. In fact, many of the articles on the market today were unknown just a few years ago.

Discussion Questions

2. *Explain how mechanization, automation, and productivity are interrelated.*
3. *Explain how specialization in manufacturing is related to the geographical location of certain industries.*

PRODUCTION MANAGEMENT AS A SYSTEM

As we have already observed, not only has production been a key factor in promoting the growth of this nation, but the progress that has been made in developing our national economy has been due largely to the high competence and effectiveness of our production managers. Their role is one of *planning, programming, controlling, and coordinating production techniques,* using costly materials and capital.

In a broad sense, *production* includes any activity that involves the process of increasing the availability of goods capable of satisfying human wants. As a study in economics, however—and production is an important part of economics—it is generally considered that the utility of material goods to satisfy wants is a function of (1) a time utility, (2) a place utility, (3) a form utility,

PRODUCTION DEPARTMENT ORGANIZATION CHART

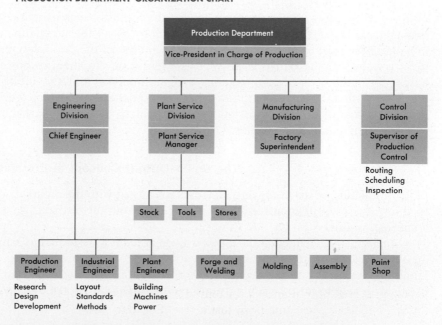

and (4) a possession utility. It is only when the capabilities of production make goods available at the appropriate time, in a place where they can be used, in the proper form, and for immediate use that production contributes an economic value to society.

The Function of Production

Every business is in some way involved in two operative functions that promote a higher standard of living: (1) the actual physical creation of goods and services (production), and (2) the placing of these goods in the possession of people (marketing). If goods or services have time, place, form, and possession utility that satisfy a need of some customer, they may have the necessary value that a customer is willing to purchase. According to formal organization theory, form utility is a line function that is directly concerned with the responsibility of providing goods and services. Much of this chapter is concerned with this line function as it operates in the production-management system.

Systems Concept Applied to Production Management

Since production management is responsible for the preparation of products that evolve through the production processes, management must make many decisions. Accuracy in decision making may be increased by the "systems approach," which is a rather new concept that emphasizes the interrelationships among the various elements that comprise the system. When we apply this concept to a business firm, it means we must view the entire enterprise, with all its functions, as a whole. Each function of the business, such as marketing, management, finance, or production, is influenced by all the other functions in making the total business operative. This total view of the firm by management is known as the *systems concept*. It is a recent development in business, having been used earlier in weapons systems analysis and the biological sciences. With the use of computers, it is now possible to develop various models, such as of a firm, a production department, or a selected market area, to study their inputs and outputs.

The Input–Output Concept in Production

Production organization as a system is concerned with the processes used to transform a set of input resources into a set of output resources to yield a specific product.

Input may be defined as the use of a given amount of resources to achieve an objective. In industry the chief inputs are in the form of raw materials and labor. In business it is the managers, workers, suppliers, creditors, and the public who help to turn these inputs into products. *Output,* on the other hand, refers to the end products obtained from the system of production, derived from applying a given amount of energy and resources. It is these products or services that the company sells to generate its income. Whenever resources are used in proper proportions in an efficient process under desirable standards, it is possible to maximize the total outputs in relation to the total inputs.

Another way to explain this concept is to express input and output in monetary units, such as dollars. Production management seeks a situation in which the monetary value of output is greater than the monetary value of input. If this occurs, the net difference is net profit; and conversely, if the value of input exceeds that of output, there is a loss. Such relationships may be expressed by the formula: $I < O =$ Profit or $I > O =$ Loss, in which I stands for input and O for output. Systems analysis normally provides for a built-in flow of information to determine if there is an optimum relationship between input and output. In most cases, this can be observed in automated factories that are controlled by computers.

The illustration below shows the relation of input resources, as contributed by managers, workers, and others, to the output resources resulting in goods and services. Notice that the flow of labor, materials, capital, and energy is into production and that they are combined by the production facilities and technology to produce outputs.

The lumber business is typical of the industry that relies on a mechanical technology in which raw materials are put through a manufacturing or production process in order to change their form. When raw timber is run through successive steps (saws, planes, and kilns), inputs are changed to outputs to achieve a profit. Thus by measuring input and output, it is possible to determine if a profit has been made.

INPUT-OUTPUT CONCEPT SYSTEM

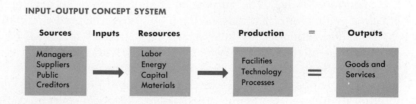

Sources	Inputs	Resources		Production	=	Outputs
Managers Suppliers Public Creditors		Labor Energy Capital Materials		Facilities Technology Processes	=	Goods and Services

---

Discussion Questions

4. *What is meant by the phrase "production management as a system"?*
5. *Explain what we mean when we say that "input" and "output" refer to the means and the end in production.*
6. *What happens when $I > O$?*

THE SCIENTIFIC-MANAGEMENT MOVEMENT

Although people had for many years talked about ways to improve their work procedures, few persons really examined human work movements until late in the nineteenth century. A Frenchman by the name of Henri Fayol, who managed a coal mine, analyzed the basic process of management and is generally credited with giving us the fundamental management principles upon which others built.

The Influence of Frederick W. Taylor

Some of the contributions of Frederick W. Taylor have already been discussed in earlier chapters. Since most of his work was done in factories and shops, scientific management first made its greatest headway in manufacturing. Taylor's observations and research were responsible for instituting new methods and procedures that greatly increased the productivity of workers.[1] He also developed the first wage-incentive plan, which bears his name.[2] His work also formed the basis of contributions of men like Frank B. Gilbreth, Henry Gantt, Harrington Emerson, and Carl Barth, some of whom were colleagues and collaborators of Taylor.

Time and Motion Study

Among the earliest efforts in scientific management were studies that timed man's movements and observed his work with the view of eliminating unnecessary or wasted activity.

Motion Study. The purpose of motion study is to develop the most effective method of performing each job by discovering and eliminating waste motions. The motion-study analyst, who is a trained specialist, breaks each job down into all the elementary motions that the worker uses, such as reaching, selecting, picking up, putting together, and replacing on the conveyor belt. Then the analyst studies both the separate motions and the operations as a whole in order to discover the rhythm of movement, distances covered, coordination, and sequence. After he has completed his study, he recommends that certain distances be shortened and that certain movements be eliminated. He tries to advise the worker on the most desirable rhythm and timing, and helps him to work out the proper sequence of steps.

Time Study. Time study is usually associated with motion study. When the observer breaks down the whole operation into the elementary motions

[1] Review our discussion in Chapter 7.
[2] See earlier discussion in Chapter 9.

that the worker goes through, he also determines the time required for each motion by using a stopwatch. He selects a location that permits him to see every action of the worker. Each time the worker makes a motion, the observer times it and records the time on an observation sheet. He also records all work stoppages and delays, and anything else that seems to be significant. Every elementary motion that the worker makes during the completion of one unit of work (that is, during what is referred to as the "job cycle") must be timed many times. Then the average of all these timings for a single movement becomes the base time for that motion, and the total of the averages for all the separate motions involved on one operation becomes the standard time for the complete job cycle.

Sometimes the worker's motions are so rapid that the observer cannot do an accurate job with a stopwatch. Then he uses cameras to make what are called "micromotion studies." A large clock having a face divided into hundredths of seconds is placed behind the worker, and a motion-picture camera records both the movement and the position of the clock's sweep hand. By studying the series of pictures, the analyst can calculate with great accuracy just how long the movement took.

As you can see, success in time and motion studies requires the full cooperation of the worker being studied. If he is not in sympathy with the idea, the results are very likely to be invalid. Then, too, he should be a typical worker and not one who is exceptionally slow or fast, efficient or inefficient.

It is a good practice to invite labor representatives to participate in time studies. Workers must be given assurance that a study will not be used to force more work from them in less time just to save production costs. If they feel that the result will be higher standards for them to meet for the same pay, they are not likely to be very cooperative.

Discussion Question

7. *How are time and motion studies used to increase efficiency in manufacturing?*

CONTROL IN MANUFACTURING

The purpose of production control is to maintain a smooth, constant flow of work from raw material to finished product, so that the product will be completed in the shortest possible time and at the lowest possible unit cost. This requires careful coordination of all the factors that enter into the production process—materials, machines, men, and methods.

Procedural Control

There are four steps in production control: (1) *planning,* (2) *routing,* (3) *scheduling,* and (4) *dispatching.*

Planning. Efficient production is rooted in proper planning. Everything that comes afterward in routing, scheduling, and dispatching, reflects the quality of the planning that has taken place in the early stages. In order to plan effectively, management must have a realistic knowledge of the plant's limitations and must be constantly informed on the total amount of work in process.

Planning is more than setting up overall procedures and objectives. It calls for close attention to specific details. For example, the type and quantity of materials that will be needed must be determined in advance by the production foreman and his assistants. When a large quantity of material is involved, it is necessary to check the inventory records to see if a sufficient amount is on hand. Second, if finished parts manufactured by other firms are to be used in the assembly process, the number of each kind needed must be determined by the executive in charge of production, and ordered in time to have them when they are needed. Purchase requisitions for these parts, and for any materials needed that are not on hand, must be issued by the production department to the purchasing department.

In addition, the work must be distributed to the different departments, the number of men needed must be determined, the number and types of machines required must be decided upon, and the time for the completion of each stage must be assigned. All this is the responsibility of those in charge of the production department.

In a small industrial plant that employs only a few workers, the foreman often handles this detailed planning in an informal manner, particularly where the production processes are standardized. On the other hand, in a large industry such as the automobile industry, where dozens of different materials and scores of finished parts from other factories are assembled, management usually sets up a planning department. The complexity of the operation makes such a department a necessity. Each model manufactured is a separate planning problem, and many different operations are performed simultaneously. Although some pass through only one process, others go through several operations before they are completed.

Routing. Control over the sequence of operations that are performed in the manufacture of a particular article is called *routing.* When you realize that some articles involve the use of several machines, and that some machines must be used for several different processes, you can see how important routing is in a modern plant. To complicate matters even more, several different jobs are "in process" at the same time.

The person responsible for routing determines the order in which different operations are to be performed, which personnel are to do the work, and which machines, tools, and supplies are to be used. He must indicate the route for each individual part produced, and its relation to the other parts in process. He then issues route cards to each department, showing the sequence of operations for each part that passes through that department. Detailed drawings are sometimes prepared to chart all necessary production processes and assemblies.

Scheduling. The purposes of scheduling production work are to ensure a smooth flow of work through the production process, to avoid conflicts and delays in the use of men and machines, and to set time-tables for the arrival of needed materials and the shipping of finished goods in such a way as to keep costs to a minimum. Scheduling is necessary in order to finish stock items at a rate that will avoid the depletion of items on hand, and in order to meet time limits on job-order work.

The person responsible for scheduling must prepare a master schedule that shows the number of items he expects to be completed during each week or month. For job-order work, the schedule can be worked backward from the desired delivery date; he determines a definite time as the date on or before which each operation or part must be completed. Since he makes known to the supervisors the schedules for the different jobs, rush orders can be accommodated, and jobs that permit an extra allowance of time can be used to avoid idle periods, thus keeping costs down.

The person responsible for schedules must keep in mind the amount of plant capacity already committed to jobs in process, and he must maintain a balance of work assignments to different departments, thus avoiding overloading. He is responsible for coordinating the delivery of parts from other plants with the completion of parts within the factory and for avoiding overloaded periods for the most frequently used transportation facilities (to avoid delay in delivery of raw materials and finished goods).

Dispatching. The issuance of work orders for each job is necessary for the planning to be carried through, for proper routing to be arranged, and for the schedule to be maintained. The preparation and issuance of these work orders, which entails a good deal of clerical work, is known as *dispatching*. The dispatcher must prepare requisitions for needed materials and supplies and see that the required tools are assembled.

The dispatch clerk must use follow-up routines to keep abreast of the progress of each task. He must record the times of starting and completing each task. He must deliver work orders and submit reports of completed work. The dispatch clerk uses messengers, pneumatic-tube conveyors, and dispatch boards for delivering and receiving records. He must have a systematic filing plan for each type of record. The dispatcher is also responsible for seeing that work progresses in accordance with the routing cards and time schedules. He must avoid idle time for machines and men by issuing new work orders as

Boston firm nearly doubles production—through Wassell scheduling. Without adding either equipment or men, Barnstead, Still & Sterilizer, a large Boston manufacturing firm has increased production through better scheduling of manpower and order control. Manpower is scheduled on the two VU-9074 Wassell VU-boards and order control is tracked on three 100-200 85P Produc-Tol Boards, one of which is visible at the far right of the picture.

soon as they have completed their tasks. The dispatcher has a responsible job, for he determines how effectively planning is translated into actual output.

Performance Control

Performance control utilizes many techniques. Among the most commonly used are the *planning board, progress charts, standards,* and *inspection.*

The Planning Board.   When several types of work are in progress, involving dozens of different types of machines, management must use some system for exercising overall control. Many modern industrialists set up a visual display called the *planning board.* This shows in detail the plans for three classes of work: jobs in progress, jobs to be started when the work in process is completed, and job orders not yet scheduled. The planning board also provides a separate record for each machine. The shop foreman can see at the beginning of each day or week exactly what management has planned for his department.

Progress Charts.   A progress chart serves much the same purpose as a bar graph. Posted on the bulletin board or on a wall, it shows at a glance the dates on which each job is to begin, the number of units to be produced, and the date by which each job is to be finished. Lines on the chart indicate whether each job is on, ahead of, or behind schedule.

Standards. No production-control system can function effectively without standards. This part of the control system does not have to be an elaborate one, but it must provide standards for operation, standards for quality, and standards for working conditions. Operating standards, which are expressed in terms of time and procedure, indicate the amount of time needed to perform a particular job and thus to provide the data needed for scheduling. The quality-control department establishes apparatus for use in comparing parts or products with established quality standards. Good standards for working conditions include good ventilation, adequate light, noise control, clean working areas, and freedom from hazards. Periodic lubrication of machines and equipment and a constant supply of materials to all work stations are essential to the proper functioning of this part of the control program.

Inspection. The most important function of inspection is to enforce standards. Carefully prepared plans and carefully observed schedules are of no value if the finished product proves unacceptable, and establishing standards is useless unless you take steps to ensure that they are met.

In addition to maintaining quality standards, inspection serves three other functions:

1. If you can catch defective materials or workmanship early in the production process, you can prevent the waste of additional labor later on.
2. Careful inspection at various stages during the completion of a product helps you to discover points of weakness in the manufacturing process.
3. Thorough inspection of the finished product helps prevent the shipping and delivery of defective or substandard products, and helps you to maintain goodwill and a good reputation among your customers.

Inspection enters the picture even before the production process begins. For example, the receiving department inspects raw materials before accepting them, and the supervisor inspects tools and gauges at regular intervals to make sure they are still up to standard. Since one of the chief purposes of inspection is to see that set standards are being upheld, the worker must be held responsible for poor-quality workmanship. In fairness, however, he must be supplied with sound materials and effective machinery; otherwise he cannot be held accountable.

How thorough the inspection is to be, at what stages it is to take place, and who is to conduct it are matters of company policy that depend on the nature of the articles being manufactured and the production processes involved. For example, if you are manufacturing parts for precision machinery that have to be accurate to within .005 of an inch, your inspection will be far more elaborate and meticulous than if you were turning out toys, pencils, or paperweights. For most products, a sampling inspection is all that is necessary, but in some cases every item must be inspected (this is called 100 percent inspection).

Through experience, most manufacturers have found that it is better to make the inspection crew responsible to the production manager than to the shop foreman. Since the foreman is intent on keeping schedules and pushing production ahead, he sometimes shows a tendency to treat quality standards rather loosely. After all, a high rejection rate would slow up production and would reflect adversely on the foreman and his department.

There are two types of inspection: *centralized inspection,* in which the inspectors are grouped together in one area, and *floor inspection,* in which the inspectors are scattered along the assembly line.

Testing is one phase of inspection; it is especially useful for inspecting completed products. For example, cans are tested under pressure at high temperatures, and automatic washing machines are put through test runs before being crated for shipment.

Discussion Questions

8. *What is the difference between procedural control and performance control?*
9. *What type of control is being employed through the use of each of these: dispatching, inspection, routing, and standards?*

Inventory Control

If shortages are to be avoided, if production is to be kept moving, and if investment in inventories is to be kept at a minimum, there must be wise management and a sound accounting for all raw materials and goods in process. This management of goods on hand is known as *inventory control.*

If the supply of raw materials falls too low, the result is production delays. If inventories are maintained at too high a figure, company funds are tied up that might be used more advantageously elsewhere. Also, too large an inventory enhances the chance of loss due to a price decrease.

When materials are received, accurate records must be prepared and systematic procedures followed so that management will know the amount of materials in the factory and their progress through the production operation. The information kept on raw materials must include descriptions of the materials, the amounts in stock, when new orders should be placed, the period of time needed for their delivery, and the amount of goods already in transit.

The simplest way to take an inventory is by actual count of all materials on hand. But it is impossible to make such a count often enough, so day-by-day records are kept of receipts of new materials and their issuance to be placed in production. Such a day-by-day record is called a *perpetual inventory*. But even when perpetual inventories are maintained, they should be verified at regular intervals by an actual physical inventory count.

One common practice in inventory control is to issue both raw materials and supplies only upon written requisition. Each requisition should be dated and signed, and should show exactly what was issued, to whom, and for what purpose. Standardizing materials when practicable, and establishing the limits within which the inventory is to be maintained, are also helpful control procedures.

Discussion Question

10. *Why is control over inventories necessary?*

THE USE OF COMPUTERS IN INDUSTRY

Computers are used in many different ways, but in manufacturing operations their chief uses are in the areas of design and control.

Product Design

The computer is in reality the heart of the scientific research laboratory. Here the computer is used to simulate in detail hypothetical operations. The design engineer furnishes the creative ideas, and the computer expedites the handling of repetitive routine details. We might say that the designer and the computer work as a team. The designer who is strong on creativity can hold a "conference" of sorts with the computer, which is strong on detail.

For example, the General Motors Research Laboratory uses a computer system, built to their specifications, called the DAC-1 (Design Augmented by Computer). The DAC-1 can display a video picture of an image that has been stored electronically in its memory component. It can change this picture, both on the screen and in the storage component, as the designer makes alterations in the sketch by using a light-pen. It can also develop, for remote viewing, a 35 mm. transparency of any image in storage. And it will even "read" original drawings of key lines and convert them to machine language. As a matter of fact, using a blank screen and his light-pen, the designer can have the DAC-1 recall a sketch from storage and have it prepare an enlargement of a particular segment of the drawing. And he can rotate the image like a three-dimensional model and, again through the use of his light-pen, make changes in the original design!

Under traditional procedures, many new detailed drawings had to be made, and then numerous tedious mathematical analyses had to be calculated, in order to make any change in design. The computer eliminates both the manual drawings and the calculations. The versatility and speed of the computer makes possible its acceptance of a variety of design factors, such as wind resistance and road conditions, and quickly evaluate their effects on the problem at hand. Auto makers feel that as they gain more experience, and as computers become more sophisticated, as much as a year may be cut from the time formerly required to make the necessary dies to stamp out a body shell for a new car.

At the Lawrence Radiation Laboratory in Livermore, California, is one of the largest computer facilities in use in laboratory research. The computers simulate the behavior of nuclear devices as part of their work in evaluating how these devices will pan out in practice. This laboratory made the breakthrough that made possible the development of the Polaris missile warhead. The Atomic Energy Commission states that this accomplishment would not have been possible without the use of computers.

PHYSICAL FACTORS OF PRODUCTION

Every manufacturing business requires physical facilities to carry on its production operation. The kind of facilities used vary in accordance with the type and size of product or service that is being manufactured. As a result, there are certain factors that management of either a new or an established concern must consider.

Location Factors

The principal factors of plant location are based on the theory that the geographical point selected must serve to maximize the total business objectives most advantageously. This means that consideration must be given to several factors that management must evaluate. These factors are summarized in the following chart.

Virtually all the factors shown in this chart can be evaluated from the standpoint of their economic or cost feasibility. For example, what is the cost of shipping the finished products to the market by water as compared to truck shipment? Can adequate rail facilities be made available to provide spur tracks? Will the employees transferred be able to find suitable housing at a price they can afford to pay?

The early history of the location of manufacturing plants was one of *concentration.* Factories were concentrated in or near urban centers like New York, Chicago, or Los Angeles. The concentration of population living in these

SELECTION OF PLANT LOCATION

Site Factors

Proximity to sales markets
Proximity to related industries
Vulnerability to natural
  disasters

Resource Factors

Availability of skilled personnel
Availability of unskilled
  personnel
Availability of raw materials

Cost Factors

Cost of land
Cost of utilities
Construction costs
Cost of taxes
Cost of power, water, and fuel

Service Factors

Educational facilities
Fire and police protection
Health and medical services
Transportation facilities
Tax regulations and local laws

Miscellaneous Factors

Library facilities
Religious facilities
Public facilities

Employee shopping facilities
Adequate employee housing
Adequate business facilities

cities provided a nearby market and a readily available labor supply. New England was naturally the nation's first important industrial region. But as the population of the Middle Atlantic states increased, these states first equalled, then surpassed New England as a manufacturing region. In later years, the rapid population growth of Los Angeles enabled it to become one of our leading manufacturing centers.

Currently, *dispersion* in manufacturing is the order of the day. By building branch factories in different geographical areas, a company can be near several separate market centers, lessen the threat of destruction from atomic warfare, avoid paying the high cost of land for industrial sites in older cities, and facilitate the diversification of product manufacture.

Community and Government Attitude

Some companies have indicated that community attitude toward industry is the highest-ranking factor they consider when seeking a favorable location. In addition, these firms seek land at reasonable prices, and favorable building and zoning ordinances.

In some communities, foundations have actually been set up for the express purpose of attracting new industry. They buy large tracts of land approved or zoned for industry. They build access roads and railroad spurs to facilitate the physical movement of raw materials into plants and finished products out. Water and sanitary sewers are piped into the area, and in some instances the land is annexed to the city in order to provide the best police

Courtesy Continental Oil Company

The platforms are part of a Continental Oil Company complex used to produce oil.

and fire protection available. Land tracts are then made available to new industries.

City governments sometimes offer to bestow immunity from local property taxes on new industry for a period of from one to five years. The reasoning is that the entry of new enterprises into the area will increase the amount of taxable property, by bringing the factory property itself to the tax rolls and by encouraging the building of new homes and the establishment of new retail stores.

Discussion Questions

11. *Why is dispersion of manufacturing plants desirable?*

12. *Give examples of industries where nearness to raw materials is especially important.*

13. *In what way does the attitude of the people and of the government authorities in a local community become important in selecting a plant site?*

CAREER OPPORTUNITIES
IN PRODUCTION MANAGEMENT

One of the chief characteristics of production management is that there are many different types of positions within this field. Probably no other area of business offers the variety or number of supervisory jobs found in production—both line and staff positions. Line positions range from that of department foreman to plant superintendent. Staff positions include positions dealing with all types of supervisory functions, job analysis, time study, and inspection. Large companies require highly specialized personnel to fill certain staff positions.

In addition to the large number of different positions, there is also a variety of types of industries. This means that those persons interested in production management have a wide choice in selecting a career well suited to their interests and abilities.

Opportunities for advancement in production are quite good. In addition to strictly industrial engineering functions, production requires the same types of specialized services available in nonmanufacturing enterprises: cost accounting, statistical analysis, personnel management, merchandising, and advertising.

In short, production industries offer most of the career opportunities available in retail merchandising and service businesses, and in addition offer opportunities in production management, planning, development, and plant management.

Most large corporations send their personnel recruiters to college and university campuses to select graduates who have the potential for succeeding in middle- and top-management positions. College courses in industrial management, personnel administration, and marketing management provide the type of background suited to modern industrial management. This college preparation speeds the trainee along the advancement trail.

SUMMARY

American citizens are living today in an era of abundance that has come to be an accepted way of life. Consumers enjoy such a wide selection of goods that they seldom stop to question where they come from or how they were made. This mass of available goods has been made possible through wise production-management procedures that coordinate the raw materials, human labor, and machine technology in an efficient manner.

Manufacturing is the cornerstone of American business, because it employs directly approximately one-fourth of all gainfully employed people, and in addition supports many other closely related business activities.

Manufacturing is characterized by the practices of specialization, standardization, mechanization, and mass operations. The machine is the key to modern industrial processes, while manpower is utilized to supervise, maintain, operate, and coordinate mechanized operations. An ever-increasing number of production processes and machines are becoming automated in today's factories. Continuous engineering and developmental research is required to perfect the current methods, machinery, and products, and develop the new ones.

Today's scheme for manufacturing utilizes planning, programming, and control as a system or unit. The systems concept also looks at all the functions of a business enterprise—production, marketing, and finance—as a unit or whole.

The scientific-management movement originated with the work of Frederick W. Taylor toward the end of the eighteenth century. He was one of the first to introduce the use of time and motion studies in industry.

Procedural production control is secured through planning, routing, scheduling, and dispatching. Performance control is obtained by time and motion studies and comparisons of outputs with expected standards. Inspection is used to maintain standards, catch defective material and workmanship, and discover areas where improvement in the manufacturing processes are needed. Most operations utilize both centralized and floor inspection.

Testing is one phase of inspection. Samples of raw materials are tested to assure quality products; the completed products are also examined carefully. Mechanically operated products are usually put through test runs as the final production phase prior to being packaged for shipment.

Most persons do not realize the importance of control over raw materials. Since raw materials constitute, along with labor, the principal ingredients of the finished product, they must be conserved, protected, and utilized wisely, or the cost of finished goods increases considerably.

Every factory needs a location, and for each type of plant some locations are preferred to others. There are several factors that help to determine the best possible location, such as proximity to raw materials or to markets, adequacy of transportation facilities, and availability of labor, fuel, power, and water. For a given industry, one of these factors may outweigh all others, whereas for another industry it may be much less important. The attitude of the public and the local government officials is very important in setting a climate in which a manufacturing enterprise can prosper. The factory furnishes employment for the workers and they in turn are a strong determinant in the degree of efficiency attained. Their combined efforts are directed and coordinated by the production managers.

VOCABULARY REVIEW

Match the following vocabulary terms with the statements below:

a. Automation
b. Concentration
c. Dispatching
d. Dispersion
e. Floor inspection

f. Input
g. Inventory control
h. Location factors
i. Motion study
j. Perpetual inventory

k. Routing
l. Scheduling
m. Specialization
n. Standardization
o. Systems concept

1. The use of uniform methods in the performance of production jobs
2. The narrowing of one person's effort to one type of operation
3. Control of machine operations automatically, without using human labor
4. The synchronization of all the functions of a business enterprise and adoption of a total view of all business functions as a whole
5. The resources used to make a finished product
6. The breaking down of a job into its various motion components
7. The ordering of production processes into a logical sequence of activities
8. The setting of specific times for the carrying out of manufacturing operations
9. The preparation and issuing of work orders to carry out planned schedules
10. Placement of inspectors at various points along an assembly line rather than all in one place
11. A plan to make sure that adequate materials are always on hand and that they are not wasted, lost, or stolen
12. A list of materials on hand that is kept up to date on a day-by-day basis
13. The various items considered when choosing a factory site
14. The practice of locating several manufacturing plants in one place
15. The scattering of a company's factories, placing them in various locations

PROBLEMS AND PROJECTS

1. Assume that a manufacturer of stoves and refrigerators wishes to locate a factory in your home state. Name your state and name two cities (or towns) that you would recommend as excellent locations. List the reasons that they would be good locations. Describe the nature and adequacy of the truck and railroad terminals available. Is it a policy of the local government to give any tax concessions to new industry? If so, what is the nature of this incentive?
2. A local wholesale warehouse stores and ships cartons of canned goods and related grocery products to 75 retail grocery stores. In order to be sure it has sufficient goods on hand and on order to fill its deliveries, it must maintain an up-to-date inventory count at all times. Explain or describe the record scheme you would recommend for this purpose.

BUSINESS CASES

Case 12-1   Inventory Control

The Carter Corporation is a specialized tool and die manufacturer that makes tools and dies to specifications. Each job is different from all others. The present practice is to allow all workmen who need raw materials or supplies to enter the storerooms, take whatever they need for the work they are doing, and simply write out a list of the supplies and/or materials taken. The cost of materials is very much out of proportion to other costs when compared to the published norms for similar types of businesses. The company management has concluded that some of the men are wasting too much material and that others are taking material home with them for their personal use. The following procedures have been proposed:

a. All workers must check out materials and sign a requisition sheet.
b. Each requisition must be approved by a supervisor.
c. A perpetual-inventory card will be maintained for each type of material.
d. Once each week, the inventory clerk will report to the purchasing department the amount of materials on hand.
e. One clerk will record the additions on the inventory card and another record the subtractions.

Comment on the desirability of each of the five suggestions.

Case 12-2 Stabilizing Output

The Rogers Company manufactures refrigerators and airconditioners, which it markets largely through small chains of department stores that handle furniture and appliances. Their products are sold under several different brand names.

Rogers buys its electric motors from Hercules Motors and its cabinets from the Southern Fabricating Company. During the past two years, Rogers has had difficulty in meeting its delivery dates because labor and material problems at both these plants have caused delays in their delivery of parts to Rogers.

Rogers has made good profits over the years, and has accumulated a significant surplus in relation to its capital investment. However, its profits for the past two years have been low because of inability to secure motors and cabinets on time from its suppliers.

The questions before management are these:

a. Shall we try to purchase these two companies that serve as our principal suppliers?
b. Shall we switch to new suppliers?
c. Shall we build a new plant and produce our own motors, or our own cabinets, or both?

1. What do you see as the important factors that enter into the problem of restabilizing production and providing protection against spotty future delivery of parts?
2. Are there alternatives other than the three we have mentioned?

financial
management
and
risk functions

long-term financing and investments

CHAPTER THIRTEEN

Because the average businessman probably knows less about finance than about any other aspect of business administration, obtaining adequate capital financing is often one of the most difficult problem areas faced by business owners. Unless one or more owners are wealthy enough to place money in the business, funds—especially for long-term financing—are likely to be limited.

The amount of capital that a business needs and the sources from which these funds can be obtained depend largely on whether the firm is a sole proprietorship, partnership, corporation, or some other form of ownership that we studied in Chapter 5. The specific financial needs largely govern the method used to raise the necessary capital.

From the standpoint of its duration, capital financing may be considered long term or short term. Short-term financing is used to acquire working capital to cover current operating costs. In Chapter 14 we shall learn that commercial banks are among the principal suppliers of short-term funds to business.

In this chapter we are largely concerned with the sources of long-term

321

financing, which include funds obtained from owners, loans that mature in several years, and equity funds from the sale of securities to the public. Because of their importance, attention is devoted to the role of securities exchanges which are the financial centers that make available billions of dollars of new capital annually for American business.

DETERMINING CAPITAL NEEDS

A course of action for the owner who is either just starting a business or expanding an existing one is to make a careful study of the amount and kind of capital required, and then to investigate what sources of funds can best meet his needs. If the owner decides to borrow, he must go into debt, which may require putting up collateral. In this case, he decides whether the loan is needed for a short term, intermediate term, or long term. Short-term credit loans are usually one year or less. Intermediate-term credit generally represents a span of one to about ten years. Term loans are commonly used for intermediate financing. A *term loan* is actually a type of installment loan with repayments ranging from three to five years. Long-term credit is usually for ten or more years.

Types of Capital Requirements

The actual financial needs of a business, regardless of its size, normally involve two types of capital: fixed and working. The distinction between these is mainly in the way they are used.

Fixed capital is money invested in fixed assets to be used over a long period of time. For the acquisition of fixed capital items—land, building, and machinery—long-term financing is normally used. They are part of the total permanent capital structure, and therefore do not change their form in the short run.

Working capital is the money invested to meet daily operations.[1] This includes various kinds of short-term expenses. As such, working capital becomes a part of the funds used up and replaced in the normal operating cycle of a business. Indeed, there is a continuous flow of current assets in the direction of cash as merchandise inventories are sold and receivables are collected.

Discussion Questions

1. *What is long-term capital, and how is it used in business?*
2. *Explain the difference between fixed capital and working capital.*

---

[1] Accountants define "working capital" as the excess of current assets over current liabilities. This concept is explained in Chapter 16. Still another name for working capital is "short-term capital," when it is capital that is borrowed for a period of less than one year.

SOURCES OF
LONG-TERM CAPITAL

Today's financial manager must be alert to the sources of capital that are available to him. The most practical source of new funds for the individual proprietorship or partnership is personal savings, but corporations may make use of other means, among which are the following:

1. Sale of securities (stock and bonds)
2. Equity capital (owner's money)
3. Profits (reinvested in the business)

Financing by Sale of Bonds and Stocks

The strategy of corporation finance for the past several years in obtaining long-term funds was to issue as little common stock as possible and rely heavily on generating capital from profits and on the sale of bonds. This strategy seemed to make sense. For one thing, interest on bonds is tax-deductible, while common-stock dividends come out of profits. Financing through bonds made more money available for distributing dividends to stockholders.

There were also a growing number of pension funds and insurance companies that preferred to invest in bonds because of their high degree of safety, making it easy to sell bonds. Between 1961 and 1970, U.S. corporations raised $96 billion by selling bonds and only $8.6 billion from the sale of stock. The accompanying chart indicates the popularity of bonds over common stocks as a source of funds for corporations.

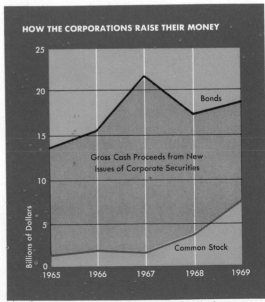

HOW THE CORPORATIONS RAISE THEIR MONEY

Gross Cash Proceeds from New Issues of Corporate Securities

Bonds

Common Stock

Billions of Dollars

Source: Securities and Exchange Commission

A new strategy has now developed. Corporations are still selling bonds to raise long-term funds, but not at the volume followed during the 1960's. Equity financing is increasing in popularity because of the continuing high bond-interest rates and growing inflation. Even smaller corporations are turning in greater numbers to the securities markets for new financing. Investors are turning away from bonds and expressing more interest in buying common and preferred stocks.

The following boxed list shows a comparison of stocks with bonds as a source of funds.

Stocks	Bonds
1. Stocks represent direct ownership.	1. Bonds represent a direct debt with interest.
2. Dividends are distributed from profits.	2. Bond interest represents a direct expense.
3. Dividends are payable at discretion of directors.	3. Interest payments are mandatory.
4. No maturity date is involved and there is no obligation to repay.	4. Principal must be repaid at specific dates.

Pros and Cons of Equity Financing

Use of equity financing offers several advantages:

1. There is the avoidance of interest charges normally paid on borrowed capital.
2. The business is financially stronger and more able to withstand a business recession because there are no fixed interest charges.
3. Assuming that the business is well financed in the beginning, the ability to borrow funds at a later date is enhanced by a strong underpinning of equipment investment.

The chief disadvantage of equity financing, except during periods of high business activity, is the difficulty the owner may have in providing sufficient funds to meet the financial requirements. The owner may also have difficulty in keeping his capital working; if part of it remains idle in cash balances, it will not be earning income for the firm.

Reinvestment of Profits

Reinvesting profits is also a satisfactory source of new capital, although there are times when funds from this source are not adequate. Some large and successful corporations prefer to borrow heavily to finance their growth, rather than retain substantial amounts of profits. This makes it possible to pay larger dividends. But financing by debt can obviously be a risky business. In the final analysis, first consideration must always be given to the nature of the firm's financial management policy and objectives.

Depreciation of Assets

Depreciation is another means of retaining funds in a business. In every business there are certain costs of operation that are not readily apparent, but that must be taken into account in the long run. One of these costs is *depreciation,* which is the amount of economic loss of a fixed asset, such as a building or machine, as a result of its use. The theory of this concept is that fixed assets begin to lose their value from the day they are put into use, and therefore some provision must be made for the allocation of these depreciation costs to the business operations during the life of the asset.

Discussion Questions

3. *What are some of the advantages that stocks offer as a source of long-term financing as compared with bonds?*
4. *Why is business turning more to equity financing and away from bonds?*

LONG-TERM DEBT FINANCING: BONDS

Debt financing is obtaining capital by borrowing. It is the financial practice of most businesses to use borrowed funds for purposes other than payment of monthly bills. Permanent debt financing by a corporation generally takes the form of issuing bonds or long-term promissory notes.

Trading on the Equity

In general, it is considered wise to borrow if the borrowed funds can earn more than those funds cost in interest. To borrow at 6 percent and earn 10 percent is a profitable way to finance a corporation. This principle is known as *trading on the equity.* In other words, the corporate directors elect to use borrowed funds rather than ownership capital. The effect, if successful, is to increase the return to the stockholders over what the return would have been had the loan not been made. The difference between what the company pays for borrowed capital and what it earns by using those funds belongs to the equity holders—hence, the term "trading on the equity."

Just how much trading on the equity is proper depends upon what constitutes a proper capital structure. When, for example, does the proportion of debt to equity financing become too high? The answer depends mainly on income. If, for the 6 percent bonds, the corporation had substituted 6 percent cumulative preferred stock, the effect on the common shareholder's return would be the same, except there would be less risk. If the directors feel that the company is reasonably sure to earn more on borrowed money than it pays out in the form of interest on the debt, the company can profitably borrow and continue to do so.

Advantages and Disadvantages of Bond Financing

Financing by bonds has several advantages:

1. The sale of bonds does not affect management control, since bondholders, unlike stockholders, have no voting rights.
2. Bond interest is a deductible expense under federal income tax laws.
3. By the practice of borrowing instead of issuing more stock, the shareholders' equity is not diluted, because there are no additional owners to share the earnings.

The chief disadvantages of issuing bonds to raise capital are that the principal must be repaid at a specific date to avoid foreclosure, and the fixed interest charges may become a financial burden during periods of little or no earnings.

Procedures for Issuing Bonds

Trust Indenture. Corporation bonds are generally issued with a *trust indenture,* which is a covenant (contract) between the lender and borrower. This indenture indicates all the various provisions of the bond issue, including limiting clauses and rights of the borrower. It also contains a list of responsibilities required of the borrower. Finally, it stipulates appointment of a third party, the *trustee,* (often a bank), to look after the interests of the bondholders, who may be widely scattered.

Trustee. Among his duties, the trustee must certify that the bonds are as described in the trust indenture and verify the signatures of the parties. He may hear bondholders' complaints and also may bring action against the corporation.

Classes of Bonds

Most corporation bonds are sold in $1,000 denominations. But in other respects, they may differ in several ways, according to their purpose. These differences are usually to make bonds more acceptable to the needs of individual corporations, and they may give issuing corporations an opportunity to pledge various assets of the business as collateral.

Among the classes of bonds are mortgage bonds, collateral trust bonds, income bonds, equipment trust bonds, and debenture bonds. Bonds may be either secured or unsecured. For example, a mortgage bond is one that is secured by a mortgage on the real property of the corporation. If the principal cannot be paid when due, the bondholders have a legal right to foreclose on the mortgage and sell the property to recover the loan. An example of a mortgage bond is Consolidated Edison's 5 percent Series N mortgage bonds that mature in 1987. These bonds were issued in the amount of $60 million, secured by a mortgage on the corporation properties.

When one series of mortgage bonds ranks ahead of others, they are known as first-mortgage bonds. Later issues are referred to as second-mortgage bonds, third-mortgage bonds, and so forth. Public utilities frequently issue bonds in this manner.

Bonds secured by collateral rather than by real property are called *collateral trust bonds,* because securities in the form of stocks or other bonds are pledged, with a trustee as backing for the bonds.

Bonds are sometimes issued with the provision that interest at a certain rate will be paid, provided it is earned in excess of other fixed charges. Bonds issued under this provision are called *income bonds.* During the reorganization of a corporation, income bonds may be issued to replace fixed-interest obligations that have proved too burdensome for the company to pay. Income bonds have maturity dates, as do other bonds, but the interest payments are contingent on company earnings.

Equipment trust bonds or *certificates* are used mainly by railroads to raise funds to buy new equipment. For example, a railroad may want to buy 25 new locomotives but cannot assemble enough cash to make the purchase without impairing its cash position. So it makes a down payment of 15 or 20 percent of the total cost, and finances the balance by selling equipment trust bonds to insurance companies and trust companies, under an equipment trust agreement with a trustee named in the agreement. Interest is paid at fixed periods to the trustee, who in turn pays the bondholders. When the bonds are fully paid, title to the equipment reverts from the trustee to the railroad company.

Debenture bonds are the type backed solely by the general credit of the company, and not by a mortgage or any pledged assets. They have been popular in business as a means of refinancing old debts. Since 1946, the American Telephone and Telegraph Company has sold nearly $5 billion worth of debenture bonds for its equipment expansion program. Of this total, $3.2 billion was raised by selling debenture bonds that could be converted into common stock under certain conditions. The Standard Oil Company of New Jersey, Consolidated Edison of New York, and the Coca-Cola Company have sold huge sums of debenture bonds at low interest rates. It was easy to find buyers for these bonds because of the sound financial condition of these corporations. As a rule, debenture bonds carry a slightly higher interest rate than other bonds because they are not secured by a mortgage; therefore, the risk to the investor is greater.

Bonds convertible into other securities, such as common stock, are known as *convertible bonds.* Terms of conversion are noted in the bond indenture.

When a single issue of bonds is divided into several groups with different maturity dates, they are called *serial bonds,* because the groups in the series mature at intervals in succeeding years.

A *registered bond* is issued in the owner's name, which is shown on the bond and on records kept by the corporation, thus affording protection against loss to the owner. *Coupon bonds,* on the other hand, are payable to bearer, and do not show the owner's name on the certificate. When bond interest is due, the holder simply clips a coupon from the bond and presents it to the bank that the corporation has authorized to make interest payments.

A coupon bond differs from other types of bonds. The principal is payable to the bearer of the bond, and the interest is payable to any one who detaches the coupon, as shown in the photograph, and presents it to a banking institution for payment.

Courtesy Merrill Lynch, Pierce, Fenner and Smith

Methods of Retiring Bonds

As part of the bond indenture, the issuing corporation is required to include one or more plans for the repayment of bonds at maturity. Three general plans are used: the serial plan, the sinking fund, and the call option.

Serial Plan. This plan stipulates that a certain number of bonds will be retired annually, based on the sequence of the number shown on the bond certificate. While this plan is an orderly procedure for amortizing corporation indebtedness, it may place a financial burden on the corporation to retire part of its bonds at a time when either the net profit is down or the company is short of cash. Investors sometimes dislike buying bonds to be retired under the serial plan because the maturity dates vary from short term to long term.

Sinking Fund. This plan calls for periodic deposits with the bond trustee of an amount that will assure availability of sufficient money to retire the debt when it becomes due. The sinking fund is commonly used by industrial corporations issuing bonds and is included in the indenture. In many respects, sinking-fund allocations are similar to installment financing.

Call Option. Although bonds are normally retired at maturity date, the debtor corporation may include a clause in the indenture that permits payment at the option of the issuer, usually at a premium. This provision, that allows an earlier date of redemption than the date of maturity, is called a *call option.* Bonds having this feature are known as *callable bonds.*

Bond Premium and Discount. A bond that sells at a price higher than its face value (the amount of its denomination) is said to be sold at a *premium.* If the sale price is less than face value, this is a *discount* sale. For example, a $1,000 bond currently selling at $1,025 has a bond premium of $25. When this bond is matured, the holder ordinarily receives only $1,000 (face value). In the same way, if the bond were sold at a discount, at maturity the holder would receive the face value.

Bond Ratings

Investors, and in fact government regulatory commissions, prefer to leave the matter of rating bonds to bond-rating agencies specializing in this type of analysis.

In appraising the merits of a bond, however, the investor should consider such factors as safety, income, and maturity. Standard & Poor's and Moody's are two of the principal rating agencies for industrial bonds. A bond rated AAA by Standard & Poor's service is considered to have the ultimate degree of safety with negligible risk of default. A bond rated AA is also a high-grade issue but not quite as free of default risk as triple-A. Bonds rated A and BBB by S & P's designation are generally referred to as medium-quality obligations in terms of income and maturity (ability to meet interest or sinking-fund payments). Bonds rated BB or B are speculative and suffer from low earnings and only narrow interest coverage during depression and recession periods.

---

5. *What are the advantages of using bonds for long-term financing as compared with the disadvantages?*
6. *Since a corporation does not have to repay funds from the sale of stock, why does it bother to issue bonds, which must be repaid?*

EQUITY FINANCING: STOCKS

The second basic method used by corporations to obtain long-term capital is the sale of capital stock. Unlike bondholders, who expect to be repaid, purchasers of stock become owners of the business; as such, they usually have a voice in its operation. The ownership of stock, whether common or preferred, is the main source of equity financing for corporations, and ownership is evidenced by a stock certificate.

Common Stock

Common stock is the best known of corporate securities. The term *common stock* is also frequently used to refer to capital stock when there is only one type of stock outstanding.

Financing by selling common shares involves several factors that affect both the shareholders and the corporation. From the viewpoint of the corporation, management may use at its discretion all money obtained from this source. There is no legal requirement for the company to pay back to the investor the value of the stock or to guarantee a dividend. Nor are the dividends cumulative—but if they are cut, they may or may not be made up the next year.

It is a common practice for corporations to issue either par value or no-par value stock. The term *par value* denotes an arbitrary value placed on the certificate. Par value is also stated in the corporate charter and can not be changed except by an amendment. Moreover, par value stock can not be legally issued for less than par. More often it is sold originally for more than par. (When it is sold above par, the difference is called *paid in surplus.*) Some states use par value as the basis for the state incorporation franchise taxes. Par value carries no general significance in the determination of a stock's market value.

When no stated value appears on the stock certificate, it is known as *no-par value* stock. The total ownership of the corporation is simply divided into shares, and dividends are paid at the rate of so many dollars or cents per share.

Common stock has other values too. *Market value* is the price of the shares on the market. *Book value* is the value of the stock carried on the company records; it is much more important than par value. Book value is computed by dividing the number of common shares outstanding into the total assets less all debts and minus the value of preferred stock, if any has been issued. Some investors calculate the book value of common stock by dividing the net worth by the number of shares outstanding. The book value is important mainly because it gives the investor some idea of the dollars per share that would be available if the company were liquidated. Investors also compare book value with market value.

Stockholders' Rights. In addition to the rights of the stockholder discussed in Chapter 5, each common stockholder has the privilege of exercising his preemptive right to subscribe to his proportionate part of any new stock. This is known as his *subscription right,* or sometimes as his *privileged subscription right.* It is the purchasing privilege of the stockholder to receive one right for each share of old stock owned by him.

As an illustration, if common stock is to be increased by 20 percent through the sale of additional shares, each shareholder in the corporation would receive the right to subscribe for one new share for every five old shares he owned. On a similar basis, a 50 percent increase in the number of shares would allow each existing stockholder to buy one new share for each two old ones. This principle—that one right represents one old share—never varies. When it is time for the stockholder to exercise his subscription right, he knows exactly how many shares of new stock he is entitled to buy; and if he does not want to subscribe, he may sell his subscription rights to other shareowners who wish to obtain sufficient rights to buy a full share of stock. Fractional shares of stock are not traded.

Stock-Purchase Warrants. Earlier in this discussion the term "subscription right" was used to identify the stockholder's preemptive right to subscribe to shares of new stock to be issued.

If a shareholder has not waived his preemptive right in a new stock issue, the corporation mails him one certificate—called a stock-purchase warrant—which shows the number of rights to which the shareholder is entitled. The rule is that one right is allotted to each share of old stock, but several rights are customarily required to buy each new share at an agreed price. Suppose a corporation having 500,000 shares of common stock outstanding decides to sell an additional 100,000 shares. In this situation, each existing stockholder needs five rights in order to buy one share of new stock at a stipulated price. Each shareholder owning 100 shares of old stock receives a stock-purchase warrant entitling him to buy 20 shares of the new issue.

In order to entice the old shareholder to exercise his stock-purchase warrant—or to get him to sell it to someone else—the price of the new issue should be somewhat lower than the current market price.

Some warrants expire on a given date; others are issued for the lifetime of the company or until exercised. If the stock to which a warrant is linked is listed on an exchange, the warrant has value in the market and may fluctuate in price. For example, a warrant entitling its holder to buy a share of XYZ stock at $25 has a basic value of $5 if that stock is selling at $30 on the market. Depending upon the price of the stock, the $5 basic-value warrant may sell at a premium (above $5) or at a discount (below $5). Currently, five corporations have warrants trading on the New York Stock Exchange.

Stock Options. During the past several years many large corporations have requested their stockholders to vote in favor of eliminating their pre-emptive right on a stated number of shares in order to install a stock option plan for key executives. A *stock option* is a privilege granted to certain executives enabling them to buy stock of the company under conditions favorable as to price and time. For example, certain executives are allowed to take advantage of an option to buy 5,000 shares of the company's stock at a time when it is selling for $25 a share. Subsequently the price advances to $60 a share and those executives each have a paper profit of $175,000. This plan has been heralded as an effective means of attracting and holding able young executives.

Stock Split. Companies often vote stockholders a *stock split,* which may be defined as the division, into additional units, of common stock outstanding. In other words, the total ownership "pie" is simply cut into smaller pieces without changing the value of the original portions. If you owned 30 shares and receive a two-for-one split, your 30 shares become 60; each new share is worth now half of the original share. The usual reason for a stock split is to bring the market price of each share into a trading range or price that more investors can afford to pay. If a stock selling for $200 a share has a four-to-one split, the new price "when issued" would be set at $50 a share. Each holder now has four shares for each one he held previously. Naturally, shareholders hope the price of the stock after the split will rise again.

Had you owned 100 shares of General Electric during the mid-1920's, it would now amount to 4,800 shares, owing to stock splits. If there had been no splits, with the stock continuing to rise as it did in market price, each share of GE would now be quoted at about $5,000.

Stock Dividend. A cash dividend is a distribution of earnings among stockholders. A stock dividend is a dividend paid in shares of capital stock. The declaration of a stock dividend does not increase the net worth of a corporation. Instead, each share of outstanding stock henceforth represents a smaller proportion of the total net worth, which has not changed. The directors may vote a stock dividend, if the surplus is available, without putting it to a vote of the shareholders. Stock dividends are more frequently paid on a percentage basis. For example, a 10 percent stock dividend means that one new share will be issued for each 10 shares outstanding. If a shareholder holds 12 shares at the time a 10 percent stock dividend is declared, he is entitled to receive $1\frac{1}{5}$ (or 1.2) new shares. Since fractional share certificates are normally not issued, the shareholder can buy on the market enough additional fractional shares to equal a full share, or he can sell his $\frac{1}{5}$ share at the current market price.

Distribution of stock, rather than cash, permits the retention of cash for use in the company. But then, sometimes a corporation will pay both a cash *and* a stock dividend. The company's dividend policy depends on the corporation's choice of whether to plow back all the earnings to avoid borrowing, or to issue part in new stock or part in cash.

The chief distinction between the stock dividend and the stock split is that the former requires a transfer from surplus to the capital account, whereas the surplus account is not affected by a stock split.

Preferred Stock

In addition to issuing common stock, many corporations raise additional capital by selling *preferred stock,* which is defined as stock that carries certain preferences over common stock. These preferences are stated in the corporation charter. Here are some of the special features of preferred stock (although these are not necessarily found in all preferred stock):

1. Preference as to assets
2. Preference as to dividends
3. A predetermined, stated dividend rate
4. No dilution of ownership of common stockholders
5. Right of conversion into common stock (not in all corporations)

Dividends on preferred stock may be either *cumulative* or *noncumulative.* Should a company's directors decide not to pay a dividend one year, the dividend on cumulative stock carries over to the next year or until it is paid. Dividends omitted in previous fiscal periods must be declared before any action can be taken on a distribution of earnings to common stockholders. Non-cumulative stock, however, provides that if the dividends are not paid during the year in which they are earned, the company is not obligated to pay the dividend later.

Financial Decision Guidelines

As we may observe from this discussion, financial managers have several choices of sources of long-term debt financing. But there is a question of the amount of debt a company can support. Furthermore, when does the proportion of debt to equity financing become too high for safety? The answers to these two questions rest mainly in how stable, how large, and how secure the firm's income is likely to be in the future. Firms that can reasonably predict long-range stability and security of the company's income can carry substantial fixed interest charges under a long-term contract debt.

The following guideline may be used when choosing a type of security as a source for long-term financing:

1. Bonds are appropriate when earnings are expected to be maintained well above the fixed interest charges and amortization requirements.
2. Preferred stock may be used when one can predict—with a relatively high degree of accuracy and over a period of several years—that earnings will remain well above the prevailing dividends to be paid.
3. Common stock is suitable for the raising of capital when one cannot predict with certainty that earnings will cover interest and sinking-fund deposits.

Discussion Questions

7. *Explain the difference between a stock dividend and a stock split and state how each is used.*
8. *What are some of the principles that serve financial managers in helping them to select the types of securities to use for long-term financing?*

STOCK EXCHANGES AND SECURITIES MARKETS

Thus far in this discussion, we have dealt with the problems of determining long-term capital needs, the sources of funds, and the types of securities—preferred and common stocks, and bonds—that are used. Because there is a widespread use of and interest in stocks and bonds by individual investors, as well as by business firms seeking capital, more than a dozen large and small securities markets, referred to as stock exchanges, have been organized in the United States to provide centers for trading (buying and selling securities at auction).

These markets are meeting places where those seeking capital can negotiate with the representatives of those who have capital to invest.

The New York Stock Exchange

The New York Stock Exchange is the largest market for trading in listed stocks and bonds in this country. It is a corporation governed by a 33-man

TABLE
13.1

**THE 10 MOST WIDELY HELD CORPORATION COMMON STOCKS
AND THE NUMBER OF THEIR SHAREHOLDERS,
1971**

Company	Number of Shareholders
American Telephone and Telegraph Co.	3,052,000
General Motors Corporation	1,334,000
Standard Oil (New Jersey) Company	809,000
International Business Machines Corporation	587,000
General Electric Company	521,000
General Telephone & Electronics Corporation	472,000
Ford Motor Company	382,000
United States Steel Corporation	356,000
RCA Corporation	330,000
Texaco Inc.	284,000

Source: Financial World Stock Factograph, *1971.*

board. The exchange membership has been 1,366 since 1953. "Seats" (evidences of membership) owned by members may be transferred subject to approval of the board of governors. The record price for a seat is $625,000, which was paid in 1929. Membership carries the right to act for clients as a broker or dealer on the floor of the exchange. As you can see from Table 13.1, there are several corporations listed on the New York Stock Exchange whose shareholders number in excess of one-half million.

To be a listed company on the exchange, a corporation must meet certain requirements, which are considered stringent as compared with those of other exchanges. Each company applying for initial listing must agree to furnish to the public—including its stockholders—earnings statements, dividend notices, and other information that may be considered pertinent and useful in influencing investment decisions. The company must have demonstrated earning power under competitive conditions of $2.5 million before federal income taxes for the most recent year and $2 million for the preceding two years. In addition, the company must have a total of $14 million in common stock publicly held, and out of each million shares outstanding in common stock, 800,000 must be common shares. All listed companies must give their shareholders the privilege of voting and must issue proxies for stockholders' meetings. The New York Stock Exchange also imposes other requirements for continued listing.

A reorganization of the New York Stock Exchange, and possibly others in New York City, is predicted for the near future. A recent study made by William McChesney Martin, Jr., the first salaried president of the New York Stock Exchange and a former chairman of the Federal Reserve Board, recommended a consolidation of national exchanges into a single exchange, which would involve a reorganization of the New York Stock Exchange as well as new regulations and controls for more efficiency. Table 13.2 lists the ten corporations whose common stocks have the highest market value among those on the New York Stock Exchange.

TABLE
13.2

**THE 10 COMMON STOCKS LISTED
WITH THE HIGHEST MARKET VALUE ON THE NEW YORK STOCK EXCHANGE
DECEMBER 31, 1970**

Company	Listed Shares (In Millions)	Market Value
International Business Machines Corporation	114.5	$36,393
American Telephone and Telegraph Co.	549.3	26,846
General Motors Corporation	287.6	23,151
Standard Oil (New Jersey) Company	226.6	16,627
Eastman Kodak Company	161.5	12,217
Sears, Roebuck & Co.	154.6	11,785
Texaco Inc.	274.3	9,566
General Electric Company	92.0	8,633
Gulf Oil Corporation	211.9	6,860
Xerox Corporation	77.8	6,734

Source: New York Stock Exchange, Fact Book, *1971, p. 32.*

The American Stock Exchange

The second largest organized stock exchange is the American Exchange, which also is located in New York. It is organized in much the same way as the New York Stock Exchange but has a smaller membership—approximately 500 seats with full membership and about 400 associate members. This exchange also has listing requirements, but they are not as stringent as those of the New York Stock Exchange. The American Exchange is the leading national market in foreign securities. Many of the nation's leading corporations are members of this exchange.

The National Stock Exchange

The National Stock Exchange is the third national exchange located in New York. It began operation on March 7, 1962 and by recent count has a total of 145 companies listed for trading. Most them have come from the over-the-counter market.

Regional and Local Exchanges

Regional and local stock exchanges also furnish a securities marketplace for many geographical areas. The Midwest Exchange in Chicago, the Philadelphia-Baltimore-Washington Stock Exchange, all of which are regional exchanges, generate almost 7 percent of the total volume of the regional and local exchanges. The remaining exchanges are located in the following cities (in no particular order): Boston, Detroit, Cincinnati, Pittsburgh, Spokane,

Honolulu, Salt Lake City, Richmond, Wheeling, and Colorado Springs. Each regional exchange lists approximately 500 companies, while the smaller local exchanges list about 100 companies each. The prices of shares traded on local exchanges is usually low. Seats and fees for memberships are relatively inexpensive, although there is no direct relationship between stock prices and membership fees.

Foreign Stock Exchanges

One of the oldest exchanges in the world is the London Stock Exchange. Known as the "Stock Exchange," it lists and trades about seven times the number of issues listed on the New York Stock Exchange. The Paris Stock Exchange (*Bourse*) is an important European exchange. Security markets are closely regulated in France dating back to Napoleonic times. Stock exchange markets in Switzerland, listed in the order of their importance, operate in Zurich, Geneva, Basel, Lausanne, Berne, Neuchâtel. These markets also work on a system of auction, with traders located around a circular shaped platform (pulpit). Swiss banks are allowed to transact business on the stock exchanges. Daily papers publish stock quotations. The Toronto Stock Exchange has over 1,000 listed issues. Since World War II, the stock exchanges in Japan have become important. There are nine exchanges in Japan with the largest in Tokyo.

The Over-the-Counter Market

In addition to the system of organized stock exchanges, there is also a market known as the over-the-counter market (OTC) where unlisted stocks are bought and sold. This market is not really a place. Rather, it is a method of doing business by negotiation. On organized exchanges, securities are traded by the auction method, with offers to buy and sell being quoted openly. Suppose, as an investor, you want to buy 50 shares of a hypothetical company—Zero Corporation. You consult your broker who does not have this particular stock. So, in turn, he consults with other brokers or dealers. When your broker finds a seller, and provided you are willing to buy at the lowest price he has found, he will place your order. As you can see, over-the-counter transactions are usually more time consuming than those on an organized exchange.

Approximately 55,000 securities, including stocks, corporate bonds, and government bonds, are traded over the counter. Shares are sold in any number by brokers and dealers. Just as a retail merchant buys and sells for a profit, the securities dealer buys securities for resale to prospective customers. Securities brokers act as agents for buyers and sellers. In the case of a large brokerage firm that attempts to make a market for OTC stocks, the brokerage will act as a principal and sell the shares from its inventory. If the broker does not have the shares to sell, he will attempt to buy them from a dealer at the best possible price for resale to his client.

The "Third Market"

There is no law that says listed stocks have to be traded exclusively on an exchange— a stockholder can sell his shares to anyone, provided he arranges for the proper transfer. In recent years, many "off-the-board" or nonmember firms that do not charge regular listed commissions on sales have offered their services to large institutional investors, insurance companies, and mutual and pension funds who buy and sell large blocks of stock as investors. These nonmember firms comprise a relatively new and growing securities market called the "third market." By using this market, institutional investors are able to save on commissions for large blocks of securities because the commission rates are negotiated.

To meet this competition, some brokerage firms have bought a membership on regional exchanges that also trade in stocks listed on the "Big Board." These regional exchanges permit commission cutting on large blocks, whereas the New York Exchange does not. This makes the brokerage firms more competitive with the third-market firms.

Function of the Securities Markets

Within the framework of our economic system, securities exchanges operate as marketplaces where buyers meet sellers through agents who are authorized to do business on the exchanges. It is possible for two persons in widely separated areas of the United States, through their brokers, to trade with each other without personal contact. You may wonder why you cannot buy a stock directly from a corporation listed on the exchange, just as you buy an automobile from your dealer. This is because a corporation has only so many shares outstanding. Whether you want to buy 10, 25, 100, or 1,000 shares listed on the exchange, you must buy from someone who owns (or a combination of several who own) that number of shares. You must buy from a broker who is the agent for each party.

There are certain facts that are worth keeping in mind concerning buying or selling stock on an exchange:

1. When you buy stock, you buy from another person through a broker.
2. When you sell stock, you sell to another person through a broker.
3. The exchange provides the marketplace for the sale.
4. The exchange neither buys, sells, nor sets the price of your stock.
5. Through their daily operations, the exchanges provide a continuous market with a constant release of market information.

Stock Quotations. Most daily newspapers publish, on the financial page, prices paid in stock transactions on the New York Stock Exchange and the American Exchange. This report is an alphabetical listing of stocks, showing

Tuesday's Volume, 13,330,000 Shares

Volume since Jan. 1:	1971	1970	1969
Total sales	3,261,425,975	2,392,902,891	2,388,124,731

ACTIVE STOCKS

	Open	High	Low	Close	Chg.	Volume
Am Tel&Tel	42⅛	42⅜	41⅞	42⅛	....	215,500
IntTelTel	49⅞	50¼	49⅞	50⅛	− ⅛	146,900
FstNCtyCp	41¼	41⅜	40¾	41¼	− ⅜	135,700
IntT&T pf N	62⅛	62¾	62⅛	62¾	+ ¼	126,000
Polaroid	89⅞	90½	89¾	90	....	125,900
Ronson	6	6⅛	5	5¼	− ¾	106,300
Athlone Ind	13⅝	13⅞	13½	13⅞	+ ⅜	102,300
Gen Elec	56½	57⅞	56¼	57¼	+ ½	100,000
Sundstrnd	23⅜	23⅜	23	23	− ¾	85,600
Fairch Cam	24	25⅜	24	25	+ ¾	82,500

Average closing price of most active stocks: 41.06.

A-B-C

−−1971−−			Sales in					Net
High	Low	Stocks Div	100s	Open	High	Low	Close	Chg.
18¾	13	AbacusF .74g	18	15¾	15¾	15¾	15¾	.....
85⅜	54	AbbtLb 1.10	66	59⅛	59½	58⅞	59	− ⅛
60	45¼	ACF Ind 2.40	284	50½	50½	50	50	− ½
17½	12½	AcmeClev .80	16	12½	12⅝	12½	12½	− ⅛
64¾	42½	Acme Mkt 2b	21	50⅜	50⅜	49¾	50	− ¾
14¾	12¼	AdmsEx .86g	60	12¼	12½	12⅛	12¼	− ¼
19⅝	10	Ad Millis .20	23	10¾	10¾	10½	10¾	− ¼
49¼	23⅞	Address .60g	150	30	31¼	29¾	30¾	+ ¼
21	8	Admiral	57	15¾	16⅛	15⅝	16	+ ¼
70⅛	45⅝	AetnaLfe 1.60	109	58⅜	60⅜	58⅜	59¼	+ ¾
13¼	8⅜	Aguirre Co	2	8⅜	8½	8⅜	8½	....
29½	20½	Aileen Inc	114	23⅜	23½	22⅞	23	− ½
57¾	44⅞	Air Prod .20b	33	50⅝	51½	50⅝	51½	+ ⅝
26½	16¼	AircoInc .80g	122	16½	16⅞	16⅜	16⅝	+ ¼
5⅜	2⅞	AJ Industries	6	3⅜	3½	3⅜	3⅜	.....
46¾	34¼	Akzona 1a	12	37¼	37½	36½	36½	− ½
17⅞	15¼	Ala Gas 1.10	22	17⅝	17¾	17½	17¾	+ ⅛
29⅛	16⅞	Alaska Inters	136	17½	17⅝	16⅞	16⅞	− ⅞
46	26⅛	AlbertoC .32	31	27	27½	26⅝	27½	+ ½
15¼	11	Albertsns .36	15	11⅞	12⅛	11⅞	12	+ ⅛
24¾	16	Alcan Alum 1	95	16⅜	16⅝	16¼	16⅜	....
24¼	15½	AlcoStand .30	20	15¾	15¾	15	15	− ½
46⅞	41⅝	Alcon Lab .26	16	41⅝	41⅞	41½	41½	− ¼
31⅜	22	Alexndrs .30r	13	22	22	21⅜	21⅜	− ⅝
17⅛	12½	AllAmLf .24g	13	14¼	14⅜	14¼	14¼	....
18½	11⅛	Alleg Cp .10g	34	11½	11¾	11⅜	11¾	+ ⅛
32½	17⅛	AllegLud 1.40	112	17½	17½	17	17⅛	− ½

Courtesy The Wall Street Journal, *Dow Jones & Co., Inc.*

the volume of sales and the price of each stock. The accompanying illustration is a partial list of stock quotations reported daily by *The Wall Street Journal.*

You will observe from this list that sales are recorded in lots of 100 shares, "round lots," on stock exchanges. "Odd lot" sales (less than 100 shares) are usually listed in a separate section of the newspaper. Price quotations are in dollars and fractions of dollars ranging from ⅛ to ⅞. Hence, a quotation of 25⅝ indicates the price is $25.625 per share. Following the name of each stock is the amount of the dividend paid to date, or other information, such as a footnote reference to a key shown below the list of stocks.

The diagram on page 340 explains in detail how to read a stock market quotation. (Your newspaper may not carry the various columns as shown in the illustration from *The Wall Street Journal.*)

Bond Quotations. In addition to stock prices (common and preferred), many newspapers list bond prices similar to the one shown on page 340 from *The Wall Street Journal.* Most bond quotations are in denominations of $100, although the usual face value is $1,000. For example, a bond quoted at 95

HOW TO READ THE FINANCIAL PAGE OF A NEWSPAPER

Final Prices for the Day

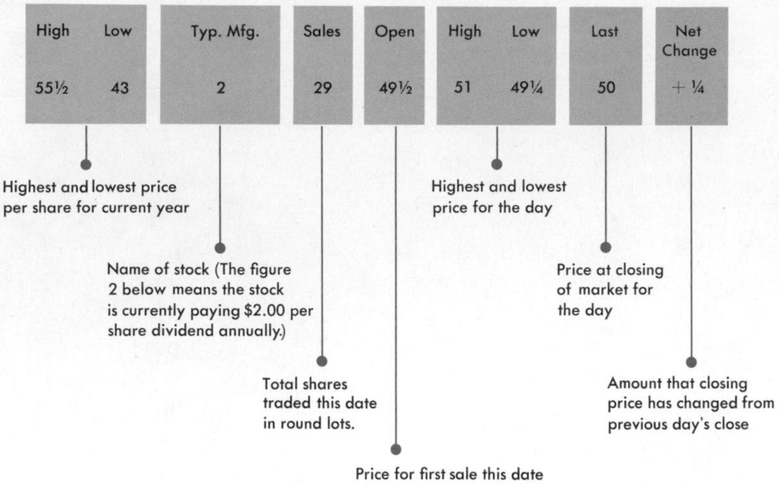

High
Low
Typ. Mfg.
Sales
Open
High
Low
Last
Net Change
55½
43
2
29
49½
51
49¼
50
+ ¼
Highest and lowest price per share for current year
Name of stock (The figure 2 below means the stock is currently paying $2.00 per share dividend annually.)
Total shares traded this date in round lots.
Price for first sale this date
Highest and lowest price for the day
Price at closing of market for the day
Amount that closing price has changed from previous day's close

Courtesy The Wall Street Journal, *Dow Jones & Co., Inc.*

American Stock Exchange Bonds

VOLUME, $3,120,000

SINCE JANUARY 1

	1971	1970	1969
Total sales	$741,170,000	$537,081,000	$777,493,000

	Tues.	Mon.	Fri.	Thur.
Issues traded	98	98	93	94
Advances	30	27	31	30
Declines	31	38	32	47
Unchanged	37	33	30	27
New highs, 1971	1	2	3	2
New lows, 1971	2	6	3	4

——1971—— High	Low	Bonds	Sales in $1,000	High	Low	Close	Net Chg.
148	100	Allson M 7s90	26	134	132	134	−1⅛
61	51	AllegA 5½s87	5	57½	57½	57½	.....
126½	75	Al Art 8¾s90	8	80	79½	80	.....
59⅞	49½	AlloyU 4½s93	4	50⅛	50⅛	50⅛	.....
138	100	A CentM 7s90	55	126	124	126	.....
102½	94	A CeM 6¾s91	27	96	94	96	+2
146	84	Banstr 6½s89	842	151	135¼	149	+10
72	54	BartM 6½s88	5	60½	60½	60½	.....
79	61	Bel El 6¾s84	21	75¾	75½	75¾	+ ¼
79¾	60½	Boothe 5¾s88	20	63½	62½	62½	−1¼
89¾	62½	Butt 5½s88	12	71½	71	71½	− ½
120	87	Cabl cv6½s90	36	89	88	89	−1
134	120	Cabot 6¾s91	15	120¼	117½	119	−3
98	92⅝	Chri Cft 7s72	7	98	98	98	+ ½
62	43	Cobrn 5½s87	22	60	59	60	+1
64	45	Condec 5s93	48	50	49	49½	+ ½
119	94	Con Tl 5¼s86	7	95	95	95	.....
122	78½	Crys Oil 7s84	20	81	80	81	.....
62¼	46	DProd 5¾s95	9	48½	48	48½	.....
81⅝	60¾	Daylin 5s89	3	68½	68	68	− ½
90½	54	DCADev 6s88	9	60	60	60	.....
99½	66	Dearb 5¼s88	20	92	92	92	.....
105¾	84½	East Air 8s88	25	98½	98½	98½	+1
106	87½	Ehren 4¾s87	3	100	99¾	100	+1
68	54	Elecsp 5½s83	2	59⅝	59⅝	59⅝	−1⅝
80⅝	63	Elgin 6⅞s82	2	66	66	66	−1⅞
68½	55⅝	Elgin 6¾s88	10	61⅛	61⅛	61⅛	− ⅛
113	90½	FidMg 7¾s85	16	108	107	108	+ ½
66	54	FstNR 6½s76	1	58	58	58	.....
106	82	FischPtr 6s86	29	101	101	101	.....
73¼	55	Fisch 5½s87	5	70	70	70	−1⅝

Courtesy The Wall Street Journal, *Dow Jones & Co., Inc.*

means the trading price is $950 as of that quotation date and that it is selling for 95 percent of par, or the price of its denomination.

Whereas stocks are traded and quoted in dollars per share and in fractions of $\frac{1}{8}$, $\frac{1}{4}$, $\frac{3}{8}$, $\frac{1}{2}$, $\frac{5}{8}$, $\frac{3}{4}$, and $\frac{7}{8}$, trading unit price variations for corporation bonds and foreign government bonds are quoted in eighths of a point expressed as a percent of par. U.S. government and state bonds listed on the New York Stock Exchange or on the over-the-counter market are quoted in thirty-second points. Thus a federal Treasury obligation quoted at 102.12 is the same as $102\frac{12}{32}$, or $102\frac{3}{8}$. The interest rate on bond quotations is also shown in a percentage of par; thus "$6\frac{1}{2}$s" means that interest payments are 6.5 percent of par value of the bond per year.

In determining the calculation of bond yields, the fulcrum around which the yield varies is the interest rate, which is fixed for the life of the bond. It is stated as a rule as a percentage of the par value of the bond. Thus a 6 percent rate on a $1,000 is $60 ($60 ÷ $1,000). If the market price of the bond drops to $900, the yield goes up and if the market price increases, the yield goes down. However, if we know the current market price and interest rate, we can calculate yield by using bond yield tables, such as in the *Basic Book* published by the Financial Publishing Company, Boston, Massachusetts. Otherwise, computing the yield involves a complicated formula.

Discussion Questions

9. *Explain the functions of the organized stock exchange.*

10. *Discuss the importance of regional and local exchanges.*

INVESTMENT ANALYSIS
AND FINANCIAL MANAGEMENT

Having explored the scope of long-term financing, the various sources, and the functions of the securities markets, let us turn to the role of the investment broker.

Role of the Stockbroker

Whether you live in Cheyenne or Chicago, if you desire to buy or sell stocks or bonds, you consult with your local stockbroker who is likely to be an employee of a brokerage firm. He is often referred to as a "registered representative" or "account executive." His primary function is to act as his client's agent to buy and sell both listed and unlisted securities. The stockbroker should not be confused with the term "dealer" sometimes called "trader," who buys and sells stocks for his own account, hoping to make a profit. The odd-lot dealer, for example, deals in less than 100-share lots.

Many brokerage offices are equipped with a large Teleregister board, which automatically records price changes of each of several hundred stocks. This board shows the symbol for the stock, the price changes as they occur, and the number of shares for each transaction. A sample ticker tape is illustrated below.[2] Only the price is shown when the sale is for 100 shares (a "round lot"); for multiples of 100, the number of hundreds is given. For sales above 1,000, the exact number is printed.

Investment vs. Speculation

Among Americans, common stocks are perhaps the most popular investment. They are easy to buy, may be bought in small lots, and are quickly converted into dollars.

Definitions. *Investment* is the purchase of securities, based on analysis, that appear to offer safety of principal and a satisfactory yield commensurate with the amount of risk over a period of time. This definition suggests that the investor should have a clearly defined investment objective and not just speculate in an effort to make a large profit quickly. *Speculation* means the deliberate assumption of risks in ventures that appear to offer anticipated gains. It is an exercise in reasoning, however; the difference between investment and speculation is only a matter of degree of risk. When investors speculate heavily on "tips" or hearsay, this is gambling.

It is often suggested that before buying any stock, one should have a savings account, which may be used if necessary to meet an emergency, and a reasonable amount of life insurance for personal protection.

Choosing Your Investment Objective. It is the wise investor who invests to achieve one or more of the following objectives: (1) safety of principal, (2) income, and (3) growth of capital.

Stocks and bonds differ in the way they satisfy these objectives. If safety of principal is the most important objective, good-quality bonds and preferred

$$\text{J} \quad \text{SOM} \quad \text{T} \quad \text{BSP}_r \quad \text{F}$$
$$50\tfrac{7}{8} \quad 3\text{s}49 \quad 108\tfrac{1}{2} \quad 146\tfrac{1}{4} \quad 1000\text{s}82\tfrac{1}{2}$$

[2] Only a small portion of the tickertape is included in this illustration, which shows the following sales of common stocks: J—Standard Oil Company (New Jersey), 100 shares at $50.87½ per share; SOM—Socony Mobile, Inc., 300 shares at $49 per share; T—American Telephone and Telegraph Company, 100 shares at $108.50; BSP$_r$—Bethlehem Steel Corporation, 100 shares preferred at $146.25; and F—Ford Motor Company, 1,000 shares at $82.50 per share.

TABLE
13.3
INVESTMENT OBJECTIVES

Security	Safety	Growth	Income
Common stocks	least	best	varies
Preferred stocks	high	varies	steady
Bonds	highest	very little	very steady

stocks are most likely to achieve it, because there is far less risk in these than in some other types of securities. Those seeking high dividend income with less emphasis on safety often favor common stocks. Common stocks of some companies are better in this regard than others. Public utilities, for example, tend to pay out a relatively high percentage of their earnings in dividends. For those seeking mainly growth of capital and willing to sacrifice high dividend income, common stocks in growth companies may be selected. Among the current growth industries are the electronics, oil, chemical, and drug companies. There are some growth companies in almost all industries. A relationship of these objectives to the three classes of securities is expressed in Table 13.3.

Selecting Your Company. One way to determine whether a particular corporation is a growth, income, or speculative investment is by charting over a long period of time the dividends, earnings, and sales volume record. The accompanying chart of the J.C. Penney Company is an example of the *growth*

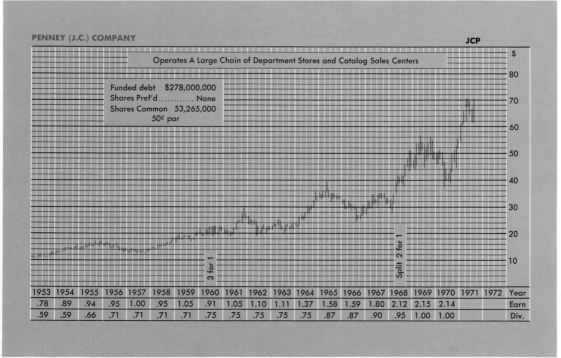

PENNEY (J.C.) COMPANY   JCP

Operates A Large Chain of Department Stores and Catalog Sales Centers

Funded debt $278,000,000
Shares Pref'd .... None
Shares Common 53,265,000
50¢ par

Year	1953	1954	1955	1956	1957	1958	1959	1960	1961	1962	1963	1964	1965	1966	1967	1968	1969	1970	1971	1972
Earn	.78	.89	.94	.95	1.00	.95	1.05	.91	1.05	1.10	1.11	1.37	1.58	1.59	1.80	2.12	2.15	2.14		
Div.	.59	.59	.66	.71	.71	.71	.71	.75	.75	.75	.75	.75	.87	.87	.90	.95	1.00	1.00		

Courtesy M.C. Horsey & Company, Inc., Salisbury, Maryland

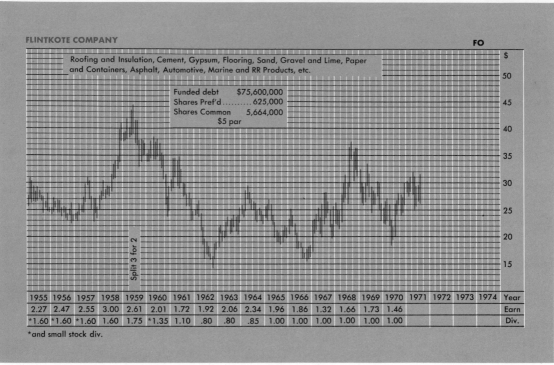

FLINTKOTE COMPANY   **FO**

Roofing and Insulation, Cement, Gypsum, Flooring, Sand, Gravel and Lime, Paper
and Containers, Asphalt, Automotive, Marine and RR Products, etc.

Funded debt $75,600,000
Shares Pref'd 625,000
Shares Common   5,664,000
               $5 par

Split 3 for 2

Year	1955	1956	1957	1958	1959	1960	1961	1962	1963	1964	1965	1966	1967	1968	1969	1970	1971	1972	1973	1974
Earn	2.27	2.47	2.55	3.00	2.61	2.01	1.72	1.92	2.06	2.34	1.96	1.86	1.32	1.66	1.73	1.46				
Div.	*1.60	*1.60	*1.60	1.60	1.75	*1.35	1.10	.80	.80	.85	1.00	1.00	1.00	1.00	1.00	1.00				

*and small stock div.

Courtesy M.C. Horsey & Company, Inc., Salisbury, Maryland

type of investment. Notice that both earnings and dividends have increased over a long period, whereas the record of the Flintkote Company, also shown in a chart, reveals sharp earnings and dividend fluctuations. Companies with this kind of record are known as *cyclical companies;* as a rule, they tend to benefit from periods of general prosperity and suffer from economic recessions.

The chart for the Pacific Gas and Electric Company, a public utility, illustrates an *income stock.* Income stocks are noted for their dividend incomes, with growing earnings from year to year.

Small investors are often advised to build their portfolios on either growth or a combination of growth and income stocks. Table 13.4 is a selected list of common stocks noted for their growth prospects. Observe that these stocks have a high price–earnings ratio but a low dividend yield. This may be due to the fact that investors are willing to pay more for growth stocks because of the possibilities for gain. The price–earnings multiple (P/E ratio) is computed by dividing the market price by its actual or indicated annual earnings per share. A stock selling at 30 with annual earnings of $2 a share has a P/E ratio of 15.

Table 13.5 is a list of common stocks noted for their high incomes. These

TABLE
13.4

SELECTED COMMON STOCKS WITH PROMISING GROWTH PROSPECTS

Stock	Recent Price	Dividend	% Yield	EARNINGS 1971*	EARNINGS 1970	EARNINGS 1969	P/E Ratio
Coca-Cola	101	$1.58	1.6	$2.80	$2.48	$2.20	36
Eastman Kodak	77	1.32	1.7	2.60	2.50	2.49	30
Xerox Corp.	113	0.80	0.7	2.70	2.40	2.08	42
Polaroid Corp.	102	0.32	0.3	2.20	2.20	2.16	29
Standard Brands Paint	64	0.40	0.6	1.80	1.36	1.13	36
Texas Instruments	104	0.80	0.8	3.00	2.71	3.06	35

*Estimate
Source: Financial World Stock Factograph, *1971.*

companies have high dividends and high yield with a low P/E ratio. Yield is computed by dividing the annual dividend by the market price. A stock that costs $50 a share and pays a $2 annual dividend will yield a 4 percent return ($2 ÷ $50).

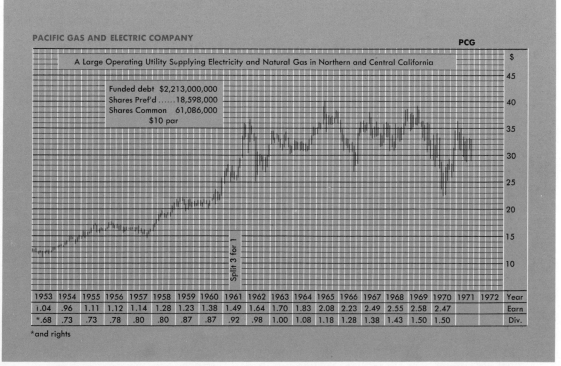

Courtesy M.C. Horsey & Company, Inc., Salisbury, Maryland

TABLE
13.5

SELECTED COMMON STOCKS WITH RECORDS OF HIGH INCOME

Stock	Recent Price	Dividend	% Yield	EARNINGS 1971*	EARNINGS 1970	EARNINGS 1969	P/E Ratio
American Electric Power	28	$1.70	6.1	$2.40	$2.30	$2.20	12
Atlantic City Electricity	22	1.36	6.2	1.90	1.83	1.83	12
Baltimore Gas & Electricity	32	1.82	5.7	2.85	2.77	2.60	11
Pacific Gas & Electricity	32	1.64	5.1	2.65	2.47	2.85	12
Standard Oil (N.J.)	77	3.80	4.9	6.50	5.90	5.78	12
Chesapeake & Ohio	59	4.00	6.8	6.50	5.42	6.05	9

*Estimate
Source: Financial World Stock Factograph, *1971.*

Evaluating Company Management and Its Record. One way to evaluate a company's record is to study management's performance by asking the following questions:

1. Has the management been able to maintain a strong earnings and sales record, and have dividends increased or decreased for the past several years?
2. What rating does the company have as shown in investment manuals?
3. Are the company's products or services widely accepted by the public?
4. Does the company have a program for development of managers that prepares them for promotions?

Dividends

Dividends are paid in cash or stock, or both. Even if the company has not earned a profit in the period for which the dividend is due, providing there are sufficient funds in the surplus account, it may be paid from that source. From the company's point of view, a stock dividend makes sense because it helps to conserve cash, which may eliminate a need for additional financing in the future.

From the investor's angle, stock dividends offer a tax advantage. Cash dividends are taxes in the year they are received, but stock dividends are not taxed until you sell your shares, and a profit may receive capital-gains treatment at that time.

At the time dividends are declared, there are four important dates: (1) the declaration date, (2) record date, (3) ex dividend date, and (4) payment date.

Declaration Date. This is the date, established by the directors, that the dividend is declared, either as a "regular" or "extra" dividend.

Record Date. This date (usually a few weeks after declaration date) is used to determine which shareholders will receive the dividend, based on their ownership up to and including this date. All shareholders whose names are registered by the record date will receive the dividend. Were you to buy a stock up to five business days prior to the record date, you would still have time to obtain delivery of your stock through regular channels and have your name placed on the books as a stockholder of record.

Ex Dividend Date. Ex dividend means "without a dividend." When a dividend is declared, the directors also set a record date. Any stockholder whose name is on the records as owner on that date will receive the dividend, even if he sells the stock between the record date and the date of the dividend payment. However, after the record date passes, the stock is said to be ex dividend. With regard to cash dividends, the ex dividend date precedes the record date by five business days.

Payment Date. On the payment date you are paid the dividend.

Securities Analysis Sources

There are two general categories of securities analysis sources: *financial services and annual reports,* and *professional investment counseling services.*

Financial Services and Annual Reports. Two of the most complete security services are Moody's *Investors' Service* and Standard & Poor's *Industry Surveys.* Standard & Poor's offers *Dividend Records, Called Bond Record,* and *The Outlook.* Each is available by subscription.

Investment Services. The services sold on subscription include the following: *United Business Service,* 210 Newbury St., Boston, Mass.; *Babson's Investment and Barometer Letter,* Wellesley Hills, Mass., and *The Value Line Investment Service,* 5 East 44th St., New York, N.Y.

Stock Market Indicators

To understand the securities market behavior by analyzing hundreds of daily transactions would be impossible for most persons. Accordingly, there are several indexes and stock averages that supply information for a quick answer to the question, "How did the market do today?"

Two of the most frequently used statistical averages are the Dow Jones (DJ) and the New York Times averages. The DJ averages, published by *The Wall Street Journal,* consist of four different groups of stocks and five bond price indexes. The stock groups are 30 industrial stocks, 20 transportation stocks, 15 public utility stocks, and a composite average of all 65 stocks.

The New York Times stock average, used since 1911, consists of an average of 25 industrial companies, an average of 25 rail stocks, and a 50-stock composite average. Changes in daily quotations on the exchange are reflected by the average for that day.

Standard & Poor's Index of Stock Prices is a system of indexes consisting of 425 industrials, 55 utilities, 20 railroad companies, and a 500-stock composite index. The Standard & Poor's Index is used by the Federal Reserve Board, the U.S. Department of Commerce, and other federal agencies.

In 1966, the New York Stock Exchange began publication of its own common-stock index, which measures the price trends of all the common stocks on the Big Board.[3]

Dollar Averaging

When to invest is a difficult decision for most investors, since it is nearly impossible to anticipate the behavior of the market from day to day. Experience shows that a satisfactory solution to investment timing is a plan known as dollar averaging (sometimes called dollar-cost averaging). Under this plan, the investor determines in advance that he will invest a sum of money at regular intervals in a given stock or a group of stocks over a long period of time, usually many months. Since most stocks move up and down cyclically, by investing the same amount each time he will buy more shares when prices are low than when they are high. Over a period of time this plan assures the investor that he will buy his stock at a favorable average price, unless the market trend for his stock is down for a long time. The plan is not a fantastically profitable one, but it prevents his making the bulk of his investment at high market prices.

Selling Short

The market technique of selling short as a means for making a profit accounts for about 6 percent of the total New York Stock Exchange transactions, yet it is widely misunderstood. A short sale is the reverse of a regular transaction. Instead of buying shares—and then selling them later at a higher price—*selling short* may be defined as selling shares now that you do not own but with the expectation that you will borrow the required number later for delivery to the buyer. When you make the sale, you expect to repurchase the same number of shares at a lower price thus enabling you to make a profit. However, if the price advances so that you pay more for the shares than you originally sell them for, then you have a loss. From whom do you borrow the stock? One source is your own broker who may have a margin account customer who owns this stock and is willing to lend it. If not, then your broker makes arrangements with another broker to obtain it. Short selling is subject to the

[3]For a fuller discussion of stock averages and indexes including the Dow Theory, see Frederick Amling, *Investments: An Introduction to Analysis and Management,* 2nd. ed. (Englewood Cliffs, N.J.: Prentice-Hall, Inc., 1970), pp. 553–588.

same rules that apply to margin buying. It is a common technique in a period of market decline when, as an investor, you decide a certain stock will drop in price along with other issues on the exchange.

Securities Market Commission Charges

A part of an investor's expense in buying and selling securities is the commission charged by brokerage firms. The commission schedule, which became effective March 24, 1972 for transactions on the New York Stock Exchange and the American Stock Exchange, applies a dollar-amount formula to both odd-lot and round-lot orders. The following is a summary of the basic rate schedule used to compute commissions on stocks, warrants, and rights for either a purchase or sale at $1 per share and above:

For 100 Share Orders and Odd-Lot Orders

Amount of money involved in order	Minimum commission rate
$100—but less than $800	2.0% of money plus $6.40
$800—but less than $2,500	1.3% of money plus $12.00
$2,500 and above	0.9% of money plus $22.00

(For each odd-lot transaction, subtract $2.00 from the money involved.) In the case of 100 share orders, the minimum commission shall not exceed $65.

For Orders Having a Total Value of Less than $100

The commission is 6% of the total money involved or as mutually agreed.

For Multiple Round-Lot Orders

Amount of order for 200 shares or more	Minimum commission rate
$100—but less than $2,500	1.3% of money plus $12.00
$2,500—but less than $20,000	0.9% of money plus $22.00
$20,000—but less than $30,000	0.6% of money plus $82.00
$30,000 to and including $500,000	0.4% of money plus $142.00

In addition, for each round lot from first to tenth round lot, add $6 per round lot and from eleventh round lot and above add $4 per round lot to money involved.

The minimum commission for each round lot within a multiple round lot order should not exceed the commission on the single round lot order based on the rate used for 100 share orders.

Commissions for various prices of stocks for odd-lot and round-lot sales are shown in Table 13.6 based on the new schedule.

The following examples show how commissions are computed:

(1) For an odd-lot order of 10 shares at \$10 per share, the amount of money involved is \$100. The commission of \$6.40 is computed as follows:

$$.02\% \times \$100 = \$2.00$$
$$\text{plus} \qquad \underline{6.40}$$
$$8.40$$
$$\text{less} \qquad \underline{2.00} \text{ (for an odd-lot order)}$$
$$\$6.40$$

(2) For a round-lot order of 100 shares at \$10 per share, the amount of money involved is \$1,000. The commission of \$25 is computed as follows:

$$1.3\% \times \$1000 = \$13.00$$
$$\text{plus} \qquad \underline{12.00}$$
$$\$25.00$$

TABLE 13.6

SECURITIES COMMISSIONS FOR SELECTED PRICES

	Odd Lots					
Number of Shares Bought or Sold	Price of stock					
	\$5	\$10	\$20	\$40	\$75	\$100
10	(a)	\$6.40	\$8.40	\$12.40	\$19.40	\$23.00
20	\$6.40	8.40	12.40	20.40	29.50	36.00
40	8.40	12.40	20.40	30.80	47.00	56.00
50	9.40	14.40	23.00	36.00	53.75	65.00
70	11.40	18.40	28.20	45.20	65.00	65.00
90	13.40	21.70	33.40	52.40	65.00	65.00
99	14.30	22.87	35.74	55.64	65.00	65.00
	Round Lots					
100	16.40	25.00	38.00	58.00	65.00	65.00
200	32.80	50.00	70.00	106.00	130.00	130.00
400	62.00	82.00	118.00	190.00	260.00	260.00
1000	127.00	172.00	262.00	362.00	502.00	602.00

(a) Negotiated rate.
On transactions of more than \$300,000, commissions on the portion over \$300,000 are negotiated. Eventually, transactions over \$100,000 may be negotiated.

(3) For a round-lot order of 100 shares at $100 per share, the amount of money involved is $10,000. The commission of $65 is computed as follows:

$$0.9\% \times \$10,000 = \$90.00$$
plus   22.00
$112.00 (Because this amount exceeds $65 for a 100 share order, the $65 applies.)

(4) For a round-lot order of 200 shares at $40 per share, the amount of money involved is $8,000. The commission of $106 is computed as follows:

$$0.9\% \times \$8,000 = \$72.00$$
plus   22.00
94.00
plus   12.00 ($6.00 per each round lot)
$106.00

In addition to commission charges, the federal government and the state of New York levy a stock transfer tax to the seller on shares traded in New York. The nonresident tax rate is 2.5¢ per share on a selling price of $20 per share or more from July 1, 1973 and thereafter. The minimum tax is 0.625¢ after July 1, 1973 on shares selling for less than $5 per share. The New York State stock transfer tax on residents ranges from 1.25¢ to 5¢ per share depending on the selling price of the shares. In addition, there is a Securities and Exchange Commission fee of 1¢ for each $500 value or fraction thereof on all security sales on a registered exchange. The fee is not collected on purchases. The state of Florida also charges a transfer tax of 15¢ per $100 par value regardless of selling price and 15¢ per $100 of actual value of no-par value stock, but not to exceed 15¢ per share.

The new commission schedule, a product of nearly four years of study by the New York Stock Exchange and others, is the first major change in securities commissions since 1958 except for the addition of volume discounts in 1968 and the adoption of a service charge of $15 in 1971.

Since 1969 brokers were hard hit by rising costs. For many, office rents increased about 70 percent and clerical and administrative salaries advanced over 80 percent. There was an ever increasing volume of paper work that raised costs. As a result, some brokerage firms failed and others merged.

The chief objective of the new commission schedule was to put the securities industry back on a sound financial basis, not only for the present but also to meet future needs.

Features of the New Schedule

For orders of 1,000 shares or less, the rates of the former schedule were based on the total money involved in one round lot—generally 100 shares. For example, the commission on 700 shares was seven times the single round lot rate. Recognizing the potential economies of volume, the rates now are based on the value of the total order. Consequently, the commission on an order consisting of several round lots is lower per round lot than for a single round lot at the same price per share.

In the case of orders of 1,000 shares or more involving a stock priced at $20 a share or higher, the commission is lower than previously. Stocks selling for $40 and $50 now cost more for those buying 700 shares or less, while orders over 800 shares will have commissions lowered by between three and 13 percent. Finally, for stocks selling at $75 or above, the new commissions are higher. For example, a 500 share order at $75 per share jumped from $247.50 commission to $322. Managements of companies whose stocks are selling for $75 or above, are expected to become more split conscious in an effort to bring prices down to levels where commissions are lower.

It is likely that many individual investors will be influenced by the new rates in their choice of investment preferences.

Discussion Questions

11. *What are the differences between growth stocks and income stocks? What is their relationship to your investment objective?*
12. *What are some of the factors to be considered in evaluating corporate management in determining your investment in a corporation?*
13. *Explain how dollar averaging and selling short are used by an investor.*

REGULATING SECURITIES TRANSACTIONS AND MARKETS

Control over securities markets and broker-dealers is a responsibility of both the states and the federal government. It was not, however, until federal legislation was passed in the early 1930's that any degree of success was achieved in detecting and prosecuting market manipulators and swindlers. The collapse of the securities market in 1929 revealed further weaknesses and abuses in securities trading.

State Regulations

Today, practically all states require registration of securities brokers and dealers. Starting with Kansas in 1911, states began to pass what were popularly dubbed "blue-sky laws," from the idea that these laws were intended to stop the sale of fraudulent securities that had nothing of substance—"nothing but blue sky"—to back them up. Today, all states except Nevada have blue-sky laws that provide (1) supervision over stock registration, (2) require dealers to register, and (3) protect the public against fraud in the securities market at the state level.

Federal Regulations

The need for stronger controls over the interstate sale of securities produced a flow of federal legislation starting in 1933.

Federal Securities Act of 1933. This act is intended to ensure that the investing public will have adequate information to make accurate and intelligent decisions about securities offered for sale. It is often called the "information law" because full disclosure of pertinent financial facts is the main requirement of the law. A registration statement containing extensive details about the company and its proposed issue of securities is required; also a prospectus, a condensed version of the information, must be available to each prospective purchaser of either stocks or bonds offered for sale.

Federal Securities Act of 1934. This law, in addition to establishing the Securities and Exchange Commission (SEC), required all brokers, dealers, and securities exchanges to file periodic reports with the SEC. Credit restrictions through control of margin requirements for stock purchases were established subject to SEC jurisdiction.[4] Brokers selling listed securities were required to pass an examination.

Under the Securities Act Amendments of 1964, OTC markets were also placed under the control of the SEC. Written examinations are now imposed on new salesmen selling OTC securities.

---

[4] The main advantage of buying on margin is to increase the number of shares that can be bought with the same amount of money. For example, if you have $1,000 to invest, you will be able to buy 100 shares at $10 per share on a cash basis. But if you bought the shares on 50 percent margin at $10 per share, you would be able to borrow, in effect, $1,000, which would give you $2,000. Now you can buy 200 shares at $10 a share. Should the stock increase in value, you will have a gain on twice as many shares. In a ruling effective May 15, 1972, the Federal Reserve Board has stipulated that OTC stocks printed below an average of $5 per share cannot be bought on margin.

Maloney Act of 1938. This act, which is an amendment to the Securities Act of 1934, authorized investment bankers to form associations for self-regulation. The National Association of Securities Dealers was created and became the self-regulatory arm of the OTC securities business. This association has the authority to limit price concessions and discounts, and to act against members who fail to abide by the rules.

Investment Company Act of 1940. This law provides the framework within which the mutual fund industry now operates, by requiring investment trust companies to register with the SEC. At the time this act was passed mutual funds had less than $500 million in assets. These funds are expected to grow to $100 billion in assets by 1975.

Securities Investor Protection Act of 1970. In 1969 and 1970 a number of brokerage firms, overwhelmed by the ever-increasing volume of paper work and the effects of a general market decline, either failed or were forced into voluntary liquidation or merger. In an effort to minimize losses of securities and cash held by brokers for their clients, the securities industry sought a remedy through legislation. In December of 1970, Congress passed the Securities Investor Protection Act. This act provides for the creation of a new nonprofit corporation—the Securities Investor Protection Corporation (SIPC, pronounced *sip-ic*)—to be financed by the securities industry and designed to protect individual securities accounts in the event of a broker's liquidation. If a member broker or dealer becomes insolvent, SIPC is authorized, within prescribed limits, to ask the court to appoint a trustee to be responsible for settling customers' claims for each account up to $50,000. However, losses arising from fluctuations in securities prices are not covered.

SIPC, the corporation, became fully organized and, hence, operational in November, 1971. At that time, the act became effective for all brokers and securities dealers holding membership in SIPC and registered with the Securities and Exchange Commission. SIPC started with an initial fund of $75 million supplied from existing stock exchange trust funds, member assessments, and bank loans. The fund is expected to increase to $150 million by 1977.

Discussion Questions

14. *What kinds of securities market violations are regulated by blue-sky laws?*

15. *What are some of the safeguards now provided by federal and state legislation to protect investors in securities?*

OTHER SOURCES OF LONG-TERM CAPITAL

Although large sums of capital for long-term use are obtained from retained earnings, and from stocks and bonds sold through the securities markets, long-term capital is also supplied by other institutional sources in increasing amounts.

Life Insurance Companies

Money at work, as represented by the assets of U.S. life insurance companies, reached nearly $207.3 billion at the beginning of 1971. Most of this was invested in stocks, corporate bonds, mortgages on real estate, and real estate. Life insurance companies are one of the most important sources of capital used to finance shopping centers, commercial buildings, and housing developments.

Pension Funds

Many American businesses, and also labor unions, provide some form of retirement pay from pensions funds contributed to by either the employee or the employer, or by both. (This is in addition to Social Security.) These funds are invested chiefly in common stocks and corporate bonds.

Mutual Funds

Mutual funds, also known as investment companies as a result of the Investment Company Act of 1940, are another kind of institution supplying long-term capital for business and industry. A mutual fund is an investment company which combines the investment funds of many investors whose goals are similar, and in turn invests these funds in a variety of securities. The selection of these securities and management of the funds is under the supervision of professional investment managers. A commission is paid by the investor on most funds each time an investment is made. This is added to the cost of the fund shares and helps to pay for the management fee and other expenses.

The main objective of a mutual fund is to make the investment profitable to the investor. This is achieved in various ways. Some funds invest in growth industries anticipating substantial market appreciation of the stocks. This can be passed on to the investors as long-term capital gains usually paid annually. Other funds concentrate mainly in investments paying a high income. The investor reviews each fund's objectives and buys the one that best suits his own investment objective.

The three basic ways to invest in mutual funds are by (1) one-time purchase, (2) monthly or quarterly purchases for an indefinite period, and (3) under a contractual plan for a specified period of time. Mutual funds must qualify under subchapter M of the Internal Revenue Code in order to avoid paying income tax on dividends and interest received by the fund from its corporate investments when distributed to fund shareholders. Investors, however, are subject to the income tax on dividends and capital gains. There are

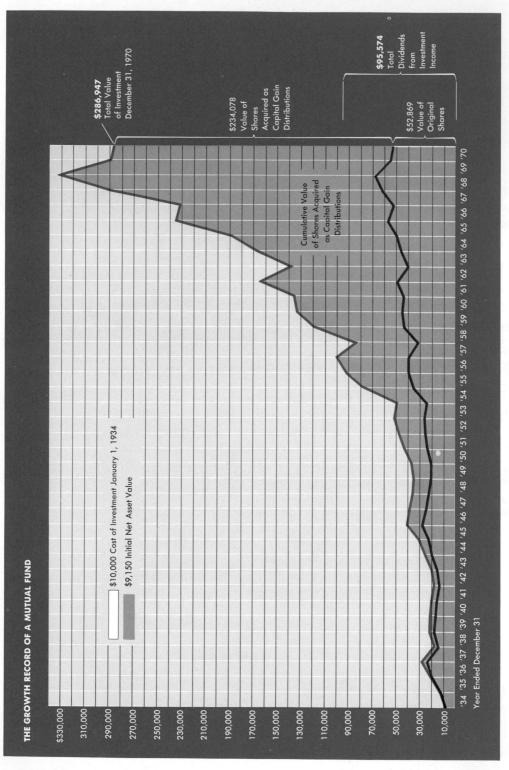

THE GROWTH RECORD OF A MUTUAL FUND

$286,947
Total Value
of Investment
December 31, 1970

$10,000 Cost of Investment January 1, 1934

$9,150 Initial Net Asset Value

$234,078
Value of
Shares
Acquired as
Capital Gain
Distributions

Cumulative Value
of Shares Acquired
as Capital Gain
Distributions

$95,574
Total
Dividends
from
Investment
Income

$52,869
Value of
Original
Shares

$330,000
310,000
290,000
270,000
250,000
230,000
210,000
190,000
170,000
150,000
130,000
110,000
90,000
70,000
50,000
30,000
10,000

'34 '35 '36 '37 '38 '39 '40 '41 '42 '43 '44 '45 '46 '47 '48 '49 '50 '51 '52 '53 '54 '55 '56 '57 '58 '59 '60 '61 '62 '63 '64 '65 '66 '67 '68 '69 '70

Year Ended December 31

An assumed investment of $10,000 in a stock fund from December 31, 1934 to December 31, 1970. The loading charge was 8½ percent. No adjustment was made for income taxes payable by the shareholder on capital gains and dividends reinvested. The original investment was $9,150 and by December 31, 1970 the total value of the investment reached $286,947. The cumulative value of shares acquired from capital gains distribution was $234,078. The original shares increased in value to $52,869.

over 500 mutual funds in approximately 21 foreign countries. The largest concentration of these funds is in Great Britain, Japan, Switzerland, Australia, Canada, and West Germany.

Discussion Question

16. *What is there about the securities market that appeals to life insurance companies and pension funds as a source of investment?*

SUMMARY

Every business, regardless of its size, must be financed, at least in part, by equity funds—the funds provided by the owner or owners. A business needs funds not only for the initial operation but for financing over a long period. Funds for fixed capital expenditures (buildings, land, and machinery) generally come from sources that will not demand immediate repayment, such as long-term loans.

Sources of long-term working-capital financing include capital furnished by owners (sale of stock), sale of bonds, accumulated profits, and depreciation allowances on fixed assets.

A corporation has the advantage over the proprietorship in being able to raise money by selling stock. Bonds may be sold, but unlike shares of stock, they must be repaid when the bonds mature. Meanwhile, interest is payable periodically and the bondholder may foreclose if the borrower defaults. Bonds offer a tax advantage in that bond interest is deductible as an expense while dividends are not. Bond issues may be secured or unsecured, registered or coupon, callable and convertible. They may be secured by equipment, such as an equipment trust certificate or equipment trust bond. Bonds may be sold at a premium (higher than the face value) or at a discount (less than face value).

Corporation securities are sold in a local market over the country by local brokerage firms. These are unlisted securities. Or they may be sold through an organized exchange using brokerage firms that hold membership on an exchange. The privilege of subscribing to additional stock is a stock right, which is evidenced by a stock-purchase warrant used to exercise this right.

The cost of capital is a factor that must be weighed. Other factors involve the prevailing tax rate, availability of money, and the interest rates.

Both the Securities Act of 1934 and the Securities and Exchange Act of 1934 provide for strict regulation of securities exchanges and brokers and dealers doing business locally and in interstate commerce. All corporations listing stocks and bonds on these securities markets must register and file periodic statements. Other restrictions pertain to "margin" buying and the requirement of a license for brokers and dealers.

VOCABULARY REVIEW

Match the following vocabulary terms with the statements below:

a. Bookvalue
b. Call option
c. Debenture bonds
d. Fixed capital

e. Market value
f. Par value
g. Preferred stock
h. Registered bond

i. Stock split
j. Stock dividend
k. Term loan
l. Working capital

1. Money invested in fixed assets used over a long period of time
2. A provision that allows for an earlier redemption date for bonds
3. Money invested in a business to meet daily operations
4. An arbitrary value placed on the stock certificate
5. Stock that carries certain preferences over common stock
6. Division of the common stock outstanding into additional shares
7. A type of installment loan with repayments ranging from three to five years
8. Bonds backed solely by the general credit of the company
9. The value of stock carried on the company records
10. A bond issued in the owner's name which is shown on the bond and on the records of the corporation
11. The price of shares on the market
12. A dividend paid in shares of capital stock

PROBLEMS AND PROJECTS

1. The Exide Corporation lists assets of $6 million and total liabilities of $4 million. A total of 200,000 shares of $100 par-value common stock is outstanding. The market value of the common stock was recently quoted at $40 a share. Calculate the book value of the common stock. Why is the market value different from par value in this case?

2. Three years ago, Frank bought 100 shares of American Car common at $30 per share. This stock is listed on the American Stock Exchange and is now quoted at $100 a share. The company has paid a $2 annual dividend for the last two years and has earned $4 a share.

    a. Calculate the current price–earnings ratio.
    b. What is the current yield on the common stock?
    c. Do you consider this stock an income, growth, or speculative stock?
    d. If the directors declared a 20 percent stock dividend, how many shares would you have then?

3. The Well-Right Corporation needs $100,000 capital for expansion. One official recommends a five-year term bank loan at 5½ percent. Another executive wants to sell some more common stock, which could be sold for about $10 a share by a local broker. Which plan would be the more expensive in the long run, assuming the company had sufficient earnings to pay 50¢ annually per share? Which plan would give management the greatest amount of managerial freedom?

A BUSINESS CASE

Case 13-1   Capital for Business Expansion

You are a director and business consultant for a leading furniture manufacturing company with annual sales of $20 million, mostly in twelve southern states. For several years the company has earned 14 percent after taxes. The company is a close corporation with 100,000 shares held by five of the officers, including you. The stock was issued at $30. Dividends have been paid annually at 20¢ per share from earnings of $2.8 million. Now the company wishes to raise capital to finance more equipment in order to double output. One plan being considered is to issue $400,000 worth of mortgage bonds at 8 percent to mature in 10 years, using a sinking-fund formula. Another plan under consideration is to sell, over the counter, 30,000 shares of common stock at $14 per share.

1. Which plan would you propose to the board of directors? What are your reasons?
2. If you were not a shareholder, would your recommendation be any different?

short-term financing

CHAPTER FOURTEEN

In the preceding chapter we observed the need for long-term capital to finance the purchase of fixed or permanent assets such as new equipment, added manufacturing facilities, land, and warehouses. But virtually all types of businesses also need a second kind of capital: short-term or working capital. Funds of this nature are used to finance payrolls, to carry customers until they pay for the goods they have bought, and to meet various kinds of emergencies.

This chapter deals with the uses and sources of short-term financing. Short-term loans are for a year or less and they can be classified as either secured or unsecured. Secured obligations are those that require the pledging of an asset as collateral for a loan. Warehouse receipts, order bills of lading, and accounts receivable are commonly used as security. Unsecured obligations involve the use of promissory notes, drafts, and trade acceptances. All these transactions involve either specialized financing or special financial institutions that have developed as part of our business system.

CREDIT AND CREDIT INSTRUMENTS

Credit touches the lives of everyone, in many different ways. It is so much an integral part of our business system that its real significance is often taken for granted. Yet it is doubtful that many businesses could exist for long without it. An understanding of its uses, therefore, is essential for businessmen and consumers alike.

What Is Credit?

The word "credit" is derived from the Latin *credere*, "to trust." (*Creditum* means "a loan.") When associated with business transactions, *credit* is defined as *the power or ability to secure goods or services* (or money) *in exchange for a promise to pay later.*[1] Popular usage of this term, however, has turned its meaning around, until it denotes something that the seller and not the buyer gives. In the strict sense, it is incorrect for the seller to state "we give credit," for it is the prospective buyer who actually extends the credit in exchange for the goods purchased or services obtained.

From certain points of view, credit may be better understood if it is explained rather than defined. Credit necessarily involves two characteristics. First, there is the element of *faith* on the part of the creditor in the willingness and ability of the debtor to fulfill his promise to pay. When such faith is present, the creditor is willing to give goods, services, or money in consideration of the debtor's ability to pay. The second element of credit is *futurity:* In every credit transaction, the seller or lender accepts some risk over a period of time. Credit instruments always involve a *time* during which the creditor's confidence is placed in the debtor's promise to pay, and until payment is made, there is always a *risk* that it will not be made. It is by these characteristics that credit instruments are distinguished from other commercial documents that resemble them.

Functions of Credit

Credit serves business in several ways. It makes capital available that would otherwise be idle. In exchange for payment for the use of their funds, thrifty people entrust their personal savings to banks and other financial institutions that, in turn, lend these savings to business. A direct result of the use of credit has been the development of enterprises of all sizes.

Credit also serves as a medium of exchange. Through its use, transactions can be accomplished quickly, with a minimum of work, and without the exchange of money. Without credit, the high level of economic activity enjoyed

---

[1] For a more complete discussion, see Ernest W. Walker, *Essentials of Financial Management,* 2nd ed. (Englewood Cliffs, N.J.: Prentice-Hall, Inc., 1971), pp. 119–141.

by business would disappear. The development of large-scale enterprise is the result of credit.

Third, credit is a tool of business promotion that enables the entrepreneur to adjust his volume of capital to the varying needs of his business. By borrowing additional capital, he may be able to increase production during peak periods of business activity. By extending credit, he can induce a desired class of customers to buy, thus gaining a competitive advantage over the entrepreneur who does not give credit.

Trade Credit

Trade credit differs radically from other forms of short-term credit, primarily because it is not obtained from a financial institution. This type of credit is an obligation typified by the common "open-book account" extended by credit managers. It has become the most common source of working capital. In accounting language, it comes under the heading of accounts receivable for the seller, and accounts payable for the buyer. It starts when goods are sold to the buyer on a 30-, 60-, or 90-day credit. Other than the invoice, no formal instrument is involved.

Reasons for Trade Credit. From a creditor's point of view, a firm is willing to grant credit in order to increase sales. If a firm's sales volume can be raised without spending large amounts on production equipment, it is possible to spread the fixed costs over a larger number of units and so reduce the unit cost of production.

From the debtor's viewpoint, firms make use of trade credit largely because they are unable to obtain adequate financing from other credit sources, such as banks and finance companies. Commercial banks are either unable or unwilling to assume the costs or the risk inherent in many trade-credit sales. On the other hand, the seller can assume both, because trade credit is about the only avenue open to him to stimulate sales without resorting to long-term credit of some kind. Many firms would find it most difficult to maintain suitable inventories in the absence of trade credit.

Credit managers estimate that *open-book accounts,* a form of short-term credit, constitute about 85 percent of the total volume of retail and wholesale sales in the United States. The seller enters into no formal written agreement acknowledging the debt, but relies instead on the buyer, whose integrity he respects, to pay for the goods at the appropriate time. However, since the seller's record alone does not constitute the best type of legal evidence of debt in the event of dispute, it is common practice to support these credit transactions with sales slips or delivery receipts.

Trade-credit debt accounts are traditionally payable in 30 days. Wholesalers, jobbers, and manufacturers may sell goods on such terms as "2/10, net 30," which means that a discount of 2 percent on the amount of the invoice will be allowed the buyer if he pays his bill within 10 days, and that the entire amount is due in 30 days. The buyer's ability to take his discount promptly is evidence of his satisfactory financial condition.

Credit Instruments

Each of the several types of credit instruments common to short-term finance possesses certain attributes. These instruments may be divided into two broad categories: those based on *promises to pay,* and those based on *orders to pay.* The former group (promises to pay) comprises promissory notes. The latter classification includes drafts of all kinds, and the general category of trade acceptances. These instruments involve two things in common: the element of time during which the creditor's confidence is placed in the debtor's promise, and the degree of risk until payment is made.

Promissory Note.   The legal instrument in the promise-to-pay category used to make a short-term loan is the negotiable promissory note.

Section 3-104 (1) of the UCC defines a negotiable promissory note as *an unconditional promise in writing made by one person to another, signed by the maker, engaging to pay on demand, or at a particular time, a sum certain in money to order or to bearer.*

In the illustration of a negotiable promissory note shown below, Joseph Doe, Jr. (the maker) agrees to pay to the East End State Bank (payee) $100, with interest at 6 percent, 60 days from the date of the note. A promissory note is preferred to an open-book account because it represents prima facie evidence of the debt. (The term *prima facie evidence* denotes that the evidence is sufficient to establish the fact in question unless rebutted.) An advantage of the promissory note over the open-book account is that when signed by the debtor, it acknowledges the accuracy of the debt at the time he agreed

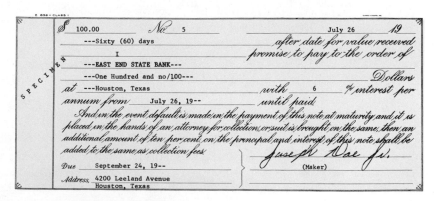

Courtesy East End State Bank, Houston, Texas

A negotiable promissory note

to it. The note may be written so that it bears interest either at maturity or at specified intervals during the life of the debt, or it may be a discounted note, in which case the interest is deducted from the principal at the time the note is made.

For example, Tom Jensen wishes to borrow $1,000 from his bank at 6 percent interest for 60 days. The money is to be used for a short-term business debt. When he signs the note, the bank accepts it and pays him the money. If he used a discounted note, the bank would subtract $10 interest immediately from the face of the note and pay him $990, and he would pay $1,000 to the bank at the end of 60 days.

When a firm accepts a promissory note from a customer, the note is carried on the firm's books under "notes receivable." But if the firm needs cash before the note is due, it may be indorsed and sold to a commercial bank at a discount. Discounting promissory notes is one of the services of commercial banks.

Drafts or Bills of Exchange. Thus far we have discussed the use of promise-to-pay credit instruments. Turning now to the order-to-pay type, the one used for short-term credit is the draft, or bill of exchange. (The terms are used interchangeably.) A *bill of exchange* is an instrument drawn by one person ordering a second person to pay a sum of money to a specified person on sight or at a future date. Bills of exchange or drafts are used extensively in foreign trade. The person drawing the draft and the one to whom it is to be paid may or may not be the same. A *bank draft,* also a form of bill of exchange, is a written order of one bank on another bank to pay to a person named on the draft a sum of money upon demand. It differs from a promissory note in that it is classed as an order rather than a promise to pay. If the draft is payable on demand, it is a *sight draft.* If payment is for a designated date, it is a *time draft.*

In the accompanying illustration, Richard B. Brown is the drawer of a sight draft payable to Joseph Doe, Jr., from funds in the drawer's account at

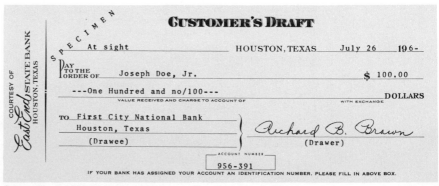

Courtesy East End State Bank, Houston, Texas A sight draft, payable when presented for payment

the First City National Bank (drawee). This draft is issued to the drawer through the courtesy of the East End State Bank as an accommodation to Brown.

A time draft is called a *trade acceptance,* particularly when used by manufacturers and wholesalers. The usual form of trade acceptance is drawn by the seller (drawer) on the buyer (drawee), payable to the seller at a future time, for the price of a shipment of goods. The seller sends the draft to the buyer, who "accepts" it. The word "Accepted," the date, and the name of the drawee are then written across the face of the instrument. The buyer, having agreed to pay the amount, then returns the draft to the seller, who, as payee, may discount it by selling it to the bank or may use it as collateral for a loan. The trade acceptance enables the seller to extend credit to his customer and at the same time to collect his money immediately. The use of this instrument is explained more fully in the discussion of an international trade transaction in Chapter 23.

In domestic trade, the bank draft may be used in the following situation. A merchant in San Francisco sells goods to someone in Chicago on credit. The seller requests the Chicago buyer to pay his account with a bank draft. The buyer goes to his own bank in Chicago and buys a draft from that bank drawn on its San Francisco correspondent bank, and forwards this draft to

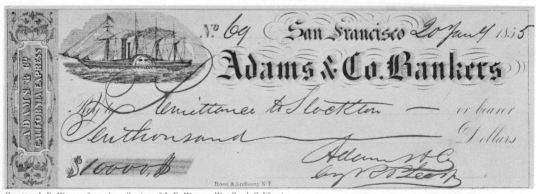

Courtesy J. E. Weaver, from the collection of J. E. Weaver, Woodland, California

A bank check that is over 100 years old. This check is payable to a named payee or bearer rather than to his order. The named payee may deposit it without a required indorsement.

the merchant in San Francisco. This method of payment has an advantage over others in that the draft does not have to be returned to the drawer bank in Chicago before it is actually paid. Consequently, the firm that is being paid with the bank draft (payee) has quicker use of the money than if it were paid with an ordinary bank check that must first clear through a distant bank before it can be drawn against by the payee.

Cashier's Check. For the kinds of transactions in which people do not know each other and are therefore reluctant to accept personal checks, the *cashier's check* is used. It is a check drawn by a bank against its own funds

SHERMAN OAKS OFFICE

CROCKER NATIONAL BANK

14720 VENTURA BOULEVARD, SHERMAN OAKS, CALIFORNIA

CASHIER'S CHECK

90-2563
1222

№ **4190499**

DATE July 26, 19--

PAY TO THE
ORDER OF: JOSEPH DOE, JR. $ 999.99

060 CROCKER
    NATIONAL   CANCELLED   **DOLLARS**

Brown
AUTHORIZED SIGNATURE

⑆1222⑉2563⑆ 419 000027⑈

Courtesy Crocker National Bank, San Francisco, California

A cashier's check—a check drawn by a bank against itself. This type of check may be purchased from a bank for remittance purposes.

and signed by the cashier or some other official of the bank rather than by a depositor. Cashier's checks are also used by a bank to pay its own debts. Almost anyone will accept this form of check because it is guaranteed by the bank. A cashier's check is illustrated above; notice that it differs from a bank draft in that it is drawn on the bank that issues it instead of on a correspondent bank. A correspondent bank is one that acts as a representative for another bank.

Among the services that a correspondent bank will perform for other banks are collecting checks, drafts, and other credit instruments; making credit investigations of firms; and accepting letters of credit and travelers' checks. Today, banks in New York are acting as correspondents for banks in hundreds of other American cities. Banks in other large cities are acting as correspondents for banks in smaller cities. Some banks maintain accounts that may be drawn on in other correspondent banks.

Certified Check.   If a bank's customer desires to make payment to a person who might otherwise refuse to accept a personal check, he could obtain a certified check. A check is certified when the bank on which it is drawn officially deducts the amount of the check from the drawer's account before the check is mailed. The bank officer stamps the word "Certified" on the face of the check and signs it. Almost anyone is willing to accept this check now bank guarantees payment. A certified check is shown at the top of page 367. Joe D. Smith is the drawer of the check, Jennie Smith is the payee, and the bank is the drawee bank, which has certified the check. Certified checks are used principally in real estate and securities transactions in which cash payment is required. The drawer of a certified check cannot stop payment on it. If a

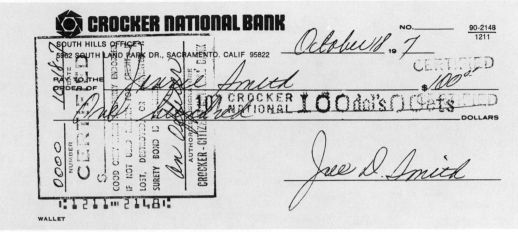

Courtesy Crocker National Bank, San Francisco, California

A certified check is safe because the bank guarantees payment.

bank certifies a check in error, it may withdraw the certification provided it acts promptly and the holder has lost no rights.

Time Certificate of Deposit. Growing in popularity is the time certificate of deposit, which is a nonnegotiable and nontransferable interest-bearing instrument. The illustration of a time certificate of deposit (see page 368) certifies that Joseph Doe, Jr., has deposited with the Crocker National Bank the sum of $10,000. The deposit bears interest at the rate of 5 percent per annum, compounded daily and payable quarterly until maturity date. This certificate cannot be assigned except to a bank. Commercial banks issue time certificates of deposit against time deposits, usually at a higher interest rate than regular passbook accounts. Savings and loan associations issue "savings certificates" against time deposits.

Negotiable Certificate of Deposit. Commonly known as a CD, the negotiable certificate of deposit is an interest-bearing obligation of a commercial bank, similar in most respects to the time certificate of deposit, except for the negotiable feature. Since it is in part an acknowledgement of receipt of money, it is distinguished from a promissory note, which is a promise-to-pay instrument. A CD is negotiable if it meets the requirements for negotiability in Section 3-104 of the UCC. From the banks' standpoint, CD's are useful because they are a means of attracting large time deposits from business corporations; a corporation may have a large sum of money that is idle for a brief period, and during this time it can be drawing interest if put into a CD account.

A bank is allowed to negotiate the rate of interest it will pay on CD's. If money is scarce, banks offer a higher interest rate. Interest is forfeited if the certificate is cashed prior to its maturity date. CD's are normally issued

CROCKER NATIONAL BANK

SPECIMEN

Current Income Certificate

INTEREST PAYABLE QUARTERLY

825542

ISSUED AT-OFFICE AND CITY

One Montgomery Street Office, San Francisco ,California July 26 ,19 --

This certifies that there has been deposited with Crocker National Bank the sum of

Ten thousand dollars and ---------------------------------- 00/100 Dollars ($ 10,000.00),

payable to _____ Joseph Doe, Jr. _____, Depositor, upon the final maturity date or any earlier multiple maturity date, as herein specified, and upon presentation and surrender of this Certificate, properly endorsed, at the above Office.

The initial maturity of this Certificate is three months after date hereof and such maturity shall be automatically extended for successive three-month periods until__2__years from date hereof (final maturity date), at which time this Certificate shall finally mature; unless prior thereto, and within 10 days after the end of the initial or any succeeding three-month period (multiple maturity date), Depositor has presented and surrendered this Certificate for payment.

The deposit bears interest at the rate of __5.00__% per annum, compounded daily, and payable quarterly until the final maturity date or earlier withdrawal.

This Certificate is a Time Certificate of Deposit, and may not be assigned except to Bank, and is subject to all present and future applicable and governing laws and regulations.

SPECIMEN

CROCKER NATIONAL BANK

By: *Richard Brown*

AUTHORIZED SIGNATURE

**NON-NEGOTIABLE
AND
NON-TRANSFERABLE**

02-618 (REV. 3-71)

Courtesy Crocker National Bank, San Francisco, California

Time deposit certificates are interest-bearing deposits in a commercial bank that have a fixed maturity date. This instrument is nonnegotiable and nontransferable.

in units of $1 million when corporations are involved; in any case, seldom is the unit below $100,000. Securities dealers may buy and sell CD's, and for a period in the early 1960's, some corporations became interested in them as a form of short-term investment.

Discussion Questions

1. *What is credit, and how is it used in business?*
2. *How do "promise-to-pay" instruments differ from "order-to-pay" credit instruments? Give an example of each.*
3. *What distinguishes a promissory note from a bank draft?*
4. *What is a trade acceptance, and when might it be used?*

OUR BANKING SYSTEM

An efficient banking system is a primary requirement for providing the financial needs of business. Owners and managers rely heavily on banks for the great pool of capital funds consisting of accumulated savings that people and organizations invest in various financial institutions. In some countries, wealth is highly concentrated in few hands and is not put to use on a large scale. In the United States, wealth—including resources—is put to active use to create more wealth. As a result of the widespread ownership of wealth among the middle-income group, much of the risk capital comes from those of modest incomes. In this kind of people's capitalism, funds move freely from one venture to another. Large sums used by business for short-term financing are generated by our banking system.

Types of Banks

Unlike the government-owned central banks in some European countries, the system of banking institutions in the United States is composed of several types of banks, classified mainly according to their primary functions— commercial, savings, investment banks, and trust companies. Much of the stability of our system is due to the Federal Reserve System, which we shall study in some detail later in this chapter.

Banks that receive their charters from the Comptroller of the Currency, U.S. Treasury Department, are known as *national banks*. They are corporations whose stock, like that of the state banks, is owned by stockholders. Their operations are supervised by national bank examiners who periodically audit their books to make certain that laws and regulations are being complied with and that there are no defalcations. All national banks are subject to the National Banking Act of 1863, the Federal Reserve Act of 1913, the Gold Reserve Act of 1934, and bank holding-company legislation.

Each state maintains its own system of banks, chartered by a state authority and identified as *state banks*. State banks are subject to both state laws and the provisions of the Federal Reserve System and the Federal Deposit Insurance Corporation.

For obtaining either type of charter, it must be established that a real need for a bank exists in the community, and before the charter is granted, a complete analysis is made of the personal qualifications, experience, and character of the organizers.

Table 14.1 gives you some idea of the total number of national, state, and mutual savings banks in the United States. By far the largest number of banks are commercial banks, both members and nonmembers of the Federal Reserve System, of which there are 7,919 nonmember commercial banks and 5,767 member commercial banks. Then there are approximately 500 mutual savings banks, not members of the Federal Reserve. The term "mutual" means that the bank's capital is obtained from the depositors rather than from stock issued by the bank. There are no proprietors, partners, or shareholders in mutual savings banks.

TABLE
14.1
NUMBER OF BANKS IN THE UNITED STATES

Federal Reserve member banks:		
National banks	4,620	
State banks	1,147	
Total		5,767
Nonmember banks:		
Commercial banks	7,919	
Mutual savings banks	493	
Total		8,412
Total, all banks		14,179

Source: Federal Reserve System, 1970.

Commercial Banks

Commercial banks are the best known of all financial institutions that serve business and industry. Directly or indirectly, they supply the bulk of short-term credit requirements of business. Although a number of small borrowers receive credit furnished by trade creditors, cooperative associations, and lending agencies, for financial help with larger loans they generally rely on commercial banks.

Commercial banks differ from other types of banks in two respects: They accept demand deposits—that is, deposits that the depositor may withdraw at any time without giving prior notice to the bank—and they specialize in making loans to businessmen and individuals for short periods of time. These loans are called *short-term loans* because they are in effect for a period of one year or less. If you needed a personal or business loan, perhaps for a short duration, you would probably go to a commercial bank in your community.

The list of services provided by commercial banks is a long one. Obviously, not all these services can be listed here, but you should be aware of the following:

1. A depository for money
2. A collection agency of negotiable instruments
3. A source of loans
4. A source of credit information and advice
5. A trustee of funds
6. An administrator of estates and trusts
7. A source of letters of credit
8. A dispenser of travelers' checks
9. An agency to handle foreign-trade transactions

Commercial Bank Loans.   Of the many banking functions performed, perhaps the most important to business is that of supplying short-term capital in the form of loans. Borrowing from a commercial bank generally requires some acceptable form of collateral. *Collateral* involves marketable assets—goods, land, equipment, or negotiable instruments—used as security for a loan. Among the common collateral instruments used are (1) stocks or bonds, (2) warehouse receipts, (3) trust receipts, (4) mortgages, and (5) order bills of lading.

1. Since *stocks* are evidence of ownership in a corporation, they are considered acceptable security provided they are marketable and may continue to be so for the duration of the loan. *Bonds,* such as corporate or municipal, are acceptable if they, too, are sound and marketable. Stocks are not used as extensively for commercial loans as they are for personal loans.

2. A document that serves as a receipt for goods stored in a warehouse is called a *warehouse receipt.* This receipt may be either negotiable or nonnegotiable. Negotiable warehouse receipts are used as collateral for loans against goods held in storage. When properly indorsed, the receipt entitles the holder to take possession of goods listed on the document in the quantity and condition specified. In the event of default by the borrower, the goods can be seized and sold at auction to benefit the lender. This type of financing has been encouraged by the provisions set forth in the Uniform Commercial Code.

3. Loans made on *trust receipts* are similar to those secured by warehouse receipts. When a bank is in possession of a warehouse receipt or a bill of lading, it is impossible for the merchant concerned to obtain possession of his goods before paying the loan. But under a trust-receipt agreement with his bank, the merchant can obtain the goods so that he may sell them to pay off the loan. Under this arrangement, the bank pays for the goods and the borrower agrees to hold in trust for the bank both the goods and the proceeds until the loan is repaid. When this type of financing is used, a letter of credit is first sent to the vendor, stating that the bank will honor drafts up to a certain amount for the borrower. Such a draft is called a *banker's acceptance.* Titles to automobiles may be transferred to a bank on a trust receipt while remaining in the dealer's showroom. Then, as the cars are sold, the dealer pays off portions of the loan. This practice, commonly called *floor-plan financing,* is used by most automobile dealers.

4. A *real estate mortgage* is the most widely used security for a debt. In case of default, the trustee acting for the lender can foreclose on the mortgage and seize the property for the unpaid claim. In addition to the real estate mortgage, a *chattel mortgage* may be used as security for a bond. It represents a mortgage on personal property (movable) in contrast with real property. Automobiles, agricultural equipment, and household appliances are commonly used for chattel mortgages. There are some states that do not recognize a chattel mortgage on personal property. Instead, a

conditional bill of sale is used. Even under this arrangement, how-ever, title remains with the seller until the debt is paid.

5. When goods are shipped by rail or truck, the shipper receives either a *straight* or an *order bill of lading*. The straight bill of lading is nonnegotiable; it conveys title to the goods and must be surrendered to the transportation company before the goods can be delivered to the buyer. The order bill of lading is a negotiable instrument.

   With respect to *intrastate* shipments, bills of lading in most states are governed by the Uniform Commercial Code; in those states that have not adopted the UCC, they are governed by Article 7 of the Uniform Bills of Lading Act. Bills of lading used in *interstate* trans-portation are regulated by the Federal Bills of Lading Act.

Savings Banks

A second type of bank, not nearly as common as the commercial bank, is the *savings bank*. These banks accept deposits on savings accounts and use the funds primarily for making loans. The deposits in excess of total cash reserves and loans may be invested in real estate, mortgages, government bonds, and corporation stocks and bonds, if approved by law.

Savings banks are of two types: *stock companies* and *mutual companies.* The former are owned by stockholders, who receive dividends from net profits. Mutual savings banks are owned by depositors, to whom the net profits are prorated on the basis of the size of each deposit. At present, mutual savings banks operate in only 18 states and the Virgin Islands. Since they are chartered by state governments, the amount of interest they may pay and the ways in which they may invest their funds are regulated by the state.

Each savings bank deposit may be insured under the Federal Deposit Insurance Corporation for up to $20,000. For persons of small or moderate wealth, the savings banks perform a most useful service in protecting their savings and earning for them a fairly dependable income. (Business firms rarely use savings banks for this purpose.) Most savings banks are located in New England and other northeastern states.

Investment Banks

The *investment bank* is a highly specialized financial institution. It does not accept deposits from the public. It serves business by helping corporations sell long-term securities. Many firms that might otherwise find it difficult to market stocks and bonds make use of these banks, which are often called "security houses" because they underwrite the securities issued by corporations. In a broad sense, the total structure of the investment banking industry includes commercial banks, broker–dealer firms, and investment banking firms that engage primarily in underwriting and distributing public corporate securities. Commercial banks are mentioned because they are important underwriters of local, state, and federal-agency bonds. However, in this discussion we are concerned mainly with investment banking firms engaged primarily in underwriting securities.

In underwriting securities, the investment bank takes a stock or bond issue at an agreed price and pays the corporation the total cash value before the securities are sold. The bank then assumes the risk involved in selling these securities to the public. If the issue represents a large sum of money, several investment banks may join together and form a syndicate. Each bank in the syndicate agrees to take a portion of the total securities offered for sale and distribute them through the regular channels. In 1954, when Ford Motor Company stock was offered to the public, over 700 firms participated in underwriting the sale of it. These firms included broker–dealers as well as investment banks.

The investment bank makes its profit by charging a commission for selling securities or by bidding for stocks or bonds at a discount and later selling them at a slightly higher price. If the market price drops before the entire issue is sold, the bank must take a loss on some of the securities. Of the New York security brokers, such as J. P. Morgan & Co., and Kuhn, Loeb & Co., few are willing to handle a securities issue of less than $1 million, since the expense of selling a small issue is almost as great as the cost of marketing a large one.

Trust Companies

Originally, trust companies were authorized by state laws to serve as trustees of funds and estates. In this capacity they acted to safeguard the property entrusted to them. In recent years, however, their services have been extended to include the role of registrar and transfer agent for corporations. As transfer agents, they record changes in stock ownership, and many even issue dividend checks to stockholders. As registrars, they accept the responsibility of certifying to the public that the stock issues are correctly stated and in accordance with the provisions of the corporation charter. Some states allow commercial banks to perform certain functions that are ordinarily performed by trust companies. Thus you may see a commercial bank with the title "_____ Bank and Trust Company."

Discussion Questions

5. *What are the kinds of banks that comprise our banking system, and what government agency authorizes each kind?*
6. *Contrast the kinds of services that commercial banks render to business with those provided by investment banks.*
7. *Explain the difference between trust receipts and warehouse receipts.*

THE FEDERAL RESERVE SYSTEM

The early banking history of this nation displays little of which to be proud. The United States had a central bank from 1791 (First Bank of the United States) until 1811, and from 1816 to 1836 (Second Bank of the United States). From 1836 to 1863 there were no national banks, no federal regulations, and virtually no controls by the states. It was during this time that "wildcat" banking was at its height. Banks were started without proper financial backing, and quite naturally many failed, resulting in heavy losses to stockholders and depositors. Finally, following the nationwide money panic of 1907, Congress decided that federal action was needed to bring order out of chaos. In 1908 it authorized a National Monetary Commission to study banking needs. The outcome was a proposal for a Federal Reserve System, which resulted in passage of the Federal Reserve Act in 1913.

In the United States, the Federal Reserve System serves as the central bank. In Europe, the well-known central banks include the Bank of France, the Bank of England, and the Reichsbank in Germany. Central banks in most foreign countries are owned and operated by the national government. In the United States this is not the case. The Federal Reserve System is owned by member banks, and the employees of the Federal Reserve are not government employees. They are paid out of earnings of the Federal Reserve instead of from federal funds. The law was purposely written to provide this kind of separation. As a result, the Federal Reserve has not been subjected to the kind of political pressure that other federal agencies frequently experience.

Organization

The law that created the Federal Reserve System was entitled, "An Act to provide for the establishment of Federal Reserve Banks, to furnish an elastic currency, to afford means of rediscounting commercial paper, to establish a more effective supervision of banking in the United States, and for other purposes."

At the time of publication of this book, the Federal Reserve System is composed of 5,767 member banks, 12 Federal Reserve Banks, and 24 branch banks. There are in conjunction with it three important groups: a Board of Governors, the Federal Open Market Committee, and the Federal Advisory Council, all of which are shown in the illustration on page 375.

The Board of Governors is appointed by the president of the United States with approval of the Senate. Each of the seven members on the board is appointed for a 14-year term, unless the appointee is replacing a member whose term has not expired. Every second year, the term of one member expires and he is replaced. Anyone serving a 14-year term is not eligible for reappointment. This board is regarded as autonomous and nonpolitical, in the sense that it is free from control by any executive branch of the federal government.

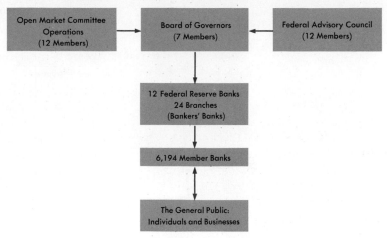

Source: Adapted from *The Federal Reserve System,* 1963, p. 22

Functions

The Federal Reserve System performs two major functions. One is to supply certain basic banking services, such as acting as a clearing-house for checks, serving as a fiscal agent for the government by distributing currency and coins, and supervising the operations of the member banks. The second function is a dual one: to maintain a sound credit policy for all member banks (by controlling the volume of credit in circulation so as to avoid sharp fluctuations in the business cycle), and at the same time to promote a high level of consumer buying. This is a very significant function because it serves the entire economy. (The methods by which credit and the circulation of money are regulated are described later in this chapter.)

Federal Reserve Banks

The United States is divided into 12 Federal Reserve districts (see the map on page 376) each with its own Federal Reserve Bank, located in the cities shown in Table 14.2.

TABLE
14.2
THE FEDERAL RESERVE BANKS OF THE UNITED STATES

District	Bank location	District	Bank location
1	Boston	7	Chicago
2	New York	8	St. Louis
3	Philadelphia	9	Minneapolis
4	Cleveland	10	Kansas City
5	Richmond	11	Dallas
6	Atlanta	12*	San Francisco

*Includes Alaska and Hawaii.

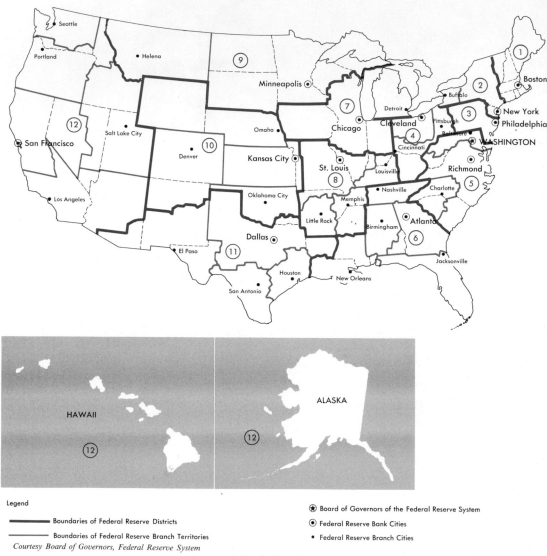

THE FEDERAL RESERVE SYSTEM

Boundaries of Federal Reserve Districts and Their Branch Territories

Legend

▬▬▬▬ Boundaries of Federal Reserve Districts

─────── Boundaries of Federal Reserve Branch Territories

⊛ Board of Governors of the Federal Reserve System

⊙ Federal Reserve Bank Cities

• Federal Reserve Branch Cities

Courtesy Board of Governors, Federal Reserve System

A map of the Federal Reserve System, which is composed of 12 district banks and 24 branch banks

Each of the 12 Federal Reserve Banks (one in each district) is a corporation organized and operated for public service. These banks differ from privately managed banks in that profits are not the object of their operations; furthermore, their stockholders, which are the member banks of the system, do not have the powers and privileges usually assigned to stockholders of privately managed corporations. (See Chapter 5.) Each Federal Reserve Bank has nine directors who conduct its business.

Branch Banks. Within the 12 districts, there are 24 branch banks. For example, in District No. 12, the Federal Reserve Bank is located in San Francisco, and the branch banks are in Los Angeles, Portland, Salt Lake City, and Seattle. These four branch banks, together with the Federal Reserve Bank of San Francisco, serve the member banks of their district.

Contributions of the Federal Reserve System to the Economy. Federal Reserve Banks are called "bankers' banks," because they provide financial services to the total monetary operations of this country. They play a vital role in helping to maintain a sound banking system and a stable economy. Although the Federal Reserve System is only one of several forces affecting business conditions, it has managed to eliminate many of the banking evils that existed prior to the enactment of the Federal Reserve Act. Over the years, the system has provided a second line of defense against bank runs by enabling the member banks to discount commercial paper in order to meet demands for cash. The Federal Reserve System and the Federal Deposit Insurance Corporation have made banks much safer than they used to be.

Member Banks. All national banks must be members of the Federal Reserve System. State banks may become members, provided they can meet the requirements. Most state banks are nonmembers, probably because their volume of business does not require the Reserve's services.

On the basis of a classification established by the Board of Governors, member banks are divided into three sizes: small, medium, and large. Member banks in each size elect one Class A member and one Class B member of the board of directors of their Federal Reserve Bank. Class C directors are appointed by the Board of Governors.

Among the advantages to member banks of belonging to the Federal Reserve are the following:

1. Currency can be obtained immediately from a Federal Reserve Bank.
2. Drafts may be drawn on the Federal Reserve Bank.
3. Deposits may be transferred by telegraph between one bank and another through a Federal Reserve Bank.
4. Eligible commercial paper may be discounted and advances obtained from the Federal Reserve Bank.
5. Deposits up to $20,000 for each depositor are insured in each member bank by the Federal Deposit Insurance Corporation.
6. Federal Reserve Banks may be used to collect checks and clear other negotiable instruments.

Operational and Credit Functions
of the Federal Reserve System

From the viewpoint of the national economy, the most important function of the Federal Reserve System is the regulation of the volume of bank credit—that is, the amount of demand deposits, or checkbook money, that banks create by making loans. The system uses several different methods to accomplish this function. These may be identified as follows: (1) open-market operations, (2) legal reserve requirements, (3) the rediscount rate, and (4) margin requirements for the sale of securities.

Open-Market Operations. The Open Market Committee increases or decreases the amount of bank reserves by directing the Federal Reserve System to buy or sell U.S. government securities in the open market. Buying or selling in the open market involves buying from or selling to the general public. Briefly, it works like this. Suppose business gives evidence of slowing down. The Open Market Committee may direct the Reserve to buy $1 billion worth of government bonds. The persons who sell these bonds deposit the money in their banks. By buying these bonds, the Federal Reserve puts that much more money into the banking system and thereby increases bank reserves. This enables the banks to increase their loans.

Conversely, if business seems to be expanding too rapidly because there is too much "easy" money in circulation, which could have the adverse effect of reducing the purchasing power of the dollar, the committee can direct the Federal Reserve System to sell government bonds. If, for example, banks are directed to sell $1 billion in bonds, the persons who buy the bonds pay for them by drawing checks on their banks. This reduces the amounts on reserve in the member banks. Thus, the cash reserves of the banking system are reduced by $1 billion and its lending capacity is likewise reduced. As a result, credit becomes "tighter," banks make fewer loans, business firms find it more difficult to obtain credit for expansion, and the dangers of overexpansion of business activity are prevented.

Legal Reserve Requirements as Against Demand Deposits. In addition to the requirement that every member bank must subscribe to a certain amount of stock in the Federal Reserve Bank in its district, each member bank must maintain a minimum legal reserve. The amount of this legal reserve can be increased or decreased by the Board of Governors when in their judgment there is a need to increase or decrease the amount of money member banks have available for credit financing. The boxed exhibit at the top of the following page shows how the Federal Reserve operates to increase the supply of money by using the multiplier capability of added reserves for demand deposits.

The effectiveness of changes in reserve requirements depends on much the same conditions as open-market operations. Increasing excess reserves when

The Federal Reserve and the U.S. Money Supply

The total supply of money consists of demand deposits (checking accounts) of commercial banks and currency in circulation. Currency is used mainly in small retail transactions. Most of the larger transactions are paid for by check.

While the level of demand deposits is determined mainly by the lending and investment activities of banks, these are influenced by Federal Reserve policies. The Federal Reserve may stimulate or slow the economy by increasing or decreasing the reserve of demand deposits. By law, a certain percentage of deposits stipulated by the Federal Reserve must be set aside as "required reserves." The remaining reserves become the basis for additional loans. As these excess reserves expand, they have the potential to increase demand deposits on a multiplier basis, and thereby add to the money supply.

To show how this works, let us assume that the prevailing member-bank reserve requirement is 20 percent. Bank No. 1 receives $100 in demand deposits (checking account).

a. Bank No. 1 accepts the $100 deposit, withholds $20 for its reserve, and is allowed to lend or invest $80. This conforms to the 20 percent reserve requirement.

b. The $80 is lent to another depositor and becomes a credit to his account.

c. The depositor writes a check for $80, giving it to a new recipient who deposits it in bank No. 2, which now has $80 in new reserve funds.

d. Bank No. 2 immediately withholds $16, or 20 percent, as required reserve and lends the remaining $64 to one of its customers.

This process can be continued until $500 becomes the grand total in all banks with the total of $400 for all loans, and until the full amount of $100 has been set aside as reserves. The $100 original deposit has now increased to $500 of demand deposits. Table 14.3 is a summary of all the transactions that have occurred.

the supply is already excessive encourages banks to put idle money to work by making more loans. If the increase in reserve requirements tends to reduce excess reserves to a dangerously low point, then the reserves will be decreased in order to curtail bank lending. This is a blunt and general means of credit control compared with the open-market operations, and when used it has

**TABLE
14.3**

MULTIPLYING CAPACITY OF RESERVE MONEY THROUGH BANK TRANSACTIONS[a]

Transactions	Deposited in Checking Accounts	Money Lent	Set Aside as Reserves
Bank 1	$100.00	$ 80.00	$ 20.00
2	80.00	64.00	16.00
3	64.00	51.20	12.80
4	51.20	40.96	10.24
5	40.96	32.77	8.19
6	32.77	26.22	6.55
7	26.22	20.98	5.24
8	20.98	16.78	4.20
9	16.78	13.42	3.36
10	13.42	10.74	2.68
Total for 10 banks	446.33	357.07	89.26
Additional banks	53.67	42.93[b]	10.74[b]
Grand total, all banks	500.00	400.00	100.00

[a]Based on an average member-bank reserve requirement of 20 percent of demand deposits.
[b]Adjusted to offset rounding in preceding figures.
Source: Federal Reserve Board: The Federal Reserve System—Purposes and Functions.

proved to be most effective in discouraging or encouraging bank credit. It is used only infrequently.[2]

The Rediscount Rate. There are times when a member bank needs money for a short period. These banks may borrow from Federal Reserve Banks in two ways: They may rediscount, or sell, the promissory notes or other commercial paper they hold, or they may borrow on their own secured notes in much the same way a customer borrows from a commercial bank. The former transactions are called *rediscounting,* the latter, *advances.* When a bank obtains an advance, eligible commercial paper (negotiable promissory notes, for example) or government securities must be offered as collateral. Reserve authorities are inclined to raise the rediscount rate to discourage member-bank borrowing from a Reserve bank, and lower the rate to encourage it.

If the Federal Reserve decides that easy credit is contributing to inflation, it can raise the rediscount rate so that borrowers will have to pay a higher interest rate. Raising the rediscount rate tends to raise interest rates, so that borrowers find it too expensive to borrow money either to expand their businesses or to make additional purchases.

Regulation of Margin Requirements. As has already been mentioned in our discussion of the New York Stock Exchange in Chapter 13, the Board of Governors by law has the power to set minimum margin requirements. Regulating margin requirements is a means of encouraging or discouraging

[2]For a further treatment of the subject of open market operations and legal reserve requirements for Federal Reserve member banks, see George Leland Bach, *Economics: An Introduction to Analysis and Policy,* 7th ed. (Englewood Cliffs, N.J.: Prentice-Hall, Inc., 1971).

lending. The smaller the margin required of the buyer, the more he can borrow against the purchase price; the higher the margin that is required of him, the less he can buy against the price of the stock. Consequently, buying on margin makes it possible for a person to buy more stocks with less money. The current margin rate is 55 percent. This means that a person buying stock may borrow up to 45 percent of the purchase price.

Besides direct controls over margin borrowing, the Federal Reserve for many years had the power to set limits on installment-sales contracts. During the years of the Korean conflict, the Federal Reserve established a regulation requiring buyers of cars, household goods, and other items under "Regulation W" to pay up on charge accounts before buying more goods on credit. This regulation was very effective in controlling credit, but it became unpopular, and when the Korean crisis ended, this power of the Federal Reserve was permitted by Congress to expire.

Clearing Bank Checks. Another function of the Federal Reserve System is to establish procedures for clearing bank checks. About 90 percent of the total dollar volume of business involves payments by check. Most checks are drawn on one bank and deposited in another. When the banks involved are located in the same community, the clearance is conducted by the local clearinghouse association of local member banks. This procedure involves tabulating, accounting, and exchanging local checks, with account differences being paid to the appropriate bank each day. When banks are not local but are in the same Federal Reserve District, handling the checks is called the *clearing process.* When there is an exchange of checks between banks located in two or more Federal Reserve Districts, the check-clearing process is known as the *transit process.* Any bank that acts as a representative of another bank is a *correspondent bank.*

In the accompanying illustration, the transit process is indicated step-by-step, involving check clearance concerning banks located in two Federal Reserve Districts. In this example, Mr. Jones in Richmond, Virginia, writes a check on his bank in Richmond and mails it to C Company in Atlanta, Georgia. That company then deposits the check to its account in an Atlanta

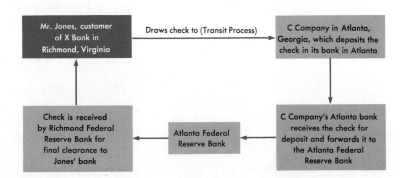

bank. This bank sends the check, together with other out-of-town checks, to the Atlanta Federal Reserve Bank, which sorts the checks by districts and sends Mr. Jones's check back to the Richmond Federal Reserve Bank. All checks are again sorted by cities, and the various checks are returned to each drawer's bank. In this case, Mr. Jones's check is received, and the amount is deducted from his account.

Discussion Questions

8. *Explain the origin of and reason for the Federal Reserve System, and its relationship to commercial-bank members of the system.*
9. *What are the main functions of the Federal Reserve System? How does the system help to stabilize the economy?*
10. *What is the purpose of the Open Market Committee operations?*

OTHER FINANCIAL INSTITUTIONS

The need for additional working capital or for special credit services not ordinarily provided by commercial banks, savings banks, and investment banks causes many establishments as well as individuals to turn to other financial institutions. Some of these institutions provide short-term credit to individuals but not to companies. Others buy short-term credit loans from large companies that sell their merchandise on an installment plan. Some specialize in purchasing accounts receivable.

Commercial-Paper Dealers

In the financial world, *commercial paper* refers to unsecured promissory notes issued by companies of good credit standing that sell on the open market. Commercial-paper dealers or houses buy these short-term notes, usually in units of from $2,500 to $10,000, and resell the paper as quickly as possible to banks and other investors. The buyer has a time option of 10 to 15 days to investigate the paper. These dealers receive a commission for rendering this service.

Finance Companies

Although there is diversity of activities among finance companies, their main purpose is to supply short-term financing. The two major classifications are sales finance companies and personal finance companies. *Sales finance companies* specialize in financing automobiles and household appliances sold under an installment sales contract. Such contracts are sold by retailers, such as automobile dealers, to sales finance companies at a discount. Thus the dealer is able to obtain cash immediately from the sale of an automobile. More than half of all new automobiles and about 70 percent of all used cars sold are financed by sales finance companies or other financial institutions. The General Motors Acceptance Corporation (GMAC) does financing for General Motors cars sold through dealers. Ford dealers are served by the Commercial Investment Trust (CIT). There are also many smaller, privately owned sales finance companies. Sales finance companies obtain their capital by borrowing from commercial banks, despite the fact that they may be in direct competition with banks for this kind of financing.

Personal finance companies, or *consumer finance companies,* are engaged primarily in making personal loans, usually for from three months to two years. These are mainly signature loans with no cosigners, although household furniture is sometimes used as collateral. Higher interest rates are charged by these companies than by other financial institutions, because the risk is greater, and the loan is often smaller. These companies are subject to the Federal Consumer Credit Protection Act (known as the Truth-in-Lending Law) when the loan does not exceed $25,000. This law is discussed in more detail later in this chapter.

Factoring Companies (Factors)

Another specialized type of business finance organization is the factoring company. *Factoring* involves the purchase of a company's accounts receivable without recourse against the seller—that is, the factor assumes the risks of collecting the accounts. Factors confine their services mainly to companies that manufacture furniture, glassware, textiles, and shoes. A continuing agreement is made between the manufacturer and the factor whereby the latter contracts to buy all the accounts receivable as they arise. Most factors operate on a notification basis, by requiring the manufacturer to send the invoice for the goods to the factor, who forwards it to the customer. The invoice says that payment is to be made to the factoring company. For many years, 6 percent was the traditional rate charged by the factor for advancing cash against receivables. In 1965, insurance companies and commercial banks began entering the factoring business by buying smaller factors, after the Comptroller of the Currency ruled that factoring was a proper area for national bank expansion. In 1960, the total factoring amounted to $5.45 billion; by 1970 it had increased to $11.88 billion.

Industrial Banks

Industrial banks operate under several different titles, such as industrial banks, Morris Plan banks, finance and thrift companies, and industrial savings and loan companies. Industrial banks, such as the Morris Plan, make loans to individuals and businesses. They obtain their funds from individual savers who make deposits or buy individual deposit certificates. The borrower from an industrial bank will sign a note agreeing to repay the loan in monthly installments to be deposited to his account or to a certificate account. The Morris Plan avoids the usury laws by the device of selling installment "investment certificates" to borrowers. Technically, the advance of money is not a loan.

Credit Unions

Credit unions are nonprofit cooperative associations that function as specialized savings and consumer finance institutions. They may be chartered by the federal or state government. Since credit unions are not banks, they are not allowed to refer to their accounts as deposits. Instead, the savings of members are called shares or share deposit accounts.

Credit unions make loans to their members, who may borrow up to $2,500 on the basis of required collateral or a cosigner of a promissory note. Loans are also made to buy automobiles and appliances. Interest rates charged for loans are below those charged by other lending agencies, such as banks and savings and loan associations.

Under the Federal Credit Union Act, which became effective in 1970, the National Credit Union Administration (NCUA) was established as an independent agency outside the Department of Health, Education and Welfare, to administer federal credit unions. The NCUA is also charged with administering a National Credit Union Insurance Fund: Under the law, the Administrator insures the member accounts of all federal credit unions and of credit unions organized under the laws of any state, the District of Columbia, and territories, provided these state credit unions can qualify for this protection. The maximum insurance provided is $20,000 for each member account. In 1971 there were 12,553 federal and 11,206 state credit unions, with total loans outstanding amounting to $15 billion. Any group of persons having a common bond, such as the same employer, may organize a credit union by applying to the NCUA for a federal charter or to the state credit union association at the state capital.

Discussion Questions

11. *What are the three types of consumer credit, and in what ways does it help merchants and consumers?*
12. *Explain the differences between sales finance and consumer finance companies.*
13. *What are factoring companies, and how do they differ from industrial banks?*

REGULATING FINANCIAL INSTITUTIONS

During the course of our discussion of various fields of business, we have noted several illustrations of government control. Both the state and federal governments have enacted legislative measures to control financial and credit-type institutions.

Regulatory Measures

Congressional authority to regulate money and credit is chiefly based on Section 8 of the Constitution of the United States. Under this provision, Congress has certain rights, among which are those of borrowing money on the credit of the United States, of coining money, of paying debts, and of performing certain other responsibilities vital to the common defense and general welfare of this nation.

For many years, financial institutions such as banks, savings and loan companies, investment trusts, finance companies, and stock exchanges were subject to very little federal control, and often to even less state control. As early as 1900, however, it became evident that government supervision of our national banking system was needed. During the boom period of the late 1920's, the public was victimized by dishonest schemes and abuses involving overvalued corporation stocks. Even more significant was the number of bank failures that occurred, most of which could have been avoided had there been proper legislation to provide for greater controls. Fortunately, corrective legislation such as the following was eventually enacted.

The Federal Reserve Act. One of the four purposes of the Federal Reserve Act of 1913 was to provide supervision of banking in the United States. The Board of Governors of the Federal Reserve System makes general monetary credit policies as a whole, and formulates rules and regulations necessary to carry out the purposes of the Federal Reserve Act. Their control of credit conditions and supervision of Federal Reserve Banks and member banks is indeed important to the general welfare of the nation.

The Federal Reserve Board has the power to examine Federal Reserve Banks and to control the admission of state banks or trust companies to membership in the Federal Reserve System. It may also terminate membership, approve or disapprove bank mergers or consolidations, and pass upon applications of national banks for authority to act in the fiduciary capacity (a special duty of care and confidence between the parties). In addition to its credit operations, the Federal Reserve can establish or discontinue branch Reserve banks and exercise supervision of those banks in their relations with foreign banks or bankers. In this chapter we have already noted many of these areas of control, particularly over practices that affect banking operations and over credit policies toward business. The value of this legislation is self-evident.

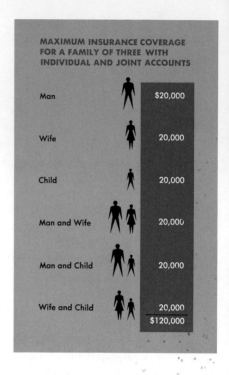

MAXIMUM INSURANCE COVERAGE
FOR A FAMILY OF THREE WITH
INDIVIDUAL AND JOINT ACCOUNTS

Man		$20,000
Wife		20,000
Child		20,000
Man and Wife		20,000
Man and Child		20,000
Wife and Child		20,000
		$120,000

The Federal Deposit Insurance Corporation. Few people today worry about the safety of their money on deposit in national and state banks that are insured by the Federal Deposit Insurance Corporation (FDIC). One reason for this public confidence is that the FDIC Acts of 1933 and 1950 require all national banks to insure their deposits with the FDIC. State banks are also eligible to participate, provided these institutions can pass a careful examination conducted by the FDIC. The maximum amount for which each account is insured was recently increased to $20,000. Funds for this program are obtained by assessing each member bank an annual fee on all deposits in that bank. The illustration shows how a family of three with individual and joint accounts can have insured savings up to $120,000.

The Truth-in-Lending Law. The Consumer Credit Protection Act (otherwise known as the "Truth-in-Lending" bill) was passed by Congress in May 1968 with an effective date of July 1, 1969. This law requires loan companies, banks, retailers, and other businesses engaged in installment consumer selling to publish—in terms of an annual rate—the cost of consumer credit charged the buyer. Where a store formerly listed the cost of a revolving charge account as $1\frac{1}{2}$ percent per month, it must now state the cost as 18 percent (the cost per year). The law covers loans and credit purchases up to $25,000 and home mortgages of any amount. It does not apply to commercial or business transactions.

This act in no way attempts to set maximum finance charges on a transaction. It merely states the kind of information to be released to borrowers and how detailed it must be.

Fair Credit Reporting Act. Your name is probably on file with the credit bureau in your community. It may include facts about your buying and paying habits and other information about your character and employment. Until recently, there has been little you could do about verifying the information in your credit file.

The Fair Credit Reporting Act enacted by Congress became law in April 1971. This law gives you access to your credit-information file. If a person discovers what he considers inaccurate or incomplete facts in his file, he can require the bureau to recheck the facts. If the bureau is unable to verify these facts, it must delete them. If a person and the bureau disagree as to the accuracy or completeness of specific data, the person is allowed to write his own statement, not to exceed 100 words, and it is added to the file.

Credit files may be released only for purposes of credit appraisal, employment, insurance, government licenses, or for other legitimate business purposes. People who can prove that a credit bureau deliberately wronged them may sue for court costs and actual damages.

This law denies the Federal Trade Commission power to write effective enforcement rules. Moreover, some of the vague wording and imprecise definitions will make court suits by consumers difficult to win. On balance, this is not regarded as a strong or forceful law.

Holding-Company Legislation

Bank Holding Company Act of 1956. As you will recall from our discussion in Chapter 5, holding companies have been a controversial matter beginning in 1888, when New Jersey passed a law permitting one corporation to buy stock in another. Holding companies in general have been subject to federal legislation since 1935. The Bank Holding Act of 1956 was designed to restrict the kind of nonbanking activities available to bank holding companies. The purpose was to keep the banking industry separate from other businesses. This act, however, specifically exempted one-bank holding companies, which have increased so greatly in number that they now control much of the banking assets. Beginning in 1968, Congress started to study this problem.

Bank Holding Company Amendment of 1970. This law is an attempt to set new standards of permissibility for the operation of one-bank holding companies, many of which have been organized since 1960. Under the new standards, one-bank holding companies are required to divest themselves of business affiliates if the Federal Reserve finds this ownership caused undue concentration of resources or diminishes competition. A business now acquired or started by a one-bank holding company will have to be "so closely related to banking or managing or controlling banks as to be a proper incident" to banking. These companies will not be allowed to own and run factories, mines, shoe stores, and other firms clearly unrelated to banking. Spokesmen for the banks say, however, that they interpret the law to allow one-bank holding companies to sell life insurance when it is related to bank loans and to buy and lease airplanes to the airlines or rail cars to the railroads. Critics of one-bank holding companies regard this legislation as leaving much to be desired.

Discussion Questions

14. *Explain some of the major control powers exercised by the Federal Reserve Board over banks. State how these controls help the banking system.*

15. *What are the purposes of (a) the Consumer Credit Protection Act, and (b) the Fair Credit Reporting Act?*

CAREERS IN FINANCE AND BANKING

Over the years there has developed in this country a variety of financial institutions that fill short-term financial needs. These organizations offer many different kinds of employment, requiring various levels of career preparation. Banks are among the largest employers in the field of banking and finance.

Qualifications for Banking Positions

Since banks are constantly handling large sums of money belonging to other people, honesty and integrity are important personal requirements for holding banking positions. Of course, bank employees must be able to keep confidential any information about their customers. Under the sponsorship of the American Institute of Banking, a series of courses to help bank employees is offered in most large and small city banks. Banks are hiring more college-educated persons—especially those with business education at the college level. Employment for women in banks is increasing.

Nat S. Rogers, president of the American Bankers Association and president of the First City National Bank of Houston, Texas, speaking before the annual convention of the National Association of Bank Women, said, "One out of every ten bank officers in the United States is a woman. In the seventies you will have the same opportunity to reach top management as any other banker."

Employment Opportunities in Banking

In the past, the low starting salaries offered by banks tended to discourage young people from entering this business. More recently, however, starting salaries have been increasing, and banks are doing a better job of informing young people of the advantages and opportunities of a career in banking.

Several kinds of employment are open to beginners in banking. The bank operations department is a good place to learn mechanical operations and accounting procedures. Other good opportunities for advancement are to be found in the loan department and in the department responsible for new-business development and public relations.

Larger commercial banks have trust departments to handle estates and administer trusts; legal training is essential in these activities. Some banks maintain a foreign or international trade department to handle trade documents used in foreign commerce (described in Chapter 23). And in every bank, no matter what its size, there are numerous clerical positions that may serve as stepping-stones to higher levels. These positions include machine operators, messengers, typists, clerks, and secretaries. In Chapter 18 you learned that a new field, that of the electronic computer, requires specialists in computer programming.

There are also positions as tellers, personnel managers, auditors, economists, tax specialists, and loan officers. The American Institute of Banking reports that out of every 100 jobs in banking, 17 are filled by administrative officers and 10 by senior supervisors.

The highest position in most banks is that of the chairman of the board of directors, who is promoted from the office of president. The regular officers are the president, vice-president (usually several), secretary, and cashier. Large banks assign each of the vice-presidents the responsibility for directing the functions of certain departments. Some banks have several assistant cashiers. One of the most interesting and responsible positions is that of loan officer, who is in charge of all loans. In very large banks, every loan is ultimately approved by a loan committee after the application has been analyzed and prepared by the loan officer.

The Investment Banker and the Stockbroker

The *investment banker* is a specialist who advises corporations on the most profitable methods of marketing their securities. He provides information about the proper timing of a sale, about what type of securities can be distributed at a minimum cost, and about legal and technical matters; and he also provides general economic information. He is actually the intermediary between two parties—the issuer and the investor.

When the corporation officials have decided to sell the firm's securities through the investment banker, he assumes the responsibility for marketing these securities. Planning the sale of corporate securities requires months of careful preparation and entails a knowledge of legal procedures, government regulations, stock market operations, and current economic conditions. All of this necessitates a broad background in finance and banking.

Closely identified with the investment banker is the *stockbroker,* who as agent executes orders for his clients. To qualify for this position, you must pass an examination conducted by the Securities and Exchange Commission. Virtually all the larger brokerage firms conduct special training programs for beginners in this field. Training in business finance, economics, law, accounting, mathematics, and investments will provide you with a good background for one of these positions.

Career Opportunities in Other Finance Fields

There are career opportunities open in many other fields of finance. These include employment in the Federal Reserve System and the Small Business Administration, and in insurance companies, savings and loan associations, commercial-paper houses, and mortgage companies. Positions with any of these organizations should pay well and offer good future expectations. The study of business administration is considered a valuable part of one's preparation for a career in all fields of finance and banking. There are additional opportunities for those with a knowledge of computers.

SUMMARY

In addition to funds for permanent financing, every business requires other forms of capital for short-term financing. Our business system is such that credit is the basis for all loans. Credit enables the proprietor to adjust his volume of capital to meet changing financial needs.

Credit instruments used in financing working-capital needs are based on either promise-to-pay or order-to-pay negotiable instruments. Credit instruments that are promises to pay are the open-book account, the promissory note, and order-to-pay instruments such as drafts and trade acceptances.

Other forms of short-term credit are pledging of accounts receivable, bank loans, installment credit, factoring, and loans for short duration made by finance companies, credit unions, and industrial banks. Security for short-term loans may be corporation stock, order bills of lading, or warehouse or trust receipts.

Commercial banks are the main source of short-term credit. They also supply business with other financial services: They accept demand and time deposits, discount negotiable instruments, issue letters of credit, service foreign-trade transactions, and collect payments on negotiable instruments.

Commercial banks are classified as either state or national. Those that are chartered by a state government are state banks. National banks receive their charters from the federal government. Federal charter requirements are considered more stringent than are most state regulations. All national banks must be members of the Federal Reserve System and the Federal Deposit Insurance Corporation. State banks may be members of the FDIC if they meet its requirements.

The broad objective of the Federal Reserve System is to control the supply of money and credit in such a manner as to contribute to high-level employment, promote price stability, and encourage economic growth. During periods of inflation or deflation, the Federal Reserve is especially active. Three devices—regulation of bank reserves, regulation of the discount rate, and open-market operations—are used.

In addition to the controls over commercial banks by the Federal Reserve Board, loan companies, finance companies, and credit unions are also subject to federal regulation. The Consumer Credit Protection Act requires finance companies and companies engaged in installment consumer selling to publish, at the time of the credit sale, such information as the terms of annual interest rate, the cost of consumer credit charged the buyer, and any finance charges. The Fair Credit Reporting Act, also a federal law, permits people to see information about them that is on file in retail credit bureaus. If the credit bureau is unable to verify the facts, it must delete them from the record.

Few fields offer greater career opportunities to college graduates than banking and finance. There are also many opportunities for promotion, since for every 100 jobs in banking, there are 17 administrative and 10 supervisory positions.

VOCABULARY REVIEW

Match the following vocabulary terms with the statements below.

a. Bank draft
b. Bill of exchange
c. Cashier's check
d. Collateral

e. Correspondent bank
f. Credit
g. Investment banker
h. Payee

i. Sight draft
j. Short-term loan
k. Time draft
l. Warehouse receipt

1. The ability to secure goods or services (or money) in exchange for a promise to pay later
2. A draft payable at some designated future date
3. A draft payable on demand
4. A written order of one bank on another bank to pay to a person named on the draft a sum upon demand
5. A check drawn by a bank against its own funds and signed by the cashier or other official and not the depositor
6. A document serving as a receipt for goods stored in a warehouse
7. A loan for a year or less
8. The person to whom a check is made payable
9. An instrument drawn by one person ordering a second person to pay a sum of money to a specified person on sight or at a future date
10. A bank that acts as a representative for another bank

11. Marketable assets, such as goods, land, equipment, or negotiable instruments, used as security for a loan

12. A specialist who advises corporations on methods of marketing their securities

PROBLEMS AND PROJECTS

1. Calox Mills, Inc., a textile manufacturing company, needs $60,000 additional working capital to carry it to the end of the season, but it has exhausted its credit with commercial banks. Name the other sources of short-term borrowing that are open to this company.

2. Homer Jackson owns a variety store in a shopping center. He recently bought a new car for $3,600, which he paid for from an inheritance. After using it three months, he moved to a neighborhood three blocks from the shopping center. Now he walks to work. He also owns an older car, which is probably worth about $300. Homer would like to sell his new car because he has an opportunity to buy at a good price an order of toys from Japan. He needs $2,700. He was offered $3,100 cash for his new car by a dealer. His bank will lend him $2,800 on the car, repayable in 15 monthly installments of $212.50. What should Homer do?

3. An invoice in the amount of $1,000 dated April 1 has terms of 2/10, net 30. Suppose the bill is paid April 21; how much should be remitted? What is the last date that the discount may be taken? When is the bill regarded as delinquent?

A BUSINESS CASE

Case 14-1   The Bell Brothers Glass Company, Inc.

The Bell Brothers Glass Company was organized as a corporation in 1925 to manufacture glass jugs and bottles. In 1927 the company added glass jars for home canning. The corporation is family-owned, with offices in Chicago. Jugs and bottles are sold directly to food-processing companies as containers for juices, syrup, cider, and vinegar bought by hotels and restaurants; the glass jars are marketed at retail by grocery stores. Bell Brothers markets mainly in the widwestern states.

The production of jars takes place mainly during the first five months of the year, to make them available to retailers for summer sales. During this period, the employment of additional workers results in increased labor costs. During other months of the year except December, the company maintains production of jugs and bottles and a few jars of special sizes.

Last year the company earned 7 percent on sales of $1 million, and paid a dividend of 50 cents per quarter on 25,000 shares of common stock. A shortage of working capital during the peak production period always requires the negotiation of one or more short-term loans from the bank. The new treasurer of the company is critical of this practice of borrowing working capital. He contends the company should use other sources to obtain funds, in view of the company's financial condition, shown below as a recent simplified balance sheet.

BELL BROTHERS GLASS COMPANY, INC.

Assets		Liabilities	
Cash	$ 25,000	Notes payable	$ 10,000
Accounts receivable	775,000	Accounts payable	190,000
Merchandise inventory	100,000	Common stock (25,000 shares,	
Machinery	50,000	par value $2 per share)	50,000
Land and building	100,000	Surplus	800,000
Total assets	$1,050,000	Total liabilities and capital	$1,050,000

1. Do you agree with the critical attitude of the company treasurer?

2. By what method can the company obtain more working capital, other than by a short-term loan? Explain the reasons for your suggestion.

3. In your opinion, does this financial statement reflect a need for improving the company's financial management policies?

risk management and insurance

CHAPTER FIFTEEN

Every aspect of living carries with it one or more risks of varying degrees. Therefore, within our economic system, every business venture and its related activities involve some amount of risk.

In business, some risks can be insured against; others can be reduced by good business practices. In some cases, businesses adjust or absorb the losses that cannot be shifted to an insurance company or removed entirely. But even assigning the risks to an insurance company, while it may minimize the loss to an acceptable degree, does not entirely relieve the business or individual from the responsibility of the loss.

In this chapter, our purpose is to discover how insurance in its various forms, through the practice of risk management, is used to shift the burden of risk from a business or individual to an insurance company.

In addition to insurance, we will examine other methods that are used to distribute or transfer some of the burdens of common business risks. It is the role of the risk manager in a business to see that the profits of the firm are not destroyed by the occurrence of a risk that can be either removed or shifted.

CONCEPTS OF RISK

One of the characteristics of our environment is the presence of risk and uncertainty. *Risk* is the exposure to losses or injuries. It is caused by the occurrence of an unfavorable or undesirable event. The loss may appear in several forms, such as loss of life, property, or health. The burden of some types of risk can be shifted. The risk manager must know when and how to shift them.

Types of Risk

The two broad categories of risk are speculative risk and pure risk. A distinction needs to be made, because only one of these types is insurable.

A *speculative risk* is a situation in which there is either a chance of loss or a possibility of gain. Wagering is an example of a speculative risk, because in a wager you may either win or lose. A certain type of speculative risk may be shifted by hedging, a subject we shall examine later in this chapter.

Pure risk is the type that involves only a chance of loss. The uncertainty is usually whether the destruction will happen at all, and in the case of death, the uncertainty is when. It is against this kind of risk that insurance offers protection. The diagram following shows the kinds of pure risks that are insurable.

Many people regard the terms "risk," "hazard," and "peril" synony-

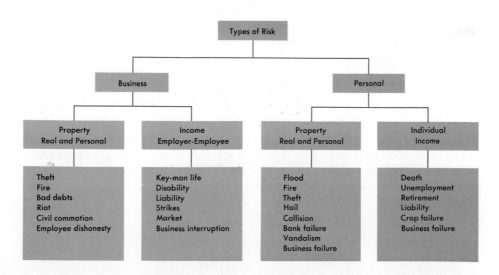

mously. In fact, they have different meanings. A peril is really a contingency that may cause a loss, while a hazard is the condition that makes the occurrence of the peril more likely. Certain occupations are hazardous; that is, the occurrence of the peril is more certain. Moral hazards are created by the mental attitude of a person; two common moral hazards are dishonesty and lack of integrity. On the other hand, physical hazards are created by certain physical aspects of property. A frame building is considered to offer a greater physical hazard than a concrete and steel building.

Methods of Dealing with Risk

One individual alone cannot reduce his risk unless he is able to control enough factors that have direct bearing on the risk. After all, each of us has but one life; most of us own no more than one house; and only a small percentage of the population owns two or more automobiles. Each of these possessions is insufficient to give one control over the variety of factors that endanger it.

What, then, are the methods of meeting risk? There are five ways to meet risk: (1) reduction or elimination of the hazards; (2) self-insurance—establish a reserve for unforeseen contingencies; (3) practicing good management to prevent risk causes; (4) shifting risk to insurance carriers; and (5) hedging—a special procedure for minimizing inventory price risks.

Reduction or Elimination of the Hazard. It is possible to reduce or remove the chance of loss by taking preventive or protective measures, such as installing safety equipment or using fireproof materials. Installing an automatic sprinkler system is a protective measure. Safety campaigns among workers tend to decrease accidents, and regular inspections of equipment will help to avoid injuries.

Self-Insurance Reserve Fund. This method assumes that it is more profitable for a businessman to accept his own risks than to insure against them. To do this, it is necessary to set aside a certain sum annually as a reserve fund to be used if property is destroyed by certain perils, such as fire or wind. This plan requires the business to carry an excessive amount of risk during the early years of the plan, because during this time the fund is low.

This method is often more successful when used by large companies with widely scattered operations. The chance of a severe loss to property at several locations during any one year is remote, and if each unit in the company contributes to the fund, the total amount would ordinarily be adequate to compensate for any loss that might occur.

Practicing Good Management to Prevent Risk. An effective way to meet certain kinds of business risks is to practice good managerial techniques. For example, be alert to price changes or sharp variations in the economic index; and recognize product obsolence as early as possible, before losses result. Many companies maintain a research department to study economic trends. It is the job of the risk manager to see that management practices are conducive to prevention of risks.

Insurance. Although all the methods of meeting risk discussed thus far offer partial protection against risks, the most universal method is to transfer the risk to professional risk bearers, such as insurance companies. We shall study this method in greater depth later in this chapter.

Hedging. Hedging is another method of shifting economic risk. It may be defined as the process of trading in futures on commodity exchanges in such a way as to gain protection from loss owing to price fluctuations during the time the same spot commodity item is being processed for delivery. Commodity markets are centers where staple commodities (wheat, cotton, hides, etc.) are traded for "cash" or "futures" contracts. The main difference between the two types is in the sales contract. "Cash" or "spot" trading calls for immediate delivery—on the spot. "Futures" refers to contracts with the selling of the commodity made through an organized exchange for future delivery. This contract specifies grade, price, amount, and delivery date (by naming the month—for instance, "May wheat"). The Chicago Board of Trade has the largest volume of trade in grains. The New York Cotton Exchange specializes in cotton. The subject of commodity exchanges, which are part of our marketing system, are discussed in depth in Chapter 19.

As an example of hedging, you are a flour miller in Illinois and you have accepted an order from a large bakery company in Chicago for several tons of flour, to be delivered at two month intervals starting four months hence. You had to give the bakery company a fixed price for the flour. You figure you will need 100,000 bushels of wheat to mill the required amount of flour to fill this order, but you cannot afford to buy all the wheat now. In fact, you have enough space to store only 25,000 bushels at one time. So you must buy wheat from farmers several times before you mill the complete order.

As an experienced miller, you know that it is impossible to predict accurately the price of wheat during the next four months. But you have agreed to a fixed price to charge for the flour. By hedging, you can minimize your risk so that you can make your normal trade profit from milling flour.

If wheat advances 10 cents a bushel on an average over the next four months, you stand to lose $10,000. So you hedge by telling your commodity broker to buy you 100,000 bushels of May wheat (futures contract), which at the moment is 10 cents a bushel cheaper than cash wheat. Regardless of what the price is—it would make no difference if May wheat were up or down—you would still hedge.

When you buy your futures contract, you pay in cash for only a small part; this is known as buying on margin. Your commodities broker will arrange for the transaction. You now have a contract for 100,000 bushels of wheat for

May delivery. However, you know that you will sell this contract before delivery date.

The day you are ready to mill the first part of the wheat to make delivery of so much flour, you place an order with your broker for 25,000 bushels of spot wheat; and at the same time, you direct your broker to sell 25,000 bushels of the May futures wheat at the market price. Now you have engaged in a hedging process. But there is still the matter of price. Assume that the price of spot wheat had advanced 10 cents a bushel, as you feared it might. For the 25,000 bushels of spot you lose $2,500, because you had to pay more for it. But since spot and futures prices almost always advance or drop together, the price of May wheat will go up 10 cents too. So, although you paid more for the spot wheat, you made the same amount as profit on the sale of futures wheat, and you came out even. Each time you need another 25,000 bushels of spot wheat to mill, you simply repeat this hedging operation, unitl you have filled the full order of flour. When you quoted the bakery company your price on flour per hundredweight, you included in that price all your expenses— broker's commission, storage, margin of profit, etc. Without hedging, it would have been virtually impossible for you to accept this risk as a flour miller without taking a loss.

Discussion Questions

1. *What is the difference between a pure risk and a speculative risk, and which is insurable?*

2. *Besides insurance, what other means can a businessman use to reduce or eliminate risk?*

TYPES OF PRIVATE INSURANCE COMPANIES

Most insurance is sold by two types of insurance companies—stock companies and mutual companies—and both are privately owned.[1]

[1]Lloyd's of London, one of the oldest insurance associations in the world, is sometimes classified as a third type. It is operated as a corporation composed of members, in much the same way as the New York Stock Exchange. Insurance contracts are written by individual member underwriters. If any single risk is too great for a member to carry alone, one or more of the other members share the contract. Lloyd's has approximately 1,400 members, many of whom have joined together in syndicates. Lloyd's transacts business in all parts of the world and insures extremely varied risks, such as the birth of triplets or changes in the weather. Lloyd's of America is organized like Lloyd's of London, but it has no connection with the English company.

Besides stock and mutual companies, life insurance is also sold by other organizations, such as savings-bank life insurance plans (Massachusetts, New York, and Connecticut), the National Service Life Insurance (a part of the Veterans Administration), and fraternal organizations. These organizations and companies are commonly referred to as *life insurance carriers*.

Stock Companies

The stock company is a corporation owned by stockholders, who need not be policyholders. The purpose of the company is to earn a profit. The initial capital subscribed by the stockholders constitutes the company's working capital, and the company's main source of income is from premiums paid by those who buy insurance policies. The *premium* is the amount paid periodically—monthly, quarterly, semiannually, or annually—by the insured for the protection. Stock companies usually write their business through local agents, paying them a commission on the amount of insurance they sell.

An important feature of stock companies is that they do not assess policyholders when losses are greater than anticipated. The stockholders must bear the loss. Stock companies seek to earn a profit in two ways: (1) by charging premiums that exceed the business expenses and costs of claims, and (2) by investing their assets in the stocks and bonds of prosperous companies. Stock companies write about 75 percent of their business in fire insurance. They are also dominant in other lines, with the exception of life insurance.

Mutual Companies

Mutual insurance companies are nonprofit corporations, organized under the code of each state, owned by policyholders. There are no stockholders, and any excess income goes to the policyholders as a dividend, which may or may not be used to reduce premiums. Policyholders elect a board of directors to manage the company. By-laws may provide for assessments to policyholders to meet losses.

The Institute of Life Insurance has reported that by mid-1970, of the 1,819 life insurance companies in business, 1,664—or about 90 percent—were owned by stockholders as stock companies, and the remaining 155—or 10 percent—were mutual life companies. However, mutual life companies, which are generally older and larger, own about two-thirds of all life insurance company assets in the United States and account for about 52 percent of the total life insurance in force.

Fraternal Societies. These are also nonprofit organizations, usually identified with lodges or societies. They write mostly life insurance, and some sickness and accident insurance. In 1955, the National Association of Insurance Commissioners adopted a Uniform Fraternal Code to regulate fraternal life insurance societies. The requirements in this code are similar to those for mutual and stock companies selling life insurance.

Class Mutuals. These are mutual companies each of which insures only a specific class of property, such as lumber mills, farms, or factories.

3. *How does a mutual insurance company differ from a stock insurance company? Which type of company offers policyholders a dividend?*

PRINCIPLES OF INSURANCE

Since the purpose of insurance companies is to accept risks that otherwise would be carried by individuals and businesses, these companies become professional risk-taking organizations. As such, their methods of operation are unique among modern business enterprises. Insurance companies use such bases as the principle of insurable interest, the principle of insurable risk, and the law of large numbers in computing costs of insurance (premium rates) and setting policy provisions.

Common Policy Parts and Stipulations

Most insurance policies contain a statement of risks covered and exempted, the amount of insurance to be paid in event of loss, the amount of premium, basis for paying premium, period of coverage, and limitations of the insurer's liability.

Insurable Interest. A fundamental principle underlying insurance contracts is the principle of insurable interest, which simply means that the policyholder must demonstrate a financial loss to himself in order to collect amounts due him as described in the contract. Without the use of this principle, a person could insure the life of any other person and subsequently take his life in order to collect the insurance benefits. An insurable interest is always said to exist when a person insures his own life, as long as it is not done to evade antigambling laws. A man has an insurable interest in his wife and other members of his family, or even in a business partner, because their death would be a loss to him. The insurable interest must exist at the inception of the policy, but not necessarily at the time of death of the insured. A secured creditor, such as a mortgagee, has an insurable interest in property on which he has lent money. A businessman has an insurable interest in the profits of his business, which he expects to earn from the use of his property. Therefore, he can insure the property.

The Principle of Insurable Risk. A second basic principle of insurance is the principle of insurable risk, which involves the conditions under which a risk can be economically insured. This principle states: *If the requisites of insurability are not met, the risk is not economically insurable.*

From the standpoint of the insurer, the following requisites of insurability must be satisfied for a risk to be insurable:

1. *It should be the kind of loss that is purely accidental and not merely unintentional.* If such losses are not accidental, there is no uncertainty involved and insurance serves no useful purpose.

2. *The nature of the loss must be determinable and measurable.* The loss must be capable of calculation and be predictable, such as by the use of mortality tables for life insurance.

3. *The loss should not be in the nature of a catastrophic hazard.* Perils, such as those caused by a nuclear-energy explosion, are difficult to insure initially because the catastrophe hazard causes possible losses to be unpredictable.

4. *The risk must be spread over a sufficient number of cases.* In computing fire losses for rate-making purposes, it would be improper to group commercial buildings with private residences because the hazards facing these classes of buildings are different.

The Law of Large Numbers. Has it ever occurred to you how an insurance company can afford to assume a $50,000 risk for an annual premium of $1,000?

The explanation lies in the application of the law of large numbers, often referred to as the *law of averages.* According to this mathematical law, if you use a very large number of similar risks, only a certain number of losses will occur. For example, if you study the number of fire losses annually of, say, 25,000 similar types of buildings over a three-year period, it is possible to predict with surprising accuracy how many of these structures will be destroyed by fire during a given year. The important factor in predicting losses by this principle is the use of large numbers of cases.

The law of large numbers, therefore, may be stated as follows: *The larger the number of cases used, the more nearly will the actual experience approximate the probable outcome.* This law uses the application of probability to past experience. Consequently, when past experience reveals the total losses, the share to be assigned to each individual insured during the next period can be equitably calculated by actuarial methods. This is the basis of all mortality-table calculations used by life insurance companies. In a similar manner, fire insurance companies study fire losses, using large numbers of cases in order to predict losses.

The Principle of Indemnity. This principle states that a person may not collect more than his actual cash loss in the event of damage caused by an insured peril. Thus, a person may insure property in excess of its actual value, but he cannot collect damages for more than his actual loss. As a general rule, only contracts for property and liability insurance are subject to the indemnity principle. Contracts for life insurance and most health insurance are not indemnity contracts.

Fraud or Misrepresentation.   Even though it is unnecessary, many insurance contracts state that misrepresentation or fraud will void the contract. Failure to reveal facts about the risk that are material but known only to the insured will invalidate the policy.

Cancellation.   All contracts of insurance specify the conditions under which the policy may or may not be cancelled. Property and liability contracts may be cancelled by either party upon written notice. In life insurance, income disability policies, and credit insurance, no cancellation privilege is given the insurer.

Discussion Questions

4. *What does the term* insurable interest *mean, and how does it differ from the principle of insurable risk?*
5. *Explain how the law of large numbers is applied to life insurance or fire insurance.*

PROPERTY AND CASUALTY INSURANCE

The types of insurance protection available to businesses and individuals are numerous and varied. Each year, real and personal property valued at more than $1 billion is destroyed despite the use of fire-protection methods. The risk of such losses can be shifted to fire insurance companies.

Fire and Allied Lines

For centuries, fire has been one of man's most useful devices, but it can be one of his most destructive enemies. Fire insurance indemnifies (pays for loss or damage) the insured (the policyholder) for the actual loss or damage to property due to destruction by fire or lightning, up to the full value of the property.[2]

Standard Fire Policy Form.   To simplify and provide uniformity in fire insurance contracts, many states have adopted a standard fire contract. By the addition of a rider or indorsement to the contract, the company will add coverages including destruction by windstorm, riot, smudge, water, hail, civil commotion, or explosion. This added coverage is known as *allied lines.* Any of these additional coverages requires an additional premium.

---

[2]Except where there is a coinsurance clause. See explanation of this clause below.

The Coinsurance Clause. Businessmen as well as individuals are in-clined to underinsure their real property against fire. The records show that few fires actually result in total loss of the property, mainly because communi-ties now have better-trained fire department personnel and more effective equipment. Therefore, fire insurance companies are allowed by state laws to insert the coinsurance clause, which limits the liability of the fire insurance company and at the same time specifies how much insurance is required based on a percentage of the property's total value. The most common provision is that insurance protection equal to 80 percent of the value must be carried for the insured to obtain the full advantages of this clause.

A typical clause reads: "In the event of loss this company shall be liable for no greater proportion thereof than the sum hereby insured bears to ____% [usually 80 percent] of the cash value of the property described herein at the time when such loss shall happen." Therefore, if a building is insured for substantially less than its actual value, the owner must bear part of the loss from fire. But in return, a reduced rate is given on the policy.

If a building is valued at $50,000, a policy with an 80 percent coinsurance clause would require the owner to carry at least $40,000 (80% × $50,000) of fire insurance.

How much could the owner collect if he carried only $30,000? On losses, he would collect only the proportion of the loss that the amount of the policy ($30,000) bears to the required amount ($40,000). If a $10,000 fire loss resulted, the owner would collect $7,500 [($30,000/$40,000) × $10,000]. The formula to determine the amount to be collected is as follows:

$$\frac{\text{Amount of Insurance Carried}}{\text{Amount of Insurance Required}} \times \text{Loss} = \text{Amount of Recovery}$$

In the following examples, you can see the amount of fire losses that would be paid on an 80 percent coinsurance contract.

Example I

> Value of building = $30,000
> Insurance required (80% × $30,000) = $24,000
> Insurance carried = $24,000

Since the owner carried the agreed amount of coverage (80% × $30,000 or $24,000), total losses up to $24,000 would be paid.

Example II

> Value of building = $30,000
> Insurance required (80% × $30,000) = $24,000
> Insurance carried = $26,000

The amount of all losses up to $26,000 would be paid.

Example III

    Value of building = $30,000
    Insurance required (80% × $30,000) = $24,000
    Insurance carried = $18,000 (less than the 80% required by clause)

Should a $20,000 loss occur, the amount to be recovered is $15,000.

$$\left(\frac{\$18,000}{\$24,000} \times \$20,000 = \$15,000. \text{ See formula above.}\right)$$

In Example III, regardless of the loss, the owner could collect no more than $18,000, which is the amount of insurance carried. As a rule, coinsurance clauses do not apply to residences, household furnishings, or other personal property in a building.

Consequential Loss.   Normally, the standard fire contract reimburses the insured only for losses that can be traced directly to the fire. Indirect losses—those which are a consequence of the direct loss are not covered. Any losses suffered by the insured from fire that results in his inability to carry on the business are *consequential losses.* These can be covered under a consequential loss clause.

Other kinds of consequential losses related to fire are loss of rental income if the building has previously been rented, extra expenses incurred in obtaining temporary quarters to carry on the business, and continuing expenses in the business after the fire loss is sustained, such as salaries and rent on equipment.

Automobile Insurance

Automobile insurance is a universal need for businesses and individuals. As a separate branch of the insurance industry, it represents the largest single classification of property-liability protection under the general heading of casualty insurance, which is a generic term applicable to various kinds of insurance other than life, marine, and the hazards of fire and windstorm. The term *casualty* means an accident—a mishap that occurs unintentionally.

Casualty insurance is the type of insurance that is primarily concerned with losses caused by injuries to persons or property and losses arising from the legal liability imposed upon the insured for such injuries sustained by others. It includes robbery, burglary, fidelity and surety, theft, public liability, accident and health, and so on. Automobile liability insurance protects the insured against financial disaster when he injures others or damages their property. Premiums on automobile liability insurance amount to nearly 50 percent of all casualty premiums.

The U.S. Department of Transportation recently sponsored a two-year study costing $2 million to learn what is wrong with the automobile insurance industry. Almost any motorist could have provided the answer for the price of a postal card. The conclusion reached after the study was completed by some government officials was that the automobile insurance industry as a whole needs help.

Types of Automobile Insurance Coverages. As either a business owner or an individual, you can buy car protection for any of the six basic insurance coverages shown in Table 15.1.

If you want protection against the perils of fire, theft, flying objects, or theft of your car or the articles locked in it, you would be covered by a *comprehensive fire and theft policy.* If your car is upset or damaged from a collision with another moving vehicle or a stationary object, you need *collision insurance.* Most collision policies provide for a deductible amount ranging from fifty to several hundred dollars, which the insured pays. If your car causes injury to a person outside the car or to a pedestrian, this comes under the category of *bodily-injury* (public liability) *protection.* For this kind of accident, the minimum protection is $10,000 for one person and $20,000 for two or more persons injured. The trend now is to buy $100,000/$300,000.

If another car or property of others is damaged by your car, you need *property-damage liability protection* (the minimum is usually $5,000). Personal injury to you or to others in your car is covered by a *medical-payments indorsement.* The *uninsured-motorist indorsement* covers the policyholder and his family if they are injured by a hit-and-run motorist or a driver who carries no liability insurance, if the other driver is at fault.

No-Fault Automobile Insurance. Automobile owners suffering from lengthy delays for claim settlements, cancellations, continuing rate increases, and high costs of car repairs are being offered in some states a no-fault insurance policy. More than half the states are considering or have already passed a new kind of no-fault automobile insurance.

In general, these new laws require that each motorist carry liability

TABLE
15.1

SIX BASIC AUTOMOBILE INSURANCE COVERAGES

Type of Automobile Insurance Protection	Coverages on Persons		Coverages on Property		
	Insured and Members of Family	Others Than Insured	Insured's Car Only	Cars Other Than Insured's	Property Other Than Cars
Comprehensive-damage losses			X		
Collision or upset			X		
Bodily-injury liability		X			
Property-damage liability				X	X
Medical payments for injury	X	X			
Uninsured-motorist protection	X	X			
No-fault liability	X	X			

insurance to cover medical payments and income losses from accidents involving the insured and any passengers in his car. Payments for claims are made to the policyholder by his own insurance company and not by the company of the driver held to be at fault, as it is at present under other types of policies. Most plans allow each claimant to collect up to $2,000 for medical expenses, lost wages, and incidental costs. Other plans provide no limits. Lawsuits for such intangibles as "pain and suffering" are prohibited under this plan unless the medical bills total more than $500, or where the injury results in death, loss of limb, or disfigurement. Damages to cars or to other property are not affected by the proposed plan. Advocates of the plan are contending that it will slash legal costs by reducing the number of lawsuits, thereby making it possible to reduce premium costs. James S. Kemper, Jr., president of the Kemper Insurance Group, a major auto insurer, predicts that "a substantial majority" of American motorists will be covered by some form of no-fault insurance within two years. Saskatchewan and Puerto Rico introduced no-fault insurance long before any of the 50 states. A federal no-fault law is under consideration in Congress.

Workmen's Compensation Insurance

Workmen's compensation insurance offers protection to cover medical expenses and partial wages lost by workers suffering from occupational injury or disease (arising from the job). Also, upon the worker's death, the beneficiary is paid a lump-sum benefit. This is the only type of social insurance under-written by commercial insurance companies. State laws supporting this type of protection vary widely: Some permit employers to use self-insurance, but few companies find it suitable. A few states offer a state insurance fund, but this is not mandatory. In the majority of states, the employer may insure with a commercial insurance company.

Premiums for workmen's compensation average a certain percentage of the company's payroll. The rate for clerical help is low; for welders or bridge painters it is much higher. Since the employer pays the premium costs, it is to his advantage to conduct safety campaigns to reduce or prevent accidents. *Experience rating* plans are used in workmen's compensation insurance, in accordance with the theory that if an employer has some control over his loss ratio, he is entitled to a credit for a good loss-prevention record, but that he should pay a higher rate if his loss record is above the average. Present state laws require that almost all employers carry workmen's compensation insurance. In 1970, premiums exceeded $3.2 billion.

Public-Liability Insurance

Public-liability insurance (other than automobile) provides protection against claims caused by injuries to others, or damage to property of others.

Liability insurance can be bought for specialized types of risks. For example, a theater owner may be held liable if a patron is injured on the premises, or a customer may fall while going upstairs in a department store. *Product-liability insurance* is coverage for damages occurring from the use of a firm's product away from the company premises. A suit against a food canner for damages caused by food poison found in the can indicates the need for products liability protection for manufacturers.

Accident and Health Insurance

Many business firms offer accident and health insurance to their employees as part of the fringe benefits. In general, the purpose of accident, health, and medical insurance is to indemnify the insured for his employment time lost because of accident or illness and also to reimburse him for a part, if not all, of his costs of medical care and hospitalization. Some policies also provide death benefits, or lump-sum payments for permanent injuries caused by accident. Many firms carry a major medical policy covering an entire group of employees. This policy pays all costs that are in excess of a deductible amount stipulated in the contract. A widely used supplementary health plan is Blue Cross and Blue Shield, a nonprofit organization that cooperates with the medical profession and hospitals. Accident and health insurance is used in connection with workmen's compensation, since the latter protects workers from losses caused by accidents occurring on the job.

Discussion Questions

6. *What advantage is there to the insured in using a standard fire insurance contract?*
7. *What is the difference between accident and health insurance and workmen's compensation?*

INSURANCE AGAINST DISHONESTY AND HUMAN FAILURE

Not only are crimes against property among the most serious perils causing loss to property, but these losses are among the more underinsured perils. Crimes against property, reported by the Federal Bureau of Investigation as shown in Table 15.2, have been increasing at a greater rate than have crimes of violence such as murder and rape. Losses from embezzlement alone exceed $5 million a day to business.

TABLE
15.2
NUMBER OF CRIMES AGAINST PROPERTY

Year	Robbery	Burglary	Larceny
1960	107,390	897,400	506,200
1961	106,210	934,200	528,500
1962	110,390	978,200	573,100
1963	115,980	1,068,800	648,500
1964	129,830	1,193,600	732,000
1965	138,100	1,261,800	792,300
1966	157,320	1,387,200	894,600
1967	202,050	1,605,700	1,047,100
1968	261,730	1,828,900	1,271,100
1969	297,580	1,949,800	1,512,900

Source: Federal Bureau of Investigation.

Burglary, Robbery, and Theft

As used in insurance contracts, the terms *burglary, robbery,* and *theft* have different meanings among the states. However, they are carefully defined by contracts for insurance purposes. If a proprietor leaves the door of his business unlocked at night, and a thief hides in the building and under the cover of darkness carries off property, this is a crime, but it is not burglary or robbery. It is a theft.

Burglary. *Burglary* is usually defined as the unlawful taking of property from premises closed for business, entry being made by force. Visible marks showing the forcible entry must be indicated.

Robbery. The unlawful taking of property from another person by force or threat is *robbery.* There must be some kind of personal contact exhibited to demonstrate robbery. Some companies write robbery protection both inside and outside the premises and apply a higher rate for outside robbery.

Theft. *Theft* represents the act of stealing. Policies which cover theft do not usually define the term because it is intended to include all losses caused by burglary, robbery, and theft. This is the most expensive of the crime coverages.

Fidelity, Surety, Title, and Credit Insurance

Businessmen use fidelity and surety bonds as a means of protecting themselves against losses caused by dishonest acts of a third party, or losses resulting from a third person's failure to perform an obligation or contract.

Fidelity and Surety Bonds. The purpose of the fidelity bond is to reimburse an employer should his employee misappropriate money entrusted to him. This bond may be purchased to cover one employee or all. The object of the surety bond is to guarantee that the terms of a contract will be fulfilled. For example, contractors for buildings are frequently required to post a surety bond (sometimes called a "performance bond"); if the contractor fails to complete the construction as agreed, the insurance company assumes the financial responsibility for completing the job.

Credit Insurance.   A type of coverage that protects a seller from abnormal credit losses of his firm is called *credit insurance.* Prohibitively high premiums would have to be charged for policies covering all losses from bad debts.

Title Insurance.   Risks attending ownership of land, such as losses resulting from title defects, are not uncommon. *Title insurance* is a device by which the buyer of real estate can protect himself against losses arising from a defective title or claims of others to the title. Title defects may be caused by forgery of records by prior owners, by defective probate procedures involving titles, by debts against property, or by errors in court records. A title company will not issue a policy to the new property owner without first making a search of the records.

Marine Insurance

Marine insurance is the oldest type of insurance; its use dates back some five thousand years. Originally it covered only loss of vessel and cargo at sea. Nowadays, two distinctly different types of policies are issued: ocean marine and inland marine.

Ocean Marine.   Ocean marine insurance covers all kinds of hazards to the vessel and cargo in port or on the high seas. The perils include sinking, capsizing, stranding, collision, and theft. Each contract is "custom-made." It may be written for a specific period of time or for a single voyage.

Inland Marine.   *Inland marine* insurance includes coverage of all forms of transportation on land; on rivers, lakes, canals, and coastal waters; and in the air. The perils include fire, lightning, wind, hail, theft, flood, and collision. Of special interest to businessmen is the form of inland marine insurance that covers shipment by parcel post. Generally, risks such as theft, robbery, riot, and strikes are covered only if indorsed.

Discussion Questions

8. *What is the essential difference between the terms* burglary *and* robbery *as used by the insurance industry?*

9. *To what extent may businessmen protect themselves by using insurance against the following risks: accounts receivable bad debts, acts of a dishonest employee who misappropriates money belonging to the business, damage from steam-boiler explosion, and protection of cargo on the Mississippi River.*

LIFE INSURANCE

Unlike any other form of insurance you have been studying in this chapter, life insurance is the only form designed to cover the loss of future income as a result of death. People buy life insurance for various reasons, but the main one is to obtain financial protection for members of the insured's family. It should not be concluded, however, that the death of the insured is necessary for the insurer to pay the face value of the policy. Some policies contain certain features that provide either retirement income, paid-up insurance, or cash savings.

Life insurance is also used by business to accomplish several purposes. It can be used to furnish funds to replace invaluable employees or partners who have been lost by death. Life insurance can be used to furnish pension funds. Money can be borrowed on life insurance policies to meet an emergency.

Life insurance in force in the United States with legal-reserve companies (companies operating under state laws requiring specific minimum reserves) reached $1.4 trillion by the end of 1970. If this total of life insurance were divided equally among all American families, each would have $20,900 worth of protection. The average size of the ordinary policy sold increased from $10,700 in 1969 to $11,000 in 1970.

Basic Types of Life Insurance Policies

The three basic types of life insurance policies are term, straight life, and endowment. By combining the features of these three types, the nation's insurance companies are able to offer a dozen or more different insurance contracts.

A brief description of each type will help make clear some of the differences among them. Term policies offer protection for a certain number of set years at a fixed premium. The term policy has the lowest premium but, at the end of the prescribed number of years, the policy must be renewed at the insured's then current age and at a higher premium. As a general rule, term insurance offers no savings feature.

Straight life or whole life is lifetime protection with limited savings values. Premium rates are constant throughout the life of the contract and are payable as long as the insured lives. The advantage of the straight life policy is that maximum protection can be bought at the lowest cost, term insurance excepted. Disadvantages of the straight life policy include the fact that the insured must die before full payment is made; also, premiums may have to be paid after the insured's earning capacity has ceased. The accumulated savings attached to this type of policy remain with the company (unless the policy is canceled) and provide what is known as the cash surrender value. If the insured desires, he may borrow this value or he may receive it if the policy is allowed to lapse.

Endowment life insurance combines protection and savings features. Premiums are paid for a limited number of years, similar to the limited-payment policy. Because premium rates are high, the cash surrender values increase at a faster rate. At the end of the endowment period, the insured receives the full face value of the policy or—if he dies during the contract period—the face value is paid to his estate or his beneficiary.

The following three diagrams convey the basic concept that different life insurance contracts offer varying proportions of protection. For example, protection is highest for term insurance and lowest for endowment policies. On the other hand, premium costs are lowest for the term policy and highest for the endowment policy. Straight life policy premiums are higher than for term policies but lower than for endowment policies.

The Mortality Table. Like some of the other forms of insurance we have studied, life insurance premiums are based on the principle known as the "law of large numbers." For life-insurance companies to have an accurate method for determining the premium rates, they must have some means to calculate accurately the risks they assume. The major risk, of course, is death. The only way by which it is possible to determine the number of deaths annually is the experience of the past. This determination is embodied in a so-called "mortality table," which is a statistical analysis of deaths for a given group beginning at birth and extending until all members of the group are dead. The table which all companies use in the life insurance industry is the Commissioners' 1958 Standard Mortality Table (CSO).

This table compiled by the National Association of Insurance Commissioners, is based on ten million persons beginning at their birth and continuing to age 99. The table shows the probability of death in terms of the number of deaths per thousand and in terms of expectation of life for each age. It is important to note that the probability of death is expressed per thousand and that the table is based on insured lives (those who meet the physical examina-

COMPARISON OF THE THREE BASIC LIFE INSURANCE POLICIES—CASH VALUE PER $1,000 OF FACE AMOUNT
(Issued at Age 25)

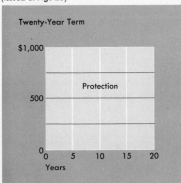 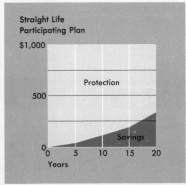 

Source: Based upon data courtesy of Cal-Western Life Insurance Company, Sacramento, California

tion standard), and not the whole population of the U.S. Therefore, the death rate is generally overstated in order to take care of contengencies such as a disease epidemic or disaster.

Table 15.3 shows that a person age 20 has a life expectancy of 50.37 years. And at age 20, 179 persons in every 100,000 are expected to die before they reach 21. The probability of death then at age 20 is .179 percent. At age 99 the table shows the number living is 6,415 out of the total group and the number of deaths during the year is expected to be 6,415. Mortality tables are revised from time to time since medical science is helping people to live longer. Different tables are used for different purposes, such as for annuities. Table 15.4 also shows life expectancy at birth and for various ages. The data are for 1969 including both male and female and white and other colors. Since Tables 15.3 and 15.4 were compiled during different years and involved different groups the life expectations are not the same.

Business Uses of Life Insurance

Many kinds of businesses use different types of life insurance plans to promote financial security or to meet financial emergencies. Life insurance can be used by sole proprietorships, partnerships, and corporations. Some of the adaptations of insurance policies to business include the following:

1. Group life insurance
2. Key executives or owners
3. Credit life insurance
4. Retirement and pension funds

TABLE
15.3
COMMISSIONERS' 1958 STANDARD ORDINARY MORTALITY TABLE (CSO)
(SELECTED AGES)

Age	Number Living	Deaths Each Year	Deaths Per 1,000	Expectation of Life
0	10,000,000	70,800	7.08	68.30
1	9,929,200	17,475	1.76	67.78
10	9,805,870	11,865	1.21	59.58
15	9,743,175	14,225	1.46	54.95
20	9,664,994	17,300	1.79	50.37
25	9,575,636	18,481	1.93	45.82
30	9,480,358	20,193	2.13	41.25
35	9,373,807	23,528	2.51	36.69
40	9,241,359	32,622	3.53	32.18
45	9,048,999	48,412	5.35	27.81
50	8,762,306	72,902	8.32	23.63
60	7,698,698	156,592	20.34	16.12
90	468,174	106,809	228.14	3.06
99	6,415	6,415	1,000.00	.50

TABLE
15.4

EXPECTATION OF LIFE AT BIRTH IN THE UNITED STATES (SELECTED YEARS)

Year	White			All Other			Total		
	Male	Female	Total	Male	Female	Total	Male	Female	Total
1900	46.6	48.7	47.6	32.5	33.5	33.0	46.3	48.3	47.3
1910	48.6	52.0	50.3	33.8	37.5	35.6	48.4	51.8	50.0
1920	54.4	55.6	54.9	45.5	45.2	45.3	53.6	54.6	54.1
1930	59.7	63.5	61.4	47.3	49.2	48.1	58.1	61.6	59.7
1940	62.1	66.6	64.2	51.5	54.9	53.1	60.8	65.2	62.9
1950	66.5	72.2	69.1	59.1	62.9	60.8	65.6	71.1	68.2
1960	67.4	74.1	70.6	61.1	66.3	63.6	66.6	73.1	69.7
1965	67.6	74.7	71.0	61.1	67.4	64.1	66.8	73.7	70.2
1966	67.6	74.7	71.0	60.7	67.4	64.0	66.7	73.8	70.1
1967	67.8	75.1	71.3	61.1	68.2	64.6	67.0	74.2	70.5
1968	67.5	74.9	71.1	60.1	67.5	63.7	66.6	74.0	70.2
1969	67.9	75.1	71.4	60.7	68.4	64.5	67.0	74.3	70.5

Source: U.S. Department of Health, Education, and Welfare, National Center for Health Statistics.

Group Life Insurance. This is one of the popular forms of coverage sold to business as part of a fringe-benefit program for employees. The policy is written under a single master policy, with or without medical examinations. The plan may be either term, straight life, or some combination of the two. Very often this program uses a one-year renewable term plan. The employer usually pays only a portion of the premium, especially when the plan includes group health insurance. Rates are lower than for individual policies, since the employer pays the premium in one check. Group life is increasing in popularity each year.

Key Executives or Owners. Since the prosperity and growth of a business depends so much on his continued existence, it has become a custom for the firm to buy life insurance on the owner or manager—the top executive. This is called "key-man insurance." The company pays the premium and is the beneficiary. If a sole proprietor dies, the business may have to be sold to pay existing debts. A term life or straight life policy, payable to the estate, may help to avoid the necessity for a quick sale of the business. Partners also may buy life insurance. A term life contract payable to the surviving partner can provide funds with which to buy the deceased's interest in the firm. Partners may execute a buy-and-sell agreement, spelling out in detail the authority to use life insurance funds to buy the partnership interest from the estate of the deceased partner. Premiums on partnership or key-executive insurance are not deductible as a business expense.

Credit Life Insurance. The wide use of installment buying has created a demand for a credit life insurance policy that has become widely used since

1950. Credit life insurance is used to repay debt in case the borrower dies. It is really term insurance which decreases in amount as a loan is repaid. It protects both the borrower's family and the lender, against a debt that may be left at death. Commercial banks, financing companies, and credit unions are among the chief buyers of credit life insurance. Today the amount of credit life insurance in force is $87.9 billion and most of it is issued under group master policies.

Retirement and Pension Funds. Many business firms provide retirement or pension programs to their employees above and beyond that available through the federal social security system. Frequently such programs use a life insurance plan.

There are three life insurance plans in use. The plan most often used by business, known as the *deposit administration* plan, involves establishing a fund with an insurance company to cover all employees. As an employee retires, money is withdrawn from the fund to buy the retiree an annuity policy. A second plan requires the annual purchase of a paid-up annuity for each employee. Smaller companies use a pension-trust plan that requires the purchase of a life insurance policy, to be placed in trust, for each employee. Profit sharing plans are frequently used, instead of life insurance, to finance pension funds. In such instances, employees usually make a cash contribution to the fund to be added to the company's contributions. Upon retirement, the worker receives either a lump sum or a monthly check.

President Nixon has proposed to Congress a sweeping pension-reform program including income tax deductions for those desiring to establish their own pension or retirement plan. It is estimated that as many as 14 million taxpayers might claim deductions for retirement contributions under the proposed law. The President has also asked Congress to enact legislation that will preserve the pension rights of employees who leave their jobs before retirement. Minimum standards are to be established to make sure employees do not lose benefits if they are discharged, laid off, or if they resign or move to another job after a certain period of time.

Life Insurance in Foreign Countries

The development of life insurance in a given country can be traced to the need created for it by the rate of social and economic progress of that country.

The use of insurance started early in the growth of Western countries in Europe, North America, and the major part of Australasia. As each country raised its economic level, insurance became a more important part of its prosperity and culture.

Without an index, any direct comparisons of the use of life insurance

Other Uses Of Insurance Protection By Business

1. *Boiler and machinery policy*—insures against damage from steam-boiler explosion and loss of machinery due to accident.

2. *Plate-glass insurance*—protects against losses caused by breakage of glass in the plant.

3. *Power-interruption insurance*—covers loss from interruption of operations, and loss from damage to property of the insured through spoilage.

4. *Furnace-explosion insurance*—covers losses resulting from the explosion of furnaces (as opposed to explosion of the steam boilers they may serve).

5. *Rain insurance*—intended to cover loss of profits or fixed charges owing to either abandonment or postponement of public events in the event of rain, hail, snow, or sleet.

6. *Accounts-receivable insurance*—covers losses brought about owing to the inability of the business to collect from open-account (unsecured) debtors when a fire has destroyed accounts-receivable records.

7. *Rent insurance*—covers insurable interest in rents that must be continued even though the premises have been partially or wholly destroyed by fire.

8. *Comprehensive general-liability insurance*—insures the businessman against such classes of liability as elevator accidents, product liability, liability arising out of use of premises, and contingent liability (imposed on the insured by law for actions of his independent contractors).

9. *Water-leakage insurance*—covers damage from a broken waterpipe or water accidentally discharged from a sprinkler system.

in this country with that in other Western countries would have little meaning. These nations have varied economic conditions, living and health standards, and personal-income levels. An index that reduces the influence of these differences is the ratio of the amount of life insurance in force to the national income. By this statistical measure, Canada continues to lead all other countries in the use of life insurance. New Zealand and the United States rank second. The five other countries in which life insurance in force exceeded national income in 1969 were Japan, Sweden, the Netherlands, Australia, and the United Kingdom. Ecuador and Portugal rated lowest among the 23 countries included in a survey made by the Institute of Life Insurance.

10. *Explain the principle upon which the mortality table is based. How is the table used in life insurance?*

11. *What are the uses of life insurance that a sole proprietorship and a partnership may make?*

12. *What is the purpose of credit life insurance, and who uses it?*

REGULATION OF INSURANCE COMPANIES

The U.S. Supreme Court in 1868 (*Paul* vs *Virginia*) held that insurance is not interstate commerce, and therefore that the federal government should have no regulatory power over insurance companies. This decision was upheld repeatedly until reversed in 1944, by the Supreme Court in the *South-Eastern Underwriters Association* case. But despite this reversal, Congress has left regulation of insurance companies pretty much to the states since states grant the charters.

The main responsibility to which states are committed is to assure the continued solvency of each insurance company. Each company is expected to discharge its obligations to policyholders and not engage in unfair discrimination or overcharge for the premium.

In life insurance, state laws require the inclusion of the grace-period and incontestability clauses. The use of a standard fire policy or a modified version is also required by law. Most states demand a standard workmen's compensation policy. The rising clamor for a better way to deal with automobile accident and health claims, plus the demand to stop the skyrocketing of premiums and long delays in settling claims, will eventually lead to a new and improved system of automobile insurance. Several states have already enacted no-fault insurance as part of automobile protection.

Discussion Questions

13. *Why are insurance companies regulated primarily by state law?*

14. *What would be the advantages for enacting a federal no-fault automobile insurance law?*

CAREERS IN INSURANCE

Careers in insurance generally fall into two broad categories: selling (or production) and administration. Under each of these two classifications, there are

TABLE
15.5

**NUMBER OF PERSONS EMPLOYED IN ALL FORMS
OF INSURANCE IN THE UNITED STATES**

Year	Annual Average
1950	800,000
1955	900,000
1960	1,105,000
1965	1,225,000
1967	1,310,000
1969	1,410,000
1970	1,460,000

Source: Institute of Life Insurance.

many kinds of employment specializations. The two main areas of employment are the home office and the field office. Insurance companies in the United States currently employ approximately 1.5 million and as shown in Table 15.5. This number has increased substantially since 1950.

Home-Office Occupations

Every insurance company has as its administrative nerve center a home office. Its operational structure is generally organized along departmental lines in order to furnish administrative direction to those working in the field. The home office uses the services of statisticians, lawyers, mathematicians, investment analysts, economists, computer programmers, and many clerks, typists, and secretaries.

The Agency Section.   Persons employed in this section supervise field agents (salesmen), determine commission rates, and supervise the issuing of directives to field agents.

Underwriters.   Underwriters specialize in different types of risk. They work in companies that write life, fire, casualty, liability, automobile, and marine insurance. They collect many kinds of facts having to do with physical and moral hazards, and they compile summaries of the company's experience pertaining to premiums received, accidents reported, and losses paid. In life insurance, the underwriter reviews the applicant's medical record and background; it is upon his recommendation that you are approved or rejected as a policyholder.

Actuaries.   In life insurance, one of the most complex and indispensable occupations in the home office is that of the actuary. He collects, compiles, and analyzes mortality statistics. He helps to plan new types of policies. To become a fully qualified professional actuary, it is necessary to pass a series of written examinations for membership in the Society of Actuaries.

Field-Office Occupations

The field office of an insurance company is similar to the branch office of a manufacturing company. The personnel of this office make direct contacts with prospective purchasers of insurance.

Field Agents. By far the largest number of persons employed in the field offices are the agents (salesmen). As a rule, an agent represents only one life insurance company. This is known as the "American Agency System" in life insurance. However, some life insurance agents share or *broker* their business with other companies, mainly because the business is not acceptable to their own company. Brokerage is not as common in life insurance as it is in other lines, because most life companies prefer to build up their own agency force.

In property insurance, the field middleman most comparable to the wholesaler is the *general agent,* while the retailer is called the *local agent.* Very often, a general agent handles all types of property and casualty insurance on his own, not as an employee of any particular company. In life insurance, the general agent is also an independent businessman.

Training for an Insurance Career

The insurance industry has long recognized the value of education for all classes of employees. As evidence of educational qualifications, two professional designations have been established by the industry. The C.L.U. (Chartered Life Underwriter) designation is granted by the American College of Life Underwriters to salesmen and administrative personnel who acquire sufficient knowledge about life insurance from study of special C.L.U. courses to pass a rigorous examination. A similar educational program of courses is conducted by the American Institute of Property and Liability Underwriters, Inc., which awards the C.P.C.U. (Chartered Property and Casualty Underwriter) upon satisfactory completion of a series of examinations. These organizations encourage colleges to conduct similar insurance courses.

SUMMARY

Risk, in business parlance, is the possibility of the occurrence of an economic loss. Since risk imposes an economic burden, it becomes important to businessmen to find a way to handle it. Insurance is one method and it does this by spreading the consequences of loss among a large number of persons subject to a similar risk. But insurance is not the only way; it is possible to remove the risk or its cause—for example, by a reserve fund in anticipation of the loss; hedging to shift the risk; or, one of the best ways to meet certain risks, by the practice of good management.

Some risks are speculative in nature, which means there is a chance of either loss or gain; risks of this type are not insurable. A pure risk, one in which there is no chance of gain but only of a loss, may be insured.

Stock insurance companies are owned by stockholders, who need not be policyholders. Mutual companies are owned by the policyholders, since there are no stockholders. Mutual companies pay dividends to the policyholders if the amount collected is in excess of that required to operate the company.

A person must have an insurable interest in what he is insuring. This doctrine prevents insurance from becoming a gambling contract. The principle of indemnity states that a person may not collect more damages than the amount of his actual cash loss.

The two major types of insurance coverage are (1) property and (2) life. As part of property insurance, coverage that provides workmen's compensation, unemployment compensation, and automobile liability is known as casualty insurance. Property insurance includes fire, marine, surety, and liability. The purpose of life insurance is to provide protection against death. Business uses life insurance for various purposes including pension funds, protection for borrower and lender (credit insurance), insurance for key executives, and individual retirement benefits.

VOCABULARY REVIEW

Match the following vocabulary terms with the statements below.

a. Burglary
b. Casualty
c. Consequential loss
d. Credit insurance
e. Hedging

f. Law of large numbers
g. Mutual company
h. Product-liability insurance
i. Premium
j. Pure risk

k. Risk
l. Robbery
m. Speculative risk
n. Title insurance

1. Exposure to losses or injuries
2. The process of trading in futures on commodity exchanges in such a way as to gain protection from loss owing to price fluctuations during the time the spot commodity is being processed for delivery
3. Losses suffered by the insured from fire resulting in his inability to carry on a business
4. The amount paid periodically by the insured for insurance protection
5. A principle stating that the larger the number of cases used, the more nearly will the actual experience approximate the probable outcome
6. An accident—a mishap that occurs unintentionally
7. Insurance coverage for damages occurring from the use of a firm's product away from the company's premises
8. Unlawful taking of property from premises closed for business, entry being made by force
9. Unlawful taking of property from another person, using force or threat
10. A device by which the buyer of real estate can protect himself against losses that arise from a defective title or claims of others to the title
11. A type of coverage that protects a seller from abnormal credit losses of his firm
12. A nonprofit insurance corporation organized under the code of each state and owned by the policyholders

13. A situation in which there is either a chance of loss or a possibility of gain

14. A type of risk that involves only a chance of loss

PROBLEMS AND PROJECTS

1. Milby and Boxby are active partners in a hardware store doing both wholesale and retail business with approximately $500,000 in net sales annually. Profits range between $45,000 and $50,000 after taxes. The partners are married and each has a family. The partners are aware that the death of a partner automatically dissolves the partnership. There is no provision for this matter in the present partnership agreement. Milby is very concerned about this matter. One partner is 36 years old and the other 41. The firm owns its own building and equipment but has a long-term lease on the land. There is no long-term debt against the firm. What is the problem about which Milby is concerned, and what should they do about it?

2. Select two local businessmen who own their own businesses. Ask each one what he considers to be the five most important risks in his business, other than death, and how he deals with each of these five risks.

3. Describe the purposes for which the following types of insurance are used by business: (a) automobile bodily-injury liability, (b) workmen's compensation, (c) surety bond, (d) product-liability insurance, (e) consequential loss, and (f) credit life insurance.

A BUSINESS CASE

Case 15-1   Does Charley Brown Have a Problem?

Charley Brown owns and operates a well established service station. He has an excellent location and does a volume of business requiring ten full-time employees. His station sells about 52,000 gallons of gasoline each month. He has a monthly contract for maintenance with a local telephone cooperative on their eight trucks. In addition, he does a good retail sales volume in accessories, tires, and batteries. Recently his station was held up, resulting in a loss of $2,500 in cash and merchandise. He had no insurance to cover this type of risk. He carries only workmen's compensation and fire insurance on the business and a $10,000 G.I. policy on himself as a veteran. Charley realizes his business is not adequately insured, but he does not know just what kind and how much protection is the most important. Of course, he does not want to spend a lot of money each month on insurance premiums.

1. What are the more common risks to which his business is exposed for which he now has no insurance protection?

2. As a risk manager, advise Brown as to the minimum insurance protection he needs that will provide him with adequate protection.

quantitative controls for decision making

accounting
as a tool
of management
CHAPTER SIXTEEN

Assume that you are interested in buying a business that has been advertised for sale by the owner at a price of $20,000. How would you determine whether the price is too high or too low?

One way to appraise its total worth is to place a value on all the things owned by the business, such as cash, merchandise, equipment, and buildings. This method, however, does not take into consideration the rate of return you would get on your investment.

A second way is to appraise its worth in terms of the rate of return you would receive from the business profits above the salary you earned for your labor and management ability.

In order to obtain the necessary information about the business and its financial condition, you would need access to certain records, called accounting records. The recording of business transactions and organization of them into usable form comprise what is known as the *accounting system*. Accounting records are concerned with such transactions as the receipts and disbursements of cash, the sale and purchase of goods and equipment, the collections from customers, and the payments to creditors. Today it is almost impossible to find a business that does not maintain accounting records on a uniform and approved basis. These records are important to business owners, managers, outside investors, labor unions, and government, because such parties cannot make intelligent decisions unless these records are available.

Let us examine some of the basic principles and procedures used in keeping accounting records; for without an understanding of these, it is virtually impossible to determine the meaning of the accounting data. Moreover, we need to know how to interpret accounting records as they appear in the annual reports and statements published by businesses.

THE FUNCTION OF ACCOUNTING IN BUSINESS MANAGEMENT

The function of accounting in modern-day business management can best be illustrated by discussing the need for accounting data, and by explaining the various ways in which different persons utilize accounting reports.

Need for Accounting Data

Consider the case of Roy Aleksa, who has inherited his father's business. Unfortunately, although Roy had worked in the store as a sales clerk on Saturdays and during rush periods, his father had never discussed the financial affairs of his business with him. But rather than close the store or sell it, Roy chooses to operate it for a while, at least until he can decide upon the most prudent course of action to follow. What are some of the cold financial facts Roy must know about this business to keep it going?

To begin with, there is a sizable weekly payroll, so he must know the amount to be paid in salaries; and in addition, he must know the number and dollar amounts of deductions to make for each employee. There are federal income and Social Security tax deductions, and those for group hospital and insurance protection. There is also the state income tax to be withheld, and the local payroll tax. Are there any employees buying savings bonds through a payroll deduction plan? Does the business have a private pension plan to which the employees contribute?

There are also other matters. How about the cash balance shown on the bank statement? The checkbook stub record shows several checks outstanding. Is there enough money in the bank to pay the salaries and also the unpaid bills that are in one of the desk drawers? Other bills, too, will undoubtedly arrive on the first of the month. On which are discounts allowable? Will there be enough money coming in from customers to meet current obligations?

In the midst of wondering about all these things, Roy discovers that many of the customers' accounts are long past due. It would really be helpful if he knew which customers had already been sent statements, and what efforts had been made to collect accounts that are past due. Would it be advisable to place some of these, together with the past-due notes, in the hands of an attorney or a collection agency? Should he continue to sell on credit to customers who already owe large amounts? Have they always paid up?

There are periodic reports that must be made to the government, too—quarterly payments of Social Security taxes; payment of income taxes withheld; payment of property taxes, state unemployment taxes, state and municipal sales taxes. Where does one get the information needed for all these reports?

The problems continue to mount. Inventory, or stock control, has to be considered. Which items are in greatest demand by customers? Is there an adequate supply on hand? Are there up-to-date records of merchandise stored in the warehouse? In what quantities should items be ordered? Do the records show any departmental breakdown on sales? Which goods have been on hand so long that they should be sold out and discontinued?

These are but a few of the many typical business questions concerning accounting data that Roy will have to answer—and their answers are to be found only in the accounting records. So it should be clear, even from the brief example given here, that the need for accounting data is crucial.

Groups Interested in Accounting Data

Several groups are directly concerned with the financial records and reports of any business enterprise: owners, creditors, governments, and labor unions.

Owners. We have already seen the degree to which the owner of a retail business depends on accounting records. This same dependency exists for all sizes, types, and forms of business organizations—proprietorships, partnerships, and corporations. Owners need accounting information to make decisions leading to remedial action, or for the improvement of business operations.

In the case of the corporation, there are two groups of persons interested in accounting reports: stockholders and management. Stockholders depend on the interpretation of financial reports as their chief means of checking on the effectiveness with which the business is being run. (*Prospective* purchasers of stock are also interested in the firm's financial reports.) And much of the work of the accounting department is aimed at assisting management in operating the business—in buying merchandise, borrowing money, investing surplus funds, raising capital, and distributing profits.

Creditors. Accounting reports normally prepared at the close of the business year are the most reliable source of information on the financial condition of any business. If a business wants credit with a bank, the loan department of the bank analyzes the firm's financial statements in considering whether or not to grant the loan.

How does a creditor (a person to whom the business owes money) measure a firm's ability to pay? He can use any of the "three C's" of credit—character, capacity, or capital—but chances are he will look closely at the firm's capital as revealed in its accounting reports. Financial reports may, of course, reveal a firm's capacity as well as its capital, but creditors have more confidence in an actual statement of capital. Credit losses are usually high in cases where adequate accounting data are not available.

Financial statements also serve as the basis for a firm's financial rating by such agencies as Dun and Bradstreet and banks making loans to the business. People who invest in stocks and bonds almost invariably review a firm's financial reports when they are considering purchasing its securities.

Governments. Various government agencies have a great interest in the accounting records of a business enterprise. For tax purposes, both federal and state laws require private businesses to file financial statements. State and federal income taxes are calculated from the amount of profit a business earns. Moreover, contributions by business for the Federal Old Age and Survivors Insurance Program and to the state and federal unemployment compensation programs are based on a firm's payroll records. Computation of state sales taxes and federal excise taxes also requires that accurate accounting records be kept by private business.

Accounting records such as time cards and payroll analyses enable the government to determine whether a business is complying with minimum-wage laws and government regulations pertaining to working hours and overtime payments. All corporations whose stock is listed on a nationwide stock exchange are required to file reports of their financial operations with the Securities and Exchange Commission quarterly, and also prior to offering new capital stock to the public.[1] When the federal government is purchasing goods on a cost-plus contract, it requires detailed accounting reports from the vendor, covering production operations and costs.

Labor Unions. Financial information reflected by a firm's income and expense statements is the basis for demands made by labor during collective-bargaining sessions. Demands for wage increases and added fringe benefits are usually accompanied by arguments and data based on the firm's profits. Labor unions give more attention to a company's financial statements today than ever before. Union officials often know as much about the factors that affect a firm's profits as does the firm's management. Increases in rates of productivity, reductions in unit costs, and trends in profits are among the factors that union management studies carefully.

In a close corporation, financial statements may not be readily available to labor union leaders, and this of course puts labor at a disadvantage when negotiating for wage increases. However, corporations that have stock listed on an exchange are required to publish financial reports, and labor unions do have access to this information.

[1] The provisions of the Securities and Exchange Act are discussed in Chapter 13.

Discussion Questions

1. What are the various types of data that an accounting department furnishes to business management?
2. Why is it that the creditors' interest in the financial statements of a business is similar to that of the owners?

HOW DATA ARE REPORTED
BY THE ACCOUNTING DEPARTMENT

We have seen that the prime function of accounting is to furnish management with information it can use in making financial decisions. Many such decisions are necessary in the day-by-day operation of a business and in planning for the future. Management, whether it be the owner–manager of a small business or the management of a large corporation, is interested in having information regarding:

1. Total net income earned during a given period
2. Factors that influence the amount of profit
3. Total value of the assets owned, and changes taking place in them
4. Amount of liabilities and net worth

The Accounting Period

Profits and losses are generally computed for a given period of time, such as one month, six months, or one year. This is known as the *accounting period*. For tax-paying purposes, the accounting period is one year. A year other than the calendar year may also be used for accounting, however, and this is called the *fiscal year*. At the conclusion of this period, financial reports and other records are prepared for the owner. For example, a business that is normally at its peak of sales from December through February, then experiences a drop for the next few months, may start its fiscal year on April 1 and end it on March 31. Hence, the accounting period may be based on either a period beginning with January 1 and ending on December 31, or some other twelve-month period. Most government units use as their fiscal year the period from July 1 to June 30. When a period shorter than a year (such as a month or a quarter) is used as the accounting period, this is known as the company's *fiscal period*.

Accounting for Cash and Receivables

The inflow and outflow of cash is important to a business operation. The inflow is known as *cash receipts* and the outflow is called *cash disbursements*.

Because most businesses operate on the *accrual*[2] basis, a business enterprise may find its cash balance decreasing even though its operations are profitable. *Cash control* is also important; management must plan to have money on hand when it is needed to make the necessary payments as they fall due.

Accounting records of cash inflow and outflow and the balance of cash on hand reveal the liquidity of a company's resources. Accounting also helps assure the safe and proper handling of an organization's cash assets, preserving their availability and protecting against their being wasted, misused, or embezzled.

The Cash Forecast. The purpose of the *cash forecast* is to present an estimate of the amount of cash to be received during a given period of time, the amount needed to meet anticipated disbursements, and the cash balance expected to be on hand at the end of that period. Here, much as in the estimating of income, it is desirable to prepare cash forecasts for the entire accounting period as well as for shorter periods. The cash record for past fiscal periods, anticipated receipts from operations (both cash sales and short-term credit operations), interest to be received and paid, and estimated expenses all have a bearing on the cash forecast.

Receivables. *Short term receivables* (amounts due from customers) are closely related to cash, for every business hopes to collect on its credit sales

[2] Some income and expense items belong to one fiscal period but are actually not paid or received until a future period. Under the *accrual* method, an attempt is made to record these in the period to which they belong, rather than in the one in which the cash actually changes hands.

THE ACCOUNTING PROCESS

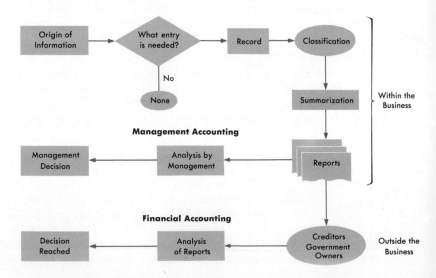

as accounts come due. However, regardless of the care exercised in granting credit, every business suffers some losses on its credit customers. It is the responsibility of the accounting department to estimate these losses and set up appropriate reserves for them. (Records of past experience are important here.) In addition, one of the usual practices is to age the accounts, applying the greatest loss against those longest overdue. Such a computation might appear as follows:

Age analysis of accounts receivable, December 31, 197___

Age in Months	Amount of Receivables	Percentage Loss Expected	Amount of Anticipated Loss
0–1	$30,200	0.2	$ 60.40
1–2	6,300	1.0	63.00
2–3	1,800	4.5	81.00
3–6	1,050	20.0	210.00
Over 6	760	50.0	380.00
Totals	$40,110		$794.40

This analysis shows an expected loss of $794.40 from inability to collect on receivables. This, therefore, is the amount of reserve to be set up.

Accounting for Inventory Purposes

Retail-store operators are familiar with the term *merchandise inventory* because they keep records of goods bought for resale. Manufacturing firms, of course, keep inventory records for their raw materials used in production. Some kinds of businesses maintain records of daily changes in inventories, which keep management informed as to when to reorder.

For purposes of inventory record keeping, the records should show three kinds of information: (1) the source of the goods and the date on which they were purchased; (2) their cost, including discounts allowed or received; and (3) partial shipments from stock, showing the amount, the price, and the buyer. With this information, it is possible to maintain an adequate inventory-control system by the use of stock ledgers and stores records.

The usual starting point for pricing inventory items is their *invoice cost,* which is the price paid for the goods at the time they were entered in the inventory system, less, of course, the amount of discount allowed by the seller.

Methods of Valuation of Inventory Costs

Among the most commonly used methods of valuation of inventory items are (1) average cost,[3] (2) first-in, first-out (FIFO), and (3) last-in, first-out (LIFO).

[3]Average cost would be determined by taking an average of the amount of goods on hand during the period at the purchase price.

FIFO Inventory Control. FIFO is based on the assumption that the goods first acquired are the goods first sold, which is typical retail-store practice. This scheme prices merchandise on hand at the cost of the most recent acquisitions equal to the quantity on hand. If goods are continually turned over and then immediately replaced, inventory values tend to increase in times of rising prices.

LIFO Inventory Control. This method assumes that the units sold are those most recently acquired—the reverse of the FIFO method—and that the units still on hand are those first acquired. As you can see, this method produces less profit than the FIFO method in periods of rising prices, and more profit in periods of declining prices. Occasionally, a retail chain that has been using LIFO will change in order to gain higher prices during periods of rising inflation.[4] To the stockholder, this is likely to result in a larger dividend for the next accounting period.

Perpetual Inventory. Some businesses attempt to keep a *perpetual inventory* of goods on hand—that is, a complete, up-to-date count of the number of each item on hand at all times. You may have noticed price tags on articles in a furniture store; the number of units of that item still in stock is usually recorded on the back of these tags. You have also noticed salesclerks in hardware and clothing stores recording item code numbers on their sales slips. These data make it easier for office clerks to keep accurate records of the quantity of items sold and the quantity remaining in stock.

Inventory Control. The problem of inventory control is relatively easy to deal with in retail stores. However, in manufacturing operations where expensive raw materials are used, it is more difficult. Usually, some scheme is used whereby the person checking out materials signs for them; or a record is kept of the quantity of material furnished each worker and the amount he uses. An actual count of goods on hand is made periodically, even when perpetual-inventory records are maintained. It is also desirable to have different persons handling the receiving records and the issuing of the materials.

In all these instances, an accounting staff prepares the records system and keeps daily records as business is transacted. It also prepares internal audits from time to time to verify the accuracy of its records.

Accounting for Payables

The amount of money owed by a business constitutes its *payables.* Sums owed on open account are called *accounts payable,* while debts evidenced by written documents are *notes payable* or *mortgages payable.*

---

[4] Any change in the method of figuring inventory would need to be reported and justified to the Internal Revenue Service. A business could not keep changing its method continually.

The accounting department must devise some plan for paying invoices within the discount period. Furthermore, care must be exercised that credit is not overextended. Therefore, payables must be controlled so that the cash on hand will be adequate not only to pay all debts, but to do so within the discount period allowed.

REPORTS TO STOCKHOLDERS

Corporations whose stock is listed on national exchanges are required to send a copy of their financial reports to each stockholder each year, soon after the books are closed at the end of the year. The backbone of these reports is the income statement and a statement of the financial condition of the business. The latter is usually called a *balance sheet,* or a statement of *owners' equity.*

At one time, the emphasis in such reports was on the *net worth* of the business. This was determined by subtracting the total debts from the total assets. Now the emphasis is on equity. The equity of the owners is the amount of value of a property above the debts against it. Examples of such reports, those of the General Electric Company for the year 1971, are shown on pages 433 and 435.

The Income Statement

A typical stockholder's first interest is in the statement of income, which shows him the financial results of the year's operations,—that is, the amount of profit that has been earned. Most companies report net income both before and after federal income taxes, as well as net income per share of common stock and dividends paid per share. The income statement for the General Electric Company for the year 1971 is shown on the next page.

In addition to the earnings statement, a brief explanation is included for each of the major items reported. For example, an explanatory paragraph pertaining to the methods used in calculating depreciation accompanied the earnings statement of the General Electric Company, as follows:

> An accelerated depreciation method, based principally on a sum-of-the-years' digits formula, is used to depreciate plant and equipment in the United States purchased in 1961 and subsequently. Assets purchased prior to 1961, and most assets outside the U.S., are depreciated on a straight-line basis. Special depreciation is provided where equipment may be subject to abnormal economic conditions or obsolescence.

The income statement is important to current and prospective stock-holders, because it gives a comparison of present accomplishments with those of previous fiscal periods. Most corporations, in their periodic reports to stockholders, compare earnings during the past quarter with those of the corresponding quarter of the previous year. In some cases, reports are included showing the accumulations for all quarters so far during the current fiscal year. For example, at the end of the third quarter, results may be given for both the three-month period and the nine-month period.

Income. As we noted in Chapter 1, the chief purpose of a privately owned business is to make a profit. This is achieved by selling products at prices greater than their cost, thus producing *income;* and income increases the owners' equity in the business.

In the case of a retail establishment, the income must exceed the combined cost of goods purchased and the expenses incurred in operating the business. *Net income* is the amount left after subtracting all costs and expenses. In order to have a net income, a manufacturing enterprise must sell its products at a price that exceeds the combined cost of raw materials, labor, overhead, selling, and shipping costs. Today it is customary to report both net income before federal taxes and net income after subtracting federal taxes. Income earned from the normal course of business operations—the manufacture and sale of goods—is sometimes shown under the caption of *operating income.* Income from interest earned or discounts taken on bills payable is shown as *nonoperating* or *financial income.*

Expenses. When payments are made for services received, they result in a direct decrease in the owners' equity in the business. These decreases are called *expenses* and are frequently classified as administrative, operating, or selling expenses. *Administrative expenses* include management costs and the various office expenses. *Operating expenses* include the depreciation of equipment and machinery, factory labor, and utility expenses. *Selling expenses* include salaries, commissions, and traveling expenses for salesmen, advertising costs, and shipping expenses. Management must keep total expenses well below the gross income earned in order to show a profit for an accounting period.

The Statement of Financial Position

Besides the statement of income earned during an accounting period, another equally valuable report is the statement of the financial status of the business, called the *balance sheet*—a statement of the financial condition of

Statement of Current and Retained Earnings

General Electric Company and consolidated affiliates *(In millions)*

For the year	1971	1970
Sales of products and services to customers	$9,425.3	$8,726.7
Other income . *Real State*	152.0	106.8
	9,577.3	8,833.5

Costs

Employee compensation, including benefits	3,885.3	3,776.4
Materials, supplies, services and other costs	4,484.0	4,073.9
Depreciation	273.6	334.7
Taxes, except those on income	101.8	88.8
Interest and other financial charges	96.9	101.4
Provision for income taxes	317.1	220.6
Deduct increase in inventories during the year	(56.4)	(96.0)
	9,102.3	8,499.8

Not Earnings

Earnings before interest of other share owners	475.0	333.7
Deduct interest of other share owners in net results of affiliates	(3.2)	(5.2)
Net earnings applicable to common stock	471.8	328.5
Deduct dividends declared	(249.7)	(235.4)
Amount added to retained earnings	222.1	93.1
Retained earnings at January 1	1,874.1	1,781.0
Retained earnings at December 31	$2,096.2	$1,874.1

Earnings per common share *(In dollars)*	$2.60	$1.81
Dividends declared per common share *(In dollars)*	$1.38	$1.30

Per-share amounts have been adjusted for the two-for-one stock split in April 1971.

management

The 1971 Financial Summary beginning on page 26 and ending on page 35 is an integral part of this statement.

a business on a specific date. The completion of only one new business transaction would entail making minor changes in this report. A balance sheet is like a physician's report on the physical condition of a patient: The picture may change in a relatively short time, but the report is quite accurate at the time it is prepared.

The balance sheet is in reality a statement of assets and equities, the latter showing the equity of the creditors in the assets and also the equity of the owner or owners. It shows the present balances in cash, receivables, inventory, and payables.

Divisions of Balance Sheet. The main sections of the balance sheet are:

1. *Assets:* items of value owned by the business
2. *Liabilities:* debts owned by the business; *equity of the creditors*
3. *Capital:* stockholders' equity of ownership

The statement of financial position for the General Electric Company for the year 1971 is shown on the next page.

One of the explanatory paragraphs accompanying the statement relates to the pricing of inventories, as follows:

Inventories in the United States are substantially all valued on a last-in, first-out (LIFO) basis, and substantially all those outside the U.S. are valued on a first-in, first-out (FIFO) basis. Such valuations are not in excess of market and are based on cost, exclusive of certain indirect manufacturing expenses and profits on sales between the parent and affiliated companies. The LIFO basis values inventories conservatively during inflationary times.

Discussion Questions

3. *Which of the following appear on the statement of financial position, or balance sheet? Assets, cash, expenses, inventory, payables, receivables, sales.*
4. *What is the chief difference in purpose and content between the balance sheet and the income statement?*
5. *How may a factory exercise control over its supply of raw materials?*

USE OF ACCOUNTING REPORTS BY MANAGEMENT

Regardless of how accurately records are kept or how complete summary statements are, the value of most accounting data lies in their analysis and interpretation. In a small business, the bookkeeper prepares the financial

Profit & Loss

Statement of Financial Position

General Electric Company and consolidated affiliates *(In millions)*

December 31	1971	1970
Assets		
Cash	$ 250.1	$ 190.8
Marketable securities	35.9	15.0
Current receivables	1,741.3	1,573.7
Inventories	1,611.7	1,555.3
Current assets	3,639.0	3,334.8
Investments	714.3	630.9
Plant and equipment	2,025.7	1,749.4
Other assets	508.8	483.4
Total assets	$6,887.8	$6,198.5
Liabilities and equity		
Short-term borrowings	$ 569.8	$ 658.1
Accounts payable	454.6	431.3
Progress collections and price adjustments accrued	656.5	599.3
Dividends payable	63.6	58.8
Taxes accrued	331.5	239.6
Other costs and expenses accrued	764.4	663.2
Current liabilities	2,840.4	2,650.3
Long-term borrowings	787.3	573.5
Other liabilities	255.1	249.3
Miscellaneous reserves	160.8	130.5
Total liabilities	4,043.6	3,603.6
Interest of other share owners in equity of affiliates	42.4	41.3
Preferred stock	—	—
Common stock	462.3	460.9
Amounts received for stock in excess of par value	368.8	330.0
Retained earnings	**2,096.2**	**1,874.1**
	2,927.3	2,665.0
Deduct common stock held in treasury	(125.5)	(111.4)
Total share owners' equity	2,801.8	2,553.6
Total liabilities and equity	$6,887.8	$6,198.5

*The 1971 Financial Summary beginning on page 26 and ending on page 35
is an integral part of this statement.*

Courtesy General Electric Company

Balance Sheet at a definite date

statements and the owner interprets them. In a large business, however, accountants prepare the statements and the chief accountant and administrative officers interpret them.

Appraising the Results of Operations

Comparative Statements. One of the ways in which accountants prepare financial reports for interpretation by the officers of a business is through the use of *comparative statements*. Figures for the current year are shown side by side with those of the previous year or two; thus the current statement may be compared directly with the past record. This comparison shows clearly and succinctly trends in business operations. Comparative statements are used for both the balance sheet and the income statement.

A comparative balance sheet is shown on the next page. Notice that each breakdown shows a comparison with the preceding quarter. The trend may be seen for each type of asset as well as for the totals of assets. Comparisons are also shown for liabilities and ownership.

The term *current assets* refers to items owned by the business that will be converted into cash within a reasonably short time. *Prepaid expenses* includes such items as insurance premiums that have been paid in advance and supplies that will be consumed within a relatively short time. *Fixed assets* refers to items representing major capital investments that will be used for a long period of time. Most businesses consider items that extend beyond one year as fixed items. The same distinction is made between current and fixed liabilities.

The term *accrued liabilities* usually refers to items in connection with services that have been received or rendered but not yet paid for. An example of an accrued liability would be interest earned on a note payable but not yet paid because the note is not yet due. Another example of an accrued liability would be wages for labor rendered but not yet paid for because the payroll usually covers a whole week and the accounting period ended in the middle of the week. Taxes payable is yet another example of an accrued liability.

Use of Percentages. Another statistical tool that management uses to interpret financial reports is *percentages*. For example, various items in the income statement, such as cost of goods sold, administrative expenses, and selling expenses, are shown in both dollar figures and percentages of income from sales. Such percentages are included in the income statement, page 437.

Even a quick glance at the income statement shows that the cost price of the merchandise sold was 62 percent of the selling price, making the gross profit 38 percent of the selling price. Both the relative amounts and the percentages of the administrative and selling expenses are clear. The net income of $9,900 represents a profit rate of 9 percent of sales.

The two methods of interpretation we have just explained—comparison by fiscal periods and use of percentages—may be combined in a single report

Balance sheet at a definite date (handwritten)

THE FINCH COMPANY
Statement of Financial Position

account listed in degree of liquidity (handwritten)

			June 30 Current Quarter	March 31 Previous Quarter
ASSETS				
Current Assets:				
Cash			$ 22,500	$ 20,000
Accounts Receivable			72,200	68,500
Notes Receivable			7,600	6,500
Merchandise Inventory			12,800	13,800
Prepaid Expenses			2,400	2,100
Total Current Assets			$117,500	$110,900
Fixed Assets:	Current	Previous		
Equipment (Cost)	$15,800	$15,800		
Less Allowance for Depreciation	(3,000)	(2,600)		
Buildings (Cost)	56,700	56,700		
Less Allowance for Depreciation	(13,600)	(11,200)		
Total Fixed Assets			$ 55,900	$ 58,700
Total Assets			$173,400	$169,600
LIABILITIES				
Current Liabilities:				
Accounts Payable			$ 12,200	$ 13,800
Notes Payable			2,000	3,000
Accrued Liabilities			800	1,600
Total Liabilities			$ 15,000	$ 18,400
OWNERSHIP				
Mr. Alford Finch, Capital			$159,400	$151,200
Total Liabilities and Capital			$173,400	$169,600

ratio analysis (handwritten)

THE FINCH COMPANY
Income Statement, March 31, 19___ to June 30, 19___

			Percentage
Net Income from Sales		$110,000	100.0
Cost of Goods Sold		68,200	62.0
Gross Profit on Sales		$ 41,800	38.0
Operating Expenses:			
Administrative Expenses	$15,400		14.0
Selling Expenses	16,500		15.0
Total Operating Expenses		$ 31,900	29.0
Income		$ 9,900	9.0

to management. These methods were presented separately here for the sake of simplification and clarity.

Sometimes the income-and-expense statement is broken down according to departments. In this way, management can see at a glance how the various departments compare with one another in total sales, costs, and profits during the period covered by the statement.

Use of Ratios in Statement Interpretation

Businessmen and prospective stock purchasers frequently interpret financial statements through the use of ratios. We shall explain three ratios commonly used by modern business management: the current ratio, the working-capital ratio, and inventory turnover.

The Current Ratio. One of the most commonly used ratios utilized in preparing financial statements is the current ratio. It is found by dividing the amount of current assets by the total of current liabilities. This ratio gives management an indication of the solvency of the business and of the firm's ability to pay its debts. What constitutes a desirable current ratio depends on the nature and type of business. In a business where the turnover of merchandise is slow—for example, a jewelry store—there will be a greater need for cash and a larger current ratio than in a business where the turnover is rapid, as it is in a supermarket. A department store might have one current ratio and a public utility quite a different one.

In the balance-sheet report of the Finch Company, shown on page 437, the current ratio improved from 6.0 to 7.8:

$$\frac{110,900}{18,400} = 6.0 \qquad \frac{117,500}{15,000} = 7.8 \qquad \text{dollar Figure}$$

A recent study of the current ratio for selected types of retail stores appears below.

Type of Business	Number of Stores	Current Ratio
Automobile dealers	128	1.9
Building materials	96	2.5
Clothing—men's and women's	75	3.0
Department stores	202	3.4
Farm and garden supplies	88	2.7
Furniture	175	3.2
Groceries and meats	156	2.0
Hardware	99	3.6
Jewelers	63	2.9
Lumber yards	140	3.7
Paint, glass, and wallpaper	39	4.6
Women's specialty shops	208	2.5

Working Capital. Working capital is closely related to the current ratio, since it is the same information stated in terms of dollars rather than as a ratio. It is the excess (in dollars) of current assets over current liabilities. Working capital indicates a firm's ability to meet its operating expenses and to purchase additional merchandise for resale. If a firm has enough capital on hand, it can take advantage of attractive buying propositions that it would otherwise have to pass up. The working capital of the Finch Company is $92,500 for the quarter ending March 31 ($110,900 − $18,400), and $102,500 for the quarter ending on June 30 ($117,500 − $15,000).

Stock-Turnover Ratio. Businessmen feel it undesirable to have large sums of money tied up in merchandise stock. When the merchandise manager discovers that inventories are too large, he determines which goods are not moving, and makes plans for selling them.

We discussed inventory or stock turnover in Chapter 6, in connection with determining capital needs. We pointed out that the usual method of calculating stock turnover is to divide the average inventory into the total sales, using the cost price of the goods sold. The average inventory may be found by adding the beginning and ending inventories together and dividing by 2. Using the figures appearing on the income statement for the Finch Company, we would calculate as follows:

$$\frac{\text{Beginning Inventory} + \text{Ending Inventory}}{2} = \text{Average Inventory}$$

$$\frac{\$13,800 + \$12,800}{2} = \frac{\$26,600}{2} = \$13,300$$

$$\frac{\text{Cost of Goods Sold}}{\text{Average Inventory}} = \frac{\$68,200}{\$13,300} = 5.1$$

The inventory or stock turnover is 5.1.

A recent study of selected types of retail businesses showed the following average stock turnover for selected types of stores:

Type of Business	Number of Stores	Inventory Turnover
Automobile dealers	128	8.8
Building materials	96	7.7
Clothing—men's and women's	75	4.4
Department stores	202	5.4
Farm and garden supplies	88	9.3
Furniture	175	4.8
Groceries and meats	156	16.6
Hardware	99	3.4
Jewelers	63	2.9
Lumber yards	140	5.0
Paint, glass, and wallpaper	39	4.8
Women's specialty shops	208	6.7

These ratios have been discussed here as illustrations of the ways in which ratios are used in interpreting financial reports. Accountants use other ratios also, such as the ratio of net profit to sales and the ratio of inventory to accounts and notes receivable—but since we are illustrating how ratios are used, and not trying to give a comprehensive treatment of them, we shall not discuss them here.

Discussion Questions

6. *What is the value of showing financial records for a previous quarter as well as for the current quarter?*
7. *What does the "working capital" for a business actually show?*
8. *Why is the inventory turnover for a jewelry store so much lower than that for a grocery store?*

THE USE OF BUDGETING

We have observed from time to time that planning is one of the most significant aspects of business management. Much of the financial planning of business is based on budgets. A *budget* may be defined as a financial plan showing anticipated income and outlays for a given period of time. Budgets are usually prepared for both individual departments and the business as a whole. If the expenditures for any one department equal the amount appropriated, we say that its budget is *balanced*. When the expenditures exceed the amount budgeted, we say that the department has operated at a *deficit*.

Purposes of Budgets

A well-prepared budget helps management in several ways. Perhaps its primary function is to serve as a guide in planning financial operations. A second purpose is to establish limits for departmental expenditures. Although budgets are at best only estimates, they are usually accepted as the limits within which a department is to operate. If there must be an overexpenditure in one area, an attempt is made to curtail expenses in other areas.

Another important purpose of a budget is to encourage administrative officials to make a careful analysis of all existing operations. On the basis of their analysis, present practices may be justified, expanded, eliminated, or restricted. Budgets are also used for control purposes—an activity that is discussed more fully on page 442.

Types of Budgets

Perhaps the most important budget to be prepared—certainly the first one—is the *sales budget*. This is an estimate of the total anticipated sales during the budgetary period. One method of preparation commonly used is to have each salesman estimate the sales increase he can effect in the territory he serves. As a rule, these estimates are broken down by principal lines, or in some cases, by individual items.

Another approach to the preparation of the sales budget is to begin with a line graph of sales for recent years, and project it for the budgetary period. Any factor or new development must be taken into account that is expected to increase or decrease future sales as compared with past performance. In this way, management can make a fairly accurate forecast of total sales and sales by products, and can then go on to determine the expected gross income.

In this same manner—that is, comparing past performance with anticipated operations and interpreting these in terms of new developments, such as changes in equipment installations or office procedures—budgets are prepared for production operations, raw materials and supplies, sales expenses, advertising, labor, plant expansion, and any other activity that requires an important expenditure.

Steps in Budgeting

The first step in budgeting is to make preliminary plans for the period ahead. All the important phases of the business operation must be studied, with the records of past performance as the starting point. Finally, estimates for the budgeting period are prepared.

The second phase is the planning and maintenance of records of expenditures during the budgetary period. These records should be broken down into several budget categories. They must be accurate, up to date, and relatively easy to interpret. Records of this sort enable management to make periodic comparisons to see whether actual expenses are falling into line with the estimates that were prepared.

The third step is to study any departure from the original estimates. In some cases, management may decide to alter the budget. Such a situation might be created by unusual capital costs, such as building enlargement or modification that had not been anticipated, or by the unavoidable replacement of heavy equipment that suddenly becomes obsolete. However, in most cases management will take steps to bring expenditures into line with the original estimates.

Budgets are generally prepared in the accounting department from data furnished it by the heads of other departments. In some cases this procedure is reversed, and the respective department heads prepare their departmental budgets from data supplied them by the accounting department.

CASH BUDGET

Item	Monthly Average for 1972	1973 January	1973 February	1973 March
Receipts:				
Accounts receivable collections	$12,000	$11,700	$12,200	$12,000
Disbursements:				
Accounts payable paid	$ 2,300	$ 2,500	$ 2,800	$ 3,000
Direct labor	2,200	2,400	2,700	2,700
Indirect labor	850	850	850	850
Variable manufacturing expenses	1,000	1,100	1,200	1,300
Insurance and taxes	150	150	150	150
General and administrative expenses	2,800	2,800	2,800	2,800
Selling expense	500	500	600	600
Total disbursements	$ 9,800	$10,300	$11,100	$11,400
Initial cash		$ 6,500	$ 7,900	$ 9,000
Cash change resulting from operations		1,400	1,100	600
Cumulative cash	6,500*	7,900	9,000	9,600
Desired level of cash		6,400	7,600	8,400
Cash excess		$ 1,500	$ 1,400	$ 1,200

* December 31

BUDGETARY CONTROL

If there is to be a fully effective cost-reduction program in the administration of an office, constant pressure must be applied by means of a continuing cost-control program. And budgets are the tools that management uses for control purposes. When they are well prepared and based realistically on past performances, they serve to reveal weaknesses in office organization, make it easier to fix responsibility, make possible comparisons that show trends in office performance, and help to maintain balance among the divisions of the office organization.

Budgetary control helps shape overall plans, set performance standards, and coordinate activities into a unified whole. It is achieved through the use of forms that show at a glance both the budget estimates and up-to-date records based on actual performance. If there should be any deviations from the budgetary plan, they are called to the attention of management through the budget committee. For example, if materials or supplies are being consumed at an abnormal rate, out of proportion to the amount of goods being produced, immediate attention is given to improving the materials-control procedures. And if sales of a particular product are declining rapidly, or if sales are falling off in a given territory, immediate conferences and investigations are held to correct this situation.

Budgetary control includes the development and use of three basic budgets: income, cash, and capital.

The *income budget* includes estimates of both gross and net income. The *gross income* estimate is premised on forecasts of sales. The net income esti-

442

mates result from subtracting anticipated expenses from the estimated gross income. The preparation of this budget requires perception and analysis of factors outside the business itself. The trends for the industry as a whole and the general economy of the region play an important role. Even the best and most accurate forecasts may prove invalid because of unforeseen price competition or research developments. Or a sudden shortage of essential raw materials may curtail operations severely.

Earlier in this chapter, we mentioned the *cash budget* or forecast. It represents a combination of the financial position of a business at the beginning of the fiscal period and the expected results of operations during the period. Basically, it states two things: the cash available for the period, and an itemized list of expected demands for funds.

The *capital budget* indicates how the sums allotted for capital expenditures are to be allocated to the major departments. Like all budgets, the estimates for capital expenditures must be kept flexible. Changes in market operations may cause changes in plans for expansion. Labor difficulties, even those of suppliers, may force a delay into a future fiscal period. Also, the use of surplus funds in terms of what they could earn by employing them in a variety of ways might become an important consideration.

The income and capital budgets are primarily the responsibility of the operating departments, but the cash budget is solely a financial function. The income and capital budgets represent a coordinated plan of action to achieve company objectives. But the cash budget is a reflection of the anticipated results of those plans.

Notice that although budgetary estimates and performance records focus attention on areas where action is needed, the actual control over funds, materials, expenses, and so on, must be exerted by individuals. The budget as a control tool is no better than the knowledge and understanding of the people who prepare it or of those who live with it. Management should create a climate that stimulates interest in budgets, and a desire to utilize them as guides against which to measure actual performance.

Discussion Question

9. *What purposes do budgets serve?*

CAREER OPPORTUNITIES IN ACCOUNTING

No matter which area of business you choose to follow as your specialty, you should certainly study accounting for at least two semesters. You will find it of great value in understanding the financial condition and operation of any business. In addition, a mastery of the basic principles of accounting will make your study of economics, finance, and business management far more meaningful. As you advance to junior executive and executive positions in business, you will find yourself using your knowledge of accounting principles and applications over and over again.

Fields of Accounting

Accounting practice may be divided into three areas: private, public, and governmental.

In *private* business, the accountant usually starts as a junior accountant or clerk. In proprietorships, partnerships, corporations, schools, and hospitals, accountants may serve as business managers, financial managers, comptrollers, treasurers, auditors, cost analysts, credit managers, and tax specialists.

The *public* accountant offers his services to the general public for the purpose of installing accounting systems, preparing income tax returns, or auditing accounting records.

The accountant in *governmental* service takes an examination administered by a civil service commission or a state merit system. Then he is assigned to some government agency or bureau. As a government employee, you might work as an accountant, a cost analyst, an auditor, or an income tax specialist.

Specialization in Accounting

In addition to the three main fields of accounting, you will find more highly specialized areas. Specialization in accounting, just as in any other field, usually leads to higher salaries. If you decide to specialize in accounting, you may choose among several important fields:

1. Systems installation
2. Cost accounting
3. Governmental accounting
4. Research
5. Teaching
6. Property appraisal
7. Budgetary control
8. Auditing (manufacturers, retailers, eleemosynary institutions, governments)
9. Taxation (income, estate, Social Security, sales, property)
10. Management consultant

From time to time, certain areas of specialization offer more job opportunities than others. At present, systems analysis and work related to the processing of data using computers are in the forefront. Auditing that includes the verification of a firm's records is always popular. Because income taxes are based on profits, management is interested in securing at least an internal audit before tax time, and of course corporations have an external audit made at the end of each year in order to include audited reports in the annual report to the stockholders.

During income tax season, most accounting firms are swamped with work and often add extra help for this period. People who have special competence in both accounting and law are always in demand, as are accountants with expertise in data processing.

We can illustrate a combination of specialization and the general fields of accounting with the following chart:

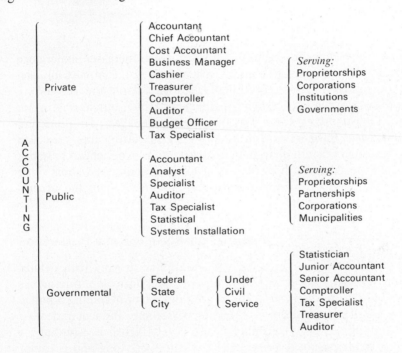

Employment and Promotional Opportunities

If you decide to concentrate on accounting, chances are you will find opportunities for employment immediately upon graduation from college. Later on, if you possess desirable executive qualities, your training will serve as an excellent stepping-stone to executive positions. One advantage of a career in accounting is that you can find suitable positions in all areas of the country. If you succeed in this type of work, and if you have broad training and experience, you will be eligible for promotions within the accounting department or in other departments of the business organization.

PROMOTIONAL OPPORTUNITIES FOR ACCOUNTANTS

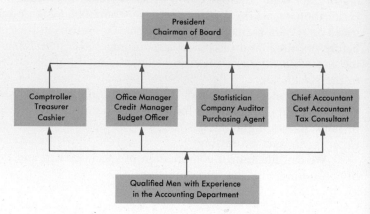

Some of the positions in accounting toward which increased experience will lead you are those of chief accountant, cost accountant, company auditor, tax consultant, treasurer, and comptroller. Positions outside the accounting department for which you may become eligible are cashier, purchasing agent, sales analyst, budget officer, office manager, credit manager, vice-president, and president. Most business organizations prefer to start young men and women who have had accounting training as assistants to experienced or senior accountants, and to advance them according to their ability and their value to the company. Promotional opportunities are summarized in the accompanying chart.

Personal Qualifications and Preparation

To be a success as an accountant, you should like to work with details, enjoy studying mathematical records, and have a knack for comparing names and numbers quickly and accurately. If you are thinking of becoming a public accountant, you will need in addition a pleasing personality and tact in dealing with clients and employees. The ability to use good English is essential for preparing final written reports. You must be able to work long and irregular hours without becoming nervous; you must possess good health, and especially good eyesight. Since you will be working with the intimate facts of the business, you must possess a high degree of personal integrity and the ability to handle confidential information properly.

Most colleges of business administration offer enough advanced courses in accounting for you to devote a large part of your study program to the field. In order to major in accounting and to prepare for the CPA examination (see below), you will need one or two accounting courses each semester, or quarter, after you have taken elementary accounting. For this reason, you will want to begin your study of accounting as early as possible. Specialized courses include accounting systems, cost accounting, corporation accounting, auditing, income taxation, petroleum or mine accounting, government accounting, and CPA problems.

In addition to specialized training in accounting, you will also need a knowledge of business law, especially the details of contracts and negotiable instruments. You would also do well to take several courses in economics, management, finance, quantitative analysis, marketing, and communication. Of course, you will find practical experience an invaluable part of your equipment in preparing for accounting work.

The *certified public accountant* is among the top members of his profession. Before you can lay claim to the title of CPA, you must meet certain requirements in education and experience, and pass a state proficiency examination. Requirements vary from state to state, but in general a candidate must meet the following qualifications:

1. He must be a United States citizen
2. He must be at least 21 years of age
3. He must sit for and pass the CPA examination given in the state in which he wishes to be certified
4. He must have practical experience in the field of accounting
5. He must be a high school graduate and, in some states, a graduate of some recognized college of business administration

The examinations are relatively uniform, since most states use those prepared by the American Institute of Accountants. The candidate is examined in business law, auditing, accounting theory, and accounting practice. It is not necessary for you to have a CPA certificate to practice private accounting, but without it you cannot practice as a public accountant and certify accounting statements.

Discussion Question

10. *What opportunities are there for specialization in the accounting field?*

SUMMARY

The accounting department of a business enterprise serves managers and owners by supplying financial data about finances, sales, operations, and profits. The results of operations are stated in terms of profits or income, and the financial condition of the business is reported on the balance sheet. Reports to stockholders usually go beyond the income statement and balance sheet and include a history of earnings per share, dividend trends, and reinvestment in capital additions.

In addition to company managers and owners, certain other groups are interested in the accounting reports of a business enterprise. Chief among these are the creditors, prospective purchasers of company stock, and the government.

In appraising the results of operations, the financial reports usually show comparisons with previous accounting periods, percentage distribution of the sales dollar among the major expense categories, and ratios that indicate the degree of liquidity enjoyed by the business. Some of the more commonly used are the current, working-capital, and inventory-turnover ratios.

Budgeting is an important management function that is dependent upon data prepared by the accounting department. Some budgets are prepared by that department, while others are prepared in other departments from accounting and other statistical data supplied to the heads of those departments. There are several different types of budgets normally prepared by a business enterprise, but budgetary control is centered around the income, cash, and capital budgets.

Accountancy is an excellent career choice for persons who like to work with figures. It offers employment opportunities at beginning positions and is also rich in opportunities for promotion. Accountants are needed by every medium-size and large business enterprise, by service institutions, and by the government. The CPA certificate is the ultimate objective of people who make accounting their lifework.

VOCABULARY REVIEW

Match the following terms with the statements below.

a. Balance sheet
b. Budget deficit
c. Capital budget
d. Cash forecast
e. Creditor

f. Current assets
g. Current ratio
h. Fiscal period
i. Income
j. Income statement

k. Inventory
l. Liabilities
m. Public accountant
n. Receivables
o. Working capital

1. A person to whom the business owes money
2. The period of time covered by a financial report prepared by the accounting department
3. An estimate of the amount of cash that will be on hand on specified future dates
4. Money due the firm from its customers in payment for goods purchased
5. A list of the merchandise on hand that was purchased for resale
6. An increase in the owners' equity resulting from a business transaction
7. The financial report that shows the result of operations as stated in terms of the profit earned
8. An accounting report that gives a picture of the financial position of the business on a given date
9. Those items of value owned by the business that will be turned into cash within a relatively short time
10. The subhead under which the equity of the creditors appears on the balance sheet
11. The ratio found by dividing the sum of the current liabilities into the total of the current assets

12. The amount by which the total of the current assets exceeds the amount of the current liabilities

13. The amount by which a group of expenditures exceeds the amount anticipated

14. An estimate of the amounts to be spent by various departments for capital improvement

15. An accountant who offers his services to any person or business who wishes to employ him

PROBLEMS AND PROJECTS

1. The accounting department has supplied the following data. Using these data, answer the questions below.

Cash	$ 20,220	Accounts payable	$17,950
Accounts receivable	25,330	Notes payable	8,250
Merchandise inventory	80,210	Fixed liabilities	60,000
Total assets	208,200		

    a. What is the current ratio?
    b. What is the total of fixed assets?
    c. What is the working capital?
    d. What is the amount of the owners' equity?

2. The Harper Furniture Company had an inventory of $14,000 on January 1 of the current year. On July 1 it was $16,000, and on December 31 it was $18,000. Sales for the year were $160,000 (selling price). If the merchandise cost on the average 60 percent of the selling price, what was the inventory turnover?

3. Accounts receivable for the Rogers Corporation were $64,250 at the end of the year. Of this sum, $48,350 was current (less than 30 days old); $9,810 was from 30 to 60 days old; $3,100 was 60 to 90 days old; and $1,870 was between three and six months old. The balance was more than six months past due. Using as percentages for expected losses those used in the illustration given in this chapter, prepare a similar table calculating the anticipated bad-debt losses.

BUSINESS CASES

Case 16-1 A Capital Expenditure

A national bank with 150 employees and total resources of $50 million, purchases four new accounting machines at a cost of $5,000 each. The machines have an estimated useful life of four years and a trade-in value of 15 percent of their cost. The purchase is regarded as an expense, and is so entered in the records. At the end of the month, when the income statement is prepared, it shows that the bank operated at a net loss of $2,150. But the president knows this conclusion is misleading.

An analysis of income and expenses for the month reveals that the loss can be traced to the expense entry for the purchase of the new machines. Their entire cost has been charged as an expense to the month in which they were purchased.

Assume you are an executive officer of the bank. Prepare the report you will make to the Board of Directors suggesting an alternative method of accounting for the purchase of these machines.

Case 16-2   Allocation of Profits

The Rogers Co. makes a profit of $300,000 for the current year. If the entire net income for the year is paid out in dividends, the stockholders would receive a return on their investment of 15 percent for the year.

The company must modernize and enlarge its plant facility, at a cost of $2,250,000. The company president recommends that only a 5 percent dividend be declared, and that the remainder of the profits earned be allocated to plant expansion.

Assume that you are a member of the Board of Directors. What factors would have a bearing on your decision in this case?

research
and
statistical
methods

CHAPTER SEVENTEEN

Decision making is a chief function in business management and government administration. It is basically a process of choosing one course of action in preference to all other alternatives. And sound decisions are based on factual data that are often collected from a variety of sources.

One of the elements that distinguishes top-level business management from the lower-level positions is the responsibility for decision making. Business executives must live with their decisions, so naturally they keep abreast of any new developments that result from new policy decisions. In other words, decision making is a continuous process, with earlier decisions being modified, in addition to the new ones being made. And this constant vigilance over results requires all kinds of data, for the wisest decisions, far more often than not, are based upon and evaluated in terms of a variety of types of business information. The scientific process of seeking new information, applying it to problem situations, and interpreting interrelationships in groups of data is called *research*.

Research, which is utilized by business management in the areas of product design, packaging, consumer wants, and marketing techniques, is carried on in a variety of ways. Some decisions are based on interpretation of numerical data regarding past performance. For example, an analysis of sales for previous years gives some indication of what might be expected this year. The science of working with this sort of numerical data is known as *statistics.* Essential in certain types of decision making, statistics is also one of the most valuable all-around tools used by business management. Statistical data are most useful when presented in a form that is easy to read and interpret—and thus the wide usage of the chart, the graph, and (to a lesser extent) statistical tables.

In this chapter we shall study the processes and methods of making business decisions, and the ways in which research and statistics are used to guide managers in making them. We shall also study major sources of business and economic information, statistical measurements of various kinds, and graphic methods for presenting data in statistical form.

DECISION MAKING

For the purposes of this discussion, we shall restrict our definition of decision making to the process of choosing, by a scientific process, a specific course of action from among several possible alternatives. Businessmen are generally considered to be pragmatists; that is, if something works, it is good. But this is not the same as saying that if something works, it has been chosen by a scientific process.

Categories of Decisions

Decisions may be grouped under two broad categories: policy decisions and administrative decisions. *Policy decisions,* as applied to business, are deliberate and specific decisions of managers that establish a policy—that is, a planned course of action by which goals may be pursued by all persons involved in the action. The larger the organization, the more important it is to see that policies are applied by other levels of the organization.

Administrative decisions translate company policies into action by determining how policy is to be carried out. For example, assume that top management decides to build a new plant to produce a new product. This is a policy decision. Selecting the employees and managers to run the plant becomes an administrative decision.

Steps in Decision Making

The decision-making process in business involves selecting from among several alternatives the one that appears best suited to the desired course of action. The complete process of decision making, however, includes the following five steps:

1. Defining the problem
2. Gathering pertinent data
3. Analyzing the data
4. Presenting the data
5. Choosing a course of action

It is essential to perform each step in the order listed in order to maintain a logical, orderly, and careful analysis of all the facts. Moreover, it is important to make certain no step is omitted.

A business's objectives determine its areas of decision. For example, assume that the demand for a certain factory's products dictates an enlargement of production facilities. The objective is to construct new facilities. The first basic decision that must be made is whether to build an addition to the present plant or to construct a new plant. If the latter is decided on, many other decisions will need to be reached regarding size, design, location, equipment, and so on. In each of these decisions, many alternatives may be feasible, but specific choices from among them must be made.

Defining the Problem and Suggesting Solutions. A clear-cut definition of the problem and an immediate identification of several plausible alternative courses of action toward its solution constitute the first step. (Since the two activities are practically concurrent, and since no firm course of action need be decided on yet, these two steps may be regarded as one.) It is most desirable to define the problem in such a manner that quantitative-measurement methods can be applied in its solution; the best decisions are usually supported by numerical-data analyses. Frequently there are several practicable alternative courses of action that obviously may be taken, and it may even be decided to pursue more than one alternative. In some cases these alternatives may be followed separately, and in others they may be combined.

Gathering Pertinent Data. The sources of data may be characterized as either primary or secondary. *Primary sources* are the original sources. For many kinds of data, such as census data, the government is the original source. Other primary sources include experiments, surveys, and questionnaires. Company reports and records are also regarded as primary sources. *Secondary sources* are those that report data that are already in published form in such documents as abstracts, magazines, almanacs, yearbooks, and encyclopedias. The important consideration is to obtain as much data as possible from primary sources in order to assure that more than a partial enumeration has been collected. A complete enumeration is often referred to as a census report.

Sources of business data will be covered in more detail in a later section, beginning on page 464.

Analyzing the Data. The data collected must be classified into "groups" of related information. Actually, this step is one of organizing the information so that it may be studied. After the data are classified, the relative importance of each "group" must be decided on. The proper study and interpretation of data will go a long way in determining its usefulness in decision making by persons responsible for formulating policy.

Presenting the Data. The chief purpose in analyzing and interpreting data is to select the information most pertinent to the problem's solution; a second purpose is to choose the method of presenting data to management. (These methods are discussed later in this chapter.)

Choosing a Course of Action. After all alternatives are evaluated, a course of action must be decided on—for here, too, the proof of the pudding is in the eating. Only the actual tryout of the chosen course of action proves the wisdom of the decision made. Of course, decision making is not an independent function of management. Decisions are always made in the context of one or more of the true management activities: planning, organizing, staffing, directing, controlling, or innovating.

Discussion Question

1. *What are the principal steps in making business decisions?*

METHODS OF COLLECTING DATA

There are several different methods used in collecting data when doing research, but the most common are the observation and the survey methods. Experimentation, which is the chief research method used in science, is also used to some degree in business. It may be used for evaluating advertising techniques or for measuring relationships among working environmental factors, attitudes, and production accomplishments.

The Observation Method

In the observation method, the researcher studies the behavior of people while they are shopping or at work. It is used by drugstores and retail establishments, for example, in the study of customer buying habits and preferences. It is especially valuable in determining desirable locations for retail stores, for the observer can take an accurate check of the number of cars passing selected locations, or the number of people walking past during specified periods of the day.

Observation is the basic method employed in job analysis and in time and motion study, where motion pictures are often used to supplement direct observation. The chief advantage of the observation method is its accuracy and objectivity; it collects facts rather than opinions.

The Survey Method

In the survey method, the researcher gathers his information through the use of questionnaires or uniform interview forms—by asking people questions. This research method is often used in gathering information related to marketing. Purchasers are asked about their buying habits, income level, size of family. Businessmen are surveyed regarding plans for plant expansion, intentions of opening new territories, employment practices. Researchers using the survey method may be interested either in factual data or in people's opinions.

One common survey technique is the mail *questionnaire.* This is especially useful when information is wanted from a large geographical area. The questionnaires are mailed either to a sample of the public at large or to a selected group of individuals. Although the percentage of returns is never large, this device is still the most economical way to cover a wide area.

When designing questionnaires, one should keep both the form and the questions short. Naturally, in order to yield helpful information, questions should relate to the kinds of factual information that the persons being surveyed would be expected to know. Questions should be very carefully worded so as not to suggest certain answers. Both questionnaires and interview forms should be pretested before the final copy for the instrument is decided upon. And one should avoid surveying for information that is already available elsewhere.

The *interview* is another commonly used survey technique. In recent years, the telephone has been used extensively for collecting information on consumer preferences and on radio and television listening habits. The telephone is also used to locate potential customers for special types of services, such as photographs or home repairs.

Face-to-face interviews are used to gather information in both homes and offices. Naturally, this type of interview is more costly than either the telephone interview or the mail questionnaire, and largely for this reason is used most often with a select group of people. Advertising agencies use the personal interview to check on reader attention and reaction to magazine advertisements.

Discussion Question

2. *What are the comparative advantages and disadvantages of the questionnaire and the interview as data-gathering techniques? Why?*

BUSINESS USES OF STATISTICS

The various departments of a business organization make many uses of statistics. Statistical data may be used to study such functions as operational planning, establishment of standards, and control. Standards might relate to quantity limitations, quality, or rates of output. Control is usually attained by comparing accomplishments against previously set standards.

In a production department, statistics are employed in establishing quality control, in testing newly developed products, in time and motion studies, and in the determination of needed capital expenditures.

In a personnel department, statistical techniques are utilized in measuring the reliability and validity of employment tests and in formulating bases for merit evaluations or wage incentives.

In accounting, statistics are used in analyzing and calculating depletion and depreciation figures, in sampling procedures used in connection with the preparation of inventories, and in price changes caused by price and other economic fluctuations.

In marketing, statistical procedures are employed in evaluating sales surveys, trend analyses, supply and demand studies, or new market areas, or in determining volume potentials in established marketing areas.

In finance and investment, management uses statistics in computing ratios, estimating future interest rates or borrowing needs, or forecasting economic trends. As an example of this last use, see the Forbes Index illustration on page 17. The various factors used in establishing the Forbes Index trend are named immediately below the Index, which is published in *Forbes* magazine each month.

Discussion Question

3. *Why do statistics make such a strong contribution to business management?*

RESEARCH AND DEVELOPMENT

It is through research and development (R&D) that new and better products become available in this country for industrial use, for the government, and for consumers. According to the National Science Foundation, which began to compile official data on research and development in 1953, U.S. businesses spent $3.6 billion (including government-supplied funds) on R&D in 1953. Since then, these expenditures have increased each year; they amounted to $22 billion in 1971, with a forecast of more than $25 billion by 1975. Expenditures for research and development in this country amount to between 3 and 4 percent of our gross national product.

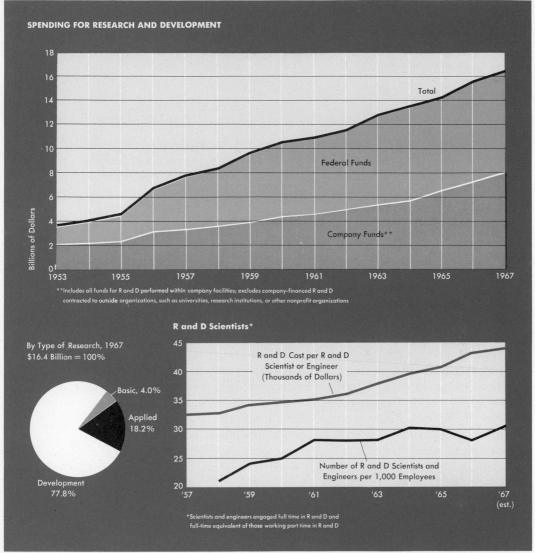

SPENDING FOR RESEARCH AND DEVELOPMENT

Billions of Dollars

Total

Federal Funds

Company Funds**

**Includes all funds for R and D performed within company facilities; excludes company-financed R and D
contracted to outside organizations, such as universities, research institutions, or other nonprofit organizations

By Type of Research, 1967
$16.4 Billion = 100%

Basic, 4.0%

Applied
18.2%

Development
77.8%

R and D Scientists*

R and D Cost per R and D
Scientist or Engineer
(Thousands of Dollars)

Number of R and D Scientists and
Engineers per 1,000 Employees

'57   '59   '61   '63   '65   '67
(est.)

*Scientists and engineers engaged full time in R and D and
full-time equivalent of those working part time in R and D

Source: The National Industrial Conference Board, No. 1623, August 1, 1969

The National Science Foundation (NSF) defines research and development as *original investigation aimed at discovering new scientific knowledge.* In American business, research is said to be *basic research* if it does not have a specific commercial objective; it is called *applied research* if it does. The NSF says that the term *development* refers to engineering or other technical activity concerned with translating scientific knowledge into new products or processes.

R&D is vital in the science- and technology-oriented industries, such as drugs, chemicals, electronics, and aerospace. Intensive competition forces consumer-goods companies, such as food packagers, soap makers, and toy manufacturers, to create a flow of new products. At the opposite pole, retailers largely depend on their suppliers to develop new things.

457

In addition to the development of new products, research and development includes quality control, troubleshooting, testing, and market and economic research.

Product Research

Product research is largely concerned with the improvement of present products and the development of new ones. It is for the most part experimental research carried on in research laboratories. Most large businesses maintain research labs devoted to the discovery, development, and testing of new materials and products.

A considerable proportion of the funds supplied by the federal government has been channelled into research concerned with the military and space programs. The government contributes heavily to experimentation in the biological and physical sciences and in aeronautics, in both state and private universities. It also subsidizes most of the research and development done by private businesses in the aircraft and electronics industries.

Market Research

Market research includes all studies of marketing for both products and services. Concerned with analyzing marketing methods and consumer buying habits, its purpose is to secure information useful in increasing company sales, and thus in improving sales position in relation to the total potential market. It is most essential in those areas where competition is keenest, for it helps a company to remain successful by keeping abreast of consumer preferences regarding its product lines. Although some companies carry on their own market research, many employ advertising agencies to perform this service.

Discussion Question

4. *Why is R&D so vital to business and industry?*

FORECASTING

Many decisions are based on estimates of what is likely to happen in the future. Such decisions are made almost daily both by businessmen and by economists employed by governments. These estimates of future economic conditions or trends, based on thorough analyses of the past and present, are called *forecasts*. Both *short-term* and *long-range forecasts* are used.

Business forecasting rests on analyses of statistical data: economic, political, and market information that is obtained to reduce the degree of risk in making business decisions. Business forecasting is important because it can mean profits and growth or financial loss and failure. Management decisions in the areas of production, purchasing, borrowing, inventory accumulation, capital spending, and marketing all depend on statistical data collected and its interpretation through forecasting.

Three basic assumptions undergird all business forecasting:

1. The economic factors such as levels of production, income, salaries, interest rates, prices, and consumer buying are all bound together in a system that has a high degree of stability over a period of time.
2. Future changes in the relationships among these factors will be determined largely by present causes, or may be deduced from symptoms presently discernible.
3. The nature of these causes (or systems) may be discovered by studying the past, and interpreting historical data in relation to probable future happenings.

Types of Forecasts

There are many different types of forecasts undertaken by business management, but most of them can be classified as forecasts regarding *supply, control,* and *demand. Supply forecasts* are concerned with the purchase and use of resources that represent cost factors to the company. Forecasts designed to aid in *control* may relate to either materials or financing. *Demand forecasts* are those anticipating the amount of future sales.

Supply Forecasts. The establishment of production schedules must be preceded by forecasts of both the supply and the cost of labor. Two factors relating to available labor and scheduling are the need for overtime work and the efficient use of expensive machinery.

The demand for raw materials and supplies must be forecast as accurately as possible. If there is a likelihood of shortages of materials or difficulties in delivery owing to possible labor strikes against suppliers, orders must be placed well in advance. The forecast of market costs of materials plays a significant role here. If a rising market is anticipated, early purchasing will be ordered and a large inventory maintained. If a falling market is forecast, inventories will be maintained at a minimal figure.

Control Forecasts. In the preceding chapter, the use of budgets for control purposes was discussed and illustrated. The cash forecast and controls on expenses are essential. If interest rates are likely to rise, management will favor long-term loans, while a forecast of future decreases in the cost of borrowed funds would dictate borrowing for short periods of time.

Demand Forecasts. Sales budgets are actually forecasts of the consumer demand for company products. Estimates of income must be based on forecasts of the market demand.

Sales budgets are greatly affected by forecasts of the economic trend for business in general. Also, the outlook of the particular industry must be studied;

the past sales record must be interpreted in the light of current and future company policies that might increase sales volume—development of new products, diversification of product lines, expansion of territory, increase in advertising, and so on. Other factors must also be considered, such as changes in consumer income or tastes, the strength of competitors, or the marketing of substitute products.

Techniques of Forecasting

The method to be used in forecasting will depend somewhat on the purpose of the forecast and the way it is to be used. There are many methods (such as opinion polling and econometrics, which you would study in a full course in statistical method), but here we shall discuss only three of those most commonly used: *trend analysis, correlation,* and *composite estimate.*

Trend Analysis. Business activities are not static; production, prices, sales, purchases, and profits all fluctuate over a period of time. Trend analysis, or time series, is a sequence of values expressed at regular recurring periods of time. It is possible from these time-series studies to detect regular recurring movements that are likely to take place as an aid in predicting future events.

Forecasting by trend analysis actually consists of interpreting the historical sequence of the past and applying the interpretation to the immediate future. It assumes that the rate of growth or change that has persisted in the past will continue. Historical data are plotted on a graph and a trend line is established. Frequently a straight line is extended for the future. However, if certain known factors indicate that the future rate will increase, the line may be curved upward. As a general rule, there may be several future projections, depending on the length of the historical period selected. Excellent examples of forecasting by trend analysis are the line graphs of population growth and production shown in earlier chapters of this book. The accuracy of forecasting by historical sequence or trend analysis depends on good judgment in interpreting those changing factors that may keep history from repeating.

In many time series, statisticians are able to detect whether the changes are in the nature of seasonal fluctuations, cyclical variations, or secular trends. *Seasonal fluctuations* are those that may occur, say, at Christmas, during summer vacations, or in winter. For example, sales in department stores peak in December and are low in January. And, again, it is more difficult to sell bathing suits in December than in July.

The up-and-down movements pertaining to business conditions are called *cyclical variations* or *business cycles.* These changes do not recur regularly, but at irregular intervals. For example, steel companies are greatly affected by business conditions. When business is booming, the sale of steel is high. A drop in the economy will cause a slump in sales. Automobile manufacturing and home building are other cyclical industries.

Secular trends are long-range movements up or down. Usually, definite forces cause a secular trend in a particular industry. Population growth has affected the need for the building of retirement homes. Government expenditures follow what is called a secular trend.

Correlation. Correlation is simply a matter of establishing a pattern of relationship between two or more variables. The closer or greater the relationship, the higher the degree of correlation. This relationship may be either positive or negative. For example as the total volume of manufacturing increases, the number of gainfully employed workers grows larger. In other words, there is a direct relationship between the volume of production and the number of workers employed. This is a positive relationship, because as one increases, so does the other. So we call it a *positive correlation*.

However, as the amount of money available for investment increases, the earning power of money (usually expressed in terms of interest rates) decreases. When the money supply is plentiful, increased competition among lending institutions forces interest rates down. On the other hand, when money becomes more scarce, the competitive bidding among people who want to borrow money brings about higher interest rates. In other words, the availability of money has a direct effect on prevailing interest rates; there is obviously some kind of relationship between the two. Since one decreases as the other increases, the correlation is *negative*.

In the same way, a decrease in the number of bushels of corn produced would probably cause an increase in the price of corn, other things being equal. Here again there is a definite relationship between the two and therefore a degree of correlation; and again the correlation is negative, because as one increases the other decreases.

When using correlation for forecasting purposes, one must keep in mind that a relationship that has been present in the past may not continue to exist in the same ratio. Unusual weather conditions, international tension, or labor–management troubles may disturb the relationship. Correlation forecasting is most useful when one factor in the relationship always occurs prior to the second factor. For example, the demand for most consumer products in any given area varies in direct proportion to the population change. An unusual increase in the number of houses being constructed because of the influx of new industries would signal an increased demand for products sold at retail. In such situations, statistical correlations may be established and rather accurate forecasts made.

Composite Estimate. The composite estimate is largely used in forecasting future sales volume. Each district manager is asked to report his best estimate of the future demand for his territory. (It is assumed that he knows more about the potential market for his area than anyone else, and that he will present an accurate forecast.) The total of all district estimates becomes the prediction of total sales for a given future period, such as six or twelve months. This total is then checked against the judgment of the person at the head of the sales department for the whole organization.

The Forecasting Process

Forecasting changes in business activity involves more than statistical analysis. It includes an understanding of why changes have occurred in the past, for the historical record serves as the basis for future projections. Another important aspect is that of choosing the items to be measured. Some factors bear directly upon a particular problem, whereas others may be only indirectly related to it. For example, the U.S. Department of Commerce, in determining the gross national product, uses a carefully selected group of factors.

After these steps have been taken, it is necessary to decide upon the measuring devices to be employed—trend analysis, cyclical fluctuations, index numbers, and so forth. Then, all data that seem to have a bearing upon the forecast projection must be interpreted in terms of anticipated alterations in future events or planned courses of action. For example, in the forecasting of the gross national product for 1971, the greatest increases in expenditures were anticipated to be in consumer spending and that of state and local governments.

The Prudential Insurance Company's *Annual Economic Forecast* for 1972, which is based on seven major components, is shown in the table below. Supporting graphs are also shown for four of the seven components on which the GNP estimate is based.

TABLE
17-1

COMPONENTS OF THE 1972 FORECAST

	1971	1972 est.	CHANGE
	(In Billions of Dollars)		
Consumers			
Consumer spending for goods and services	665.5	725.0	+ 59.5
Housing outlays	40.5	45.0	+ 4.5
Business			
New plant and equipment	107.0	116.0	+ 9.0
Inventory investment	3.5	9.0	+ 5.5
Government			
Federal purchases	97.5	103.0	+ 5.5
State and local purchases	135.5	150.0	+ 14.5
Net Exports	1.5	4.0	+ 2.5
Total GNP	**1051.0**	**1152.0**	**+101.0**
Real Growth	3%	6%	
Price Inflation	4¾%	3½%	

Source: The Prudential Insurance Company, Annual Economic Forecast for 1971.

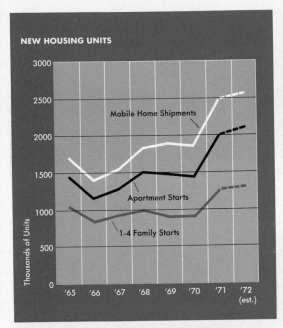

NEW HOUSING UNITS

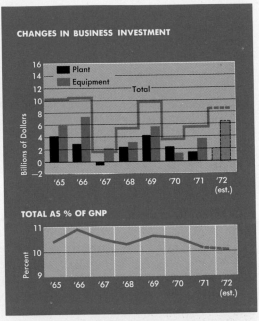

CHANGES IN BUSINESS INVESTMENT

TOTAL AS % OF GNP

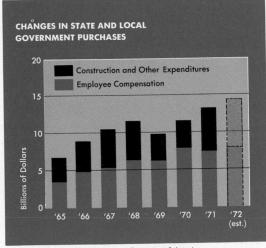

CHANGES IN STATE AND LOCAL GOVERNMENT PURCHASES

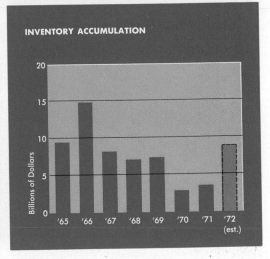

INVENTORY ACCUMULATION

Courtesy The Prudential Insurance Company of America

Discussion Questions

5. *Suggest several ways that forecasting is used in business.*
6. *What factors must be considered when using the trend analysis?*

SOURCES OF BUSINESS INFORMATION

There are many sources of data that are extremely helpful to business management. We have just discussed research, which is categorized as a *primary source,* since it gathers data not previously available. *Secondary sources* report information assembled from primary sources. The Bureau of Labor Statistics of the U.S. Department of Labor and the Bureau of the Census of the Department of Commerce collect and publish in report form data covering a wide variety of topics. Their reports are primary sources of data. On the other hand, much of these data from the original reports are repeated or condensed in the *Economic Almanac* or the *Statistical Abstract of the United States.* These are secondary sources of such data.

Private organizations such as the Brookings Institution and the National Industrial Conference Board publish reports and issue statistical charts and graphs dealing with a variety of topics of value to persons engaged in business. Most of their reports are based on primary sources, but some are merely graphic and succinct presentations of data collected originally by another agency, such as the Department of Commerce or Department of Labor.

Since both private and governmental agencies provide much valuable business information, the business student should become familiar with some of them. Every student of business administration should learn the best places to look when seeking specific types of business information.

Business Periodicals

Many general and specialized periodicals are of interest and value to the businessman and the business student. Among the general publications are *Business Week* (issued weekly), the *Prentice-Hall Report on Business* (issued weekly), *Fortune* (issued monthly), and the *Economic Almanac* (issued annually). Some representative publications dealing with the principal specialized areas of business follow.

Advertising. Among the periodicals that discuss research being carried on in the field of advertising, and that report news about agencies, methods, and trends, are *Advertising Age, Broadcasting, Editor and Publisher, Printers' Ink,* and *Tide.*

Finance. The leading periodicals in the field of finance are *Banking, Barron's National Business and Financial Weekly, Financial World, Moody's Stock Survey,* and the *Wall Street Journal.* These publications discuss economic trends, new financial policies of business and government agencies, and the overall financial condition of the economy.

Information Handling. Publications in this field include *The Office, Office Appliances and Administrative Management,* and *Systems.*

Insurance. *Best's Insurance News, Insurance Field,* and *The National*

Underwriter are among the best sources of current news and trends in the field of insurance.

Labor Relations. Three important publications dealing with labor and labor–management relations are *Labor, Monthly Labor Review,* and *Industrial and Labor Relations Review.*

Management. *Fortune, Business Week, Modern Management, Nation's Business,* and *Business Review and Forecast* contain current information about processes, new equipment, and automation in production.

Marketing. Excellent sources of information about current marketing trends, and reports on marketing management, are provided by *Industrial Marketing, Purchasing, Sales Management,* and *Journal of Marketing.*

Personnel Management. The leading periodicals of interest to persons in personnel and industrial relations work include *Personnel, Personnel Administration,* and *Personnel Psychology.* These publications contain articles dealing with employment practices, fringe benefits, employee training, and wage negotiations.

Retailing. Some of the periodicals of interest to those engaged in retailing are *Department Store Economist, Chain Store Age,* and *Women's Wear Daily.* They deal with current fashion trends, store management, and consumer-research reports.

Publications of the U.S. Bureau of the Census

Census of the United States. Published every ten years. In addition to statistics on population, with which you are probably familiar, census reports cover unemployment, business, manufacturing, distribution, agriculture, and state and local governments.

Census of Manufactures. Published biennially. Contains detailed statistical reports for different industries, such as textiles, paper products, and food products. Includes statistics for the various industries in each of the fifty states.

Census of Business. Covers, on an area basis, retail trade, wholesale trade, service businesses, construction, and distribution of manufacturer's sales.

Statistical Abstract of the United States. Published annually. Contains a summary of statistics of the industrial, social, political, and economic organizations of the United States.

Other Government Publications

Foreign Commerce Yearbook. Series of annual compilations of foreign economic statistics. (*Foreign Commerce Yearbook* alternates from year to year between statistics on the United States and those on foreign countries.)

Domestic Commerce. Published monthly. Includes articles on business trends, census releases, and reports of important legislation affecting markets and prices.

Survey of Current Business. Published monthly. Presents articles and statistics on current business situations for the major fields of activity in trade and industry. Summarizes data relating to trends in economic conditions. A supplement to this periodical is published weekly.

Foreign Commerce Weekly. A series of reports and discussions on world trade and commerce.

Market Research Sources. Published biennially. A guide to sources of information on domestic marketing. Lists recent publications on marketing.

Consumer Market Data Handbook and *Industrial Market Data Handbook.* Published every 10 years. Present statistical data on general consumer market, farm market, and industrial market, upon which the public can base economical marketing or sales operations.

Monthly Labor Review. Published by the Bureau of Labor Statistics. Deals with trends and status of employment and unemployment, labor legislation and court decisions, wages, retail prices, and wholesale prices.

Federal Reserve Bulletin. Published monthly by the Federal Reserve Board. Presents articles pertaining to business conditions and has approximately 55 pages of statistical tables dealing with finance, industrial production, construction, employment, and cost of living.

USING MEASURES TO SUMMARIZE DATA

The thousands of items of information that the researcher collects must be tabulated and analyzed before they can be put to use. In recent years, machine methods of tabulation have greatly reduced the time required for this step. After all the data have been tabulated, the experienced statistician is ready to analyze them. Actually, he has planned, or helped to plan, the whole research project beforehand. Thorough preparation in systematic planning will make his analysis easier. It is in the analysis and summarization of data that the statistician draws on his knowledge and experience in fitting the facts together into an orderly and meaningful picture. Usually, data are grouped together so that some type of measure may be used.

Statistical Averages

Perhaps the most frequent use of statistical data is some form of average. The most commonly used forms of average are the mean, the median, and the mode. These are measurements of central tendency representing the central values around which groups of data tend to cluster. They identify the distribution of the data.

The Mean. The mean is sometimes called the *arithmetic mean* or *arithmetic average.* It is calculated simply by adding a group of numbers and dividing the total by the number of items in the group. It is the most commonly used average in business.

Let's assume that you are the manufacturer of a line of electrical appliances. You are interested in knowing not only your total sales and your total profit for each month, quarter, or year, but also how the current figures compare with those for previous periods. You might discover, for example, that although your total sales for all products are lower this year than they were last year, still the sales of one product (Product Good in the following table) have been unusually good. As a basis for comparison, you might gather together sales data for the last five years as follows:

Year	Total Sales of All Company Products	Sales of Product Good
Current year	$7,300,000	$420,000
Last year	7,600,000	400,000
2 years ago	6,900,000	380,000
3 years ago	7,000,000	375,000
4 years ago	7,300,000	360,000
5 years ago	7,200,000	335,000
5-year average	$7,200,000	$370,000

With these figures, you can compare this year's record with other years during the past five-year period and also with the average for the period. Here are some of the pertinent facts that such a comparison would bring home to you:

1. *Total sales for this year are below those of last year.*
2. *Total sales for this year were exceeded only once during the previous five-year period—last year.*
3. *Total sales for this year exceed the yearly average for the five-year period by $100,000.*
4. *This year's sales of Product Good were the greatest of any year during the five-year period.*
5. *This year's sales of Product Good exceed the average by $50,000.*

If you had compared this year's record with that of last year only, you would have an entirely different picture from that shown by a comparison with the five-year period. This year's sales, when compared with last year's, fell off; but when compared with the five-year period, this year's total sales are good. When we examine the record for Product Good sales, we see that this year's increase is about the same as that for any other previous year—$20,000 seems to be the normal increase.

When the record of Product Good sales is compared with the total sales, we see that whereas the total sales have fluctuated from year to year, the sales for Product Good have shown a continuous increase. With this information, management is in a position to determine why the sales of Product Good vary so greatly from the total sales. By making a similar analysis of other products, management may be able to determine the cause of the fluctuation of the total sales, and which products should be dropped from the line of goods handled.

The Median. Another type of average that is sometimes used in business is the median. This is determined by arranging a series of numbers in ascending or descending order; the middle number is the median number in the *series*. In other words, there are as many numbers in the series that are smaller than the median as there are numbers that are larger. Here is how we would find the median if we used the same series of numbers that we used in solving for the arithmetic mean:

	Total Sales	
	$7,600,000	The median number in this
	7,300,000	series is $7,200,000,
Median ⟶	7,200,000	which is exactly the same as
	7,000,000	the arithmetic mean.
	6,900,000	
	Sale of Product Good	
	$400,000	In this case, the median
	380,000	number is $375,000,
Median ⟶	375,000	whereas the arithmetic mean
	360,000	was $370,000.
	335,000	

In these two cases, both the mean and the median are meaningful—either one could be used. On the other hand, here is an example involving the costs of five different possible plant sites, any one of which would meet the needs of the business:

$$
\begin{array}{rl}
& \$\ 97,000 \\
& 32,000 \\
\text{Median} \longrightarrow & 24,000 \\
& 20,000 \\
& 17,000 \\
\hline
\$\ 190,000 & \div\ 5 = \$38,000 = \text{Arithmetic mean}
\end{array}
$$

In this case, the median ($24,000) would be far more meaningful than the arithmetic mean ($38,000). None of the properties is valued at $38,000; only one exceeds that amount, and it exceeds the mean by a considerable sum. However, one piece of property is actually valued at the median price of $24,000, and there are as many pieces of property priced higher than $24,000 as there are lower. In this illustration, you can see that there is a tendency for the prices to be grouped about the median, whereas there is no tendency for them to be grouped about the mean.

The Mode. A third measurement of averages that is sometimes used is called the mode. This is the point of greatest concentration—in other words, the figure that occurs the greatest number of times in a series. Let us consider the hourly wages paid to a group of men who are performing similar work but who, because of differences in seniority and skill, receive different wage rates. The wage distribution is as follows:

	Hourly Wage	Number Earning That Wage	Calculation of Arithmetic Mean
	$2.20	2	(2.20 × 2) = $ 4.40
	2.10	6	(2.10 × 6) = 12.60
	2.05	10	. . . . 20.50
Median ⟶	2.00	12	. . . . 24.00
Mode ⟶	1.90	14	. . . . 26.60
	1.75	8	. . . . 14.00
	1.70	4	. . . . 6.80
		56	$108.90 ÷ 56 = 1.94 = Arithmetic mean

In this example, we found the arithmetic mean by multiplying the hourly wages by the number of men earning each wage; then we added all these figures together and divided by the total number of wage earners. The arithmetic mean turns out to be $1.94, the median is $2.00, and the mode—that is, the point of greatest concentration—is $1.90.

You can see from these examples that different types of averages show different values. The value of an average lies in the degree to which it conveys a real meaning to the data. If the distribution of data is relatively concentrated about the average, the *mean* is significant. When the data are distributed over a wide range, the *median* may be more meaningful; at least it indicates that there are as many cases distributed above the median as below it. There are times when it is important to know which figure occurs most frequently, and the *mode* gives this information.

Index Numbers

In many situations, figures that show relationships are much more significant than absolute figures would be. One of the most common ways to show relationships is by means of index numbers. An index number indicates the changes that have occurred in groups of related data on different dates or for different periods of time. Index numbers are used in business probably more frequently than any other statistical device. They are used to measure a variety of business activities, such as agricultural and mineral production, manufacturing, wholesale and retail trade, employment, construction, finance, and general business activity.

A common use of index numbers is in relation to the cost of living. In fact, perhaps the best-known index is the Consumer Price Index. Prepared and published by the federal government, this is in effect a method of showing from one month to another the average price of selected articles considered to be basic in determining the cost of living of American families. In order to show comparisons, a base period is chosen and assigned a value of 100. The data for other years is shown as a percentage of this base period. In Table 17.2, the period from 1957 to 1959 is the base period.

The Consumer Price Index, often called the cost-of-living index, measures the average change in prices of goods and services purchased by urban wage-earner and clerical-worker families, and by single persons living alone. The weights used in calculating the index are based on studies of actual expendi-

TABLE
17.2
CONSUMER PRICE INDEX: MAJOR COMPONENTS

Index numbers, 1957–1959 = 100

Year	All Items	Food[a]	Housing	Apparel and Upkeep[b]	Trans-portation	Health and Rec-reation
1947	77.8	81.3	74.5	89.2	64.3	—
1950	83.8	85.8	83.2	90.1	79.0	—
1951	90.5	95.4	88.2	98.2	84.0	—
1952	92.5	97.1	89.9	97.2	89.6	—
1953	93.2	95.6	92.3	96.5	92.1	89.7
1954	93.6	95.4	93.4	96.3	90.8	90.7
1955	93.3	94.0	94.1	95.9	89.7	91.4
1956	94.7	94.7	95.5	97.8	91.3	93.6
1957	98.0	97.8	98.5	99.5	96.5	97.0
1958	100.7	101.9	100.2	99.8	99.7	100.3
1959	101.5	100.3	101.3	100.6	103.8	102.8
1960	103.1	101.4	103.1	102.2	103.8	105.4
1961	104.2	102.6	103.9	103.0	105.0	107.3
1962	105.4	103.6	104.8	103.6	107.2	109.4
1963	106.7	105.1	106.0	104.8	107.8	111.4
1964	108.1	106.4	107.2	105.7	109.3	113.6
1965	109.9	108.8	108.5	106.8	111.1	115.6
1966	113.1	114.2	111.1	109.6	112.7	119.0
1967	116.3	115.2	114.3	114.0	115.9	123.8
1968	121.2	119.3	119.1	120.1	119.6	130.0
1969	127.7	125.5	126.7	127.1	124.2	136.6

[a] Includes restaurant meals and other food bought and eaten away from home.
[b] Formerly apparel; redefined in 1964 to include laundry, dry cleaning, and other apparel upkeep services.
Source: U.S. Department of Labor, Bureau of Labor Statistics, Monthly Labor Review; *and unpublished data.*

tures by wage earners and clerical workers. The quantities and qualities of the items in the "market basket" remain the same between consecutive pricing periods, so that the index measures the *effect of price change only* on the cost of living of these families. The index does *not* measure changes in the total amount families spend for living expenses.

Table 17.2 shows the trend in consumer prices for selected commodity groups, 1950 to 1969. Alaska and Hawaii were included for the first time in 1964.

Let us take an example in relation to the cost of living to show how the index numbers are calculated. In our example we shall assign a value of 100 to the base period 1957–1959, since this was used as the base in Table 17.2. The calculation would be made as follows:

Item	Average Yearly Cost, 1957–1959	Index Number	Cost for 1969	Index Number
Food	$1,750	100	$2,205	126
Housing	1,386	100	1,760	127
Apparel	584	100	742	127
Transportation	568	100	704	124
Health and recreation	314	100	430	137
Other living expenses	1,004	100	1,335	133
Total	$5,606	100	$7,176	128

The index number in each case was found by dividing the figure for the year to be compared (1969) by the figure for the base period.

For food: $\dfrac{\$2,205}{\$1,750} = 126$

For housing: $\dfrac{\$1,760}{\$1,386} = 127$

Another way to state this would be in terms of proportion, as follows:

For food: $\dfrac{\$1,750}{100} = \dfrac{2,205}{x}$ $1,750x = 220,500$
                                         $x = 126$

For housing: $\dfrac{\$1,386}{100} = \dfrac{1,760}{x}$ $1,386x = 176,000$
                                         $x = 127$

The cost-of-living index has become extremely important in recent years. Many labor agreements provide for automatic adjustments in wage rates as the cost-of-living index fluctuates. Likewise, management considers this when deciding on increments (increases) for salaried workers; in addition to merit raises, a cost-of-living adjustment is also included. Other important indexes are the *wholesale price index* and the *index of industrial production*.

·

7. *Describe a situation in which the mean would be preferable to the median and one in which the median would be better than the mean.*

8. *What important information does the consumer price index show?*

PRESENTATION OF STATISTICAL DATA

In most organizations, top management does not want to be burdened with masses of unorganized data or to waste valuable time in attempting to interpret them. After the data have been collected, tabulated, and organized, they should be presented clearly and concisely. The devices most commonly used for presenting data are numerical tables, charts, maps, and graphs. There are several kinds of graphs; the ones you will meet most often are line, bar, and circle graphs. Although most data may be presented in various ways, usually one method of presentation is more effective than the others. Just to show you why this is true, in the following paragraphs we shall present data in several different ways.

Line Graphs

The line graph is one of the most commonly used types of graph. It is especially useful when the variations to be presented are a time series. The time factor is nearly always plotted horizontally and the variation data vertically. The points plotted are then connected by either solid or dotted lines. When it is desired to illustrate several series on the same graph, different-colored lines are drawn. Economic trends, and growth factors such as population increases or increased sales volume, are common examples of the sort of data that can be illustrated in an easy-to-understand fashion by means of line graphs.

In order to illustrate the differences between a numerical table and a line graph, compare the price index as shown in Table 17.2 with the line graph on page 473. Although the base period for the table is 1957–1959 and that for the graph is 1967, one can see that relationships are more readily observed in the graph while exact figures are easier to obtain quickly from the table.

Bar Graphs

In bar graphs, which are also widely used, the bars may be drawn either vertically or horizontally. The horizontal bar graph is useful in comparing

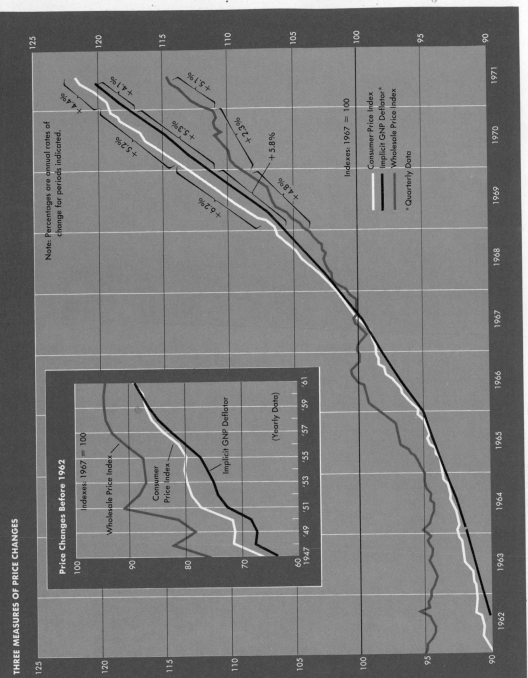

THREE MEASURES OF PRICE CHANGES

Note: Percentages are annual rates of change for periods indicated.

+4.4%

+4.1%

+5.1%

+5.2%

+5.3%

+3.3%

+2.2%

+6.2%

+5.8%

+4.8%

Indexes: 1967 = 100

Consumer Price Index

Implicit GNP Deflator*

Wholesale Price Index

* Quarterly Data

125 120 115 110 105 100 95 90

1971 1970 1969 1968 1967 1966 1965 1964 1963 1962

Price Changes Before 1962

Indexes: 1967 = 100

Wholesale Price Index

Consumer Price Index

Implicit GNP Deflator

(Yearly Data)

100 90 80 70 60

1947 '49 '51 '53 '55 '57 '59 '61

125 120 115 110 105 100 95 90

Source: The National Industrial Conference Board, No. 1673, September 1, 1971

MONEY INCOME OF HOUSEHOLDS, 1970

By Age of Head

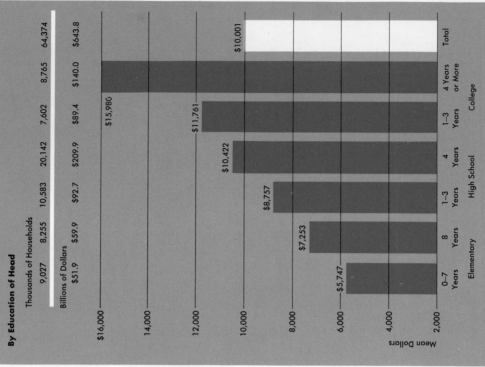

Thousands of Households	4,707	11,847	11,739	12,509	10,952	12,620	64,374
Billions of Dollars	$33.5	$122.2	$143.1	$160.8	$115.8	$68.4	$643.8

Mean Dollars

	14-24	25-34	35-44	45-54	55-64	65 and Over	Total

Age in Years

$7,115 — $10,313 — $12,193 — $12,858 — $10,573 — $5,418 — $10,001

By Education of Head

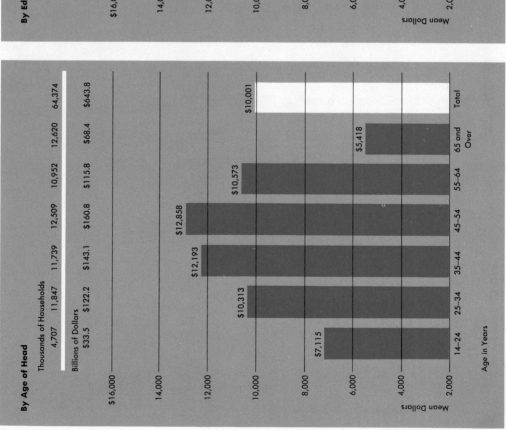

Thousands of Households	9,027	8,255	10,583	20,142	7,602	8,765	64,374
Billions of Dollars	$51.9	$59.9	$92.7	$209.9	$89.4	$140.0	$643.8

Mean Dollars

	0–7 Years	8 Years	1–3 Years	4 Years	1–3 Years	4 Years or More	Total
	Elementary		High School		College		

$5,747 — $7,253 — $8,757 — $10,422 — $11,761 — $15,980 — $10,001

Source: U.S. Bureau of the Census

different data for the same time interval; the vertical bar graph is excellent for comparing data for different time intervals. Bar graphs are easy to interpret, for the lengths of the bars show the relative quantities. Sometimes the sort of data that can be most easily illustrated by two sets of bars are shown side by side, with different shadings used to distinguish them. In another variation, different shadings are introduced to show a breakdown of the total figures being presented.

Interesting data on the money income of households are shown in the bar graphs on page 474. Other examples of bar graphs are shown on pages 251 and 257.

Circular Graphs

The simplest type of statistical graph is the circular graph, or *pie graph,* which is especially valuable for presenting a breakdown of items expressed in dollar values or as percentages. The complete circle represents 100 percent, and each segment shows a percentage of the whole. Circle graphs are frequently used to show the distribution of the tax dollar—both the sources of income and the items of expenditure. They may also be used to show the breakdown of a company's sales dollar—see the circle graph at the bottom of this page.

Statistical Maps

Sometimes you may find it appropriate to present statistical data pertaining to one state, to an area of several states, or to the country as a whole, on a map of the geographical area being discussed. For example, on an outline map of the United States you can enter the figures for each state, or else use symbols to represent the numbers. Another method is to group the states into three or four divisions; by shading the states in each group differently, you can readily suggest the comparisons that are to be made—see page 476.

THE BUDGET DOLLAR — ESTIMATE FOR FISCAL YEAR 1971

Where It Comes From

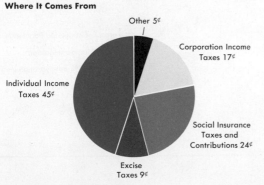

Other 5¢
Corporation Income Taxes 17¢
Individual Income Taxes 45¢
Social Insurance Taxes and Contributions 24¢
Excise Taxes 9¢

Where It Will Go

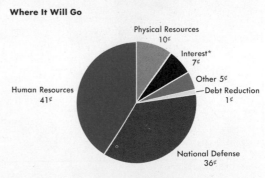

Physical Resources 10¢
Interest* 7¢
Other 5¢
Debt Reduction 1¢
Human Resources 41¢
National Defense 36¢

*Excludes interest paid to trust funds

Source: U.S. Bureau of the Budget

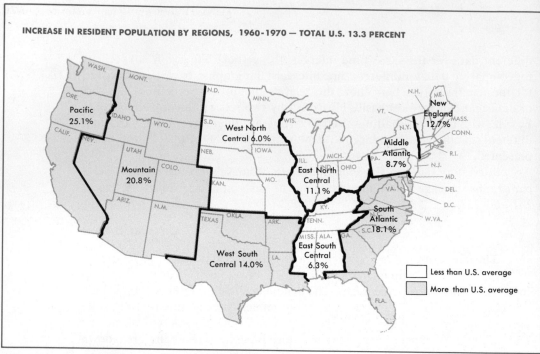

INCREASE IN RESIDENT POPULATION BY REGIONS, 1960-1970 — TOTAL U.S. 13.3 PERCENT

Pacific 25.1%

Mountain 20.8%

West North Central 6.0%

East North Central 11.1%

West South Central 14.0%

East South Central 6.3%

South Atlantic 18.1%

Middle Atlantic 8.7%

New England 12.7%

Less than U.S. average

More than U.S. average

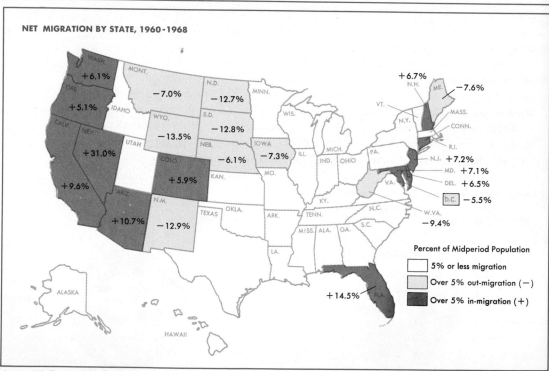

NET MIGRATION BY STATE, 1960-1968

+6.1% (WASH.)
+5.1% (ORE.)
−7.0% (MONT.)
−12.7% (N.D.)
−13.5% (WYO.)
−12.8% (S.D.)
+31.0% (NEV.)
−6.1% (NEB.)
−7.3% (IOWA)
+5.9% (COLO.)
+9.6% (CALIF.)
+10.7% (ARIZ.)
−12.9% (N.M.)
+6.7% (N.H.)
−7.6% (ME.)
+7.2% (N.J.)
+7.1% (MD.)
+6.5% (DEL.)
−5.5% (D.C.)
−9.4% (W.VA.)
+14.5% (FLA.)

ALASKA

HAWAII

Percent of Midperiod Population

5% or less migration

Over 5% out-migration (−)

Over 5% in-migration (+)

Source: U.S. Bureau of the Census

476

9. *Under what circumstances is each type of graph—line, bar, and circle—the best way to depict statistical data?*

RESEARCH AND STATISTICS
AS A CAREER

In recent years there has been increasing recognition, both in business and government, of economic problems that can best be studied through statistical procedures. As a result, there has been a marked growth in the use and application of statistics.

The present demand for statisticians and statistical workers is greater than the supply. Graduates of collegiate schools of business administration who are trained in statistics experience little or no difficulty in securing desirable positions. There is also a shortage of individuals who are qualified to teach statistics in colleges and universities. Probably the supply of statisticians will be insufficient to meet the demand during the next half-century, because the field of statistics is not sufficiently glamorous to attract large numbers of individuals.

Manufacturers, retailers, and advertising agencies spend millions of dollars each year to determine consumers' preferences, habits, opinions, and attitudes as a basis for making business decisions; both sampling and polling methods are used extensively. Statisticians with training and experience in scientific sampling find the fields of advertising and market research an important source of employment. Moreover, there is a shortage of actuaries in the field of insurance.

Your initial employment in the field of statistics might be as a statistical clerk, statistical draftsman, assistant statistician, or statistical analyst. It might be work in some related field, such as that of computer, accountant, tabulating-machine operator, or research assistant. There are also secretarial positions that require a knowledge of statistics. The statistician's salary is not usually high, but employment is steady in this field, and increases in salary are commensurate with the increasing value of the statistician to the growth and development of the business.

Positions in government agencies under civil-service tenure vary from junior statistical clerk to principal statistician. Promotions to other fields are also common; you may become head of the department of accounting or finance, director of statistical research, or administrative consultant. Advancement depends on native ability, breadth of training, and experience.

Qualifications and Preparation

It is obvious from what we have said so far that statistical work is largely mathematical. Measurement of data must be accurate and orderly, and the statistical worker must like to work with figures. Artistic ability and originality are necessary in order to determine the types of charts or graphs that should be used. A certain amount of manual dexterity is essential, because the statistical worker is frequently called on to prepare charts and graphs requiring lettering and other drafting techniques. He must be able to operate calculating machines and to perform moderately complex statistical computations. He must develop a knack for reading and understanding charts and tables. and must learn to distinguish between essential and unimportant data. Above all, he must possess the kind of mind that is apt at visualizing relative values from masses of data.

Statistics is a tool in research. It is necessary to know how to gather data and present them in such a way that the results will be reliable, valid, and objective. To be reliable, the results must be dependable; to be valid, the material must be accurate; and to be objective, the results must be free from personal judgments.

SUMMARY

Decision making is practiced at every level of management, from the top executive to the supervisor. Almost every phase of business from production to sales must be planned in advance. This calls for schedules in production, budgets for financial planning, and sales forecasts. The steps in decision making are very similar to those used in the scientific method of problem solving.

Research aids in making business decisions because research is based on the interpretation of facts and on projections of historical trends into the future. Experimental research characterizes research laboratories. Observational research is used in the factory through job analyses and time and motion studies. It is also useful for determining desirable locations for retail enterprises. The survey technique is most common in market research.

There are many useful sources of business information. Both private organizations and the federal government publish many books and periodicals that are very helpful to business management. The various statistical reports of the Bureau of the Census, the Economic Almanac, *and the* Statistical Abstract of the United States *are considered standard works. There are special periodicals for almost every area of specialization in business—accounting, personnel, advertising, industrial management, and sales.*

Both business and governmental economists employ a variety of measures such as the mean, median, mode, and index numbers. Almost every business publication and economic report makes use of statistical tables, charts, and graphs of all types. The most commonly used graphs are the line graph, bar graph, and circle graph.

There is a growing demand for research and statistical workers in business and government. Statistics is an attractive field for young people who are accurate in working with figures and who enjoy doing research or the preparation of statistical reports.

VOCABULARY REVIEW

Match the following vocabulary terms with the statements below.

a. Administrative decision
b. Composite estimate
c. Consumer Price Index
d. Correlation
e. Decision making
f. Forecast

g. Index number
h. Mean
i. Median
j. Observation method
k. Primary data

l. Product research
m. Statistics
n. Supply forecast
o. Survey method
p. Trend analysis

1. The process of analyzing problem situations in relation to numerical data
2. The reaching of a conclusion as the basis for establishing a course of action by choosing from several plausible alternatives
3. A decision having to do with the choice of procedures in implementing policy
4. A research method in which events are watched and recorded as they occur
5. The collection of data through the use of the questionnaire or interview
6. Research concerned with the development of new and improved goods
7. An estimate of future economic situations, conditions, or trends
8. An estimate of the future availability of needed labor
9. An interpretation of historical performance as the basis for making estimates for the future
10. The degree of relationship between two or more variables
11. The combining of several estimates to secure a picture of future expectations
12. The original source of business information
13. The arithmetic average of a group of related numbers
14. A figure used to indicate the degree of change that has taken place in relation to a base period
15. The middle number in a series of related figures
16. An index prepared by the federal government showing how the average price of selected cost-of-living factors at a given time compared with that of a selected base year or period

PROBLEMS AND PROJECTS

1. The Robert Cutter Company has five departments, with sales for one quarter as shown below. Compute the percentage of the total sales accounted for by each department and show this information as a circle graph.

Clothing	$300,000	Appliances	$150,000
Furniture	250,000	Household supplies	100,000
Cosmetics and jewelry	200,000		

2. The monthly sales figures for the Jake Rogers Company are:

January	$62,000	May	$72,000	September	$80,000
February	65,000	June	70,000	October	82,000
March	68,000	July	70,000	November	86,000
April	70,000	August	74,000	December	92,000

Determine:

    a. Average monthly sales
    b. Sales for each quarter
    c. Months that fell below average
    d. Months that exceeded the average
    e. Slowest quarter
    f. Best quarter of sales

3. Plot a line graph showing the month-by-month sales of the Jake Rogers Company.

4. Which type of graph would you recommend for depicting the following types of data?

    a. The gross national product and its various components
    b. The trend in wholesale prices for a period of five years
    c. Company sales, costs, and profits for one year
    d. Company sales, costs, and profits for a six-year period
    e. Distribution of the company sales dollar among raw material purchases, wages and salaries, tax payments, other operating expenses, payments to stockholders, and retained earnings

A BUSINESS CASE

Case 17-1 An Interview Study

The Henry Burton Company, located in Phoenix, Arizona, processes and packages a variety of dried foods. It employs thirty-five salesmen, to whom it pays a straight salary and expenses. The salesmen call on wholesale grocers and chain-store food buyers. The company has been awarding three small prizes to the three sales leaders each month. However, management has observed that all salesmen sell about an equal volume of goods and that their sales are fairly constant from month to month.

The vice-president in charge of sales has recommended that the company change to a scheme of paying only commissions. The salesmen are asking for a combination plan of salaries plus commissions. As a research assistant to the president, you have been asked to make a survey of other similar companies to determine their practices and how well they are working.

1. Draw up a research plan designed to obtain the kind of information you think would help the vice-president make a decision on this problem.

2. Prepare a set of questions you would ask if you used the interview technique.

information management and data processing

CHAPTER EIGHTEEN

Since management decisions are based on up-to-date data, it is essential that a business's management-information system be an effective one. And the rapidly increasing availability of business information, together with the ever-growing complexity and variety of data to be analyzed, requires some modern scheme for processing business information.

The same information is used in many different departments of a typical business. Therefore, business data must be organized and stored systematically so that it may be retrieved immediately when needed. So the mechanization and automating of records handling is a business "must." Many companies have installed their own high-speed electronic equipment. Other businesses secure the services of such equipment by contract or on a shared-time basis from service centers. As more mini-computers come on the market, many additional companies will be able to install their own data-processing equipment.

THE SYSTEMS CONCEPT APPLIED
TO RECORDS MANAGEMENT

Most people ordinarily view any activity as consisting of only the single action that they readily observe. Closer scrutiny of what is taking place, however, reveals that the activity includes several minor actions, operating together in an orderly fashion. These minor actions are an integral part of the activity as a whole, and operate in meaningful relation to one another; acting together in unity, they give "system" to the activity. For the purpose of our discussion here, we shall use *system* to refer to any series of related items or events whose interrelation is woven into an organizational pattern, together with some means of securing, storing, transferring, transmitting, controlling, and retrieving data concerning these related items.

The utilization of the systems-and-procedures approach has modernized the way office records are managed, bringing with it much sought-after time and dollar savings. A records-management system includes a whole group of integrated related procedures that are coordinated for efficient handling of business information.

The use of computers in processing business information has become quite commonplace. At first they were employed to handle the routine tasks formerly performed by records clerks and calculating-machine operators—such as payrolls, inventory reports, and accounts receivable. Later, computers were used for such operations as ordering goods and parts, making travel reservations, scheduling production operations, and assisting in design and control of manufacturing operations. Today, businesses have well-integrated systems for using computers in processing data that cut across departmental functions and boundaries. In 1971 there were over 100,000 computers in operation throughout the world, representing a capital outlay of about $25 billion. The Diebold Group, Inc., concluded from one of its recent research surveys that approximately 10 percent of new plant and equipment expenditures were for computer systems.

Steps in System Development and Utilization

Organizing for developing a business-information management system consists of the following five stages:

1. Assessment of problems and needs. The department manager determines the types and quantities of information that need to be handled. (In all probability, programming consultants from the equipment supplier would assist in this assessment.)
2. Preparation of system proposals by the staff, allocation of resources, and recommendation of an operating budget.
3. Design, implementation, testing, and conversion of the systems-development project.

4. Development and procurement of hardware, installation, system testing, and completion of plans for operation and maintenance.

5. A "try-out" operation, evaluative comparison of expected and actual outcomes in terms of costs, benefits, etc., and a determination of improvements and/or future systems development.

Some of the major applications of the records-management system in the office are the planning of office methods and procedures, forms design and control, quantity and quality of work (routing, scheduling, dispatching), cost control and budgeting, and space utilization and procedures.

Discussion Questions

1. *What do we mean by the term "system" as applied to the management of company records?*

2. *What are the steps in developing an information system?*

WHAT IS DATA PROCESSING?

Most persons who use the term *data processing* probably have in mind the handling of large amounts of numerical information by machine at a very rapid rate. However, data processing in its simplest form includes any process of information handling: When a clerk prepares invoices for payment, when a records clerk sorts checks, or when a typist prepares statements of account to send to a customer, this too, is data processing.

We can process information by hand or by machine. In every office, a great deal of information is processed by hand. In fact, most data must be processed by hand to a certain degree in order to get it first into the proper form to be processed later by a machine. Today we handle most accounting and statistical data by machine, thereby saving time. A typical office force can now provide management personnel with information that was not even available to them a generation ago. If both mechanical and electronic equipment are used, the term *automatic data processing* (ADP) is applicable; if all the processing is done electronically, the term *electronic data processing* (EDP) is the more descriptive term. Data processing generally includes coding, communicating, computing, recording, storing, summarizing, and reporting.

An Example of Data Processing

One of the best ways to explain how business data is handled is to show the treatment of a typical business transaction involving merchandise. Let us consider as our example a quantity of goods being ordered, received, and paid for.

Every purchase order describes and states the amount of the items wanted and lists the item cost and the total cost of the goods ordered. This latter figure is arrived at by multiplying the price per unit by the number of units. (This figure may, however, differ from the total cost of purchase; other changes may be added.) So *computation* is a necessary operation.

After the order form is prepared, it is sent to the company from which the goods are to be purchased. This operation can be called *communication.* At a later date, there will be other instances of communicating information—such as when the goods are shipped by the seller, and when a check is issued in payment for the shipment.

There are several records to be made in connection with the transaction we are using as our illustration: a record of the order, of the receipt of merchandise, of the obligation to pay for the goods, and of the payment that is made later. So the process of *recording* is another essential operation in the proper handling of a business transaction. And records do not just float around; they must lodge somewhere, so they are usually filed according to some prearranged plan. When records are systematically arranged in specially prepared storage cabinets, we usually call this *filing.* But when data are recorded by a computer, the term *storage* is commonly used. So the filing or storing of information is another operational function in handling data.

And before they are stored, most records are classified according to the nature of the transaction involved. It is easier and faster to record information by machine if it is stated numerically than if words are used. So the goods to be ordered in our illustration need to be classified—assigned an identification number. This is usually called *coding,* and it speeds up the operation when large quantities of data are involved.

If you were responsible for paying for merchandise purchased, how would you know to do this on or before the particular day that the invoice falls due? One way would be to write yourself a note on your desk calendar pad. You might actually make the note on the sixth of the month, but you would write it on the page of the calendar pad that is dated the sixteenth, the date the bill is to be paid. A better way might be to file the invoice in a bellows file under the date of the sixteenth, and then on the sixteenth issue your check. In fact, however, you would at the same time have to prepare checks to pay *all* the invoices previously filed in the bellows file as due on that day. So it is clear that, using the bellows file system when preparing several invoices for filing, you would arrange them in order according to their due dates. This is called *sorting,* and it is another important function in data processing. (Note that whereas in our illustration we sorted invoices and prepared them for filing by hand, in electronic data processing, cards would be sorted rapidly by machine.)

The final phase of data processing is vital, because it is important to know how many invoices are paid each day and the total amount spent in order to pay them. A list of all invoices paid on a particular date, the amount of each invoice, and the total paid would constitute a summary of this group of business transactions. Thus, *summarizing* is yet another essential function in handling large quantities of data.

The seven operations we have discussed here—coding, computing, communicating, recording, sorting, storing, and summarizing—make up the basic elements involved in data processing. We might define *data processing* then as *that group of operations performed in handling units of business data from the original entry to the final entry.* A *data-processing system* would be the total method used to carry out the seven basic elements of data processing to accomplish the accounting, statistical, and reporting functions of business management.

Advantages of Computers in Processing Business Data

The two primary advantages of electronic computers in handling information are their incredible speed and their high degree of accuracy. Information is more complete and more immediately available than when processed by hand or mechanically. By operating the computer center during the night, management may have reports that are as up to date as the close of business operations the previous day. And without the aid of computers, management might not be able to have these reports at all.

Computers can do a complete accounting job, and they can handle as many as five separate accounts simultaneously—and the limits of their versatility have not yet been reached. New electronic typing calculators combine the electric typewriter with a high-speed electronic computer. They are used to process material in which mathematical calculations are part of the typing operation. Any typist can type in the correct information and numbers, and these machines automatically calculate and then type out the answer.

Electronic data-processing machines are used in the following activities: payroll, inventory, expense accounting, sales statistics, accounts receivable, computation of commissions and dividends, property accounting, and invoicing. The use of electronic machines in processing information saves time and money through the elimination of duplicated effort.

The typical sales-order entry can serve to illustrate this point. As a rule, an order for goods is originated by a salesman who writes out a sales order and mails or telegraphs it to the home office. When this order is received, a production order is typed. It repeats the name and address of the purchaser and most of the other information written on the sales order by the salesman in the field. A copy of much of this information is included in the report that goes to the accounting office, and it is typed out again in the billing and shipping departments.

Actually, less than 10 percent of the information typed on the sales invoice and on the bill of lading is new information—that is, different from that first typed when the production order was prepared. With electronic data-processing equipment, as much as 80 percent of the information on the sales invoice is written automatically from a magnetic or punched tape. A separate record is prepared on tape for each regular customer, bearing his name and address and all other information needed for any sales invoices issued to him. This information is typed only once; thereafter it is reproduced automatically through the use of the tape. New information, such as the purchase-order number, date of order, quantity ordered, unit price, and total amount, are added to the tape by the machine operator.

Discussion Questions

3. *Explain how a data-processing system utilizes the various operations of coding, communicating, sorting, etc.*
4. *What are the advantages of processing data by computers over doing it by hand or by mechanical means?*

THE COMPUTER

For centuries, mathematicians have sought a machine capable of performing arithmetic calculations rapidly. About 1880, W. H. Adhner invented the pinset calculator, capable of performing arithmetical operations mechanically, and in 1885 William Burroughs developed the first mechanical adding machine for use in business. During the same year, Herman Hollerith introduced the electronic punch-card calculating system. In 1946, the University of Pennsylvania perfected the first electronic computer, called the Electronic Numerical Integrator and Calculator. Five years later, UNIVAC I, the forerunner of the modern computer, was built for the U.S. Department of Commerce, to be used in the office of the Bureau of the Census.

Perhaps the work of the computer may be best illustrated by comparing it with an adding or calculating machine. As with these simpler machines, *the three basic elements involved are the input, processor, and output units.* But the similarity stops there, because in the calculating machine, the keyboard is inevitably the means of putting information or data into the machine; the internal machinery is largely composed of gears, racks, and counting wheels, and the output is achieved through some type of simple printing mechanism, the report usually being printed on a paper tape of limited further use.

There are two types of computers—the analogue computer and the digital computer. An *analogue computer* carries out its calculations by making measurements. It deals with continuous quantities; it translates such physical conditions as temperature, pressure, or voltage into related mechanical or electrical quantities. Its chief function is in structural-design calculations for seeing how new models would work. Analogue computers are used in industry to make scientific computations, solve scientific problems, or control manufacturing processes.

Digital computers deal solely with numbers. Whereas analogue computers measure physical relationships, digital computers count numbers. Their absolute precision makes them best suited to business-problem calculations, and they have larger storage capacities than analogue computers. The discussion in the remainder of this chapter pertains to digital computers, since they are the type most commonly used in business.

The Binary Number System

Digital computers operate by opening and closing electrical circuits. The circuit is either open, permitting the electrical impulse to go through, or it is closed. Therefore the binary number system is used instead of the more familiar decimal system. A comparison might be made to an electric light bulb—it is either on or off. Similarly, within the computer, transistors are held in either a conducting or a nonconducting state, and specific voltage potentials are either present or absent. These binary modes of operation are signals to the computer in much the same way that light or the absence of light is a signal to a person. Since an electric current can indicate only an "on" or an "off" situation, only two symbols are registered by the computer—either a zero (for the "off" position) of a 1 (for the "on" position). In any single position of binary notation, the zero represents the absence of any assigned value and the 1 represents the presence of an assigned value.

The memory component might consist of electronic rods, screens, thin film, or magnetic cores. These memory components serve as a sort of electronic filing cabinet. They have the capacity for storing huge amounts of information in a small space, and for reading this information out of storage *automatically* and at electronic speeds.

Computer Hardware

Hardware is computer terminology for the machinery that makes up the various aspects of a computing center. There are five components that constitute the computer hardware: the input unit, the storage unit, the arithmetic unit, the control unit, and the output unit.

The Input Unit. The input unit feeds data into the computer system. Its purpose is to enable the operator to "communicate" with the computer. It performs its function by translating codes from the external form (cards,

THE BINARY NUMBER SYSTEM

Unlike the decimal system, which employs the digits 0 through 9, the binary system employs only two digits—0 and 1.

64	32	16	8	4	2	1...value of each position
0	0	1	0	1	0	1 equals 21

The lowest-order position in the binary system is called the *1-bit* and it can have only two conditions, 0 or 1. The next position is called the *2-bit*; the next, the *4-bit*; the next, the *8-bit*; etc....each of which can have one of two conditions, 0 or 1.

Another example:

64	32	16	8	4	2	1...value of each bit
1	0	1	0	0	1	1 equals 83

This is just another way of writing the quantity 83. Sixty-four ones, plus sixteen ones, plus two ones, plus one one, equals eighty-three units.

magnetic tape, or punched paper tape) to the internal form in which data are stored in the memory unit. The data translated might be numbers to be used later in arithmetic calculations, instructions that tell the computer what to do, or numbers and letters to be used in names and addresses.

The *card reader* converts holes in cards into electrical impulses and transmits the information to the memory unit of the computer, ready for processing. Similarly, the *tape reader* performs this function when the input medium is paper tape instead of cards. The important factor here is that this "reading" of data by the card or tape reader is done independently of human attention.

Instead of a card reader or tape reader, the *optical scanner* may be used with the input medium. The optical scanner reads each character from some input medium and translates it into electrical impulses that are then transmitted to the computer for processing. Scanning devices are programmed to read and evaluate certain numerals, characters, and symbols. Rays of light scan a field on a document, form an internal image, and compare it with an image that has been programmed into the scanner's memory component. If the scanner finds the corresponding image, it accepts it and moves on to the next figure. The optical scanner makes possible the use of journal records, adding-machine tapes, and accounting-machine tapes as input media, instead of the usual punched card or punched tape. Ordinary pencils may be used on specially prepared forms for reading by optical scanners.

The optical scanner represents the coming thing in data processing. The Internal Revenue Service and the Social Security Administration are already using scanners to collect employee-earnings data that employers submit quarterly. The Bureau of the Census used optical scanners for processing the data

INPUT MEDIA

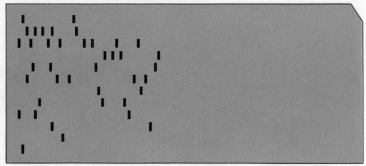

Punched Cards

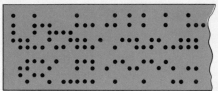

Punched Paper Tape

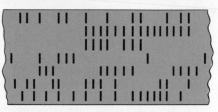

Magnetic Tape

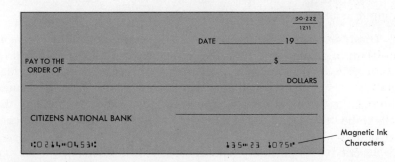

DATE _____ 19 _____

PAY TO THE
ORDER OF _____ $ _____

_____ DOLLARS

CITIZENS NATIONAL BANK _____

90-222
1211

⑆0214⑈0453⑉   ⑆35⑈23 ⑈075⑈

Magnetic Ink
Characters

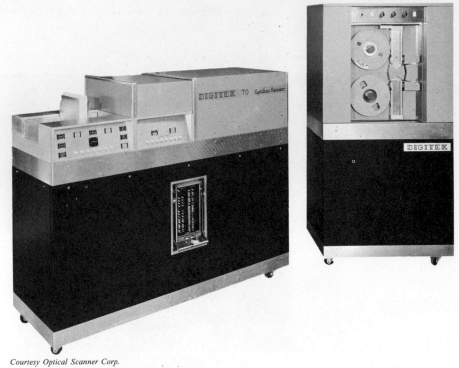

Digitek Optical Reader can read pencil-marked data from source documents at a basic speed of 2,500 sheets an hour, and transfers this information directly to magnetic tape.

it collected in the last census. In the future, many systems will be converting to optical scanners; but until recently they have been very expensive and have lacked a high degree of sophistication.

The Control Data Corporation announced its CDC 955 Optical Character Reader in January 1971. This machine reads material from typewriters and high-speed line printers, and journal tapes from cash registers and adding machines. It accepts characters at the rate of 750 per second. A single reader can input as much data as 90 keypunch stations.

The Memory or Storage Unit. The memory unit is the distinguishing component of a computer, the center of operations. All data being processed by the computer pass through it. By means of this unit, immense quantities of data are immediately available to the commands of the computer. The memory holds the input data, the intermediate result of calculations, the final results to be "read out," and the *program of instructions* telling the computer what to do.

Several types of memory units are used in computers. One is the *magnetic core,* which is used in most of the high-speed computers. Magnetic cores are made of special magnetic material shaped into circles or "doughnuts" the size of pinheads. Each core can be magnetized at any time in one of two directions, one standing for the binary 0, and the other for the binary 1. Thousands of these cores are strung on criss-crossed wires, arranged like the strings of a tennis racket, inside a square frame. The frames are stacked one on top of another to make a basic memory unit. A large-scale computer may have as many as eighteen basic units, each with more than 150,000 cores.

TYPES OF COMPUTER STORAGE OR MEMORY

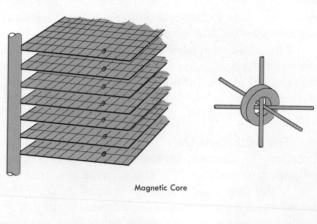

Magnetic Core

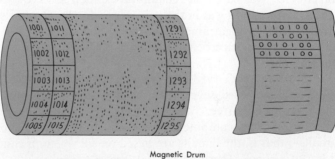

Magnetic Drum

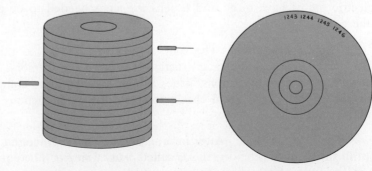

Magnetic Disk

The stacking arrangement places the cores in columns. Each of the columns is assigned an *address,* which is a specific location within the memory unit. Each column of cores can store either one fact or one instruction, expressed in binary code. The stored data can be instantly "read out" from any address and used in working a problem. If desired, the data can be erased from any address and replaced with a new fact or instruction.

There are other types of memory units, such as electronic rods, disks, drums, and magnetic tapes, but in each case the computer performs the same basic operation. It converts data according to instructions into a series of magnetic charges and stores these charges.

The capacity of a memory unit is measured in *words.* A *word,* which is a technical term, is defined as a group of binary digits that is treated as a unit and is stored in one location. A *location* is a unit-storage position in the main internal storage, in which one computer word may be stored or from which it may be retrieved.

The Arithmetic Unit. The arithmetic unit of a computer performs the operations of addition, subtraction, multiplication, and division, as well as comparison operations. It is also referred to as the *processing component.*

In this unit, which forms the heart of the computer, is found the circuitry that performs the mathematical operations. In the first generation of computers, the circuitry was based on vacuum tubes, such as were used in radio sets. The speed of operations was in the neighborhood of 500 additions a minute. These units took up a great amount of space, cast off a great deal of heat, used a large amount of electricity, and were plagued by the problem of the tubes burning out.

Starting about 1958, the vacuum tubes were replaced by transistors and speed was increased sevenfold. The new units were much smaller, cheaper, and more trouble-free.

Since 1965, computers have been built using "monolithic integrated circuits"; that is, the circuits are based on silicon chips much smaller than the eraser of a pencil. These tiny circuits are so advanced that just one can replace 15 transistors and 13 resistors. Their tiny size both shortens the distance the electric pulses have to go and lessens the steps needed to tie elements into one circuit.

The Control Unit. The control unit, or *console,* has the function of interpreting the program or instructions stored in the memory. It directs the various processing operations, issues proper commands to computer circuits to execute instructions, and checks to see that the instructions are properly carried out.

The Output Unit. After information has been processed, it is printed out in the form of a report; this is called *printed output.* The equipment used is in the form of a high-speed printer, and several printers can be placed on

High speed UNIVAC 490 Real-Time computing system manufactured by the Sperry Rand Corporation's UNIVAC Division. This is the installation at the Keydata Corporation, Cambridge, Mass., one of the nation's first on-line, real-time, and time-sharing computer centers.

the line with the central processor simultaneously. Printers are capable of printing up to 2,000 lines of numeric data per minute, and somewhat fewer lines of alphameric data. (*Alphameric* means consisting of both numbers and letters.)

In connection with a printed report, the output may take the form of a punched tape or a punched card, magnetic tape, magnetic disk, or video tube, depending on the type of output. It is desirable to have a record of the report on magnetic tape when there is a need to process the data further by the use of computers, or to prepare a new copy of the report at a later date.

The output report is the end product of the computer. Some of the types of information that can be produced by a printer are statements of accounts, journals, trial balances, financial statements, bills, invoices, checks, payroll reports, or just lists of names and addresses.

Computer Software

Software is the term used to refer to the instructions to the computer. The control panel merely controls the mechanical operations of the machinery. The instructions to the machine telling it what to do are in the form of a *program*. The person who writes these directions is called a *programmer*. A program consists of a set of coded instructions that inform the computer which data are to be picked up to be used, where the data is stored, what mathematical computations are to be performed, the order in which each operation is to be done, and what is to be done with the output. This program is first written

493

out by hand or on a typewriter, then transferred to cards or tape so that it may be fed into the computer.

There are four basic considerations in the preparation of a program:

1. Defining the problem to be solved
2. Outlining each logical step required to reach the solution
3. Writing the program in machine or symbolic language
4. Translating the program into machine language, if the program has been written in symbolic language

Programs must be written in a language that the machine "understands." Each step is written out in a carefully prepared sequence. There are several languages used when preparing programs. One common language is called Common Business Oriented Language (COBOL) and another is called Formula Translation (FORTRAN). COBOL resembles English and may be used by different types of computers. It utilizes the numerals 0 through 9, the 26 letters of the alphabet, and a dozen or so special characters, such as the dollar sign, the asterisk, and parentheses.

Discussion Questions

5. *Why do digital computers use the binary number system?*
6. *Distinguish between computer software and hardware.*

BUSINESS APPLICATIONS OF DATA PROCESSING

Industry

As one example of how computers serve business management, consider the General Electric Appliance Park operation in Louisville, Kentucky. Here, in a single location, are grouped together what might have been built in several widely separated communities. In one large building, washing machines and dryers are manufactured; in another, electric refrigerators are produced; and in still another, stoves are made. And small appliances, such as disposal units, dehumidifiers, and mixers, are fabricated under their own roof, too. In fact, seven major operations are carried on, each in a separate building.

In one central office at the Park, there is a computing center, and smaller installations of electronic equipment are located in several of the other buildings. By having all these manufacturing operations located in close proximity, all may utilize the services of the computer center. With a small office crew operating the computers during the night, an up-to-date inventory can be ready for use by management the following morning. Here is dramatic proof of what we have already said: The speed of the computer makes possible the preparation of reports that otherwise would take so long to prepare that they would be of little or no value when finally ready.

As another example, REA Express has a data-processing operation called "Projex." It is an electronic computer system used to speed up receipting and accounting procedures. REA Express moves approximately 100 million pieces of freight a year. These shipments originate and terminate in their more than 8,000 offices located throughout the nation. Each office sends its receipting documents to a "feeder city"—a transmitting point in its area. This city transmits shipment data to designated central receiving stations. The receiving stations prepare machine-printed and -punched delivery cards and make them available to their "satellite" cities, pending arrival of the actual shipments. Thus each office is served by a transmitting city for outbound shipments, and by a receiving station for inbound traffic. The advantages to the public are lower costs resulting from increased efficiency, improved service, and a better utilization of the work force employed by the company.

Government

The Treasury Department provides us with another illustration. The National Computer Center in Martinsburg, West Virginia, the hub of the Internal Revenue Service automatic data-processing system, began computer processing of tax data from their Southeast Regional Service Center in Chamblee, Georgia, in 1961. The Chamblee center was the first of ten regional service centers established to convert individual and corporate income tax data to a magnetic tape format.

The Internal Revenue Service's vast Automatic Data Processing System at the National Computer Center in Martinsburg is in operation 24 hours a day, 7 days a week. The National Computer Center updates, maintains, and analyzes a centralized master file of more than 100 million accounts, one for every business and individual taxpayer in the country. The major data processing equipment utilized in this vast undertaking consists of five I.B.M. System 360 computer systems, one I.B.M. 1401 computer system, and two Stromberg-Datagraphix 4440 magnetic tape to microfilm converter systems. This equipment, and its operation, is supported by a permanent staff of 265 employees and a magnetic tape library of over 60,000 reels of tape.

Taxpayers file their returns with the ten Regional Service Centers where the information is transcribed from the returns and documents, validated, key verified, and converted to magnetic tape through a direct data entry system.

Magnetic tape output files from the service centers are used as input data to the National Computer Center where the information is applied against the master file to update taxpayer accounts. From this operation, tape files are generated which will be converted to microfilm and distributed to the service centers for use as research material; refund data on tape is sent to Treasury Disbursing Offices where refund checks are printed and mailed to taxpayers; and tape files of bills, notices, and mailing labels are forwarded to service centers to be printed and sent to taxpayers.

By having data on all taxpayers in the national master file at Martinsburg, IRS can easily check on their failure to file returns and can ascertain whether a taxpayer owes anything for a prior year before paying him a refund claimed on his current year's return. In cases where tax credit from prior years has been forgotten or overlooked, IRS can remind the taxpayer of his good fortune. It can also match information relative to wages, dividends, and interest on taxpayers' returns with information received from employers and financial institutions reporting to the Service. In fact, businesses can now file their tax returns on magnetic tape, provided they use tape that is compatible with IRS equipment. The IRS is already receiving millions of taped returns a year. Most of these are No. 1099 (dividend-payment) or W-2 (tax-withholding) report forms.

In addition to the Internal Revenue Service and the Bureau of the Census, nearly all areas of the federal government use electronic computers for data processing. The Defense Department is one of the largest users, having almost a thousand computers in use today.

Financial Institutions

The banking field is very greatly dependent upon data processing by computers. There are already 22 billion checks written and processed yearly in this country, and this figure should climb to 43 billion by 1980. These checks are sorted and cleared many times—first by the banks where they are originally deposited, then by one or more clearing houses, and finally by the banks where the persons who wrote the checks maintain their accounts.

To facilitate sorting, identification numbers are printed in magnetic ink in the lower left-hand corner of the checks. The large banks in this country and the Federal Reserve Banks now sort electronically the checks they handle.

In many a large city bank, branch banks are wired to a central computer for *"on-line processing."* Under this plan, deposits or withdrawals by customers are entered on the keyboard console in the branch bank. The branch is connected by leased telephone line with the computer in the home bank, where each customer's account information is stored in the memory unit of the computer. In seconds, the transaction performed at the branch is recorded in the main bank, and its results reported back to the branch bank.

But the real breakthrough is an approach to an almost completely cashless society. The financial institutions in this country are moving toward a nationwide electronic payment-transfer system. Utility bills and installment payments would be made automatically by the banks for their customers. An automated clearing system would shift funds from one bank to another without checks. Combined, the Master Charge card and the Bank Americard have more than 50 million card-carrying customers.

This nationwide payment-transfer system would include all types of financial institutions, not just banks. The stock exchanges are working on a scheme that would give stock purchasers a report of the number and type of certificates they own, rather than issuing individual stock certificates for each purchase.

Insurance Companies

Most insurance companies find the electronic computer ideal for keeping policyholder information up to date. Information regarding premium payments, loans against policies, cash reserves, and dividend payments can be made available at a moment's notice. The data-processing service has made this possible for even the small companies, through shared-time facilities. The mini-computer is also making it possible for the small company to handle its records electronically.

The loan departments of insurance companies have also found magnetic tape and the automatic typewriter helpful in the study of financial reports. When a business applies to an insurance company for a loan, it is asked to submit a copy of its financial report. If the loan application involves a large amount of money, the financial report is investigated thoroughly; and the report on the application may be updated many times. As new data are reported, the financial report is revised and reprinted—under the traditional method, the entire report had to be checked each time for accuracy in copying. By using magnetic tape that reproduces verbatim all the old data in the report, only the changes that are made need to be verified. Since the automatic typewriter prints copy from the tape, this saves time in two ways: The work is done at speeds much faster than that of the highest-skilled human typist, and the old data in the report need not be proofread for accuracy.

Other Uses

You are probably familiar with the way airlines agents check with the computers to see if space is available and to confirm prior reservations for specific flights.

The Strategic Air Command uses computers to keep track of all elements of its missiles and bombers. An airborne component is now being developed whereby computers in the sky can direct and redirect retargeting operations.

Assignments previously made to knocked-out areas can be reassigned to surviving stations.

Universities are using computers for scheduling and for student records, as well as for business and financial operations.

Large oil tankers use computers in their docking procedures. A 250,000-ton tanker is more than 1,000 feet in length, and it must approach a dock or jetty with great caution and at a very low speed. A computer installed aboard a ship improves safety in tanker operations in berthing, position fixing, and avoiding collision. Data fed in from radar and sonar equipment are processed by the computer and the results shown on a screen, giving the navigator an instantaneous and continuous report on the ship's position.

An example of a successful management-information system (MIS) exists at RCA's parts and accessories operation in Deptford, New Jersey. This operation is responsible for providing replacement parts for all the commercial equipment built and distributed by the other RCA divisions and for merchandising accessories for use with this equipment. These parts and accessories are distributed through the same channels as the parent equipment.

Orders for parts and accessories are received from over 8,000 customers, at the rate of over 300 orders per day. These orders average about 10 items each and are filled from an inventory of over 70,000 stock parts that represents an investment of approximately $10 million.

It was determined early in the planning stage that the MIS would be a decision-making system and not a reporting system. It was not designed to generate reports that would go to clerks or analysts for manual review in order for decisions to be made, because there were very few decisions made by these clerks and analysts that couldn't be programmed, no matter how complex, unique, or varied these decisions were.

The necessary logic for decision making is incorporated in the system, so that instead of an inventory-control analyst's determining from a report which items and what quantities are to be ordered, this type of work is now performed in the computer system. Decisions are reviewed by analysts on an exception basis, and from time to time, the computer's decisions are revised by a human being who is "on-line."

But basically, the routine decisions are being successfully made by the computer system. Reports were designed to include only those items that required specific action by someone. Comprehensive status listings and other reports of a detailed nature are also produced; however, these are intended for reference and audit-trial purposes only and are not distributed to operating personnel for routine day-to-day decision-making purposes. For example, a complete listing of all items on open order is distributed to the purchasing group. This listing is issued both in part-number sequence and in purchase-order-number sequence, and it is also grouped by specific buyer and vendor.

The flow chart on page 499 shows how information is fed into and through the system.

DATA FLOW IN ORDER PROCESSING

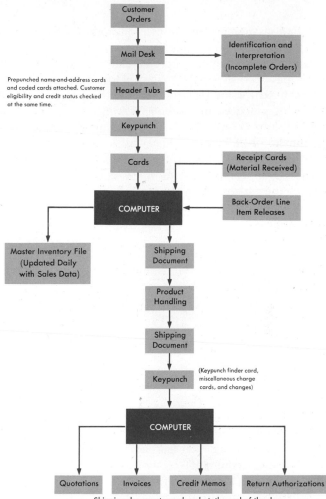

Prepunched name-and-address cards and coded cards attached. Customer eligibility and credit status checked at the same time.

Shipping documents produced at the end of the day reenter the system with additional data the next day.

Source: Reprinted from *Business Automation*, November 1967. © Business Press International, Inc.

Discussion Question

7. *Explain how some business with which you are familiar utilizes a computer in processing its records.*

DATA-PROCESSING SERVICE CENTERS

Although the recent trend in computers has been toward small units as well as huge systems, the development of the small unit has not led to as many installations in small businesses as one might imagine, largely because hundreds of thousands of businesses cannot afford to buy or lease even the cheaper computer equipment; it would actually be used very little, and thus might not even "pay its own way," as every worthwhile piece of equipment should. Out of the need for the part-time use of computers has developed *time sharing,* which, as practiced in *computer service centers,* enables several businesses to use the same computer. These service operations (or bureaus) have complete equipment installations and a full staff of specially trained personnel. In addition, they maintain a depository of hundreds of different types of programs—even complete data-processing accounting systems. Through these centers, the advantages of electronic data processing are available to businesses, educational institutions, and hospitals that cannot afford even limited computer installations. This aspect of data processing is expanding rapidly.

Discussion Question

8. *What do you see as being the key to the future success of the data-processing service center?*

THE ACCOUNTANT
AND DATA PROCESSING

In previous chapters, you learned about the work of accountants. Here let us consider the accountant's relationship to data processing. It is the accountant who determines the choice of data to be fed into the computer, who establishes an organizational pattern for that data, and who takes over where automation ends. Machines process basic data accurately and rapidly according to the program given them, but their tabulations must be interpreted by and for management. Machines calculate, but they do not think; and therefore they cannot replace the accountant–management relationship. A machine may show the amount a business has lost during a given period, but it cannot tell the causes of the loss. The machine's report may show that overhead is too high, but it will not tell how it should be reduced. Machines can calculate tax liabilities, but they cannot advise on legal ways to minimize them. The accountant is the interpreter of the machine's findings.

You will recall that one type of work accountants perform is setting up accounting systems. Systems analysis and design is an integral part of installing a computer program. An accounting system must be developed in terms of the firm's specific objectives and of the requirements that records management poses. The systems analyst must have a knowledge of accounting applications, of programming, and of the types of reports the equipment is capable of producing.

The transfer from a traditional basic accounting system to one based on the use of electronic computers is a gradual process, requiring a period of several months. Time is needed to plan the program and prepare key personnel to use it. But even then, as certain operations are put on tape for use on the computers, some types of records are continued for a period on traditional equipment. There are several reasons for this. Not all new equipment is added in a single stroke, and of course personnel cannot be properly trained to operate new pieces until they are installed. Also, exactly how many and which kinds of additional machines are needed depends to some degree on how equipment already purchased works out. It is a time of developing transition, called *conversion.*

The traditional accounting activities, such as accounts receivable, accounts payable, or payroll, are organized in a department separate and distinct from data processing. It is generally held that accounting is the *functional responsibility* of the financial system and that a computer system is essentially *method* rather than functional. In other words, the computer system is the method whereby the general ledger is brought up to date, the payroll is processed, and other special reports are produced for management. Computing services are not reserved solely for the accounting department, but are used for other functional areas as well, such as marketing, production, and financial analysis.

Since accounting is a functional responsibility, members of the accounting department need a working knowledge of the data-processing method used to process the financial information. They would need at least a basic knowledge of the computer system in order to supply the necessary input data to update the general ledger, and also to control the input data and interpret the output. A knowledge of data-processing methods, therefore, is very much a part of modern accounting.

COMPUTERS AID IN MANAGEMENT DECISIONS

Up to this point, our emphasis has been on the services that a data-processing system renders a business enterprise in a specific location. Now we shall see how and why large corporations utilize centralized computer systems to coordinate a wide (and widespread) variety of activities.

Prior to the introduction of electronic data processing to their business equipment, most large corporations were obliged to use the relatively unsophisticated telephone or telegraph leased-wire services to provide a complete communications network between and among their far-flung industrial plants and offices. Now, with an electronic data-processing system hooking them up, such traditional intracompany communications networks can be rung in as an integral part of a modern centralized computing center's operations. When production, sales, and financial data are all communicated into a company's home office, management has available up-to-the-minute information on which to base its decisions.

In addition to the vast assortment of general intracompany communications, the central telecomputer center often handles conventional inventory and payroll records. Then, too, there are customers' orders. Because the central computer's storage component always has the latest information on exactly how many units of every type of product are on hand in every warehouse, all orders, together with shipping instructions, can be sent immediately to the warehouse that is nearest the customer and that stocks the wanted items.

The cash analysis is an item of real interest and significance to management. Extremely large corporations have funds deposited in hundreds of different banks throughout the country. A centralized telecomputer system can, in a matter of minutes, make available to management a complete status report on the corporation's cash balance.

Sales records and customer billing may also be kept current. Under conventional records systems, there is a five- to ten-day delay in entering company records of sales, and in customer billing. The computing center provides instant information and makes possible simultaneous recording and customer billing. In addition, company management may have a daily report on total company sales, broken down by products, by regions, or in any other way that management would want such data.

Such data handling improves decision making at all levels. It frees divisional accounting managers from mountains of paperwork and enables them to function as true financial planners.

Discussion Question

9. *How do computers improve the decision-making process for management?*

CAREER OPPORTUNITIES

Job opportunities in data processing and records management are currently as promising as in any area of business. The classified-ad section of any metropolitan newspaper includes notices of such employment needs. There are positions open for people to operate various types of equipment, for programmers, and for systems analysts. In addition, there are opportunities for promotion to supervisory and management positions.

> The *data-processing manager* is responsible for the planning, coordinating, and direction of data-processing activities of the entire organization. He must supervise the work of others and should possess high managerial as well as technical skills.

The *manager of computer operations* directs the computer installation, plans the scheduling of computer time, allocates personnel, maintains the program library, and controls operations within the computer center.

The *tabulating supervisor* is responsible for the preparation and processing of punched cards in the unit-record section. He must supervise machine-room operations, including the design of punched-card systems, the allocation of machine time, and the assignment of operating personnel.

The *systems analyst* is responsible for creating an ordered system for data collection, processing, and the production of useful information. His objective is to improve controls and decision making, and at the same time make the most efficient use of available data-processing equipment. The largely abstract nature of his work, like that of the computer programmer, requires strong logical and creative abilities.

The *computer programmer* must work closely with the systems analyst to define the problem, analyze data and report requirements, prepare a detailed flow chart of the logical solution to the problem, convert this logical diagram to coded instructions understandable to the computer, and test the program to remove errors. Programmers must understand completely the business or scientific problem they are attempting to solve. They must be able to work with a team or alone and be able to communicate with management personnel. They must be sticklers for detail, be logical thinkers, and have no end of patience.

The *computer operator* is in command of the computer during a program run. He must load programs, prepare input data for entry, and be on hand to monitor error messages and keep the machines operating smoothly.

The *tabulating operator* works with unit record equipment, transferring the cards being processed and controlling the operation of various accounting machines.

Keypunch operators transcribe input data from the original documents to cards, using keypunch equipment. Keypunch supervisors schedule activities in the keypunch section and instruct operators on procedures for keypunch applications.

Actually, in data processing, a person's title does not delineate clearly just what his work is. One person with the title of programmer may spend most of his time writing out specific directions for the computer. Another person who is called a programmer may spend his time developing problems and even doing systems design.

Accounting firms are now installing computer equipment and offering programs and information-system services to their clients. All the types of positions discussed above would exist here, as well as with businesses that have their own installations.

Educational Qualifications

People who wish to enter data-processing positions should prepare themselves broadly in the area of business administration, including the study of courses in business management. They would do well to pursue accounting and statistics to some depth. They should be competent in their ability to rationalize, and to see and understand mathematical relationships. The field of information management is one of the more promising areas for young educated people who plan to make a career in business management. In preparation, courses in records management and computer systems are essential.

SUMMARY

The ever-increasing load of records work has made machine processing of information a necessity. The use of computers for handling a wide variety of types of business information is quite commonplace—payroll functions, inventory records, accounts receivable, communication, manufacturing design, and control. The computer has made available to management up-to-the-minute information that was not previously possible.

The basic elements of information handling, or data processing, are coding, computing, communicating, recording, sorting, storing, and summarizing. In addition to speeding information handling, electronic data processing is more accurate than the work done by human beings, and it eliminates considerable duplication of effort in records management.

The digital computer works solely with numbers and employs the binary number system. It consists of the input unit that feeds data into the system, the memory or storage unit, the calculator, the control panel, and the output unit.

Almost every aspect of modern business operation—finance, manufacturing, and selling, as well as government—utilizes electronic computer services. Businesses that are too small to have their own installations may contract with data-processing centers for selected computer services. A variety of programs and systems is available at these centers.

Career positions are available for college-educated men and women who have the right preparation, interest, and competencies. The top position would be that of the office manager. To qualify for this position, one would of course need practical experience in addition to his college preparation.

VOCABULARY REVIEW

Match the following terms with the statements below.

a. Address
b. Binary system
c. Coding
d. Computation
e. Computer
f. Conversion
g. Data processing
h. Digital computer
i. Hardware
j. Optical scanner
k. Processor
l. Program
m. System

1. A related series of items, with interrelationships organized into a discernible pattern
2. The process of working with or handling information
3. Working with different number calculations
4. Assigning identification or classification numbers to goods or accounts
5. A very high speed electronic calculator that utilizes the input, processor, and output units as its basic components
6. A computer that works only with numbers
7. An arithmetic system that employs only two digits, zero and 1
8. The various types of machines that make up the computer center
9. A machine that reads input characters and translates them into electrical impulses
10. A specific location within the storage unit
11. The part of a computer that performs the arithmetic computations
12. A set of coded instructions that tells a computer what to do
13. A transition period during which a business is changing from one records system to another

PROBLEMS AND PROJECTS

1. Assuming that a computer is available for use, describe the types of information one would need in order to maintain a perpetual inventory of electrical appliances on hand in a wholesale warehouse where appliances are continually being received and shipped.
2. Suppose that the home office of the electric utility that serves your community wished to calculate and print its bimonthly statements to its customers by using a computer. What data would the computer need to use, and what would be the sources of that data?
3. Examine the numbers encoded in magnetic ink in the lower left-hand corner of a bank check form. What are the numbers written there and what do they represent? Why is it important that these numbers appear in the same place on all checks?

A BUSINESS CASE

Case 18-1   Shipping Schedules and Routes

W	Warehouse
F	Factory

F^1	Detroit	W^1	Boston
F^2	New York	W^2	Baltimore
F^3	Charleston	W^3	Jacksonville
F^4	Louisville	W^4	Atlanta
F^5	Fort Worth	W^5	Kansas City
		W^6	Chicago

The Acme Stove Manufacturing Company has factories and warehouses at the various locations in the eastern part of the United States as shown above. The capacity of each plant varies, as do the demands from the different warehouses. The company manager responsible for scheduling and routing shipments from factory to warehouse and from warehouse to customers has access to a company computer on a shared-time basis. His problem is that of moving the finished products at the lowest transportation cost, without letting them accumulate at the factory and without depleting the supply at any of the warehouses.

What are the information factors that must be programmed into the computer in order that he can know when to ship to or from the respective warehouses?

PART SIX

marketing functions

our marketing system

CHAPTER NINETEEN

As they do with the production of goods, consumers tend to accept as commonplace the finished product that is delivered to their doors. Seldom do they ask questions about the kinds of activities that make it possible for them to choose from among several makes and styles of merchandise immediately available. Yet on every trip to the shopping center, one can observe trucks, large and small, moving finished goods from producers to consumers. This exchange of goods and services, including the physical movement of goods, is the heart of the marketing process.

The underlying reason for this mass movement of merchandise lies in the geographical specialization of production that we discussed in an earlier chapter. Specific types of crops are grown where the climate is best suited to them. Iron and steel are processed in those areas where this can be done most advantageously and economically. Ceramics are produced where high-grade clays are found. But the consumers who want certain types of goods may be located hundreds of miles from where those goods are made. So it becomes important to move goods, regardless of where they are manufactured, to those persons who desire to purchase them, regardless of where they are located. This general movement or distribution of goods is called *marketing*.

The term *market* is used to refer to several different things; sometimes its scope is quite narrow, and at other times it includes a wide range of activities. For example, some cities have what is generally referred to as "the farmers' market," a trading place where all types of fresh fruits and vegetables are sold. The Chicago "livestock market" refers to both the stockyards, the nation's largest marketplace of its kind, and the sales that take place there daily. Sometimes we say that the "automobile market" is picking up or that the "cattle market" is down, meaning that customer demand is strong or weak. The term "stock market" is used to refer to the sale of corporation stock on the stock exchanges. To the economist, the market for a specific economic good (or service) is *the sum of all exchange transactions between buyers and sellers of that good at any designated time. And therefore, to constitute a market there must be a buyer and a seller, a commodity or service, an exchange, and an agreed-upon price.*

In this chapter we shall study the nature and scope of marketing, the role of management in marketing, the basic types of goods distributed, the "value added" concept in marketing, and the functions of marketing. In succeeding chapters, we shall take a closer look at some specific aspects of marketing.

Courtesy Board of Trade, City of Chicago

Trading on the floor of the Chicago Board of Trade

THE NATURE AND ROLE
OF MARKETING

The first thing one observes about marketing is motion or movement. The whole marketing process is concerned with the flow of goods from farms, forests, and mines to mills and factories, and from there to the different marketing establishments—warehouses, wholesalers, and retail stores. To bring about this movement, goods must be bought and sold—their ownership transferred from one group of persons to another. This continual movement of goods and services (the marketing system) is an integral subsystem of the overall economic system that is concerned with meeting people's needs and wants.

A committee of the American Marketing Association defined marketing as *the performance of business activities that direct the flow of goods and services from producer to consumer or user.* This includes all the activities concerned with the processing, sale, and physical distribution of goods that take place after they are manufactured (or harvested, or mined) until they are delivered to their ultimate users. It includes marketing research, transportation, product packaging, and also the use of advertising and credit as means of influencing consumer patronage.

The mere building of a good product is not in itself the formula for success, because the product must be marketed to consumers before its complete value can be determined. Actually, the marketing function begins before goods ever enter the manufacturing process. The emphasis in marketing today is no longer centered on *things;* rather, it is largely concerned with *people.* A business that is truly marketing-minded concentrates on creating goods of value that satisfy potential patrons' needs. So we shall define marketing for the purpose of our discussion as *the system of interrelated business activities that pertain to designing, promoting, pricing, and distributing goods and services to potential users.*

This definition presents marketing as a comprehensive term, which encompasses merchandising, promotion, selling, and transportation. It emphasizes the management function of marketing, and the concept that the whole scheme of business activities should be customer-oriented. It presents marketing as a coordinated and integrated function rather than one of fragmentation.

Discussion Questions

1. *Based on what you have read thus far and your personal observations and experience, how would you define the term* marketing?
2. *How broad is the scope of marketing—what does it include?*

THE ECONOMIC IMPORTANCE
OF MARKETING

Marketing as a system is a twentieth-century development. During the nineteenth century, marketing was actually a by-product of production. Much of the goods manufactured were made to order, so that marketing consisted of little more than delivering the goods produced. But as manufacturing output increased, there was an accompanying shift from made-to-order manufacture to production in anticipation of orders. As output increased, the market for these goods had to be expanded beyond what could be absorbed in the local and nearby communities. During the agrarian period in the United States, the quantity of manufactured goods usually met, but seldom exceeded, the demand for them.

But early in the twentieth century, it became apparent that marketing was becoming an increasingly important mechanism for moving goods from areas of surplus to areas of scarcity. By the early 1930's, the quantity of manufactured goods being produced exceeded the demand for them. Mass production techniques were forcing the development of mass marketing procedures. Today the basic needs of most consumers have been satisfied. Improved agricultural methods have produced surpluses of nearly every type of farm product. The economy of abundance has made necessary a marketing system that motivates consumers to become buyers. Furthermore, the employment of large numbers of persons is being shifted from the production of goods to the provision of services. However, the basic concept of marketing still holds. Whether it be goods or services, marketing is concerned with making them available to persons who want them, in those places where they are needed, at a time when they are desired.

To move the mountains of goods that make up our gross national product to the persons who want them requires the services of between one-fourth and one-third of the employed civilian labor force. This includes all employees in wholesaling, retailing, warehousing, and transportation.

Creating Time and Place Utility

Economists use the term *utility* to denote the idea of meeting people's needs and wants. The movement of goods from a place of abundance to a place where they are needed creates *place utility*. Moving them at the time they are needed or storing them until such time creates *time utility*. These are essential services, for they play an important role in satisfying human needs at the time and place they are wanted.

The Value-Added Concept

On the average, about one-half the final sales price of an article goes to pay for the assorted marketing services required to get a finished good to the consumer at the right time and in the right place. This was once referred to as the *cost of marketing*. But the word *cost* gives it a negative connotation. The current idea is to consider this the *value added* to the good by the performance of marketing services. Just as raw materials are enhanced in value by processing them, a finished product has little value until it is in the possession of the person who can use it. The money spent in marketing goods adds to the value of those goods. The value-added concept is a more realistic way to measure the cost of marketing than the use of only such factors as advertising, transportation, and other direct selling costs.

Sometimes, what seems to be an increase in distribution costs is really the result of including a broader classification of business expenses as part of marketing costs. Consumers today are asking for various kinds of services that add to the cost of distribution. Housewives seem to prefer small packages that will fit into the refrigerator rather than large containers. Nonreturnable containers add to the cost of marketing packaged goods. Consumers demand many more assortments and styles of items from which they may make their choices. As long as consumers demand these special considerations, it is not likely that manufacturers can cut marketing costs materially.

Discussion Questions

3. *What is the greatest contribution marketing makes to the overall economic system?*
4. *What do we mean by* place utility *and* time utility?
5. *Do you accept the cost-of-marketing or the value-added concept? Why?*

MANAGEMENT'S ROLE IN MARKETING

The thing that makes a marketing program successful is what has been termed the proper "marketing mix." By *marketing mix* we mean a combination of four basic elements: the product, the channels of distribution, the pricing policies and practices, and the methods used in promotion. A company may manufacture a single line of products or several lines. Its products may be packaged singly or in groups; by brand or unbranded. They may be distributed through wholesalers only, through jobbers, directly to retailers, or by a combination of methods. It is management's responsibility to see that all these variables are combined in the right marketing mix.

In a previous chapter we learned that management is a distinct and separate skill, not to be confused with technical operating skills. It was also pointed out in earlier chapters that management is involved with setting objectives, organizing, planning, coordinating, staffing, directing, analyzing, making decisions, and evaluating. The term *marketing management* refers to the carrying out of these management functions through marketing processes. The ways that they are performed vary from company to company.

As an example of how one company administers its marketing management program, let us consider the brand-management practices of Procter & Gamble. This firm manufactures a wide range of consumer products, many of which are familiar to you—Ivory soap, Tide detergent, Crest toothpaste, Folger coffee, and Duncan Hines mixes, to name only a few. Each marketing manager at Procter & Gamble is responsible for his own brand (company product). In many ways, P&G brand managers enjoy much the same freedom in decision making and in administration as they would if they were in business for themselves. They set marketing goals and formulate marketing budgets. They develop the strategies to be used in achieving these goals. They stimulate and coordinate the total marketing package that supports their respective products. Of course, they are free to draw upon the competencies of company personnel in the areas of copy editing, television programming, and other specialities. However, they have the task of synthesizing all the marketing efforts (pertaining to their respective brands) that are focused on stimulating and satisfying the consumers' wants.

Planning and operating decisions applied to marketing must be in line with the goals set by general management. For example, if the goal is to saturate a mass market in order to achieve broad coverage, a predetermined policy must be set by management as to how much money is to be spent and what media of advertising are to be used. The decision to market only through department stores requires a different policy approach from that of utilizing all types of retail outlets.

Marketing-Management Organization

In a small company, the marketing department would be relatively small, with those in responsible positions handling a wide variety of duties. But in a company with a large marketing department, there would be a number of specialists—in research, planning, advertising, selling services, brand management, and so forth. Under this system, the department personnel would probably be classified into three groups: marketing services, personal selling, and product management. The chart illustrates how these three groups would be organized to serve under the chief marketing manager.

The marketing-services personnel would largely have staff responsibilities. Those working under the direction of the general sales manager would probably follow a line-organization pattern, while those under the products manager would have both line and staff responsibilities. They would most likely be in charge of a particular product or brand line.

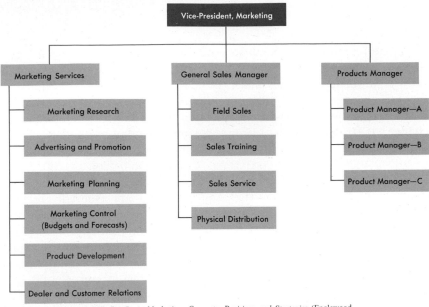

Source: Cundiff, E., and Still, R., *Basic Marketing: Concepts, Decisions and Strategies* (Englewood Cliffs, N.J.: Prentice-Hall, Inc., 1971).

Discussion Questions

6. *What is meant by the term* marketing mix?
7. *Why are persons whose responsibilities are in marketing services considered to be in a staff relationship?*

Marketing Decision Making

Management's basic marketing decisions are influenced by two groups of forces. One group can be determined and somewhat controlled within the business; however, the second group is outside the business and therefore beyond the control of management. These factors are summarized below.

Controllable Forces	Outside Forces
Advertising programs	Competition from other businesses
Distribution channels	
Brands management	Economic developments
Internal organization	Government directives
Pricing	Local legal regulations
Product development patterns	Sociological forces
Shipping media	Technological innovations

The forces beyond the control of management constitute the economic or business environment within which a business must operate. Management must manipulate the forces that may be controlled within the framework of this business environment. For example, the manager may choose the means of transportation to be used from among those available to him, but he cannot change the structure of the distribution system serving his market. His choice of marketing channels is limited by the number and variety of types of middlemen available.

Within his own company, the marketing manager can exercise some influence over production models and costs that are especially relevant to pricing decisions, but he does not have direct control over them. This means that his marketing decisions must be correlated with decisions made in other departments of his company. A dynamic manager will continually adjust the controllable factors in marketing to the shifts that occur among the uncontrollable forces that make up his business environment and climate.

Production–Marketing Interlock

Marketing is very definitely interlocked with production and product development. A business can market a product only after it has been produced, and there is no point in producing a good that cannot be marketed.

Although a business must produce goods for "the market," few companies produce goods that exactly match market demand, largely because individual customers have specific needs. Yet most companies must standardize in their production in order to effect the economies that come from mass production. Thus the management decision is usually one of producing goods that fall somewhere between the specific preferences of individual customers and what can be produced at a low unit cost. In other words, the idea is to design products that will be acceptable to as many customers as possible, but at the same time to sacrifice as little as possible the economies that accrue from volume production.

Marketing research must furnish the production department with data relative to the qualities and characteristics desired by the various groups of customers and prospective customers. Potential markets must be determined and developed. Ideas for new products may come either from within the company or from outside, but in both instances market research furnishes needed market information. Actually, company management works at both ends of the problem—goods are produced for which there appears to be a ready market, and markets are sought and/or created for promising goods developed through production research. The forces over which management has control—advertising, pricing, personal selling, and so on—are manipulated to hold and enlarge markets for established products and to gain markets for both established and newly developed goods.

The two subsystems of production and marketing are so interlocked that the efficiency of either one is strongly dependent on the other.

PRODUCT PLANNING AND DEVELOPMENT

Consumers tend to become more and more selective in their choice of products. New products are constantly appearing on the market and advertising is designed to urge the consumers to buy them. As the disposable income (income after taxes) has increased in recent years, the demand for variety in new goods has also increased.

Meaning of "The Product"

Today a consumer is buying more than just a product; actually, he is buying want satisfaction. As Elmer Wheeler, a well-known sales consultant, once advised salesmen, "Don't sell the steak, sell the sizzle." Any product represents a variety of attributes that the consumer wants—including style, design, utility, color, size, prestige, and service. For example, a Cadillac provides different attributes of an automobile from those of a Pinto. Because of these differences in attributes, we have different products. Mennen's shave cream, Rise, became three products when the company created Rise with lanolin and Rise with menthol, in addition to regular Rise. Thus, any different combination of attributes can create a different product. An article that cannot satisfy the maximum number of consumer wants is not likely to be as popular as another that can.

Scope of Planning

What happens when management attempts to engage in product planning and product development in terms of the decision-making process? The scope of product planning and development entails the following:

1. Which product is to be produced?
2. What attributes will this product provide?
3. How does it differ from competing products?
4. What product size will satisfy the most customers?
5. Is the proposed quality right for the market to be served?
6. How should the product be priced in relation to other, similar products?
7. What new uses can this product offer?

Whether a company is developing a new product or redesigning an old one, the development process must be preplanned, so that the company will not be left behind either by its competitors or by changes in consumers' fancies. Some companies have special departments for this work, while others carry it through as a part of the marketing function.

Stages in Planning

There are eight stages in product planning. Although they normally follow one another, some steps may be performed simultaneously.

1. The first step is a *market forecast* to estimate the size and type of product to introduce.
2. The basic *market study* attempts to make an assessment of consumers' needs. This tends to establish the overall market potential for the product itself, not specifically for the product of a particular company.
3. The *product concept* is concerned with the specific qualities of the product. This is vital to the overall product development and must be kept in constant review during all remaining stages.
4. The *product objective* sets out the product's dimensions as to sizes, colors, prices, and quantities.
5. This is followed by an *evaluation* or feasibility study, which is done by the engineering staff. It answers the question of whether the product will perform the functions planned for it.
6. *Consumer reaction* is needed at this point, in order to prevent the waste that would result from proceeding too far in the wrong direction. This is a preliminary sounding of consumer acceptance.
7. *Models* or prototypes are then tested in a limited market.
8. *Tooling up* for production is the final stage. At the time this is done, consumer testing is continued on a broadened scale. Attempts are made at this time also to perfect the product, eliminating all possible defects before full-scale marketing begins.

Discussion Question

8. *How does product development relate to the marketing function?*

THE FUNCTIONS OF MARKETING

One of the best ways to develop an understanding of how goods are marketed in our modern economy is to examine the functions that are performed as goods move from producer to consumer. These functions may be listed as follows: *buying, selling, transporting, storing, risk bearing, standardizing, grading, pricing, financing,* and *market information.*

Each of these functions is essential to the success of the overall marketing activity. To illustrate: The marketing of the shoes you are wearing began the moment they were completed at the factory. First they had to be stored at the factory and then in the retail store where you bought them. Sales efforts were expended by the manufacturer, the wholesaler, and the retailer through whose hands they passed. The retailer spent time and money selecting his stock of shoes; they had to be shipped to him; someone had to assure that they conformed to certain standards of size and color. The wholesaler extended credit to the retailer, thus assisting him to finance his business. And at every step along the way, efforts were made to keep abreast of information on the leather market and on fashion trends.

Buying

For the consumer who walks into a retail store, the buying function is usually a simple enough matter, but in a business concern it involves several distinct activities. First the buyer must determine his needs, based on his knowledge of the preferences of customers. Customer taste in one locality may differ greatly from that in other communities, and the buyer must be able to predict whether the goods he chooses to sell in any particular area will appeal to the tastes of his customers there. Such prediction is a fine art that demands extensive experience and is one of the key functions in successful buying at the retail level.

After the buyer determines what his customers' wants are likely to be, he must select his sources of supply. A buyer normally deals with the representatives of dozens of different companies; he must decide which one or ones will give him the best terms—quality merchandise at reasonable prices. This is true whether he represents a wholesale or a retail business enterprise.

The third phase of the buyer's task is negotiating with the suppliers for the delivery of the merchandise. Generally, these negotiations are most successful when detailed specifications can be given, helping to assure that exacting quality standards will be met. Purchase-order and delivery schedules must be arranged and clearly understood by both parties engaged in the negotiation procedures. Through all this, the buyer is constantly concerned with maintaining the correct inventory balance within the minimum and maximum limits necessary to keep business going.

Selling

Selling is the very heart of the marketing function. It includes locating customers whose wants can be satisfied by the kinds and quantities of goods that are being sold. A significant aspect of selling is promotion. Advertising, window displays, sales demonstrations, special prices for limited periods of time, trade movies, trade exhibits, and samples are all important aspects of promotion. The selling of industrial goods differs somewhat from that of consumer products, just as the selling efforts at the wholesale level differ from those of retailers. (The discussion in Chapter 20 discusses in considerable detail the various channels of marketing.)

Transporting

Transportation of goods is essential in any marketing activity. Of primary concern to both buyer and seller are the speed and cost of this service. Although cost is usually the determining consideration in choosing the method of transportation, speed and special services (such as refrigeration) determine the method of shipment of certain goods—perishable commodities, for example.

A highly developed system of transportation enables us to benefit from large-scale operations and regional specialization. Thus we are able to produce goods here and there, according to where the most favorable conditions are, and yet make them available in all parts of the nation. Improvements in transportation service also broaden the market for goods. For example, the inauguration of air freight extended the market for California strawberries to many distant parts of the United States.

Storing

Adequate storage is essential to marketing because of the lag between the production and the ultimate consumption of a product. In certain marketing situations, it is necessary to store reserve supplies of goods that are produced seasonally but consumed regularly throughout the year. In other situations, it is necessary to store goods that are produced regularly but are consumed irregularly from one season to another.

Clearly, the physical location of storage facilities is of paramount importance in the successful performance of this function. Reservoirs of consumer goods must be maintained and made readily accessible in the vicinity of retail outlets, since the retailer can profitably store only enough goods to supply the needs of his customers for a relatively short period of time. Instead of using his valuable display space as a storage area, the retailer insists that goods be kept on hand in the wholesale house, the chain-store warehouse, the manufacturer's branch warehouse, or a public warehouse.

The storage of agricultural products requires an especially complex set of facilities, organized in an elaborate geographical pattern. In the producing areas, for example, middlemen must operate extensive storage facilities to care for the commodities they purchase from farmers. Then the commodities must be transported and stored in tremendous elevators and warehouses located in or near the large centers where the commodity is widely traded. Other storage facilities must be available in areas where commodities are processed, and at seaports and railroad terminals where they await shipment to their destinations.

Risk Bearing

The ownership of valuable stocks of industrial or consumer goods carries with it a heavy burden of risk, for the major portion of the capital at the command of most marketing firms is tied up in their physical inventories. Fire, storms, and theft are common types of risk that may be covered by insurance, but other risks cannot be guarded against by this means. Sudden shifts in styles of dress, for example, may result in severe losses to dealers in fashion goods. The only way this risk can be reduced is through careful market analysis. Also, every marketer is faced with the possibility that price levels may decline sharply, leaving him with a warehouse full of goods on which he must take a loss. Careful control of inventory is the usual way of minimizing this risk, but even that will not eliminate the danger entirely.

Controlling the costs of bearing these risks is a test of the skill of the marketer. The cost of risk bearing varies widely with the type of goods handled, but some loss is inescapable in almost every business that distributes goods.

Standardizing

Standards must be firmly established before merchandise can be accurately catalogued and described in a way that is meaningful to the buyers and sellers of goods. A *standard* is a constant physical characteristic that gives uniformity to a group of products. For example, when a plumber orders a length of ¾-inch pipe and the fittings necessary to use it in an installation, he has no doubt that all the critical measurements will be uniform. Because electric light bulbs are standardized, we have no hesitancy in ordering by telephone a quantity of 60-watt bulbs. Manufacturers observe an industry-wide standard in designing the bases of bulbs, making it possible for us to screw any ordinary bulb into virtually any light socket. Moreover, when you see a bulb labeled "60-watt," you know without experiment just how much light you can expect to get from it.

During the early days of trading, when the "let the buyer beware" attitude was accepted by buyer and seller alike, there was little need for standardization. Buyers inspected the merchandise and made their own selections, and descriptions were unimportant. But now, when the buyer and seller are often far apart, sales transactions must be based on mutually accepted standards. Life would be primitive indeed if goods were not standardized.

Grading

Grading is another process that improves marketing efficiency. This is the process of sorting goods into a number of classes, or grades, according to quality. The term is most commonly applied to agricultural products, such as grain, fruits, eggs, and meat. For each grade of a commodity, certain specifications have been established, usually by federal agencies. The Agricultural Marketing Service of the Department of Agriculture has developed standards of quality for approximately 100 commodities.

In most cases, grading eliminates the necessity of inspecting the product at the time of sale. Thousands of bushels of grain are sold daily, completely on the basis of grade. Trading in the futures market would be impossible were it not for a universally accepted system of graded products. Furthermore, grading improves marketing efficiency by channeling different qualities of goods to the markets best suited to them. Only grade-A eggs can be sold successfully in certain stores, while lower grades may be quite satisfactory for processing as powdered eggs. The cost of grading is negligible compared with the economies and improvements it makes possible.

Pricing

The degree of freedom that a seller has in setting prices varies according to several factors. To begin with, the cost of the product sets the absolute floor for pricing. But one tries to sell for more, of course, because a sale at cost price results in a loss of sorts, since that sale does not bear its proportionate share of the overhead expenses. There was a time when one could charge whatever the traffic would bear, but this is hardly possible any more. Actually, the price ceiling varies according to the keenness of the competition. In some industries, a few giant businesses may try to set pricing patterns and force the smaller companies to "follow the leader" in raising or lowering their prices. But government pressure is often exerted in these cases to prevent pricing practices that will lead to monopoly or increase inflation. In the absense of competition and where government pressure is not required, consumer demand limits the price

Financing

Regardless of the sales policy (cash or credit) followed by the retailer, someone must finance the marketing function. Because large sums of capital are required to provide marketing services and maintain an adequate inventory of goods in stock, credit frequently has to be extended all along the marketing line: by the retailer, by his wholesaler, and even by the manufacturer. If credit were suddenly discontinued, the economic system would suffer dire effects.

Retailers are usually engaged in keen competition with one another in their attempts to offer credit terms attractive to customers. Now, a liberal credit policy, although a powerful force in attracting customers, also increases materially the capital requirements of the business. Nevertheless, a variety of credit plans are offered by retailers today. Many offer credit either on a 30-day payment basis or by means of a "revolving" plan of payment. Under the latter plan, the customer makes regular monthly payments of a previously agreed-on amount, and may make additional purchases as long as the account does not exceed an agreed-on maximum balance. Retailers also offer the installment plan of credit, which is evidenced by a conditional sales contract with payments extending over a period of several months.

Discussion Question

9. *Describe five important marketing functions.*

COMMODITY-EXCHANGE MARKETS

One of the important marketing agencies within our total economic system is the *commodity exchange*. This may be defined as an organization or association of individuals that provides a place for its members to buy and sell commodities both for themselves and for nonmembers. Commodity exchanges do not actually exchange commodities per se; instead, all transactions are made "on the floor" by persons who have a membership in the association similar to membership in a stock-market exchange. Many commodities are traded in these markets, including raw materials like rubber, hides, silver, tin, and copper; such grains as wheat, barley, and oats; cotton, soybeans, sugar, and potatoes; and certain frozen foods.

There are over 40 such exchanges in the United States. On 15 of these, "futures trading" is conducted in about 30 commodities under regulations set by the Grain Futures Act of 1922 and the Commodity Exchange Act of 1936. The Chicago Board of Trade has the largest volume of trade in grains. In New York and New Orleans, there are exchanges specializing in cotton.

Types of Trading

The dealing in grain that occurs on the larger exchanges is of two types: cash (or spot) and futures. *Spot transactions* are purchases or sales of commodities in specific amounts, requiring immediate delivery of the commodity and payment in cash. The seller either owns, or has the assurance of being able to deliver, the commodity. *Future transactions* are purchases or sales that call for future delivery, contingent upon the payment of presently agreed-upon prices. The futures market provides insurance to warehousemen, millers, and farmers against loss due to price fluctuations in the future.

A typical futures transaction may be as follows: In March, a commodity speculator named Hensen decides that May wheat is low, so he had his broker buy 5,000 bushels (a unit of trading) of May futures at $2.06 a bushel. Hensen is taking a "long" position in making this purchase. He does not expect delivery, however. If he had ordered his broker to sell 5,000 bushels of May wheat, this would have been a "short" sale. (You will recall the explanation of selling short in Chapter 13's discussion of the stock market.) In April, the price of May wheat reaches $2.12 a bushel. So Hensen decides to take his profit by selling his 5,000 bushels of futures-contract wheat. The first transaction offsets the second, and the $300 difference becomes his gross profit, from which he must pay his broker his commission.

Commodity Specification and Prices

The commodity exchange specifies the unit of trading for purchases and sales. Most grain transactions are in multiples of 5,000 bushels, known as a "round lot," similar to the stock-exchange round lot of 100 shares. A "job lot" consists of 1,000 bushels, or multiples thereof, for all grains except oats, the lot for which is 2,000 bushels.

The exchange also designates certain months to identify futures prices contracts. For wheat, corn, oats, and rye, these months are September, December, March, May, and July. It is interesting to know why these months were selected. December represents the end of the harvest period and the beginning of winter storage (navigation is closed on the Great Lakes). March is the time when many southern-hemisphere crops come on the market in volume. May is the "clean-up" month prior to the harvesting of small grains, and the month when the Great Lakes are again fully navigable. July is the time of heavy movement of winter wheat and some oats, barley, and rye to the markets. September is the month when new spring wheat begins to come to the market.

The spot price of wheat is affected both by consumption demand and by supply from marketing channels or from storage. If the current demand increases, the spot price generally rises. This has a tendency to induce storers of wheat to sell more to consumption channels.

The difference between spot and futures prices for grains is called the *basis,* a term widely used by the trade in quoting prices. Much of the trading by grain speculators is done in the belief that the basis will either widen or become narrower in the future, and a transaction is made to take advantage of the direction the basis seems to be taking. The difference between the spot price and the futures commodity-trading price is the *spread,* which is often less than the average of storage costs. It is important to note that futures and spot prices, over a short period, tend to move up and down together by more or less the same amount.

Under normal conditions, the futures price tends to exceed the spot price at any given time by the average of storage costs for the commodity from that time to the delivery date of the futures. It is through this process of pricing that it becomes possible to shift the risk of loss (on commodity manufacturing or processing) to the professional speculator who deals in futures contracts.

Discussion Question

10. *What purpose does trading in "futures transactions" serve?*

REGULATION OF MARKETING PRACTICES

Pricing and labeling practices in marketing have been of concern to the federal and state governments for many years. Legislation at both levels of government is aimed at preserving competition in marketing and providing protection for consumers.

The Robinson-Patman Act

The Robinson-Patman Act was passed in 1936 as an amendment to the Clayton Act, for the purpose of prohibiting certain types of price discrimination in selling. It prohibits price discrimination between different purchasers of goods of like quality if such discrimination would lessen competition with either the person (or company) who grants or the one who receives the benefits of such discrimination. The act includes an interesting provision—the buyer, as well as the seller, is guilty if he *knowingly* accepts an unlawful discrimination.

However, the act did legalize price differences resulting from attempts to meet competitors' prices, and differences resulting from fluctuating market prices or the threatened obsolescence of a perishable product.

The Miller-Tydings Act

The Miller-Tydings resale Price Maintenance Act was passed in 1937 to amend the Sherman Antitrust Act of 1890. Prior to the Miller-Tydings Act, vertical price agreements between a manufacturer and a middleman were illegal in interstate commerce. The Miller-Tydings Act made it lawful for a manufacturer to make vertical price agreements with resellers in those states that had such laws.

Although the act, as well as various state "fair-trade" acts passed later, applies only to trademarked or branded goods, it still covers a wide variety of merchandise. The Miller-Tydings Act actually changed public policy on resale price agreements, from an attitude of opposition to the government view to one of complete support of it.

One of the most controversial features of the Miller-Tydings Act was a provision permitting a manufacturer of brand-name products to enter into contracts with retailers in a given state; the retailers would agree not to sell the products below the list price set by the manufacturer. Furthermore, such a contract would be binding on all sellers in that state, whether they signed a contract or not. In 1951, however, the Supreme Court declared that part of the law affecting nonsigners to be unconstitutional. Other parts of the Miller-Tydings Act still remain in force.

The McGuire Act

No sooner had this Supreme Court decision been announced than manufacturers and retail associations again put pressure on legislators to pass a new price-maintenance law that would cover nonsigners of these agreements. So Congress enacted the McGuire Fair-Trade Act of 1952, which specifically declared that fair-trading under the nonsigner agreement was not illegal provided it was approved by the state legislatures concerned.

But the controversy was not over. Many state legislatures made nonsigner arrangements legal, and immediately several state courts declared these clauses unconstitutional. Fair-trade laws incorporating nonsigner clauses are now in effect in about three-fourths of the states.

Many large retail outlets, like Macy's and Gimbels in New York, have challenged fair-trade legislation on the grounds that such laws, both state and federal, restrain competition and open the door to monopolistic activity. Trade associations can use these laws as legal authority for collective action by going through the motions of making a "cost survey" and then establishing a minimum retail price below which competitors are forbidden to sell.

Effects of Fair-Trade Laws

The items most commonly subject to *fair-trade price agreements* are food, drugs, tobacco products, soaps, photographic supplies, and electrical appliances. From the consumer's viewpoint, fair-trade laws prohibit retailers from cutting prices on popular brand-name goods. Some merchants, in an effort to free themselves from price controls, have resorted to promoting private-label brands (brands sold by only one firm) as substitutes for the much better known, nationally advertised articles on which there is some kind of price control.

Manufacturers complain that they cannot police all retailers to make sure that set prices are being maintained. Furthermore, neither the Department of Justice nor the Federal Trade Commission has the necessary personnel or the funds to detect and prosecute violators. And state agencies are reluctant to take action against large companies about which complaints have been received. Faced with the futility of trying to maintain price agreements on a national scale, a growing number of manufacturers have abandoned price agreements on many lines of merchandise.

Laws Regulating Labeling Practices

In the interest of public welfare, the federal government has enacted laws to protect consumers from those who would sell inferior goods not appropriately marked.

The Pure Food and Drug Act. The Pure Food and Drug Act of 1906 considers an article "misbranded" if its labeling is false or misleading. The term *labeling* includes both written and printed matter that appears on the article or the container. In 1938, the Copeland Act amended the Pure Food and Drug Act by requiring that the Commissioner of Food and Drugs approve all new drugs before they are marketed. The Copeland Act also prohibits the interstate shipment of misbranded or adulterated foods, drugs, cosmetics, and therapeutic devices. The penalty for violating this law is a fine of up to $1,000, or imprisonment for one year, or both. More serious violations involve a fine of $10,000 and imprisonment for three years.

The Wool Products Labeling Act. Food, drugs, and cosmetics are not the only items whose quality is subject to federal regulations. Consumers are protected against the misbranding of woolen fabrics by the Wool Products Labeling Act of 1950. If you purchase a nationally advertised woolen blanket, you can be sure of its condition and wool content, because this law requires the manufacturer to show how much new and how much used wool has been used in the blanket. Other kinds of materials used with the wool must also be indicated on the label, along with the manufacturer's name. (Carpets and upholstery materials are exempt from this law.)

Fair Packaging and Labeling Act. This act, passed in 1967, states that the label on packaged goods must show the identity of the product, the name and location of its manufacturer, packer, or distributor, and the net amount of its contents (weight, measure, or numerical count). Furthermore, this net-quantity statement must appear on the main display panel in sufficient size and close to the main printing of the trade name.

Discussion Question

11. *Why does the government regulate marketing practices of businesses?*

CAREERS IN MARKETING

People who have a strong interest in the field of marketing should have little trouble establishing a career suited to their aptitudes and abilities. Among the fruitful areas of specialization are selling, statistical work, research, copywriting, and art. Some areas of opportunity in marketing require technical training— product design, product development, and testing. The position of purchasing agent also requires technical training.

Market research is a good possibility for those who have a solid preparation in statistics, for it involves market analysis as well as sales procedures. It supplies information for the marketing manager and serves as a guide for judging sales performance. Sales promotion and advertising occupations are highly rewarding to people with imagination, initiative, and resourcefulness.

Selling is the most common marketing vocation and offers opportunities on almost every educational level. The sales force is the group charged with the responsibility for producing the revenues of the firm and is usually rewarded liberally if successful. Accordingly, compensation is higher in the sales field than most areas of business. The amount sold is the usual measure of success in selling, but the satisfaction that comes from successful selling is also very rewarding.

Young people with college preparation are often given initial employment in selling not only because they are promising salesmen but because selling provides valuable preparation for attacking many types of problems common to all business, and good experience for managerial responsibility.

Many young people look forward to owning their own business; some day *you* may be the owner of one of the 5 million small businesses operating in the United States. With a steadily expanding population and a continuing rise in per capita income, there will be excellent opportunities for industrious young men and women who set out on their own in marketing.

SUMMARY

Marketing is primarily concerned with the movement of goods and services from areas of surplus to the places where the goods are in demand, and of finished goods from the manufacturer to the consumer. Marketing adds to the value of goods by giving them place utility and time utility.

Marketing management is concerned with integrating and coordinating the various marketing services and functions into a unified system. Consumer goods are those produced directly for the general public. Industrial goods are produced for use by business and industry. Almost one-half of all goods manufactured are for industrial use.

The marketing of goods is accomplished by the performance of a number of activities or functions. Buying and selling are the key functions, because they effect changes in ownership until the goods are in the hands of the consumer. Other essential functions are transporting, storing, standardizing, risk bearing, pricing, financing, and providing market information. All these functions must be performed even when the goods are sold directly by the producer to the consumer.

Control over marketing practices has been a concern of state governments and the federal government for many years. The two main purposes of government legislation are to prevent monopolies and preserve competition in business, and to protect consumers from fraudulent marketing practices.

VOCABULARY REVIEW

Match the following vocabulary terms with the statements below:

a. Fair-trade agreement
b. Futures transaction
c. Grading
d. Market

e. Marketing management
f. Marketing mix
g. Place utility
h. Risk bearing

i. Robinson-Patman Act
j. Standardizing
k. Time utility

1. A place where goods are exchanged between a buyer and a seller
2. The value of goods that is created by delivering them to the places where they are needed
3. The combination of the four basic elements in marketing
4. The value of goods that is created by placing them in a customer's possession at the time when they are needed
5. Carrying out the functions of organizing, planning, coordinating, directing, and decision making in the area of marketing
6. The process of establishing constant physical characteristics for manufactured goods
7. Classifying products according to size or quality
8. Taking the chance that goods may be lost, destroyed, or stolen
9. Business agreements whereby goods will be purchased at some future time at today's price
10. Legislation prohibiting price discrimination that lessens competition with those who grant or receive the benefits of such discrimination
11. Contracts that prohibit retailers from reducing the prices of brand-name products

PROBLEMS AND PROJECTS

1. List the various types of marketing activities that occur from the time that wool leaves the ranch in the western United States until the delivery of a new wool coat to your home.
2. Assume that you recently bought four articles for your home, for which you paid $18, $24, $36, and $42 respectively. Assuming that the ratio of manufacturing cost to marketing cost was 55/45 in each case, what was the value added by marketing services for each product?
3. Assume that you are contemplating entering some phase of marketing by becoming an entrepreneur. Assume that you have sufficient capital and that you are free to choose your role in marketing. Would you enter some type of transportation, a retail store that handled merchandise, or a service type of business? Which would you choose, and why?

BUSINESS CASES

Case 19-1 Trading Stamps, Sales, and Profits

An independent grocer was making a profit of 3.8 percent of his gross sales, which were $350,000 annually. He adopted a trading-stamp plan to try to stimulate sales. The cost of the stamps to him was $1.80 per $100 of sales. After a trial period of six months, he analyzed the results of his experience, which were as follows: His sales increased by 20 percent, his profit (before trading stamps) increased to 4.2 percent. He found that since some customers did not take stamps, stamps were issued on only 80 percent of his sales.

1. What were his gross sales for the six months?
2. What was his profit before paying for his trading stamps for the six months?
3. What was his net profit for the six months (after paying for his stamps)?
4. What would his sales and profit have been had he not issued the stamps? (Use his former experience record for sales and profit margin.)
5. Would you recommend he continue the issuing of trading stamps? Give reasons to support your decision.

Case 19-2 Will Book Customers Buy Candy?

A college bookstore manager has been visited by a representative selling a well-known line of candy packed in one-, two-, and three-pound boxes. The manager is undecided about whether or not to add the line. He estimates that a stock suitable for his store would consist of 100 one-pound boxes, 50 two-pound boxes, and 20 three-pound boxes, to retail at $1.50, $2.75, and $3.75 respectively. A third of the money taken in would represent the store's margin of profit. The average margin of profit in the store (based on retail prices) is 23 percent. The college is coeducational, with an enrollment of 4,000 students.

1. What information about the student body should the manager have to help him reach his decision?
2. Is the location of the bookstore a factor?
3. What information about competitors would be helpful?
4. Is a line of candy a suitable kind of merchandise for a college bookstore?

marketing channels: wholesaling and retailing

CHAPTER TWENTY

In our modern economy, where production is not for self-consumption but for sale to others, marketing channels are the means by which goods are distributed. In the preceding chapter we noted that the heart of the marketing process includes transferring ownership from seller to buyer and delivering goods to the buyer at the time and place he wants them. This process may be simple and direct or it may be complex and indirect. The farmer who sells his produce at a roadside stand uses a simple and direct distribution system. In contrast, some manufacturers sell to jobbers, to agents, or to wholesalers, who in turn sell to retailers.

In this country, business has developed a highly complex system for marketing goods, which functions as efficiently as our system of mass production. Marketing decisions are concerned with more than just choosing some type of distribution channel. The number of middlemen to use, the maintenance of communication channels between the different levels of middlemen, the selection of specific middlemen, the geographic deployment of inventory stock, the location of distribution centers—all are a part of the problem. Furthermore, these factors are interlocked and interrelated, thus making the management decisions complex and difficult.

In this chapter we shall study the major types of middlemen—retailers as well as wholesalers—and the kinds of services they perform.

Goods that are bought by individuals for their personal or household use are called *consumer goods.* Goods that are consumed by businesses, and those used in the manufacture of other goods, are *industrial goods.* The distribution channels employed for marketing consumer goods differ from those used for industrial goods, so we need to examine in some detail the ways in which both types of goods are marketed.

CHANNELS OF DISTRIBUTION FOR CONSUMER GOODS

The channel of distribution (often referred to as trade channel) is the route taken by the product as it travels from the producer to the ultimate consumer or industrial user. This trade channel does not include the use of transportation companies, banks, and other companies that make no direct contribution to the sale. For example, the channel for furniture may begin with the lumber mill, move on to the manufacturer, then to the manufacturer's agent, to the retailer, and ultimately to the consumer. A channel always includes both the producer and the final consumer.

It is important to note that not all products and services use the same channels of distribution. Some consumer goods are sold direct to the consumer by the producer or manufacturer, but more commonly they are handled by a wholesaler, by a retailer, or by both. Because of intrinsic differences among products and even among various producers of the same product, there are countless variations in the manner in which goods are distributed in our economy.

From Manufacturer Direct to Consumer

At first glance, this channel promises to be very simple and extremely economical. But actual experience has shown it to be relatively costly. Only a few types of manufactured goods, such as Fuller brushes, have been successfully marketed in this manner. The milkman still makes his rounds, but what with improved refrigeration, a great portion of our fresh milk is sold by food stores. Farmers still make limited use of the direct channel to sell small quantities of fruits, vegetables, honey, poultry, and eggs; but here again we find that most farm produce reaches the market through a more circuitous route. Manufacturers using this direct-selling channel ordinarily employ one or more of the three methods we shall now discuss: *manufacturer-owned retail stores, house-to-house selling,* and *direct mail.*

Manufacturer-Owned Stores.   The most widely used method of selling "direct" from manufacturer to consumer is through the manufacturer-owned store. A limited number of manufacturers operate their own stores, both in order to take full advantage of the profits from the retail sale of their products and to promote the greatest possible volume of sales. We find manufacturer-owned stores in the shoe, paint, and men's clothing industries, for example. The basic items in these stores are produced in the plants of the owner—although, in order to carry a complete stock, many items are purchased from outside sources. You may have observed manufacturer-owned shoe stores that carry hosiery, handbags, and gloves purchased in this manner. Few manufacturers enter into this sort of marketing activity, however, since it requires considerable amounts of capital and demands experience in the operation of retail stores.

House-to-House Selling.   House-to-house selling has proved successful for only a few products—mainly brushes, mops, brooms, vacuum cleaners, silverware, cookware, and cosmetics. The success of this sales method depends largely on the company's ability to develop highly effective salespeople, carefully trained to present a well-planned demonstration. The principal drawback of this approach is that it is extremely costly, for a salesman must spend a great deal of time with a single customer—or, at best, with a few customers gathered in a private home. Moreover, most housewives lack confidence in the door-to-door salesman and refuse to give him the time he needs to make an effective presentation. The system will, however, undoubtedly continue to be used for products that lend themselves to convincing home demonstrations. After all, at least *some* consumers will always be attracted by the opportunity of buying direct from the manufacturer. And most certainly there will always be people willing to try their hand at this type of selling because of the attractive commissions it pays.

Direct Mail.   Another means of selling direct to the consumer is through the use of magazine ads and direct-mail brochures. This method has sometimes proved quite successful in marketing neckties, food specialties, and similar

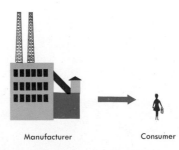

Manufacturer   Consumer

commodities. It has been especially effective in selling books and recordings to customers who contract to buy a specified number of items over an extended period of time. But this channel of distribution is generally regarded as costly and relatively inefficient, since only a small percentage of returns can be expected from even an expensive mailing piece. Moreover, it is difficult for the small-scale seller, who typically uses these techniques, to generate public confidence.

From Manufacturer to Retailer to Consumer

Many kinds of goods, such as automobiles, furniture, appliances, and shoes, are sold through this channel. Certain manufacturers prefer it because they are anxious to retain a high degree of control over the manner in which their product is retailed. And by selling directly to the retailer they are able to influence the training of salespeople and see that the retailer's service staff provides consumer satisfaction. Some manufacturers even follow a policy known as *exclusive distribution*, under which each manufacturer deals directly with a restricted group of retail stores, instead of seeking wide distribution of his goods through as many stores as possible.

Since speed is important in the marketing of fashion goods, for instance, buyers from retail stores often prefer to go directly to the sales offices of the manufacturer to place their orders, instead of working through middlemen. And to expedite their dealings with retail buyers, frequently several manufacturers will join together to show their samples and take orders at a show or fair, such as the semiannual furniture show at the Chicago Furniture Mart.

Manufacturers who distribute their goods over a wide area sometimes establish branch warehouses in which they maintain a stock of goods adequate to meet regional demands. By shipping orders directly to retail stores, they render much the same service as does an ordinary wholesaler. Although these manufacturers incur many of the expenses inherent in wholesaling, they have more freedom to conduct an aggressive selling program than they would if they depended exclusively on wholesalers to distribute their goods to retail outlets.

Notice that although this channel of distribution bypasses the wholesaler,

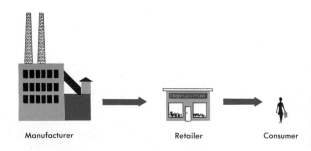

Manufacturer   Retailer Consumer

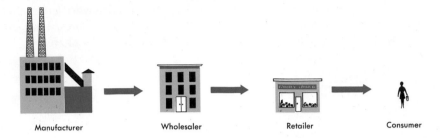

| Manufacturer | Wholesaler | Retailer | Consumer |

it does not eliminate any of the marketing functions discussed in Chapter 19. Every one of these functions must be performed, either by the manufacturer or the retailer. This means that the wholesaler must justify his position in the marketing system by competing successfully with this more direct method of distributing commodities.

From Manufacturer to Wholesaler to Retailer to Consumer

This is probably the most widely used channel to market the goods we buy most frequently. Most convenience goods, such as drugs, hardware, groceries, and bakery goods, move along the route from the manufacturer to the wholesaler, to the retailer, and then to the ultimate consumer.

Wholesalers purchase goods in large quantities from numerous manufacturers. From their collection of a wide variety of types of goods, they supply the needs of retailers. Thus the wholesaler reduces the number of accounts that the manufacturer deals with, and the manufacturer saves the expense of having to service thousands of individual businesses.

The wholesaler likewise saves the retailer money and time. An independent grocer normally stocks his shelves with thousands of different items. Instead of contacting hundreds of manufacturers, he does business with just a few wholesalers.

From Manufacturer to Chain Store to Consumer

The chain organization performs most of the functions that wholesalers render. The chains have buyers who specialize in particular lines of goods. Chains buy in large quantities, have their own storage facilities, and in some instances own their own trucks for delivering goods to their outlets. (The delivery problem alone can be enormous, for a single warehouse might serve as many as 50 different company-operated retail sales outlets.) Safeway, Kroger, and A&P are well-known grocery chains that maintain warehouses.

Independent retailers sometimes group together to form a *voluntary chain* organization. These merchants pool their buying and certain other distribution functions in much the same manner as the large chains. In many instances, the voluntary chain group is organized by a wholesaler who serves them by supplying their most important items. The Rexall drug stores, IGA grocers, and Ben Franklin variety stores are well-known voluntary chains.

Discussion Questions

1. *What middlemen are eliminated in house-to-house selling?*
2. *What types of goods normally follow the pattern from manufacturer to wholesaler to retailer to consumer?*

MARKETING INDUSTRIAL GOODS

There is no single market for industrial goods, but several markets. Some dealers sell to a very restricted market, while others handle a wide variety of products. The chief types of industrial goods are:

> Raw materials
> Industrial equipment and machinery
> Industrial supplies
> Tools and accessory equipment
> Processed materials
> Parts and subassemblies

Industrial goods are sold to farmers, mines, lumberers, fisheries, construction contractors, factories, governments, institutions, wholesalers, and retailers. Some marketers will specialize, calling on only one type of market, while others will cover several different types.

The distribution channels through which industrial goods travel are markedly different from those followed by consumer goods. No retailers are needed, and fewer middlemen are used. Consequently, the marketing of industrial goods is usually a simpler process. The most commonly used channels are these:

1. Direct from factory to industrial user, sometimes by way of a factory sales branch
2. From factory to agents (or brokers), to industrial user
3. From factory to industrial distributor (wholesaler), to industrial user

Approximately two-thirds of the total volume of industrial goods marketed is sold direct from the factory by the manufacturers to the users. An additional 12 to 15 percent is sold to industrial users through the sales branches of manufacturers. One reason for this short distribution channel is the technical nature of products that require expert installation and maintenance service; the best way for the purchaser to insure getting this service is often through face-to-face dealings with the manufacturer. Another reason is that when most of a manufacturer's important customers are concentrated in a small geographic area, there is simply no reason to work through a middleman. Finally, many orders for industrial goods are so huge that the cost of direct negotiations between manufacturer and buyer is negligible.

CONTRASTS IN MARKETING OF INDUSTRIAL AND CONSUMER GOODS

A look at the markets and marketing techniques commonly associated with industrial and consumer goods reveals a number of clearly identifiable contrasts.

1. There is a very narrow market for many kinds of industrial goods. For example, the market for certain industrial chemicals or for automobile-body hardware is limited for the most part to a small group of manufacturers. The consumer-goods market, on the other hand, often has millions of potential customers for a product. A narrow market simplifies the task of marketing because it facilitates the making of sales directly from the producer to the industrial user. On the other hand, such a restricted market makes it impractical for the producer to employ a sales organization large enough to contact all potential customers. When these conditions exist, it is not uncommon for industrial consumers to seek out the seller of the goods. For this purpose, the industrial user's purchasing department usually has an assortment of catalogues and an index of suppliers, such as Thomas' Register. This four-volume set has 500,000 listings of manufacturers under thousands of product classifications.

2. It is more difficult to discover in the industrial market the party who actually makes buying decisions than it is in the consumer-goods market. Retailers can usually assume that any person who visits their stores and shows an interest in their goods is a potential purchaser. On the other hand, it is often difficult for the salesman of industrial goods to determine which persons in the customer firm really make buying decisions. In the purchase of an item used in manufacturing, for example, the decision may be made by the purchasing agent, the plant superintendent, the foreman, the product engineer, or the plant manager. Sometimes the salesman finds it very difficult to get a candid answer when he asks who has the final authority over purchases.

3. Reciprocity of orders between buyer and seller is a common practice in the industrial market, but relatively unimportant in the consumer-goods market. Many companies buy goods or services produced by their customers. For example, a steel producer may buy

its chemicals from the chemical manufacturer that buys its steel. The steel producer may adopt this practice because it makes the chemical firm a more loyal customer. A salesman of industrial goods may therefore attempt to influence the purchasing department of his firm to patronize his potential customers.

4. A single sale of industrial goods often represents a large sum of money. The sale of a single machine, for example, may amount to thousands of dollars, and a contract for materials and parts may run into millions.

5. Buyers of industrial goods are usually well informed and make their purchasing decisions on the basis of the product's proved performance.

6. The demand for certain types of industrial goods is extremely sensitive to changing business conditions. The demand for machines, for instance, drops precipitously when business slows down. In fact, the entire industrial market suffers more than the consumer market during periods of declining business activity. But in normal and boom periods, the demand for machinery, equipment, and parts is greatly accelerated.

7. Industrial goods are commonly sold directly by the producer to the user without the intervention of the middleman that is characteristic of the consumer market. Engineers representing both the buyer and the producer may work together in setting up specifications for the product. And the producer often furnishes expert advice, machine installation, and repair service after the goods have been sold. A relationship of this sort increases the likelihood that future dealings will be kept on a direct, face-to-face basis. Approximately 80 percent of the industrial goods manufactured in this country are sold directly to the industrial user.

The channels of distribution used in marketing industrial goods and consumer goods are contrasted in the diagram on page 539.

Discussion Question

3. *In what ways does the marketing of industrial goods differ from the marketing of consumer goods?*

WHOLESALERS' FUNCTION IN MARKETING

There are more than 300,000 wholesale businesses in the United States. Most of them limit their active selling to an area within a 150-mile radius, but some cover the entire nation.

FOR INDUSTRIAL GOODS

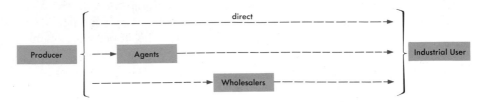

FOR CONSUMER GOODS

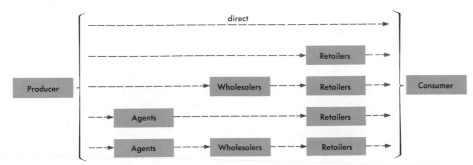

The Nature and Importance of Wholesale Trade

Almost all manufacturers sell their goods on a wholesale basis. In other words, manufacturers engage in wholesale trade, but they are not regarded as wholesalers because their primary function is manufacturing. It is also important to recognize clearly the distinction between a retail sale and a wholesale sale. The former type consists of any sale of goods to an ultimate consumer for his own personal satisfaction. A wholesale sale, on the other hand, is any transaction in which the purchaser desires the goods for either resale purposes or for use in his business. Notice that neither the price of the goods nor the quantity purchased necessarily distinguishes the retail sale from the wholesale sale. Often the sale of a single item is a wholesale transaction. Wholesale sales are commonly made to manufacturers, wholesalers, retailers, public utilities, railroads, hotels, schools, colleges, and governmental units.

Surprisingly enough, wholesale establishments do a larger dollar volume of business than retailers. In fact, in recent years the wholesale sales volume in the United States has been 50 percent greater than the total sales of all retailers. Clearly, the activities of wholesale establishments include far more than simply supplying goods to retailers. True, retailers are their biggest customers, but they absorb only 38 percent of total wholesale sales. Industrial users account for 35 percent of the sales of all wholesale establishments, while other wholesale establishments, and also exporters, are responsible for the remaining 27 percent.

The wholesaler is the most important source of supply to many retailers. The small retailer especially could scarcely operate without his services. And for some kinds of goods—especially convenience goods—the wholesaler is the principal supplier to both small and large retailers. The importance of this middleman in our marketing system can best be understood by investigating the ways in which he serves the manufacturer and the retailer.

How the Wholesaler Serves the Manufacturer

Why is it that so many manufacturers depend on wholesalers to distribute their products? There are several good reasons:

1. Most manufacturers are small firms with limited resources. They must direct their main effects toward production and cannot afford to spend time and money coping with the difficult problems of marketing. Because of their lack of know-how and capital, these firms are perfectly willing to rely on wholesalers to sell their output.
2. Since the wholesaler is in intimate contact with retailers, he is able to keep the manufacturer informed about such matters as desirable package styling, advertising appeals, and product features. Without assistance from the wholesaler, every manufacturer would be forced to make his own market surveys to keep abreast of changing market conditions.
3. The wholesaler provides the manufacturer with thorough coverage of virtually every retailer who might be interested in stocking his product. The wholesaler counts among his regular customers all kinds of stores, large and small, in the city and in out-of-the-way country towns. This is an especially valuable service for manufacturers whose products, such as tobacco and groceries, need wide distribution.
4. The services provided by the wholesaler enable the manufacturer to keep at a minimum his selling cost per unit. The manufacturer of food products, for example, would have to maintain enough salespeople to call on thousands of retail stores and restaurants in order to serve the grocery trade himself. But by selling only to wholesalers he can get along with relatively few salesmen taking orders for large quantities of goods.
5. A manufacturer can also minimize his clerical costs by selling only to wholesalers, because he needs to carry only a few accounts on his books and to make only large bulk shipments.

How the Wholesaler Serves the Retailer

In order to appreciate the importance of the services rendered by wholesalers to retailers, let us compare what happens when a retailer purchases from wholesalers with what happens when he purchases direct from producers.

1. Purchasing from wholesalers saves the retailer much time in the buying process. Imagine what would happen if every grocer had

to buy direct from the 50,000 manufacturers of the goods he stocks. If only half these manufacturers called on the grocer once every three months, he would be visited by approximately 400 salesmen daily! Obviously the retailer in most lines of trade could not deal with all the manufacturers who produce the goods he might be interested in stocking.

2. The wholesaler carries a complete line of goods from which the retailer can replenish his stock easily and swiftly. This means that the retailer need not keep a huge supply of goods on hand, and it saves him from tying up large amounts of capital in inventory.

3. Freight costs are reduced when the retailer buys goods from nearby wholesalers. Few retailers enjoy a large enough volume of business to order carload lots from the factory, but goods are often shipped in carload lots to wholesalers.

4. The nearby wholesaler is in a better position to grant credit to the retailer than is a distant manufacturer. Even the small merchant, who would order only small quantities from an individual manufacturer, may provide a valuable source of business for the wholesaler. The high costs of making credit investigations and carrying on clerical work make it expensive for a manufacturer to carry a host of small credit accounts on his books.

5. The retailer regards the sales representatives of wholesalers as a valuable source of information and advice. For example, they may give suggestions on display and sales promotion of the goods they sell. They suggest new items that might be added to his stock and keep him informed about trends in merchandising. The wholesale representative is, in fact, the principal business adviser to many small retailers.

Discussion Question

4. *Discuss the various ways that wholesalers serve the manufacturer and the retailer.*

TYPES OF WHOLESALERS

The three major types of wholesale middlemen are (1) merchant wholesalers, (2) limited-function wholesalers, and (3) agent middlemen. The main distinctions among wholesalers, aside from the kinds of products they distribute, involve (1) the number of functions they perform, (2) whether they take title or possession of the goods, and (3) the type of commission, fee, or regular income they receive.

Merchant Wholesalers

Merchant wholesalers—sometimes called wholesalers or jobbers—are the most numerous of all wholesalers. They take title to goods, store, deliver, and assemble it, and maintain a regular place of business. Their income is derived from the sale of the goods rather than from commissions or fees. This is the most common and most familiar type of wholesaler, distributing about 45 percent of all consumer goods. Merchant wholesalers who provide a wide variety of services, such as granting credit, making deliveries, and giving out current trade information, are appropriately called *service wholesalers.*

Limited-Function Wholesalers

As their name implies, limited-function wholesalers render fewer marketing functions than do merchant wholesalers. For example, the truck wholesaler, who combines the marketing functions of selling and delivery, does not grant credit, but collects for each sale. Another example is the *drop shipper,* who sells merchandise that is delivered directly from the manufacturer to the customer, which is called a "drop shipment."

Agent Middlemen

Agent middlemen, a third category of wholesalers, do not take title to the goods they sell, and they perform relatively few services. Their main function is to make a sale for the manufacturer or distributor; they are usually compensated by a percentage commission based on volume of sales. Brokers, selling agents, and manufacturers' agents are classed as agent middlemen. *Brokers* negotiate transactions without having either title or possession of goods. *Selling agents* often handle an entire production or season's output, serving an unrestricted territory. *Manufacturers' agents* may sell only a part of a producer's output and are limited to a specific sales territory.

Commission merchants, unlike the agents we have discussed so far, actually take possession of the goods they market. They usually arrange for the shipment of goods, store them temporarily, sell them, and deliver them to the buyer. At times they grant credit to the buyer. For all these services they charge their clients a commission—a percentage of the sales price—and sometimes

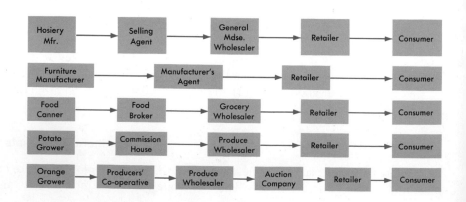

add the expenses they incur in the handling and storing of the goods. The majority of commission merchants deal in agricultural products, such as melons, fruits, vegetables, and livestock. Since these products must be sold quickly once they reach the market, it is customary for the owner to instruct the commission merchant to sell at the best possible price.

The diagram on page 542 shows how the agent or broker fits into the distribution channel for selected products.

Discussion Questions

5. *What are the chief differences in the way a merchant wholesaler and an agent middleman operate?*

6. *How does the commission merchant differ from other types of agents?*

MARKETING AGRICULTURAL PRODUCTS

Since most farm products are neither consumer goods nor industrial goods, they are marketed differently from both types of products. Farm operations are carried on in every state, with most farmers producing on a relatively small scale, and in most instances an individual farm operator raises more than a single type of produce. Thus, farm produce must be assembled and concentrated in order to make it available to manufacturers, processors, and consumers.

To do this job, we have in this country approximately 14,000 individuals or companies who assemble farm products. Some of them are small operators with a minimum amount of invested capital and little in the way of specialized equipment. Others own and control a whole chain of elevators, warehouses, or packing plants.

Fruits, vegetables, milk, and eggs are ready for consumers with little or no processing, but they must be distributed quickly. Grains, cotton, wool, and livestock must be processed or manufactured into products before being sold to consumers.

There are three basic types of middlemen engaged in marketing farm products: wholesalers, brokers, and commission merchants. The physical transportation of farm products is done largely by trucks, railways, and water carriers.

Marketing Grains

Although the value of the corn produced in the United States is about twice that of wheat, much of it is fed to livestock right on the farms and in feeder pens. So from a marketing viewpoint, wheat is the chief grain raised, transported, and processed into manufactured goods. It requires some 7,000 elevators in this country to handle wheat and other grains. In earlier years, most grains were moved by rail, but currently, trucks and water carriers are being used on an ever-increasing scale.

Marketing Livestock

Farmers currently sell approximately one-third of their livestock on consignment to commission merchants in central markets, about one-fourth through local auction markets, about one-sixth to local buyers, one-sixth to packers at their processing plants, and the remaining tenth to other farmers. Animals are purchased at more than 700 concentration yards, most of them owned and operated by the meat packers. There has been a significant shift in transporting livestock by rail, until today most livestock are transported by trucks.

Marketing Fruits and Vegetables

Because of the perishable nature of fresh fruits and vegetables, they are usually moved by truck to nearby canneries and processing plants. A small amount is sold directly to retail stores, again delivered by truck. Also, a small amount is sold to truck jobbers who sell to nearby markets. Trucks provide much faster delivery than rail and are much more versatile.

Farmers in California, Florida, and southwestern Texas ship fresh produce the year around, using refrigerated trucks or refrigerated rail cars if the market is some distance away.

When farmers sell fruits and vegetables through cooperatives, the produce is usually sold to wholesalers or chain-store buyers. Such produce may be shipped either by truck or by refrigerated railroad cars.

The 1970 census reported that there are almost a thousand brokers who sell fruits and vegetables, and slightly more than 2,200 businesses that assemble fruits and vegetables, approximately half of which are packers.

Cooperatives

A *cooperative* is a business enterprise organized and owned by a group of people in order to serve their marketing needs. Each member has an equal voice in the control of the firm, which is sometimes operated without profit. If profits do accrue, they are distributed to members in proportion to their patronage.

Agricultural Marketing Cooperatives. Agricultural marketing cooperatives are associations operated by the growers or producers of a single product, or a group of closely related products. Sunkist Growers, Inc., to name a familiar example, markets oranges and lemons, and Land-O-Lakes Creameries, Inc., markets dairy and poultry products. These middlemen are important agencies in the marketing of several kinds of farm products. They market the grain, dairy products, fruits, vegetables, nuts, and livestock of more than 4 million producers. In addition to actual selling, these associations have several other purposes: (1) to improve merchandising practices; (2) to create demand through the use of brand names and advertising; (3) to promote more orderly marketing; (4) to extend financial assistance to members; and (5) to encourage the growing of higher-quality products.

Agricultural Purchasing Cooperatives.   A second type of cooperative association that serves farmers is the agricultural purchasing cooperative. These associations purchase and resell to members and nonmembers alike such commodities as fertilizer, seeds, gasoline, feeds, and farm machinery. Many of them also stock household appliances, but they do not attempt to handle most kinds of consumer goods. The principal objective of these associations has been to enable their members to obtain their farm needs at lower prices. Their business has increased with the trend toward farm practices that require many kinds of equipment, seeds, and supplies. Membership is open to any farmer willing to buy one or more shares of stock in the association. Dividends, in cash or stock, are distributed on the basis of the patronage of members. Each member has an equal voice in controlling the affairs of the association.

Discussion Question

7. *What are the chief types of middlemen who handle agricultural products?*

THE ROLE OF RETAILING IN MARKETING

The two major groups of merchant middlemen are wholesalers and retailers. When a person argues for the elimination of middlemen, he is usually speaking of the wholesaler, because most people recognize that they cannot get along without retailers.

Retailers are businessmen who purchase goods from manufacturers and wholesalers and sell them to final customers. Retailing is a heterogeneous business carried on in stores that differ as to the lines and quality of goods sold, services provided, price ranges, and types of locations. Each store has its own personality, layout, and customer-service policy. In the field of retailing are to be found small-, medium-, and large-scale enterprises, some individually owned and others operated as corporations, cooperatives, or manufacturers' retail sales branches.

In recent years, Americans have spent approximately two-thirds of their disposable income (income left after paying taxes) for goods and services purchased in retail stores. Of the approximately 8 million nonagricultural businesses in the United States, approximately 2 million are retail establishments, employing some 10 million people.

Retailing Is Easy to Enter

You can start a retail store with a relatively small amount of initial capital—far less, for example, than is normally required to establish a wholesale or manufacturing business. Moreover, you will be subject to relatively few legal requirements. Experience, although important, is not a mandatory prerequisite. Manufacturers seeking new outlets for sale of their products may even prove willing to provide you with some financial assistance and merchandising advice.

Retailing Is Typically Small Business

There are many large-scale retail chain organizations in existence. But it is interesting to note that even the largest of the retail chains are not the largest businesses in this country. *Forbes* magazine publishes each year a directory of the 500 largest corporations in the United States. They feature three groupings: the largest corporations according to gross revenues, according to value of assets, and according to amount of net profits. For the year 1970, when measured by the value of corporate assets, there was not a single retail chain in the top 20 companies, and when measured by net profits, only Sears, Roebuck, which ranks ninth, is in the top 20. But when measured by gross revenues, five retailers rank among the top 20.[1] They are:

Retail Chains	Rank	Revenues (millions)
Sears, Roebuck	5	$9,262
A&P	12	5,754
Safeway Stores	14	4,860
J. C. Penney	18	4,151
Kroger	19	3,736

By far the greatest number of retail stores are small, owner-managed concerns. As a rule, the independent retailer serves as both owner and manager of the business, especially if the operation is on a small scale. In about one out of every three retail stores, there are no paid employees outside the owner's

---

[1] The largest company according to revenues received is the General Motors Corporation, and AT&T is the largest in total assets and in net profits.

family, and considerably less than 1 percent of all retail firms employ over 100 persons. About one-third of all retail stores sell less than $25,000 worth of merchandise a year. The fact that those entering retailing as proprietors usually start as independents accounts for the large number of small enterprises in retailing. It also contributes to their high rate of failures.

Retailing Is Highly Competitive

Retailing is one of the most competitive segments of our business economy. Competition is especially keen among grocery stores, restaurants, liquor stores, service stations, and automobile dealers. You will often find gas stations located on opposite street corners. If people were aware of the high degree of competition that exists in these lines, they would probably be more reluctant to risk their money and time in starting such enterprises.

Retailing Is Highly Specialized

Like so many other segments of our economy, retailing has become highly specialized. The great majority of all retail business is carried on in stores. Many of these stores specialize in a particular line of merchandise—men's clothing, ladies' ready-to-wear, shoes, luggage, hardware goods. Later in this chapter we shall note some of the trends of the various types of retail operations.

Discussion Question

8. *What is meant when we say that retailing is typically small business?*

THE FUNCTIONS PERFORMED BY RETAILERS

The purpose of our marketing system is to help fill the needs and wants of every consumer. This is also the general function of the various middlemen, one of whom is the retailer. His principal functions are buying, dividing, pricing, storing, selling, and delivering.

Buying Merchandise for Resale

This function involves selecting the goods that will be offered for resale, determining the prices at which they will be offered, marking the goods, and planning sales activities. Many observers regard these as the most critically important activities of all the retailer's functions.

To do an effective job, the buyer, who may be the owner if the store is small, must have not only an intimate knowledge of the markets from which he will obtain these goods, but an awareness of his customers' needs and tastes. He must carefully determine the quantity and quality of stock to buy—the right sizes, colors, and styles. Otherwise, he may find himself disastrously overstocked at the end of the season or year. Good buying comes only through meticulous planning, and the buyer must draw on every available source of information—his own sales staff, manufacturers' catalogues, and general market conditions—before making his final choices.

Except in stores that cater exclusively to the "carriage trade," proprietors should stock merchandise that appeals to medium-income groups, with perhaps a limited number of items for low- and high-income buyers.

Dividing and Pricing

The second retailing function involves getting the goods into the store and preparing them for resale. For example, some goods cannot be displayed until they have been unpacked and processed. Moreover, since consumers usually buy in small quantities, stock clerks have to divide case lots, cartons, boxes, and other shipments of goods into small quantities.

Receiving and processing goods in retail merchandising make several demands on management. For example, the retailer must work out an efficient method for checking incoming goods against invoices, and set up a quick, accurate system of marking the goods with prices. Moreover, he must ensure that the stockroom is run efficiently. Effective housekeeping in the stockroom requires providing a clean storage place with readily accessible shelves or bins, maintaining systematic arrangements for locating stock quickly, and making economical use of all space.

In order to enjoy the profits that go with a large volume of sales and in order to keep fresh supplies of goods on hand, retailers try to maintain a rapid turnover of stock. Various dating codes are used on price tags as a means of keeping a record of the age of goods. Perhaps the most common code is simply to indicate, by means of a letter or a numeral, the month in which the merchandise was received. For example, January might be indicated by the letter A or the numeral 1; February, by B or 2; and so on.

In pricing goods, the retailer works on the basis of a *markup*. The markup is the difference between the retailer's cost and his selling price. Hence, if a product cost the merchant $20 and is marked to sell for $30, his markup is $10. Markup is generally expressed in terms of percentage of selling price.[2] Here, for example, the markup would be 33⅓ percent. Many retailers use a markup table similar to that in Table 20.1.

---

[2] To find the percentage of markup when both the cost and selling price are known, first find the profit (difference between cost and selling price), and then divide that by the selling price.

TABLE
20.1
MERCHANDISE MARKUP TABLE

Percentage of Margin Based on Selling Price		Percentage of Margin Based on Cost Price
10		11.1
11		12.4
12		13.6
13		15.0
14	is equivalent to	16.3
15		17.7
20		25.0
25		33.3
30		42.9
33		49.1
35		53.9
40		66.7
50		100.0

In lines where competition is not severe, or where the rate of turnover is low, the retailer's markup may be as high as 50 percent. Many merchants begin a selling season with their standard markup, and then toward the end of the season reduce their prices in order to clear out any remaining stock.

Normally, markup covers both the cost of the goods and an amount for expenses and profit. It may also include an estimated amount to allow for an anticipated markdown in the future. This is often the case with highly seasonal merchandise; at the end of the season, quantities may remain on hand that must be reduced in price in order to ensure a quick disposal. *Markdown* is simply a reduction in the original selling price. It is generally expressed as a percentage, just as markups are. As a rule, the chief reasons for having to make markdowns are overbuying, poor selection of quality, shopworn goods, selecting too many units of a given size, unpopular colors, or just weak sales effort.

Storing Merchandise

Storage is often regarded as a problem peculiar to warehousing, but actually it is as important in retailing. Retail stores use a great many different systems for storing merchandise. If space permits, the retailer may set aside part of his building or shop exclusively for storage; otherwise, he may store goods under counters and on open shelves. A good storage system ensures ready accessibility to the stock, a means of filing and classifying goods according to the different departments in the store, and protection against fire, breakage, deterioration, and theft. Large department stores maintain separate warehouses; or if the main building is large enough, they reserve entire floors for storage purposes.

Selling

Since the core of the retail operation is the volume of merchandise that passes over the counter, the selling function is of paramount importance. Selling involves every aspect of sales promotion, including advertising, store displays, special sales, and service to customers, as well as actually selling the goods.

The services provided by a retail store vary widely with the size of the store and the attitude of the retailer. The following services, designed to increase sales, are commonly offered by retail establishments, particularly department stores and household-goods stores:

Personalized Customer Service	*Credit Service*
Personal shopper	Open-account credit
Mail-order service	Layaway privileges
Prompt delivery	Installment credit
Presale announcements	COD deliveries
mailed to customers	Goods on approval
Nurseries	Return privileges
Style shows	

Delivery Service

The customers of today's retail stores expect free delivery on many purchases, and they insist that the service be prompt and efficient. In many stores, delivery service is just as much a part of retailing as cash-and-carry transactions are. Prompt, efficient, and courteous delivery service is an effective bid for customer goodwill. What many consumers fail to realize, however, is that "free delivery service" is a deceptive term. Theoretically, each customer should pay more for goods in a store offering free delivery service than in one that does not, because the cost of delivery must be in the markup.

Discussion Question

9. *When pricing goods, when does a merchant mark goods up and when does he mark goods down? What price base is used for markup and markdown?*

TRENDS IN RETAILING

Since the early days of the itinerant peddler, retailing has undergone many and constant changes. The general store finally gave way to specialized types of stores, mainly because these outlets could render better service, provide customers a wider choice, and attract more customers with increased advertising and other sales-promotion aids. Continued expansion of suburbs and the increased use of automobiles for shopping not only has promoted the development of more suburban shopping centers, but also has multiplied the number of different lines of merchandise carried by these stores. Suburban stores now provide a full third of department-store sales, as against only 5 percent a decade ago. And many downtown department stores are constructing suburban stores in shopping centers located away from the central business district.

The giant supermarket, with its multiple lines of goods, is cutting down the number of small neighborhood stores. Supermarkets have also helped to promote the trend toward more self-service-type stores.

Variety stores, notably those in the "five-and-dime" category, are carrying higher-priced goods. Many outlets have been remodeled to provide for more self-service and at the same time to reduce selling costs by eliminating some clerks.

Drug chains are expanding their hard-goods and housewares lines. And former "cash only" chains have joined the credit-customer parade.

The introduction of electronic data-processing equipment promises to improve stock-control and record-keeping operations, as well as to reduce clerical costs.

The Discount House

The discount house is a relatively recent development in the retailing field. A *discount house* is a business that offers lower prices than those normally found in the traditional type of retail store. They started in the mid-1950's, selling appliances at discount prices. They soon added furniture and other types of durable goods. Experiencing success, they later added drugs, a wide variety of soft goods, sporting goods, and automotive supplies.

Discount houses are now operated in every large and middle-size city. Some of them are operated by chains, but many are independently owned and operated. The most modern discount houses, currently being established by chains in suburban shopping centers, are almost complete department stores.

Whereas most discount houses are open to the general public, a few of them sell only to members or card holders. These are referred to as *closed-door discounters.* Members must identify themselves upon entrance before they are permitted to shop. The majority of the closed-door discount houses are operated for one or more specialized groups, such as a company's employees, union members, or persons in some type of government service, such as state or federal employees, postal workers, or teachers.

Franchising

In many lines of business, retailers operate under a franchise. A *franchise* is a relationship between a producer or manufacturer and a retailer whereby the franchising grantor supplies the retailer with a brand name or image, equipment layout, marketing procedures, and organization know-how. The franchiser may assist in choosing a desirable location, planning and erecting buildings, and training the first employees. The franchiser helps the retailer get launched and provides advice and supervision on a continuing basis as needed.

Franchising has been an important part of the retail field for many years in the marketing of petroleum products. Its recent rapid growth has been with retailers of the short-order food, or fish-and-chips, variety. For example, almost everyone is familiar with McDonald's hamburgers, Colonel Sanders Kentucky Fried Chicken, and H. Salt's fish and chips.[3]

A franchise differs from a leased department. A franchiser operates in his own building, whereas a leased department operates in the same building with the lessor; and the leased department usually uses certain services in common with the lessor, such as accounting, billings and collections, and delivery service.

Discussion Question

10. *In what lines of retailing is franchising most popular?*

CAREERS IN MIDDLEMAN MARKETING

The career opportunities in wholesaling and retailing are excellent. Nearly 10 million people work in the latter field alone. The college graduate is in demand, with excellent opportunities open to both men and women, especially in department stores. Although a majority of the higher executives today are men, an increasing number of women are holding positions as manager, buyer, and personnel director.

If you are interested in wholesaling or retailing as a career, there are two types of opportunity you may consider: self-employment (that is, owning your own business), and working for a small-, medium-, or large-size establishment.

Regardless of your area of specialization in college, you will find an opportunity in wholesaling or retailing. Majors in business administration with training in such fields as marketing, advertising, accounting, personnel administration, and statistics are especially well equipped. Many of the larger stores, regardless of the employee's major, will train candidates for high-level positions in their own executive-training programs.

[3] A more detailed discussion of franchising was given in Chapter 6.

Opportunities in Self-Employment

The fact that a large percentage of the retail stores in the United States are small establishments suggests that there are many opportunities for owning your own business. But it also suggests that you will have to be prepared to cope with strong competition in this area. At one time, selling goods to consumers was a simple process. But now, giant organizations have entered the field with large-scale capital outlays and complex merchandising methods, thus creating a highly competitive situation.

Opportunities in Working for Others

Some people have the idea that the only jobs in retailing are those that involve direct selling. But the fact is that retail stores offer a great variety of career opportunities in nonselling activities. At the executive level, for example, the merchandising division of a large department store must be staffed by specialists such as these:

Department buyers	Divisional merchandise managers
Department managers	General merchandise coordinators
Comparison shopping managers	General merchandise managers
Fashion coordinators	

And the field of general management offers additional opportunities to talented young people with managerial and selling experience:

Store managers	Training directors
Store supervisors	Adjustment managers
Employment managers	Delivery-department managers
Personnel directors	Receiving-department managers

SUMMARY

In this chapter we have examined the different ways that consumer goods, industrial goods, and farm products are moved from producer to user. These are called distribution channels. The chief movers in the distribution of most goods are the wholesaler and the retailer. However, agents, brokers, and commission merchants also play important roles.

Wholesalers and retailers serve both the manufacturer and the consumer by making goods that are produced in one location available to users who reside in many locations. They do more than assemble and disperse goods; they process, package, grade, store, label, and price goods while they have possession of them.

In the marketing of consumer goods, most of them are handled by both the wholesaler and the retailer. The marketing of industrial goods is done largely by manufacturers' agents, brokers, or wholesalers who handle only industrial goods. Farm products are assembled usually by small operators who truck them to elevators, *processing, or packing plants. The middlemen who handle agricultural products are chiefly brokers, commission merchants, or wholesalers. The cooperative plays an important but minor role in distribution, serving principally in agricultural areas.*

The discount house and the franchiser are the most rapidly growing elements among retailers today. Although both have been in existence for many years, they have relatively recently come to the forefront in retailing.

VOCABULARY REVIEW

Match the following vocabulary terms with the statements below.

a. Broker	f. Distribution channel	k. Markup
b. Commission merchant	g. Exclusive distribution	l. Middleman
c. Consumer goods	h. Franchise	m. Retailer
d. Cooperative	i. Industrial goods	n. Service wholesaler
e. Discounter	j. Markdown	o. Voluntary chain

1. The route by which a product moves from the producer to the consumer
2. A person or business enterprise that buys and sells goods in the distribution process
3. The marketing of goods by manufacturers through a restricted group of retailers
4. Goods purchased by individuals for their personal use
5. A group of independent merchants who collaborate and pool their purchasing and advertising efforts
6. Goods that are used in the process of manufacturing other goods
7. A wholesaler who renders a full range of marketing services
8. A middleman who negotiates the sale of goods that belong to his client but who does not take possession of the goods
9. An agent who takes possession of the goods he sells for another for a percentage of the sales price
10. A marketer in the distribution channel who buys from manufacturers or wholesalers and sells to consumers
11. Setting the sales price of a product, by adding a certain percentage to the cost price
12. A reduction made in the price originally asked for goods offered for sale
13. A business enterprise organized and owned by a group of people for the purpose of serving their marketing needs
14. A retail merchant who sells goods at a price below that charged in other stores
15. A relationship between a producer and a retailer whereby the retailer uses the grantor's brand name and receives service from him

PROBLEMS AND PROJECTS

1. List three types of middlemen, and after each one named, describe briefly the kinds of marketing functions the type performs.

2. Name five types of products that can be marketed satisfactorily without the services of a wholesaler.

3. What are the advantages to retailers of using trading stamps? Customers think they are getting ''something for nothing.'' Why is this not true?

A BUSINESS CASE

Case 20-1 How to Market the Goods

The Hope Processing Company has specialized in processing, packaging, and distributing cereal products, cat food, and dog food. The cereals are all sold in cardboard boxes, the cat food and dog food in tins with paper labels around the cans. Their special identifying insignia has been the use of black and red stripes around the packages. They have been marketing their products using their own salesmen, who call upon wholesalers and who are paid on a commission basis.

A chain-store buyer has offered to sell for the company its entire cereal line, but he is not interested in the cat food or dog food. The cereal line accounts for the larger sales volume, but the canned products have a greater profit margin.

If the company should accept the chain store as its marketing middleman on cereals and retain its salesmen, the salesmen would need larger territories in order to receive the same amount of commissions as they have previously earned.

The company wants to keep the black and red stripes for its pet-food products, but eliminate them on the cereal boxes should they be sold through the chain store.

1. What advantage would there be to the chain of continuing the identifying black and red stripes?

2. Why should the Hope Company not want to continue the stripes on the cereal packages?

3. What are the chief advantages and disadvantages to the Hope Company in letting the chain store market its cereal line?

4. Since the same wholesalers have been buying both the cereal and the cat and dog food, how can the Hope Company best market its noncereal products if it makes a deal with the chain-store company?

advertising and personal selling

CHAPTER TWENTY-ONE

A marketer communicates directly with his market chiefly through advertising and personal selling. Advertising seeks to appeal to masses of people who are potential buyers—in other words, using the "shotgun" approach to communicate with market segments. Personal selling tends to use the rifle-like approach, aimed at an individual prospect.

Business has found that advertising is an effective aid to salesmen because it informs consumers about products well before they are ready to buy, priming them to make the "right" choices when they are confronted by the salesman. It makes the final selling job less difficult and often speeds up the process.

In this chapter, we shall examine the ways in which advertising and personal selling are used as tools of marketing managers. For purposes of clarity, advertising and personal selling will be treated separately so that the problems of each can be better understood. Such highly specialized aspects of advertising as copywriting, layout, illustrations, type styles, and detailed psychological appeals are not included in this discussion, since they are part of a regular course in advertising.

WHAT IS ADVERTISING?

To the housewife, advertising may mean the grocery ad in Wednesday's local newspaper, informing her of the weekly specials that will help her save money. To the sales manager, it is a method of communicating with the public to make the selling job easier. To the accountant, advertising is one of the costs of doing business, and to the economist it may be an economic waste.

All of us at one time or another have yielded to the persuasive powers of some form of advertising. It is universally recognized that advertising conveys selling messages and appeals better than any other technique for most businesses. Yet an advertisement that appears before adquate product distribution is achieved can be wasteful.

Advertising Defined

The Definitions Committee of the American Marketing Associations defines *advertising* as "any paid form of nonpersonal presentation and promotion of ideas, goods, or services by an identified sponsor." Two characteristics are significant in this definition: the requirement of payment for the advertisement, and the presence of a sponsor who pays for it. There are times when it is possible to advertise without cost to the sponsor—for example, through editorial comments by newspapers or magazines about a firm or a product. This type of information is considered publicity rather than advertising. The public relations department is responsible for the company's publicity, and, in most businesses, public relations is more concerned with building and maintaining an image or favorable relations with the public than with promoting directly the sale of a specific product.

Publicity is information made available to the public through various media about a firm, a product, or an event, because such information is regarded as news. For example, a news release about a new automobile model is publicity. The news announcement about the discovery of a new product as a possible cure for cancer would be a publicity item.

The Purposes of Advertising

The overall purpose of advertising is to influence the level of product sales and thereby increase the profits of the advertiser. Sometimes, a firm is forced to advertise because of the actions of competitors. Under such circumstances, the opportunity to increase profits may be slim, yet failure to advertise could result in reduced sales and less profit.

As a tool of marketing, advertising generally serves the following purposes sometimes called "the 3 R's of advertising"):

> **1.** *Retain "loyal" customers:* Persuade present customers to keep buying.

2. *Reduce "lost" customers:* Slow down the flow of present customers away from the proffered brand.

3. *Recruit "new" customers:* Increase the flow of customers toward the advertised product; replace those lost to competitors; widen the total market.

How Advertising Actually Serves Business. In addition to the three broad purposes of advertising shown above, a study of advertising indicates that it provides a wide variety of services to a business firm's marketing program in the following ways:

1. *Advertising has altered living habits.* So powerful is the influence of advertising that it is constantly changing our daily habits and attitudes. It has created public acceptance of new styles in clothes, automobiles, personal appearance, and homes. Family eating habits have been changed—housewives are buying more prepared and frozen foods, and are preparing fewer at home.

2. *Advertising helps to lower unit costs by increasing sales.* By increasing consumer desires, advertising enables a business to sell more units. This in turn allows the manufacturer to increase product output, which in turn decreases the cost of each unit.

3. *Advertising can help to associate a whole family of products under one brand name.* Manufacturers often find it more economical to produce a group of products, usually in a related field, than to specialize in one item. For example, soap companies produce soap flakes, toilet soap, and toothpaste. Thus it is possible to promote the sale of an entire line in single advertisements.

4. *Advertising helps to publicize changes in the price of an article or an announcement of a new model.* This type of advertising is used by a manufacturer to tell the public about a new low-priced dishwasher or a new and improved toothpaste.

5. *Advertising simplifies the task of personal selling.* In fact, advertising may even on occasion replace the salesman, although this may not be the primary purpose the advertiser had in mind. Advertising may be used to pave the salesman's way among new and unfamiliar prospects.

Types of Advertising

Advertising can be classified into certain types, depending upon the use and purpose.

Product Advertising. This type of advertising is designed to sell one or more definite and identified products or commodities, and usually it describes and lauds their features and good qualities and may even emphasize their prices. Product advertising is used to sell both consumer and industrial goods. (You will recall that consumer goods are more or less finished goods in such forms as to be readily usable by the general public; industrial goods are items destined for further use in industry in the manufacture of other goods.) Because consumer and industrial goods possess different marketing characteristics, the two types are sold in different trade channels to different markets, under different pricing policies, and by dissimilar selling methods. Consumer goods, therefore, are generally advertised by using appeals different from those used in advertising industrial goods.

Institutional Advertising. This type of advertising is intended to create a proper attitude toward the seller and to build goodwill, rather than to promote a sale. For example, a manufacturer may run an institutional advertisement to tell the public about the firm's efforts to reduce air pollution. Large corporations can afford to spend money on institutional advertising; small companies can seldom afford it.

National Advertising. This type of advertising is used to sell nationally distributed brands; therefore, *national advertising* is defined as any form of advertising using a medium with nationwide circulation. It is generally associated with the advertising of a manufacturer or wholesaler, in contrast with that of a retailer or local advertiser. Moreover, national advertising refers only to the *level* of the advertiser and has no relation at all to geographic coverage. If a manufacturer places an advertisement in only one city, it is still called national advertising.

Local Advertising. Sometimes referred to as retail advertising, *local advertising* is advertising placed by a local retailer. It usually differs from national advertising by being more specific in terms of price, quality, and quantity. In local advertising the stress is on the store where the product is sold while in national advertising the purpose is to build a general demand for a product which may be sold in many stores.

Effects of Advertising on Price and the Public

Advertising by itself will not persuade the consumer to pay what he regards to be an unreasonable price. Yet consumers are often inclined to believe that a nationally advertised brand is worth a higher price than an unadvertised brand, because they are more confident that they are buying what they want. For example, customers are willing to pay a little more for Armour's canned ham than for an unknown brand, because their experience leads them to think that it will taste the way they expect it to taste. The consumer may determine this added value by prior use, or he may accept the claims of the advertiser. However, if the advertised brand has no important differences, obvious or otherwise, its price may be no higher than those of similar products of unadvertised competitors.

Is Advertising an Economic Waste? For years, economists have questioned the value of advertising to society. For one thing, these critics claim that advertising fails to create new demands, and merely results in brand-switching. Evidence shows that in the case of such consumer goods as toothpaste, cosmetics, detergents, and gasoline, whose advertising is highly competitive, the total per capita consumption has risen steadily over the years. To say that all advertising is purely competitive and therefore wasteful suggests that competition itself is wasteful. From the standpoint of the advertiser, to justify advertising a brand, the potential dollar sales should be of an amount that will produce enough gross margin dollars—the excess of sales over cost of goods sold—to pay the advertising costs. Advertising is expected to pay for itself in added sales. If it does not, it may be regarded as wasteful and will probably be discontinued.

Although it may be difficult to prove scientifically the economic value of advertising to the public, the weight of evidence is that mass advertising is essential in order to maintain both mass consumption and mass production.

Does Advertising Promote Brand Monopolies? It is sometimes said that brand monopolies are promoted through excessive amounts of advertising, and that when this happens it is difficult to sell other, competing brands for which there has been little advertising. There is little if any reliable evidence that this claim is accurate. Whether a manufacturer is able to hold much of the market by continuing to make large advertising expenditures is questionable too.

Jules Backman, in his study *Advertising and Competition,* concluded that there is little evidence that advertising encourages monopolies.[1] In determining if a product should be advertised, the important question is, "Is the brand capable of satisfying the consumer's needs?" If the product is incapable of satisfying at least a reasonable amount of consumer needs, excessive advertising is not likely to change the demand for the product. Despite the large sums spend by Eastman Kodak on advertisement of its products and by General Motors to promote Frigidaires, there is no proof that either firm has gained a monopoly owing to these large advertising expenditures.

Truth in Advertising. There are, of course, dishonest advertisers, just as there are dishonest men in other walks of life. As the watchdog to protect the American public, the FTC is constantly battling with companies about their alleged exaggerations or untruths. What do we mean by "tell the truth"? Is the advertisement expected to tell the literal truth, or merely to give a reasonably accurate impression? On this subject, the Supreme Court has made these statements:

> Advertising as a whole must not create a misleading impression even though every statement separately considered is literally truthful.
> Advertising must not obscure or conceal material facts.
> Advertising must not be artfully contrived to distract and divert readers' attention from the true nature of the terms and conditions of an offer.

[1]Jules Backman, *Advertising and Competition* (New York: New York University Press, 1967), p. 157.

The Federal Trade Commission is now embarked on the biggest truth-in-advertising campaign in the history of that agency. It is demanding that advertisers be prepared to substantiate most of the advertising claims they make. A resolution adopted by the FTC stated that advertisers are not voluntarily meeting the public's needs for more objective information about their advertising claims.[2] The resolution added:

> Public disclosure can enhance competition by encouraging competitors to challenge advertised claims which have no basis in fact . . .

In another area of concern, the FTC is seeking to prevent deceptive price advertising. Typical practices that the commission warns advertisers to avoid

[2] *U.S. News & World Report,* June 21, 1971.

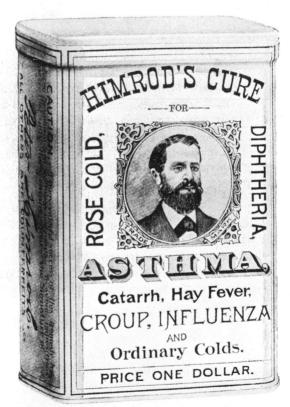

Courtesy The Bettmann Archive

Advertisements appearing around the turn of the century, such as the one above, were not regulated by any public agencies. As you may observe, claims made in some old-time advertisements had little respect for truthfulness. Nor were advertisers required to prove their claims as they are now.

are contained in its publication, "Guides Against Deceptive Pricing," now available to businessmen in cooperation with Better Business Bureaus everywhere.

In New York City, Consumer Affairs Commissioner Bess Myerson is pushing for a citywide regulation forcing manufacturers to keep records to use in supporting advertising claims that are apparently based on objective or clinical evidence. It is also proposed that theater, movie, and book advertisements be prohibited from using out-of-context words and phrases in advertising, if the words distort the opinions of the reviewer.

A study published by the Harvard Business Review recently disclosed that only one in three business executives reported that advertisements really give a true picture of the product, and two in five believed that the general public's faith in advertising is at an all-time low. Nine out of ten executives felt advertisers should be required to prove their claims.

Although most advertising can be considered truthful, there are still too many unscrupulous advertisers who make misleading or half-true statements about their products. Exaggerated claims for killing germs, curing colds, and producing sleep have been challenged by government agencies. Fortunately, a great deal has been accomplished to correct these false claims.

In 1938, Congress passed the Wheeler-Lea Act, amending the Federal Trade Commission (FTC) Act of 1914 and giving the FTC power over "unfair or deceptive acts or practices." Several statutes aimed at specific industries grant the FTC the authority to act on matters related to labeling and advertising; among them are:

> The Wool Product Labeling Act of 1939
> The Fur Products Labeling Act of 1951
> The Flammable Fabrics Act of 1953
> The Textile Fiber Production Identification Act of 1968

The Federal Communications Commission also has regulatory power over radio and television stations and network operations, and maintains a watchful eye over the merits of advertising broadcast by these two media.

In 1965, Congress passed the Highway Beautification Act, prohibiting billboards and other signs within 600 feet of the interstate and primary road systems, but this law has not had total enforcement in all the states.

On January 1, 1966, cigarette manufacturers were first required to place on each cigarette package a health warning reading, "Caution: Cigarette smoking may be hazardous to your health." Again in 1970, Congress made this warning notice stronger, requiring that each package contain this statement: "Warning: The Surgeon General has determined that cigarette smoking is dangerous to your health."

What has come to be the most-far-reaching federal law affecting advertising is known as the Public Health Cigarette Smoking Act, effective January

2, 1971. This law prohibits cigarette advertising of any kind on radio and television broadcasts.

Printers' Ink, a marketing magazine, and the Better Business Bureaus are well known for their efforts to protect consumers. For years, these two organizations have worked to improve advertising standards and prevent false claims.

Discussion Questions

1. *How does advertising differ from personal selling? In what way does advertising differ from publicity?*
2. *What are the purposes of advertising and how do these purposes differ from the services advertising provides for business?*
3. *Discuss what is meant by the question, Is advertising an economic waste? Do you believe that advertising often forces you to buy things or act in making a product choice against your will? Explain.*

ADVERTISING MEDIA

The *advertising medium* (plural: *media*) is the means chosen by the advertiser to present his message—newspaper, magazine, or radio, for example.

Advertising media may be classified in the following manner. (Their relationship to each other are shown in the chart, top of page 564.)

Newspapers	Radio	Transportation
Magazines	Television	Point-of-purchase displays
Direct mail	Outdoor signs	Specialty

Media Characteristics

Some large companies use almost all of these media, but small ones, for financial reasons, may use only one or two of them. Many factors must be evaluated by the advertiser in selecting the proper media, including the cost, extent of coverage (circulation), amount of selectivity provided, degree of flexibility, timeliness, and nature of coverage (geography).

Newspapers. In terms of expenditures, the newspaper is the leading medium, accounting for nearly 30 percent of total dollars spent. Newspaper advertising is popular with consumers. It is an effective one when the advertiser is seeking geographical selectivity. Advertisements may be prepared and submitted only a few hours before press time, although most newspapers specify that copy be turned in several days in advance. However, the short life of each

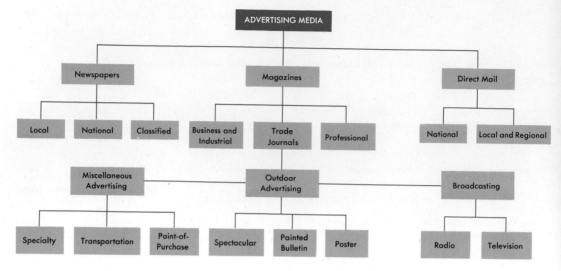

Advertising media possess characteristics which affect media choices.

newspaper edition and the lack of quality reproduction of illustrative materials are two limiting factors. Studies show that the average length of time a person reads a newspaper is only about 20 minutes daily. Almost all newspapers quote different rates to local and national advertisers, with local rates lower than national.

Magazines. Magazines are an effective medium when the aim is to reach special-interest groups, such as physicians, engineers, educators, farmers, or business executives. Magazines are printed on top-quality paper that permits creative typography and extensive use of color. Compared with newspapers, magazines permit little flexibility in submitting copy, which is usually required several weeks in advance. The cost of reaching 1,000 readers (cost-per-thousand circulation) can be compared by the space buyer among magazines in the following way:

$$\frac{\text{Page rate} \times 1,000}{\text{Circulation}} = \text{Cost-per-thousand.}$$

If the cost for a black-and-white full page is $24,000, and the average net paid circulation is 4 million, the formula will look like this:

$$\frac{\$24,000 \times 1,000}{4,000,000} = \$6$$

A magazine with a rate per page of $11,000 for a black-and-white ad and a circulation of 2 million would have a cost-per-thousand of $5.50.

Direct-Mail Advertising. The main advantage of direct-mail advertising is that it reaches a selected audience, providing more precision than is possible through any other medium. It is especially good for advertisers with a limited

564

budget, and it can serve a local, regional, or national market with a broad geographical flexibility.

Radio. Once an important medium for reaching mass audiences, radio stations today specialize in appealing to selective audiences—including news fans, music lovers, sports fans, and teen-agers. Advertisers usually take care to select the kind of programs that they believe will attract the largest audiences. Radio advertising can be used in saturation campaigns, and time costs are low. In addition, there are some products that can be sold best by the human voice without a visual impression to accompany it. Radio advertising ranks fifth in total dollar expenditures.

Television. Television is a mass medium. It can be used either on a nationwide or regional basis, or concentrated on the local market. (Also true of radio, if to a lesser extent.) As with radio, television has the advantage of immediate reception, providing timeliness to an even greater extent than do newspapers. A magazine or newspaper may be in print several hours or days before it is read by the subscriber, but the advertising message on TV is received by the listener at once. Its greatest advantage is that it combines sight, sound, and motion, a unique combination for advertising. On the other hand, its message is short-lived and production costs are high. Expenditures for TV advertising are the second largest of those for all separate media. Table 21.1 shows the top 15 TV advertisers, ranked according to their expenditures.

TABLE
21.1

TOP 15 TV NETWORK ADVERTISERS, 1970

In millions of dollars

Company	Expenditures
1. Procter & Gamble Company	$128.4
2. Bristol-Myers Company	57.0
3. R. J. Reynolds Industries	52.4
4. Colgate-Palmolive Company	46.5
5. Warner-Lambert Pharmaceutical Company	46.2
6. General Foods Corp.	44.6
7. Sterling Drug, Inc.	41.3
8. American Home Products Corp.	40.8
9. Lever Bros.	38.5
10. Philip Morris, Inc.	36.6
11. General Motors Corporation	32.9
12. Ford Motor Company	31.3
13. Miles Laboratories, Inc.	28.9
14. S. C. Johnson & Son	28.8
15. American Brands, Inc.	28.0

Source: Television Bureau of Advertising, Inc.

Outdoor Advertising. The three principal categories of outdoor advertising are posters, painted bulletins, and spectaculars. A poster is the standardized "billboard," with the advertising message printed or painted on sheets of heavy paper that are glued onto the poster. Poster signs are located along routes traveled by large numbers of automobiles or pedestrians. The painted bulletin is usually more elaborate than the poster and somewhat longer. The spectacular is a custom-made sign constructed to fit a specific space, using elaborate color and illumination to attract your attention long enough to see it. The main disadvantage of outdoor advertising is that it must be restricted to short, simple messages. Drivers or pedestrians have little time to look at a long or complex advertisement. Outdoor advertising must comply with local, state, and federal regulations when located along a main highway.

Miscellaneous Media. In addition to those media already mentioned, there are others used by advertisers. *Point-of-purchase displays* consist of advertising displays mounted inside stores where consumers shop. These are intended to stimulate impulse buying—purchases made on sudden inclination or unpremeditated urge to buy. *Catalogues* are also used for advertising. *Car cards,* located in subways, buses, taxis, and suburban trains, are widely used forms of advertising mainly in large cities.

Advertising in Foreign Countries

No longer is advertising used almost exclusively in the United States. American companies doing business abroad, many as multinational firms, have generated increasing interest in the use of advertising. Table 21.2 lists the eleven

TABLE
21.2

LEADING FOREIGN COUNTRIES IN
ADVERTISING EXPENDITURES, 1968

In millions of dollars

Country	Expenditures
West Germany	$2,152.2
Great Britain	1,705.0
Japan	1,478.0
Canada	902.1
France	890.0
Italy	550.0
Sweden	418.0
Switzerland	405.9
Australia	385.1
Netherlands	285.0
Spain	276.0

Source: Advertising Age, *Sept. 22, 1969, p. 51.*

foreign countries that lead in advertising expenditures. During 1968, these countries spent a total of nearly $10 billion for advertising, compared with $18.3 billion spent in the United States. The relative amount of advertising expenditure abroad is closely identified with the country's stage of economic development. West Germany, Great Britain, and Japan spent almost one-third as much for advertising as the United States. Several American advertising agencies have established branch offices abroad. Advertising in Russia is directed by two organizations, Vneshtogreklama and Soyustorgreklama.

Discussion Questions

4. Why is it important for the advertising manager to select the proper media? What are some of the factors that advertisers consider in choosing media?

5. Compare the advantages of newspaper advertising with those of direct mail if you want to sell the following products: (a) farm machinery, (b) electric toasters, and (c) rare coins.

PERSONAL SELLING

We know from the preceding discussion that advertising can do much to stimulate market demands by bringing a product to the attention of buyers. But without a personal presentation by salesmen, few sales may be closed. Personal selling is a form of salesmanship. The salesman alone does not control the market, but he plays an important role through inducing others to purchase.

Salesmanship may be defined as the power to influence others to buy what the seller has for sale. Salesmanship is an art that is based on some scientific principles. There is a growing body of knowledge dealing with selling methods and with human behavior as it responds to selling methods. The principles of selling can be taught and learned, the same as other academic subjects. This is why companies are constantly conducting sales training programs for new and inexperienced salesmen.

Selling and the Merchandising Mix

When Emerson said, "He is great who can alter my state of mind," he was in a sense referring to salesmen. A true salesman does influence people to act. He stands as an indispensable link between producer and consumer.

The oldest and most effective method of selling is through *personal selling,* which is generally defined as the activities of both the inside and outside salesmen involving direct contact of the seller with the buyer. It can take the form of house-to-house selling, as practiced by Fuller Brush Company repre-

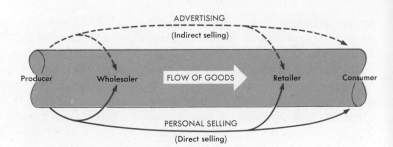

Personal selling and advertising expedite the flow of goods through the marketing channel, which involves—in most cases—the wholesaler and the retailer.

sentatives. A study of the accompanying diagram shows the parallel relationship of advertising to personal selling in promoting the flow of goods through the channels of distribution. This combination of advertising, personal selling, package design, dealer promotion, and marketing research comprises the merchandising mix. There is no set formula for determining the best combination of these ingredients. The mix varies among firms. Some emphasize advertising; others use more personal selling.

Types of Personal-Selling Employment

According to the U.S. Census Bureau, about 5 million persons work directly in selling occupations, representing a ratio in the total population of one salesman to every 42 people. Although the nature of these selling jobs varies, it is possible to identify them for purposes of this discussion under five headings: (1) manufacturers' salesmen, (2) wholesale salesmen, (3) retail salesmen, (4) technical salesmen, and (5) door-to-door salesmen.

Manufacturers' Salesmen. These are the salesmen who sell to wholesalers, retailers, and other manufacturers. They sell machinery and semimanufactured products to industry. The two types of manufacturers' salesmen are the sales engineer and the missionary salesman. The sales engineer is not only employed to sell; because of his technical knowledge, he is expected to be competent on technical matters and therefore to give advice about them. His financial rewards are higher than those of other types of salesmen.

The missionary salesman usually does not actually "sell" his employer's products; instead, his job is to help his firm's customers. For example, the salesman for a chemical manufacturer may call on a retailer to acquaint him with a new product that can be obtained from a local wholesaler, who is the manufacturer's direct customer. The pharmaceutical manufacturer employs a "medical detail man" (salesman) who calls on doctors to tell them about new drugs that can be bought from a wholesale drug company.

Wholesale Salesmen. These salesmen sell to retailers as a rule. Like manufacturer's salesmen, they perform low-pressure selling—selling based on the idea of giving service without high-pressure techniques. The alert wholesale salesman makes sure the retailer is well stocked with his firm's goods.

Retail Salesmen. These are the people from whom you buy merchandise at retail. Retail selling differs from other types of selling in that the buyer seeks out the salesman instead of the salesman calling on a prospect. To some extent, a retail salesman is an order taker. In large retail stores, salesmen generally specialize in selling goods found only in one department. The trend toward self-service tends to decrease the relative number of retail selling positions.

Technical Salesmen. The technical salesman's purpose is to increase the volume of sales by providing technical knowledge about the product to his company's customers. In this type of selling, the ability to analyze and solve customers' problems and needs is important. To this extent, the technical salesman is similar to the missionary salesman. Formal education in engineering or a science is generally required.

Door-to-Door Salesmen. Those manufacturers who sell directly to consumers use door-to-door salesmen. A vigorous sales presentation beyond that required in regular retail selling is often necessary. The list of companies selling from door to door is long, but the failure rate is high. Magazines, brushes, cosmetics, detergents, vacuum cleaners, books, aluminumware, and dairy products are commonly sold directly to the home. This method of selling has acquired a poor reputation because some door-to-door salesmen have been nuisances or even used fraudulent methods. This method of selling also runs counter to other buying habits, such as the desire to choose from a wide assortment of goods or to compare price and quality.

Discussion Questions

6. *What is the difference between personal selling and advertising?*
7. *How does the job of a salesman representing a manufacturing company differ from that of a retail salesman?*

IMPORTANCE OF BEHAVIORAL APPROACH IN SELLING

In recent years, marketing executives have received from the behavioral scientists an increasing amount of information regarding human behavior in the market place. A study of behavior starts with an understanding of motivation. The term *motivation* may be defined as the inner urge resulting from stimuli that move a person to act in a certain way. Thus, motivation involves a three-stage cycle consisting of a need, a drive, and a goal. The need may be psychological, such as hunger or thirst. The drive is the stimulation to act, which is created by the need. The third stage, attainment of the goal that satisfies the need, is the result of the behavioral drive.

An earlier theory of behavior held that human responses were based on instincts common to all human beings. Psychologists developed a list of inherent traits, and marketing experts, including sales managers and advertising authorities, tried to determine which ones influenced people to buy. For some years now, psychologists have recognized that human behavior is also motivated by environmental conditions arising from social and economic needs. The reasons consumers buy specific goods and services are called *buying motives.*

Consumer Buying Motives

In personal selling as well as in advertising, specific motives are used to appeal to consumers for their patronage. The shrewd salesman knows that "if you want to sell John Doe, you must know something about what makes him tick." So in order to understand the consumer, we must recognize the motives that cause him to act.

Buying motives are classified as emotional or rational. *Emotional motives* are subjective and impulsive in nature, produced without the advantage of logical thinking. A woman buys a new dress not because she needs it but because she wants recognition. Emotional motives include hunger, pride, status, safety, and comfort. Sellers of tangible articles like musical instruments, sporting goods, or furniture rely heavily on emotional buying motives, such as pleasure, comfort, or distinction. Oftentimes, emotional buying motives are the stronger appeals.

Rational motives are those produced by a logical reasoning process. A product that is sold only after the buyer weighs all its advantages and disadvantages is not purchased on impulse. Some of the commonly used rational motives are economy, dependability, fair price, and quality. Watch salesmen know that fair price and dependability are far more convincing buying motives than are such emotional motives as security, recognition, or superiority.

A typical buyer may respond to both emotional and rational motives. As an example, a decision to buy a certain style of automobile may be entirely emotional, but the decision as to the brand may well be rational. It is not unusual either for a buyer to express a rational motive as the reason for buying an article that was actually purchased for emotional motives. Sellers sometimes recognize this type of individual behavior, and often use advertisements carrying rational motives as well as emotional appeals. The study of consumer buying is complicated. What may be purely a rational motive to one person may be emotional to another. In the final analysis, the distinction is generally determined by the amount of time and consideration given to making the purchase.

The company that uses as part of its marketing strategy a combination of buying motives is more likely to be successful in personal selling than one that fails to recognize the effectiveness of buying motives at all. It is the clever salesman who counteracts customer objections with positive buying motives.

Steps in Making a Sale

Despite the fact that there are different types of selling jobs and numerous motives in a selling strategy, the process of selling may be broken down into specific steps. Although these steps cannot always be timed precisely nor distinguished from one another because they tend to blend, they do occur in the following order: (1) locating the prospect, (2) meeting the prospect under favorable conditions, (3) presenting the product, (4) creating the prospect's desire to buy, and (5) closing the sale.

The actual presentation by the salesman may begin with his attempt to obtain the prospect's attention. He will then attempt to hold the customer's interest. This may entail giving a demonstration or a detailed explanation of the product's uses. The final step is to close the sale. A question, "When do you want delivery?" implies a straightforward request, and if the salesman has not received an objection by now, the prospect generally buys. A good salesman is always a good closer. The salesman who fails to close is like the sprinter who trains all season and leads in the race, only to fall down three yards from the finish line.

Selling Techniques

A successful salesman will admit he uses various techniques. Several pages could be used to explore all of them in detail. However, among those most often used are these:

1. Know all about your product and what it can do for your customer. Product knowledge is a "must" in personal selling, because it creates customer confidence, builds enthusiasm, and gives a professional touch to the situation.
2. Size up your prospect. Ask him questions about the kind of product or service he wants; this incites his interest. Make him feel that he is important. Listen and let him tell you what he wants or does not want.
3. Present a positive rather than a negative approach. The salesman is more effective when he says, "May I help you?" than when he says, "You wouldn't like to see our new model, would you?" A negative approach calls for a negative answer.

4. Train yourself to handle objections. If the prospect says the price is too high, you might reply ''Yes, the price may be a little higher than you planned. However, in the long run you'll save money because of the superior quality of this product.'' In any event, don't argue with your prospect about whether a price is too high.

ADVERTISING AS A CAREER

Since the services performed by people working in advertising agencies vary from artistic skills to marketing research, it is difficult to be specific as to the personal qualifications that are required. These depend largely on the type of work to be performed. However, in addition to the qualifications ordinarily needed for a career in business (as discussed in earlier chapters), there are at least four essential personal qualifications.

One is the ability to create—to visualize and come forth with new ideas. It helps to be an innovator. Another qualification is adaptability. The third is the ability to sell, and the fourth is patience. One who has studied college marketing, advertising, statistics, and other basic business-administration subjects has an advantage. And the study of written and oral communication is most essential.

Positions in Advertising Agencies

Most of the work in advertising is performed by advertising agencies. Because agencies tend toward a division of labor, qualified specialists are always in demand. The following positions are commonly found in an advertising agency.

Media Director. This person selects the best media to achieve the client's objectives. He must be able to choose from among the nation's 1,600 daily newspapers, 800 weeklies, 900 consumer magazines and farm journals, 2,600 business and professional magazines, and 4,000 radio and 500 TV stations. Then there are outdoor signs, direct mail, transportation, and miscellaneous types of media.

Production Man. This position requires a knowledge of printing processes. The production man's primary job is to keep the project—pamphlet, booklet, or ad—moving through the various processes. All told, agencies employ about 1,000 production men. A smaller number work in publishing firms, for printers, and in company advertising departments.

Art-and-Layout Director. This person, who must possess talent and skill as an artist, is responsible for the quality of the art work. He confers with the client, and with the account executive and others in the agency, to determine the best possible layout and art for the ad.

Copywriter. Often called the "idea man," the copywriter prepares the copy—the message the advertiser wishes to present. In the final stages of the copy, he works with various specialists, including the art-and-layout director and the account executive. Recent figures reveal that about 4,600 persons in advertising agencies are copywriters.

Account Executive. This person occupies one of the most important and "sensitive" positions in an agency, because he is responsible for keeping his client satisfied with the agency's work. Besides being a creative person and a good salesman, the account executive must be familiar with business practices and have an understanding of marketing, merchandising, and advertising.

PERSONAL SELLING AS A CAREER

A good salesman is rarely without employment. Also, for him every day is different; selling is not a monotonous occupation but one that offers a challenge and interesting experiences.

Based on average compensation, personal selling pays a high income to those who are successful. Famous Americans like Walter P. Chrysler, Marshall Field, and Charles Walgreen worked as salesmen before they started their own businesses.

Selling is difficult work. It is known to cause mental strain because of the pressure that is often placed on the salesman. Only people with a strong personal desire to achieve and a positive and enthusiastic attitude toward their jobs are likely to succeed. But it is a stepping stone to higher-level positions in large firms. It can be very rewarding both in terms of monetary benefits and personal satisfaction.

Discussion Questions

8. *What are buying motives, and how do they relate to personal selling?*
9. *What is meant by the "steps in selling," and how do these steps differ from selling techniques?*

SUMMARY

In marketing, there are two common methods by which goods are sold: advertising and personal selling. Advertising seeks to appeal to the masses, while personal selling involves an oral presentation by the seller to the prospect.

As a tool of marketing, advertising serves to retain loyal customers, to reduce lost customers, and to recruit new ones. As a social force, advertising has altered our living habits and helped to raise living standards. Economically, it has promoted the growth of industry, lowered unit costs, and served to identify in the minds of consumers, families of products under one name or brand.

The more popular advertising media are newspapers, radio and television, magazines, direct mail, and outdoor displays. Transportation advertising and point-of-purchase displays are effective, but they are used less frequently. Direct-mail advertising is the most selective and radio and television advertising the most flexible. Newspapers are widely read, but the average reading time is less than for magazines. Outdoor advertising offers geographical selectivity, because it is directed to a given locality.

The ability to sell involves both a personal selling strategy and an understanding of consumer buying habits. For instance, there are five steps identified in the selling strategy: (1) locating the prospect, (2) meeting the prospect under favorable conditions, (3) presenting the product, (4) creating the prospect's desire for the product or service, and (5) closing the sale.

VOCABULARY REVIEW

Match the following vocabulary terms with the statements below.

a. Advertising	e. Motivation	h. Publicity
b. Advertising medium	f. National advertising	i. Rational motives
c. Impulse buying	g. Point-of-purchase displays	j. Salesmanship
d. Local advertising		

1. Any form of advertising using a medium with national circulation
2. Information made available to the public through various media about a firm, a product, or an event, because such information is regarded as news
3. Any paid form of nonpersonal presentation and promotion of ideas, goods, or services by an identified sponsor
4. Advertising placed by a local retailer
5. The power to influence others to buy what the seller has for sale
6. Motives produced by a logical reasoning process
7. The means chosen by the advertiser to present his message
8. Promotional materials mounted inside stores where consumers shop
9. Purchases made on sudden inclination or unpremeditated urge to buy
10. An inner urge resulting from stimuli that moves a person to act in a certain way

PROBLEMS AND PROJECTS

1. Choose from a current magazine two advertisements: an example of an institutional ad, and an example of a product ad. From each of the two ads determine the following:

   a. The nature of the appeal used
   b. The basic function of the ad (the 3 R's of advertising)
   c. Whether the copy appeal is rational or emotional

2. Given the following media—newspaper, television, direct mail, outdoor display, and magazine—rate each according to the following qualifications:

     a. Degree of flexibility—5 points
     b. Timeliness—4 points
     c. Cost—3 points
     d. Amount of selectivity—2 points

3. Carter Jackson is president of the United Can Company, the second largest producer of tin containers. At a meeting of the board of directors, he was instructed by the board to make a recommendation on the most effective ways to increase sales, either with an expanded advertising budget of $400,000 or the same amount of money with which to employ as many new salesmen as the budget could provide. Your problem is not one of recommending what to do, but of analyzing the nature of the problem and what it is that Jackson is trying to accomplish.

A BUSINESS CASE

Case 21-1 L/C Cola

The Lone Star Beverage Company has just announced a new cola drink. The L/C Cola Company in Dallas has the franchise to bottle and market this cola drink in the Dallas-Fort Worth area. The drink is sold in a 10-ounce bottle, which is a throwaway glass bottle requiring no deposit. The franchiser plans to spend $1 million for advertising the first year. Tentatively, the advertising will either be divided among radio and television spot commercials and in local newspapers, outdoor signs, and direct mail, or it will take the form of retail-store demonstrations. In the latter case, the product would be sampled in grocery stores in a crash program, completed in two months and employing a team of 20 women, each assigned to a grocery store for a two-day period.

1. Which type of campaign (using the various media or store sampling) would you recommend?
2. Explain how your recommendation will accomplish the desired objectives best.

physical distribution and transportation
CHAPTER TWENTY-TWO

The distribution system for any enterprise is developed for the purpose of moving goods from the producer to the purchasers. It must be concerned with the flow of raw materials as well as of completed products. A good distribution scheme helps to create a demand for goods as well as to deal with the problems of time and space.

Distribution is sometimes referred to as "the other half of marketing," since approximately half the total cost of the marketing process, it has been estimated, is generated by the physical-distribution aspects of marketing.

There are a number of interrelated components in the physical-distribution network: size of shipment, inventory size and control, storage, transportation, and materials handling. The management of the total physical-distribution mix is complex; in some cases, even the internal components are in opposition to one another. For example, the production department may wish to have a large run in order to keep the unit cost low, marketing may want a large inventory in order to fill deliveries fully and promptly, while finance may want small inventories in order to minimize the amount of capital tied up in unsold goods.

ORGANIZATION FOR DISTRIBUTION

The various components of the logistics of most businesses have historically been fragmented and distributed among several different departments. Naturally, control over physical distribution is next to impossible when this situation exists. The problem is one of seeing that the right products are available in the right quantities, in the right places, at the right times; and this requires coordination, direction, and control.

The National Council of Physical Distribution Management has defined *physical distribution* as

> . . . the broad range of activities concerned with efficient movement of finished products from the end of the production line to the consumer, and in some cases includes the movement of raw materials from the source of supply to the beginning of the production line. These activities include freight transportation, warehousing, material handling, protective packaging, inventory control, plant and warehouse site selection, order processing, market forecasting, and customer service.[1]

One way in which many firms have put an end to fragmentation and established control over the logistics of physical distribution is to give full responsibility for it to the vice-president for marketing. (He may have a director of physical distribution answering directly to him.)

Another scheme that has proved effective is to centralize the most basic components of physical distribution while leaving production schedules and inventory control in the production department.

A third arrangement establishes physical distribution as a line-and-staff function on the same level with production, finance, and marketing. Under this arrangement, physical distribution is responsible for materials flow, inventory control, warehousing, customer service, order processing, packing, and shipping.

The centralization of the various aspects of physical distribution can best be accomplished when a firm's operational activities are similar among its different product lines. When the production processes, the materials handling, the marketing channels, and the modes of transportation are identical or similar for the various products manufactured, overall control is much more likely than when these components vary widely.

---

[1] Definition by the National Council of Physical Distribution Management, Executive Offices, Chicago, Ill.

Should the similarity described above exist for either the raw materials or the finished goods but not for both, the logistics pattern may consist of two different schemes—one for inbound materials and another for outbound finished goods.

Discussion Question

1. *Describe briefly three ways that control over the logistics of physical distribution can be effected.*

LOGISTICS DECISIONS AND PLANNING

The breadth and variety of a manufacturer's product line are usually determined before plans are made for solving physical-distribution problems. In other words, the logistics system is usually adapted to the product rather than the product to the logistics plan.[2] However, the extent and level of service to be given one's customers is a variable over which management has control. Some of the factors that enter into the service picture are the degree of concentration or dispersion of customers; the size of a typical order; how frequently orders are received and processed; the extent to which the manufacturer must provide storage, as against the assistance he might receive from others in the distribution channel; and the variety and quality of transportation media from which a choice may be made.

Decisions on Inventory

We may think of inventories as reservoirs of goods being held available for filling orders. At intervals, products are added to the reservoir as they come off the production lines, and goods are withdrawn from the reservoir as sales are made.

The decision that management faces is to determine at what level goods should be allowed to accumulate, and to what level they should be permitted to fall—setting the upper and lower limits. These control limits are partially determined by the forecast sales volume. The more accurate the sales forecast, the more economical the management of the inventory.

The level of customer service considered to be acceptable is an important factor in setting inventory control limits. One writer estimates that "approximately 80 percent more inventory is needed in a typical business to fill 95

[2] Logistics embraces the details of supply, storing and transport of materials and finished goods.

The *Skycrane* is used to transport heavy freight

percent of customers' orders out of stock than to fill only 80 percent."[3] The question to be decided then would be to what degree the revenues from 15 percent additional volume would offset the storage and handling costs of almost doubling the inventory.

This all points up again the importance of all components of the marketing mix working together. The question of how much inventory to maintain is closely related to the regularity of flow of finished goods, to promptness in handling goods by transportation agents, and to the time required to process orders, as well as to the sales forecast. Inventory maintenance must be determined by types of products, not on total volume of sales. Sometimes a relatively few items make up a significant percentage of the total sales.

Cost Considerations.   Control of inventory costs is largely determined by the output factors. There are three major categories of cost factors: holding costs, costs due to shortages, and replenishment costs.

[3] John F. Magee, "The Logistics of Distribution," *Harvard Business Review,* 37:92 (July–August 1960).

Holding costs include warehousing expenses, finance costs arising from capital investment in inventories, losses resulting from price changes due to market conditions, insurance on inventory, and losses resulting from spoilage or obsolescence. *Shortage costs* arise from failure to have sufficient goods on hand to fill orders at the time they are received; they include special clerical and handling costs, loss of income because of losing the sale, and in extreme cases, loss of customers. *Replenishment costs* are usually tied closely to manufacturing costs—overtime required to make up shortages, loss of production time caused by equipment breakdowns, and so forth.

Distribution Centers and Storage

It is inevitable that finished goods must be stored in some quantity in selected locations. The amount to be stored and the locations of facilities are closely linked to the sizes and types of inventories maintained and to the "acceptable level" of customer service to be given.

Historically, in discussing a logistics system we have talked largely in terms of warehousing. But unfortunately, "warehousing" has taken on the connotation of depositing goods for an extended period of time, implying a lack of movement. The term *distribution center* puts the emphasis on the movement of goods and is therefore a more modern and a more acceptable usage. Moreover, it also seems to express better than "warehouse" the concept of broad and prompt service to customers. Warehousing becomes one of the important aspects of the distribution center.

By including the use of major distribution centers in its physical-distribution system, a company improves efficiency through savings in shipping charges, larger delivery packages, shorter delivery time, and increased sales effectiveness, because the products sold are in close proximity to the market.

Both costs and the acceptable level of customer service are paramount in determining the practicability of establishing a number of distribution centers. But the availability of a variety of types of transportation media is a very important and limiting factor.

To illustrate, today's facilities are such that it is possible to reach a third of the U.S. consumer market within one day, using only five distribution centers. However, to reach four-fifths of the total consumer market in one day would require five times as many distribution points. Thus management can combine the available options in many different ways. Management might choose, for example, to service one-third of the market through five distribution centers and reach some fraction of the remaining market by a number of centers above five but fewer than the total of 25. The best choice of number and location of distribution centers would be determined by the relation of costs to revenues and profit margins.

Materials-Handling Decisions

Improvements in handling goods have made rapid strides in recent years. Railroad cars are brought completely within the warehouse to facilitate loading and unloading. Hand labor has been almost eliminated, through the use of pallets on which many boxes of goods are placed, forklifts for moving pallets, and docking plates that bridge the gap between the warehouse floor and the railroad car, enabling the forklift to enter the car.

Conveyor-belt systems have reduced the time and labor costs of handling goods. Containerization is now so widely accepted that it has also greatly reduced handling costs.

Containerization. The idea of *containerized shipping* embodies the practice of placing goods in a sealed container, which is transported by more than one type of carrier between the shipper and the consignee. It might travel first by truck, then by rail, then on a ship, and finally by truck again on the last leg to its destination.

The original plan for containerization, introduced by the New Haven Railroad and approved by the Interstate Commerce Commission in 1954, involved nothing more than the transporting of the trailers of common-carrier trucks on railroad flatcars. Then in 1958, the railways began offering the shipper the choice of using his own trailer or one owned by the railroad. The use of standardized containers—which are easily handled, are completely inter-

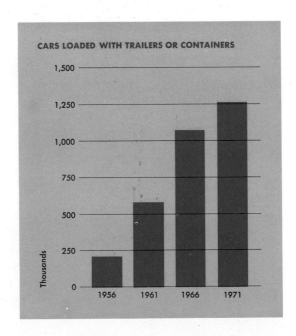

changeable between trucks, railroads, and barges, and can be coupled together to make a single unit—holds great promise for future operations.

Shippers prefer "piggybacking" (trailer-on-flatcar rail hauling) because of convenience and economy. A long haul by piggyback requires approximately 40 percent fewer man-hours than it does by highway, and offers great savings in wear and tear on the equipment as well. Containerized operations are not only cheaper than conventional truck shipment for long hauls, but require less effort on the part of the shipper, because he has to deal with only one organization instead of with connecting truck lines in different cities. Piggybacking also reduces damage and theft, because the cargo remains sealed in the container throughout its travels.

At the beginning of 1971, there were 293,000 trailers and containers registered for intermodal service in the United States. Slightly more than one-fourth of these were trailers and the rest were containers. They play their biggest role in rail and ocean shipping.

The European maritime industry has built modern port facilities for handling containerized cargo, and European shipping lines have converted ships to specialize in carrying it. It has been estimated that containers can reduce port costs by as much as 50 percent. They can also reduce the time required for loading, transporting, and unloading cargo; the time required between England and Chicago, for example, can be reduced by several days. More than half of all transatlantic cargo is now being carried in containers.

Courtesy The Port of New York Authority

Containerized shipping-loading dock in New York City

Courtesy Pan American World Airways

747 cargo containers are loaded at Kennedy International Airport aboard a Pan American World Airways aircraft destined for London's Heathrow Airport.

The airlines are also shipping containers in their large jets. The A container fills the entire semicircular hold of a DC-8 or Boeing 707. This container accepts 10,000 pounds of weight and 457 cubic feet of bulk. B-size containers are half the size of A; C-size, half the size of B; and D-size, half the size of C. Combinations of B, C, and D containers build up to the size of an A container.

WAREHOUSING

Warehousing is an important part of physical distribution. Storage is essential if production and consumption are to be coordinated in relation to time, because, for one thing, not all goods can be consumed as they are produced. For instance, the growing of crops is seasonal, yet farm produce is in demand at all times. Therefore, produce such as orange juice must be canned or frozen in season, although it is sold throughout the year. The proper use of warehousing services thus enables the producer to store his surplus goods for the present and market them later. And the proper use of transportation in conjunction with warehousing helps the producer adjust his operation to fit the time, place, and rate of consumer demand.

The reverse of this situation also exists. The demand for Christmas toys and outdoor sporting goods is seasonal, yet manufacturers wish to maintain their operations the year around. Here, warehousing again helps the adjustment that must be made: to gear year-round production to meet peak seasonal demands without the added cost of overtime or around-the-clock operations.

Types of Warehouses

There are essentially two types of warehouse operations: private and public. *Private warehouses* are owned or leased and operated by individual enterprises—manufacturers, wholesalers, and retailers—for their own use. They may maintain storage and distribution centers near their plants, or they may maintain branch operations at other locations.

Public warehouses make their storage and handling facilities available to any businesses wishing to use them. Patrons of public warehousing facilities pay for the services they receive on the basis of space and time requirements. Some warehouses store all types of general merchandise; others store only special commodities, such as farm produce or frozen foods. Public warehouses are in operation in all principal market areas in the United States. A recent U.S. census of business showed that there are more than 1,600 general warehousing and storage operations in the United States. In addition, there are many specialized storage facilities, such as those for cold storage, frozen produce, and bulk liquids.

Warehousing Services

All too frequently, people are inclined to think only of storage in connection with warehousing. It includes storage, of course—in fact, this is its primary service—but warehousing is much more than storage. For instance, among other services offered by public warehouses are the dividing of bulk shipments and reshipping. They receive carload shipments, divide them into smaller units, and ship them to a number of customers in different geographical locations. Some of the large shipments may be stored for future demand and the rest divided and shipped immediately. And in some instances, the goods may be processed or packaged according to customer's specifications before being reshipped.

Warehouses may help the owner of goods being stored to finance his operation. A receipt is issued to the owner, showing the kinds and amounts of goods he has in storage. This warehouse receipt, as we saw in Chapter 14, may be used as security for a loan at a bank. When the goods are sold, the loan from the bank is paid and the goods are released and shipped to the new owner.

Because they are specialists, warehousemen can advise business management regarding specialized aspects of physical-distribution services. They can suggest ways in which available facilities may be used to the best advantage of both buyer and seller.

2. *Explain how the level of customer service helps to set the control limits on inventory.*

3. *Why is the term* distribution center *preferred to* warehouse?

4. *What are the advantages of containerized shipping over not using containers?*

THE ECONOMIC IMPORTANCE OF TRANSPORTATION

We share in the benefits of transportation in so many ways that we tend to take it for granted. Our homes and businesses are equipped with merchandise and equipment that comes from every corner of the globe. Perhaps the severest tests of transportation's effectiveness come in times of emergency. For example, when a snowstorm buries the western plains, aircraft must be used to fly in emergency rations and medical supplies, and to airlift hay to stranded cattle. And when a hurricane batters the Gulf Coast, railroads and trucks must be pressed into action to rush food and clothing to the area. But we are concerned with the ways in which businesses use the various modes of transport in everyday commerce. In brief, transportation does the following basic things:

1. Moves raw materials from source to point of use
2. Conveys partially processed goods to other factories
3. Transports manufactured goods to warehouses for storage
4. Ships goods from a company's main factory to its branch operations
5. Routes goods from storage to wholesalers, retailers, and consumers
6. Carries people from one place to another

Now let us consider in more detail four aspects of transportation that follow from the performance of these fundamental accomplishments.

Transportation Widens the Market

A bushel of corn on an Iowa farm may be fed to farm animals or processed into meal for human consumption. But by the use of transportation facilities, it may be sold throughout the country. Steel made into sheets or bars at the mill may be shipped to any factory that wishes to use it, anywhere in the world. Furniture manufactured in Michigan, Indiana, or North Carolina is available in short order to homes and offices wherever it is in demand, because it may be swiftly transported to those places. By enlarging the market for raw materials and processed goods beyond the boundaries of the local communities where they originate, our transportation system contributes materially to the soundness and the successful functioning of our national economy.

Transportation Enhances the Value of Commodities

Transportation increases the value of commodities in two ways. It enables us to move merchandise from a location of surplus where it is not needed to an area of scarcity where it is in demand. Also, because our transportation system works efficiently and rapidly, goods can be shipped from one location to another quickly and at a small unit cost. You will recall that we call this *giving place and time utility to goods.*

Transportation Enhances Specialization

We studied mass-production techniques in an earlier chapter. Mass production is possible only because of modern transportation facilities for shipping raw materials to factories, and finished products to markets. Transportation also makes possible manufacturing specialization. To illustrate, automobile-parts manufacturing can be concentrated in the Detroit area, with the parts shipped to assembly plants in other sections of the country. Steel production is concentrated in Pennsylvania and Ohio; textiles in New England and the Southeast.

Efficient transportation enables a geographical region to specialize in producing those crops best suited to its land and climate. For example, the western plains can devote its entire grassland area to sheep and cattle, and its cultivated lands to wheat. The South can best raise cotton, peanuts, and soybeans, while citrus fruits grow best in Arizona, California, and Florida.

Transportation also enables different countries to specialize by producing those things they can make best and most profitably. Because of the worldwide transportation system, petroleum is shipped from eastern Mediterranean countries to Europe and Asia. We buy coffee from Brazil, bananas from Guatemala, tin from Indonesia, and transistor radios from Japan.

Because of modern transportation facilities, individuals, states, countries, and regions can specialize. By trading with one another, all benefit, and everyone can have more of the articles he needs and wants. Without an efficient transportation system, this high degree of specialization would be impossible.

Transportation Reduces the Need for Large Inventories

There was a time when many business firms were required to maintain large inventories because movement of goods from one point to another required relatively long periods of time. This situation no longer holds true, since it is now possible to ship goods posthaste. Today, many concerns that sell to a national market maintain decentralized warehouses, strategically located to supply wholesalers and retailers efficiently. This reduced delivery time eliminates the need for the small wholesaler and the retailer to maintain large inventories, as was formerly necessary.

The degree to which the centralized distribution center is replacing the former pattern of decentralized warehouses may be illustrated by the Corn Products Company, which has replaced its 221 consignment warehouses with 16 distribution centers. General Foods has replaced more than 100 warehouses with 17 regional distribution centers. The Scott Paper Company has so coordinated its distribution processes, through the use of strategically located shipping centers and by effectively coordinating traffic control with order processing and shipping, that whereas eight days were once required to process an order, it now takes only overnight.

Discussion Question

5. *What are the economic contributions of transportation?*

MODES OF TRANSPORTATION

During recent years, we have seen in this country the use of large jet airliners in the development of airfreight service, the growth in containerized shipping by railroads and ships, the creation of an increasing number of expressways, and the building of large truck fleets by motor freight lines. As a result, practically every major city in the United States provides manufacturers and wholesalers with a wide selection among transport alternatives.

Under any given set of conditions, some mode of transportation has an advantage over the others. Airfreight and air express are preferred for shipping goods that possess a high dollar value but small bulk, for perishable produce, and where distances are great but delivery time is short. Shipment by truck provides door-to-door service and reaches into small communities as well as large cities. Trucks play a most important role when shipping in less-than-carload lots, and trucking is perhaps the most versatile transport method one might choose. The railroads dominate, of course, where the haul is long, where shipments are in carload lots, and where the size or weight is large. Water freight rates are the cheapest, so shipping by water is a good choice when the bulk is large and where time is not of the essence.

Until well into the 1950's, railroads were this country's most important type of transportation carrier. In 1930, three-fourths of all freight shipments were carried over the rails. By 1950, the fraction had dropped almost to one-half. Today, considerably less than half the intercity freight shipments are carried by the railroads. Figures released by the Bureau of Railway Economics, Association of American Railroads, show that the percentage of domestic intercity freight for selected years was distributed as follows:

TABLE
22.1

INTERCITY DOMESTIC FREIGHT SHIPMENTS
(in ton-miles)

Type of Carrier	Percentage of Total				
	1930	1940	1950	1960	1970p
Railroads	74.3	61.3	56.2	44.1	40.8
Motor trucks	3.9	10.0	16.3	21.7	21.0
Oil and gas pipelines	5.3	9.6	12.1	17.4	21.8
Inland waterways (Great lakes, rivers, canals)	16.5	19.1	15.4	16.8	16.2
Air carriers					.2
	100.0	100.0	100.0	100.0	100.0

p = preliminary

Petroleum is the largest item in U.S. port traffic, making up as much as 50 percent of the water freight shipments in Houston, Savannah, Jacksonville, and Philadelphia; 70 percent or more for New York, Los Angeles, San Francisco, and Boston; and over 90 percent for Providence, Rhode Island.

Pipelines now carry about half of all crude oil and refined petroleum products. Limited quantities of powdered coal and wood pulp are also transported by pipeline.

You will note as you study Table 22.1 that the proportion of all freight shipped by rail is continually decreasing, the proportion by motor truck and pipelines is increasing, and the proportion by water is holding fairly constant.

Railroads and Passenger Traffic

Coal, ore, grains, and steel are the principal products shipped by rail, although they are also shipped in large quantities by water. Based on tonnage, coal alone makes up 24.8 percent of all shipments by rail. Each year an average of $1 billion is spent on new freight cars, and in addition, 80,000 existing cars are rebuilt. Freight cars currently being retired have an average capacity of 61 tons; the new cars built to replace them average 81 tons.

Amtrak. Most railroads have lost money on their passenger service over the years, and consequently the quality of passenger service has deteriorated. In October 1970, Congress enacted the Rail Passenger Service Act, which created the National Railroad Passenger Corporation, popularly known as Amtrak, for the purpose of saving intercity passenger-train service.

THE SCOPE OF AMERICA'S BOOMING WATERWAYS

- 26,000 miles of inland and coastal waterways of which all but a few hundred miles are in the Eastern half of the country.

- 20,000 barges plying the waterways—with the number rising steadily.

- 200 billion ton-miles of freight carried yearly—two thirds more than just a decade ago.

- 10 per cent of all intercity freight in the U.S. now moved by water, including: 40 per cent of all U.S. petroleum, 68 per cent of all grains, 86 per cent of coal, 75 per cent of chemicals and 50 per cent of all bulk shipments.

Source: Transport Association of America; U.S. Corps of Engineers

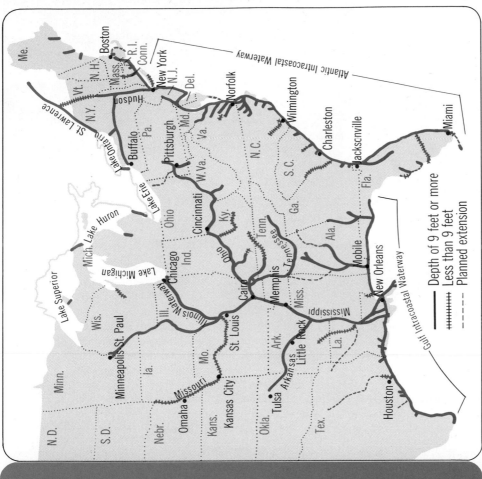

Ten percent of all intercity freight in the United States is now moved over our 26,000 miles of inland and coastal waterways.

Source: Reprinted from *U.S. News & World Report*, September 20, 1971, p. 67. Copyright 1971, U.S. News & World Report, Inc.

Courtesy Nippon Oil Staging Terminal Company, Ltd.

Kiire Terminal, as of February, 1971, the world's largest. This new Caltex-interest crude oil transshipment facility in Japan is so huge that giant super-tankers seem toylike.

A 15-member board of directors and the corporation president are responsible for operating the trains through contractual agreements with existing railroads. Each member rail system company contributes either money or equipment to the company and receives stock or a tax deduction in return. Any railroad not joining Amtrak must run all passenger trains on their schedules for five years as of October 30, 1971. Operations began in 1971 and nearly all major railroads signed a contract to join Amtrak.

Originally Congress envisioned that Amtrak, after an initial injection of federal funds, would soon be in the black, thus relieving Congress of the problem of granting government subsidies to support passenger traffic. Congress appropriated $140 million[4] as a start, but the corporation requested $170 million in additional funds six months later.

Amtrak estimated that it would collect approximately $333 million in revenue during its first two years of operation. However, it faced the immediate task of spending about $150 million for modern equipment to attract passengers back to railroad travel and anticipated that expenditures for equipment and operation during the first two years would exceed $600 million.

At this writing it is too early to foresee how this new development will work out. Congress had hoped that it would be successful, but the experience of the Canadian National Railway offers little encouragement for the realization of this hope.

---

[4] A grant of $40 million, plus a $100-million federally guaranteed loan. Amtrak also received almost $200 million from the railroads and, in return, the railroads received stock or a tax deduction as a price for abandoning their passenger service.

Advantages of Truck Transportation

Trucks can reach all communities, many of which are inaccessible to trains or water transportation. They are very flexible and can be adapted to serve a variety of purposes; manufacturers will, in fact, build a truck to suit the needs of the purchaser. And the relatively low cost of a truck makes it possible for many individual businesses to operate trucks which they either own or lease.

One of the greatest benefits of truck transportation is the quick and convenient delivery service it makes possible. Retailers rely heavily on free deliveries to stimulate buying; they have found that increased sales more than compensate for the added expense. Most retail stores that offer free delivery service maintain their own fleet of trucks or hire the services of local delivery companies that specialize in consolidating deliveries for several stores in the city.

More than 90 percent of all U.S. business firms use the services of trucking companies that operate as public carriers; the rest operate trucks which they own or lease. The arguments given by companies owning and operating their own trucks are:

1. They save the company money.
2. There is better control over merchandise.
3. The driver is a company employee and better able to meet customer problems right on the spot.
4. Trucks may be loaded at odd hours when this seems desirable.
5. During peak traffic periods the shipper, not the transportation company, sets the priorities.
6. The company reaps on advertising value, since the company name goes everywhere the truck goes.

Truck Leasing. Full-service leasing companies provide approximately a quarter of a million trucks annually to business enterprises throughout the United States. (Full-service leasing provides the trucks, their financing, maintenance, insurance coverage, and licensing.) Leasing eliminates the direct operating costs, frees working capital, saves record-keeping costs, and provides cash savings on procurement, maintenance, insurance, and licensing expenses. It also takes the company out of the transportation business and frees administrative personnel from many problems that demand their attention when the company owns its equipment.

A study conducted by the University of Chicago Research Center made a cost comparison of the ownership of a single truck, ownership of an eight-truck fleet, and full-service leasing, based on an operation of 15,000 miles per year for a vehicle of 17,000 pounds gross weight, costing $5,720. The annual costs for the three types of operation were:

Single truck ownership	$4,452.60
Eight-truck fleet operation	4,233.60
Full-service leasing	4,210.00

This would indicate that the decision of whether to own or lease must be made on factors other than cost. The number of miles driven per year, convenience, and flexibility of operation are factors that must be taken into consideration.

The Internal Revenue Service holds that automobile and truck rental payments under a lease arrangement are deductible only if they represent ordinary and necessary cost figures attributable directly to the operation of the vehicle for business purposes. No deductions are allowable when so-called lease expenses constitute payments toward the purchase price of the vehicle.

The Airlines as Carriers

The relative percentage of total freight shipped by air is small, but its role in freight shipments is important. Containerization, large jet aircraft, and improved equipment for materials handling are causing airfreight shipping to come into its own.

At first, packages shipped by air could not be very large or heavy, but modern jet airliners can carry almost any size and weight of container. The Boeing 747B can carry 120 tons of freight; the Lockheed L-500 can carry 150 tons—as many as 120 compact cars, or 75 standard-size cars. To illustrate what this means, one Detroit car manufacturer points out that the daily quota of its automobiles consigned to Los Angeles (450 cars per day) could be transported aboard seven L-500's, in contrast to 35 railroad cars or 60 tractor trailers.

Air cargo among the free-world nations is expected to approximate 55 billion ton-miles by 1980, and to reach more than 100 billion ton-miles before 1985. As large as the latter figure appears to be, it will still amount to less than 1 percent of all intercity freight traffic.

Advantages of Air Transport. Air shipments are fast and safe, and save on manpower. Air shipping cuts down time for delivery, and, for perishables and goods that have great value but little bulk, offers rates that are competitive with those of other types of shipping. It enables producers to maintain fewer distribution centers and lower inventories. And it saves on packaging costs, since most goods can be shipped in inexpensive, lightweight containers.

The development and use of standardized containers will undoubtedly help the airlines continue to increase their share of freight shipments in the future. The economy of jet planes compared to engine aircraft has given airfreight transportation an important boost; the construction of airports near all major cities is also strengthening airfreight shipping; and the building of distribution centers near air terminals will enhance it even more in years to come.

Choosing Transportation Media

It should be clear to the reader by this time that the selection of modes of transportation cannot be made only on the basis of comparative costs.

Shipping costs constitute only one of the factors in the physical-distribution mix. The savings in freight costs might very easily be offset by costlier packaging, storage costs, or handling expenses. The appropriate mode of transportation in any given situation is the one that maximizes the efficiency in the total physical-distribution scheme. Whereas airfreight may be the best choice in those cases where time is especially important, for other goods the greatly reduced rates for water transport may be the best choice.

TYPES OF CARRIERS

Transportation firms are classified by law as *common carriers, contract carriers,* or *private carriers.*

A *common carrier* offers its services to the general public to transport property for a stated rate and in accordance with standard rules. It is expected to give the same service and charge the same rate to all shippers. Examples of common carriers are railroads, bus lines, intercity freight motor lines, some airfreight lines, most airlines, most domestic water carriers, all freight-forwarding companies, and REA Express. Common carriers are subject to various kinds of state and federal regulations, which are discussed later in this chapter.

A *contract carrier* sells its transport services on the basis of individual agreements or contracts that specify the carrier's liability. Some contract carriers specialize, transporting only specific types of goods. Automobile trucking companies, household moving vans, and chartered buses and planes are examples of contract carriers.

A *private carrier* is one who transports his own goods. Manufacturers, wholesalers, and retailers who make their own deliveries in their own trucks are classed as private carriers. Since they are usually small companies operating in small geographical areas, they are subject primarily to local and state regulations.

Discussion Questions

6. *Name one major advantage of each mode of transport: rail, truck, water, and air.*
7. *How do you account for the trend in intercity freight shipments as shown in Table 22.1?*
8. *What is the distinction between a common carrier and a private carrier?*
9. *What are the advantages of airlines over other types of carriers?*
10. *What is the advantage of leasing trucks over buying them?*

REGULATION OF TRANSPORTATION

Because transport companies operate in specific territories by government franchise, they are subject to special government regulations pertaining to routes, consolidation with other companies, rate structures, and curtailment of services. In many instances, regulations are needed to protect the general public and the best interests of transport companies as well.

Most states have commissions that regulate *intrastate* transportation operations—those that occur entirely within the state. These commissions were first concerned with railroads, then later with motor carriers; now it is airport facilities.

Because most transport companies cross state lines, and a state regulatory body has jurisdiction only within its own state, the federal government is responsible for the rules governing *interstate* transportation operations. The passage of the Interstate Commerce Act in 1887 was largely for the purpose of providing railroad regulation. This law created the Interstate Commerce Commission, which dealt with rate discrimination. The law required that the tariffs or rates to be charged were to be reasonable and just. It further provided that railroads could not charge a higher rate for a short haul than for a long haul under similar circumstances.

As both transportation traffic and the number of types of transport companies have continuously increased since 1887, there have been several laws passed broadening the jurisdiction and responsibilities of the Interstate Commerce Commission. The commission was given jurisdiction over interstate pipeline shipments in 1906 and over water transportation in 1940. Now it not only has jurisdiction over the tariff schedules of railroads; it is concerned with the appraisal of the value of properties, and with methods of accounting, curtailment of services, financing, and consolidations.

The Motor Carrier Act

In 1935, with the passage of the Motor Carrier Act, the federal government officially recognized its responsibility to regulate motor transport companies that send their trucks across state lines. This act provided that the regulation of interstate motor transport lines, both common carriers and contract carriers, should be under the jurisdiction of the Interstate Commerce Commission. Its supervision and control of interstate motor transport carriers is very similar to its overseeing of interstate railroad carriers.

Regulation of Air Transportation

Although the construction and operation of airfields and terminals is largely up to municipal and state governments, the federal government makes available funds for construction and establishes and enforces safety regulations for airports and landing fields. The Federal Aviation Agency is the watchdog of airline safety, and the Civil Aeronautics Board is concerned with rate structures, routes, consolidations, air traffic, and the investigation of accidents. The Civil Aeronautics Board has jurisdiction over both domestic and international carriers; it is an independent agency reporting directly to Congress, as does the Interstate Commerce Commission.

TRAFFIC MANAGEMENT

Every manufacturer, wholesaler, and retailer has his own traffic problems. A major problem, shared by all three, is how to select the most advantageous shipping routes. This task is usually assigned to the traffic department, in a company large enough to employ one.

The Traffic Manager

The person who heads the traffic department is called the *traffic manager*. Most of his routine work consists of collecting accurate, up-to-date information about tariff rates; selecting common carriers to be used in transporting foods; preparing claims of overcharge, damage, or loss; and auditing freight bills. He is also expected to trace lost shipments, supervise the actual handling of freight, and maintain control over back orders.

In addition to these routine duties, the traffic manager helps consolidate small orders into carload shipments, arranges systematic warehouse distribution points for less-than-carload lots, studies and perfects ways of reducing losses in shipments caused by improper packaging and handling, and selects the most advantageous or strategic destination points for shipments. The traffic manager must know when to use rail, water, truck, or air to transport goods to customers. It is also his job to seek adjustments on overcharges caused by discriminatory rates; he actually prepares cases and presents them before commissions and government bodies. And he helps to select plant and warehouse sites that will ensure desirable transportation service.

In a large oil company, for example, transportation functions may be combined with supply functions. The person in charge, who is called the Manager of Supply and Transportation, advises the company president and furnishes functional guidance to department heads regarding supply coordination, transportation, traffic, buying and warehousing, and purchasing activities.

The Use of Electronic Computers

Railroads.   One way to please a customer is to tell him when he may expect his shipments to arrive. The railroads, through the use of electronic computers and modern communications systems, help shippers to do just this.

A railway can advise a shipper of the location of any shipment within a matter of minutes.

Many large railway companies own tens of thousands of freight cars, and operate in a dozen or more states over thousands of miles of track. Since a shipment may originate at almost any point along the line, supplying data to the computer is as important as processing it. A teletype network is used for this purpose. Details regarding freight shipments are sent by teletype from the yard offices directly to the computer center as trains are made up. Computers sort the information according to the code numbers of the cars in which each shipment is loaded.

In modern yards, the most important time-saving tool is the computer. It can "see" and "think" faster—and "remember" more—than any human. Automatic Car Identification (ACI) scanners can be used to "read" color-coded labels on incoming cars. Because the scanners can "read" very fast, an incoming train can travel at 15 miles an hour—three times faster than when a man had to read and write down the car numbers. The computer's memory banks can also store the exact location of every car in the yard and make this information available almost instantly.

As a series of cars approaches the apex of the "hump"—over which they will roll freely to the proper track—scanners transmit the number of each car to a screen in the yardmaster's office. As the car rolls down the hump, the computer automatically retards its speed to prevent it from damaging the cars it is to join. To do this, the computer must calculate the car's gross weight, the curvature of the track, the distance the car must travel, and even the prevailing weather conditions. Among other things, this means the car may be weighed while in motion.

When the cars are classified, the computer can produce lists of trains ready for departure, along with the total tonnage.

As the trains leave the yards, more scanners check the equipment. The computer compares the information with train lists and waybills. If errors are spotted, the next station on the line is notified.

Airways. In a similar manner, by linking an electronic computer to a high-speed communications network, airline traffic management can ascertain information on seat availability in a hundred different cities within a few seconds. Also, reservation agents can be supplied with up-to-the-minute flight arrival and departure information almost as soon as the data come into existence. Computers help perform these airline operations:

1. Check on seat availability on as many as eight to ten separate flights simultaneously.
2. Sell or cancel seats on any flight up to six months in advance.
3. Determine the number of seats already booked out of any particular city for a specific flight.
4. Examine any flight schedule for delays and cancellations.

Pipelines.   Automatic equipment is also used to manage traffic through pipelines. Today, most new pipeline installations are being equipped to electronically guide products most of the way from the well or refinery to the market. Valves are opened and closed, pressure and temperature gauges are read, and engines turned on and off by a remote-control system combining electronic computing equipment and a modern telemetering communications system. An example of this operation is the Transwestern Pipeline Company's Texas-to-California line, which uses five large compressor stations along 1,800 miles of pipe. Whereas nonautomated stations require an operating crew of from five to 75, these stations operate without the aid of a single crewman.

SUMMARY

Physical distribution is far more than transportation. It encompasses inventory controls, the level of customer service desired, storage, and materials handling. The systems concept of physical distribution means that the movement of raw materials into the plant, the handling of materials and finished goods within the plant, and the movement of finished goods from the plant are all organized into a coordinated flow. Logistics decisions by management must be made so as to bring about economies in distribution costs and at the same time provide an acceptable level of service to the customers.

Each method of transport has advantages over other means of shipping in terms of time, cost, and degree of service. Rail and water shipping seem ideal for products of large bulk and for distance hauling; trucks serve all communities; and air transport is the most rapid.

The use of containers has grown rapidly and helps to coordinate shipping by truck, rail, and water.

Almost all goods spend some time in a warehouse or in storage. Ingress and egress must be carried out efficiently, and materials must be handled systematically and effectively.

Because transport companies have exclusive rights to certain routes and territories, they must be regulated and their tariff schedules approved by the government.

In large businesses, transportation problems are managed by a traffic department under the direction of a traffic manager. The transport company that serves a large geographic area keeps track of its equipment through the use of computers.

VOCABULARY REVIEW

Match the following terms with the statements below.

a. Common carrier
b. Containerization
c. Contract carrier
d. Distribution center

e. Intrastate
f. Logistics
g. Physical distribution
h. Private warehouse

i. Time utility
j. Transport medium
k. Traffic manager

1. The whole range of activities concerned with coordinated movement of goods from production line to consumer
2. The general concept of storing and moving goods
3. A storage and supply facility that serves customers by moving goods
4. A storage facility owned and operated by a manufacturer, wholesaler, or retailer for his exclusive use
5. The placing of goods in containers where they remain until delivered to their ultimate destination
6. Moving goods to the place where they are in demand at the time they are wanted
7. Any means of shipping products from one geographic location to another
8. A transport company that serves the general public
9. A transportation company that works according to individual agreements that specify the extent of the carrier's responsibilities
10. Working within the boundaries of a single state
11. The person who is responsible for directing and coordinating the work of the traffic department of a business enterprise

PROBLEMS AND PROJECTS

1. Divide the country into the following geographic regions: Pacific, Mountain Plains, North Central, Southeast, Middle Atlantic, and Northeast. Choose the area in which you live and name the cities in it that lead in air, water, rail, and truck shipping.
2. Which cities in Canada and the United States have been helped the most by the St. Lawrence Seaway?
3. An automobile manufacturer has an assembly plant in St. Louis, Missouri. Indicate the geographical areas to which automobiles might profitably be shipped from St. Louis by waterway.
4. We now have a Department of Transportation in the U.S. president's cabinet.

   a. What do you see as the chief advantages of having such a department?
   b. What will probably determine how effective and how helpful this department will be?

5. Name the factors you consider to be of greatest importance in determining the most desirable location of a public warehouse.

A BUSINESS CASE

Case 22-1   Locating an Assembly Plant and Warehouse

A manufacturer of stoves and refrigerators is considering Toledo, Ohio, and Louisville, Kentucky, for the location of a new assembly plant and a distribution center. Motors are now manufactured in the Detroit industrial area, and the pressed-steel panels for cabinets in Cleveland, Ohio.

1. Would both Louisville and Toledo qualify as far as land and water transport are concerned? In what order would you rank them, and why?
2. How would you rank Louisville and Toledo as far as labor costs for warehousing and materials handling are concerned? Why?
3. How would you rank Louisville and Toledo as far as proximity to markets is concerned? Why? Would both qualify?
4. Considering all factors, which location would be your number one choice? Would both locations be fully acceptable?

international business

CHAPTER TWENTY-THREE

Thus far, our analysis of modern business has been confined to domestic transactions, with only passing references to international business. But some business activities involve the crossing of national boundaries.

Both domestic and international business involve the same purpose, and many of their transactions are concerned with the same kinds of functions. Since "business is business," this is to be expected. However, doing business abroad merits special study because these transactions are conducted in a different environment. Foreign transactions are subject to different laws and involve different monetary systems. In some cases, the need for a given product is just beginning to develop—if we are to sell industrial machinery in a foreign country, there must be some kind of industry in that country that can make effective use of such machinery.

Our task in this chapter requires starting with the assumption that foreign trade is a two-way street. We shall analyze the mechanics of international trade; foreign exchange; the "principle of comparative advantage," which states what kinds of trade will take place and why; the balance of international payments; tariff duties on imports, and import quotas; financing exports; and finally organizations committed to international cooperation. And we shall use the terms *international business, international trade, world trade,* and *foreign trade* interchangeably.

THE DYNAMICS OF WORLD TRADE

Considered in its broadest sense, world trade covers not only merchandise, but services, and also financial investments and monetary transactions between residents of different countries. However, the bulk of international economic transactions involve merchandise exports and imports.

Since there is an unequal world distribution of resources, food, wealth, population, and technology, the need for international trade is crucial. Fortunately, there is good reason to believe that as the nations of the world continue to develop economically, world trade *will* increase, not only because of the growing demands of peoples achieving a higher standard of living, but also because of the expansion of productive activity and the tendency for nations to achieve specialization.

What is *world trade*? It may be described as *business transactions between citizens, companies, and governments, conducted on an international scale.* Just as some persons possess skills not held by others, some nations have resources not found in abundance elsewhere. For instance, if one country has tin and another coal, it becomes mutually advantageous for them to exchange these materials with each other as long as an economic need exists in both countries. Domestic producers often stand to gain from international trade by way of importing, in that imports can do much to satisfy their constant need for low-priced raw materials. Oftentimes, imported raw materials are cheaper and more readily available than the same items supplied by domestic sources, whose prices reflect higher all-around costs and whose deliveries may be erratic as to time or content, owing perhaps to dwindling natural resources. Domestic producers stand to gain also from international trade by way of exporting. Exporting affords them a profit on sales and a larger production scale that may result in lower unit costs. Thus export markets offer means of additional economic growth that can enable domestic producers to compete more effectively with one another. So we see that international trade is indeed a two-way street.

Composition of International Trade

Despite the versatility of American business, this nation is completely dependent upon other countries for supplies of specific commodities, such as bananas, coffee, and tea. A list of such items, although by no means a complete

INTERNATIONAL TRADE IS A TWO-WAY STREET

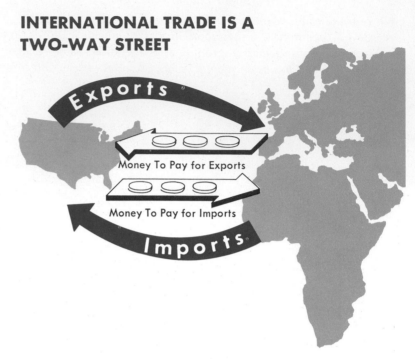

The United States is not self-sufficient. Importing goods from other nations encourages them to import goods from us.

one, is given in Table 23.1. Notice that several of these commodities are basic to our industrial needs, and many are important to us as food. Similarly, a host of American industries are greatly dependent upon foreign markets. Several segments of agriculture rely heavily on foreign markets to buy American-grown rice, wheat, and cotton.

Goods and services that are produced in this country and sold abroad are called *exports*. Raw materials and manufactured products shipped into this country are known as *imports*.

With only slightly less than 6 percent of the world's population and about 7 percent of its land area, this country produces and consumes about 30 percent of the total world supply of goods and services. American industry exports annually from 4 to 6 percent of its production and imports about 5 percent of the goods consumed in this country. (These percentages fluctuate somewhat from year to year, depending upon economic conditions here and elsewhere.) Table 23.2 shows the major commodity exports and imports of the United States. As we can see from this table, many of the imports are raw materials. Some of the items listed are produced in very limited quantities here; others are not available at all in this country and must be obtained abroad. This is

TABLE
23.1

**MAJOR IMPORTS TO THE UNITED STATES
AND THEIR USES**

Item	Use	Percentage of U.S. Consumption Imported
Alpaca	Clothing	100
Bananas	Food	100
Cashmere	Clothing	100
Cacao	Food	100
Coffee	Food	100
Copra	Manufacturing	100
Diamonds	Gems	100
Spices	Food	100
Tin ore	Manufacturing	100
Tung oil	Varnish	100
Tea	Food	100
Jute	Textiles	78
Lapidary work	Jewelry	65

Source: Bureau of International Commerce, U.S. Department of Commerce.

particularly the case with several of the basic raw materials and metals named in the accompanying illustration.

International trade is especially vital to certain segments of the American economy. We depend upon foreign markets to absorb about 35 percent of our milled rice and its by-products, 30 percent of our cotton-farm products, and about 32 percent of our mining, construction, and tractor production. The chemical, automobile, and machine-tool industries market significant portions of their output abroad.

TABLE
23.2

UNITED STATES EXPORTS AND IMPORTS OF LEADING COMMODITIES, 1970

(In millions of dollars)

Exports	Value	Imports	Value
Machinery and equipment	$17,875	Other manufactured goods	$13,281
Other manufactured goods	7,638	Machinery, transport equipment	11,171
Crude materials and fuels	4,609	Transportation vehicles	5,797
Chemicals	3,826	Raw foods and live animals	5,379
Grains and milled flour	1,112	Aircraft and parts	3,719
Coal	961	Petroleum and petroleum products	2,770

Source: Bureau of International Commerce, U.S. Department of Commerce.

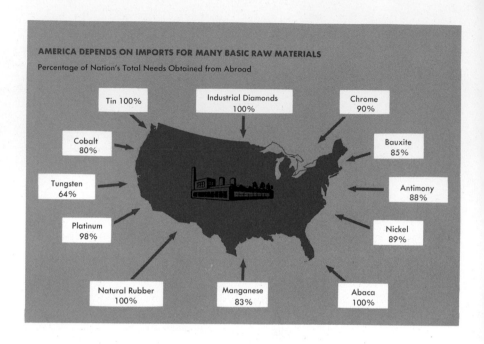

AMERICA DEPENDS ON IMPORTS FOR MANY BASIC RAW MATERIALS

Percentage of Nation's Total Needs Obtained from Abroad

Tin 100%

Industrial Diamonds 100%

Chrome 90%

Cobalt 80%

Bauxite 85%

Tungsten 64%

Antimony 88%

Platinum 98%

Nickel 89%

Natural Rubber 100%

Manganese 83%

Abaca 100%

Among the major specific products exported by American companies are the following:

Agriculture equipment	Fine paper	Pen and pencil sets
Automobiles	Fruits and nuts	Phosphate rock
Canned sardines	Inedible tallow	Soft coal
Chemicals	Leaf tobacco	Textile machinery
Cigarettes	Milled rice	Synthetic rubber
Corn	Newsprint	Tractor parts
Cotton cloth	Oil-drilling equipment	Turpentine

Who Carries on Trade with the United States? The largest volume of world trade is among countries having a highly industralized economy, able to produce a surplus and to use large quantities of the materials they obtain from other nations. Therefore the United States trades mostly with the countries of the Western Hemisphere—Canada, South America, and Mexico—Europe, and Japan. (See Table 23.3.) The developing countries of Africa are beginning to engage in world trade because they have products desired by other nations.

Our leading imports from Canada are paper pulp, agricultural products, and lumber. From Germany we buy automobiles, precision instruments, musical instruments, and textiles. Wines, automobiles, and textiles are some of our major imports from Italy. Japan, our largest customer in Asia, ranks second

TABLE
23.3

**UNITED STATES EXPORTS AND
IMPORTS BY CONTINENTS, 1970**

(In millions of dollars)

Continent	Exports	Imports
Western Hemisphere	$15,118	$16,930
Europe	14,819	11,401
Asia and Oceania	11,292	10,520
Africa	1,498	1,088

*Source: International Trade Analysis Division, U.S. Department
of Commerce.*

to Canada in export and import trade with the United States. Japan is a leading
world manufacturer of radios, televisions, automobile parts, and steel products.
Because of the high labor costs in the United States, most American radio and
television parts are made in Japan under the trade names of American brands
and returned to this country for assembly.

When we analyze the dependence of the American economy, on both
imports and exports, it becomes clear that this nation must continue to promote
trade with other countries. Approximately 4.5 million jobs in this country alone
depend directly on import and export trade. Because the needs of our constantly
growing population require ever more materials, many of which are not available here, we must seek foreign sources. If we are unable as a nation to obtain
these scarce materials, it becomes necessary to substitute inferior goods or
reduce our production. And in the area of exporting, foreign markets often
make the difference between profit and loss for some American companies
operating in this country.

Discussion Questions

1. *Why is trade with other nations considered essential to the welfare of this nation
   and to American businesses?*
2. *How does world trade promote a higher international standard of living?*

**ECONOMIC THEORIES
OF INTERNATIONAL TRADE**

Many textbooks have been devoted exclusively to the economic theories of
international trade, or "international business" as it is sometimes called, and

new books on the subject are appearing periodically, so we shall not discuss these theories in great detail. Rather, we shall deal only with the essential aspects of certain basic theories pertaining directly to our analysis of why international trade takes place.

Why Nations Trade

Through international trade, a nation is able to obtain, more cheaply than if it were to produce them at home, certain goods that are needed to satisfy the desires of its population. International trade also enables each nation to combine its factors of production more efficiently, by its specializing in the production of those goods that it can make so economically and so well that, all factors (including tariffs) considered, they will outsell similar foreign goods domestically. Under this concept, nations tend to export their specialties and import the specialties of other nations. World trade thus enables each nation to achieve a higher degree of specialization by allowing it to make full use of its peculiar advantages—low labor costs, favorable climate, mass-production techniques, deposits of scarce minerals, high educational level, and so on.

If all nations suddenly discontinued their foreign trade, their production would be limited by their own resources. But by engaging in world trade, they can exchange part of their production with other nations for goods that the other nations are best able to make. As a result, each country can have a larger national income than would be possible without the trade, and each country can attain a higher living standard than if it tried to supply all its own needs itself.

Principle of Comparative Advantage

What determines the products a country will decide to specialize in? One answer may be found in the principle of *comparative advantage*. In general, this principle implies what we have been stressing in this chapter: that it is to the economic advantage of a country to specialize in producing goods that it can produce more cheaply than can other countries; that nations should refrain from producing those items they can buy more cheaply elsewhere. Comparative advantage may be due to such factors as a well-trained labor force, an abundance of raw materials, modern and efficient plants, and favorable climatic conditions. David Ricardo, one of the great classical economists, explained the principle of comparative advantage like this:

> Two men can make both shoes and hats, and one is superior to the other in both employments. But in making hats, he can only exceed his competitor by one-fifth, or 20 percent, and in making shoes he can excel him by one-third, or 33⅓ percent. Will it not be for the interest of both that the superior man

should employ himself exclusively in making shoes, and the inferior man in making hats?[1]

The principle of comparative advantage may be explained further by a hypothetical example. Suppose there were but two countries, the United States and Russia, and that, in isolation, each country produced but two commodities of mutual interest, wheat and textiles. Assume further that the cost ratios between wheat and textiles differed between the two countries as follows:

Unit cost (price)	United States (Dollars)	Russia (Rubles)
Unit cost (price) of wheat	1.00	5.00
Unit cost (price) of textiles	2.00	1.00

Disregarding the exchange rate between the two currencies, in the United States the cost ratio of wheat to textiles is shown to be 1:2, and for Russia, 5:1. These ratios indicate that the United States would have a comparative cost advantage in the production of wheat and a comparative cost disadvantage in the production of textiles. In Russia, the converse situation would exist. *Gainful trade would occur when the United States exported wheat and imported textiles while Russia exported textiles and imported wheat.* The real cost of one unit of wheat in the United States would be half a unit of textiles. In Russia, the opportunity cost of producing one unit of wheat would be five units of textiles. It is obvious that the United States would have a lower opportunity cost of producing wheat and would export it because of the comparative advantage in that commodity.

At this point you might ask: Why shouldn't the United States sell both wheat and textiles to Russia, bringing the dollars home without buying anything from them? The answer is that there would be no dollars in Russia with which to pay for American wheat and textiles, and therefore no dollars to bring home, unless Russians could obtain dollars by selling something to the United States. In other words, we cannot be paid for our goods and services unless we take payment in the form of foreign goods and services—all of which tends to reemphasize the fact that foreign trade travels on a two-way street.

Principle of Absolute Advantage

Specialization in foreign trade is also encouraged under the principle of *absolute advantage,* which recognizes that the costs of producing commodities differ from country to country. According to this principle, a nation should specialize in an article when it enjoys the advantages of low costs that are due

---

[1]David Ricardo, *Political Economy* (London: Everyman's Library, 1911), p. 83.

to a natural monopoly or some unusual technical development. As an illustration, Brazil can produce coffee more cheaply than the United States; so as a coffee producer, Brazil has an absolute advantage over this country. On the other hand, we have an absolute advantage over Brazil in making automobiles. Both countries will gain from the exchange of American automobiles for Brazilian coffee.

To compare the absolute advantage with the comparative advantage: It often pays a nation to import goods even when that nation can make them for lower labor costs than can another—that is, even though it enjoys an *absolute advantage* over the other country. Whereas a nation may have a greater absolute advantage, its *comparative advantage* may dictate that it should specialize in the production of a second good, using the income from this production to pay for the first good bought from another country. In other words, unless we buy from other countries, they cannot buy from us.

(Although these economic laws make sense to most economists, governments sometimes ignore them by erecting trade barriers in the form of tariffs and import quotas, making it possible to increase prices of imports so they cannot undersell goods produced domestically and thereby eliminating any advantages a foreign country may have.)

Advantages of International Trade

Aside from these broad aspects of international trade, a high level of commerce with other countries provides individual businessmen with several specific advantages.

Advantages to Importing. Business firms in this country import goods because (1) foreign prices may be lower than domestic prices on similar goods; (2) certain goods are not available in this country—or, if they are available, the supply is not sufficient to meet the demand; and (3) ordering goods from foreign firms may encourage them to buy goods from more American firms. Moreover, some lines of foreign mechandise are considered to offer more style and prestige than are domestic products, and consequently will command higher prices in the United States.

Advantages to Exporting. Many American firms engage in exporting because (1) selling to foreign customers is often less expensive than expanding a new home market; (2) foreign markets are a means of absorbing surpluses that might otherwise be sold at a loss in the home market; (3) some mass-production industries cannot earn a satisfactory profit without foreign markets to maintain their volume at a high level—even a 5 percent increase in foreign sales may enable a company to reduce its unit cost; (4) industries with high fixed costs can, by exporting, spread these costs over a larger total volume, and thus reduce the average cost per unit, even on items produced for the domestic market; and (5) for some firms, exporting is the one remaining source of new business the company has not attempted to develop. A large American integrated oil company recently decided to "go international" because that was the only way left to them to achieve new growth.

Difficulties in International Trade

Aside from the problems arising out of tariffs and trade agreements, which will be discussed later in this chapter, there are several barriers in foreign trade.

The Language Barrier. Fortunately, more and more countries are encouraging the teaching of English in their schools, and in these places the language barrier is disappearing in our favor. However, in many countries there is still a language barrier for those who come from another country to trade.

Differences in Social Customs. Each nation has its social customs and business practices that are different. The Latin American *siesta*—the long lunch hour that makes the workday longer—is not common to other ethnic groups, and many foreigners working in Latin American countries find it somewhat difficult to follow. Driving an automobile on the left-hand side of the road is confusing. Removing your shoes to enter a residence or religious center is another unique custom. Strange and exotic foods sometimes create a diet problem for the newcomer abroad.

Differences in Laws. A *cartel* is an association of individual companies whose purpose is to control prices or the conditions of sale; hence, cartels are price-fixing monopolies which are illegal in the United States. But in most other countries, the cartel is legal. Price-fixing by cartels abroad can lead to critical situations in international commerce when an American firm finds it must compete with foreign firms. *Patent laws* of various nations differ more widely than do laws relating to other industrial property. Some countries decline to grant patents on certain products—for example, chemical compounds. Others issue patents immediately upon application, but these give protection for different periods of time. And Russia is not even a signatory to the International Patent Agreement. In some countries, *copyright laws* are not respected as they are in the United States. Requirements for copyrights in foreign companies also vary. Some nations require that a certain number of resident stockholders be maintained by foreign corporations.

Differences in Currencies and Availability of Dollars. When you travel abroad, you find that monetary systems differ. The United States and its possessions use the dollar, which until recently was accepted widely as the medium of exchange in foreign trade. The franc is the currency unit of France, while England uses the pound and Italy the lira. An American pencil manufacturer who sells his product to an Italian merchant expects to be paid in dollars, because his employees demand dollars. The process to obtain lira for dollars is carried out by foreign exchange (see page 620). At one time gold was the common denominator for all currencies; but for several years the gold standard has been nonexistent. Now it is not possible to obtain gold when dollars are not available or in scarcity. The fluctuations of these currencies in their exchange values does not help to simplify the situation.

Discussion Questions

3. What determines the kinds of products a nation will decide to sell abroad?

4. What are some of the difficulties in international trade?

ORGANIZING FOR INTERNATIONAL BUSINESS

When an American firm decides to sell abroad, it may do so by choosing one of two methods. One method of marketing is to engage in direct selling by using the company's own export department or division. This is commonly referred to as using direct-exporting marketing channels. The other method is to sell through independent middlemen located in the United States who specialize in export selling. Among these latter middlemen are export merchants, export agents, and buyers for export. As you will observe from the following discussion, these marketing channels differ widely.

Using Direct-Export Marketing Channels

Companies that engage in a substantial amount of foreign commerce find that it pays to have their own marketing outlets. These companies may own one or more factories.

Foreign Branches.   These are divisions of a domestic company, located in a foreign country. These operations range from foreign sales, storage or warehouse operations to foreign assembly plants or manufacturing plants. The object is to provide as much customer service as possible.

Foreign Subsidiaries.   These may resemble foreign branches, but in fact they are virtually separate companies owned and controlled by a parent American corporation. One advantage of the subsidiary over the foreign branch is the ability of management to control both cost and profits, because all revenues and expenses are separated from domestic operations. The subsidiary may be a separate corporation. There is another advantage in that the subsidiary can handle a complete line of products because of its size rather than one single line.

In recent years, many foreign subsidiaries have grown into global operations, and the multinational corporation has evolved. This *multinational business* is a firm that has a number of directly controlled operations in different countries, and that tends toward a worldwide perspective. Among these large multinational companies are such firms as International Business Machines, with its IBM World Trade Corporation; John Deere, a farm-machinery maker with subsidiaries in nine countries; Procter & Gamble, with four international divisions; Ford Motor Company, with plants in 20 countries; and National Cash Register, which operates worldwide. It is estimated that of the 20,000 American companies engaged in international business, about 3,000 have subsidiaries and branches established in foreign countries.

The Built-in Export Department. Aside from the two methods of marketing abroad using direct-export marketing channels, a third method is the built-in export department. Where such a system is in effect, export activities are assigned to certain personnel in the company, consisting of an export manager and one or two clerks. The export manager does the selling or directs it. The traffic department handles documents and transportation along with other traffic matters for the company. Such other functions as credit and accounting operations for foreign sales are performed by these two departments which at the same time handle domestic activities for credit and accounting. The built-in export department is generally small. It is well adapted to the manufacturer whose export volume is likewise small in comparison with the total volume of the business.

Using Indirect-Export Marketing Channels

Indirect exporting involves the use of outside organizations located in the home market. These are export middlemen, willing to assume the major portion of details involving foreign trade. Some of these middlemen take title to goods.

The Export Merchant. The export merchant is an independent middleman who buys and sells abroad on his own account. He does both exporting and importing. In exporting, his firm is often known as a trading company, because it buys and sells such a variety of products from many companies.

The Export Agent. The export agent generally represents several non-competing American firms on a commission basis. Sales are made by the export agent for the manufacturer, who finances and ships the product to the buyer.

Buyers for Export. These are also independent middlemen who canvass American markets in search of goods needed by foreign consumers. Buyers for export take orders from foreign clients and are paid on a commission. The main advantage in selling through export buyers is that there is little marketing expense for the seller.

5. *Explain two channels for marketing goods abroad?*
6. *What is a multinational corporation?*

TARIFFS AND GOVERNMENT TRADE POLICIES

Within this country, goods can be shipped from one state to another with little or no government interference; but in international trade, the same shipment of goods is subject to various kinds of controls established by governments of the trading nations. These controls are in the form of tariffs, quantitative restrictions (quotas), embargoes, and price-fixing agreements that in one way or another interfere with the free play of economic forces.

Definition of Tariff

A *tariff* is a tax or customs duty levied by a nation on goods imported from other countries. In the United States, Congress may levy import duties in accordance with the authority contained in Article I, Section 8, Paragraph 1 of the U.S. Constitution. Depending upon which political party was in power, this nation has had high or low tariffs from the early days of our republic until the early 1930's. The Smoot-Hawley Tariff Act of 1930 achieved the highest tariff on record. Then, in an attempt to combat the economic depression of the 1930's, a Democratic Congress in 1934 passed the Reciprocal Trade Agreements Act, which reversed this trend of more than a century. This act and its numerous amendments since then (providing for further reductions of tariffs) are discussed later in this chapter.

Kinds of Tariffs

The two broad categories of tariffs are (1) revenue tariffs, and (2) protective tariffs. Each type is designed for a different purpose. A *revenue tariff* is a tax on imports to produce revenue. A *protective tariff* is a tax on imports to protect domestic producers against competition from foreign producers.

The *specific duty* tariff, usually intended to produce revenue, is levied on imports at so much per pound, gallon, or unit. For example, the specific duty on imported champagne is $1.50 per gallon, and on chestnuts it is $.06½ per pound.

The *ad valorem* ("according to value") *duty* is a protective tariff that is based on the value of the imported goods rather than on some quantity. Examples of ad valorem duties are the 15 percent tax on imported gold bags and the 25 percent duty on imported leather gloves. *Compound duties* are a combination of specific and ad valorem duties. For example, the chemical compound ethylene glycol, used as an antifreeze for automobiles, has for years carried both a 15 percent ad valorem duty and a three-cent-per-pound specific duty.

Arguments For and Against Tariffs

The very first Congress debated the tariff issue in 1789, and Congress has taken it up at one time and another ever since. Some people advocate complete "free trade," which would abolish all tariffs. Others argue for "protection" or for quotas.

The Infant-Industry Argument. This is the oldest pro-tariff argument of all. It holds that a new and struggling young industry should be protected from foreign competition by a protective tariff until the industry has had time to become established. True, it is sometimes difficult for a new industry to get started in the face of foreign competition from other countries where labor costs are low. Too often, however, even after the infant industry has grown up, new arguments are advanced to retain the high protective tariff.

Arguments for Free Trade. Free-traders urge the elimination of tariff barriers because it will promote a free flow of goods between countries. They rest their case on the benefits from the worldwide specialization of production that free trade would promote; all nations, they say, would be able to raise their standards of living.

The Wages Argument. Labor unions use this argument because they seem to see in it an immediate short-term gain for labor. The gist of the argument is that by prohibiting entry of goods made by lower-paid (foreign) labor, goods made by higher-paid (domestic) labor can be sold thereby maintaining higher domestic wages. There are several points to be considered regarding this logic. Keeping out imports produced by lower-paid labor does help to maintain higher domestic wages, but higher-priced goods result. The necessity for consumers to buy goods at the higher prices leaves them with less money to buy other goods. When foreign competition is eliminated, some industries become less efficient, and then consumer prices go up. Furthermore, keeping out competition restricts our volume of exports; if many foreign producers are unable to sell to the American market, they lack the necessary funds to buy from us.

Foreign Trade Legislation

The Reciprocal Trade Agreements Program. Although the present tariff policies of the United States are based on the Reciprocal Trade Agreements Act of 1934 (RTA) and its 11 amendments passed by Congress since, it was not until 1947 in Geneva that the United States and 22 other nations agreed upon a system of procedures and rules for studying tariffs. This was the General Agreement on Tariffs and Trade (GATT). Despite its technical complexity, with tariff schedules listing thousands of negotiated tariff concessions, the basic elements of GATT are to provide the rules of nondiscrimination in trade relations, to agree on commitments to observe negotiated trade concessions, and to approve prohibitions against the use of quantitative restrictions on exports and imports. The member countries of GATT meet annually to review recommendations, to settle disputes, and to study ways to reduce tariffs.

Despite the progress made under GATT, Congress in 1962 passed the Trade Expansion Act, which the late President Kennedy signed into law on October 11, 1962. Unlike the previous 11 amendments of the original RTA of 1934, the TEA of 1962 provided for a completely new approach, and one unprecedented for the United States. This legislation gave the president the power to cut tariffs by 50 percent in negotiating new trade pacts during the five years following its inception. The purposes of the TEA, as expressed in the language of the act, are these:

1. To stimulate the economic growth of the United States and maintain and enlarge foreign markets for the products of United States agriculture, industry, mining, and commerce
2. To strengthen economic relations with foreign countries through the development of open and nondiscriminatory trading in the free world
3. To prevent communist economic penetration

Some people are critical of the reciprocal-trade laws because, they say, tariff making has been removed from the direct control of Congress in favor of presidential control. The fact remains, however, that Congress has the power to modify or abolish the program if it is not satisfactory. The full impact of the law really depends upon the extent of cooperation between or among nations involved.

Kennedy Round of Tariff Negotiations. The most sweeping tariff reductions in the history of this country were concluded in June 1967, involving over 50 member nations of GATT. During the negotiations, called the Kennedy Round of Tariff Negotiations because they were initiated by President Kennedy under the 1962 Trade Expansion Act, tariff duties were cut on some 60,000 items. Only a few items, such as zinc, lead, watches, and rugs were not affected by these agreements.

Although the purpose of these tariff cuts was to promote U.S. exports by removing trade barriers, much of the impetus to total world trade can be credited to the spread of international commerce that resulted from these reductions.

Nontariff Restrictive Measures

In addition to tariffs, additional kinds of restrictive measures have been used over the years by the United States and other world-trading nations to slow down the movement of foreign trade:

1. Import quotas
2. Export controls
3. Embargoes
4. Buy-American regulations

Import Quotas. What is a quota? A quota is a device for directly regulating the flow of goods between countries. An *import quota* is defined as a quantity control on imported merchandise for a certain period of time. The aim of an import quota is to permit the importing country to determine the exact amount of a given commodity which it considers to be to its advantage to import, and to levy either absolute or relative limits on imports in excess of the quota. When import quotas are used by the United States, prices tend to rise, since competition is reduced. In the current mood of protectionism, a movement to protect American markets or workers from foreign competition, there has been a strong demand for trade quotas on imports. There is essentially little difference between tariffs and quotas. But nonprohibitive tariff at least gives revenue to the government; a quota, on the other hand, puts profits in the hands of the importer who is lucky enough to get a quota license. It is curious and difficult to understand why the AFL-CIO, as an example, proclaiming its opposition to wage and price controls because they interfere with freedom of action, can support quotas, as they have recently done on behalf of textile manufacturing companies in this country.

Export Controls. Controls to prevent the shipping of certain kinds of goods to unfriendly countries are known as export controls. Countries behind the Iron Curtain have been subjected to export controls by the United States to prevent the shipment of militarily strategic items to them.

Embargoes. The term *embargo* means any prohibition by a government upon the movement of goods in commerce. The term also refers to the refusal of transportation companies to accept or move freight in the case of a strike or because of tariff congestion. For moral reasons, the United States maintains an export embargo on certain drugs, gambling devices, and lottery tickets. President Kennedy in 1962 ordered an embargo on all imports from Cuba to the United States, to keep the Castro regime from getting U.S. dollars with which to promote communism in the Western Hemisphere. (The president left unchanged, however, the policy allowing limited exports of foods, medicines, and medical supplies to Cuba, for humanitarian reasons.)

Buy-American Regulations. Buy-American regulations aim to give special priority and privileges to domestic producers in preference to foreign producers seeking a market for their goods with government agencies. The restriction that prohibits the use of foreign steel in U.S. highways is an illustration of this regulation.

Discussion Questions

7. *What is the purpose of a tariff, and how does a protective tariff differ from a tariff to produce revenue?*

8. *In what way did the Kennedy Round of Tariff Negotiations help or discourage trade with other countries?*

THE BALANCE OF INTERNATIONAL PAYMENTS

The most useful tool to explain the interrelations created by foreign-trade transactions is a statistical statement, prepared annually by the U.S. Department of Commerce, called the *balance of international payments*—known also as the balance of payments. It resembles a profit-and-loss statement rather than a balance sheet, because it shows the nation's sales (exports) and purchases (imports), together with the other forms of receipts and expenditures derived from foreign-trade transactions and foreign relations. An examination of a country's balance of payments would show that country's ability to pay for goods bought from other countries and to pay its debts to other nations. On balance, a country is either a debtor or a creditor nation.

Transactions between domestic and foreign residents are entered in the balance of payments as either debits or credits. Debit transactions involve payments by domestic residents to foreign residents for imports. Credit transactions are dollars received by domestic residents from foreign residents for exports.

In addition to the income received by the United States from its exports and the payments made for its imports, the balance-of-payments statement also includes other items. Among these are capital outflow when residents of this country invest abroad, and capital inflow when a foreign resident invests in the United States. Another section shows gold movements, representing gold exports and imports. For years the United States has experienced a deficit in the balance of payments, and gold was used to offset this deficit. Still other transactions include money spent by tourists abroad, military-aid payments, dividends, and grants.

Favorable Balance of Trade

When a nation's exports exceed the value of its merchandise imports, it is said to have a favorable balance of trade. Conversely, when a nation's imports exceed the value of exports, it has an unfavorable balance of trade. The idea conveyed by the terms "favorable" or "unfavorable," as used to describe a balance of trade, is misleading, because it implies that a nation should always work to export more than it imports.

The trend in the U.S. balance of trade between 1960 and 1970 is presented in the accompanying chart; as you can see, our merchandise exports exceed our imports. While this is considered a favorable balance of trade, it is an unsatisfactory balance of payments. This is caused by the fact that the export surplus has not been sufficiently large to offset other expenditures such as grants, loans, gifts, and military expenses. Thus a deficit results. Persistent deficits in our balance of payments reflects deficiencies in the economy. For example, it can drain our gold reserves to a point of danger to our monetary system. It can destroy confidence in the dollar, jeopardize the stability of the economy, and help to create a dollar shortage.

It is not surprising under these circumstances that the money markets of Europe turned to the use of *Eurodollars* as a source of funds. Eurodollars are dollar-denominated deposits in commercial banks outside the United States, including foreign branches of U.S. banks. These deposits may be owned by U.S. residents or foreigners, and in recent years their volume has increased significantly because of this nation's high balance of payments deficits. As this nation continues to spend more than it takes in, the hoard of foreign-based

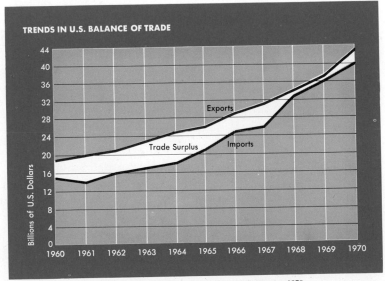

Sources: Bureau of International Commerce; U.S. Department of Commerce, 1970

dollars piles higher and higher. Consequently, dollars flow into the Eurodollar market because the return is better than on most alternative forms of investments.

Declining Value of the Dollar

Since World War II, the dollar had been considered sound and acceptable as a medium of exchange in international trade. But by 1970 international trade began to indicate that the dollar was no longer acceptable. Our economy was suffering from a high rate of unemployment, inflation, a dollar shortage, and a continued deficit in the balance of payments. In 1971, President Nixon announced a temporary 10 percent surcharge on U.S. imports, the purpose of which was to increase the price of imported goods and thereby make American-made products more competitive with imported goods. It was also hoped that this action would widen the gap between merchandise exports and imports. At the same time, there was a demand in Congress for trade quotas on imports. Table 23.4 shows how much American imports have increased for certain items between 1961 and 1971.

President Nixon's surcharge of 10 percent was unpopular with such foreign governments as Japan, Canada, and the Common Market countries, since these must raise the prices of the goods they export to the United States. Immediately, there was talk of retaliation against this nation and the possibility of starting a trade war by imposing high tariffs and trade quotas on American goods. It was also proposed that the United States devalue its dollar.

TABLE
23.4
INCREASE IN FLOW OF IMPORTED GOODS INTO THE U.S.:
SOME SPECIFIC EXAMPLES

| | (In millions of dollars) | | |
Imported Goods	1961	1971*	Percentage Increase
Automobiles	$307	$5,159	1,580%
Clothing	259	1,263	388
Iron, steel products	422	2,380	464
Meats	385	932	142
Motorcycles	17	546	3,112
Musical instruments	54	494	815
Machinery, nonelectrical	471	3,401	622
Office machines, computers	95	528	456
Scientific instruments	46	346	652
Shoes, other footwear	126	777	517

*Covers January–May, annual rate.
Source: U.S. Department of Commerce.

U.S. Dollar Devalued

President Nixon, following a conference with leaders of the world's ten leading non-communist countries, announced that an agreement had been reached to devalue the U.S. dollar by 8.57 percent. At the same time, the 10 percent import surcharge was dropped, and the price of gold was to increase from $35 an ounce to $37.80. This was the first dollar devaluation and change in the price of gold made by the United States since 1934 at which time a 41 percent mark-down in the value of the dollar was made. On April 3, 1972, a new federal law fixed gold at $38 an ounce.

What Does Devaluation Mean to Americans and Foreign Businesses? To begin with, the value of the dollar in terms of both gold and other currencies dropped. Prices of goods made in this country and consumed here remain the same. But prices of many imported goods will rise. For example, Scotch whisky; French, German, and Italian wines; British woolens; Danish cheese; and Canadian bacon will cost more in this country. The cost of Japanese cameras, radios, and TV sets coming into the country will also increase. Foreign cars and "brand name" American products made abroad will be more expensive in this country. Some foreign producers whose goods will cost more on the U.S. market after devaluation may cut their prices and be willing to take less profit on sales here. Americans traveling in any foreign country where the currency was revalued upward against the dollar will pay more dollars.

What about stock-market prices? The stock market already has largely discounted devaluation of the dollar according to financial authorities. Personal debts and home mortgages will remain the same for the number of dollars required in repayment.

Discussion Questions

9. *How is a balance-of-payments statement like a profit-and-loss statement? What is the purpose of such a statement?*
10. *Why did President Nixon devalue the American dollar and how is this related to international trade?*

FINANCING INTERNATIONAL TRADE

As we have mentioned, one of the complications of international trade is the fact that although the seller of goods or services expects to be paid in the kind of money he can use in paying his debts, not all nations have the same currency system. English pounds, for instance, must be converted into dollars before an English buyer can pay his American business associate.

Fortunately, buyers and sellers need not meet in order to complete transactions. In this and other countries are banks that buy foreign currencies (or claims to them) for sale by exporters, and also sell foreign currencies to importers who want to make payments in foreign money. These banks charge a commission for buying and selling the currencies or handling the negotiable instruments used in foreign exchange. Later in this chapter, when we discuss the use of various negotiable instruments, we shall see how the services of a bank are used in carrying out the details of a foreign-trade transaction.

The Foreign-Exchange Market

The term *foreign exchange* may be defined in two different ways. In one sense, it is *a financial asset involving a cash claim held by a resident of one country against a resident of another country,* and is represented by a variety of credit instruments, the most common of which is the bill of exchange, or bank draft (previously discussed in Chapter 14). As a negotiable instrument, the bill of exchange has three parties: (1) the *drawer,* who orders payment and initiates the draft; (2) the *drawee,* who is ordered to pay; and (3) the *payee,* to whom payment is to be made. When a bill of exchange is drawn against a commercial debtor (usually an importer), it is called a *trade bill.* When it is drawn against a bank, it is a *bank bill.* As a rule, trade bills are drawn by exporters and other trade creditors, whereas bank bills may be drawn by banks or commercial creditors. Thus, a bill of exchange becomes foreign exchange when it is a claim held by a domestic resident against a foreign resident.

In another sense, *foreign exchange* is *the process by which balances resulting from foreign transactions are settled.* Under either definition, a rate of exchange is established—and consequently, any nation's exports should (theoretically, at least) pay for its imports. By selling to foreign nations, a country earns the necessary foreign exchange to buy from those nations.

You have already observed that the balance-of-trade status of the United States is reflected in the amount of its foreign exchange, or in other words, in the value of deposits that American banks, business firms, and individuals have in foreign banks, as compared with the value of deposits on the part of foreign countries in American banks. Our supply of foreign exchange in the market is increased when we sell goods and services to foreign customers and corporate securities to foreign investors, and when we ship gold and currency out of the country. It is decreased when other nations obtain American dollars by selling us goods or services, and when we buy foreign securities or receive gold or currency from abroad.

Foreign-Exchange Rates. Market values for most of the world's currencies fluctuate almost daily. It is the function of foreign-exchange dealers located in large commercial banks in the major financial centers to buy and sell foreign exchange, based on the prevailing rate for a given day. An American importer, for example, who expects to buy a foreign article must keep in mind not only the price he must pay for his item abroad, but also the price of whatever foreign currency he must buy to pay for his import. This

Foreign Exchange

Friday, March 10, 1972

Selling prices for **bank transfers** in the U.S. for payment abroad, as quoted at 4 p.m. (in dollars). (Par value or central rate in parenthesis.)

Country	Friday	Prev. Day
Canada (Dollar)	1.0029	1.0035
Great Britain (Pound, 2.6057)	2.6412	2.6440
30-Day Futures	2.6424	2.6450
90-Day Futures	2.6424	2.6450
Australia (Dollar, 1.21600)	1.2100	1.2100
New Zealand (Dollar, 1.21600)	1.2200	1.2200
South Africa (Rand, 1.3333)	1.3600	1.3370
Austria (Schilling, .042918)	.0440	.0440
Belgium (Franc, .0223135)	.022800	.022840
Denmark (Krone, .143266)	.1443	.1442
France (Franc)		
Commercial rate (.195477)	.1991	.1996
Financial rate	.2058	.2055
Holland (Guilder, .308195)	.3151	.3154
Italy (Lira, .00171969)	.001732	.001735
Norway (Krone, .150480)	.1528	.1530
Portugal (Escudo, .0366972	.0376	.0374
Spain (Peseta, .0551021)	.0154	.0154
Sweden (Krona, .207775)	.2106	.2110
Switzerland (Franc, .260417)	.2619	.2627
West Germany (Deutschmk, .310318)	.3171	.3173
LATIN AMERICA:		
Argentina (Hard Peso)	.1050	.1055
Brazil (Cruzeiro)	.1760	.1769
Chile (Escudo)	.0370	.0370
Colombia (Peso)	.0472	.0472
Ecuador (Sucre, .0400)	.0385	.0383
Mexico (Peso, .0800000)	.0801	.0801
Peru (Sol)	.0235	.0235
Uruguay (Peso)	.0023	.0023
Venezuela (Bolivar, .227272)	.2285	.2285
NEAR EAST:		
Iraq (Dinar, 3.04000)	3.10	3.10
Israel (Pound .238095)	z	z
Lebanon (Pound)	.3210	.3210
FAR EAST:		
Hong Kong (H.K. Dollar, .179143)	.1820	.1820
India (Rupee, .137676)	.1400	.1400
Japan (Yen, .00324675)	.003320	.003320
Pakistan (Rupee, .2100)	.2125	.2125
Philippines (Peso)	.1560	.1560
Singapore (Dollar, .354666)	z	z

Source: First National City Bank, New York.

Prices for **foreign banknotes**, as quoted at 4 p.m. (in dollars):

	Buying	Selling
Argentina (New Peso)	.08	.12
Australia (Dollar)	1.14	1.22
Austria (Schilling)	0.40	0.45
Belgium (Franc)	0.20	0.25
Brazil (New Cruzeiros)	.13	.18
Canada (Dollar)	.98	1.01
Chile (Escudo)	.01	.03
Colombia (Peso)	.03	.06
Denmark (Krone)	.13	.15
Egypt (Pound)	1.23	1.62
France (Franc)	.19	.21
Great Britain (Pound)	2.60	2.67
Holland (Guilder)	.30	.32

Courtesy The Wall Street Journal, *Dow Jones & Co., Inc.*

price is called the *foreign-exchange rate,* and it may be defined as *the rate at which one currency is exchanged for another.* For example, assume that the exchange rate for Mexican pesos is one peso to the dime. An American wishing to obtain a foreign-exchange credit of 1,000 pesos for use in Mexico City would pay $100 for these pesos.

In all the great financial centers of the world—New York, London, Paris, Tokyo, and Hong Kong—the daily rates are quoted by commercial banks and listed in the major metropolitan newspapers. The preceding illustration, page 621, lists the daily quotation rates for foreign exchange.

Rates of exchange fluctuate in response to the supply and demand of international money transfers. If our total foreign sales are greater than our total foreign purchases, the foreign demand for dollars to make payments rises. This is because dollars would sell at a premium in terms of foreign currencies. But if our imports exceed our exports, the dollar will be at a discount in terms of foreign currencies. This illustrates the effect of our balance of trade. Actually, money is rarely shipped to another country to settle a debt. Instead, drafts or bills of exchange are used. These are provided through a bank as part of its service to its customers.

Financing Exports

Financing is more complicated in international trade than in domestic trade, because there is greater risk in extending credit to buyers abroad. The parties may be unknown to each other. Or the seller may wish to be paid immediately. A variation on cash terms is the requirement of part payment with the order, and the balance payable on receipt of the shipment.

As a rule, when an exporter sells goods abroad, he takes the initiative in obtaining payment by drawing a draft for the amount of his invoice. This instrument is drawn directly on the buyer (importer), who is the debtor. It may be drawn to become due at sight, on arrival of goods, or at a designated future time. It is customary in such a case to use the services of a commercial bank that offers exporting services.

Export Documents. The export documents that generally accompany drafts are of the following types:

1. Ocean bill of lading, usually indorsed in blank (lists goods shipped and terms of the contract under which goods are shipped by the transportation agency)
2. Commercial invoice (shows quantities, terms, and prices)
3. Marine insurance certificate
4. Special customs invoice (shows weight, value, destination, and class of goods)
5. Inspection certificate
6. Certificate of origin

On receipt of an order from a foreign customer, the American exporter draws a draft (either in dollars or in the foreign currency) against the importer and takes them, together with the documents listed above, to the bank for further handling.

Customer's Draft. The following example illustrates the steps involved in financing a foreign sale by the use of a draft. (The use of drafts in domestic trade was discussed in an earlier chapter.)

The Tejas Manufacturing & Equipment Company of Houston, Texas, sells certain items of equipment to Colombiana Importadora, S.A., Bogotá, Colombia.[2] On receipt of an order, the Houston firm (the seller) draws a customer's draft (shown below) made payable to itself, in the amount of $3,500, on Colombiana Importadora. This instrument instructs Colombiana (drawee and buyer) to pay the amount of the draft to the holder at a specified future date—that is, 30 days from the date of the draft.

The draft is presented to the buyer (drawee) for his acceptance. If the drawee chooses to accept it, he writes across the draft the word "Accepted," followed by the date and his signature, and returns it to the drawer. This actually transforms the draft into a trade acceptance. It is customary for American exporters to draw drafts similar to this illustration, in dollars. Such a draft is often referred to as a *dollar draft*.

The buyer (drawee) cannot obtain physical possession of the goods that have been shipped to him until certain documents, such as the bill of lading, commercial invoice, and any others required to be attached to the draft, are released to him by the bank. Actually, these documents are released to the buyer when he accepts the draft for payment. If the Tejas Company decides not to keep this draft the full 30 days for payment, but sells it to its Houston bank, it must take a discount on the $3,500 face value in order to receive the cash immediately. This discount rate, which the bank charges for paying the

---

[2] The abbreviation S.A. used as part of the company title is derived from the Spanish term *sociedad anonima,* which means "corporation."

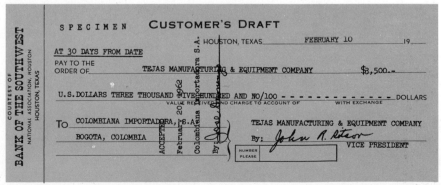

Courtesy The Bank of the Southwest, Houston, Texas

A customer's draft used in foreign trade transactions

draft before it is due, is normally the amount that would be charged for a 30 day, $3,500 loan to the Tejas Company.

Letters of Credit. Another method of payment used in international business is by means of letters of credit. The rather common use of the letter of credit stems from the weakness of the bill of exchange, or draft, under which the exporter (seller) must bear the entire risk of collecting from the importer (buyer). However, letters of credit have one disadvantage—they are not standardized, and each document must be carefully read. The money to be paid under a letter of credit is obtained by a bill of exchange drawn on a bank.

Letters of credit may be classified as either *irrevocable* or *revocable*. If the letter of credit contains an express waiver of the right to revoke or cancel the credit prior to a specified date, the document is regarded as irrevocable. On the other hand, if the opening bank reserves the right to withdraw from the transaction by stating that the credit is "good until canceled" or "unless sooner revoked," the letter of credit is regarded as revocable. In addition to their use in commercial transactions, letters of credit may also be used by travelers going abroad.

The illustration opposite is an irrevocable letter of credit issued by The Bank of the Southwest, Houston, Texas, authorizing payment to the firm of Cafetero Manizales, Colombia, not to exceed 160,000 U.S. dollars. This amount is to be charged to the account of the Houston Coffee Importing Company, Houston, Texas, for the purchase of coffee by the Houston company.

This letter of credit is used on the assumption that the seller is not willing to ship without complete assurance that he will be paid, and that the buyer is unwilling to make payments in advance. It assures the Colombian firm that it will receive payment from the Texas bank for coffee purchased by the Houston firm. The steps involved in the transaction occur in the following order:

1. The Houston buyer arranges through his bank the issuance of a letter of credit that describes the nature of the transaction and directs the drawing of a draft against the bank for the amount of the purchase.

2. The letter of credit is then forwarded by the Houston bank to the seller in Colombia through a correspondent bank in Manizales, Colombia. The Colombian firm ships the coffee to Houston according to the conditions of the credit and presents to the Colombian bank the draft supported by the documents specified in the letter of credit.[3]

[3] Notice that among the specific documents to accompany the letter of credit in this illustration is a "Full set clean on-board ocean bills of lading." This term means all the original copies of the bills of lading that are issued. Having them protects the buyer because he knows that no one else has a full set and might present one of the copies and claim the goods. The term "clean" means there are no restrictions to the condition of the goods and that nothing has been lost or damaged owing to a broken bag. (The possibility of loss or damage from any method of shipping always exists.)

BANK OF THE SOUTHWEST

NATIONAL ASSOCIATION, HOUSTON

IRREVOCABLE COMMERCIAL CREDIT

S P E C I M E N

HOUSTON, TEXAS

NO. 9600

UP TO US$160,000.-

CAFETERO MANIZALES
Manizales, Colombia

February 25, 19

GENTLEMEN:

WE HEREBY AUTHORIZE YOU TO DRAW ON - - - - - - - O U R S E L V E S - - - - - - - -

FOR ACCOUNT OF - - - - - - HOUSTON COFFEE IMPORTING COMPANY, Houston, Texas - - - - -
UP TO AN AGGREGATE AMOUNT OF - U.S. DOLLARS ONE HUNDRED SIXTY THOUSAND AND NO/100 - - -

AVAILABLE BY YOUR DRAFTS AT - - - - - - - - - - - - SIGHT - - - - - - - - - - - - - -
ACCOMPANIED BY - Commercial Invoices
                - Special Customs Invoices
                - Full Set Clean On-board Ocean Bills of Lading issued to the order
                  of BANK OF THE SOUTHWEST, N.A. HOUSTON, Houston, Texas notify
                  HOUSTON COFFEE IMPORTING COMPANY, Houston, Texas - - - - - - - - - -

Evidencing Shipment: - - - - - - - - not later than April 25, 196* - - - - - - - - -

From: - - - - - - - - Colombia - - - - - - To: - - - - - - - - Houston, Texas - - - - -

Of Merchandise Invoiced as: - 2,500 bags "WASHED COLOMBIAN COFFEE" - - - - - - - - - -

Special Stipulations: - Partial shipments are permitted. - - - - - - - - - - - - - -
                      - Insurance is covered by buyers. - - - - - - - - - - - - - -

DRAFTS MUST BE DRAWN AND NEGOTIATED NOT LATER THAN - - - - - May 5, 19 - - - - - -
EACH DRAFT MUST BE MARKED "DRAWN UNDER LETTER OF CREDIT NO. - 9600 - OF THE BANK OF
THE SOUTHWEST, N. A., HOUSTON, DATED February 25, 19 AND THE AMOUNT OF EACH DRAFT SO
DRAWN ENDORSED BY THE NEGOTIATING BANK ON THE REVERSE SIDE HEREOF. WHEN PRESENTED BY
THE MAKER DIRECT TO THE DRAWEE BANK, THE DRAFTS MUST BE ACCOMPANIED BY THIS LETTER OF
CREDIT FOR THE PURPOSE OF SUCH ENDORSEMENTS BEING MADE THEREON.
     WE HEREBY AGREE WITH THE DRAWERS, ENDORSERS AND BONA FIDE HOLDERS OF DRAFTS DRAWN
UNDER AND IN COMPLIANCE WITH THIS CREDIT THAT SAME SHALL BE DULY HONORED UPON PRESENTA-
TION TO THE DRAWEE BANK AS SPECIFIED ABOVE.
                         YOURS VERY TRULY

SPECIMEN John H. Doe   SPECIMEN Joseph P. Doaks
          AUTHORIZED SIGNATURE   AUTHORIZED SIGNATURE
               A.V.P.   V.P.

FORM 22506.

Courtesy The Bank of the Southwest, Houston, Texas

A commercial letter of credit

3. The bank in Colombia forwards the draft, along with the supporting documents, to the Houston bank.

4. According to the terms of the commitment with its client, the Houston bank pays the Colombian bank, which in turn credits the Colombian exporter's bank account.

5. As per the contractual obligation between the buyer and his Houston bank, the buyer becomes legally obligated to reimburse the Houston bank for the amount of the credit used.

You will notice that the letter of credit also indicates that partial shipments are not permitted and that insurance is carried by the buyer.

Government and International Banks

Our present high volume of import–export trade could not be maintained without the indirect support of certain government and international banks. A general discussion of several of these organizations follows.

The Export-Import Bank.   In 1934, the Export-Import Bank of Washington (D.C.) was established as an agency of the U.S. government. It provided help in the financing of American exports to ease the domestic unemployment problem common during the 1930's. The bank tries to supplement, rather than compete with, commercial banks by lending only to those ventures in which the ordinary commercial bank is not interested. It tends to confine its loans to those for productive capital equipment for export, such as special machinery used in mining, industry, and agriculture. The capital stock is subscribed to by the U.S. Treasury.

The World Bank.   More properly named the International Bank for Reconstruction and Development (IBRD), this bank finances exactly what its title says it does. Conceived in July 1944 at the wartime Bretton Woods (New Hampshire) Conference at the same time that the International Monetary Fund (IMF) was created, the bank began operating early in 1946 with slightly more than $9 billion of subscribed capital. Since then, the number of countries supporting the bank has grown from 43 to 116, with $24 billion in capital stock subscribed to (but only $2.4 billion paid in; the remainder is due only if needed to cover guarantees the bank has granted on loans). To date the bank has encountered no defaults on its loans, and is not likely to call on its members for additional payments of capital.

The bank was organized to solve the problem of long-term capital movements. This can be done in three ways: (1) by lending its own funds to needy countries for development purposes; (2) by underwriting loans to developing countries from other sources; and (3) by borrowing money itself from member countries in order to finance loans. The fine reputation of the bank for screening its projects has enabled it to sell part of its loans to private banks and insurance companies. Initially, IBRD guaranteed the repayment of the loan to the purchasers, but that practice is no longer followed in all instances.

The International Finance Corporation.   In 1956, a group of 55 nations (by 1971 the number had reached 96), all members of the World Bank, subscribed capital to form the International Finance Corporation (IFC). In association with other investors, the IFC provides risk capital, although without government guarantee, for productive private enterprises. The corporation makes direct investments, usually on a mixed loan and equity basis. The IFC is an affiliate of the World Bank.

The International Development Association. This organization was started in 1960 by several member countries of, once again, the World Bank, with which it is also closely allied. The association's aim is to make long-term loans, without interest, to underdeveloped countries, on terms more flexible and bearing less heavily on the balance of payments of recipient countries. Funds are used to build sanitation and water-supply systems, pilot-housing developments, and other community projects. The loans have been made largely for 50 years, with repayments generally beginning after 10 years. A service charge of $\frac{3}{4}$ of 1 percent per annum is made, but no interest is charged.

The International Monetary Fund. With over $29 billion in gold and national currencies, the International Monetary Fund (IMF) is the world's largest source of quickly available international credit. The purposes of the fund are to promote international monetary cooperation, to help eliminate restrictions on foreign trade, and to provide funds to meet temporarily unfavorable trade balances between nations. If country A desires to buy goods from country B but lacks the currency to make the purchases, it can borrow the money from the fund in the currency of country B. Country A pays back its debt to the fund in gold or currency received through transactions with other nations. The IMF was established, effective December 27, 1945, at the aforementioned Bretton Woods Conference.

The United States Tariff Commission. In 1916, Congress created the Tariff Commission, a nonpolitical agency of the government, consisting of six members appointed by the president of the United States. The main function of the commission is to investigate, study, and submit to the president recommendations on tariffs and other matters pertaining to the foreign trade of the United States.

Before entering into negotiations with a foreign nation about tariff changes, the president must, under the terms of the 1962 Trade Expansion Act, furnish to the commission for study and recommendation a list of contemplated tariff concessions. Prior to such negotiations by the president to lower the tariff, the commission investigates to determine a *peril point* for each tariff item. The peril point is the tariff level below which, in the commission's opinion, the tariff cannot be cut without threatened or actual damage to a domestic producer. If the president exceeds this point in reducing a rate (he has the power to do so), he must explain his reason to Congress. Congress may then reverse him by a two-thirds majority vote of both houses. Hence this provision provides an escape clause by which the commission can recommend an increase in restrictions on imports if it finds that threatened or actual damage to a domestic producer would occur.

Under the Trade Expansion Act of 1962, Congress modified the use of both the peril point and the escape clause by offering tax relief, technical assistance, and loans to industries adversely affected by a tariff reduction. Employees may also receive a readjustment allowance for partial or complete unemployment caused by the tariff, or else they may receive training for new types of work, and in addition, a relocation allowance to help defray their moving costs to new regions where employment may be available.

Discussion Questions

11. *Explain the two definitions of* foreign exchange.
12. *What weaknesses does the bill of exchange have that would cause a business firm to prefer using a letter of credit to complete a foreign-trade credit transaction?*

INTERNATIONAL TRADE COOPERATION

The success of the Marshall Plan in achieving the economic recovery of Europe after World War II further demonstrated the advantages of closer economic cooperation among European nations. One effective way to promote cooperation is for the nations of Europe to remove their trade barriers by forming a customs union. A *customs union* is a geographical region embracing two or more nations, within which goods may move freely without being subject to customs duties.

World Economic Communities

The most effective customs unions in Western Europe have been the European Economic Community (EEC), known as the "Common Market" or "Inner Six," and the European Free Trade Association (EFTA), called the "Outer Seven." Similar customs unions have since been formed in Latin America.

The European Economic Community. Adopting the Common Market plan spelled out in the Treaty of Rome, signed March 25, 1957, six countries— France, Italy, Belgium, West Germany, Luxembourg, and the Netherlands— formed the EEC January 1, 1958.

The six nations had been striving to produce a full integration of their economies by 1970. Beyond this, their goal is to achieve political unity. The EEC is also working toward elimination of restrictions in insurance, banking, and labor laws, and the enactment of new laws to regulate the marketing of drugs and pharmaceuticals.

On June 23, 1971, the EEC voted to admit Great Britain, a decision in sharp contrast to those of Britain's two earlier bids to be admitted, when the late President Charles de Gaulle of France vetoed both proposals to make England a member. On October 28, 1971, Great Britain's House of Commons approved membership in the Common Market as of January 1, 1973. The British government must still have parliamentary approval of several major pieces of implementing legislation before final admission to the EEC. Meanwhile, the government of Denmark announced on January 15, 1972, that it had completed its negotiations for entry into the Common Market customs union. Ireland and Norway also plan to join the Common Market.

The admission of Great Britain to the EEC is bound to have an impact on the U.S. On the negative side, American exports to Great Britain—farm products, in particular—will compete at a disadvantage against exports from Common Market countries. This is because EEC goods will be duty-free when entering Britain. On the positive side, some 1,600 American companies operating in England will have duty-free access for their products into an expanded Common Market of, eventually, ten nations with approximately 250 million customers. Even prior to the October 28, 1971, vote of Parliament, there were signs that Great Britain was breaking away from its political alignment with the United States in order to shift its support to the EEC.

Once the EEC is expanded to ten countries, it would become an industrial giant second only to the United States. Experts predict that a host of new problems will then arise for this country. For example, the enlarged EEC would possess most of the world's gold and foreign-exchange reserves (outside communist countries), considered to be worth $36 billion in contrast to the $11 billion in gold owned by the United States. The EEC, with ten members, would account for about 30 percent of all world trade, as compared with about 15 percent for the United States. From the standpoint of overall trade, disputes between the United States and Europeans would seem inevitable as the EEC members reduce tariff walls among themselves but continue to discriminate against United States exporters. Some experts believe that Europe during the next decade will establish a common currency that could challenge the dollar. Finally, one of the most important issues confronting the enlarged EEC is how to reply to American demands that Europe contribute more to the European defense burden, thus allowing the United States to reduce its expenditures.

The European Free Trade Association.   Seeking a broader trade agreement among all European countries, seven nations—the United Kingdom, Sweden, Norway, Denmark, Switzerland, Austria, and Portugal—in 1960 formed the first industrial free-trade area outside the EEC. Finland and Iceland have since been admitted to the group.

Unlike the EEC, EFTA maintains no common tariff system with third countries. Rather, each member country maintains its own tariff and pursues its own trade policies with other nations outside of EFTA. The formation of EFTA was to set the stage for future negotiations with EEC countries to set up regional trading arrangements that would include the whole of Western Europe. President Kennedy took the position that a successful economic integration of Europe would in the long run be beneficial to all capitalistic coun-

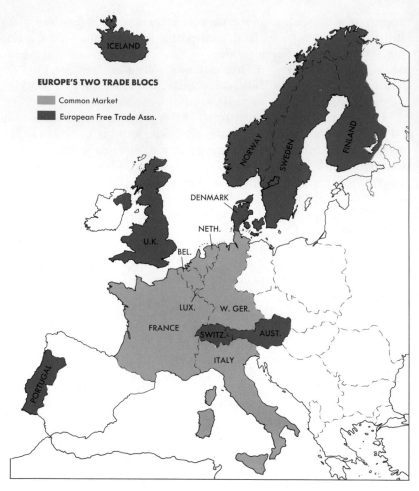

International trade organizations such as the Common Market and the Free Trade Association cut tariffs for members, but maintain duties on products from nonmember countries. Great Britain, Denmark, Norway, and Ireland have applied for membership in the Common Market.

tries. Perhaps the most significant benefit is cooperation that will result in checking inflation, reducing deficits in the balance of international payments, and increasing exports.

Economic Integration in Latin America. In the Western Hemisphere, two trading blocs have been established. The nine member countries of the Latin American Free Trade Association (LAFTA) are engaged in developing a free-trade area to serve Mexico, Argentina, Brazil, Chile, Colombia, Ecuador, Paraguay, Peru, and Uruguay. This association hopes to create a broad market that will encourage new industries. Unlike EFTA, which has established automatic tariff reductions, LAFTA follows the procedure that each round of tariff concessions depends on negotiations, and members may select the products they are willing to bargain on.

Five countries in Central America—Honduras, El Salvador, Nicaragua, Guatemala, and Costa Rica—have organized the Central American Common Market (CACM). This association is also engaged in cutting tariff restrictions and in promoting common finance with a common monetary system.

CAREER OPPORTUNITIES IN INTERNATIONAL TRADE

Today, an increasing number of American corporations are engaged in international business, and as a result, career opportunities in this field are on the increase. Or if you want to work for yourself, you may become an independent importer, exporter, broker, commission merchant, or import merchant. There are also opportunities with domestic companies engaged in foreign-freight forwarding.

Generally speaking, there are probably more positions open to the beginner in international business in domestic companies' training programs than there are for immediate employment abroad.

General Requirements

One of the important skills needed in foreign trade is the ability to speak at least one foreign language. Another is adaptability to a foreign culture, including ways of doing business that are very different from those used in the United States.

A college education, preferably with a degree in business administration, is an important general requirement. Others include such qualities as adaptability, stability, and responsibility.

Field of Employment in Exporting

The Export Manager. Experience in business is a necessary prerequisite for this position. The export manager exercises direct supervision over company agents, salesmen, and clerks. He must have an understanding of trade documents used in foreign shipments. Such documents include the ocean bill of lading, commercial invoice, marine insurance certificate, and others that were discussed under the subject of financing exports.

The Export Agent. This is an indirect-exporting position. The export agent is similar to the manufacturer's agent in domestic trade, in that he sells goods in the name of the manufacturer, who finances and ships the goods.

The export agent receives a commission. The more successful export agents are those who have lived abroad and know a great deal about foreign-trade operations.

The Freight Forwarder.   There are two types of freight forwarders. One is a domestic-freight forwarder who consolidates and combines domestic shipments in order to take advantage of the lowest freight rates. The foreign-freight forwarder prepares shipments for foreign countries, usually for companies that ship large amounts abroad and do not require combining of individual shipments. One of the most important functions of the freight forwarder is to handle documents used in finance and in transportation; both loading and unloading of shipments can be delayed if the forwarder fails to prepare the documents correctly.

Field of Employment in Importing

The Import Broker.   His function is to bring foreign sellers and American buyers together, in much the same way as the domestic broker, who finds a buyer and then locates a seller with that article. The import broker rarely takes title, but he is paid a commission and expenses. Much of the Brazilian coffee trade is carried on by import brokers in the United States who deal with export merchants in Brazil.

The Import Merchant.   This person's specialty is buying goods abroad and holding them in either a foreign or an American warehouse until he can find a buyer. This process requires that the import merchant take title to the goods until they are sold. On occasion, the import merchant sorts, grades, mixes, or blends goods where this must be done for shipment. He travels widely in foreign countries to locate goods. Diamonds, rugs, china, liquor, seeds, bulbs, and leather goods are among the many items imported into this country through import merchants.

Opportunities in Foreign-Trade Banking

As we have seen, commercial banks are important in promoting overseas trade. Many large commercial banks located in harbor cities maintain fully staffed trade departments to handle all the details involved in preparing, processing, and collecting on negotiable instruments used in foreign trade. These departments engage in currency exchange, prepare letters of credit, and handle such negotiable instruments as drafts, checks, and promissory notes. Persons interested in this phase of banking need a broad background in banking and business administration. An understanding of all the various credit instruments, such as those discussed in Chapter 14, is essential.

Discussion Questions

13. *What is the purpose of the European Economic Community? What advantages does the EEC offer American businessmen?*

14. *Compare the purposes of the EEC with those of EFTA. Why is it important for this country to cooperate with EEC and EFTA?*

SUMMARY

Although the United States is a leading producer of goods and services, it still depends heavily on other countries for many raw materials, goods, and services. Exporting is a means of selling surplus goods, which may not be easy to sell at home. Exporting also expands the market for a company's product. We import because it is impossible to produce some items in this country or because goods may be purchased abroad at lower prices than those available at home. Actually, millions of jobs (in the U.S. alone) depend directly on import and export trade.

There is an economic theory, the principle of comparative advantage, which states that a nation tends to export those goods which it can produce at relatively low costs and to import goods for which the costs are relatively high. Countries, therefore, specialize in producing certain products.

International trade is far more complex than doing business at home. There are differences in laws, social customs, and languages. Trade barriers in the form of tariffs and quotas restrict international movement of goods and services. Currencies vary both in their exchange rates and stability.

Companies that engage in a substantial amount of foreign commerce find that it pays to have their own marketing outlets such as foreign branches, factories, or even foreign subsidiaries located in other countries. In recent years, many foreign subsidiaries have grown into global operations known as multinational businesses. These use direct-export marketing channels.

Other companies find that the most efficient export marketing channels are the export merchants, export agents, and buyers for exports. Such channels are referred to as indirect-export marketing channels and are chiefly marketing middlemen serving to bring the exporter and his client together.

Goods can be shipped from one state to another in the United States with little or no government interference; but in international trade, the same shipment of goods is subject to various kinds of controls. The most frequent control is the tariff which is a tax or customs duty levied on goods imported from other countries.

The two broad categories of tariffs are revenue tariffs and protective tariffs. A revenue tariff is a tax on imports designed to produce revenue. A protective tariff is a tax on imports to protect domestic producers against competition from foreign producers. Reciprocal reductions of tariffs on a broad scale began in 1947 in Geneva resulting in the General Agreement on Tariffs and Trade. The most recent and far-reaching legislation enacted by the United States Congress was the Trade Expansion

Act of 1962 which resulted in tariff reductions on some 60,000 items. The purpose of such tariff reductions was to stimulate foreign trade by eliminating trade barriers.

A useful tool to explain the interrelations created by foreign-trade transactions is a statistical statement prepared annually called the balance of international payments. Transactions between domestic and foreign residents are entered in the balance of payments as either debits or credits. Debit transactions involve payments for goods purchased from other countries while credit transactions are receipts from export sales to other countries. A nation having more exports than imports has a so-called favorable balance of trade and, conversely, when imports exceed exports, this is an unfavorable balance of trade.

In an effort to improve the trade balance of the United States, which has deteriorated in recent years from large annual favorable balances of trade to almost no balance, President Nixon in 1971 devalued the American dollar by increasing the price of gold from $35 an ounce to $37.80. He also eliminated the 10 percent surcharge on imports. Devaluation makes goods imported into the U.S. more expensive while goods and services exported from the U.S. become less expensive to foreign consumers. (In April, 1972, a new federal law fixed the price of gold at $38 an ounce.)

The Export-Import bank makes loans to foreign countries for mining, agriculture, and industrial ventures to promote foreign trade. The International Bank for Reconstruction and Development (World Bank) has financed projects in developing countries of Asia, Africa, and Latin America.

VOCABULARY REVIEW

Match the following vocabulary terms with the statements below.

a. Ad valorem duty	e. Export merchant	i. Import quota
b. Customs union	f. Foreign exchange	j. Multinational business
c. Embargo	g. Foreign exchange rate	k. Revenue tariff
d. Exports	h. Imports	l. Tariff

1. Goods and services that are produced in this country and sold abroad

2. Raw materials and manufactured products shipped into this country

3. A firm that has a number of directly controlled operations in different countries, and that tends toward a worldwide perspective

4. A marketing middleman who buys and sells abroad on his own account

5. A tax on imports to produce revenue

6. A tax or customs duty levied by a nation on goods imported from other countries

7. A type of protective tariff that is based on the value of the imported goods rather than on some quantity of goods

8. A quantity control on imported merchandise for a certain period of time

9. Prohibition by a government upon the movement of goods in commerce

10. A financial asset involving a cash claim held by a resident of one country against a resident of another country

11. The rate at which one currency is exchanged for another

12. A geographical region embracing two or more nations, within which goods may move freely without being subject to customs duties

PROBLEMS AND PROJECTS

1. Referring to your library resources, prepare a written report on any one of the following topics:
   - a. Export-Import Bank
   - b. European Common Market
   - c. International Monetary Fund
   - d. European Free Trade Association
   - e. International Bank for Reconstruction
   - f. Kennedy Round of Tariff Negotiations
   - g. International Business Machine Corporation (World Trade Corporation)

2. Refer to an article in the August 1971 issue of *Fortune* magazine, "U.S. Foreign Trade: There's No Need to Panic," by Sanford Ross. Write a three-page summary of this article for presentation in class.

3. Beginning with the Smoot-Hawley tariff of 1930, trace the growth of the free-trade movement to the Kennedy Round of Tariff Negotiations.

A BUSINESS CASE

Case 23-1   The Jackson Company Proposes to Go International

The Jackson Company of Toledo, Ohio, is a manufacturer of household appliances—including vacuum cleaners, electric dishwashers, and electric stoves—under the trade name of Welbuilt. The company management is considering going abroad to expand sales. Last year their annual sales amounted to $30 million, with earnings at 9 percent on sales. The company is a close corporation owned by the Jackson family.

Ten weeks ago Tom Jackson, the son of the founder, Robert Jackson, attended a conference in Detroit on foreign-trade opportunities in Australia for American firms where he heard Professor Richard Simpson, a foreign-trade expert, speak on his trip to Australia. In response to Tom's invitation, Professor Simpson recently visited with officials of the Jackson Company. His recommendation was that the company establish an export department to conduct foreign trade with Australian companies. He also recommended that the firm get in contact with the International Monetary Fund, the Export-Import Bank, and the International Bank for Reconstruction, the International Chamber of Commerce, and the U.S. State Department about opportunities for trading in Australia.

1. Assume that you are assigned to make a study of how to set up an export department. Prepare a list of information you would seek to obtain to make the proposed study.

glossary
of
business terms

Absenteeism Failure of workers to be present at their work stations.

Abstract of title A summary statement based on county and other records, tracing the title of real property, including all liens, charges, and encumbrances against the land.

Accountability The liability of a person for his conduct with respect to fulfilling his obligations.

Ad valorem duty A tariff duty levied on goods according to their values.

Advertising Any paid form of nonpersonal presentation of goods, ideas, or services, presented through the various media to induce the public to buy.

Advertising medium The means or channel through which the advertising message is carried to prospective consumers.

Agency shop A shop in which nonunion employees as well as union members pay union dues.

Agent A person authorized to act for another in transactions with third parties.

Aptitude The potential ability to perform satisfactorily a specific type of work.

Arbitration Settlement of a dispute by a third party in a situation in which both sides agree in advance to abide by the decision rendered by that party.

Articles of partnership A written statement of the terms of agreement among partners.

Assets Items of value owned by a business.

Automation The process of operating machinery that controls other machines automatically without the aid of human effort.

Bailment A legal relationship created when the owner delivers goods to another person who accepts them for an agreed purpose. Upon accomplishment of the stated purpose, the goods are to be returned to the owner, as provided in the agreement.

Bankruptcy The financial condition of a person or corporation that indicates inability to pay debts. Often the term is used when a company's assets are being legally held to provide payment to creditors.

Bill of exchange An instrument drawn by one person ordering a second person to pay a sum of money to a specified third party on sight or at a future date.

Binary system A number system, based on bits instead of decimals, that employs only two digits: zero (0) and one (1).

Boycott An attempt to curtail a company's business through influencing the firm's customers to withhold their patronage.

Broker One who has authority to act for or on behalf of either the buyer or the seller in a marketing transaction.

Budget A financial plan that shows the amounts of anticipated revenues and expenditures during a specified period of time.

Business environment Those forces and activities outside and beyond the enterprise that affect the organization and its operation.

Capitalism A system of economic organization based upon the right of private ownership and on the right to work for a profit.

Capital stock Total aggregate equity ownership of a corporation as shown on the corporation's financial statement as the amount obtained from the sale of stock.

Cartel A contractual association of independent businesses in one or more countries, formed for the purpose of regulating production, prices, and marketing of goods by members.

Cashier's check A draft (bill of exchange) drawn by the cashier of the issuing bank against funds of the bank and payable to the order of the person named as payee.

Chattel mortgage A mortgage on personal property.

Close corporation A corporation that does not sell its shares to the public.

Collateral Property or securities pledged as security for a debt.

Collective bargaining Negotiations between representatives of labor and representatives of management.

Commission merchant A middleman who takes possession of, but not title to, the goods he markets. He arranges for the shipping, temporary storage, and delivery of the goods.

Commodity market A center where future-delivery contracts for staples such as wheat, cotton, soybeans, and hides are traded.

Common carrier One who offers transport services to the general public and charges uniform rates to all shippers.

Common stock Shares of ownership in a corporation, usually carrying voting rights and without a fixed rate of return, but having a residual claim to the assets and profits of the company.

Community property   Property held jointly and in equal shares by husband and wife.

Comparative advantage   Economic ability of a country to produce certain goods more cheaply than other countries can produce them.

Competition   A state of rivalry existing among several persons or business firms seeking the same or similar goods or other objectives.

Conciliation   A situation wherein a third party (a mediator) attempts to bring representatives of management and of a union together for the purpose of negotiation.

Conglomerate   A corporation that is made up, by merger, of a number of other companies that produce diverse products.

Consequential losses   Losses suffered by the insured, caused by his inability to carry on his business in a normal way due to its destruction or damage by fire.

Consideration   A payment or promise offered to bind the bargain in a contract negotiation.

Containerization   The shipping of goods in containers that permit them to be kept intact from origin to destination.

Contract   An agreement between two or more competent parties that is legally enforceable. It ordinarily provides for something to be given or done as consideration in return for compensation.

Contract carrier   One who sells transport services on the basis of individual agreements.

Cooperative   A business organization owned and operated by the persons it serves.

Copyright   The right of ownership of some written work as recognized by the federal government.

Corporate bond   A printed credit obligation acknowledging a debt of the corporation.

Corporation   A group of persons, created by statute as a legal person, authorized with powers to contract, own, dispose of, and convey property in the name of the corporation, and to otherwise transact business within the limits of the powers granted in the charter.

Correspondent bank   A bank that acts as a representative bank for one or more banks in other cities.

Craft union   A union whose members are skilled workers, usually engaged in one of the trades.

Credit   The power or ability to secure goods, services, or money in exchange for a promise to repay the debt later.

Creditor   A person or business to whom a firm owes money.

Current assets   Items of value, owned by a business, that will be converted into cash within a relatively short time.

Customs union   A geographical region composed of two or more countries, within which goods may move freely without being subject to customs duties.

Data processing   The group of operations performed in handling units of business data from the original to the final entry.

Debenture bond   A bond that is secured by the general credit of the company.

Defendant   The person accused in a lawsuit.

Discounter   A merchant who sells goods at a price below the regularly established retail price.

Dispatching   The preparation and issuance of work orders in manufacturing.

Dispersion   The scattering of factories and warehouses over a wide geographic area.

Disposable income The income that one has essential freedom in spending: income remaining after taxes.

Distribution center A building where goods are collected, stored for short periods, then shipped to customers in the area.

Distribution channel The route that goods follow as they move from the producer to the consumer or from the seller to the buyer.

Ecology The study of ecosystems and their status as a part of the environment.

Economics The study of the organization and utilization of the means of production for the purpose of meeting the economic needs of people.

Embargo Any prohibition by a government upon commerce.

Employers' association An organization of the management of similar businesses to further their mutual interests.

Endowment policy A life insurance contract that combines life protection with an investment feature. The company will pay the face amount to the insured if he lives to a certain date, or the same amount to his beneficiary should the insured die before that date.

Entrepreneur One who establishes a business and assumes the risks involved in putting capital and labor to work, in the hope of economic gain.

Ethics A set of rules of conduct that is accepted by society as being right and proper.

Eurodollars American dollars deposited in commercial banks outside the United States, which are not subject to U.S. control.

Executive A person in a business organization who occupies a position of authority over others and is responsible for their work.

Export merchant A marketing middleman (merchant), engaged in foreign trade, who buys and sells abroad on his own account.

Exports Goods or services produced in some country and sold abroad.

Factoring The buying of a company's accounts receivable without recourse against the seller.

Fidelity bond Insurance coverage that protects an employer against loss owing to acts of dishonest employees.

Fiduciary relationship A relation of mutual trust and confidence between company directors and officers.

Fiscal period The accounting period, when it does not follow the calendar year.

Fixed capital Long-term assets such as land, buildings, and equipment.

Foreign exchange rate The rate at which the currency of one country is exchanged for that of another country.

Franchising A scheme of distribution whereby an individually owned business is operated as though it were a part of a larger group of businesses, employing uniform operating procedures and a trademark name.

Fringe benefits Employee benefits or considerations in addition to wages or salary earned.

Futures transaction A purchase or sale of commodities on an exchange, where the goods are to be delivered at a future date.

Grading The sorting of goods into classes or groups, according to size or quality.

Grievance procedure The method by which an employee registers complaints resulting from circumstances that develop in his working situation.

Gross national product (GNP) The total market value of all goods and services produced by a nation's economy in one year.

Hedging The process of trading in futures on a commodity exchange in order to gain protection against price fluctuations.

Holding company A corporation organized for the purpose of owning stock in one or more other corporations.

Imports Goods entering one country from another country through regular channels of trade.

Impulse buying Consumer purchases based on sudden, unpremeditated urges to buy.

Income The revenues or earnings resulting from business operations.

Independent union A union not affiliated with any labor federation.

Industrial goods Products used by businesses in the manufacturing of other products.

Industrial union A labor group organized according to the industry involved rather than to the specific type of work providing the immediate employment.

Inheritance tax Excise taxes levied by a state on the right to receive property from one who is deceased.

Input The "feeding in" of information material, and/or effort required by an operation; also, that which is "fed in."

Insolvency The financial position of an individual or business when his total assets are inadequate to pay his debts.

Insurable interest An insurance principle that requires the policyholder to prove that he will suffer a financial loss if the insured property is lost, destroyed, or damaged.

Interstate carrier A carrier that transports goods across state lines.

Intrastate Doing business within a single state.

Investment banker A specialist who advises corporations regarding ways to market their securities.

Job analysis A study of the functions carried on in a work position, made in order that a description and classification of the position may be prepared.

Job description A statement based on an analysis of the duties to be performed on a job, and of the qualifications needed by the worker who is to hold that position.

Joint-stock company A form of business ownership that combines the unlimited liability of the general partnership with such features of the corporation as management by a board of directors, transferability of stock certificates, and the possibility of attracting a large number of shareowner investors.

Joint tenancy Real-property ownership in which two or more persons have, or are entitled to have, undivided possession of common property with the right of survivorship.

Jurisdictional dispute A controversy between unions as to which has the right over certain types of work activities or procedures.

Labor turnover The rate at which employees fill and vacate positions within a firm's working force—that is, join and quit the company.

Liabilities The debts owed by a business; the equity of the creditors in the business.

Lockout The act on the part of management of closing a plant and refusing to allow workers to enter it.

Markdown A reduction in the original selling price.

Market A place where goods or services are exchanged at a mutually agreed-upon price.

Marketing The performance of business activities to bring about the movement of goods and services from producer to consumer.

Marketing mix The combining of the product, distribution channels, pricing, and promotion in the sale and distribution of goods.

Markup The difference between the retailer's cost and his selling price.

Mean An arithmetic average of certain given numerical data.

Median The middle number in a series of related numbers that are arranged in ascending or descending order.

Mediation The offering of various suggestions by a third party assisting in labor–management negotiations.

Merchant wholesaler A wholesaler who provides a wide variety of services to retailers.

Middlemen Those who buy and sell goods as an aid in distributing them from the producer to the consumer.

Mode The point of greatest concentration; the number that appears most frequently in a series of numbers.

Monopoly The situation that exists when one or a very few firms gain control of the market in a given locality or region.

Morale The attitudes and feelings of employees toward their company and their working relationships.

Motion study The breaking down of a worker's movements and procedures into all the basic motions he uses; also, the analysis of this breakdown.

Multinational business A business firm that has a number of directly controlled operations in different countries, and that tends toward a worldwide perspective.

Mutual assent The condition when both parties to a contract agree, or have a meeting of the minds.

Mutual company A nonprofit insurance company organized under state codes and owned by the policyholders.

Mutual fund An investment company that raises its funds by selling shares to the public and investing its capital income in corporate and government securities.

Negotiability The right to transfer a good title to a legal instrument and make it legally payable to the holder.

Nominal partner A person who is not actually a partner in a business but pretends to be one.

Oligopoly A market situation in which only a few business firms compete, and where they can influence the price of a product by changing its supply.

Open corporation A corporation that sells its ownership shares to the general public.

Open shop A business enterprise in which there is no organized union.

Output The information "fed out" by a computer system, or that part of the system that prints out the reports, after data have been processed; also, the productive measure realized by a work-performing entity.

Partnership An association of two or more persons to carry on a business as co-owners.

Par value An arbitrary value placed on a stock certificate.

Patent An exclusive right to some invention, granted to its owner by the federal government.

Payee A party to a negotiable instrument to whose order the instrument is drawn.

Perpetual inventory A count of the merchandise on hand that is kept up to date continually.

Personal property   Property other than real property—movable property.

Picketing   The stationing of union members (usually carrying placards) at store or plant entrances to influence customers not to patronize the firm, and to prevent other union members from reporting for work.

Piece wages   Wages paid on the basis of the number of units produced.

Place utility   The meeting of consumers' needs by moving goods from a place of surplus to a place where they are in demand.

Plaintiff   One who brings action in a court of law.

Preferential shop   A business in which workers may choose not to be union members, but in which, because the union is the bargaining agent representing all the workers, union members enjoy certain preferences in employment over nonmembers.

Preferred stock   Corporation stock that has preference over common stock (e.g., preference in the payment of dividends). In case of bankruptcy, preferred stockholders have a preference over common shareholders.

Premium   The sum of money the policyholder pays periodically to the insurance company for the protection being purchased.

Private carrier   One who transports his own goods.

Private enterprise   A business system wherein individuals may hold legal title to property and are free to carry on business as they see fit in utilizing their property.

Procedural law   The body of rules that govern the conduct of a lawsuit.

Processor   A unit of a computer that includes the control panel, the calculator, and the memory or storage element.

Production   All activities involved in removing natural resources from the earth and processing them into finished goods.

Production sharing   Participation of workers in the distribution of profits that result from savings that accrue from a reduction in production costs.

Productivity   Efficiency of production: the amount of output in relation to input.

Profit   The return to the business owner of an amount over and above his cost of doing business.

Profit sharing   Participation of workers in the distribution of profits earned by the business.

Program   A set of coded instructions that tell a computer which operations to perform.

Progressive tax   A tax that falls most heavily on persons with the largest incomes.

Promotion   A position change that increases one's responsibility and pay.

Proportional tax   A tax that takes money from people in amounts directly proportional to their income. A tax is proportional when its rate remains the same, regardless of the size of the tax base.

Protective tariff   A tariff on imports high enough to protect domestic producers against foreign competition.

Proxy   A person appointed to represent another and to act as his agent.

Publicity   Information about a firm, a product, or an event, made available to the public without charge.

Pure risk   A type of risk that can result only in a loss should the peril occur. In pure risk, there is uncertainty as to whether the destruction of the object in question will occur.

Qualified indorsement   An indorsement that restricts the obligation of the person who transfers the instrument.

Quitclaim deed   An instrument that merely transfers to another whatever rights the grantor possesses.

Real property   Land and anything permanently attached thereto, as distinguished from *personal property,* which includes all movable property.

Recycling   Reconverting waste materials into usable products by reclaiming existing values.

Regressive tax   A tax whose rate takes a larger fraction of their pay from those with low incomes than from those in high income brackets. A sales tax is regressive because it bears most heavily on persons with low incomes.

Restrictive indorsement   An indorsement that stops further transfers of title because the indorsement limits its use to the single purpose indicated.

Revenue tariff   A tariff on imports, levied for the purpose of producing tax revenue.

Right-to-work law   A state law that prohibits union-shop contracts.

Risk   The possibility or uncertainty of loss arising from hazards such as fire, or those to credit, life, or health.

Routing   Assigning a sequence to the various steps in a manufacturing or other process; also, sending something through such a sequence.

Salesmanship   The power to influence a person or persons to buy what the seller offers for sale.

Schedule bond   A type of fidelity bond that lists many employees of the firm by name and bonds them for specified amounts of coverage. Fidelity bonds are purchased by an employer for his own protection against the dishonesty of employees.

Scheduling   Assigning times to production tasks in order to assure a smooth and constant flow of work along production lines.

Secondary boycott   The bringing of pressure upon an employer by attempting to influence other businesses to withhold their patronage.

Secret partner   A business partner who takes an active part in the management but who does not want to reveal his identity to the public.

Separation   Voluntary or involuntary severance from a job.

Sight draft   A bill of exchange constituting a written order issued by the drawer to the drawee to pay a third party (the payee) a sum of money, certain in amount, either on sight or on demand.

Silent partner   A partner in a partnership who plays no active role in the business even though he may be known to the public as a partner.

Speculation   The deliberate assumption of risk in ventures that appear to offer the chance of gain.

Speculative risk   A situation, such as a wager, in which there is both a chance of loss and a chance of gain.

Staff relationship   An organizational relationship that provides advisory or technical service to persons in line positions or performing operating functions.

Standard   A constant physical characteristic or quality that gives uniformity to a group of products.

Standardization   The use of uniform methods and procedures in manufacturing.

Statutory law   Written law, consisting of formal declarations or enactments by government bodies.

Stock dividend   A dividend paid in stock shares.

Stock-turnover ratio   The number of times per given period of time in which a business sells its entire stock inventory.

Straight life insurance   A life insurance policy on which premiums are payable for the duration of the insured's life.

Strike   The refusal of employees to report to work until management agrees to meet certain of their demands.

Substantive law   The part of the law that creates, defines, and regulates legal rights.

Surety bond   A written contract involving three parties: the principal (obligor), the one protected (obligee), and the insurer (surety,—who agrees to make good on any default on the part of the principal in performing his duties toward the obligee. In surety bonds, the obligee is concerned not only with the obligor's honesty, but also with his capacity to act.

System   A related series of items or activities, their interrelatedness being woven into an organizational pattern.

Tariff   A tax or customs duty levied by a nation on goods imported from other countries.

Tenancy in common   Ownership of real property held by two or more persons jointly with the right to share in its enjoyment or use during their lifetimes.

Trade credit   Credit granted for goods sold on an open-book account as accounts receivable, with the understanding that payment is due within a certain number of days after the date of invoice.

Trademark   The right of ownership of some distinctive symbol or title when it is registered with the federal government.

Transfer   A job change at the same level of employment, without changing the person's degree of responsibility or rate of pay.

Trust   A combination of businesses operated under trust agreements by trustees for the benefit of the members; also, an organization for holding the property of one person for the benefit of another.

Trustee   One who holds legal title to property but who uses it for the benefit of another.

Union shop   A shop in which union membership is required of all employees.

Usury   Interest charged beyond the legal rate.

Voluntary chain   A group of independent retailers who pool certain buying and distribution functions.

Warehouse receipt   A document serving as a receipt for goods in storage.

Warehousing   The storing of goods in large buildings until they are needed to meet consumer demand.

Warranty   A guarantee as to quality or title.

Warranty deed   An instrument that guarantees that property is free of debt and that the owner conveys a good title.

selected
readings

PART ONE

business and its environment

Anderson, Ronald A., *Social Forces and the Law.* Cincinnati, O.: South-Western Publishing Co., 1969.

Baltz, Howard B., and Richard D. Baltz, *Fundamentals of Business Analysis.* Englewood Cliffs, N.J.: Prentice-Hall, Inc., 1969.

Chapman, Elwood N., *Big Business: A Positive View.* Englewood Cliffs, N.J.: Prentice-Hall, Inc., 1971.

Colberg, Marshall R., et al., *Business Economics: Principles and Cases,* 4th ed. Homewood, Ill.: Richard D. Irwin, Inc., 1970.

Harter, Lafayette G., *Economic Responses to a Changing World.* Glenview, Ill.: Scott, Foresman and Company, 1970.

Heilbroner, Robert L., *The Making of Economic Society,* 3rd ed. Englewood Cliffs, N.J.: Prentice-Hall, Inc., 1970.

Inman, Raymond S., and Robert E. Murphy, *The Economic Process, Inquiry and Challenge.* Glenview, Ill.: Scott, Foresman and Company, 1969.

Salera, Virgil, *Multinational Business.* Boston: Houghton Mifflin Company, 1969.

Schnitzer, Martin C., *Comparative Economic Systems.* Cincinnati, O.: South-Western Publishing Co., 1971.

Schultz, Arnold M., *Ecosystems and Environment.* New York: Harper & Row, Publishers, 1971.

Silk, Leonard, *Readings in Contemporary Economics.* New York: McGraw-Hill Book Company, 1970.

Smead, Elmer E., *Governmental Promotion and Regulation of Business.* New York: Appleton-Century-Crofts, 1969.

Södersten, Bo, *International Economics.* New York: Harper & Row, Publishers, 1970.

Votaw, Dow, *Legal Aspects of Business Administration.* Englewood Cliffs, N.J.: Prentice-Hall, Inc., 1969.

Walton, Clarence C., *Business and Social Progress: Views of Two Generations of Executives.* New York: Praeger Publishers, Inc., 1970.

Wilcox, Clair, *Public Policies Toward Business,* 4th ed. Homewood, Ill.: Richard D. Irwin, Inc., 1971.

Wykstra, Ronald A., *Introductory Economics.* New York: Harper & Row, Publishers, 1971.

PART TWO

organization and management
of the enterprise

Bass, Bernard M., and Samuel D. Deep, *Current Perspectives for Managing Organizations.* Englewood Cliffs, N.J.: Prentice-Hall, Inc., 1970.

Broom, H. N., and J. G. Longenecker, *Small Business Management,* 3rd ed. Cincinnati, O.: South-Western Publishing Co., 1971.

Bunn, Verne A., *How to Buy a Small Business.* Cambridge, Mass.: Boston Technical Publishers, Inc., 1970.

Dale, Ernest, *Readings in Management: Landmarks and New Frontiers,* 2nd ed. New York: McGraw-Hill Book Company, 1970.

Elbing, Alvar O., *Behavioral Decisions in Organizations.* Glenview, Ill.: Scott, Foresman and Company, 1970.

Hersey, Paul, and Kenneth H. Blanchard, *Management of Organizational Behavior.* Englewood Cliffs, N.J.: Prentice-Hall, Inc., 1969.

Kazmier, Leonard J., *Principles of Management: A Program for Self-Instruction.* New York: McGraw-Hill Book Company, 1969.

Massie, Joseph, *Essentials of Management,* 2nd ed. Englewood Cliffs, N.J.: Prentice-Hall, Inc., 1971.

Mintz, Morton, and Jerry S. Cohen, *America, Inc.: Who Owns and Operates the United States.* New York: The Dial Press, 1971.

Morrisey, George L., *Management by Objectives and Results.* Reading, Mass.: Addison-Wesley Publishing Co., Inc., 1970.

Owens, Richard N., *Management of Industrial Enterprises.* Homewood, Ill.: Richard D. Irwin, Inc., 1969.

Small Business Administration, *Annual Report, Small Business Administration.* Washington, D.C.: U.S. Government Printing Office, 1970.

PART THREE

operating problems
of the enterprise

Brody, David, *The American Labor Movement.* New York: Harper & Row, Publishers, 1971.

Buffa, Elwood S., *Basic Production Management.* New York: John Wiley & Sons, Inc., 1971.

French, Wendell, *The Personnel Management Process: Human Resources Administration,* 2nd ed. Boston: Houghton Mifflin Company, 1970.

Gitlow, Abraham L., *Labor and Manpower Economics,* 3rd ed. Homewood, Ill.: Richard D. Irwin, Inc., 1971.

Heinritz, Stuart F., and Paul V. Farrell, *Purchasing: Principles and Applications,* 5th ed. Englewood Cliffs, N.J.: Prentice-Hall, Inc., 1971.

Jucius, Michael J., *Personnel Management,* 7th ed. Homewood, Ill.: Richard D. Irwin, Inc., 1971.

Lee, Lamar, *Purchasing and Materials Management,* 2nd ed. New York: McGraw-Hill Book Company, 1971.

Pigors, Paul, and Charles A. Myers, *Personnel Administration,* 6th ed. New York: McGraw-Hill Book Company, 1969.

Thierauf, Robert J., and Richard A. Grosse, *Decision Making through Operations Research.* New York: John Wiley & Sons, Inc., 1970.

Timms, Howard L., and Michael F. Pohlen, *The Production Function in Business,* 3rd ed. Homewood, Ill.: Richard D. Irwin, Inc., 1970.

U.S. Department of Labor, *A Brief History of the American Labor Movement.* Washington, D.C.: Superintendent of Documents, 1970.

Yoder, Dale, *Personnel Management and Industrial Relations,* 6th ed. Englewood Cliffs, N.J.: Prentice-Hall, Inc., 1970.

PART FOUR

financial management
and risk functions

Athearn, James L., *Risk and Insurance,* 2nd ed. New York: Appleton-Century-Crofts, 1969.

Bickelhaupt, David L., and John H. Magee, *General Insurance,* 8th ed. Homewood, Ill,: Richard D. Irwin, Inc., 1970.

Brands, L. K., *Business Finance,* 2nd ed. Englewood Cliffs, N.J.: Prentice-Hall, Inc., 1971.

Dauten, Carl A., and Merle Welshans, *Principles of Finance.* Cincinnati, O.: South-Western Publishing Co., 1970.

Dobrovolsky, Sergel P., *The Economics of Corporation Finance.* New York: McGraw-Hill Book Company, 1971.

Federal Reserve System, *The Federal Reserve System, Purposes and Functions.* Washington, D.C.: Board of Governors of the Federal Reserve System, 1963.

Huebner, S. S., and Kenneth Black, Jr., *Life Insurance,* 7th ed. New York: Appleton-Century-Crofts, 1969.

Hunt, Pearson, et al., *Basic Business Finance: Text and Cases,* 4th ed. Homewood, Ill.: Richard D. Irwin, Inc., 1971.

Institute of Life Insurance, *Life Insurance Fact Book.* New York: Institute of Life Insurance, 1971.

Johnson, Robert W., *Financial Management,* 4th ed. Boston: Allyn & Bacon, Inc., 1971.

National Consumer Finance Association., *Finance Facts Yearbook.* Washington, D.C.: National Consumer Finance Association, 1971.

Polakoff, Murray E., et al., *Financial Institutions and Markets.* Boston: Houghton Mifflin Company, 1970.

Prather, Charles L., and James E. Wert, *Financing Business Firms,* 4th ed. Homewood, Ill.: Richard D. Irwin, Inc., 1971.

Ritter, Lawrence, and William L. Silber, *Money.* New York: Harper & Row, Publishers, 1971.

Walker, Ernest W., *Essentials of Financial Management,* 2nd ed. Englewood Cliffs, N.J.: Prentice-Hall, Inc., 1971.

Zarb, Frank G., and Gabriel T. Kerekes, eds., *The Stock Market Handbook.* Homewood, Ill.: Dow Jones-Irwin, Inc., 1970.

PART FIVE

quantitative controls
for decision making

Awad, Elias M., *Business Data Processing,* 3rd ed. Englewood Cliffs, N.J.: Prentice-Hall, Inc., 1971.

Cashman, Thomas, and William J. Keys, *Introductory Data Processing.* New York: Harper & Row, Publishers, 1971.

Chisholm, Roger K., and Gilbert R. Whitaker, Jr., *Forecasting Methods.* Homewood, Ill.: Richard D. Irwin, Inc., 1971.

Craxton, Frederick, et al., *Practical Business Statistics.* Englewood Cliffs, N.J.: Prentice-Hall, Inc., 1969.

Desmonde, William H., *Computers and Their Uses,* 2nd ed. Englewood Cliffs, N.J.: Prentice-Hall, Inc., 1971.

Dipple, Gene, and William C. House, *Information Systems, Data Processing and Evaluation.* Glenview, Ill.: Scott, Foresman and Company, 1969.

Elliott, C. Orville, and Robert S. Wasley, *Business Information Processing Systems: An Introduction to Data Processing,* 3rd ed. Homewood, Ill.: Richard D. Irwin, Inc., 1971.

Kim, Thomas, *Introductory Mathematics for Economic Analysis.* Glenview, Ill.: Scott, Foresman and Company, 1971.

Lindley, Dennis V., *Making Decisions.* New York: John Wiley & Sons, Inc., 1971.

Stockton, John R., and Charles T. Clark, *Introduction to Business and Economic Statistics,* 4th ed. Cincinnati, O.: South-Western Publishing Co., 1971.

Tracy, John, *Understanding Accounting.* Englewood Cliffs, N.J.: Prentice-Hall, Inc., 1971.

Welsch, Glenn A., *Budgeting: Profit Planning and Control,* 3rd ed. Englewood Cliffs, N.J.: Prentice-Hall, Inc., 1971.

PART SIX

marketing functions

Cateora, Philip R., and John M. Hess, *International Marketing,* rev. ed. Homewood, Ill.: Richard D. Irwin, Inc., 1971.

Conference Board, *A Guide to Consumer Markets 1970.* New York: The Conference Board, Inc.

Converse, Paul D., et al., *Elements of Marketing,* 8th ed. Englewood Cliffs, N.J.: Prentice-Hall, Inc., 1971.

Gillespie, Karen R., and Joseph C. Hecht, *Retail Business Management.* New York: McGraw-Hill Book Company, 1970.

Gist, Ronald R., *Basic Retailing: Text and Cases.* New York: John Wiley & Sons, Inc., 1971.

Grayson, Robert A., and Reynold A. Olsen, *An Introduction to Marketing: A Practical Approach.* New York: Appleton-Century-Crofts, 1971.

Kerby, Joe Kent, *Essentials of Marketing Management.* Cincinnati, O.: South-Western Publishing Co., 1970.

Kramer, Roland L., *International Marketing.* Cincinnati, O.: South-Western Publishing Co., 1970.

Lazer, William, *Marketing Management: A Systems Perspective.* New York: John Wiley & Sons, Inc., 1971.

Leighton, Richard I., *Economics of International Trade.* New York: McGraw-Hill Book Company, 1970.

Lipson, Harry A., and John R. Darling, *Introduction to Marketing: An Administrative Approach.* New York: John Wiley & Sons, Inc., 1971.

Lockley, Lawrence C., et al., *Cases in Marketing,* 4th ed. Boston: Allyn & Bacon, Inc., 1971.

Moller, William G., Jr., and David L. Wilemon, eds., *Marketing Channels: A Systems Viewpoint.* Homewood, Ill.: Richard D. Irwin, Inc., 1971.

Samli, A. Coskun, *Marketing Research.* Glenview, Ill.: Scott, Foresman and Company, 1970.

Snider, Delbert A., *Introduction to International Economics,* 5th ed. Homewood, Ill.: Richard D. Irwin, Inc., 1971.

Staudt, Thomas, and Donald A. Taylor, *A Managerial Introduction to Marketing,* 2nd ed. Englewood Cliffs, N.J.: Prentice-Hall, Inc., 1970.

Still, Richard R., and Edward W. Cundiff, *Essentials of Marketing,* 2nd ed. Englewood Cliffs, N.J.: Prentice-Hall, Inc., 1971.

Warner, Daniel S., *Marketing and Distribution: An Overview.* New York: McGraw-Hill Book Company, 1969.

Wasson, Chester R., and David H. McConaughy, *Buying Behavior and Marketing Decisions.* New York: Appleton-Century-Crofts, 1968.

Wright, John S., et al., *Advertising,* 3rd ed. New York: McGraw-Hill Book Company, 1971.

Zober, Martin, *Principles of Marketing.* Boston: Allyn & Bacon, Inc., 1971.

index